The Psychology of Ageing

also by Ian Stuart-Hamilton

An Asperger Dictionary of Everyday Expressions
ISBN 1 84310 152 1

Key Ideas in Psychology
ISBN 1 85302 359 0

Dictionary of Cognitive Psychology
ISBN 1 85302 148 2

Dictionary of Developmental Psychology
ISBN 1 85302 146 6

Dictionary of Psychological Testing, Assessment and Treatment
Second Edition
ISBN 1 84310 494 6

of related interest

Spiritual Growth and Care in the Fourth Age of Life
Elizabeth MacKinlay
ISBN 1 84310 231 5

Depression in Later Life
Jill Manthorpe and Steve Iliffe
ISBN 1 84310 234 X

The Psychology of Ageing
An Introduction
4th Edition

Ian Stuart-Hamilton

Jessica Kingsley Publishers
London and Philadelphia

First published in 2006
by Jessica Kingsley Publishers
116 Pentonville Road
London N1 9JB, UK
and
400 Market Street, Suite 400
Philadelphia, PA 19106, USA

www.jkp.com

Library of Congress Cataloging in Publication Data

A CIP catalog record for this book is available from the Library of Congress

336 pp

British Library Cataloguing in Publication Data

A CIP catalogue record for this book is available from the British Library

ISBN-13: 978 1 84310 426 1
ISBN-10: 1 84310 426 1

Printed and bound in Great Britain by
Athenaeum Press, Gateshead, Tyne and Wear

To Ruth

Whither thou goest

Acknowledgements

I wish to thank my long-suffering wife and children for putting up with my long absences in the study whilst I hammered the first draft of this book into shape. I also wish to thank Dr Peter Mayer and my other esteemed colleagues at the Department of Psychology, University of Glamorgan for offering such a conducive and friendly working atmosphere, and especial thanks go to Dr Rachel Taylor for the endless supply of herbal tea.

Contents

Preface

Since the publication of the third edition in 2000, there has been an explosion of research papers in many areas of the psychology of ageing, often from longitudinal studies which, after the inevitable years of waiting, are now bearing fruit. Accordingly, nearly all areas of the book have a plethora of new references. Otherwise the status quo is largely maintained and I have generally resisted the temptation to tinker with the structure of the book after the relatively large (and, modesty aside, well-received) changes introduced in the previous edition. Also as before, I have attempted to give a judicious range of references suitable for readers from different backgrounds (though with some of the more recent research only primary sources such as journals have been included because overviews are not yet available). However, for the first time I have included references to websites where I feel they are appropriate. I have an innate mistrust of unverifiable sources (and that is what most websites are), but it makes pragmatic sense to recommend sites taken as authoritative by many researchers, such as official government statistics websites and the like.

Professor Ian Stuart-Hamilton
University of Glamorgan
January 2006

CHAPTER 1

What is Ageing?

The greying population

Ageing is not unique to the modern times, but it is only in the past hundred years that it has become commonplace. It is estimated that in the prehistoric era, old age was extremely rare, and even up to the seventeenth century probably only about 1 per cent of the population was over 65. By the nineteenth century, this proportion had risen to approximately 4 per cent (Cowgill, 1970). In Britain today, about 11 million (c.16%) of the population is aged 65 or older and this figure is expected to rise until it peaks at approximately 17 million (c.25%) in 2060, before various demographic changes cause a relative decline (Shaw, 2004). Similar proportions and growth are predicted for other industrialised nations (OECD, 1988). To take another perspective, provided the gloomiest predictions about global catastrophes are not realised, about 70 per cent of today's western population can expect to live past 65, and 30–40 per cent past 80. By 2050 it is predicted that almost half the population will live past 85. In 1900, only about 25 per cent of the population could even hope to reach their sixty-fifth birthday (Brody, 1988; Sonnenschein and Brody, 2005).

Put yet another way, the average life expectancy of a baby born in an industrialised country in 1900 was 47–55 years; today, this figure has risen by approximately 30 years. In the UK today, women can expect to live to circa 80 years and men to circa 76 years. However, there are regional variations. For women, the longest-living regional group resides in west Somerset (in the south west of England, and fairly rural) with a life expectancy of circa 83 years. The longest-lived men are in nearby north Dorset, with a life expectancy of 79 years. For both men and women, those living in central Glasgow in Scotland or central Manchester in England have amongst the lowest life expectancies at circa 76 years for women and circa 69 years for men (National Statistics Online, accessed 21 June 2005). Other countries report similar regional differences, largely associated with socio-economic status (see Griffiths and Fitzpatrick, 2001).

Arising from these considerations, the modern industrialised population has been described as a **rectangular society**. Since roughly equal numbers of people are alive in each age decade (i.e. equal numbers of 0–9 year-olds, 10–19 year-olds, etc.), a histogram plotting numbers alive against age decade appears (with a little artistic licence) like a rectangle. By comparison, a graph from 1900 looks like a pyramid (lots of people in the youngest age decade, progressively fewer in the older ones), and hence is described as a **pyramidal society**. The more rectangular a society becomes, the longer people can expect to live and hence the more 'advanced' or 'successful' the country.

However, without caveats, the above figures are misleading. To the casual reader, the information that in 1900 life expectancy was in the mid-fifties implies that everyone died before they reached 60, which is palpably nonsense. **Life expectancy** refers to the age by which half of a group of people born in the same period of time die. In other words, half the age group live longer than this (the members of a group who are left alive at any point are called the **survivors**). The reason for the lower life expectancy figure in 1900 can be largely attributed to a higher rate of infant and child mortality (i.e. a lot of the 50% who died had passed away before they even became adults). If a person survived childhood, then he or she could expect to live considerably longer than their mid-fifties. A young adult in 1900 still had a lower life expectancy than a young adult today, but the difference was 'only' about seven years. Indeed, the older the age group one considers the smaller this difference progressively becomes, until centenarians in 1900 had about as much future life ahead of them as centenarians today (Bromley, 1988; Kermis, 1983).

In other words, the longer one lives, the less modern society can extend remaining life beyond what would have been experienced in earlier times. Furthermore, it must not be supposed that the added life many modern people experience is necessarily blissful. Wilkins and Adams (1983), working from Canadian actuarial tables, calculated that for older adults, about 75 per cent of this 'extra time' is spent suffering from one or more physical disabilities and hence discomfort. Brattberg, Parker and Thorslund (1996) cite a similar figure of 73 per cent of Swedish adults in their late seventies reporting mild or severe pain. These considerations give rise to the concept of **active life expectancy** (i.e. the average number of years remaining in which people can expect to lead a reasonably active life). From birth, the average citizen of an industrialised country can expect to spend at least the final 10 per cent of their life suffering an appreciable disability (World Health Organization, 2004). And if this is not depressing enough, serious chronic illness (i.e. enough to impinge significantly on quality of life, if not immediately to disable) will probably appear several years prior to this (World Health Organization, 2004). Thus, it can be argued that the added life expectancy figures are something of a chimera – the so-called **greying population** is due more to childhood illnesses no longer being the killers they were, rather than to an 'improvement' in the way people age.

However, it should be noted that not all commentators and researchers agree with this rather gloomy outlook (sometimes called the **expansion of morbidity theory**, loosely, that on average people 'buy' extra life by suffering more). Commentators such as Fries (e.g. Fries, 2000) propose the **compression of morbidity theory**. This argues that advances in medical science mean that many previously fatal illnesses have been eradicated or brought under control, and thus the range of diseases or conditions people can die from has been reduced. Thus, probabilistically speaking, people have on average to live longer before they develop something that medical science cannot cure. Additional to this, many of the incurable diseases can be staved off with appropriate prophylactic measures such as sensible diet and exercise. Thus, with the right intervention, it is possible to avoid entering into a disabled state until very late in life. Although a final fatal illness cannot of course be prevented, Fries and others have argued that the period of severe disability and suffering can be compressed into a shorter time frame than has been known by previous generations.

Arguably the expansion of morbidity theory represents the (undesirable) current state of health for many older adults, whilst the compression of morbidity theory represents what should be the norm. Fries presents strong evidence that the goals are attainable, and this argument is supported by the observations of researchers who have noted that the proportion of reported severe disability amongst older patients has significantly declined (e.g. Gorin and Lewis, 2004; Laditka and Laditka, 2002). However, other studies have not found a clear link between healthiness of lifestyle and compression of morbidity (e.g. Hubert et al., 2002). But failure to find compression of morbidity may not represent a failure of the theory but, rather, a failure by the local health care services to treat older patients sufficiently well. This arguably points out a weakness in the theory. Since at heart it is a model of what *should* be, failure to find data that match it arguably represents a failure of treatment to reach a desired goal rather than a failure of prediction. This is rather like saying that it would be a good thing if countries were nice to each other. If country A and country B subsequently go to war, this does not represent a failure for the theory, only that the countries didn't live up to the ideal (since the theory only expressed a hope, not a prediction). Thus, whilst the compression of morbidity theory represents something entirely laudable, it does not necessarily have a particularly strong predictive power.

Furthermore, the shift in the balance of older people in the population is not without potential economic and social problems. If the proportion of older adults increases, then by definition the proportion of younger adults decreases. This means that a smaller fraction of the population is working and hence paying direct taxation (i.e. income tax, National Insurance, and similar). Such taxation forms the backbone of funding for welfare support schemes such as state pensions and (in most countries) national health care. Older people are of course pensioners and also are, along with children, the main beneficiaries of national health care. Thus, a 'grey shift' will create an increase in demand for services which are principally funded by a workforce diminishing in size. A simple method of expressing this is the **old age dependency ratio**, which is the number of people of pensionable age divided by the number of people of working age. This currently stands at about one-fifth for most industrialised nations, but is expected to rise to one-third or more by 2040. In the case of the UK, the current figure is circa 27 per cent and is expected to rise to circa 50 per cent by 2050 (OECD, 2004). This is an instance of the 'demographic time bomb' – the major and potentially catastrophic financial burden on the economies of the coming decades created by a greying population. Governments are of course aware of this (though some would argue they have been slow to act), and moves to relieve the problem can be clearly seen in the UK through measures such as increasing the retirement age for women (in the decade from 2010, it will be incrementally raised to 65). (This should also mean that, in conjunction with increased life expectancy, the proportion of one's lifetime spent not working will remain comparable with previous generations.) In addition, governments in many industrialised nations are working towards encouraging or even forcing individuals not to take early retirement. In nearly all such countries (with the notable exception of Iceland) under circa 70 per cent of the people aged 50–64 are in paid employment, so there is potentially a significant proportion of the population who could find themselves working longer than expected (OECD, 2004). Coupled with this are increased government-led incentives to prepare for later life through private pension schemes to 'top up' a small state pension.

Unfortunately, the private pensions industry is currently facing a crisis (for once the term is justified rather than being journalistic hyperbole). The relatively poor performance of the stock markets in recent years has meant that a key source of funding for pension schemes has generally fallen well short of expectations. Those reaching retirement have often received lower private pensions than they expected (or even none at all if the schemes have collapsed) and those in employment will have to pay higher premiums in order to maintain a reasonable pension in retirement. Unfortunately, this has occurred at a time when property prices in many parts of the world have reached record heights (at the time of writing, young professionals such as teachers or lecturers do not earn enough to afford even the most basic of houses or apartments in 90 per cent of UK cities). The understandable need to buy somewhere to live may force people to defer starting to save for pensions until they are practically into middle age, and this can only magnify the problem in future years. In addition, a study by Casey (2004) argues that fears about private pensions (poor stock market performance, labyrinthine regulations, etc.) not only deter individuals, but this sense of unease spreads like a contagion through others contemplating a pension. Thus, not only is there a financial disincentive to start a pension, there is also a psychological one.

However, although the demographic time bomb and the pensions crisis are serious problems, it is important to put things into perspective. First, the costs of health care of older adults may be exaggerated by current accounting methods, and the real cost may turn out to be significantly lower (Seshamani and Gray, 2004; Yang, Norton and Stearns, 2003). Second, the discussions so far have dealt with industrialised nations. It is a sobering thought that for developing countries, the figures for 1900 are more appropriate, with infant mortality being commonplace rather than the tragic rarity it is in developed countries (World Health Organization, 2004). It is also worth noting that recently commentators have begun to argue that the rise in obesity in developed countries such as the USA will lead to a marked fall in life expectancy, and that official projected figures of a high proportion of people surviving into their seventies and eighties may be wide of the mark (e.g. Olshansky et al., 2005).

Differences in life expectancy

The prevalence of ageing has thus differed within the same society across historical time and differs today between industrialised and developing countries. It also differs between individuals and groups within the same society. A striking illustration of this is the **Roseto effect** (see Egolf et al., 1992). This is named after an Italian-American community in Roseto, Pennsylvania, whose members' susceptibility to heart disease increased as it became more 'Americanised'. This neatly demonstrates that people can radically influence their life expectancy simply through which socio-economic group they belong to and the lifestyle they lead. In some instances, choice of lifestyle is voluntary; in others, regrettably, it is not. A much-cited instance of this is the effect of socio-economic class on life expectancy. Essentially, the less affluent the social group is, the lower its life expectancy and prospects of a healthy life (e.g. Kawachi and Kennedy, 1997; Luo and Waite, 2005; Macintyre, 1994; Roberge, Berthelot and Wolfson, 1995; Schwartz et al., 1995). Many reasons have been suggested for this phenomenon, not least of which are levels of stress, nutrition and access to health care services.

Another major group difference is that ageing, particularly amongst octogenarians and older, is principally an experience of women. In peaceful societies (i.e. where heavy war casualties do not distort the figures), the balance of men and women is roughly equal until about 45 years. Thereafter, men die at a faster rate, so that by 70, there are approximately six women for every five men, and by 80, this ratio has moved to 4:1. Many reasons for the earlier deaths of men have been suggested. A popular conception is that it is because men have traditionally led physically more strenuous lives. However, this seems at best a marginal explanation, since comparisons of men and women matched for levels of physical industriousness still show a strong sex difference in mortality rates. The phenomenon is seen across many animal species besides humans (Shock, 1977), implying that differences may lie at a chromosomal rather than an environmental level. However, a complex interaction of physical and environmental factors and differences in social behaviour (such as higher risk-taking amongst males) may also play a key role (see Lang, Arnold and Kupfer, 1994). Tangential to this, Tsuchiya and Williams (2005) argue that part of the gender difference may be due to unequal treatment of older men and women. They point out that the life expectancy of women from poor socio-economic groups is about equal to that of men from the richest socio-economic groups. Hence, are older men the victims of unfair treatment?

The argument may seem at first rather tendentious, but Amorim Cruz *et al.* (2002) found evidence that could be taken as qualified support for it. The researchers followed up a group of older adults living in various European countries over a ten-year period. They found that more men died than women, but also noted that the death rate of the men was significantly more influenced by the country they were living in than was the death rate of women, implying that variations in treatment may have a significant influence on male life expectancy. However, it seems unlikely that differential treatment can be the complete explanation of gender differences, since, as has been noted, it appears reliably across other species where the differential treatment argument cannot possibly apply. For example, female fruit flies live longer than male fruit flies when their environments are made more optimal for longevity (Partridge, Piper and Mair, 2005), so, if cross-species comparisons are valid, it seems probable that women are attuned to benefit from certain environments and treatments more than men. Again, in a study of care of heart disease patients, Dudley *et al.* (2002) found the bias in care to act *against* women and the oldest of elderly patients, such that the younger older adults and men were more likely to receive greater levels of treatment (though note this was a study of only one hospital). In contrast, Hubbard *et al.* (2003) found no age discrimination influencing access to critical care beds in a survey of five hospitals in the same administrative region. Neither the findings of Dudley *et al.* or those of Hubbard *et al.* can be said to support the argument that care is biased against older men.

The fact that some lifestyles are more associated with longevity than others begs the obvious question – which is the best for a long and productive life? The search for the answer to this question has led some to make extravagant claims for remote rural populations in various parts of the world. The best known of these is a group of people in Georgia (in the former USSR) where a disproportionate number of centenarians were found. Various explanations were offered (many involving health foods and abstinence), but the prosaic truth is that there were no centenarians. The older adults, to avoid conscription into the Soviet Army, had used their parents' birth certificates, thereby adding 20 or 30 years to their real ages. This draft dodging had backfired because, in later years, the Soviet authorities had seized upon the 'well-preserved' older people and used them as a tourist attraction and propaganda vehicle. Detailed medical examinations debunked the story. Other cases of long-lived communities in Pakistan and Ecuador are explained by the simpler reason that high local levels of illiteracy coupled with poor population records had led to calculations of ages which were, to say the least, fraught with errors (see Schaie and Willis, 1991a). Although some commentators still rather touchingly believe that these older people are indeed very old, the majority of evidence points to there being no 'magical' society in which people live significantly longer then elsewhere.

Indeed, for anyone looking for a lifestyle which offers the elixir of life, the answer seems to lie in the things most people hate. Namely, taking more exercise and eating and drinking less. The oft-cited **Harvard Alumni Study** found that in their sample of ex-students from Harvard University, exercise was strongly equated with longevity. However, the relationship is not consistent across all conditions. For example, regular exercise burning up between 1000 and 2000 kilojoules (kJ) per week significantly reduced the risk of stroke. There was a further reduction in risk if the exercise rate was between 2000 and 3000 kJ burnt per week. However, exercise beyond this point did not seem to confer any additional reduction in risk (Lee and Paffenbarger, 1998). In contrast, Sesso, Paffenbarger and Lee (2000) reported that the risk of getting coronary heart disease decreased with more vigorous exercise (i.e. burning 4000 kJ per week conferred on average more protection than burning 2000 kJ per week in exercise). Generally, regular exercise throughout the week seems best for longevity, but the Harvard Alumni researchers also found that 'weekend warrior' behaviour (in which an individual crams their exercise into one or two brief, rather intense periods of exercise) can also be beneficial, provided there are no underlying risk factors (Lee et al., 2004). Overall, the findings of the Harvard Alumni Study 'provide some support for current recommenda-tions that emphasize moderate intensity activity; they also clearly indicate a benefit of vigorous activity' (Lee and Paffenbarger, 2000, p.293). Almost all studies that have looked for it similarly find a strong association between exercise and health and, although there may be some dispute over what constitutes the right level of exercise (see Lee and Paffenbarger, 2000), there is little doubt that exercise is a good thing.

However, in our eulogy to the life-giving properties of exercise there is a danger in overlooking confounding factors. For example, someone with an underlying fatal condition may be predisposed not to exercise even though medical tests can find no sign of a disease waiting to strike. Similarly, those who have the leisure time to engage in exercise are also likely to be financially better off, and so forth. These counter-arguments do not create a couch potato's charter to carry on doing nothing (though anyone starting serious exercise after a long period of sloth should consult a qualified person before beginning), but they do indicate that exercise may not be *quite* as beneficial as it may first appear.

Not surprisingly, smoking (of any amount) and heavy drinking can reduce life expectancy by a decade of more. For example, excessive alcohol consumption is associated with raised blood pressure and other life-threatening conditions (e.g. Huntgeburth, Ten Freyhaus and Rosenkranz, 2005), and the strong link between smoking and numerous fatal illnesses such as lung cancer and heart disease is very well documented. However, the evidence on eating is more equivocal. Although obesity is known to reduce life expectancy (e.g. Olshansky *et al.*, 2005), discussions of what should be eaten and how much of it are open to debate. For example, it has been known since the 1930s that deliberately restricting calorific intake significantly increases the lifespan of many animal species (e.g. Masoro, 1988, 1992). However, this statement must be qualified. First, a restricted diet is only effective after a certain age – if begun too early, then ageing will be accelerated, not retarded (Aihie Sayer and Cooper, 1997; Gage and O'Connor, 1994); and second, the most reliable results are from studies of rodents and fruit flies: evidence on humans is more circumspect. Some variations of diet have also been suggested as 'life prolonging'. Recently, an increased consumption of nuts has been proposed as a prophylactic against ischemic heart disease (Sabate, 1999). Again, vegetarians live slightly but significantly longer than their omnivorous neighbours, probably because they are less prone to some common forms of illness, notably heart disease and some forms of cancer (see Dwyer, 1988). However, it is probably not a complete absence of meat which accounts for this. Similar results can be claimed for an omnivorous diet in which the proportion of meat is (by most western standards) drastically lowered, though not completely removed (see Dwyer, 1988; Nestle, 1999).

For those who reject the idea of exercise and a limited-calorie diet of lettuce leaves and tofu, and hope instead that medical science will provide anti-ageing treatments, there may be a long wait. Ageing involves changes in multiple biochemical processes, and treating one without the others is unlikely to be particularly beneficial (an analogy might be replacing the window frames of an old house whilst the unusable floor boards, wiring and utility supplies are left untouched). Thus, even if there is a breakthrough tomorrow in one area of anti-ageing research, researchers are still likely to have to wait for other areas to catch up before an effective treatment can be created (see Rose, 1999, for an excellent review of the issues involved). And if a 'cure' for ageing is found, this may create more problems than it solves, not least of which is that if everyone can avoid ageing, overpopulation to an unprecedented degree seems inevitable. In which case, anti-ageing treatments will be either rationed or banned, both of which in turn create the possibility of serious social unrest (see Chapter 8).

However, it is worth noting that environmental and lifestyle factors alone are probably not a complete explanation. In spite of some of the claims which gain wide circulation in the media, many of the strategies for prolonging life are largely speculative and based on extrapolations from laboratory studies rather than real-life observation (see

Bernarducci and Owens, 1996). Furthermore, other aspects of lifestyle may affect matters. For example, Giles *et al.* (2005) followed a group of 1500 older adults for ten years and found that those who at the start of the study reported having five or more friends were a quarter less likely to die over the period of the study than those who did not. Thus, considering factors in isolation can be an unwise policy. Potentially someone with a worse medical history may survive an apparently healthier person, perhaps because their social life ensures they have less stress. Again, findings on differing life expectancies illustrate trends across whole groups – they do not automatically dictate the fates of individuals within those groups. Not everyone who leads a healthy lifestyle will reach older age; not everyone who lives in a deprived environment will die young. The **Winston Churchill argument** can be raised here. Namely, that some individuals live long lives in spite of seemingly doing everything that modern medical advice would say is wrong. Churchill was overweight for most of his life, smoked, drank too much, had a history of cardiovascular illness and had what could be reasonably described as a stressful job in stressful conditions. Yet he survived into his nineties (compare and contrast this with Adolf Hitler, a vegetarian teetotal non-smoker). Most people can think of similar examples (e.g. in the author's case, his two grandmothers who single-handedly could keep the sweet shops of Barrow-in-Furness in business), but this is not a reason personally to adopt such a lifestyle since, first, it is possible that such people would live even longer by adopting a healthier lifestyle, and, second, for the majority, an 'unhealthy' lifestyle will almost certainly reduce their life expectancy.

In addition to environmental factors, life expectancy is to some extent determined by genetic inheritance. The most obvious manifestation of this is that longer-lived individuals tend to produce longer-lived offspring (Murphy, 1978). Again, there is evidence from studies of identical twins (who are genetically identical) that there is a strong genetic influence on both mortality and susceptibility to many diseases (Iachine *et al.*, 1998; see also Korpelainen, 1999). It is clear how genetic inheritance might influence life expectancy through relatively 'obvious' factors such as a congenitally weak heart, but other effects may also be less apparent, such as the finding that height may influence longevity (generally, shorter people have longer lives than tall people, possibly because of lower blood pressure; Samaras and Elrick, 1999). However, just as with the evidence on environmental effects, some caution must be sounded. Not least is that teasing apart the effects of environment and genetics in determining what causes increases in longevity is notoriously difficult (see Yashin *et al.*, 1999 for a review).

Thus, there is evidence that differences in ageing are attributable to both genetic and environmental causes. Readers new to the area may by now have a feeling of imminent doom, since it appears that anything pleasurable is bound to lower life expectancy, whilst anyone with short-lived relatives may feel that no matter what they do, the Grim Reaper is going to call before too long. However, it is worth stressing once again that such matters are relative. A good lifestyle generally only extends time spent in old age, and even then only by a small proportion of overall lifespan relative to an average person – there are no immortal non-smoking teetotal fitness-fanatic vegetarians.

Definitions of ageing

There is a surprising range of methods for describing the age of a person, some less obvious than others. For example, ageing can be described in terms of the processes which have affected a person as he or she has developed. These can be divided into relatively distant events (e.g. lacking mobility because of childhood polio) known as **distal ageing effects**, and those more recent (e.g. lacking mobility because of a broken leg) known as **proximal ageing effects**. Again, ageing can be defined in terms of the probability of acquiring a particular characteristic of later life. **Universal ageing** features are those which all older people share to some extent (e.g. wrinkled skin), whilst **probabilistic ageing** features are likely but not universal (e.g. arthritis). These terms may be contrasted with the similar concepts of **primary ageing** (age changes to the body) and **secondary ageing** (changes which occur with greater frequency, but are not a necessary accompaniment). Some commentators add a third term – **tertiary ageing** – to refer to the rapid and marked physical deterioration immediately prior to death.

Another method of measuring ageing is to create a division between later and earlier adult life. However, the change from one to another is gradual and continuous, so any measure must be to some extent arbitrary. This is a manifestation of a familiar problem in science – how does one divide a continuum into subgroups? For example, if we consider the colour spectrum, it is obvious that there are bands of red and orange, but that these merge into each other. At what point in this red–orange boundary do we say that the colour has changed from orange to red? Similarly, at what point does someone move from being 'middle aged' to 'elderly'? Despite the popular phrase, people do not become old overnight. Over several years one may observe a person's physical and mental characteristics change, but it would be hard to pinpoint one precise moment in this process when a threshold was unambiguously crossed. This is one reason why the commonly used measure of **chronological age** is so unsatisfactory. Chronological age is simply the measure of how old a person is. However, it is essentially an arbitrary measure. How often the Earth has circled the sun since a person was born tells us nothing about him or her unless this passage of time is correlated with other, more relevant changes. In fact, age alone can in some circumstances be a poor indicator. For example, it correlates poorly with physical changes. One can think of 70-year-olds who look like stereotypical older people (grey hair, wrinkled skin, etc.), but one can also recall 'well-preserved' individuals who lack these features (**agerasia**) and younger adults who look 'prematurely old'. An important aside is that the latter should be distinguished from (extremely rare) disorders in which ageing is grossly accelerated. These include **progeria** (or **Hutchinson-Gilford syndrome**), in which the patient begins to age rapidly in early childhood and typically dies in their early teens, and **Werner's syndrome**, which develops in the teens, with patients typically dying in their forties). In both diseases, patients develop physical characteristics and symptoms which resemble extreme ageing, but whether these are caused by genuinely accelerated ageing or whether they simply coincidentally resemble ageing is open to debate (see Bergeman, 1997; Hayflick, 1994). However, even excepting these unusual cases, chronological age by itself is a far from infallible indicator.

A common response amongst some researchers to the arbitrary nature of chronological age has been to emphasise **functional age**. Definitions of this term vary widely, but essentially it means the average age at which a particular level of skill is found. The concept has been in use for over a century in child psychology, where it is a useful and instantly comprehensible guide to a child's development (e.g. if a child is 12 but has a mental age of eight, then he or she clearly has intellectual problems). However, the term sits less comfortably in dealing with older adults. For example, it is known that some older adults' intellectual skills decline to a level on a par with children (see Chapter 2). In principle, we could label these older people as having the functional age of a child. In one sense this is accurate, but it brings with it an unwelcome set of associations about 'second childhood' and similar that question whether the use of functional age in these circumstances is appropriate. In addition, it seems contradictory to create a new method of classification intended to supplant chronological age and then use chronological age as a key part of the definition (i.e. functional age is basically the mean chronological age at which a skill is shown at a particular level). Arguably there is more mileage in defining performance in terms of a scale of measurement independent of age considerations (e.g. longest list of numbers that can be remembered, highest frequency note that can be heard), but this in effect is doing nothing more than advocating the use of test scores to grade people. A refinement of this is to argue that anyone passing a set threshold of ability can be held to be functional in that particular activity (e.g. remembering lists greater than a particular length, hearing sounds higher than a particular frequency), but ultimately this is simply paraphrasing measures of everyday competence used all the time by clinicians and nurses. The concept does not necessarily extend well into measuring everyday activities outside a clinical setting, where, apart from all other considerations of whether a simple accurate test can be devised, there is the issue of compensatory strategies (see Chapter 2) which may negate the effects of a decline in some skills.

Another commonly used measure is **social age**. This refers to societal expectations of how people should behave at particular chronological ages. In some contemporary societies and in many more historical ones, a long life is/was considered to be the reward for pious behaviour (Minois, 1989; Thane, 2000). Two of the commonest beliefs arising from this have been classified as the **antediluvian ageing myth** and the **hyperborean ageing myth** – the beliefs that in ancient times or in a far distant land, respectively, there was/is a race of virtuous people with incredibly long lifespans. Modern industrialised societies take a different view. Later life is seen not as a time of reward but of enforced relaxation. Thus, western culture expects the over-sixties to behave in an essentially sedate fashion and, not surprisingly, the onset of later life is often indicated by retirement from full-time employment. The chronological age at which 'old age' begins is thus often judged to be between 60 and 65 (though some societies have ages ranging from 50 to 70 – see Decker, 1980 – and this figure may change as mandatory retirement ages are increased). Most **gerontologists** (people who study ageing) tend similarly to select a figure of 60 or 65 to denote the age of onset or **threshold age** (e.g. Bromley, 1988; Decker, 1980; Kermis, 1983; Rebok, 1987; Ward, 1984). This is not just to fit in with western stereotypes, but also because at around the threshold age various psychological and physical changes tend to manifest themselves, as shall be seen. In this book, the threshold age will be defined loosely as being between 60 and 65. This rule of thumb is intentionally vague, to reiterate the caveats made earlier:

1. there is no single point at which a person becomes 'old'; and

2. chronological age is in any case an arbitrary and not very accurate measure, so the use of a single figure for the threshold would give it a speciously objective status.

Some commentators further divide older adults into **young elderly** people and **old elderly** people (or 'young old' and 'old old'). The precise ages involved in this categorisation can vary between writers, however. Some feel that 'young elderly' describes anyone between 60 and 75, and 'old elderly' anyone older than this, but others take different spans under the same terms (e.g. 60 to 80, or 65 to 80 or 65 to 75 for the young elderly group). Caution in reading reports using these terms is thus advised. A variant on this theme by Burnside, Ebersole and Monea (1979) proposed categories of 'young old' (60–69), 'middle-aged old' (70–79), 'old old' (80–89), and 'very old old' (90+). This seems simply to introduce new and unnecessary synonyms for 'sixties', 'seventies', 'eighties' and 'nineties'. Another method divides the over-65s into the **third age** and the **fourth age**. The 'third age' refers to active and independent lifestyle in later life, and the 'fourth age' to a (final) period of dependence on others. The terms have met with some favour, since they do not have the pejorative overtones which some people perceive in words such as 'old' or 'elderly'. However, this is a moot point, since terms such as 'third age' in effect classify people in terms of how much help they need from others. It should also be noted that the terms used by gerontologists are not necessarily the ones employed (and by implication, liked) by older people. Midwinter's (1991) survey found that the majority (72%) of older people preferred the terms 'senior citizen' or 'retired', with only 5 per cent preferring 'elderly' and 4 per cent 'older people' (these were used by 61% of younger people). Stuart-Hamilton (1998) found a similar pattern (though with far less pronounced age-group differences). An opinion poll conducted by the BBC and published late November 2004 (text copy available at the time of writing from www.bbc.co.uk/ageing) found that in general, the older the person asked, the later in life they felt the term 'old' applied. Thus, whilst 47 per cent of 18–24-year-olds interviewed thought that 'old' equated to someone older than 64, only 9 per cent of respondents aged over 65 felt the same way (51% of this group felt that 'old' only applied to those aged 75 or over). There are sound reasons why researchers (many of whom are considerably younger than 65) use terms such as 'elderly' or 'old'; they have an objectivity which is lacking in terms such as 'retired' (which can in any case be misleading, since people currently often retire before their sixties). However, there are equally good reasons why people may prefer different terms, and sensitivity to this is advised.

Regardless of how they are labelled, signs of ageing exist, and can be both physical and mental. These are measured by **biological age** and **psychological age** respectively. Since the rest of this book is primarily about psychological ageing, no further mention will be made of biological ageing here. However, it cannot be passed over without some consideration, since many bodily changes (particularly those in the sensory and nervous systems) directly impinge on the workings of the ageing brain.

Biological ageing

The term 'biological age' refers to the body's state of physical development/ degeneration. Generally, the term is used loosely to describe the overall state of a person's body. However, several more specific exemplars are sometimes used. These include **anatomical age** (the relatively gross state of bone structure, body build, etc.); **carpal age** (the state of the wrist (carpal) bones); and **physiological age** (the state of physiological processes, such as metabolic rate). In the instances cited below, the general term is usually implied.

Ageing is the final stage of development which every healthy and accident-free individual experiences. However, one must be careful not to overextend the word 'development' to imply that ageing necessarily involves an improvement. Indeed, one commentator emphasises this point by classifying later life as **post-developmental**: 'all the latent capacities for development have been actualized, leaving only late-acting potentialities for harm' (Bromley, 1988; p.30).

The body's cells are not immortal – over a period of about seven years most of them die and are replaced by new cells or are lost. Thus, a large part of the body at any one time is in effect new – it is not only newborn babies who are composed of freshly created cells. However, over time the cell replacement process becomes less efficient – some replacement cells are lost because the copying fails whilst those that are replaced may be represented by inferior copies. A loose analogy is that the process is like photocopying a complex diagram, throwing away the original, then photocopying the copy, then copying the copy, and so forth. The copies will become weaker and less distinct simulations of the original until eventually they become useless and have to be thrown away with no further copying being possible. The general consensus is that the central nervous system is an exception to this: its cells are not replaced when they die, though at least under laboratory conditions, some central nervous system neurons may be able to regenerate (see Brewer, 1999).

The general cycle of cell death and regeneration has led some commentators to argue for a **programmed theory of ageing** (i.e. that cell death is in effect programmed or intended to happen). The best evidence for this is the evidence of a limit to the number of times a cell can be replaced. The **Hayflick phenomenon** (named after its discoverer: see Hayflick, 1985, 1994, 1997) states that living cells taken from the body and raised *in vitro* will only reduplicate themselves a limited number of times before dying (the **Hayflick limit**), and the older the body from which the cells are taken, the fewer the duplications before death occurs. Why this happens is open to debate. One plausible explanation currently in great favour concerns the **telomere**, a sequence of DNA located at the end of chromosomes (for readers interested in making a human telomere for themselves, it is composed of a pattern of TTAGGG repeated several thousand times). The analogy frequently made is that if the chromosome is a shoelace, the telomere is the plastic bit at the end that prevents the shoelace fraying. The analogy is an appropriate one, because it is felt that telomeres are a key component in maintaining the structural integrity of chromosomes (see Cong, Wright and Shay, 2002). The currently favoured theory (though aspects of it are still disputed) is that each time a cell duplicates, the telomere shortens. When the telomere can shorten no more, the cell can no longer duplicate, and it dies. This seems to concur with the available evidence (see Olovnikov, 1996), and is further supported by the finding that reactivating telomeres extends cell life considerably beyond its natural Hayflick limit (see Johnson, Marciniak and Guarente, 1998). In addition, evidence is accruing that shortened telomeres are associated with a variety of harmful ageing changes to the body, such as to the cardiovascular system (e.g. Serrano and Andres, 2004). However, although much of the research on telomeres implies that it is the telomere driving the change, the reverse may also apply. For example, Gardner *et al.* (2005) demonstrated that telomere shortening was related to rising insulin resistance and an increase in the body mass index. Thus, telomeres shorten more rapidly in those who grow fat, and it seems intuitively plausible (though not logically certain) that it is weight gain that leads to telomere shortening, not the reverse.

As a postscript to this, it would at first seem plausible that if a method could be found to lengthen the telomeres, then this should extend cell life expectancy. It is known that some specific types of cells in the body (principally, sperm and egg cells) are practically 'immortal' and can replicate virtually infinitely without any sign of degradation. These cells use **telomerase**, an enzyme that in effect ensures that telomere length is maintained when the cell is copied. Telomerase, however, is not used in this way by other, 'normal' cells, which are thus doomed to die when they reach their Hayflick limit. Using telomerase as a drug to stave off cell loss would thus at first sight seem an ideal anti-ageing treatment, but, unfortunately, telomerase is also a key component in the production of many types of cancer. In essence, as the body ages, DNA sequences in cells become damaged, either through repeated errors in copying as cells die and are replaced (this is why many types of cancer increase in likelihood in later life) or through physical attack from, for example, smoking or radiation. In most cases these damaged cells die by reaching the Hayflick limit before these sequences become sufficiently aberrant to begin to cause cancerous growths, but in some instances, the damaged cells are accidentally 'repaired' by telomerase, causing the cells to be able to reproduce themselves without being halted by the Hayflick limit. Thus, simply supplying cells with telomerase may have an anti-ageing effect, but it may also create cancerous growths. This may also explain why cell life usually has a Hayflick limit and avoids use of telomerase – possibly the alternative is an unacceptably high risk of cancer.

However, it seems unlikely that the telomere length alone is responsible for the ageing of cells. For example, it has been found that in Leach's storm petrel, telomere length actually increases with age (Hausmann *et al.*, 2003). This may reflect a cunning evolutionary ploy to extend life expectancy and thus further prove the telomere case, but it may also indicate that the current view of 'long telomeres = more life left' may be overly simplistic. In any case, there are many other plausible mechanisms that could cause ageing changes at the cellular level, such as abnormal accumulation of DNA within the nucleolus (a structure within the nucleus of the cell: see Johnson *et al.*, 1998). Another theory – the **somatic mutation theory of ageing** – argues that the problem is compounded because replacement cells are not precise replicas but contain errors (a permutation of this – the **error catastrophe theory** – pins the blame on faulty protein replication). The theory predicts that the older the animal, the greater the damaged DNA in its cells, and for some (though not all) types of cell this appears to be the case (Bohr and Anson, 1995). This faulty replication may be exacerbated by factors such as environmental pollutants and poor diet (e.g. cells from rats on a restricted calorie diet repair themselves more effectively following damage – Weraarchakul *et al.*, 1989). In contrast, the **autoimmune theory of ageing** argues that ageing may be attributable to faults in the body's immune system. First, by becoming less able to combat infection and second, by incorrectly identifying the body's own cells as infectious agents, and attacking them. Yet another argument (the **cellular garbage theory**) is that ageing occurs because of toxins produced as by-products of normal cellular activity. These include a pigment called 'lipofuscin' and a set of chemicals called **free radicals**. Evidence for each of the above theories (and many others) is mixed: each may play some role, but each alone is unlikely to account for a notable proportion of the ageing process (see Bergeman, 1997; Hayflick, 1994; Sanadi, 1977). On the present evidence, it would seem that ageing at the cellular level is probably the accumulation of several processes whose effects may be greater as a sum than as parts.

Whatever the causes of bodily changes, there is no doubt that they do occur. One notable feature is cell loss. It is important to remember that this does not begin in later life, but in early adulthood, with most bodily systems showing a decline of 0.8–1 per cent per annum after the age of 30 (Hayflick, 1977). The course of this loss is very slow and, as most bodily systems have over-capacity built into them, it is only in about the sixth decade of life that the change is first apparent to the casual observer. Botwinick (1977) notes that the decline is greater in complex than in simple functions. This is probably because the simpler functions have each only declined slightly, but, when used together in a more complex action, the total effect becomes multiplicative. As shall be seen, this disproportionate loss of complex over simple functions manifests itself repeatedly in both the ageing body and the ageing mind.

Another consideration is that many changes observed in older people may be due to disease rather than ageing *per se*. It is practically impossible to go through life without succumbing to at least some illnesses, and it is thus difficult to exclude the possibility that ageing changes are at least in part due to the cumulative effects of successive infections. The effect of even minor decrements in health is demonstrated by the 'forty-seven healthy old men' study (Birren *et al.*, 1963). The researchers studied 27 completely healthy older men and 20 men who appeared healthy, but on extremely rigorous examination proved to have very slight evidence of potentially serious illnesses. This latter group showed a decline on a range of measures of mental functioning and physical measures such as brain wave rhythms. Birren *et al.* and subsequent commentators (e.g. Botwinick, 1977; Kermis, 1983) have argued that this shows that the decline was because of disease rather than ageing or the intrinsic health of the people studied, and other studies have recorded similar findings. However, the argument can be pushed further and made circular – are some older people healthy because they have never contracted a disease, or have they never contracted a disease because they are healthy? If a weaker form of the argument is taken – namely, that the rate of ageing may be affected by infection – then the case for the role of illness is far more plausible.

Evolution and ageing

The evidence presented so far implies that ageing is inevitable: a combined toll of genetics, faulty cell replication, 'self-poisoning' and illness may all make physical degradation unavoidable. However, is this planned? The **programmed senescence** theory argues that ageing is caused by evolutionary forces, and is in essence designed to happen (readers who are Creationists are advised to skip this section). The evidence for this argument is at first sight plausible. Perhaps the best-known version of this theory is that bodies have an inbuilt programme to decay and die in order to make way for younger members of the species, and thus prevent the problem of overcrowding. Other versions include the concept that individuals grow weaker so that they become easier targets for predators, thereby preventing younger species members (still capable of breeding) from being chosen as targets. Such arguments are still accepted uncritically by a few commentators, but they are undermined by one simple fact: very few animals in their natural habitat reach old age. Accordingly, because older animals are so rare 'in the wild', it is unlikely that evolutionary pressure has created a method of 'self-culling' a species – predators, disease and accident do a satisfactory job in themselves (see Hayflick, 1998; Kirkwood, 1988; Medawar, 1952).

A more plausible argument is the **mutation accumulation theory** (Medawar, 1952) which argues that ageing effects happen because they are not selected against by evolutionary forces. Let us suppose that there is a genetic predisposition to die if exposed to sunlight and this manifests itself at birth. It is highly unlikely that anyone born with such a gene would survive into adolescence and breed. Thus, such a gene would not survive and thus would not be handed down the generations. However, suppose the 'killer sunlight' gene only took effect when a person was in their sixties? For the overwhelming majority of human existence, the chances are extremely high that most people would be dead before they reached 60, so the gene first, would rarely appear, and second, if it did, would have very little effect on survival rates. Therefore, genetic mutations that only take effect in later life can accumulate without any strong evolutionary pressure stopping them.

The **antagonistic pleiotropy theory** (Williams, 1957) bears some similarities with the mutation accumulation theory in that it too argues that harmful later life changes have been created by evolutionary pressure because too few members of a species live long enough to experience them. The antagonistic pleiotropy theory argues that some genes can confer an advantage in early life and a disadvantage in later life. Thus, suppose that in younger life there was a gene creating an abundance of testosterone and an easy capacity to gain weight. This would be advantageous in a male trying to establish dominance through aggression and physical strength. But in later life, such attributes would greatly increase the risk of cardiovascular problems and might lead to an unavoidable death. Until very recent times, the downside of the deal would not have been evident. As proof of the antagonistic pleiotropy theory, there are a lot of experiments on fruit flies. If an advantage in early life is met by a disadvantage in later life, then manipulating a genetically controlled aspect of early life should affect later life. In one such study, it was found that creating a disadvantage in early life (breeding fruit flies that took longer to reach sexual maturity) was met with an advantage in later life – namely, increased life expectancy (Rose, 1984).

A further permutation of these arguments is the **disposable soma theory of ageing** (Kirkwood, 1988). Modern evolutionary theory argues that an organism is driven to reproduce as much as possible, and this takes precedence over the organism's personal survival. What matters is that the genes the organism carries survive (and which body they are in is of secondary importance). Thus, according to this theory, it would be better for a man to die at 20, having sired 30 children, than to die childless at 100 (see Dawkins, 1976). The disposable soma theory takes this argument and adapts it as follows. Body cells die and have to be replaced constantly. If they are not replaced, then the body parts concerned decline in number and efficiency. However, it is not possible to replace all cells equally effectively. The disposable soma theory argues that the best evolutionary strategy is to maintain the reproductive organs in top condition at the expense of the somatic (non-reproductive) body parts. Accordingly, the greater the energy invested in reproduction, the greater the bodily decay. Taken to extremes, this theory sounds like a Victorian homily, but at a subtler level the argument is persuasive, and Kirkwood (1988) provides strong supporting proof, to which the reader is referred.

The three theories outlined above provide three explanations of ageing based on evolutionary theory. Although distinct, their focus on the evolution and their shared assumption that old age would have been rarely seen before the advent of the developed world gives them a kinship. Arguably all three could be correct in different scenarios. If one accepts the theories, then it follows that later life is not 'planned' by natural selection to the extent it is earlier in the lifespan. In other words, when we consider an older person, it is difficult to argue that a particular change in behaviour or bodily function is 'designed' to happen. Wrinkled skin, more brittle bones, lowered memory span or lowered response speeds may never have been deliberately planned – they have arisen because there was no evolutionary pressure to prevent them (mutation accumulation theory), because they are the reverse side of processes that were advantageous in earlier life (antagonistic pleiotropy theory) or because investment in earlier life was centred on reproduction (disposable soma theory). Most individuals in 'natural' surroundings are dead before these characteristics can ever manifest themselves (see Zwaan, 1999). It is both the curse and the privilege of modern life to see evolution cheated in this way. Hayflick (1994) makes the useful analogy of the life course being, in evolutionary terms, like a satellite sent on a mission to survey a distant planet. Once a satellite has done its mission and sent back pictures of its target, it carries on into space, continuing to send back signals until eventually accident or simple decay terminate its activities. In a similar way, individuals, once they have accomplished their target of producing viable offspring, continue to live until accident or illness kills them. However, the life of the satellite after sending back the photos of the target, or of the individual after breeding, is coincidental. Enough 'over-engineering' has to be built into the system to ensure that the job can be accomplished with something to spare. We interpret this extra life afforded by the over-engineering as a 'natural' part of the lifespan, but in fact in evolutionary terms it is an accidental gift, not a right. However, in another sense the argument that old age 'defeats' evolution is inaccurate – what is being shown in effect is what evolutionary pressure thinks of old age. Namely, it is a time when in evolutionary terms the usefulness to species survival is at an all-time low, and thus it can act as a repository for all types of decay that will strike those who have 'failed' to die having successfully reproduced their genes.

The ageing body

The general picture of changes to the ageing body is not an attractive one. For example, at the level of tissue, the skin and muscles become less elastic; at the cellular level, there is a loss in the efficiency of the mitochondria (which generate energy within the cell); and at a molecular level, the somatic mutation theory of ageing and the research on telomeres have already been mentioned. Not surprisingly, these changes have a deleterious effect upon the functioning of bodily systems. For example, the urinary system becomes slower and less efficient at excreting toxins and other waste products. The gastrointestinal system is less efficient at extracting nutrients. There is a decline in muscle mass and the strength of the muscle which remains. The respiratory system can take in less oxygen. The cardiovascular system receives a double blow – the heart decreases in strength while simultaneously a hardening and shrinking of the arteries makes pumping blood around the body more energy-consuming. The result is that the average 75-year-old person's cardiac output is approximately 70 per cent of the average 30-year-old's (Aiken, 1989; Kart, 1981; Kermis, 1983).

These changes have a disadvantageous effect on the functioning of the brain and hence on psychological performance. For example, a decline in the efficiency of the respiratory and cardiovascular systems will restrict oxygen supply and thus the energy available for the brain to function. Birren, Woods and Williams (1980) suggest that the slowing of reaction times, even in apparently healthy older people, may be due to a restriction in blood supply. Cardiovascular illness, in addition to normal senescent decline, will also have a detrimental effect on brain functions (Kermis, 1983). The most notable example of this is the **stroke**, where blood supply to a section of the brain is interrupted, causing death of the affected brain tissue. At a less severe level, some older people may have an oxygen supply so constricted that they fall asleep after meals, because the energy required by the digestive processes deprives the brain of sufficient oxygen to remain conscious. Changes in other systems may have subtler effects. For example, a decline in the urinary system may mean a high level of toxins accumulating in the body, in turn affecting the efficiency of neural functioning. If an older person is receiving drug therapy, then failure to excrete the drug from the system with sufficient speed may lead to overdosing problems, including **delirium** (see Chapter 6). A decline in the gastro-intestinal system can have similar far-reaching consequences. If the decline has the effect of lowering an older person's interest in food, then malnutrition can result. This is especially serious from a psychological viewpoint if the person develops a deficiency of vitamin B12, since this can trigger dementia-like symptoms.

Another effect of ageing bodily processes is that it can cause a person to re-evaluate their state of being. This is not necessarily serious. Being aware that bones are becoming more brittle and muscles less strong may create a reluctant but pragmatic sense of caution. However, in others, these physical signs can lead to depression (Raskin, 1979). Weg (1983) argues that the majority of older people still have ample *capacity* to deal with the demands of everyday life. However, whether they *do* is another matter.

The ageing sensory systems

The senses are the brain's means of contact with the surrounding environment and, accordingly, any decline in them directly impinges on the workings of the mind. Age-related declines in perception deprive the brain of a full experience of the world, but it would be unrealistic to assume that such a loss begins in later life. Like many aspects of age-related decline, the changes often start in early adulthood, and it is important to bear this in mind when reading the sections below.

Vision

It is a frequent complaint of older people that their sight 'isn't what it used to be'. This is usually true: aside from relatively simple problems of long- and short-sightedness, about a third of people aged over 65 have a disease affecting vision (Quillan, 1999). A common problem is the decline in **accommodation** (the ability to focus at different distances), leading to **presbyopia** ('old sight' – 'presby-' indicates 'old'), characterised by long-sightedness. This is probably due to the ageing lens losing some of its elasticity and hence focusing power. The most serious visual disability most people suffer is a loss of **acuity** (variously defined as 'ability to see objects clearly at a distance' or 'ability to focus on detail'). Bromley (1988) estimates that about 75 per cent of older adults need spectacles, and many will not have full vision even with this aid. Corso (1981), in his excellent review of the literature, observes a marked decline in acuity with age, though he notes that the problem can be at least partially alleviated if visual displays have a high contrast in luminance (e.g. black on white rather than black on grey). Indeed, at such levels, older people's acuity (when wearing glasses) may be at or near more youthful norms (Haegerstrom-Portnoy, Schneck and Brabyn, 1999). But for lower levels of contrast, older people's sight may be much worse. This is borne out by studies of **contrast sensitivity function (CSF)**. Experimental participants are shown patterns of alternating light and dark parallel lines. The thickness of the lines can be varied, as can their luminance. Obviously, broader lines which vary strongly in luminance are the easiest to see. By reducing the thickness and/or contrast in luminance, it is possible to make the pattern 'disappear': the observer sees a homogeneous grey because he or she can no longer distinguish between the lines and they blur into one. The CSF is a formula which expresses the smallest difference in luminance for a given thickness of line that a person can still see as a pattern rather than as a grey splodge. The less the difference in luminance, the more sensitive the person's vision is. Sekuler, Owsley and Hutman (1982) found that the CSF declines in later life (furthermore, worsening CSF may be indicative of ophthalmic disease – see Woods, Treagear and Mitchell, 1998). For relatively broad patterns (measured in cycles/degree, 0.5 and 1 c/deg), the contrast in brightness had to be significantly greater before older people could see the pattern. A further complicating factor is that for some line thicknesses, younger participants' performance can be improved if the pattern is moving. However, no such advantage is conferred on older people by this procedure (Sekuler, Hutman and Owsley, 1980). More recent research suggests that these problems may be due at least in part to the neural system rather than receptors in the eye itself (see Pardhan *et al.*, 1996).

Another example of poor CSF in older adults is in recognising and matching pictures of faces when the contrast in luminance has been reduced. Again, acuity loss is appreciably worse when viewing a moving rather than stationary display (Fozard *et al.*, 1979). Such findings bode ill for the everyday vision of older people. Sekuler and Owsley (1982) comment that most studies of acuity are conducted in optimal lighting conditions. However in real life many items are dimly lit, visual displays rarely provide a strong contrast in luminance and, as has been seen, older people are especially disadvantaged in these conditions. Thus, standard measures of acuity may underestimate the degree of disability. In everyday conditions, on average a person in their sixties requires three times the brightness that a person in their twenties does to read everyday printed materials (Beers and Berkow, 2000). Furthermore, ability to detect low contrast patterns appears to be a key aspect of sight in later life. Schneck *et al.* (2004) followed a group of older participants over a four year period. They found that out of a range of measures of eyesight (e.g. glare recovery, flicker sensitivity, etc.) ability to detect low contrast patterns was the only measure significantly to predict visual acuity loss circa four years later. For every doubling of the pattern size necessary to make the pattern visible to an observer, there was a greater than doubling of the chance of significant sight loss four years later.

Beyond considerations of acuity, practically all other aspects of vision worsen in later life (Haegerstrom-Portnoy *et al.*, 1999). For example, the visual threshold (the dimmest light that can be seen) *increases* with age – in other words, older people cannot see lights as dim as younger people can see (Elias, Elias and Elias, 1977; McFarland and Fisher, 1955). This is probably due to a variety of factors, including a diminution in the maximum expanse of the pupil, and poorer metabolism of receptor cells (Pitts, 1982). Similarly, the rate at which people can adjust to low level lighting conditions (dark adaptation) decreases with age (Domey, McFarland and Chadwick, 1960). The converse – ability to recover from glare – is also reduced, sometimes by several hundred per cent (Carter, 1982). This clearly has practical implications (e.g. for older people's ability to drive at night; see Scharwey, Krzizok and Herfurth, 1998, who estimate 40 per cent of older adults have impaired night driving vision). Another important consideration is the change in colour perception: older adults perceive the world as being yellower. Colours at the yellow end of the spectrum (red, orange and yellow) are identified reasonably well, but greens, blues and purples become harder to discriminate between (note that this problem does not typically manifest itself before people are in their eighties). Many commentators have argued that this is due to the lens yellowing with age, but this cannot be the full explanation. Some unfortunate individuals who have had a lens surgically removed still perceive the world as having a yellow tinge. The reason is thus probably due to changes in the nervous system (Marsh, 1980).

Older adults are also slower at processing visual stimuli, and need to see them for longer before they can be accurately identified. Also, their disadvantage grows disproportionately worse the dimmer the stimulus at which they are looking. This slowing occurs in both the perceptual stages (i.e. the retina and nerves leading to the brain) and in the sections of the brain responsible for processing visual information (Moscovitch, 1982; Walsh, 1982).

The size of the visual field also diminishes. A relatively minor problem is that older people cannot move the eyeball as far up as younger adults, with the result that older people have to move their heads to see some object above them which younger adults can see with eye movements alone. A more serious problem is a loss of peripheral vision (i.e. how 'wide' the field of view is). Onset of this decline occurs in middle age, but becomes far more pronounced in the over-75s (Jaffe, Alvarado and Juster, 1986).

The above problems can be serious and annoying for older people, but they are not necessarily crippling. In addition, many of the problems in vision arise prior to later life, in some instances as early as the mid-thirties (Corso, 1987). However, it is pertinent to remember that about 7 per cent of 65–74-year-olds and 16 per cent of people over 75 are either blind or severely visually impaired (Crandall, 1980). The principal causes of this are **cataracts** (where the lens becomes opaque); **glaucoma** (excess fluid accrues in the eyeball, and the resultant pressure permanently destroys nerve and receptor cells);

macular degeneration (where the macula or 'yellow spot' on the retina, which has the greatest acuity of vision, degenerates; see Sunness *et al.*, 1999); and **diabetic retinopathy** (damage to the blood vessels of the retina as a result of diabetes). These illnesses are not confined to later life, but they are certainly much commoner (Corso, 1981; Quillan, 1999). It should be noted that they can also be either prevented, or at least the worst effects can be tempered, if they are identified early enough. For example, the longer the time since last visiting an eye specialist, the worse a discovered case of glaucoma is likely to be (Fraser, Bunce and Wormald, 1999).

Hearing

Hearing declines gradually throughout adult life so that as young as 50 many people are impaired in at least some circumstances, such as listening to faint sounds (Bromley, 1988). For some individuals, the degree of hearing loss can be a severe disability. Stephens (1982) estimates that 1.6 per cent of 20–30-year-olds have serious hearing difficulties, compared with about 32 per cent of 70–80-year-olds. This figure rises to over 50 per cent for those aged over 80 (Herbst, 1982). Other commentators, using slightly looser criteria, posit even higher estimates for hearing difficulties, with figures of 75 per cent for people aged over 75 being not uncommon. The rate of hearing loss can be exacerbated by environmental conditions. For example, a poor diet lacking in vitamin B12 may have a significant effect (Houston *et al.*, 1999). Again, deafness amongst long-term workers in heavy industry is well documented (e.g. Sekuler and Blake, 1985). Men tend to have greater hearing loss than women. Typically, their decline is at twice the rate and begins earlier (by 30) though sensitivity to low frequencies (<1000 Hz) remains better (though there is considerable individual variation in patterns of loss: Pearson *et al.*, 1995). It has been supposed that this is because men have tended to work in noisier places than women. However, evidence indicates that even amongst people in 'quiet' occupations, there is still a gender difference (Pearson *et al.*, 1995). This suggests more innate reasons for some hearing loss, and indeed there appears to be a genetic component to at least some types of hearing loss in later life (Gates, Couropmitree and Myers, 1999). However, in general it is impossible to adduce how much of hearing loss is due to ageing *per se*, and how much to the environment, though almost certainly both play a role and there is no doubt that it is a considerable problem (see Gates and Rees, 1997; Willett, Chisolm and Lister, 2001).

Working from the outside of the ear inwards, an assortment of age-related changes may be noted. One of gerontology's more esoteric findings is that ageing ear lobes increase in size by several millimetres (Tsai, Chou and Cheng, 1958). The functional significance of this remains unclear. The elderly ear canal can get blocked with wax more easily, causing hearing loss, though this is easily treated. Changes in the middle ear are more severe and usually less easily solved. The bones of the middle ear – the hammer, anvil and stirrup (or malleus, incus and stapes) – tend to stiffen with age, through calcification or arthritis. This affects the transmission of sound, most particularly for high frequencies. The problem may be compounded by changes in the inner ear, where cell loss is usually concentrated in the receptors for high frequency sounds (Corso, 1981; Gates and Rees, 1997; Pearson *et al.*, 1995). Leading from the inner ear to the brain is the auditory nerve. This bundle of nerve fibres diminishes in size with age. The atrophy is probably due to a combination of loss of blood supply, and bone growth restricting the channel for the fibres (Crandall, 1980; Krmpotic-Nemanic, 1969).

A frequent misconception about hearing loss is that all sounds are perceived as quieter and harder to hear. Some forms of hearing disability do take this form, but not all. The commonest form of hearing loss in older people is a condition known as **presbycusis** (or *presbyacusis*). This condition can occur in several forms (see Cohn, 1999), but all have in common a proportionately greater loss in perception of high than low frequency sounds. Sometimes the problem is exacerbated by a phenomenon called **loudness recruitment**: higher pitched sounds are perceived as having louder than normal intensity, often to the point of being painful and/or distorted. Presbycusis clearly impairs a sufferer. At best the auditory world becomes muffled; at worst, it is agonisingly painful.

Causes of presbycusis are severalfold. This is a heavily researched area, and explanations are legion. The loss of high frequency detection because of a stiffening of the middle ear bones has already been mentioned. Again, a lifetime in a noisy environment tends to exert greatest damage to high frequency detectors in the inner ear (which are more damage-prone than lower frequency detectors). An ingenious theory that snoring may be a contributory factor seems to be unfounded (Hoffstein *et al.*, 1999). Research on neurological functioning within the brain indicates that presbycusis may in part be a product of age-related changes in the way some nerves function (e.g. Caspary, Milbrandt and Helfert, 1995; Oku and Hasegewa, 1997). It may also be influenced by genetic factors (Bai *et al.*, 1997).

Whatever the causes, presbycusis is a serious problem. For example, sound localisation (the ability to detect where a sound is coming from) is impaired (see Rakerd, Van der Velde and Hartmann, 1998). Again, loss of ability to hear high-pitched sounds will of course make the world sound 'muffled', and this has serious consequences. Speech sounds are a composite of high and low frequencies, but it is usually the high frequency components which are crucial in distinguishing them from each other (this particularly applies to consonants). Thus, presbycusis makes following speech (particularly conversations) very difficult.

Presbycusis is not the only common hearing problem in later life. For example, there is a worsening of pitch discrimination, sound localisation and in perceiving timing information (see Marsh, 1980; Schneider, Speranza and Pichora-Fuller, 1998; Strouse *et al.*, 1998). In addition, up to 10 per cent of older adults suffer from **tinnitus**, or what is commonly (if slightly inaccurately) known as 'ringing in the ears' (Eggermont and Roberts, 2004; Kart, Metress and Metress, 1978). This can block out other auditory signals as well as causing suffering in its own right.

A further problem with hearing in later life is that the decline appears to be another manifestation of the **age × complexity effect**. Generally, the more complex the speech signal, the more older people are disadvantaged relative to younger adults (Corso, 1981). For example, this can be the case when detecting signals played against a background of noise or competing signals compared with a silent background (e.g. Bergman *et al.*, 1976; Dubno, Dirk and Morgan, 1984; Pichora-Fuller, Schneider and Daneman, 1995). However, when signals are familiar phrases or ones expressing familiar concepts, there is no or little age difference (Hutchinson, 1989). Again, Orbelo *et al.* (2005) found that comprehension of the emotional content of speech, although impaired in older adults, is unrelated to level of hearing loss (or for that matter cognitive decline – the report's authors attribute it to an ageing-related deficit in the right hemisphere).

A complicating factor in studies of hearing loss is that the degree of impairment can only be partly explained by objective measures. Thus, older adults' subjective ratings of their impairment are often at some variance with an objective measure of hearing loss, and Corso (1987, p.45) estimates that 'audiometric data explain less than 50 per cent of the variance in hearing handicap in the elderly' (for a more recent survey of self-reported hearing problems in older adults, see Slawinski, Hartel and Kline, 1993). However, whatever the 'true' size of the problem, given that hearing is such an integral part of everyday life for most people, it is not surprising to find that a loss (even marginal) is associated with lowered feelings of well-being (Scherer and Frisina, 1998), empowerment (Ryan, 1996) and even cognitive functioning (Naramura *et al.*, 1999). It should be stressed that hearing loss only has to be relatively slight for signs of impairment to manifest themselves (e.g. Kart, 1981). Herbst (1982) observes that most societies have held a grudge against deaf people since the start of recorded time. To the Ancient Greeks, the word 'deaf' was synonymous with 'stupid', and to the early Christian deafness was a curse because, in preliterate societies, it blocked the person from holy teachings. In modern times, this bias has continued. For example, deaf charities tend to receive fewer donations than those for the blind because, Herbst argues, whilst blindness cuts one off from things, deafness cuts one off from people. This is perhaps rather too tenuous an argument, but it is not without some validity.

This alienation of deaf people is of course illogical, but an encounter with a hearing-impaired person often leads able hearers into behaving like the stereotype of the Englishman abroad, complaining that the failure in communication is solely due to the natives having the temerity not to learn English. In other words, the speaker can never be at fault. The older person with hearing problems is usually well aware of this, and is often cowed into submission and silence rather than risking anger or ridicule. This removal from social intercourse can cause a person to become depressed and still more withdrawn. This may be interpreted by outsiders as evidence of antisocial behaviour or even the onset of dementia, and the person is accordingly shunned even more. This can cause further withdrawal, and thus a vicious cycle is created. It is small wonder that hearing loss is associated with loss of self-esteem, as noted above.

However, there is a danger that the social effects of hearing loss can be over-dramatised. Whilst it is right and proper that deafness-induced isolation should be carefully monitored, there is evidence that the level of social isolation is poorly correlated with the specific level of hearing loss (see Norris and Cunningham, 1981; Weinstein and Ventry, 1982). There are similar findings on hearing aid use (see Brooks and Hallam, 1998). In other words, hearing loss may trigger negative feelings, but the level of hearing loss may be relatively unimportant. Such evidence does not obviate the need for help, of course, and a variety of remedial measures are available (see Burnside, 1976). However, as Herbst (1982) argues, one of the biggest problems is getting older people to come for help in the first instance because of the perceived stigma (plus the fact that hearing loss tends to be gradual, making the change harder to detect in oneself); many people do not seek medical attention at all until they are very hard of hearing.

Other senses

Declines in the other senses are generally of less interest to the psychologist because they do not impinge as directly on psychological functioning. Nonetheless, they must be noted.

> *Taste* The tastes humans perceive can be divided into four primary types: bitter, sour, salty and sweet. Commentators are divided on the extent to which ageing causes a de-cline in sensitivity to these. For example, Engen (1977) argues that whilst there is a gen-eral decline, sensitivity to bitter tastes increases with age. However, Schiffman *et al.* (1995) found a *loss* in sensitivity to bitter tastes, whilst Cowart, Yokomukai and Beauchamp (1994) found decreased sensitivity to some bitter-tasting substances but not to others. Weiffenbach, Banm and Berghauser (1982) found a decline in sensitivity to bitter and salty tastes, but no change in sweet and sour sensitivities (though detection of sweet and sour may decline in centenarians; see Receputo *et al.*, 1996a). To further muddy the waters, Mojet, Heidema and Christ-Hazelhof (2003) found that, although there is no age-related loss in ability to judge which concentration of a taste primary was stronger than another, the ability to grade how strong a taste was on an individual basis was impaired in older adults. However, Nordin *et al.*, (2003) found a significant worsen-ing of taste intensity discrimination for some substances.

The data on detection of complex tastes is (thankfully) more clear cut, with older people showing a marked decline in detection of many everyday food items (see Bischmann and Witte, 1996; Murphy, 1985; Ng et al., 2004; Schiffman, 1977), and in detecting a primary taste when presented in a mixture of other tastes (Stevens, 1996). However, although there may be a slight decline, sweetness detection appears to be relatively well preserved (Walter and Soliah, 1996). Furthermore, Stevens et al. (1995) note that although there is an overall age-related decline, there is considerable variability between individuals (in other words, some will show more decline than others). In addition, the connections between level of taste sensitivity and food intake and preferences are far from clear cut (see De Jong et al., 1999; Rolls, 1999). With regard to the final point, irrespective of what older people can or cannot taste, they are in some instances bad at either choosing or metabolising a healthy diet. A study by Clarke et al. (2004) found that 5 per cent of their sample of 65–74-year-olds had a vitamin B12 deficiency, and this proportion rose to 10 per cent for their sample of people aged 75 and over.

Smell Sense of smell appears to show relatively little change in very healthy older adults (e.g. Corso, 1981). However, since most older adults experience illness in one form or another, it would be more demographically representative to argue that most older adults will show at least some decline (see Doty, 1990; Finkelstein and Schiffman, 1999). However, the magnitude of this decline is debatable, and declines, though statistically significant, have often been reported as slight, even in centenarians (Receputo et al., 1996b). It is worth noting that many older adults have no awareness of a decline (Nordin, Monsch and Murphy, 1995). Research has demonstrated that there is an appreciable decline in smell in the early stages of Alzheimer's disease (e.g. Moberg et al., 1997), and this may prove to be a useful diagnostic aid. In addition, a lowered level of olfactory sensitivity predicts a lowered level of some intellectual skills (e.g. memory for verbal materials) in non-dementing adults four years later (Swan and Carmelli, 2002), though it could be argued that this may be detecting very early dementia.

Touch Older adults have higher touch thresholds (i.e. firmer stimulation of the skin is required before it is detected: see Stevens and Patterson, 1996; Thornbury and Mistretta, 1981), and similarly, sensitivity to the temperature of objects decreases. However, the changes are not necessarily clear cut. For example, the effects vary greatly in their magnitude across individuals. Again, sensitivity to vibration is different across the frequency range. At relatively high vibration speeds (250 Hz), older adults are worse at estimating the strength of the vibration. However, at a lower frequency (25 Hz) there is no significant age difference (Verillo, 1982). The touch sensors are housed in the skin and, accordingly, it is tempting to link the decline in sensitivity to the obvious thinning and wrinkling in an older person's skin. This may be a partial explanation, and there is evidence that at least part of the decline is due to a decrease in the number of touch sensors in the skin (Gescheider et al., 1994). However, Woodward (1993) argues that, when changing properties of the skin are controlled for, an age difference still remains, implying that the decline may also be due to changes in the nerves conducting information to the brain.

Pain Some researchers have reported an increase in the pain threshold of older people: in other words, they can endure more extreme stimuli without perceiving them as painful (e.g. Benedetti *et al.*, 1999; Gibson and Farrell, 2004; Harkins, Price and Martelli, 1986; Lasch, Castell and Castell, 1997). This may be due to a decline in the number of sensory receptors in later life. However, some studies have failed to find any changes in pain perception, and this discrepancy may be due to where on the body the experimenters inflict the pain (Bromley, 1988). In addition, the emotional meaning of pain may differ between ages. For example, older adults tend to be less distressed about the lessening of mobility through the pain of an illness, because they may generally have lower expectations of what they can or 'should' do at their particular age (see Williamson and Schulz, 1995). Also, a study by Yong *et al.* (2001) found that older adults were more reticent about reporting pain and less willing to label an aversive stimulus as being painful. There are also serious methodological problems with pain studies. Apart from the obvious ethical considerations which curtail the range and strength of pain inflicted, there is also the problem of creating a suitably objective measure for such a subjective sensation as pain (see Gibson and Helme, 1995; Yong *et al.*, 2001). In addition, there is evidence that the range of factors which affect older adults' perception of pain may be more varied and less easily grouped together than in younger adults (see Corran *et al.*, 1997; Manetto and McPherson, 1996).

Overview

The clear message from this brief survey of the ageing senses should be readily apparent: the information reaching the brain from the surrounding environment is constrained in its range, is less detailed and, given the general slowing of the nervous system, takes longer to arrive. This hardly bodes well for the ageing intellect (see Lindenberger and Baltes, 1994); nor indeed for the personality if an elderly person's self-image is affected (it is known that illness is linked to level of depression in older people; see Williamson and Schulz, 1992). However, it should be noted that the ageing brain is in turn not making the best use of the incoming sensory information. A notable pattern of decline in the ageing perceptual processes is that the older mind is less adept at integrating several strands of sensory information into a cohesive whole (e.g. complex versus simple tastes, complex versus simple auditory signals). As mentioned earlier in this chapter, the principal age deficits appear to occur when several simple processes must be operated in tandem.

Basic anatomy of the nervous system

It is important that the reader has some knowledge of the nervous system in order to understand the psychological and neurological changes that occur in later life (particularly in the dementias). Accordingly, this section is devoted to a basic description of neuroanatomy. As far as possible, this is presented in non-technical language. Those readers already familiar with neuroanatomy can safely skip this section.

The neuron

The basic building block of the nervous system is the **neuron** (or, less accurately, the 'nerve cell'). Neurons vary enormously in shape and size, but all have the basic function of receiving signals from other neurons or specialised sensory receptors (for touch, pain, heat, etc.), and passing signals on to other neurons or sense organs. Neurons connect with each other at junctions called **synapses**, where signals are transferred from one neuron to another. When a neuron is activated, an electrical pulse passes down its length until it reaches a synapse, where two neurons meet with only a microscopic gap separating them. The activated neuron 'spits' a chemical across the gap onto the receiving neuron, causing one of four things:

1. It was dormant, and it is activated into sending a signal.

2. It was already sending a signal, but the new input causes it to fire with greater vigour.

3. It was already active, but the new input makes it either stop firing, or fire with less vigour.

4. It was dormant, and the new input prevents other neurons exciting it into firing.

In cases 1 and 2, the effect is said to be **excitatory** and in cases 3 and 4 the effect is said to be **inhibitory**. Therefore, neurons can either spur each other on, or they can suppress activity. The chemical transmitters employed to do this (i.e. the chemicals 'spat' at synapses) are called **neurotransmitters**. On some occasions, it is convenient to classify neurons according to the type of transmitter they use. For example, there is the **cholinergic system**, which uses the transmitter **acetylcholine**. About 90 per cent of the neurons in the brain are cholinergic. The other principal use of the cholinergic system is in the control of skeletal muscle. Conversely, the **noradrinergic system** (using **noradrenaline**) is primarily employed in the control of smooth muscle. Many neurons are covered with a layer of fatty substance called **myelin**, which acts rather like the insulation around electrical wires as it stops the signal from escaping and also helps to increase the speed at which the signal is sent.

Anatomy of the nervous system

The simplest division of the nervous system is into the **central nervous system (CNS)** and the **peripheral nervous system (PNS)**. The CNS consists of the brain and the spinal cord, the PNS of the neurons connecting the CNS to the rest of the body. The nervous system consists of at least 10^{10} neurons, most of which are in the brain. The 'textbook definition' of the fundamental difference between the neurons of the CNS and the PNS is that the former cannot be replaced if they die, whilst the latter can (though as noted above, see Brewer, 1999).

PNS anatomy

The PNS can be divided into subsections, according to function. **Afferent** neurons carry information into the CNS, and are said to be 'somatic' if they carry information from the joints or skin of skeletal muscle and 'visceral' if they carry information from the **viscera** (intestines). **Efferent** neurons carry commands from the CNS to the body, and are said to be motor if they send signals to the skeletal muscle and **autonomic** if they send signals to glands, smooth muscle, cardiac muscle, etc. (i.e. bodily functions over which there is little conscious control).

CNS anatomy

The **spinal cord**'s principal function is to channel information between the PNS and the brain. However, it is capable of some simple processing. By means of a mechanism called the **reflex arc** (a simple connection between afferent and efferent neurons), it can make the body respond to some forms of stimulation. Many reflexes (such as the well-known knee-jerk reflex) are produced in this manner.

The spinal cord projects into the brain, or, more accurately, the section of the brain called the **brainstem**. Many lay persons think of the brain as being a homogeneous mass of 'grey matter', but in fact the brain is a collection of distinct though interconnecting structures. For anatomical and functional reasons, the brain is often divided into four principal divisions. The first is the brainstem. Located behind this at the base of the skull is the **cerebellum**. Located above the brainstem is the **diencephalon**, or **interbrain**. Seated above and overlapping the other three segments is the **cerebral cortex** (often simply called the 'cortex'), the wrinkled 'top' of the brain. Generally, the further a structure is away from the spinal cord, the more sophisticated its functions.

The brainstem is chiefly concerned with the maintenance of 'life support' mechanisms, such as control of blood pressure, digestion, respiration, and so forth. It also receives inputs from the senses and channels them through to other systems in the brain.

The cerebellum receives somatic input, and information from the semicircular canals (the balance sensors located in the inner ear). Given this information, it is not surprising to learn that the cerebellum is responsible for co-ordinating movement.

The diencephalon is a collection of several components. Among the more important of these are the following. The **thalamus** co-ordinates and channels sensory information and the execution of motor movements. Damage to this region gives rise to Parkinsonism (see Chapter 6). The **hypothalamus** might be loosely said to control bodily needs such as hunger and satiety, sexual drive, anger, and so forth. The **hippocampus** is, in evolutionary terms, amongst the oldest sections of the brain. It is involved in emotional control, but of principal interest to psychologists is its role in memory. Some unfortunate individuals who have had this areas of the brain destroyed (by disease or accident) cannot retain any new information in their memories for more than about two minutes. Therefore, the hippocampus is in some manner involved in retaining information in a long-term memory store.

The cortex is responsible for the execution of most higher intellectual functions. It is divided into two **hemispheres**. The divide runs vertically from front to back, along the centre of the head. The hemispheres are linked by several pathways, of which the most important is the **corpus callosum**. For most individuals, the right hemisphere is principally responsible for visuo-spatial skills, the left for verbal skills. The cortex can also be divided into lobes, based upon the psychological functions which each of them controls. The **frontal lobes** extend from the front of the skull back to the temples. They are mainly involved in the control and planning of actions, such as producing sequences of movements, getting words and letters in the right order in speech and spelling and producing socially appropriate behaviour. The frontal lobes are also involved in memory, principally in identifying which events in memory occurred in the recent and which in the distant past. The **temporal lobes** are situated in the positions of the right and left temples. One of their principal tasks is in interpreting information, and in particular the left temporal lobe is vital in comprehending speech and print. The temporal lobes are also strongly involved in memory, particularly the long-term retention of information. Because of the specialisation of the left and right hemispheres, the left temporal lobe tends to store verbal memories and the right temporal lobe tends to store spatial information. The **occipital lobes** are at the rear of the brain. They are involved in reading, but their principal function is vision. Virtually all processing of visual information takes place in the occipital lobes. The **parietal lobes** are located at the 'top' of the brain, surrounded by the other three lobes (they lie roughly in the position of an Alice band or the headband of a pair of headphones). In part they are responsible for maintaining awareness of the body's state and location. Their principal intellectual role might be said to be symbol interpretation, and they are involved in object recognition and reading.

Neuronal changes in later life

Researchers agree that the brain decreases in weight by 10–15 per cent in the course of normal ageing (Bromley, 1988). This is in part is because of the death of brain cells (a high proportion of nerve cells are not replaced when they die). This obviously has potentially serious repercussions for psychological functioning. The reasons why this loss occurs are far from clear. Most probably, several factors are responsible, and the relative contribution of each may vary from person to person. One possible cause is decreased cerebral blood flow, leading to neurons starving of oxygen and thus dying. Alternatively, reduced blood flow may lead to neuronal function being severely compromised because of reduced supply, particularly at times when there is a need for intense activity (see Riddle, Sonntag and Lichtenwalner, 2004). Another explanation is that many older people suffer from miniature strokes or **infarcts**, where a minute portion of the brain atrophies because of the demise of the local blood supply. The older person is unaware of this happening, and it is worth stressing that usually the number of infarcts is small, and can be regarded as symptomatic of normal ageing. However, in some individuals they dramatically increase in numbers, giving rise to **multi-infarct dementia** (see Chapter 6). A third explanation is that the cerebral blood supply, when operating efficiently, filters out possible toxins in the blood before they reach the brain, by a mechanism called the **blood–brain barrier**. If ageing causes this to decline, then the brain might be exposed to potentially damaging toxins (see Bouras *et al.*, 2005). Generally, such declines in metabolism and cardiovascular problems mean that even if their death is not caused, the neurons are less well supplied with oxygen and blood glucose and cannot operate as efficiently (see Farkas and Luiten, 2001; Meier-Ruge, Gygax and Wiernsperger, 1980; Woodruff-Pak, 1997).

In addition to cell death it is known that, for many sections of the brain, neurons shrink in size in later life (partly because of a thinning of the myelin sheath) and decrease the number of connections made with other cells. Estimates of actual losses and shrinkage differ considerably between researchers because of the technical difficulties in taking measurements. However, whatever the size of the loss, researchers are generally agreed that cell loss may be particularly concentrated in some areas of the brain, notably the hippocampus, the cortex as a whole and the temporal lobes in particular (see Adams, 1980; Beers and Berkow, 2000; Selkoe, 1992; Woodruff-Pak, 1997); in other words, the areas of the brain most strongly linked with intellectual functions and memory. Some other brain areas are relatively unscathed. Yet note that Miller and O'Callaghan (2003) argue that cell loss may not be as severe as first supposed in some parts of the brain such as the hippocampus, and observed changes in functioning may be due to, for example, changes in neurotransmitter function.

It is important that the discussion of cell loss and shrinkage is put in its proper context. In non-dementing ageing, loss and shrinkage cannot be reliably correlated with psychological state. First, because cell loss *per se* may not be as drastic an issue as it at first appears. There are much larger cell losses in early infancy, when the growing brain jettisons millions of neurons which are not integrated into the developing networks of active neurons. However, nobody looks at this cell loss and decides that it must seriously lower intellectual functioning. Second, it seems likely that the mind can cope with considerable cell loss. The issue of how the brain stores information is hotly debated. However, it seems likely that it is spread across networks of thousands or millions of neurons (see Stuart-Hamilton, 1999a). The departure of even a reasonably large proportion of neurons should not matter, because the neurons which remain in the network hold sufficient of the 'memory pattern' for the information to continue to be stored efficiently. Therefore, one cannot assume that cell loss will automatically lead to a decline in intellectual ability.

In part the unresolved nature of this issue is due to limitations in measurement techniques. Not least of these is that current technology cannot count nerve cells in living brains – instead, it can only be done on samples from corpses. There are considerable methodological problems with this. For example, one cannot take samples from the same person across his or her lifespan, so judgements about age differences in cell counts have to be made by comparing young adults who died young with older adults who died later in their lifespans. Finding that the brains of dead younger adults have more cells may indicate that had they lived longer they too would have shown a cell loss, but it is also not inconceivable that the older adults when they were younger had fewer brain cells (see Woodruff-Pak, 1997).   Until further refinements of measurement are made, this will remain a moot issue.

Other methods of assessing ageing changes in the brain concentrate upon measurements of brain activity and relatively large-scale structures. The earliest of these is the **electroencephalograph (EEG)**. This measures the electrical activity on the scalp, and from this the activity of the brain within can be roughly surmised. The electrical pulses recorded by the EEG are transmitted across a range of frequencies **delta** (0–4 Hz), **theta** (4–8 Hz), **alpha** (8–12 Hz), and **beta** (>12 Hz). It used to be supposed that EEG frequencies simply slowed down in later life, but recent evidence shows that the situation is more complicated than this. Alpha activity is largely unaffected by ageing, whilst for other frequency bands there is 'a general desynchronization with age, characterised by decreased slowing and increased fast activity' (Duffy and McAnulty, 1988, p.274). Several researchers have observed age differences in EEG recordings made whilst experimental participants perform simple intellectual tasks, such as scanning a list of letters to see which has been presented in a previous exposure, or choosing the correct response in a reaction time task. Usually the age difference manifests itself as a less strong electrical pulse, and sometimes the pulse takes longer to be initiated (Marsh and Watson, 1980; Polich, 1997).

Research using EEG is interesting, but is being superseded by other techniques, simply because they can provide a more detailed insight into the workings of specific sections of the ageing brain. **Computed tomography (CT scan)** is in essence an X-ray of a fine cross-section of the brain. It thus provides a view of the structure of the brain. An advance on this is the **magnetic resonance image (MRI scan)** which can also provide images of cross-sections of the brain (or other body parts) and can also construct three-dimensional images of components of the brain (which the CT scan cannot do). The techniques are ingenious and very adept at detecting fairly large-scale anomalies, such as tissue atrophy or tumours. They have thus not surprisingly been used in analysing the brain structure of patients with dementias. However, the level of detail provided by scans (although improving constantly) is still insufficient to detect anything but fairly gross changes in non-dementing ageing. **Positron emission tomography (PET)** works on a different principle. It measures how the brain metabolises a (mildly) radioactive solution injected into the bloodstream. The more active an area of the brain, the greater its metabolic rate, and the more of the radioactive solution which will be used. This can be detected using a suitable scanner. Thus, whilst CT and MRI measure the brain's structure, PET measures the brain's level of activity. The **fMRI** (functional MRI) measures structure and level of activity and is likely to supersede PET, as it is both more detailed and less invasive. Conclusions from studies using such scans are nearly unanimous in noting that age-related declines in brain mass and metabolism are correlated with decrements in intellectual and memory performance (Albert and Stafford, 1988; Bakker *et al.*, 1999; Daselaar *et al.*, 2005; Metter, 1988; Wang *et al.*, 2005; Woodruff-Pak, 1997).

Summary and overview

Ageing as a widespread phenomenon is confined to twentieth-century industrialised nations, resulting from lower infant mortality rates and improvements in health care and lifestyle in earlier adulthood, rather than any intrinsic improvements in the way humans age. There is no single reliable measure of ageing. Most gerontologists, as a rule of thumb, take an age of 60 or 65 years as indicating the onset of 'old age'. About this age, declines in many physical and psychological processes (which have been taking place for most of the adult lifespan) first become readily apparent. There are many suggested causes of physical decline, which may be grouped under the larger headings of **wear and tear theories** (parts of the body gradually 'wear out' with use) and the **cytologic theories** (that the body ages through exposure to toxins, including metabolic waste products). The evolution-based theories explain why ageing may be an evolutionarily sound strategy for an individual's genes – certainly, ageing and death from 'old age' are not methods of population control, as many commentators have argued in the past. Physiological ageing typically takes the form of cell loss coupled with a decline in the efficiency of the remaining cells. A consistent phenomenon is that age-related declines are greater for complex than simple processes. The general effect of physical ageing is to provide the brain (and hence the mind) with poorer support. Perceptual changes in later life can be severe to the point of disabling many older adults. For those with less severe loss, the brain is nonetheless receiving a compromised perception of the world around it. The ageing nervous system also suffers. There is some loss of central nervous system neurons, and a decline in the efficiency of those neurons remaining.

It must be stressed that the processes of social, biological and psychological ageing do not occur independently of each other. As has been seen, changes in the physical state of the body (and the brain in particular) can have profound effects upon psychological functioning. The point is at least tacitly acknowledged by many researchers, although not often spelt out. A useful model is provided by Dannifer and Perlmutter (1990), which combines the concepts of biological, social and psychological ageing into a single framework. The researchers argue that ageing can be seen in terms of 'physical ontogeny' (essentially, biological ageing); 'environmental habituation' (the process of coming to respond to items in the environment automatically: i.e. without conscious attention); and 'cognitive generativity' (at its most basic, conscious processing of information about the self and the environment). The ageing process is made up of a combination (and interaction) of these three factors. It is argued that some aspects of ageing, such as physical ontogeny, are largely beyond volitional control, but that others (particularly cognitive generativity) are what the individual makes of them. At a basic level, this is a restatement of the old adage that people must make the best of what they are given, but the model is subtler than this, and interested readers are advised to consult the authors' work.

An older and consequently further developed model by Baltes (e.g. Baltes and Reese, 1984) argues that development is determined by three factors – purely environmental, purely biological, and mixtures of environmental and biological. These influences manifest themselves through three strands of development. **Normative age-graded development** (a.k.a. age-normative development) is the basic developmental pattern one would expect to find in a 'normal' individual (e.g. in terms of biological ageing, the onset of puberty; in terms of social ageing, the effects of retirement on behaviour). Within a particular society, the norms of 'correct' behaviour determine that everyone experience these events. **Normative history-graded development** (a.k.a. history normative development) charts the effects of historical events which have been experienced by one age group but not others (e.g. experience of food rationing would be normal for most British people in their sixties, but would be unusual for people in their twenties). **Non-normative life development** measures the effects of major events unique to an individual's life (e.g. not everyone has experienced playing soccer or winning the Nobel

Prize). The model neatly demonstrates how people's lives are made similar by the common experiences of normative development, how identification with one's own generation is shaped by historical normative development and how an individual's uniqueness is shaped by non-normative development.

In short, ageing is the result of a complex mixture of factors, and in the chapters which follow, although isolated aspects of psychological functioning have been selected for scrutiny, it must not be forgotten that they form part of a wider pattern of development.

Suggested further reading

An excellent text on ageing populations and the ageing body is *Brocklehurst's Textbook of Geriatric Medicine and Gerontology*[1] (Tallis and Fillit, 2003). It should be noted that at the time of writing, the current hardback edition retails at circa £130 (thus, for many this may be a book for borrowing from a library). For those on less generous budgets, Bromley (1988) is still often cited. It is a general textbook, is comparatively inexpensive, is well written and provides a solid (if now slightly dated) overview. The potential disadvantages are a paucity of references and an assumption that the reader is already familiar with basic medical and psychological jargon. Another often-cited book is Stokes (1992). This too is readable, and has a different format from many texts in veering towards considerations of the impact of ageing. This may be advantageous for some readers. For those interested in a more technical discussion of evolution and ageing, Gavrilov and Gavrilova (2002) is recommended. Corso (1981) is the acknowledged authority on perceptual processes in older adults, but much of his work is steeped in technical jargon. Slightly more approachable is the collection of papers on visual perception (including one by Corso) edited by Sekuler *et al.* (see reference for Carter, 1982). A good overview of neurophysiology and neuropsychology in later life is provided by Woodruff-Pak (1997). A more advanced general text is the *Handbook of the Psychology of Aging*, edited by Birren and Schaie (1990). Chapters 1–3 are particularly relevant to this chapter. The book is a flagship of gerontological scholarship (however, it is also expensive, at least in the UK). Economic, social and demographic aspects of ageing are well served by the literature. Binstock and George (1990), Jeffreys (1989) and Johnson and Falkingham (1992) may be of value to interested readers. For those interested in the history of ageing, then Thane (2000) is warmly recommended. In addition to being scholarly and informative, it is also an engrossing read. Although the

---

1   The author declares a vested interest since he has a chapter in it (though in fairness, the rest of the book is of a higher standard).

book concentrates on the history of ageing and later life in England, many of the findings will be applicable to other cultures. Finally, it is worth noting that the Internet can also provide a useful source of material. Caution is as usual advised. Whilst sites such as the National Statistics Online (www.statistics.gov.uk) by the UK government are reliable sources of data, other sites may have agendas that consciously or unconsciously bias their outlook. For example, sites on health and ageing offered by purveyors of quack anti-ageing medicines should be treated with particular suspicion. This sounds obvious but, after 20 years of teaching, the author has learnt never to underestimate what students think is a reliable source of information.

CHAPTER 2

Measuring Intellectual Change in Later Life

Intuitive beliefs about ageing and intelligence

Most people, if asked to describe the effects of ageing on intelligence, would judge that stereotypical older adults have more knowledge but are slower at thinking things through. In short, ageing is popularly characterised as an increase in wisdom at the expense of a decrease in wit. For example, Berg and Sternberg (1992) found that when asked to describe exceptionally intelligent adults of different ages, participants tended to emphasise 'ability to deal with novelty' in younger people and stress 'competence' in older adults. This reflects the finding that young and middle-aged adults have a greater tendency than older adults to associate 'wisdom' with later life (Clayton and Birren, 1980). A problem with attitude studies is that it is sometimes difficult to judge if everyone is using the same mental models in making their judgements (e.g. is the 'very intelligent' older person what the hypothetical very intelligent younger person will turn into?). A more revealing insight into everyday concepts of ageing and intelligence is perhaps to be gained from studies of works of art. For example, painters and sculptors have conditioned people to accept that a depiction of a healthy older man looking pensive is automatically a representation of the epitome of wisdom, be it temporal or spiritual. It is very difficult for anyone raised in a western culture to think of a philosopher, saint or even God, as anything other than an older man (long white beard optional). Paradoxically, older people are simultaneously portrayed as being slow thinking and dull witted. The elderly person, doddery of mind and body, has been the butt of jokes from Chaucer to television situation comedy. Dogberry's famous adage in *Much Ado About Nothing* that 'when the age is in, the wit is out' expresses the guiding spirit for centuries of ageist humour. This conflicting view is neatly encapsulated in **Dewey's paradox of ageing**, which states that 'we are…in the unpleasant and illogical condition of extolling maturity and depreciating age' (Dewey, 1939, p.iv). However, popular opinion is not necessarily synonymous with scientific fact. Is there any proof that different aspects of intelligence are differentially preserved?

Crystallised and fluid intelligence

When psychologists began to consider the issue in the early years of this century, it was generally felt that 'intelligence' was a unitary skill. In other words, no matter what type of intellectual task was set, be it verbal, numerical or visuo-spatial (i.e. shapes and figures), the same basic ability dictated a person's performance. This was christened g (for 'general intelligence') by one of the founding fathers of intelligence testing, Charles Spearman. The term 'g' or 'Spearman's g' is still in use, although it is now generally employed more loosely, to describe overall ability or score on a battery of intellectual tests which have assessed a variety of intellectual skills. Most researchers now reject the more rigid definition of g, arguing that 'intelligence' is composed of several interrelated skills. What these are is still open to debate (see Deary, 2001; Eysenck and Kamin, 1981; Kail and Pelligrino, 1985; Rebok, 1987). However, perhaps the most widely accepted theory has been the **hierarchical approach** (Cattell, 1971). This argues that all intellectual skills make use of a general intellectual ability, but they also call upon more specialised skills, depending upon the needs of the task at hand. Cattell (1971) and Horn (1978) identified two of these specialised skills, and called them **crystallised intelligence** and **fluid intelligence**.

Crystallised intelligence measures the amount of knowledge a person has acquired during his or her lifetime. Usually it is measured by simple direct questions, such as asking the person to define obscure words (e.g. 'What is the meaning of *manumit?*'), or to answer 'general knowledge' questions (e.g. 'What is or are the *Apocrypha?*'). The questions can also ask a person to solve problems based on his or her existing knowledge. They can be practical (e.g. 'What do you do if you cut your finger?') or moral (e.g. 'Why should we pay our taxes?'). Such questions can only be answered correctly if one already has the necessary information in one's head and can retrieve it. One cannot create definitions of words or knowledge of sticking plasters, antiseptics, taxation structures or fiscal policy on the spur of the moment. Fluid intelligence tests, on the other hand, draw on acquired knowledge as little as possible, and measure what might be defined as the ability to solve problems for which there are no solutions derivable from formal education or cultural practices. In other words, it is the ability of the person to solve novel problems. The most commonly used method is to ask a person to identify a rule governing a group of items (verbal, numerical or visuo-spatial) and then provide the next one in the series:

A C F J ?

or to spot the odd one out:

245   605   264   722

Typically, fluid intelligence tests have a time limit imposed on them so that to be proficient a person must not only be accurate, but fast as well.

There is also the measure of overall intelligence called (not surprisingly) g, which, according to Horn and Cattell's framework, is the aggregate of fluid and crystallised intelligence scores. In the next section whether these skills change (if at all) with age will be examined.

Age changes in general intelligence (g)

Early studies (*c.*1900–1930) of the effects of ageing on intelligence brought discouragement to anyone older than their late twenties. The typical finding was of the **classic ageing curve** – that intelligence test scores rose to a peak in early adulthood, before beginning a steady downward decline around the person's thirtieth birthday, though verbal skills were typically unaffected (see Rebok, 1987; Thompson, 1997). However, this finding was based upon flaws in the methodologies used (in fairness to the early researchers, some of them recognised the potential problems; see Thompson, 1997). Principal amongst these was an over-reliance on **cross-sectional** studies. These are experiments in which groups of people of different ages are tested and compared at the same point in time. However, if the researcher finds an age group difference, he or she cannot be sure how much of an age group difference is due to age *per se*, and how much is due to the effects of different educational and socio-economic backgrounds. The last hundred years have seen an enormous improvement in health care and standards of living. Younger adults may therefore outperform older adults not because they are less old, but because they are healthier, have had more (and better?) education and have been brought up in a culturally richer world. A difference due to generational differences in background and upbringing rather than ageing *per se* is called a **cohort effect**.

There are several ways of compensating for the cohort effect. One is to try to match the age groups for level of education, socio-economic class, and so forth; in other words, to try to ensure that the *only* difference between them is their different ages. This is problematic, because it is practically impossible to match large numbers of people in this way and, for many forms of analysis, large numbers are *de rigeur*. Again, there are some factors which simply cannot be matched, such as different historical and cultural experiences. A related method is to compare younger and older adults, and then statistically adjust their scores to account for the cohort differences which can be calibrated. This is best illustrated by example. Suppose it is found that there is a difference in test scores between an older and younger group, but that the two groups also differ in how many years of formal education they received (highly likely, because the minimum age at which a child can leave school has been raised incrementally over the last hundred years). The difference may be due to age, but it could also be due to education level (variables that distort results in this manner are called **confounding variables**). There are a variety of methods of statistically adjusting the figures to take account for confounding variables; in this instance, a statistical technique would be used to discover if there is still an age difference after the proportion of the difference due to different education levels has been accounted for. There are three possible outcomes of this procedure – either there will be no change in the finding (i.e. differences in education levels are coincidental: they have no influence on the difference in test scores); or the difference is removed (i.e. the age group difference was coincidental: it was all due to differences in education levels); or the difference is lessened, but a significant (if smaller) difference remains (i.e. education level accounts for some of the age group difference, but not all of it).

It has been known for several decades (e.g. Ghiselli, 1957; Latimer, 1963) that when confounding variables are controlled for in this way, the age difference is typically diminished but not removed (see Stuart-Hamilton, 1999b). This will be considered in detail in Chapter 7, but for the moment it is sufficient to note that at least some of the age difference found in a cross-sectional study will almost inevitably be due to cohort effects.

Although attempting statistically to remove cohort effects from a study can be effective, it is practically impossible to remove all of them, simply because some of them cannot be measured (as stated previously, how can one quantify differences in historical epochs?). Another method of measuring ageing change can cope with this problem. This is the **longitudinal study**, in which the same group of people is tested at one age, then retested as the group gets older (typically at fixed intervals of time). Suppose one wished to compare the difference between 20- and 70-year-old people on a test. Using a cross-sectional method, groups of 20- and 70-year-old people would be found and tested and their results compared. In a longitudinal study, a group of 20-year-old people would be tested, then retested 50 years later when they reached 70, and their test scores on the two occasions would be compared. There are considerable advantages to the longitudinal over the cross-sectional method. The most important is that it escapes the problems of cohort effects mentioned earlier. If an age difference is found in a longitudinal study it cannot be because the older and younger groups differ in their upbringing, since the two groups are composed of the same people. An age difference in these circumstances can only be due to growing older. When longitudinal studies have been run, then g is found to be preserved until at least middle age, and usually far longer (e.g. Bayley, 1968; Owens, 1959; Purdue, 1966; Schaie and Hertzog, 1986). Thus, a large component of supposed age differences in early studies was in fact attributable to cohort effects.

However, longitudinal studies are not without their problems. First, there is the thorny issue that a longitudinal study may only be informative about the particular cohort that is studied (e.g. following a group of people born in 1920 across their lives may uncover a different pattern of change from a group born in 1940). In other words, having removed one form of the cohort effect, we are immediately saddled with another permutation of the problem. A second issue arises from the fact that many volunteers drop out of longitudinal studies. In some cases, this is because they move to areas too geographically remote for the researchers' travel expenses. A more serious worry is that many volunteers quit for motivational reasons. No matter how hard researchers try to explain to the contrary, most participants in experiments seem to regard psychological tests as a competition. Therefore, volunteers who perceive themselves to be worsening in intellectual performance will be less willing to be retested. This means that as a longitudinal study progresses, the 'declining' participants drop out, leaving a rump of 'well-preserved' volunteers (the **drop-out effect**). For example, Riegel and Riegel (1972) demonstrated that people who refused to be retested in a longitudinal study had significantly lower test scores than those who remained, a finding echoed by Siegler and Botwinick (1979).

This problem is compounded by a **practice effect** – namely, that those participants who remain in a study often significantly improve in their performance on the tests employed (Salthouse, 1992b). To rebut the obvious criticism, this is not because the participants remember the answers from the last time they did the test (at different sessions they are usually given 'parallel versions' of the test, which use different questions whilst having the same general format and level of difficulty). Instead, the problem is probably due to several factors. Participants may become **test wise**: in other words, they are increasingly at ease with the test procedures (and hence perform better), have increased general awareness of the ways in which psychological tests operate, and so forth. For whatever reason they occur, the result of these flaws is that the longitudinal method may underestimate the effects of ageing (whilst the cross-sectional method probably exaggerates them). For example, Rabbitt *et al.* (2004) found that practice effects were significantly masking the rate of decline in their 17-year-long longitudinal study of older adults. Practice effects were even noticeable when there was a seven-year gap between test sessions. Similarly, Ferrer *et al.* (2004) found that practice effects caused longitudinal changes to be underestimated. Furthermore, the researchers noted that practice effects were stronger for some tests than others (in the case of Ferrer *et al.*'s study, memory-based tests showed a larger practice effect than measures of speed of response). This means that especial caution needs to be employed in interpreting results, since practice effects may not be uniform across all types of test.

One method of side-stepping the problems of the two approaches is to combine them in a technique called the **overlapping longitudinal study**. This essentially involves testing several age cohorts on one occasion, then retesting them at regular intervals thereafter. To take a simplified example, suppose that at the first test session there are groups of people who are 50, 57, 64 and 71 years old. They are tested, and their performances at Session 1 can be compared in the manner of a traditional cross-sectional study. At regular intervals thereafter (for the sake of argument, let us say every seven years), the participants are retested. Thus, at Session 2, the 50-year-old group is now 57, the 57-year-old group is now 64, and so forth. The age groups at Session 2 can once again be compared in a cross-sectional manner, but in addition, the members of each group can be compared with their younger selves, as in a longitudinal study (e.g. the people who are 71 at Session 2 can be compared with their 64-year-old selves at Session 1).

**Table 2.1   A conceptual table illustrating
the overlapping longitudinal study**

	Session 1	Session 2	Session 3	Session 4	Session 5
Cohort 1	50	57	64	71	78
Cohort 2	57	64	71	78	85
Cohort 3	64	71	78	85	92
Cohort 4	71	78	85	92	99

However, there are further advantages to the overlapping longitudinal method beyond simply combining cross-sectional and longitudinal methods. Consider Table 2.1, which conceptually represents this imaginary study. As can be seen, as the study progresses, the younger cohorts will become the ages the older cohorts were earlier in the study. For example, at Session 4, Cohort 1 will become the age Cohort 4 was at Session 1. Armed with such information, it is possible to gauge and control for cohort effects. Take the following (intentionally simplified) example. Suppose that at Session 4, it is found that Cohort 1 has scores 20 per cent higher than Cohort 4. Does this mean that ageing from 71 to 92 will result in a 20 per cent loss in ability, or is this change due to a cohort difference? To answer this, we can consult Cohort 4's scores on Session 1, when they were the same age as Cohort 1 is at Session 4. Suppose we find that Cohort 4 when aged 71 had scores only 5 per cent lower than when aged 92. We now have two measures of ageing decline – the longitudinal method says the change is 5 per cent, the cross-sectional method says the change is 20 per cent. Armed with such information, it is possible to tease apart how much of ageing change is due to ageing *per se*, and how much is due to cohort differences.

Adopting this design (though in a more complex and erudite form – the above is a simplified illustration), Schaie and colleagues conducted the **Seattle Longitudinal Aging Study** (e.g. Schaie, 1983, 1994). In 1956, a group of people aged between 20 and 70 were tested and then retested at seven-yearly intervals thereafter (i.e. in 1963, 1970, 1977, and so forth). Periodically new participants have been added. The principal test used was the **Primary Mental Abilities Test** or **PMA** (Thurstone, 1958). This is a **test battery** (i.e. a collection of tests with a common theme – in this case intelligence – although each test measures a different facet of the skill). The authors of the PMA claim that it measures five distinct abilities: *number* (basic arithmetic and number skills); *reasoning* (logical deduction); *space* (visuo-spatial skills); *verbal meaning* (knowledge of semantics); and *word fluency* (efficiency at producing words related to an example). However, by cross-checking the figures in a manner conceptually similar to the above example, Schaie has demonstrated that part of the age difference is due to cohort effects. Still, having allowed for this, a significant decline becomes apparent when people reach their mid-sixties. It would thus appear that the social age concept (see Chapter 1) that 'old age' begins in the sixties may have some empirical support. Equally, it rejects the earlier findings that appreciable ageing decline begins before middle age.

An important caveat must be made at this point. It should be noted that what changes with age is the *raw score* on an intelligence test (quite simply, how many answers a person gets right). The **intelligence quotient (IQ)** does not alter particularly with age. This is because IQ is calculated by converting the raw score into a measure of how intelligent a person is *relative to the rest of his or her age group*, and not adults of all ages. Generally, an individual remains at *roughly* the same level relative to his or her age peers throughout the lifespan. For example, if a person starts life as a young adult of average IQ, he or she will probably end life as an older person of average IQ. This has been demonstrated in numerous studies, including one by Deary *et al.* (2000). In 1931, ten-year-old children attending school in Scotland were given an intelligence test in (predictably enough) a survey of intelligence levels amongst Scottish children born in 1921. By curious coincidence some of this same group had been gathered together in the 1990s in a medical study of people born in 1921 and resident in Aberdeen, Scotland. Even more remarkably, the records of their test performances in 1931 were intact, and so the opportunity was taken to retest this group of now elderly people on the same test papers they had first sat as ten-year-old children in 1931 and their scores then and now were compared. It was found that with only a few exceptions (in one case alas attributable to the onset of dementia), their scores relative to each other were very much the same.

However, although people's positions relative to each other remain relatively unchanged, their raw scores will have altered. Raw scores rise through childhood, reach a plateau in late adolescence and then decline again in later life. It follows from this that to be classified as having a particular IQ score requires a different raw score depending on your age. For example, to be classified as having an average IQ, a younger person needs a higher raw score than an older adult. It is important to note this because researchers have a tendency to use 'IQ' as shorthand for intelligence. However, statements such as 'IQ declines in later life' are, strictly speaking, misleading.

It is also important to note that although longitudinal studies, when carefully controlled, are in most instances preferable to cross-sectional ones, there is the simple pragmatic consideration that longitudinal studies are expensive, take many years to produce results (obviously!) and are thus relatively rare. Although over the past few decades the number of longitudinal studies has risen (Ferraro and Kelley-Moore, 2003) they are still relatively rare and are far from being the normal method of investigation.

Age changes in fluid and crystallised intelligence

So far intelligence has been considered principally as a general measure. However, what of the crystallised and fluid skills discussed earlier? Is it the case, as was mooted above, that fluid intelligence declines whilst crystallised skills are unaffected by the ravages of time? An often-cited study by Horn and Cattell (1967) supports this notion, since they demonstrated an age-related decline in fluid intelligence, whilst crystallised test scores remained stable. However, the researchers probably underestimated the age when the decline started, perhaps because of cohort effects. Schaie's Seattle data found that components of the PMA which were crystallised remained relatively unaffected by ageing, whilst fluid skills began to decline appreciably in the mid-sixties. Subsequent studies have almost universally supported Schaie. For example, Cunningham, Clayton and Overton (1975) demonstrated that younger people had significantly higher scores on a common test of fluid intelligence (**Raven's Progressive Matrices**) than did older people, whilst age differences on a crystallised test of vocabulary were relatively insignificant. Hayslip and Sterns (1979) found similar results using a battery of fluid and crystallised tests. So did Rabbitt *et al.* (2004) who in their longitudinal study found accelerated decline in fluid intelligence, but no significant decline in the crystallised intellectual measure of vocabulary. Singer *et al.*'s (2003b) findings echo those of Rabbitt *et al.*, at least until the participants were in their nineties.

An analogous point is made by Salthouse (1992a). He reviewed a number of studies of performance on fluid intelligence tests, and re-tabulated the scores of the older participants. He found that compared with younger adults, the older people were an average of 1.75 **standard deviations** below the mean of the younger group (figures extrapolated from Salthouse, 1992a, Table 4.2, pp.175–6). This is a *very* large difference. To put it in perspective: if a child or teenager scored two standard deviations below the mean for their age group on an intelligence test, then he or she would be considered to be potentially in need of remedial education. Were the average older adult several decades younger, he or she would be bordering on candidature for special education. This point is a dramatic one, and is surprisingly infrequently aired in the research literature. We shall return to it in Chapter 7. However, it is important to state two caveats at this point. First, the studies used by Salthouse are largely cross-sectional. Therefore, part of this considerable age gap may be due to cohort effects. Second, different studies using the same test have produced rather variable results. For example, the PMA Reasoning test has, in different researchers' hands, yielded effects ranging from -1.62 standard deviations (s.d.s) to -5.19 s.d.s. Accordingly, these findings must be treated with caution.

It is important to stress that cohort effects can exaggerate cross-sectional measurements of age differences. For example, Storandt (1976) tested older adults on a component of a widely used intelligence test battery called the **Wechsler Adult Intelligence Scale**, or **WAIS**. The particular measure she used was the **digit-symbol test**. This requires participants to match up digits to printed symbols according to a preordained code (e.g. if one sees a square, write a 2 underneath it, and similarly, a triangle equals 3, a rectangle equals 4, etc.). There is a time limit of 90 seconds, during which the participant must match up as many symbols as possible. There is little doubt that changes in performance of such a task can be a useful measure of perceptual processing (e.g. MacDonald *et al.*, 2003) and that there is an age decline. However, the absolute size of the decline that can be attributed to psychological change alone is open to question. The test clearly is centred on the ability to remember and use a coding system, but because of the time constraint, it also requires rapid writing. However, older people are generally slower at writing because of physical problems (e.g. arthritis, rheumatism, simple general weakening of muscles and joints). Thus, they may perform relatively badly at the task, not because of a failure of mental processing, but because they cannot write down the answers quickly enough. To see how much time older people were losing through writing, Storandt measured how many symbols people could copy within 90 seconds, and took this as the index of writing speed. This was compared with the performance on the test itself, and Storandt was able to demonstrate that about half the age difference was due to writing speed. This clearly demonstrates that physical limitations may exaggerate psychological differences, but it should be noted that a psychological difference nonetheless remained (a finding echoed in a similar study by Tun, Wingfield and Lindfield, 1997). Indeed, even when given as long as they wanted to perform a fluid intelligence test (Storandt, 1977), or increasing the test print size to overcome eyesight problems (Storandt and Futterman, 1982), older people still performed significantly worse then younger controls.

To further confuse matters, performance on crystallised intelligence tests is not as immune to ageing as it may first appear. For example, Core (unpublished, cited Rabbitt, 1984) found that older adults took significantly longer to respond to questions on a crystallised intelligence test (the **Mill Hill Vocabulary Test**). Had a time limit been imposed on the test (significantly, crystallised intelligence tests are generally not against the clock), then older people would have performed significantly less well than younger controls. Hence, to a certain extent, the absence of an age difference on a crystallised intelligence test is because researchers have decided not to put a stopwatch to the task. Again, Botwinick and Storandt (1974) demonstrated that although there was no age difference in performance on the WAIS vocabulary subtest, the answers given by older people were less precise. However, the test marking criteria were sufficiently lax for this difference to go unchecked. Other researchers, using different crystallised tests, have found an age decline without any revision of marking scales (e.g. Kaufman and Horn, 1996). Again, although in general studies of younger age groups find a better correlation between knowledge and crystallised than fluid intelligence (Beier and Ackerman, 2001), Ghisletta and Lindenberger (2003) found that in older old (70–103 years) participants, changes in knowledge levels are, to use the authors' phrase, 'dominated' by fluid intelligence (note the same group found a decline in knowledge levels in the over-nineties in a longitudinal study of their participant group – see Singer *et al.*, 2003b). Therefore, crystallised intelligence is not as immune to ageing as might at first be supposed.

There are further examples in this chapter (and elsewhere in this book) where crystallised skills can be shown to decline with age. This is supported by Meacham (1990) who argues that 'the essence of wisdom is not in what is known but in how that knowledge is held and put to use' (p.188). This implies that once one moves beyond a straightforward recital of stored information to any form of *interpretation*, then a decline is at least possible. However, it cannot be automatically concluded from this that crystallised skills are necessarily fluid intellectual skills in disguise. There is considerable evidence that the two behave in somewhat different ways. For example, as Horn and Cattell originally argued, fluid intelligence tests are more strongly correlated with physical condition (e.g. pulmonary function – Emery *et al.*, 1998). Again, decline in crystallised skills, where observed, has tended to be far less severe than for fluid skills (see Lindenberger and Baltes, 1997), and longitudinal changes in the variability between people's crystallised test scores tends to be less than for fluid scores (Christensen *et al.*, 1999). Furthermore, in at least the early stages of dementia, certain crystallised skills may be preserved (thereby giving a reasonable indicator of pre-illness level of intellectual functioning) when fluid skills have already severely deteriorated (see Carswell *et al.*, 1997; Raguet *et al.*, 1996). Crystallised skills may not be ageing-proof, but they are perhaps rather more resistant than fluid skills.

A word of caution should be raised here. It has been argued that the 'true' size of a decline may be different from what has been measured. This is a common theme in psychological studies – since researchers cannot open up the brain and see thought taking place everything has to be inferred from behaviour and this inevitably means that some error creeps in. However, an admission of measurement error can lead the unwary into making an unfortunate mistake. Occasionally a student reads that, for example, differences between young and old test scores are partly due to a cohort effect and therefore assumes that the 'real' difference between young and old is in reality smaller than the test score implies. So for example, if the difference between the test scores of a group of younger and older adults is 20 points, and it is known that half this difference is due to a cohort effect, then the 'true' difference is ten points. This is wrong – the true difference is still 20 points. In discussing cohort effects and similar, what is being debated is the *cause* of the difference, but this does not refute the existence of the difference. As has been argued elsewhere (Stuart-Hamilton, 2003) it is like being mugged. On one level it matters little whether the mugger is a hardened criminal or someone who, had they been brought up differently would have been a nice person and thus is not 'truly' a criminal. The fact remains that the victim feels the same level of pain and loss regardless of what the 'true' cause was. Similarly, the size of the difference between younger and older adults remains the same, no matter what the cause.

Wisdom

It is also important not to confound crystallised intelligence with **wisdom**. The terms have been used interchangeably by some commentators (including this author). Because wisdom can be understood to mean 'worldly knowledge', the usage is not unreasonable. However, some researchers prefer to use the term in a more specific manner. Unfortunately, there is little direct concordance between definitions (see Coleman and O'Hanlon, 2004; Shea, 1995; Sternberg, 1996), with different researchers pursuing different aspects of what is after all a rather nebulous term. At one level, there have been attempts to define wisdom in terms of psychometric parameters. For example, Sternberg has attempted to correlate it with various essentially intellectual traits (see Sternberg, 1996, 1998). In contrast, psychoanalytic approaches have attempted to link it with a lifetime of experiences of personal conflicts and resolutions (see Shea, 1995). Again, there have been attempts based on questionnaires and interviews that have met with varying degrees of success (see Coleman and O'Hanlon, 2004). However, underlying many of these arguments is perhaps a simpler concept – that of ability at resolving real-life problems. For example, Sternberg (1998) predicates his model of wisdom on the concept that it is essentially about finding balance between conflicting forces. Baltes and Smith (1990) define it in terms of sagacity of judgements about real-life problems.

Chandler and Holliday (1990), based upon interviews with members of the public, synthesise a similar view of providing good advice, with the additional considerations of being competent and socially skilled in doing this. In most instances, researchers stress that wisdom is very much linked to 'real-world' problems where pragmatic considerations may play as important a role as pure logic (the goal of many acts of wisdom is to *resolve* an issue rather than *solve* it).

Empirical evidence on wisdom generally finds a reasonably strong correlation with intelligence, tempered by personality traits, but with a significant proportion of measurement independence (e.g. Staudinger, Lopez and Baltes, 1997; Staudinger *et al.*, 1998). In other words, although wisdom is in part a product of a person's personality and intelligence (which, given its definition, would not be surprising), it is also in part independent of these factors (i.e. it is not just another way of describing *g*). Predictably, researchers have also found that wisdom is a beneficial ability, and is strongly related to, *inter alia*, life satisfaction in older people (Ardelt, 1997, 1998).

Individual variation

It is important to note that the above findings describe what happens to age groups *as a whole* – however, there is considerable variability between individuals of the same chronological age. For example, Rabbitt (1984) divided a group of 600 people aged 50–79 into age decades (i.e. fifties, sixties and seventies) and tested them on a set of crystallised and fluid intelligence tests. The groups showed no difference on crystallised tests, but there was a significant ageing decline on the fluid measures. The instinctive supposition is that this means that *everybody* in the older groups was getting worse. However, this is not what was happening. Most people's scores declined with age, but not all. Thus, Rabbitt found that the best and the worst scores in each age group were the same (i.e. if one found a person in the fifties group with a very high score, a person could be found from the seventies group who could match it). The age difference was coming from a downward shift in a *majority* but not all of the people tested. In more technical language, there was an increased skew in the older groups' scores. Rabbitt estimated that between 10 and 15 per cent of older adults were retaining their youthful level of intellectual skills. Salthouse's review a few years later (Salthouse, 1992a) found smaller proportions of 'well-preserved' older adults. However, whatever the precise figure, the important point is that a decline in fluid skills is not inevitable for everyone. Subsequent research by Rabbitt (e.g. Rabbitt, 1993) and others (e.g. Barton *et al.*, 1975) has demonstrated that variability in test scores is greater for older than for younger people on a variety of cognitive measures, such as reaction times (see below) and measures of memory. The longitudinal study by Rabbitt *et al.* (2004) likewise demonstrated that variability increased with the age of the participants. A literature review by Morse (1993) also records similar findings on changes in variability in later life. This means that amongst themselves, older adults differ more in their performance than do younger people, and hence, in this context, it is harder to justify talking about a 'typical' older person than it is to talk about a 'typical' younger person. It should also be noted that individuals can vary in performance considerably between test sessions. For example, Nesselroade and Salthouse (2004) found that in a study of perceptual-motor performance, the 'magnitude of between-session variability was found to average between 25 per cent and 50 per cent of the between-person variability and was equivalent in magnitude to the variation that was apparent across an age range of 12 to 27 years in cross-sectional comparisons' (p.49). It is worth adding to this that it can be reasonably surmised that the size of the variability may have varied considerably had the participants been given other tasks. This serves only to muddy the waters further.

Furthermore, it appears that some fluid skills may be better preserved than others. Overall, visuo-spatial tasks generally decline at a faster rate than verbal skills (Jenkins *et al.*, 2000; Verhaeghen *et al.*, 2002) but notwithstanding this, the pattern of preservation also varies between individuals (thus, one person may have skills A, B and C well preserved, and D, E and F in relative terms may be declining, whilst for another person the opposite pattern may be true). In a six-year longitudinal study by Wilson *et al.* (2002), a group of older participants were tested annually. It was found that there was considerable variation between individuals in the pattern of decline they showed. Although decline in one sub-skill was likely to be met with a decline in another, this was not inevitable, and level of performance at the start of the study was not an indicator of the rate of decline in skills as the study progressed.

Health, intelligence and the terminal drop model

Discussion of individual variability in performance brings us to another phenomenon of cognitive ageing based upon individual rather than group performance, namely, the **terminal drop model** (of which more below). This is predicated on the basic argument that fitness and health are correlated with intelligence in older adults. This can be readily demonstrated. For example, many researchers have found that physical exercise can improve certain aspects of ageing intellectual performance. For example, Hawkins, Kramer and Capaldi (1992) demonstrated that a ten-week exercise programme resulted in a significant improvement in attention tasks, and that in some instances, this was disproportionately greater for older than younger participants. Powell (1974) found cognitive improvements in older institutionalised patients given an exercise regime. Again, people who maintain a reasonable level of physical fitness appear in general to change less over time on indices of intellectual performance, particularly fluid intelligence (Bunce, Barrowclough and Morris, 1996; Emery *et al.*, 1998). There are many reasons why physical exercise might have a beneficial effect on the intellect. For example, exercise is beneficial to the cardiovascular system and it is known that cardiovascular health is correlated with cognitive skills in older adults (e.g. Elwood *et al.*, 2002; Fahlander *et al.*, 2000; Izquierdo-Porrera and Waldstein, 2002). Again, a sensible level of exercise and diet are useful in staving off old-age diabetes, which is associated with a lowering of intellectual skills (Bent, Rabbitt and Metcalfe, 2000). A healthy body is likely to function more effectively and, as was seen in Chapter 1, a healthy body can enhance neural and hence intellectual functioning. Again, an older person who feels fit and healthy is also more likely to have greater confidence in what he or she is doing, and hence have a higher motivation to do well at mental tasks.

Aside from considerations of fitness, it can be easily demonstrated that many indices of health are correlated with aspects of intellectual functioning, such as blood rheology (essentially, the efficiency of blood flow – Elwood, Pickering and Gallacher, 2001); level of B vitamins (Bunce, Kivipelto and Wahlin, 2005; Calvaresi and Bryan, 2001); and levels of apolipoprotein E (Seeman *et al.*, 2005). However, the weight that can be placed on these findings is harder to judge than would first seem apparent. For example, suppose that it is known that a deficiency in chemical X is associated with a reduction in intelligence in later life. The apparent solution is to increase levels of chemical X, sit back and watch the intelligence test scores rise. However, there are several reasons for arguing that this may not be the case. First, there is the argument that the horse has already bolted – in other words, once the damage has been done, it is irrecoverable. Second, it is possible that the wrong horse is being backed – i.e. the lowered level of X is a symptom not the cause. Thus, a lowered level of X may be caused by a general decline in bodily functions, and treating X alone may be like offering an arts festival to a country where the population is starving – it may do some momentary good, but when it is over, the situation will be as before. A third reason is that, to continue the equine metaphors, the wrong horse has been backed. It is possible that the lowered levels of X are a product of the lowered intelligence levels. For example, people with an impaired understanding of things may be less good at looking after themselves, and indeed there is some evidence for this (e.g. intellectual status when a child is a strong predictor of health status in later life: Starr *et al.*, 2000). A fourth reason is also worth noting: namely, that aside from considerations of health, in nearly all instances studies that have looked for it have found strong effects of socio-economic status (e.g. Elwood *et al.*, 1999; Starr *et al.*, 2000.). Lower education levels are probably also associated (Bosma *et al.*, 2003). Therefore, although health is an important issue in and of itself, its role in ageing cognitive change is less easily defined.

However, what occurs when health catastrophically fails in later life, and a person enters into a terminal decline? It is known that if the average scores for the population at different ages are taken, then these inexorably decline with increasing age but the rate of decline is fairly gentle. Is this true for individuals as well – in other words, if we were regularly to measure the intelligence test scores of an older person, and plot them on a graph, would we see a similar gentle decline? The answer in some cases appears to be 'no'. Some older people display a very rapid decline in scores in the months before they die. This phenomenon has the moribund title of **terminal drop** (Kleemeier, 1962; Riegel and Riegel, 1972). The terminal drop model argues that individuals maintain the same level of performance until a few months or years before death, when their abilities plummet, as if their minds suddenly 'wind down' in preparation for death.

An immediate counter-argument to this is that if the *individual* decline is so sudden, why does the *group* decline appear relatively gentle? The answer is quite simple. The probability of dying rises from middle age onwards. Therefore, the older the age group, the greater the proportion of its members in the terminal drop stage, and hence the lower the *average* intelligence score for the group as a whole. However, because the proportion of 'drop' individuals rises fairly gently across age groups, the overall group average likewise only declines gradually. Thus, the terminal drop will not reveal itself in group averages, but only when individuals are examined.

Kleemeier (1962), working on longitudinal data, found that if, on retesting, a participant showed a large drop in intellectual performance, then there was a high probability that he or she would be dead within a short space of time. Similar evidence was provided by Riegel and Riegel (1972). They tested a group of middle-aged and older volunteers, and then retested them 10 to 20 years later. The researchers found that the volunteers who had died before they could be retested had had significantly lower scores at the initial test session. Every longitudinal study has similarly reported the terminal drop phenomenon (Jarvik, 1983), although the magnitude of the effect varies from study to study and to a certain extent is dependent upon the method of statistical analysis used (Palmore and Cleveland, 1976).

Jarvik and colleagues developed the terminal drop model to include the concept of **critical loss** (e.g. Jarvik, 1983; Jarvik and Falek, 1963). This argues that if over a period of time (ten years in the original study) there are declines in abilities on intelligence tests which exceed certain boundaries, then the probability of dying within a short period of time is dramatically increased. The extent to which a skill may decline before it is considered critical very much depends upon the skill in question. For example, Jarvik argued that the ability to detect verbal similarities can decline by up to 10 per cent without cause for concern. However, *any* decline in vocabulary size was counted as a critical loss. Blum, Clark and Jarvik (1973) conducted a longitudinal study on 62 older volunteers, and found that 15 of them had suffered a critical loss. Within five years of retesting, 11 of these were dead (compared with five of the other volunteers). Whilst accepting the general concept of critical loss, other researchers have disagreed with Jarvik *et al.* regarding what constitutes a critical decline. For example, Botwinick, West and

Storandt (1978) found that changes in verbal abilities did not predict terminal drop, whilst worsening abilities on **paired associate learning** (remembering which items have been previously seen together) and **psychomotor skills** (very loosely, mental skills with a physical skill component) did. In complete contrast, Siegler, McCarty and Logue (1982) found that verbal skills were the best predictors of the probability of imminent death. To complicate matters further, Reimanis and Green (1971) found that the *total* score on the WAIS was the best predictor. In other words, in early studies of terminal drop, although researchers agreed that something must be declining in the terminal drop phase, nobody seemed quite sure what it was. The majority of more recent studies have tended to find that decline in most areas of cognition precedes death (e.g. Bäckman *et al.*, 2002; Johansson *et al.*, 2004; Small *et al.*, 2003). However, some measures may be better predictors than others. For example, Rabbitt *et al.* (2002) found that vocabulary test scores were a better predictor (along with level of depression) than other test measures.

A further qualification to the terminal drop model concerns whether it applies to all or just some individuals. It was initially supposed that the phenomenon only applied to people who died of relatively fast-acting fatal conditions in early old age. Thus, a person gently 'fading away' in their eighties would not experience terminal drop, whilst for example a person in their sixties who suddenly developed a fatal heart condition would. Several early studies found that terminal drop was indeed seen most frequently in the 'young-old' (pre-75 or 80) and after that age, people's cognitive abilities tended to fade gradually rather than plummet (e.g. Berkowitz, 1964; Jarvik, 1983; Riegel and Riegel, 1972; White and Cunningham, 1988). However, more recent studies such as the ones cited in the previous paragraph have found terminal drop predicted in a wider age range and several studies have reported that deaths from different illness types are not preceded by appreciably different patterns of psychological change (e.g. Rabbitt *et al.*, 2002; Small *et al.*, 2003). The difference between the findings of older and newer studies may reflect the arrival in the last few years of more sophisticated computerised statistical analyses, and also perhaps changes in medical care. If the predictions of the compression of morbidity theory (see Chapter 1) are fulfilled, then future generations may expect to live relatively 'well-preserved' lives until a brief while before death, when there will be a relatively sudden decline into terminal illness. The concept of fading away (often in considerable discomfort) may become a thing of the past. The relationship between terminal drop and the type of medical treatment received by participants is a potentially interesting one which, to the author's knowledge, has never been examined. Researchers have generally confined themselves to recording when a participant died and from what. The length of incapacitating illness prior to death and the degree to which the terminal illness's symptoms are kept under control, etc., remains unknown, possibly because of the enormous logistical problems inherent in collecting such data.

However, this should not sidetrack us from the central point that physical exercise and well-being are strongly related to intellectual skills, and thus are a 'good thing'. But what of *mental* exercise?

Disuse theory

A commonly used expression is 'use it or lose it'. The more refined psychological term is **disuse theory** – the belief that age-related declines are attributable to a failure to use skills, so that eventually they fall into a decline (see Milne, 1956). The theory is not easy to prove or disprove. Finding that older people practise a skill less, and that the level of performance on that skill is lowered, is ambiguous. The skill may be worse because of lack of practice. However, the skill may have worsened, causing the older person to lose the motivation to continue practising it (motivation is known to adversely affect older participants in a variety of tasks – see Perlmutter and Monty, 1989). Or, the skill could have worsened by itself, in spite of practice. Studies of older very well-practised individuals have almost always found that there is a decline in at least some related skills spite of regular practice. For example, architects and airline pilots have shown age-related declines on spatial tasks in spite of using spatial skills every day of their working lives (Salthouse, 1992a). Before readers panic that older architects are therefore unsafe to design buildings or older pilots unsafe to fly, it should be stressed that these declines are relative to younger architects or pilots – in absolute terms, their skills are still high.

In another approach to the problem, Salthouse, Berish and Miles (2002) examined the effects of intellectual stimulation on level of cognitive skills. They began by arguing that if disuse theory is correct, then three predictions can be made. The first is that the older the person, the lower their level of intellectual stimulation. This is on the grounds that we know that older people have lower intellectual skills. By the disuse theory's reasoning that level of skill is due to level of practice/exposure to intellectual stimulation, this means that older adults should have lower levels of intellectual stimulation. Salthouse *et al.* conducted a survey of adults aged 20–91 and found that this was indeed the case – older adults had lower levels of intellectual stimulation than younger adults. This seems like proof for the disuse theory, but Salthouse *et al.* still had two further predications that they said must be fulfilled. Their second prediction was that there should be a positive correlation between level of stimulation and level of functioning. In other words, the more intelligent the person, the more intellectual stimulation he or she would report in his or her life. However, this was not found to be the case. The third prediction was that there should be an interaction between age and level of stimulation in predicting intellectual functioning. This is a rather complex point, but essentially it is arguing that if practice is helping to stave off ageing effects, then it should be especially beneficial to older people, and this would show in this analysis. However, the data collected did not support this prediction. This appears to be a heavy blow to the disuse theory, but it should be borne in mind that level of intellectual stimulation was principally gauged by an activity inventory. This is a rather unsubtle instrument that cannot detect all the incidental stimulation that can be received in daily living. A large amount of learning can take place in everyday life without the person being consciously aware of being intellectually stimulated (Schliemann, 2000). Therefore, the Salthouse *et al.* study may be overlooking key parts of the equation. In addition, it is worth noting that a study by Schooler and Mulatu (2001) found a positive correlation between the intellectual complexity of leisure activities and the intelligence of their participants aged 40–80.

The experiments cited above use relatively abstract laboratory tests. If one considers more realistic situations, then the age difference is often less. Although older people may be slower and less accurate at some 'basic' skills, their experience may be able to compensate for this. For example, Charness (1981) studied older chess players and found that they were able to play chess as well as younger adults. However, what was remarkable was that the older players often showed quite serious declines in skills that should be essential to good chess playing, such as memory. Charness found that the older players compensated for this loss by having a greater fund of experience. Because they had played (literally) thousands more games than younger opponents, they were able to tap a greater store of knowledge. Thus, when faced with practically any sort of game, they had probably been in the same situation many times more often than younger players. Greater experience thus compensated for loss of more basic skills. The same researcher found analogous results in an earlier study of habitués of bridge (Charness, 1979). More recently, Masunaga and Horn (2001) demonstrated that players of go (a Japanese board game of strategy) maintained relatively high-level skills relevant to the game, even if more generally their intellectual skills (such as fluid intelligence) showed a decline. Similarly, Salthouse (1984) compared older and younger typists. He found that the older typists generally had slower finger movements and reaction times, but showed no difference in typing speed. This was because the older typists planned longer sequences of finger movements than younger typists (with less experience) could manage. Thus, although it took an older typist longer to move a finger to a key, the move towards that key started earlier because they looked further ahead (in essence, younger typists were starting later in their sequences of finger movements and then catching up with the older typists). Bosman (1993) adds that this only applies to older typists who regularly practised their skill. A caveat to this is provided by a study by Westerman *et al.* (1998) of older and younger participants who were all practised in word processing. The researchers found evidence for a compensatory strategy, but also noted that, amongst the more skilled older participants, their abilities were associated with possession of high levels of basic cognitive capacities rather than integration of sub-skills into an overall strategy. This implies a bigger role for basic skills than other compensation studies have suggested, but it should also be noted that Westerman *et al.*'s sample was of people who had 'over 100 hours of experience in using a word processor' (p.583) as opposed to the years or decades of experience of participants in some other studies.

In another study of compensatory strategies, Hoyer and Ingolfsdottir (2003) conducted an ingenious experiment on medical laboratory technicians. They showed the participants microscope slides with the task of identifying a target structure on it. Anyone other than a biologist who has seen slides of cells and similar will readily appreciate that the difference between such slides and random blobs of ink is fairly minimal, and the task is a demanding one. Hoyer and Ingolfsdottir found that the older technicians (in their late forties) took significantly longer over the task than younger technicians (in their twenties) if just presented with the slide images. However, if they were given contextual information (i.e. orienting them to what was expected) before they started, then the age difference disappeared. In other words, given the capacity to use a compensatory strategy (20 years' greater experience of looking at slides) the age decline in basic visual search skills could be overcome.

Practice may not only preserve existing skills, but also revive supposedly lost or declining ones. For example, Plemons, Willis and Battes (1978) demonstrated that training in taking fluid intelligence tests could boost the test scores of older participants. Furthermore, this seemed generally to enhance performance of intellectual tests, suggesting that the training made participants more test wise. These findings are echoed by other researchers (e.g. Baltes and Willis, 1982; Kermis, 1983; Rebok, 1987). Salthouse (1992a) criticises these studies because often there have been inadequate control groups, and/or the success of the training has been judged on too narrow a range of tests. Again, he (and other commentators) have suggested that training may not affect the root skill, which remains in decline, but instead may offer new strategies to cope with the problem. This is analogous to taking a painkiller to mask the pain of toothache – it does not cure it, but it enables one to cope. From a practical viewpoint, this argument may seem relatively unimportant (why worry if it helps older people cope?), but the theoretical considerations are of course not trivial. More recently, Mireles and Charness (2002) have conducted computerised simulations of the effects of knowledge on factors likely to influence chess playing skills (in this instance, memory span for sequences of moves). The researchers found that knowledge appears to protect against increased neural noise (see Chapter 1), but not cell loss. This perhaps helps explain the finding by Rothermund and Brandstädter (2003), who in a longitudinal study found that compensatory strategies were increasingly used by their participants until they were circa 70 and then use decreased. Again, even in its full flowering, compensation may not be totally effective. For example, Charness *et al.* (2001) conducted a study in which young, middle-aged and older typists who were either novices or experienced were given the task of learning a new word-processing application. In the case of the novices, the younger participants were faster to learn and retained more information at the end of the training course. In the case of the experienced participants, the older group differed only minimally from the younger groups in what was learnt and retained. Thus, there is evidence that experience acts to compensate for age-related decline. However, the older group had a significantly slower learning rate. Therefore, compensation has its limits.

If disuse theory cannot provide a full explanation of cognitive change in later life, what is the alternative? The theory often set up in opposition to disuse theory argues that ageing decline is due to a biological process of the slowing of bodily functions that in turn leads to a slowing and lowering efficiency of mental processes. To understand this argument fully, we first need to take a step back and consider how this slowing can be measured.

Reaction times

The **reaction time** or **RT** is a measure of how long it takes a person to respond to the appearance of a stimulus: the *lower* the reaction time, the *faster* the person is responding (and vice versa). Obviously, having lower reaction times is advantageous. Faster reactions will aid a sports player and may mean the difference between life and death to a car driver. Other examples of reaction times are less dramatic but more central to everyday life. For instance, the speed at which one can think of the answer to a question is an example of a reaction time, as is the time taken to recognise a voice, a face or a familiar picture. Wherever there is the perception of something and a response to it, there is a reaction time. Thus, in one sense, the reaction time is the measure of the time gap between reality and one's perception of it. Most research on reaction times has confined itself to rather more mundane considerations, such as the time taken to make a simple response to a simple stimulus. Classical reaction time experiments adopt two basic formats. The first is the **simple reaction time (SRT)** study. This is a measure of how quickly a person responds when there is only one stimulus and only one response allowed. This is typically tested by requiring a person to press a button every time a light flashes (or an analogous condition). The delay between the signal and the response is the reaction time. The second measure is the **choice reaction time (CRT)**. In this instance, the participant is presented with an array of stimuli and a choice of responses. For example, there might be three lights and three buttons, and the participant is told to press button *A* if a red light flashes, *B* if a green light, or *C* if a blue light. Participants have to give more consideration to what they see in a choice reaction time experiment, and thus responses tend to be slower than in a simple reaction time paradigm. Similarly, the more choices which have to be decided between, the slower the responses become.

It is very well established that reaction times get slower as people get older. According to a review by Birren and Fisher (1995, p.329), it is 'one of the most reliable features of human life' (see also Lindenberger, Mayr and Kliegl, 1993; Rabbitt, 1996). This is not doubted. Nor is it questioned that if people are tested on a single occasion, older people are disproportionately slower on choice than on simple reaction time tasks. Furthermore, the age difference gets proportionately larger the more choices that must be discriminated between in a choice reaction time task (see Botwinick, 1973; Kermis, 1983; Salthouse, 1985). The simple explanation for these phenomena is that older people's nervous systems are slower and less efficient at conducting signals, and the disadvantage imposed by the extra choices is another manifestation of the age × complexity effect (see Chapter 1).

However, beyond this fairly superficial level lie some deeper and fascinating problems. It should first be noted that much of the disproportionate age difference on choice reaction time tasks disappears if people are allowed to practise for several days; older adults remain slower across different versions of the task, but the difference becomes a constant (Rabbitt, 1980). In other words, if an older person is x milliseconds slower on a simple reaction time task, he or she will also be x milliseconds slower on a choice reaction time task. This implies that a significant proportion of the age difference may be due to 'settling in' to the task. Once it has become sufficiently rehearsed to be automatic (in psychological terms, this generally refers to a skill rehearsed to the point where it requires no conscious control), then age differences are less important than when the task required conscious monitoring. Hasher and Zacks (1979) argue that automatic processes are relatively unaffected by ageing (see also Wishart *et al.*, 2000), although more recent commentators (e.g. Burke, White and Diaz, 1987; Myerson *et al.*, 1992) have found some instances where this is not the case.

A further consideration is that many researchers have only considered age difference in *mean* reaction times. Rabbitt (1980, 1988a, 1998b) argues that this is misleading, since it presents the impression that older people are incapable of the fast responses of their youth. In fact, if the distribution of response speeds is considered, then the fastest reaction times of older and younger people are the same. The age differences lie elsewhere. In part they are because older adults make fewer very fast responses. They are also due to older people making a much wider variety of response speeds, which increases the mean reaction time. This is particularly the case when reactions to errors are concerned (an error occurs when, e.g. in a choice reaction time task, the participant presses button B when the correct response was A). Participants are usually aware they have made a mistake, and respond by slowing down on the next trial. Younger adults then pick up speed relatively quickly, whilst older people take several more trials to return. This means that relatively speaking, younger adults 'shrug off' their mistakes quickly, whilst older adults are over-cautious. Younger adults thus can find an optimal response speed (i.e. as fast as they can go without making too many mistakes) and stick to it, whilst older people seem to lack this level of control and oscillate far more. When the average performances are considered, this age difference expresses itself more simply as a difference in mean response times. In a more recent study, Smith and Brewer (1995) have provided similar evidence. It should also be noted that increasing the preparation interval (i.e. the time gap before the start of the next trial in a reaction time experiment) also disproportionately aids older adults' reaction time performance (Bherer and Belleville, 2004).

It is well established that reaction times correlate well with measures of intellectual performance (e.g. Ferraro and Moody, 1996), and from this emerges another interesting phenomenon. Rabbitt and Goward (1986) found that if groups of older and younger adults are matched for intelligence test scores, then there is no difference in their choice reaction times. Hertzog (1991), Salthouse (1991a) and Schaie (1989) similarly report that when the effect of speed of response is statistically controlled for, differences between age groups on intellectual tasks are significantly lowered, or disappear altogether. This implies that slowing reaction times are measuring the *cause* of declining intellectual skills (e.g. Eysenck, 1985; Salthouse, 1985). If two items such as intelligence test score and reaction time are correlated, there is no simple mathematical way of proving which causes the other. However, it can be logically argued that reaction times are measuring a more fundamental process (and hence an earlier stage in the chain of causation) than are intelligence tests. *Very* crudely, reaction times measure the speed with which neurons send messages, intelligence tests measure what is done with those messages. If older people have slower reaction times, then they have slower mental processes, and this in itself could explain much of the decline on timed intelligence test scores. However, there is more to this issue than just simple speed. In tandem with the slowing comes a lowering of the general accuracy and efficiency of the system. In part this is because some mental processes may have to be executed within a certain number of milliseconds or they decay beyond recovery – a slower system means that some processes will take longer to complete than this critical limit, and so a particular mental process cannot be completed (see Salthouse, 1996). Again, a decline in speed is the result of the general physical decline of the nervous system, such as a depletion in the number of interconnections between neurons, lowered efficiency of neurotransmitters, increased neural noise (see Kail, 1997) and so forth. The reaction time may thus be not only gauging the speed of transmission, but also giving a general indication of the efficiency and health of the nervous system.

A further aspect of reaction times concerns the consistency of responses by older adults. If a person is given a reaction time task, it makes intuitive sense that they will not respond at exactly the same speed on every trial. For example, they are more likely to have responses over four successive trials of, for example, 500, 478, 520, 431, and 576 msecs than they are to have responses of 500, 500, 500, 500 and 500 msecs. Such variability in scores is to be expected. However, in older adults this variability increases, and (purely as descriptive shorthand) this is sometimes described as 'unreliable' performance. Hultsch, MacDonald and Dixon (2002) found that the more 'unreliable' the participant, the lower their cognitive test score. Rabbitt *et al.* (2001) argue that this apparently capricious behaviour may in fact be a stable characteristic and were able to demonstrate that the level of unreliability an individual displayed remained remarkably consistent over a study in which older adult participants attended 36 weekly test sessions to perform a variety of reaction time tasks (an heroic accomplishment in itself). Furthermore, the more 'unreliable' a person, the lower their intelligence test score. Thus, in addition to speed of response, the pattern of response in a reaction time study may also be revealing of cognitive status.

Returning to studies of speed of response, the attribution of an ageing decline in intellectual skills to a slowing in the speed of neural transmission (and all the related phenomena this implies) is known as the **general slowing hypothesis** (or, rather confusingly, the **speed hypothesis**). At a general level, this argument is not greatly disputed: low speed typically equals low test scores and, across time, changes in speed of processing correlate significantly with changes in fluid intelligence (Zimprich and Martin, 2002). Instead, the debate is principally about the degree to which general slowing alone predicts intellectual performance. As mentioned several times in this and the previous chapter, the age × complexity effect states that as the task gets harder, so older adults become disproportionately more disadvantaged. Underlying this may be an even simpler explanation. The impetus for this came from Cerella (1985; 1990), following earlier research by Brinley (e.g. Brinley, 1965).

If we consider the response times for harder and easier versions of the same task, we find that the times increase as the task complexity increases. Furthermore, the rate of change is bigger for older than younger adults. Thus, a graph plotting task complexity against response time shows that a younger group has a line rising less steeply than that an older group's (see Figure 2.1). However, what if we plot the response times for older and younger adults on the same tasks against each other? What we will usually find is illustrated in Figure 2.2, and is known as a **Brinley plot**. What this shows is that the underlying difference between older and younger adults is linear (note that real data rarely show a perfect straight line, but allowing for experimental error, it is argued that a straight line is the best description of the results). For those not mathematically minded, what this means is that the apparent disproportionate difference between older and younger people illustrated in Figure 2.1 is illusory; older adults *appear* to be disproportionately disadvantaged the more complex the task, but in fact they are not – the real underlying difference remains the same size. This means that complex formulae used to predict changing age differences across different levels of complexity (see Rabbitt, 1996) can be jettisoned; instead, all age differences can be expressed by a simple formula – find the mean reaction time of a younger adult on a task, multiply it by a constant, and that will be the mean reaction time for older people on the same task.

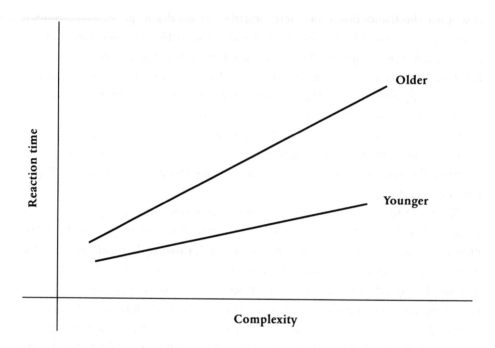

Figure 2.1 Illustration of the age × complexity effect

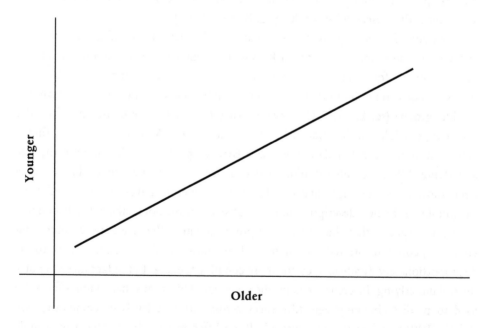

Figure 2.2 Illustration of a Brinley Plot, plotting younger v. older means on same data as Figure 2.1

Because of the beguiling simplicity of this theory, the general slowing hypothesis has understandably attracted a lot of attention. It has been established that the phenomenon is widespread: across a wide variety of tasks, where average older and younger response speeds can be compared, a linear relationship has been found (e.g. Cerella, 1990; Lindenberger *et al.*, 1993; Maylor and Rabbitt, 1994; Ratcliff, Thapar and McKoon, 2001; Sliwinski *et al.*, 1994; Verhaeghen and De Meersman, 1998). Myerson *et al.* (1992, p.266) make the important point that, within a particular domain, 'the term *general slowing* would appear to capture the fact that the degree of slowing does not appear to depend on the nature of the task or the specific cognitive processing components involved'. In other words, slowing must involve something more basic, such as changes at a neural level (Cerella, 1990).

However, there are several important caveats which limit the extent of general slowing's applicability. For example, it does not stop the old–young speed relationship being influenced by other factors, such as compensatory strategies by older people:

> Because of the compensatory effects of lifelong knowledge accumulation, for instance, some domains of cognitive functioning may be less affected by slowing than others. Recent evidence showing that slowing is less pronounced in tasks requiring lexical decisions as compared with analogous tasks requiring nonlexical decisions is consistent with this assumption. (Lindenberger *et al.*, 1993, p.207)

This indicates that some caution must be taken in reading too much into the shape of the line. It would be unwise to assume too much about ageing change on the basis of one type of task. In addition, there are some questions about the statistical and mathematical validity of the technique. For example, Perfect (1994) suggests that similar linear relationships can be generated using essentially random data. Again, Rabbitt (1996) notes that when data increase in variability with task complexity, a linear relationship can still be obtained. This is a mathematically difficult argument, but it essentially means that a considerable amount of the young–old difference may be due to more than just a simple slowing process, but the Brinley plot is masking this by 'over-simplifying' the relationship into a simple linear one. Sliwinski and Hall (1998) observe that in many cases the statistical method used to demonstrate Brinley plots (the *ordinary least squares multiple regression*, or OLS) is too simplistic and that a *hierarchical linear model* (HLM) is more appropriate. When the two techniques are compared on the same sets of data, the OLS produces Brinley plots, whilst HLM identifies rather greater variability.

If proof for the slowing hypothesis is sought away from Brinley plots, the evidence is still equivocal. For example, Salthouse and Czaja (2000) produced a plausibly argued and technically complex case that if a study shows no evidence for general slowing this is because in effect it has been taken out of context (more technically, by studying some variables in isolation their shared variance with other variables – which would indicate a common factor, such as general slowing – is overlooked). As proof of this, the authors demonstrated the presence of a common factor explaining impressively large proportions of the variance in two separate data sets of older adults' intellectual performance (see also Salthouse, 2001). However, this plea to look at the bigger picture was short lived as the following year Allen *et al.* (2001) re-analysed Salthouse and Czaja's data and found that by using a different (and arguably superior) statistical technique, although a common factor could be found, it explained less of the variance than previously claimed and, furthermore, other significant explanatory factors were present, thus denying a single factor explanation (a finding echoed in studies by Anstey, Hofer and Luszcz, 2003; Anstey, Luszcz and Sanchez, 2001; and Schmiedek and Li, 2004). Allen *et al.* demonstrated similar problems with other published studies supporting a single factor case, and, as a *coup de grâce*, showed that if simulated data sets were used (i.e. where the underlying structure was deliberately created), the statistical methods used by the single factor supporters were difficult to falsify. In other words, a single factor was likely to be produced regardless of whether it was the best fit for the data.

An assortment of disparate findings have further indicated that general slowing may not be as strong a predictor as was first assumed (see Bashore, Ridderinkhof and van der Molen, 1997 for a review). For example, Sliwinski (1997) reports that cognitive slowing did not seem to be a good predictor of counting speed in tasks of different levels of complexity. Instead, different counting tasks seemed to be mediated by different mechanisms. Salthouse (2000) reported that in a survey of responses to individual items on a variety of tests, a common age-related factor correlated across all these, but in addition there appeared to be a second factor (also related to age) that was correlated only with performance on the most difficult individual items. Salthouse and Ferrer-Caja (2003) found 'at least 3' factors underlying performance of adults (aged from their teens to their nineties) on a range of cognitive tasks. Again, Shimamura *et al.* (1995) demonstrated that a decline in skills may be offset by use of what is in effect compensation in some individuals. Furthermore, the use of reaction times as an index of mental processing has also been criticised, on the grounds that it is essentially a simplification of what are probably a series of complex and very rapid mental processes, and may thus overlook important subprocesses (Bashore *et al.*, 1997). In other words, the reaction time may be like a camera set at too slow a shutter speed for taking a picture of a particular fast event, such as the finish of a race. The picture which emerges may give a general outline, but there is too much blur to see what is really going on. Bashore and colleagues argue that EEG measures (see Chapter 1) of brain activity during mental activity may be a more fruitful way forward.

Thus, the general slowing hypothesis is probably not as strong a theory as first supposed. Although there is considerable evidence that slowing of neural functions explains much of ageing intellectual decline, there is still room for other, more specific factors to play a role in the process. Before leaving this topic, one further caveat should be raised. Because reaction times are such a 'basic' measure, there is a tendency to assume that they are measuring an inevitable, genetically ordained change. In fact, whatever the validity of the general slowing hypothesis, reaction times are not necessarily predestined to decline. Although the most parsimonious explanation is that declining processing speed results from the physical decline of nervous tissue in tandem with other physical ageing changes, decline may also in part be due to lack of appropriate practice. For example, Goldstein *et al.* (1997) demonstrated that older people who were given practice on video games improved their reaction times. Again, reaction times are strongly linked to level of health – the greater the number of serious illnesses a person has experienced, the greater the decline in their speed of response (Houx and Jolles, 1993). The same report also found significant effects for level of education. This implies that at least a proportion of the decline in speed may be due to probabilistic ageing (e.g. older people tend to have fewer activities which stretch their reactions, and they tend to have more illnesses) rather than ageing *per se*.

Given the above arguments about their utility and even allowing for counter-arguments, it is perhaps surprising to find that reaction times seem at first to be fairly weak predictors of ageing performance. Although they are statistically significantly linked to changing intellectual skills, Salthouse (1985) found an average correlation of 0.28 between age and simple reaction times and 0.43 between age and choice reaction times. For those unfamiliar with statistics, this means that ageing can only account for about 8 per cent of the variability in simple reaction times and about 19 per cent in choice reaction times. At first sight, this seems to indicate that the interest in reaction times is unmerited given that they have a relatively peripheral role to play. However, this would be an inaccurate conclusion. Salthouse has provided an ingenious, if mathematically complex, rejoinder, which demonstrates that changes in intellectual skills are *mediated* by the decline in processing speeds (Salthouse, 1985, 1991b, 1992b). In a similar manner, the chains connecting the carriages of a railway train are relatively unimportant in comparison with the power of the engine – but try pulling a train without the chains. For further consideration of this issue, see Salthouse (1992b).

The related issue of *semantic facilitation*, which uses the reaction time technique, is dealt with in the word recognition section in Chapter 4.

Thus, reaction times, an expression of speed of neural processing, slow in later life, and this has an influence on the decline in *g*. The magnitude of this difference can be influenced by practice and by the complexity of the task involved. At one level, this can be described as the age × complexity effect, at another by the general slowing hypothesis. Evidence for either theory is currently equivocal, and whether one wishes to see disproportionate slowing or a constant lag largely depends upon how one chooses to interpret the data. However, to place matters in perspective, it should be noted that reaction times, whilst important, are not the sole arbiter of intellectual change, in spite of some of the more enthusiastic claims by their supporters.

Other physical correlates with intellectual skills

The relationship between reaction time and intellectual performance is a complex one, but nonetheless, and despite the caveats, a relationship exists. It is reasonable to assume that a measure of reaction times is gauging the relationship between the physical state of the body, particularly the brain and the workings of the mind. Indeed, not only the research on reaction times, but also studies of the effects of physical exercise and health noted above, point to a good correlation between physical status intellectual functioning. Not surprisingly, therefore, researchers have examined the relationship between physical status and intelligence in older adults. As noted in Chapter 1, the brain loses volume with age (see also Coffey *et al.*, 1999). The same phenomenon has been observed for many subsections of the brain, such as the hippocampus, parahippocampal region and the amygdala (e.g. Jack *et al.*, 1997; Kaye *et al.*, 1997). Given such findings, one might reasonably expect ageing changes in the brain's structure to have psychological correlates, and such is the case. As will be noted in a later chapter, the severe loss of brain tissue in dementia has a catastrophic effect on mental functioning. However, links can also be noted in normal ageing. For example, Deary *et al.* (2003) used MRI scans to examine the brains of participants in the follow-up to the 1932 Scottish Mental Survey described previously. They found that circa 14 per cent of the variance in cognitive skills was attributable to abnormalities in the **white matter** of participants' brains. (White matter takes its name from the myelin covering the nerves. Essentially, it is the part of the nervous system responsible for transmitting information – as opposed to **grey matter**, which is the cell bodies, synapses, etc., responsible for processing information.)

In recent years, considerable interest has focused on the role of ageing changes in the frontal lobes (see Chapter 1) and their effects on intellectual functioning (see Band, Ridderinkhof and Segalowitz, 2002; Rabbitt, 1997, for overviews). It is known that the frontal lobes are relatively prone to age-related physical decline (e.g. Shan *et al.*, 2005) and it is also well established that the frontal lobes are heavily involved in many forms of complex thought processes, particularly those involving planning sequences or remembering the order in which events occurred. In many instances, brain activity produces several potential responses, and a principal function of the frontal lobes is to inhibit those responses that are not needed, allowing the correct response to be made. In other instances, several responses may be produced that need to be given in the correct sequence, and the frontal lobes ensure that it is this sequence that is given and that other possible sequences are inhibited. For this reason frontal lobe activity is often referred to as **inhibitory functioning** or similar. Evidence that older people show a decline in skills known to involve the frontal lobes is considerable (e.g. Chao and Knight, 1997; Friedman, 2003; Isingrini and Vazou, 1997; Persad *et al.*, 2002). Some commentators have argued that the age change in intellectual skills is principally the result of changes in the frontal lobes. For example, Duncan *et al.* (1996, p.257) have argued that *g* may in fact be 'largely a reflection of the control functions of the frontal lobe'. However, other research has qualified or even contradicted this argument. For example, where 'frontal lobe' deficits are reported, not all of the frontal lobe may be involved. Phillips and Della Sala (1998) persuasively argue that many of the supposed 'frontal' changes are in fact confined to one region of the frontal lobes. Namely, the dorsolateral prefrontal cortex (principally responsible for executive functions and working memory – see Chapter 3) shows decline, whilst the ventromedial region (responsible for emotional and social reasoning) is relatively unscathed. Further empirical proof is provided in a subsequent paper from the same research team (MacPherson, Phillips and Della Sala, 2002).

Again, it might be intuitively expected that if frontal lobe decline was a major feature of the intellect in later life, then older people would perform in a manner qualitatively similar to patients with damage to the frontal lobes, but, at least in some circumstances, this is not the case (Phillips, 1999). Tangential to this, Robbins *et al.* (1998) found that frontal lobe functions were certainly an important predictor of cognitive skills in later life, but they were not the sole factor, a finding echoed by Whelihan *et al.* (1997). Again, Foster *et al.* (1997) note that many executive/planning functions are not the sole preserve of the frontal lobes, but may be shared between several brain areas. Rabbitt, Lowe and Shilling (2001) note that failing to account for differences in the statistical reliability and validity of different frontal lobes tests may lead to inaccurate estimates of loss of function. Parkin and Java (1999) demonstrated that a considerable degree of the difference supposedly due to frontal lobe deficits was removed if the scores on a digit-symbol substitution test and a fluid intelligence test (the AH4) were taken into account. Removing the influence of scores on crystallised tests had relatively little effect. In other words, much of the frontal lobe deficit may be a manifestation of a general change in fluid intelligence-related skills. This may apply not just to the frontal lobes but to many supposedly 'localised' effects. Salthouse, Fristoe and Rhee (1996) studied age changes in skills associated with the frontal, parietal and temporal lobes, and found that an average of '58 per cent of the age-related variance in a given variable was shared with that in other variables' (p.272). In other words, although different areas of the brain may each contribute something unique to the patter of age-related decline, a great deal of what they do is in tandem with other ageing changes.

These findings must be put in perspective. Arguing that frontal lobes do not have the overwhelming influence which some commentators supposed does not deny the existence of frontal lobe problems. To make an analogy, a naturally clumsy man might break his leg. Seeing him struggling to get around on crutches may be ultimately part of the manifestation of his clumsiness, but that does not mean that the specific problems associated with a broken leg have gone away. In other words, whether frontal lobe problems are a cause of age-related decline, an effect, or a bit of both, does not stop them being a significant factor in considerations of ageing decline in intellectual skills. Likewise, it would be breathtakingly naive to assume that changes in brain structure might have no effect on psychological functioning (see Woodruff-Pak, 1997, for a comprehensive introduction to neuropsychology and ageing). However, it is also important to remember the caveat raised above that an apparently 'basic' decline in neural functioning is not necessarily uncontrollable. For example, Coffey *et al.* (1999) observed that brain volume was relatively preserved in people with higher levels of formal education. Again, Kramer *et al.* (1999) demonstrated that aerobic exercise (though not simple stretching and toning) had a significant improving effect on performance of frontal-lobe-related tasks.

It should also be noted that the frontal lobes are heavily involved in many aspects of attention (see below).

Discussions of changes in brain function/structure and its relationship with psychological functioning are often based on a selective view of the situation. At one level is the straightforward observation that changes in psychological functioning are too diverse and complex for a change in a single area of the brain (or indeed a single kind of change across the brain) to account for them all (see Band *et al.*, 2002). In addition, there is the problem that by only examining part of the situation at once, it is impossible to gain a picture of which changes are unique and which are shared. For example, suppose that changes in brain area X are known to cause a change in psychological skill Y. Does this mean that an age-related decline in area X is responsible for age-related changes in skill Y? The answer is at best a qualified 'yes'. Unless a complete study is done of all areas of the brain and all psychological skills simultaneously, then it is impossible to say. It is, for example, conceivable that a change in area X occurs in tandem with a change in area Z and that when skill Y changes, so do skills A, G and H. Such an in-depth analysis is in practical terms impossible given current technology and in one sense it is churlish to complain, but logic dictates that findings of simple associations between brain and behaviour only indicate strong possibilities, not certainties. It is also worth noting that old and young brains may not behave in identical manners. For example, using fMRI scans, Springer *et al.* (2005) found that whereas frontal lobe activity was negatively correlated with level of education in younger adults, it was positively correlated in older adults. Thus, it is possible that observed patterns of decline will also eventually have to come to terms with individual differences in the degree to which people change brain functions in later life.

Another aspect of physical decline that has been strongly associated with intellectual change is the worsening sensory system. In recent years, considerable attention has been paid to empirical evidence of a strong correlation between measures of sensory functioning and intelligence. For example, Lindenberger and Baltes (1997) found that under certain conditions, measures of sensory and sensorimotor skills predicted the majority (59%) of variance in intelligence test scores in older adults. This relationship appears to grow stronger through adulthood. Baltes and Lindenberger (1997) found that the variability in intelligence test scores explained by the status of sensory functioning (as measured by auditory and visual acuity) rose from 11 per cent in a group of adults aged under 70 to 31 per cent in adults aged 70 to 103. In both age groups, sensory functioning was correlated with fluid intelligence. The authors conclude that the status of the senses is a good index of biological ageing, and that this may be the main factor influencing intellectual skills in later life. Dulay and Murphy (2002) found similar results. Testing olfactory thresholds (i.e. the faintest smells that could be detected) they found a strong correlation between sensory and cognitive skills, which grew stronger the older the participants considered. These findings are echoed in a study by Finkel, Pedersen and Larsson (2001) which found a strong correlation between olfactory and cognitive skills in a sample of middle- and older-aged identical twins. The authors concluded that a significant proportion of the relationship was genetically mediated. Again, Marsiske, Klumb and Baltes (1997) found that older people's perceived level of basic competence and the degree to which they participated in social activities were both correlated with their sensory acuity (and particularly their vision).

How is this sensory decline related to intelligence? The simplest explanation is that a decline in quality of sensory input means the mind has a lower quality of materials to work with – thus, garbage in, garbage out. However, Lindenberger, Scherer and Baltes (2001) demonstrated that simply reducing sensory acuity in middle-aged people to the level of an average older person (using special glasses, muffling hearing, etc.) did not reduce cognitive performance to an older person's average level. Therefore, sensory change is about more than simply making input harder to see or hear. In any case, the finding that olfactory skills are related to intelligence makes a 'compromised input' argument implausible, since intelligence tests never assess or need olfactory skills. The explanation therefore lies at a deeper level, and must reflect a general ageing change that affects both cognitive and sensory processes to the same extent (see Li and Lindenberger, 2002; Scialfa, 2002; Stankov, 2005). In other words, we have returned to the general slowing hypothesis in another guise. Once more the explanation is presented in terms of a single gauge of decline that binds together neurological functioning from the most basic (senses and simple reaction times) to the sophisticated (e.g. cognitive skills used in complex intellectual tasks). However, can the argument be accepted at face value?

There is little dispute that these are robust findings, and that the status of the senses is a good gauge of physical and mental functioning. Once again though, caution must be exercised before one interprets this phenomenon as a total explanation of ageing-related change. For example, in Dulay and Murphy's study on olfactory thresholds cited above, the authors found that although sensory and cognitive skills were correlated, there was additional variance accounted for by chronological age, implying that the sensory deficit explanation does not account for all ageing-related changes in cognitive skills. Often such unaccounted variance is referred to as a **general ageing effect** which means that the effect is known to be linked to ageing, but its precise nature is unknown. Lövdén and Wahlin (2005) similarly reported positive correlations between acuity and cognitive skills, indicating a common factor at work. However, the correlations were not particularly overwhelming, and a high proportion of the variance was left unaccounted for. Again, Hofer, Berg and Era (2003) found no correlation between sensory acuity and cognitive change, suggesting that whether it is found or not may depend upon the technique of analysis used (they used narrower age bands in their study). Even where strong correlations are found, there is some debate about whether sensory measures are correlated with all types of cognition. Several studies (e.g. Anstey *et al.*, 2002) have found correlations between some cognitive skills and sensory acuity, but not others. In Anstey *et al.*'s case, there were significant correlations between visual acuity and fluid intelligence (even after statistically removing the effects of age) but visual acuity could not statistically 'explain' performance on a face recognition task. The finding that sensory measures only correlate with some cognitive measures and not others (and studies do not necessarily agree on which skills correlate) raises uncomfortable thoughts of the early studies searching for critical loss in the terminal drop (see earlier in this chapter). Researchers felt that something must be there, but the search never seemed to pin down what it was to everyone's satisfaction.

Another (and complementary) possibility is that older people with high IQs are likely to be better at looking after their health (e.g. going for regular eye tests) and may have had occupations which did not expose their senses to potential damage (e.g. working in a quiet office rather than on the factory floor). For example (with tongue only slightly in cheek), good senses and high IQ may be part and parcel of a more general factor of good self-preservation skills – and this returns us to the world of disuse theory ('use good self-preservation skills or lose your intelligence'). Newson and Kemps (2005) report that, in their six-year study of older adults, they found a significant correlation between sensory acuity and cognitive skills. However, a large amount of the variance could be accounted for by lifestyle activities. Therefore, a link between acuity and lifestyle may not be as frivolous as it may first appear.

Although there are doubts about the extent to which a sensory deficit measure can predict cognitive change due to ageing, there is little doubt that the issue continues to exercise the minds of researchers and it remains a key method of explaining cognitive change.

Intelligence level and its relationship with specific intellectual skills

A great many intellectual skills (particularly those reliant on fluid intelligence) decline in later life (Horn, 1982) by becoming slower and/or less accurate. For example, the following have all shown an age-related decline: memory for word lists; identifying briefly presented visual images (Walsh, Williams and Herzogs, 1979); pattern recognition (Walsh, 1982); finding solutions to anagrams (Witte and Freund, 1995); everyday problem solving (Diehl, Willis and Schaie, 1995; Sorce, 1995); and speed of planning a driving route (Walker *et al.*, 1997). This list could be continued for the rest of the book. About the only skills where the level of skill is found to be unrelated to ageing are arguably rather less cerebral, such as finding solutions to social problems (e.g. Heidrich and Denney, 1994) and time taken to give up trying to solve an insoluble puzzle (Stuart-Hamilton and McDonald, 1998). The cause of the age-related decline is usually easy to find. In a review of the literature, one author concluded that:

> Such changes in intellectual competence as may occur with ageing are much better picked up by a simple, brief, timed test of general intelligence, than by any single specific cognitive measure we have yet explored. (Rabbitt, 1984, p.113)

Rabbitt is probably deliberately overstating the case, but certainly most intellectual changes in later life are strongly tied to, if not uniquely explained by, the decline in general intelligence. We are thus once more back to a single factor explanation of ageing change and, since general intelligence has, as we have seen, been reliably correlated with reaction times and sensory changes, such a finding should not be surprising. This raises a serious problem for some researchers. Suppose that an experiment discovers that older adults are significantly worse at mental arithmetic and suppose also that this is explained by a general fall in intelligence. If one is interested in discovering what makes older and younger people different from each other, then this finding is dull, because it tells one nothing *new* about ageing – the drop in arithmetic skills has been shown to be nothing more than yet another manifestation of a general decline in intelligence which is already thoroughly documented. It is about as earth shattering as the finding that elephants have big toenails. This is not to say that the experiment is of no value at all. For example, the researchers may be able, from their results, to construct a detailed model of how ageing affects mental arithmetic (i.e. explain *why* the changes take place). If the findings are not used for model building, then the study might still be of value from a practical viewpoint. Thus, the study might lead one to exhort older adults to use a calculator when they go shopping. Throughout this book there are examples of tests of intellectual ability, many of which demonstrate that the decline in a skill is attributable to general intellectual decline, and their value must be weighed against the above considerations. It is the instances where the decline in a skill is *not* in tandem with the general pattern of changes which are often more interesting.

There are a variety of ways in which the effect of general intelligence on performance can be assessed. The two simplest are **matching** and **partial correlation**. The former involves comparing groups of people who are known to have the same level of ability at a certain skill. Thus, any difference between the groups cannot be due to that skill. For example, suppose younger and older people with the same intelligence test scores are compared on a task, and an age difference is found. This cannot be due to differences in intelligence. Matching is a useful technique, but it is often difficult to get good matches between people, especially in different age groups. In such circumstances, partial correlation may provide a solution. This is a statistical technique which is quite complex to perform, but relatively easy to explain. It assesses whether the relationship between two variables is due to the common influence of a third. To take a standard example, suppose some strange passion drove a researcher to measure schoolchildren's foot sizes and to compare these with their scores on a maths test. It is highly probable that there would be a good **positive correlation** between the two measures – that is, on average, the bigger the foot size, the bigger the test score. There is obviously not a causal connection between the two measures, so why the correlation? The answer lies in a third factor – age. Older children have bigger feet and also will perform better on maths tests. Therefore, the feet–maths correlation is the coincidental effect of the influence of a third variable (i.e. age). This can be demonstrated mathematically using the partial correlation technique. The children's foot sizes, test scores and ages are fed into the equation, and the coincidental effect of age is removed mathematically – that is, age is said to be **partialled out**. If, after this has been done, there is no longer a significant correlation between foot size and test scores then it is valid to assume that the effect was attributable to the coincidental effect of age. The partial correlation technique is an important one in gerontology, because it enables researchers, amongst other things, to test if an ageing decline on an intellectual skill is solely due to the coincidental effect of a general fall in *g*. Further information about the mathematical rationale behind the method can be found in any general statistical textbook.

Another important caveat concerns the cohort effect, which can manifest itself in several forms, and can skew results either to exaggerate or diminish ageing effects. For example, there is evidence that some cognitive skills are well preserved in later life because, although some aspects of performance (such as memory) decline, the older person's greater experience can compensate for this, as was seen in Charness's studies of bridge and chess players and the training studies in intellectual skills cited above.

Attentional deficits in ageing

Attention is the ability to concentrate on and/or remember items, despite distracting stimuli (which may have to be simultaneously mentally processed). The frontal lobes (see above) are often cited as being involved in attentional processes. Attention manifests itself in several forms. The ability simply to concentrate on the task at hand without being distracted is known as **sustained attention**. A typical test of this might be to require a participant to respond every time a particular letter appears in a continuous stream of letters presented on a computer screen. Ability on sustained attention tasks is known to be quite well preserved in later life: there is some decline, but it is not appreciable (Salthouse, 1982). Where declines are reported, they may be a product of the test stimuli being hard to detect by older participants under any conditions rather than a failure of attention *per se* (see Giambra, 1993). It is also notable that older adults prefer visual attention tasks to occupy a small rather than wide visual field (Kosslyn, Brown and Dror, 1999).

Selective attention refers to the ability to concentrate on the task at hand whilst there are other distracting stimuli present. A popular method of testing this is the **visual search task**. Participants are shown a display of (for example) letters, and are told to find a particular letter. Where age differences are found in visual search tasks, Walsh (1982) has demonstrated statistically that the slowing and loss of accuracy in older people cannot be solely due to a general slowing in neural transmission. A key aspect of visual search is the ability to ignore or demote the inessential aspects of the task at hand. This can be illustrated through the phenomenon of **negative priming**. Suppose that a participant has a task of finding a target Y surrounded by distractors X. Then the task is changed so that the target is now an X surrounded by distractors Y. The time taken to find the target should significantly slow down, because there will be inhibition from the previous trial where X had to be ignored and Y searched for. There is no doubt that negative priming is an effective way of slowing down responses, but of interest here is whether older adults show a different level of negative priming from younger adults. If older adults are *less* prone to the inhibitory effects of negative priming then it indicates that their inhibitory mechanisms are defective relative to younger adults, and this could point to a key source of age-related decline. Rogers (2000) reviewing the evidence up to that time, noted that the evidence was equivocal – some studies found that older adults were relatively less affected by negative priming, whilst other studies found no difference between younger and older adults. It all depended upon the type of experimental task used. Evidence accrued since then has failed to resolve the issue unambiguously (see Gamboz, Russo and Fox, 2002; Kramer and Strayer, 2001). The most plausible current explanation is that inhibition is affected in some processes but not others (see Rogers, 2000).

Rabbitt (1979) showed that older people did not take advantage of a feature of an experiment in which the target appeared more often in some positions than others. Older people's responses were the same speed whether the target was in an often- or rarely used position. Younger participants, on the other hand, were faster for the frequently used positions. This was not because older people were unaware of the phenomenon: at the debriefing after the test session, they could accurately identify where the target was most likely to appear. Hence, they could accrue the information but not act upon it. Furthermore, repeated practice did not seem to improve their performance (Rabbitt, 1982). Other researchers, however, have failed to replicate Rabbitt's findings. For example, Gilmore, Tobias and Royer (1985) found that older people can use information conveyed by a visual array, and Nissen and Corkin (1985) showed that, in their experiment, older adults responded relatively faster to a target appearing repeatedly in the same position. McCrae and Abrams (2001) demonstrated that older adults retain information about position relatively more efficiently than visual aspects of a target (see also Madden et al., 2004). Also, older adults' ability to ignore distracting information at fixed positions is preserved (see Einstein, Earles and Collins, 2002). Other studies have shown that the presence or absence of an effect depends upon relatively peripheral features of the experimental design, such as the size, shape and brightness of the stimuli (Albert, 1988).

Maylor and Lavie (1998) gave participants the task of identifying a **target** contained within a set of letters presented in the centre of a visual display. In the periphery was a **distracter**. It was found that relative to younger adults, the older participants were more affected by the distracter when there was a small number of letters to choose from than when there was a large number. This seems an interesting finding, but a subsequent study by Madden and Langley (2003) failed to find an age effect by altering perceptual load. At the time of writing, this matter is unresolved. However, it does appear that as for studies of effects of spatial position cited above, some findings on the effects of ageing on visual search are sensitive to experimental design to an extraordinary degree. Indeed, the literature contains more examples of how using a slightly different test method or even re-analysing the data in a different manner can yield significantly different results (see e.g. Cornelissen and Kooijman, 2000). Ultimately, this questions the degree to which some measures of attention measure genuine psychological phenomena rather than experimental artefacts.

It is known that visual search can be enhanced under certain circumstances by **visual marking**. It refers to the phenomenon that if old items can be inhibited (basically, ignored) then a search can be conducted faster. Watson and Maylor (2002) found that visual marking occurred in younger adults for both moving and stationary stimuli, whereas for older adult the phenomenon was only found if the items were stationary. The authors conclude (not surprisingly) that this cannot be attributed to a single cause hypothesis, and argue that different factors govern the attention process depending upon the nature of the array. With tongue in cheek, it is possible to argue that a simple motivational factor may play a role here, and older adults simply give up attempting to make elaborate use of information that will not stay still (as we shall see in Chapter 7, the concept that older adults may not play by the same rules is not an entirely idle speculation). Another, more specialised aid is **subitisation**. This is the ability to identify the number of items present 'at once' without counting them. Most people can instantly recognise something between two and seven items at once (there are considerable individual differences). This is known, because given a task of counting how many items are present in a visual display, people give the same response times for the low numbers they can subitize and beyond this number, the time taken to provide a response rises reliably in tandem with the number of items. For example, if the largest number of items a person can subitize is four, then their response times for counting one, two, three or four items will be approximately the same, but their response time for counting five items will be slower, and the time taken to count 20 items will be a lot slower. Watson, Maylor and Manson (2002) found that older adults could only subitize the items in a display when there were no distracter items present. However, other aspects of the skill may be relatively unaffected by ageing (Basak and Verhaeghen, 2002).

In another test of selective attention, McDowd and Filion (1992) gave participants the task of listening to a tape of a radio play, whilst a number of tones were played. In the key experimental condition, participants were told to ignore the tones and concentrate on the play. The degree to which participants succeeded in this task was measured by testing skin conductance and heart rate – if the tones were being ignored, then neither measure should show a change when they were played. After the first few tones were played, younger participants successfully ignored them, but older people could not, and their responses remained at the same high level throughout the experiment. Again, Friedman, Hamberger and Ritter (1993) found that brain potentials (electrical activity produced by the brain) were far more pronounced in older than in younger participants when presented with a repeated stimulus. Comparable results on EEG patterns have been reported by Amenedo and Diaz (1999). These findings reflect the studies of Bergman *et al.* (1976) and Dubno *et al.* (1984), which found that older people are disproportionately disadvantaged when trying to follow auditory messages played against noisy backgrounds. This is evidence of a more serious attentional problem than has been found in many visual attention tasks. However, Murphy, McDowd and Wilcox (1999) demonstrated that many aural attention experiments failed to allow adequately for hearing loss in the older participants. When the sound volume of the stimuli was adjusted to allow for this, the researchers found identical patterns of response for older and younger adults. This implies that many of the age differences in auditory attention studies may at least be inflated, if not created, by a cohort effect.

It is important to note that the influence of selective attention, like the other forms of attention, extends beyond tasks which are very obviously centred on an explicit attentional task. We use attention in a vast range of everyday tasks (for example, it would be impossible to read this sentence without being able to attend to what is printed on the page rather than the visual surroundings). Thus, research in attention is about more than how participants perform in laboratory tasks (even if after several hours of reading about the topic, this is all it seems to be to a less than fanatical observer). For example, Viskontas *et al.* (2004) demonstrated that attentional skills are strongly correlated with other cognitive skills in older adults. What happens in attention is often a guide to the general level of intellectual performance in older people.

Divided attention refers to the ability to attend simultaneously to and process more than one source of information. Many **working memory** tasks (see Chapter 3) fall into this category. The best-known method of assessing divided attention is probably the **dichotic listening** task. Using stereo headphones, the participant is presented with a different message in either ear. Typically, the participant must report what he or she heard in either ear separately. Many researchers have shown that older people are bad at this task (e.g. Horn, 1982; Salthouse, 1985). More generally, researchers have found that there is an ageing deficit on tasks requiring the sharing of attention between two or more sources (e.g. Lajoie *et al.*, 1996; Vaneste and Pouthas, 1999). Various theories have been advanced to explain this phenomenon. Salthouse (1985) argues that the effect is yet another manifestation of the age × complexity effect. This is for two main reasons. First, because on simpler attention tasks (e.g. sustained attention), the age difference is less pronounced. Second, if the information load is lessened, then the age difference is also diminished (Albert, 1988). Why the age × complexity effect should manifest itself is harder to explain. For example, it is resistant to being comfortably explained as another manifestation of general slowing (Brink and McDowd, 1999; Lowe and Rabbitt, 1997; Wickens, Braune and Stokes, 1987). Salthouse (1985) showed that older people are as able as younger people at shifting and allocating attention in a divided attention task, and thus it can be concluded that both age groups are using the same working methods. The most parsimonious explanation is that older people suffer from a general loss of processing resources: in other words, through general neural decline, they no longer have the 'mental capacity' to attend to as much at one time as they could in their youth. This explanation seems to fit the available evidence. Salthouse (1985; especially Chapter 7) provides more detail and a lengthy technical argument supporting this. However, a (again, very technical) meta-analysis of studies by Verhaeghen *et al.* (2003) argues against a single general slowing factor.

At a neurological level, the decline of the frontal lobes (strongly linked with attention) may also play a role (see Lowe and Rabbitt, 1997; Woodruff-Pak, 1997) and more generally a failure within the brain to screen neural signals effectively from each other (see Woodruff-Pak, 1997, for a review). Gaeta *et al.* (2001) conducted an experiment in which participants had to ignore the signal (a pure tone) to the left ear and only respond to the pure tone which followed it in the right ear. The tone to the left ear was usually 700 Hz, but occasionally would be slightly lower (650 Hz) or considerably lower (500 Hz). The tone to the right ear was 1500 Hz and had one of two intensities (the participants had to make a judgement on the intensity of the right ear tone). If the left ear tone was the considerably lower 500 Hz tone, this interfered with responses to the right ear tone, and performance worsened yet more if there was a short interval between the start of the left ear tone and the start of the right ear tone. These findings applied to all participants, but the older participants were disproportionately worse. The authors concluded that a deficit in performance such as this is indicative of frontal lobe dysfunction (see also Gaeta, Friedman and Ritter, 2003). Essentially, the older participants had lost the accuracy and speed of functioning necessary to maintain a youthful level of control over attentional processes.

It can also be demonstrated that anxiety level differentially affects older adults' divided attention task performance. Hogan (2003) found that older people who scored highly on a measure of anxiety levels performed significantly less well on a divided attention task. The same effect was not found in younger adults. The effect was not, however, found in a measure of motor performance, implying that the effect is a relatively specific one.

There thus seem to be several possible explanations as to why older adults' abilities at divided attention tasks worsen, and indeed there is no clear agreement as to which theory is 'top dog'. Most probably, as with much of the cognitive ageing literature, the search for a single factor has created the tacit belief that there 'must' be a parsimonious explanation for everything in the ageing intellect. It is of course perfectly possible that the decline is attributable to several more or less independent factors. For example, Glass *et al.* (2000) argued that decline may be due to three factors: a general decline, a decline specific to the task and older adults being more cautious over their use of strategies to perform tasks. However, it should be noted that age differences are only reliably found in studies where participants have had relatively little practice at the task. If people are given extensive practice (in the order of thousands of trials) then age differences are smaller or non-existent (see Rogers, 2000). The most parsimonious explanation is that practice makes, if not perfect, then at least easier to do, and the reduction in processing demands means older adults have sufficient processing capacity to perform the task. The situation is analogous to learning to ride a bike or drive a car. At first all the attention is needed for the basics of steering, etc., but with experience these become less attention-demanding, leaving spare capacity for other things.

Conceptual organisation

As reaction times measure the mind's immediate reactions to stimuli, so **conceptual organisation** describes the ability to treat items at an abstract level, in order to uncover basic rules and principles. Conceptual organisation is often measured by using shapes and symbols where the rules that classify the groupings have been experimenter-decided and it is the task of the participant to uncover these rules (e.g. 'shapes are grouped by colour irrespective of size and shape' or 'all shapes are grouped by colour and by shape' etc.). Researchers have shown that, in many instances, older people have difficulty in doing these sorts of tasks (see Filoteo and Maddox, 2004). However, classification can also be applied to the everyday world. For example, a man, a gerbil and an elephant are visually dissimilar, but at an abstract level they are all examples of mammals. Again, a proverb such as 'people in glass houses shouldn't throw stones' is of value only to greenhouse owners unless it is treated at a symbolic level. The latter might be supposed to be part of general knowledge and thus ageing-resistant. However, Albert, Duffy and Naeser (1987) found that older people were worse at interpreting the meaning of proverbs. This applied whether participants were left to provide their own answers unaided, or were given a multiple choice test. It is possible that Albert *et al.*'s results are attributable to a cohort effect. However, as has been remarked above, it is also possible that crystallised intelligence is less 'ageing proof' than most commentators believe.

Another test of conceptual abilities is the '20 questions' type of task. This is a version of the parlour game in which the participant is told that the experimenter is thinking of an object, and by a series of questions to which the experimenter can only answer 'yes' or 'no', the participant tries to elicit the name of the object. Clearly, the optimal strategy is to narrow down the field by asking questions which progressively constrict the choice of alternatives (e.g. 'Is it an animal?', 'Is it a mammal?', 'Is it a household pet?'). This is called a **constraint seeking strategy**, because the choice of possibilities is increasingly constrained by each question. Eventually, when the list is down to a small number, it is best to switch to a **hypothesis scanning** question, where a specific item is named (e.g. 'Is it a dog?'). If a hypothesis scanning question is asked when the list is still large, then this is a foolish strategy, because the chances of hitting on the right name are too remote (e.g. asking 'Is it a dog?' having only established that the animal is a mammal). Denney and Denney (1974) found that older people are far less efficient at the '20 questions' task. They had to ask more questions before getting the right answer, largely because they asked fewer constraint seeking questions. Older people are disadvantaged in an analogous fashion when they are given a range of items, and asked to divide them into groups. Clearly a good strategy would involve the grouping of items into superordinate categories (e.g. 'animals', 'items of furniture'). However, older participants tend to produce more groupings where the linkage between items is illogical to an observer (Denney and Denney, 1973). It might be argued that the decline in categorisation skills is due to an artefact of declining memory (i.e. older adults cannot simultaneously keep in mind everything they need to sort through). However, varying the memory load by varying the number of items to be categorised has no appreciable effects on performance (see Rebok, 1987). Neither can differences in education level provide a total explanation (Cicirelli, 1976; Laurence and Arrowood, 1982). Nor again can a cohort difference in knowledge of how to deal with this sort of task, since even after being shown the best strategy, older adults failed to use it as extensively as younger controls (Hybertson, Perdue and Hybertson, 1982).

Another explanation (and perhaps the most parsimonious) is that declines in classification skills are tied to a general decline in *g*. Laurence and Arrowood (1982) compared the performance of (Toronto) university students, elderly alumni from the same university and hospitalised older adults, on a classification task. No significant difference was found between the alumni and students, but both groups were significantly superior to the hospitalised group. Although no IQ data are provided, it is reasonable to assume that the alumni's intelligence levels were 'well preserved' (this would accord with studies of similar groups). Hence, classification skills probably only decline when intelligence begins to fall, as in the case of the hospitalised older adults. Laurence and Arrowood also noted that the error made most often (43%) by the hospitalised group was **sentential grouping** – items were linked together because they fitted into a sentence (e.g. 'the *bunny* ate the *carrot*'). This was rarely if ever done by the other two groups, who made errors, but these were usually due to relatively minor slips of logic. Thus, deleterious ageing can result in quantitative and qualitative changes in classification skills. Furthermore, Arenberg (1982), in a longitudinal study, showed that younger participants' performance on a conceptual formation task improved on subsequent test sessions, whilst the older participants got worse.

However, it may be observed that when people make 'errors' in a classification task, they are only 'wrong' because their classifications do not conform with what the experimenter wanted. Grouping a carrot with a rabbit is perfectly sensible; although, in a wider scheme of things, it is not the most elegant solution, it is perhaps more fun (that participants might seek amusing solutions does not seem to occur to many experimenters). Denney (1974) argues that older people make grouping mistakes, not because of any 'decline' but because they forget the accepted 'correct' way of grouping things as defined by educational practice, and instead adopt an arguably more 'natural' method of grouping. This may be coincidentally related to education level and intelligence, because higher educated and and higher intelligence people tend to enter professions and have leisure activities more demanding of formal grouping practices, and thus maintain these methods longer than other people.

If a 'failure' of grouping does occur, then the change need not be as bad as it may first appear. For example, the decline observed by Arenberg was not appreciable until the participants were in their seventies. More encouragingly, Labouvie-Vief and Gonda (1976) found that older people can under some circumstances improve their classificatory skills with practice. Also, older adults perform better if the tasks have an obvious practical slant rather than being purely abstract. For example, Arenberg found that older people were better at working on problems where items of food were grouped to produce 'safe' and 'poisonous' combinations than when given structurally identical problems of set formation using abstract shapes.

Critics might argue that the studies reported above are relatively 'gentle' classification tasks. Where there is added difficulty (e.g. being required to transfer between categorising items in one way to categorising them in another), then age differences become more pronounced, and there is good evidence that this is attributable to differences in frontal lobe functioning (e.g. Kramer *et al.*, 1995; Levine, Stuss and Milberg, 1995). However, these more difficult tasks may also be more demanding of other cognitive processes, and it is doubtful if they are testing the same genre of skill. It should also be noted that age differences are more pronounced if people try some categorisation techniques rather than others. For example, Filoteo and Maddox (2004) found that if categorisation was based around rule-based learning, then age differences were less than if categorisation was based on integrating information. Similarly, Rousseau and Rogers (2002) demonstrated that there was little difference between younger and older adults who formed hypotheses about categories and tested them out, whilst for those who tried to 'form an impression', age differences were larger. This implies that if people stick to tried and tested working methods, age differences are likely to be minimised.

Creativity in later life

Running in tandem with general intelligence is **creativity**. Researchers are divided on how best to describe the skill, but most would agree that for an act to be creative, it must be novel, and it must be appropriate to the situation. The best way to demonstrate what is meant by this is to consider a typical creativity test. The participant is presented with a house brick and is asked to think of as many uses for it as possible. There are two types of response which are classified as being 'uncreative'. The first is appropriate but conventional (e.g. 'Use it in building a house'). The second is novel but inappropriate (e.g. 'Use it to cure insomnia by knocking yourself out with it'). A creative answer would be something like 'Scrape the surface of the brick to make rouge' (i.e. something both novel and feasible). People who produce a lot of creative answers are said to be good at divergent thinking (i.e. given a simple situation they can produce answers which diverge from mainstream thought). Studies have found that older people are poorer at divergent thinking tasks. It might be argued that this is because the older also have depleted intellectual skills in general. However, the age difference persists even when older and younger participants are matched for intelligence and education level (Alpaugh and Birren, 1977; McCrae, Arneberg and Costa, 1987). Among individuals who have always been very creative, this difference may be lessened or even not be present (e.g. Crosson and Robertson-Tchabo, 1983). Again, Sasser-Coen (1993) has argued that divergent thinking becomes generally less important in the creative process as people grow older, with greater emphasis placed on items generated from personal experience. An important caveat to the findings of the above studies is raised by Simonton (1990) and separately by Hendricks (1999), which is simply that the applicability of divergent thinking tests, along with other psychometric measures, is debatable, and that they may not be reliable indicators of 'real-life' creative abilities in all cases.

Another way to consider creativity is the biographical approach. By this method, the lives of acknowledged leaders in fields of activity where originality of thought is highly prized are examined, to see what made or makes them 'better' than others. Some generalisations can be gleaned from such studies. Artists and musicians tend to display their talents early in life (e.g. Mozart), whilst scientists are usually in their twenties before they show signs of outstanding ability. In addition, scientists are often competent, but not outstanding students, until the area of specialisation in which they will become pre-eminent grips their imagination (Hudson, 1987). Charles Darwin was a classic example of this. Thereafter, most eminent persons make their major contributions to their field before the onset of old age. Most have a peak of creative output before they are 40. This applies to disciplines as diverse as mathematics, chemistry and musical composition. It is important to note that 'great' and 'routine' pieces of work tend to be produced in tandem. In other words, in a prolific period, a creative person will produce the same ratio of good to indifferent work as he or she will during relatively unproductive periods – thus, the **quality ratio** stays fairly constant (Simonton, 1990). Creativity has for *most* people relatively declined by their sixties (see Rebok, 1987). Although there have been several studies claiming that creativity continues to rise throughout life (e.g. Reed, 2005) it is notable that these often rely on self-report and self-perception, not on more objective measures. However, this is not *universally* true, and Butler (1967) has made a spirited counterattack to this view, citing numerous masterpieces produced late in their creators' lives. Titian, for example, continued to paint into his nineties, and most critics agree that his later work far surpasses his earlier output. However, Butler cites notable *exceptions*. For the majority of creative people, ageing is associated with a decline.

It can be argued that the sensory and physical declines of ageing will affect creative people especially badly, because above all others they need a precise, accurate and untiring view of the world (Rebok, 1987). Undoubtedly in some creative fields, where physical fitness is *de rigeur*, this is true. Opera singers and ballet dancers are never at their peak in old age (but equally, there are few ballet dancers over *35* who still perform on the stage). However, for the majority of creative persons, another explanation must be sought, since there is a long list of innovative people who have succeeded in spite of, or even because of, physical incapacity. For example, it is well known that Beethoven was deaf in his later years, and this fact may account for some of the innovations in his later works, when he had to rely on an imagined world of sound. Mahler suffered from a crippling heart condition, which probably contributed to the angst-ridden nature of his later work (indeed, the irregular rhythm of his heart beat is incorporated into the opening of his ninth symphony). Stephen Hawking, perhaps the most famous of contemporary theoretical physicists, is nearly completely paralysed by motor neuron disease; a condition which by his own admission has encouraged him to think about his work. In short, there is plenty of evidence that creativity need not be affected by physical declines far more severe than those experienced in normal ageing. Similarly, attribution for the effects of ageing cannot be laid upon a general intellectual decline, for two main reasons. First, because as was seen from Alpaugh and Birren (1977) cited previously, age differences in creativity exist even when intelligence levels are matched. Second, intelligence is in any case a poor predictor of creativity (Hudson, 1987). Therefore, another explanation must be sought.

One possibility is that creative people are victims of their own success. Scientists who achieve pre-eminence in their field are likely to find themselves quickly elevated to headships of departments or research groups. Once in this position, much of the running of experiments and 'hands on' experience is passed on to research assistants, whilst the head of department finds him- or herself embroiled in an increasing quantity of administrative duties. Thus, the eminent scientist's reward for success at a particular endeavour may be to have his or her future activities in the field restricted, thus causing a decline in creative output. A different set of values probably applies to people pre-eminent in the arts. First, far more than scientists, artists (of any type) rely for their success on critical and public opinion. Accordingly, the worth of an artist depends upon what is fashionable at the time, and to be considered creative, the artist must be seen as a leading interpreter of the fashion and/or to have been the creator of that fashion. A second consideration is that few artists are able to support themselves if their craft does not pay. Accordingly, if they do not achieve success in early life, they are likely to withdraw from full-time creative activity and seek other employment. It follows from these two premises that the creative person usually becomes noticed for being a skilled exponent of a current fashion at an early stage in his or her career. Obviously, the artist seeks to capitalise on this, and accordingly becomes increasingly identifiable with that fashion. However, opinions change, and almost inevitably the artist becomes a representative of a movement which is now unfashionable. The more successful he or she was, the more strongly he or she is now identified as being unfashionable. In short, successful artists are hoist by their own petard (for a brilliant fictional account of this, see the shamefully under-regarded novel *Angel* by Taylor, 1957). The only solution for most artists is to move with the fashion. Since this probably involves a radical change of style, their output is likely to suffer. The speed at which these changes occur vary from discipline to discipline. Anyone with any knowledge of pop music will know that a cycle such as the one described occurs every three or four years. However, in any field, there are very few artists who produce 'timeless' works which rise above the mercurial changes of fashionable opinion. For example, a quick perusal through a second-hand bookshop or a musical dictionary will readily reveal how many 'geniuses' of literature and music from previous generations are now completely forgotten. Thus, the reasons behind the changes in creative output across the lifespan may be due far more to the lifestyles and job demands of the gifted than to ageing *per se*. Older people may have 'lost' their creativity because they were too good at their job earlier in life.

The above arguments apply to people who are outstanding in their field, but they do not deny a role for creativity in everyday life. It is important to note that even where studies have found creativity scores to be lower in later life, nobody has argued that creativity is non-existent. This argument is not just a simple justification for older adults to pick up their paint brushes. It also counteracts the claims of some creativity advocates that mainstream psychology has claimed older adults are over the hill and lack creative powers. This is not the case – on objective measures, creative acts usually *decline* in later life. Nobody has said that they *stop*, nor that older adults should be barred from creative acts. In fact, there is considerable evidence that engaging in creative activity (e.g. painting, writing, and so on) is of considerable value to older participants, and is reported as enhancing feelings of well-being and general self-esteem (e.g. Hickson and Housley, 1997; Weisberg and Wilder, 2001).

Piagetian conservation

Papalia (1972) demonstrated that older people are bad at some of the **Piagetian conservation tasks** (named after their inventor, Piaget). This is a surprising finding, because most seven-year-old children can successfully perform them. The tasks in question test participants' knowledge that two items of equal volume remain of equal volume even when one of them changes shape. The participant is shown two balls of modelling clay of equal size and shape, and agrees that each is composed of the same amount of clay. The experimenter then rolls one of the balls into a sausage shape, and asks the participant if the two pieces have the same amount of clay in them, to which of course the answer is 'yes' (pedants note that one ignores the minuscule amount lost on the hands and table surface during rolling). It is surprising that ageing should cause people to fail what appears to be such a simple task (and indeed, Piaget thought it impossible). The decline is not limited to conservation of matter. For example, McDonald and

Stuart-Hamilton (2002) conducted a replication of another of Piaget's studies, in which participants were placed at a table on which was a model of three mountains, each with a distinct feature (one had a snow cap, one had a house on it, etc.). The participants were shown a range of pictures showing views of the model from various positions around the table. Asked to select their own viewpoint, they could do this faultlessly. However, if now asked to select a picture representing what a doll positioned at another location around the table could 'see', participants made errors. Some of these were simple errors of spatial judgement (i.e. they chose a view that was close to that of the doll's, but nonetheless inaccurate). However, circa 15 per cent of older participants chose a view that was their *own*. This type of error – called an egocentric error – is illogical and is only otherwise seen when the task is given to younger children (typically aged eight years or younger). There are similar surprising failings on other Piagetian tasks, such as moral reasoning (McDonald and Stuart-Hamilton, 1996) and animism – the erroneous belief that some inanimate objects are alive (McDonald and Stuart-Hamilton, 2000). Certainly, older people who fail Piagetian tasks are not incapable of performing them, since they can be easily retrained to do them correctly (Blackburn and Papalia, 1992).

Hooper, Fitzgerald and Papalia (1971) suggest that skills necessary to perform Piagetian tasks may be lost in the reverse of the order in which they were acquired during childhood, and may also be strongly linked with changes in fluid and crystallised intelligence. However, more recent research by McDonald and Stuart-Hamilton (e.g. Stuart-Hamilton and McDonald, 1996, 1999, 2001) suggests a more complex tale. If older people's performance on a wide variety of Piagetian tasks is measured, then it is possible to create a 'Piaget score' (i.e. the total number of tests correctly performed). This is a better predictor of participants' ages than their intelligence test scores (Stuart-Hamilton and McDonald, 1996). In turn, the best predictor of Piagetian score is a personality measure called **need for cognition** (Stuart-Hamilton and McDonald, 1999, 2001). This is a measure of the drive a person feels to pursue intellectually demanding tasks as part of their lifestyle, as opposed to their actual level of intelligence. Overall, this implies that the changes in Piagetian performance may reflect an older person's level of involvement with intellectual tasks and (for want of a better expression) an 'intellectual lifestyle'. As a person gets older, he or she may become less committed to certain intellectual pursuits, and his or her methods and styles of thinking shift (no value judgement is implied in this – see Chapter 7). Such changes will correlate reasonably well with performance on intelligence test scores, but this is in part coincidental.

To some extent this echoes the argument by Labouvie-Vief (1992), who proposed a concept of **postformal thought**. This is a stage of intellectual development, which, it is argued, occurs in adulthood, after the stage of **formal operations** (the final stage of Piaget's theory of development in which people begin to think in genuinely abstract terms). Formal operations is very systematic and relies on logical processes. However, it can be reasonably be argued that people do not spend their lives being logical, and that many important decisions are made by not only cold logic, but also considerations of emotions and other subjective feelings. Accordingly, 'postformal thought' refers to this ability to weigh up and balance arguments created by logic and emotion, and is similar in some respects to the discussion of wisdom earlier in this chapter. However, whilst this is a useful operational distinction, it is debatable whether formal and postformal thought are intrinsically different, since arguments created from an emotional source and arguments created from a logical source can be combined logically, without the need for a 'new' kind of thinking. A cynic might argue that a further danger is that the theory might be used to excuse some age-related declines in intellectual performance by relabelling failures to perform tasks as examples of alternative strategies. It is also hard to justify a stage of postformal thought when there is evidence that a significant proportion of older adults are jettisoning earlier stages of Piagetian development. More probably, some older adults lose skills because they are no longer important in their lives (see Chapter 7 for further discussion of this point). This raises potentially awkward questions for more general studies of intellectual change in later life. Many studies have assumed that participants, both younger and older, are using the same set of mental skills, albeit with varying efficiency. However, if a significant proportion of older adults are using different logical systems, then is such a comparison fair or meaningful?

Summary

Older people have traditionally been seen as retaining crystallised skills and increasing their wisdom, whilst showing a decline in fluid intelligence. Research has generally backed this conclusion, but only at a relatively broad level. *Inter alia*, it should be noted that: (a) some older people preserve their youthful level of fluid intelligence; (b) the size of the difference is in part an artefact of the experimental and analytical methods used; (c) the 'preservation' of crystallised intelligence relies on tests not being timed and/or marked less rigorously. Where an age change is noted, it can be considerable, being on average nearly two standard deviations below the mean of a younger group. However, in all of the above cases, the cohort effect exaggerates the effects. Longitudinal studies lessen age differences, but they are also expensive and (obviously) time consuming to run. There is some evidence that, in older people, a sudden decline in intellectual abilities is a harbinger of death. Various models of ageing change have been proposed, including the disuse theory (that skills decline because they are insufficiently practised) and the general slowing hypothesis (that the changes are due to a slowing in neural conduction). The former has some validity (particularly through the related issue of compensation), but has difficulty in explaining why certain well-practised older people still display a worsening of skills. The latter theory is backed by some intriguing evidence (particularly Brinley plots), but evidence also suggests that at least some variability in skills is left unexplained. Declines in more specific intellectual skills, such as attention, conceptual organisation, creativity and Piagetian task performance, have all been well documented. However, in all instances, cohort effects or lifestyle changes may strongly colour the results. Indeed, in general, it would appear difficult if not impossible to decide how much of ageing change is due to cohort effects rather than 'pure' ageing.

Suggested further reading

Perhaps the best (and most readable) summary of the study of intelligence and how it is tested is provided by Deary (2001); although a short book, it covers a lot of ground and is very readable. A more advanced text covering a lot of the areas addressed in this chapter in much greater depth is Perfect and Maylor (2000). Readers should be cautioned that, although very erudite, it assumes a high level of prior knowledge of advanced psychological and statistical techniques. The same caveat applies to Hertzog and Nesselroade's (2003) excellent critical review of methodological problems in testing older adults. Salthouse (1991a, 1991b, 1992a, 1992b) provides a suitably exhaustive (and exhausting!) critical review of the ageing and intelligence literature. These works remain required reading for anyone hoping to come to grips with mainstream psychological research on ageing and cognitive skills. Some of the classic journal papers and book chapters on the psychology of ageing, particularly cognitive ageing, can be hard to find without using an inter-library loan or similar. Lawton and Salthouse's (1998) edited collection *Essential Papers on the Psychology of Aging* contains many of the widely cited papers and is warmly recommended. A more critical consideration of problems with testing older adults is provided by the present author in Chapter 7 of this book and in another work (Stuart-Hamilton, 1999b). For readers wishing to gain an overview of changes in intellectual skills across the whole lifespan, Turner and Helms (1995) is warmly recommended. A shorter overview is provided by Stuart-Hamilton (1999a).

CHAPTER 3

Ageing and Memory

Introduction

The study of the psychology of memory has generated a large number of concepts and technical terms, and a brief survey of at least some of these is necessary before an examination of the effects of ageing on memory skills can begin. A belief held by many lay people is that memory is a homogeneous skill: that is, everything is memorised in the same way. This is erroneous, simply because physiological research has demonstrated that different types of memories (e.g. for word, pictures, physical skills) are stored in anatomically different sections of the brain (see Chapter 1). Furthermore, psychologists have found that these memory systems also behave in different ways. Accordingly, when researchers talk, for example, of 'verbal' or 'visual' memories, they can be confident that they are discussing anatomically and functionally distinct systems.

One of the simplest ways of categorising memories is by the length of time over which they are retained, and this usually means a division into **short-term memory (STM)** and **long-term memory (LTM)**. Short-term memory is the temporary storage of events and items perceived in the very immediate past: that is, events and items that occurred no more than a few minutes ago, and usually a much shorter period (i.e. the last few seconds). The classical test of short-term memory requires the experimenter to read out a list of letters, numbers or words, and get the participant to repeat it back. The longest length of list of these **to-be-remembered (TBR)** items which can be repeated back reliably is called the participant's **span**. Spans vary according to the nature of the TBR items and thus, there is usually a prefix denoting the materials used in the test. Hence, **digit span** denotes memory for numbers, **word span** memory for word lists, and so forth.

One of the problems with the classical span experiment is that it is not very realistic: people simply do not spend very much of their time learning arbitrary lists. Another point is that short-term memory is impermanent: unless an especial effort is made, the memory fades within a brief time. A popular explanation of why there is a short-term store, and how it might function, is provided by Baddeley and Hitch's (1974) working memory model. Working memory is defined as: 'the temporary storage of information that is necessary for such activities as learning, reasoning, and comprehension' (Baddeley, 1986, p.324). Thus, typical tasks involving working memory:

> are those in which the person must hold a small amount of material in mind for a short time while simultaneously carrying out further cognitive operations, either on the material held or on other incoming materials. (Morris, Craik and Gick, 1990, p.67)

This is a form of short-term memory which most people can intuitively appreciate that there is a need for. For example, in listening to speech, it is necessary to keep in mind what a person has just said in order to make sense of what is currently being said. Another example of working memory in action is mental arithmetic. All the figures of the sum have to be retained (in the right order) while the arithmetic transformation is performed on them. Note that in both these instances something has to be remembered whilst another mental operation takes place.

Full details of how the working memory model is presumed to operate are still far from finalised. However, in its basic form the system is said to be controlled by the **central executive**. This is in part a memory store (though with a limited capacity) and in part a controller of several **slave systems**. These have larger memory capacities than the central executive, and each specialises in only one type of memory. Thus, there are separate systems for verbal material, pictures and spatial position. The verbal material system is called the **phonological loop** (in some older texts it is called the **articulatory loop**). This deals with words in the broadest possible sense, and thus not only memorises letters and words, but also numbers. The central executive controls the depositing and retrieval of memories to and from the slave systems. When **concurrent processing** is required (i.e. maintaining a memory and doing another attention-demanding task at the same time) the central executive helps to co-ordinate these. It is important to note that if there are too many TBR items to fit in the slave systems (i.e. the slave systems by themselves cannot remember everything sent to them), then some or all of the items can be transferred to long-term memory, which thus acts as a back-up.

Memory traces quickly fade from short-term memory for the simple reason that the vast majority of information taken in is only of value at the time, and afterwards is highly redundant. To return to the example given above, remembering the numbers in a mental arithmetic problem is necessary at the time, but to keep remembering them afterwards would be both an irritation and a waste of memory space. However, there is obviously some information which *does* need to be remembered more permanently, and this is the role of long-term memory.

Long-term memory seeks to be a permanent store of information. Whether it has a maximum capacity and how much information is lost from it are unanswerable questions.

However, it is certainly the case that for people not suffering from amnesia, 'essential' and 'everyday' information is never lost. For example, people do not forget their native language, their names, the name of the capital of France or toilet training. In all probability, this is because such information is either very important to them and/or it is frequently **rehearsed** (i.e. the memory is recalled and thus 'practised') so that they form strong, unshakeable **memory traces**. Some information *is* lost from long-term memory, however (e.g. old addresses, telephone numbers, etc., tend to be forgotten when friends move). These lost memories tend to be information which either is now irrelevant and has been superseded, or is unimportant, so it is infrequently rehearsed. The classical test of long-term memory is the same as the short-term memory 'span' procedure, except that the participant is required to hold the TBR items in memory for a longer time (typically, anything from 30 minutes up to several days). If the reader is wondering why participants do not forget the TBR items as with the short-term memory experiment, the simple answer is that the participants are encouraged to rehearse them.

Another method of categorising memory is into **episodic** and **semantic memories** (Tulving, 1972). Episodic memories are of personal experiences (a deceptively similar concept is **autobiographical memory**, referring to memory for events specific to one's personal life). Semantic memory is for items independent of personal experiences and is a store of facts, such as general knowledge, or academic learning. A further system divides memory into **explicit** and **implicit memories** (Graf and Schachter, 1985). This refers to the distinction between a memory which is consciously sought (e.g. trying to recall the date of the Battle of Waterloo) and one which can be gleaned from memory, but which has not been deliberately stored. For example, one method of testing implicit memory is to expose a participant to a list of words in the guise of a psychological task (e.g. grading words for the level of visual images they provoke). At a later time, the participant is given a **word completion task**, in which a word must be provided, having been given its first letter or letters (e.g. 'complete FOR_ _ _'). The participant is more likely to provide a word he or she has encountered in the previous list (e.g. 'FOREST' rather than 'FORGET'), even though he or she may be unaware that these memories are being drawn upon. In other instances, implicit memory may refer to inferences which may be drawn from memories, even though the inferences themselves have not been explicitly stored. For example, people can readily answer the question 'Does Elton John have two legs?' by extrapolating the information from the memory that Elton John is a pop singer, pop singers are humans and humans are bipedal. In short, people can have a 'memory' that Sir Elton has two legs, even though it is not stored as an explicit statement of fact.

Tangential to the above domains of memory are the skills of planning and overseeing. One of the commonest uses of memory is to remember to do something in the future, or **prospective memory**. Conceptually related to this is **metamemory**, which is knowledge about one's own memory – what its capacity is, how best to remember things, and so forth.

Memory systems can also be considered in terms of how they work: for example, how memories are created for storage (**encoding**) and how they are retrieved. There is a considerable debate within psychology as to whether memories are lost through inefficient coding or inefficient retrieval. The inefficient coding hypothesis can be likened to a library where an incompetent librarian puts books on the wrong shelves, so that when a search is made for a book, it cannot be found in its rightful place. Similarly, memories that are inefficiently encoded will be lost because they cannot be retrieved. The inefficient retrieval argument is that memories are lost because although they are stored properly, the search for them is inefficient. To return to the library analogy, it is as though a person with severe dyslexia were sent to find a book. This issue is of especial importance in discussing the memories of people with dementia (see Chapter 6).

Memory can be tested in a variety of ways. The commonest distinction is between **recall** and **recognition**. The former requires a participant to report as much as possible of a list of TBR items. In an **ordered recall** task, the participant is only marked correct if all TBR items are repeated in their exact order of presentation (e.g. if TBR items are *17654* the participant must recall *17654*; *71546*, for example, is not sufficient). In a **free recall** task, the order of recall does not matter (thus, *71654*, *71546*, *56147*, or any other permutation of these numbers would be equally acceptable). A recognition task is considered to be easier than a recall task. Both begin with a presentation of the TBR items. However, in a recognition task, the participant's memory is tested by having to select the items he or she has seen (the *targets*) from a list which also includes items which were not on the original list (the *distracters*). Participants tend to remember more items in a recognition than in a recall task, because the memory load is lighter (it is also worth noting that the recognition and recall processes are almost certainly controlled by different mental mechanisms). In a **cued recall** task, the participant is in effect given a hint about the answer (e.g. he or she might be given the first letter or letters of the TBR word).

Having thus briefly considered some of the technical terms, theories and techniques employed in memory research, attention will now shift to how ageing affects memory.

Ageing and short-term memory

If a basic STM span test is administered (where the participant simply repeats back what the experimenter has just said or shown), then several studies have demonstrated a statistically significant but nonetheless rather small decline in later life (Craik and Jennings, 1992; Craik *et al.*, 1995). However, when any extra demands are placed on participants, then age effects generally become very much more pronounced (Cohen, 1996; Craik, 1986).

One method of making a STM task more complicated is the **backward span** procedure, where the participant is required to repeat the items back in reverse order of their presentation (e.g. TBR items are *75123*; participant must reply *32157*). This is clearly harder than straightforward recall, since participants must keep in store the items in their correct order whilst simultaneously working out what they are in reverse (in essence, this is a test of working memory). Bromley (1958), among others, has shown that older people are significantly worse at this task. Several causes have been suggested. One is that because the items in the forward and reverse lists are identical, it is easy to confuse the two, and thus form a garbled amalgam. This implies a failure of planning of mental materials and thus problems with frontal lobe functioning (see Thompson-Schill *et al.*, 2002). Thus, just as a decline in frontal lobe functioning may have a significant influence on other cognitive tasks (see Chapter 2) so might it do in memory. This failure to distinguish between irrelevant and necessary information is sometimes described under the heading of the **inhibitory deficit hypothesis**. The hypothesis can also be demonstrated in working memory tasks in which older participants are disproportionately disadvantaged on later trials of the experiment, because the accrued earlier lists of to-be-remembered items have not been properly 'flushed out' and thus interfere with memory of the new to-be-remembered items (Bowles and Salthouse, 2003). Hedden and Park (2001) similarly demonstrated that older adults have an especial difficulty in distinguishing between items from earlier to-be-remembered lists and items in a current to-be-remembered list.

These findings complement the working memory model. Baddeley (1986) cited the central executive as the prime cause of this age-related decline in STM. Given that the central executive is felt to be anatomically centred on the frontal lobes (see Baddeley, 1995) this makes intuitive sense. Although something of a simplification, what is being argued is that memory span is relatively unaffected by ageing – the principal deficit is in organising the material that is to be remembered and in juggling different tasks when doing something more complex than simply remembering a list of items. For example, it can be readily demonstrated that increasing the complexity of the distracting task in a working memory task disproportionately affects older people's recall (e.g. Mitchell *et al.*, 2000; Morris, Gick and Craik, 1988). Note that the distracting task does not have to be overtly cognitive. For example, Lindenberger, Marsiske and Baltes (2000) found that walking whilst memorising was sufficient to impair memory in older people, and the more complex the path to be walked, the disproportionately greater the decline in older adults' memories.

Again, altering the degree to which two tasks overlap in time also has a disproportionately disadvantageous effect on older adults (Holtzer, Stern and Rakitin, 2004). According to the working memory model, these processes are overseen by the central executive, which in older people is failing to combine memory and concurrent processing (see e.g. Craik *et al.*, 1995; though see Jenkins *et al.*, 1999 for a possible criticism). Again, Maylor, Vousden, and Brown (1999) present an ingenious model linking STM for serial order to a combination of frontal decline and response slowing. Findings such as these thus support the argument that a principal component of age-related decline in STM is in the processing of information, rather than the storage *per se*. Given this finding and the argument that both memory and other aspects of cognition both appear to be strongly influenced by the state of frontal lobe functioning, it is fairly predictable that ageing changes in STM ability are strongly correlated with fluid intelligence (Salthouse, 1991b), speed of processing (Bryan and Luszcz, 1996; Byrne, 1998; Fisk and Warr, 1996) and, more broadly, with other indices of central nervous system functioning, such as visual acuity (Salthouse *et al.*, 1996). To this extent short-term/working memory decline may be seen as little more than part and parcel of general intellectual ageing. It is thus not surprising to find that the decline in ability to inhibit is held by many commentators to be a key factor in ageing memory decline. However, as with the frontal lobe hypothesis in Chapter 2, we should be cautious about over-applying the theory. Bowles and Salthouse (2003) found it does not explain all the variance in memory scores, and Burke, Mackay and James (2000) note that inhibition can be difficult to define accurately. Maylor and Henson (2000) found that the **Ranschburg effect** was greater in older than in younger adults on a task requiring participants to recall letter lists in their correct order. The Ranschburg effect is the deterioration in memory performance when items are repeated in a list of to-be-remembered items (e.g. that ATYABF would be harder to recall than ATYMBF). It is argued that this is because inhibitory processes tend to act against repeating items. If inhibition is failing in older adults, one would expect the Ranschburg effect to be less pronounced but, as Maylor and Henson demonstrated, the reverse is true. Thus, although inhibition is a good predictor of ageing memory performance, it is not the sole predictor.

Returning to the relative difficulty backward spans present to older adults, another explanation is that, with increasing age, people might lack the mental processing capacity of younger people, and simply not have the 'processing space' necessary to manipulate the TBR items (see Morra, Vigliocco and Penello, 2001). A refinement of this is to argue that the items are transferred to LTM for rearrangement, because the slave systems' memory capacity is too inadequate. Either items are lost during the transfer process, or the LTM in some manner fails to store the items efficiently. This is supported by the findings of Morris *et al.* (1990). They gave younger and older participants a conventional working memory task, in which they had to remember a short list of words whilst simultaneously deciding if a simple sentence was true or false (e.g. 'Sparrows can build nests'). The older participants' subsequent recall of the words was significantly worse than the younger participants', and the magnitude of this difference increased the more words had to be remembered at one time. Morris *et al.* argue that this age difference occurs because the younger participants not only encode information in their working memory, but also send a copy of the memory trace to a LTM store. If the memory trace is lost from working memory, the younger participants can retrieve a spare copy from LTM. Older participants, however, are less able to make a copy, either because they lack the 'mental capacity' to do it, or because their LTM is in some manner inefficient (see next section). Thus, if the memory cannot be retained in a working memory store, either it cannot be retained at all or, at best, it is retained inaccurately. Note that the logical consequence of this argument is that it is possible that older and younger people may have equally efficient STM stores – the difference lies in the fact that older people may have poorer encoding and/or retrieval strategies.

Although STM tasks such as backwards span present compelling evidence of an age-related decline, there is an important caveat to these findings. Some researchers use the difference between forward and backward spans as a 'benchmark' gauge of ageing decline. However, Ryan, Lopez and Paolo (1996) argue that this is too variable between test sessions to be of value, whilst Gregoire and Van der Linden (1997) go further and argue that there is no age difference in the size of the effect (a finding echoed by Myerson *et al.*, 2003).

However, this is not the only problem besetting older people's memory skills. A study by Belmont, Freeseman and Mitchell (1988) suggests that older people may encode information in STM using less efficient strategies. This concerns a memory process called **chunking**. Given a long string (>4) of TBR items, a better strategy than trying to remember them as one long string is to think of them as a series of groups of three or four items. For example, instead of trying to remember *345172986142* as *345172986142*, a better strategy would be to think of it in chunks of three as *345 172 986 142*. Precisely this principle is used in the presentation of credit card and telephone numbers. Belmont *et al.* demonstrated that older people are less likely than younger people to chunk long digit lists when trying to encode them. However, it is worth noting that some older participants *did* chunk, and their spans were as good as the best of the younger participants. Other researchers have also noted that older people do not arrange TBR items, and that without prompting, they do not pay as close attention to them. In other words, they do not process the items 'deeply' enough (e.g. Craik and Rabinowitz, 1984; though note Salthouse, 1991b, argues that evidence of age differences in depth of processing is equivocal because of methodological flaws in the studies concerned). Furthermore, older adults may at a broader level change their memory strategies. For example, Brebion, Smith and Erlich (1997) argue that when given a working memory task in which a set of TBR items had to be remembered in tandem with performing a sentence comprehension task, the older participants tended to place greater emphasis on the comprehension than the memory task.

Perlmutter and Mitchell (1982) concur that older people have an especial problem in encoding material, but also note that ageing affects the retrieval and/or storage process. In support of this argument, they note that on some STM tasks the older participants were disproportionately better on the recognition than the recall tasks. Again, Marquié and Baracat (2000) found no age difference in a word recognition task. Recognition is easier than recall, because the participant does not have to possess as clear a memory of the TBR item in order to get the right answer. This can be explained conceptually as follows (though no claims that this is actually what takes place in the brain are intended!). Suppose that older and younger participants are given the following list of TBR items:

> DUCK, CLOCK, TABLE, GLASS, PHONE, PACK

Suppose also that the younger and older adults encode the items equally well, and that any problems which arise occur after this stage, in either storage or retrieval (experimentally, it is difficult to distinguish between the two processes). Finally, suppose that any errors that occur consist of forgetting letters in the words (indicated by Xs below). If the storage/retrieval of the older participants is worse than the younger participants', then the memories they retrieve may be something like this:

> Younger participants: DXCK, CLOCK, TABLE, GXASS, XHONE, PACK

> Older participants: DXCK, CLXCK, TABLE, GXASS, XHONE, PACK

In a recall task, only those items completely clearly retrieved can be recalled. Thus, the recall scores for younger and older participants would be 3 and 2 respectively. However, in a recognition task, the participants can compare their 'fuzzy' memories (e.g. DXCK) with the items in front of them. If there is a strong correspondence between the fuzzy memory and a possible answer (e.g. DXCK and DUCK), then either the participants' memories may clear (thereby recognising the X as a U) or they may make an educated guess. Either way, the older people's performance should match younger people's, because a crystal clear memory is no longer de rigeur. Following this argument a step further, it should be apparent that older people's memory for items is not so much less, as slightly but critically more inaccurate. Recognition cannot aid participants if they have no memory trace of a TBR item, or at best a very poor one (e.g. the memory trace of DUCK was XXCX). This is supported by a study by Parkin and Walter (1992), in which participants were asked to state if a word they claimed to recognise was one which they could distinctly remember, or if they 'knew' it was on the list, but had no clear recollection. The researchers found that the proportion of 'definitely know' to 'just know' answers shifted towards the latter with increasing age of participants. Furthermore, this shift was related to evidence of a decline in the functioning of the frontal lobes, thereby providing further evidence for a central role of this section of the cortex in ageing psychological change (see Chapter 2).

Belmont *et al.* and Perlmutter and Mitchell provide evidence that older people can encode and retrieve as well as younger adults, but they do not do so spontaneously. If not deliberately prodded or aided into such strategies, then they choose less efficient methods of encoding and retrieval. Waugh and Barr (1982) also noted that older people are less good at encoding if TBR items are presented quickly in succession (rather than slowly). This indicates that the encoding processes of older people are slower and less efficient. However, by Perlmutter and Mitchells' own admission, the 'younger participants' used in their (and indeed most other researchers') memory studies are college/university students, who are likely to be better versed in memory tasks (and hence using mental *aides memoires*) than community resident older people. This places a question mark over these studies – are older people worse because of their age *per se*, or because of a cohort effect? The debate surrounding this issue has yet to be resolved, but from the combined longitudinal and cross-sectional research by Schaie and others (see Chapter 2), which have included memory measures, it appears that there are genuine age differences, but that these are *in part* the result of a cohort effect.

However, there is evidence that, with training, at least some age deficits can be overcome. One method is to train older people in the **method of loci** technique. This involves memorising a series of mental pictures of familiar scenes, such as the rooms in one's house. Each TBR item is mentally placed in a scene, and then the list is recalled by making an imaginary journey, recalling what was stored in each picture. Suppose that one was given the list *15794* to recall. One might imagine entering one's house. A *1* is sticking through the letter box, a *5* is in the umbrella stand. Entering the living room, *7* is sitting on the sofa, whilst next door *9* is helping himself to a large scotch. Going into the kitchen, *4* is peeling potatoes. The purpose of the technique is to make each image as vivid as possible and, accordingly, more memorable. Smith *et al.* (1984, cited Rebok, 1987) using native Berliners as participants, found that they could increase their digit span by using familiar Berlin street scenes as loci. Herrman, Rea and Andrzejewski (1988) have also reported improvements in the memory of older participants after training, but noted that training only aided the particular memory task involved – the advantages did not transfer to other forms of memory. Improving digit span, for example, does not automatically aid recall of pictures. This effect has been noted in all age groups (i.e. it is not just a phenomenon of ageing). It must also be borne in mind that the method of loci technique is also used more efficiently by younger than older adults. For example, Lindenberger, Kliegl and Baltes (1992) found that older participants performed less well than younger controls on a method of loci task, even in comparisons of older experienced graphic designers (with good spatial skills) and younger people with no especial spatial skills. Singer, Lindenberger and Baltes (2003a) reported at best very modest gains in memory performance in older old people (75 years +) following training in mnemonic techniques. However, for younger older adults, memorisation training can be effective and retained (at least over eight months, as shown in a study by Derwinger, Neely and Bäckman, 2005), and generally training is reported as efficacious (e.g. Cavallini, Pagnin and Vecchi, 2003).

Ageing and long-term memory

As mentioned in the Introduction, the 'basic' LTM and STM tasks are identical, save that the time gap between presentation of the TBR items and the request for their recall differs. Whereas the age differences in basic STM tasks are significant but quite small, there is a very pronounced effect in the case of LTM (Albert, 1988). This may not be very surprising, since much of the information passing into LTM must first be processed by STM, and any defects in STM may be magnified over the time items are stored in LTM prior to recall. Much of the recent work on ageing, however, has moved beyond the rather arid 'laboratory studies' of long-term retention of arbitrary lists of words and digits, to more realistic everyday memory tasks, and the chapter will concentrate on these.

Remote memory

Remote memory is for non-autobiographical events which have occurred within a person's lifetime. It is usually tested by giving participants a list of names and/or descriptions of events which have been 'in the news' over the past 50 or so years, and asking them to indicate which they can remember. Several obvious precautions are taken by test designers. First, to prevent people getting full marks simply by saying 'yes' to everything, a few fictitious names and/or events are included in the list ('Prince Babylon', 'The assassination of King Marvo of Ruritania', etc.). A more pressing problem is ensuring that the participants are genuinely recognising a remote memory, and not a more recently stored piece of information. To take an example. Most English people aged over 45 can remember England winning soccer's World Cup in 1966 (they beat West Germany in the final by four goals to two). Therefore, asking a question such as 'Did England beat Germany 4–2 in the 1966 World Cup final?' might seem to be a sensible item to include in a remote memory test. However, it is very improbable that people responding correctly do so by consulting a memory laid down in 1966 and not consulted since. This is simply because highlights of the event have been replayed very frequently on television ever since. Hence, a participant could answer 'yes' to the question based on seeing a broadcast the previous week. Likewise, a participant aged under 20, who could not possibly have seen the match as a live event, would also be able to answer correctly. By analogous reasoning, any event which is 'too famous' must be excluded from a remote memory test, because it is more properly part of general knowledge.

To escape this problem more obscure names and events must be chosen. If too-obscure items are chosen, then one has the reverse problem that nobody has heard of them. Luckily, the media has an agreeable habit (as far as experimenters are concerned) of making some people very famous for a brief while, after which they sink back into obscurity once more. This is in no way to belittle their achievements – often they are considerable – but the inevitable hunger for news of the arrival of new champions in their field of endeavour causes a shifting of attention. The **Famous Names Test**, or **FNT** (Stevens, 1979) is a test which uses these 'briefly famous' names. It comprises a list of names of people such as John Conteh, Sid Vicious, Issy Bonn and Reggie Whitcombe. Any reader aged over 40 may recognise the first two names, but unless he or she is over 70, it is improbable that the reader will recognise the final two (John Conteh was a boxer, Sid Vicious a punk rocker, Issy Bonn a music hall 'comedian' and Reggie Whitcombe a golfer). The argument is made that since their period of fame, the above names have not been frequently mentioned in the media. Thus, if people recognise a name, it is because they are recalling a genuinely remote memory, and not just recalling the name being mentioned in a recent media presentation. To assess the depth of a person's remote memory, the names on the FNT can be divided into categories: namely, those famous in the 1970s and 1960s, the 1950s, the 1940s, and the 1930s (plus a group of very famous names such as Winston Churchill, whose non-recognition might indicate dementia). A number of fictitious names are included to prevent cheating.

Stuart-Hamilton, Perfect and Rabbitt (1988) tested participants aged 50–80 on the FNT, and found that for all ages, memory of recent names was better than for distant ones. This phenomenon has been observed by many other researchers (e.g. Craik, 1977; Perlmutter, 1978; Poon *et al.*, 1979), and contradicts the once popular **Ribot's hypothesis** (Ribot, 1882). This argues that, in older people, memory for recent events should be worse than for remote ones. A useful analogy is to think of the brain as a long deep tank, into which memories, in the form of water droplets, are deposited. Obviously, it takes a long time for the tank to fill, but when it does, water starts to flow over the edge of the tank and is lost. This overflow is likely to be composed of recently deposited water which is lying on or near the surface: the older deposits deeper in the tank are unlikely to be much disturbed and hence are not lost. In a similar manner, Ribot's hypothesis argues that recently deposited memories are more likely to be displaced because they are not sufficiently 'bedded in'. However, experimental evidence indicates that it is the remote, not the recent memories which are lost.

In terms of the number of names correctly recognised, the FNT is a rare example of a psychological test in which older participants outperform the younger. Having acknowledged this, there are problems in accurately interpreting what the findings mean. The most serious difficulty is that the youngest participants in the Stuart-Hamilton, Perfect and Rabbitt study were in their fifties when the experiment was run (*c.*1987), and thus would be hard pressed to remember the earliest names on the FNT (from the 1930s). In a second experiment by the authors, 20-year-olds, who could not possibly know the older names except as 'historical' figures, were given the FNT. However, they could still accurately recognise about 25 per cent from each decade group (the participants correctly rejected all or most of the false names, so they were not simply guessing). This means that a proportion of items on remote memory tests are probably recognised from semantic memory rather than as genuine 'only experienced at the time' remote memories. In short, remote memory tests may in part assess remote memory, but the answers are heavily contaminated with recollections from a store of general knowledge. Furthermore, the relative likelihood of a particular name on the FNT being recognised was relatively similar for participants of different ages. In other words, if 'Miss X' was the tenth most recognised name amongst participants in their seventies, Miss X was likely to be at or around tenth position amongst those aged 60, 50 or 20 (Stuart-Hamilton, Perfect and Rabbitt, 1988). This suggests that supposedly 'remote' names may be rather more frequently aired in the media than researchers suspect, and the similar 'league tables' of popularity for different names implies that the impact of media coverage is remarkably consistent for different age groups. Thus, whilst remote memory may exist, testing it remains fraught with difficulties, and measuring it in a 'pure' form, uncontaminated by general knowledge, is probably impossible. However, the measure can be useful in assessing patients with dementia (see Chapter 6), since notable errors can occur relatively early in the illness. For example, Storandt, Kaskie and Von Dras (1998) found that (American) participants' knowledge of the temporal order in which the last eight US presidents had held office was impaired in demented patients even in the early stages of the illness.

Eyewitness testimony

As the title suggests, eyewitness testimony refers to the ability to remember information about an incident which has been seen once. In 'real life', eyewitness memory forms the basis of many legal cases, and experimental measures of eyewitness testimony have tended to present participants with an enacted incident (either 'in the flesh' or on video tape). Generally, older people are found to be as good as younger adults at remembering the main points of an incident, but show some worsening of recall of relatively minor points, such as details of the clothing of the protagonists (e.g. Adams-Price, 1992). If a simple 'score' of overall information recalled is made, then there is an appreciable age difference (e.g. Yarmey and Yarmey, 1997). This does not bode particularly well for the credibility of older adults as eyewitnesses. Such a feeling is not enhanced by the findings of Coxon and Valentine (1997). They directly compared the responses of older and younger adults and children to a series of misleading and non-misleading questions about a crime video they had witnessed. It was found that both the older adults and children performed less well than the younger adults. Furthermore, the older adults answered fewer correct questions than the children. In compensation, they gave fewer incorrect answers, and were as relatively immune to the misleading questions as were the younger adults. However, a study by Karpel, Hoyer and Toglia (2001) found that older adults were more susceptible to misleading information surrounding a vignette depicting a theft. Not only did they subsequently report more pieces of misinformation as 'fact', but their level of certainty that the misinformation was real was significantly higher than in younger adults. In part, the problems of older people's eyewitness memories may be perceptual deficits. Certainly, when these are controlled for, then at least some age differences are reduced or removed (see Searcy, Bartlett and Memon, 1999). However, in real-life situations, these sensory deficits cannot of course be compensated for.

Specific features of eyewitness recall also show age differences. For example, Memon *et al.* (2003) showed participants a video tape of an incident and then asked participants to identify the perpetrator in a line-up. When the delay between video and line-up was half an hour, there was no difference in the accuracy of the younger and older participants. However, if the line-up was a week later, the older adults were significantly less accurate and more likely to identify someone falsely in the line-up if the real perpetrator were missing. A key feature of eyewitness testimony is remembering the source of a particular event or utterance (e.g. who said what). Ferguson, Hastroudi and Johnson (1992) demonstrated that older people have greater difficulty in remembering the source of an item (this is explored in greater detail in the section on episodic memory). The participants listened to sets of spoken words played over a stereo system and had to remember which speaker produced particular words. The older participants found this harder to do when both speakers played voices of the same sex and, although advantaged by having different sex voices in either speaker, other permutations worsened recall (although they improved the recall of younger participants). This implies that the older participants cannot make use of the same range of information as the younger adults. Although not an eyewitness memory experiment, these findings have an obvious link to issues of recall of detail from different locations and persons. Again, in a review of the literature, Cohen and Faulkner (1989) note that older people are more prone to believing that an interpretation of an event is the actual memory of the event (see also Kensinger and Schachter, 1999). This means that there may be a greater danger of the memory of an event being distorted to fit a subsequent interpretation, thereby removing the objectivity of an eyewitness account.

Such considerations paint a grim picture of the status of an older person as a witness in a courtroom. Even if he or she is correct in the main points of their testimony (which arguably may be all that matters), a lawyer may quickly discredit this by playing on weaknesses over (what are after all irrelevant) recall of details (thereby reducing the older person's self-esteem as well). Kwong See, Hoffman and Wood (2001) found that generally older eyewitnesses' testimony was rated as less credible by observers (though they did not regard older people as being any less honest). Brimacombe *et al.* found that if people read statements in which the age of the witnesses had been manipulated (i.e. there were statements which were really by younger adults ostensibly provided by older adults and vice versa) then judgements of accuracy tended to go with the perceived accuracy of the statement rather than the perceived age of the witness. In other words, it is the *content* rather than the stereotype of older people's eyewitness accounts which may provoke a negative judgement. However, Kwong See *et al.* found that the content of an older witness's statement had less effect because it was so poorly rated.

Although this section presents a rather gloomy picture, it should be stressed that the effects reported are only *average* and not applicable to *all* older adults.

Text recall

Because recall of text is strongly linked with linguistic skills, this topic is dealt with in detail in Chapter 4. A summary of the findings is that, essentially, there are no or relatively few age differences in the recall of the main points of a story (the 'gist' of the text) but that memory for details may worsen, especially in older people who are also low scorers on intelligence tests. However, there are a number of occasions when this rule breaks down, and interested readers should consult the appropriate section in the next chapter.

Semantic memory

Semantic memory might be expected to survive ageing in a fairly robust state, because memory for facts and information is part of the definition of crystallised intelligence, which is known to be relatively age-invariant (see Chapter 2). Indeed, this appears to be the case – in general, older adults are as good as, if not better than, younger adults at recalling facts and information held in semantic memory (e.g. Camp, 1988; Fozard, 1980; Sharps, 1998). However, there are some caveats to this. First, Craik *et al.* (1995) in a review of the literature concluded that, whilst this is true for existing memories, storage of new semantic memories may be somewhat worse. Again, ability to retrieve items from semantic memory may not be as fluent in later life. For example, Kozora and Cullum (1995) found that producing examples of particular semantic categories was less efficient in older adults. In a similar vein, it was noted in Chapter 2 that many older people's definitions of words, whilst correct, were less exacting. Furthermore, Hultsch *et al.* (1992), in a three-year longitudinal study, found a significant decline in general knowledge for world events (along with declines in other memory and intellectual measures). However, this may in part have been a cohort effect.

Episodic memory

Episodic and semantic memory are often compared with each other – not only because of their shared origins in theoretical models, but also because the relative preservation of semantic memory is explicitly compared with the relative decline in episodic memory. Episodic memory has already been defined as memory of personal experiences. This encompasses not only memories of everyday experience but also the relatively artificial laboratory-based tasks such as remembering lists of words over periods of time (i.e. the LTM tasks mentioned at the start of this section). There is overwhelming evidence that there is a significant ageing decline in such tasks (e.g. Naveh-Benjamin *et al.*, 2004). It is also known that older adults can improve performance if *aides memoires* are introduced into the encoding and/or retrieval stages of the process (e.g. providing the initial letters of the to-be-remembered word at the time of retrieval). However, younger adults are also advantaged by this, and as Craik (2000) has observed in an excellent review of the literature, whether older adults are differentially aided (and thus by extrapolation whether there are any appreciable qualitative features about ageing change) is as yet uncertain. It is also known that an input of glucose can significantly improve episodic memory performance (Riby, Meikle and Glover, 2004), but unless we want an elderly population of diabetics with good memories, dosing up older adults with wine gums every time they want to remember especially well seems an unfeasible solution.[1]

A key failing in the episodic memory abilities of older adults is what amounts to a failure to remember sufficient details surrounding the to-be-remembered items. Often this concerns the issue of **source memory** (essentially, remembering the context in which something was learnt). For example, McIntyre and Craik (1987) gave participants the task of remembering a new set of 'facts' (in reality false but plausible snippets of general knowledge). Over a week, the older adults showed little deficit in memory for the facts themselves, but were far worse than younger participants at remembering where they had first learnt the information (i.e. at the previous test session). Again, Simons *et al.* (2004) found that older adults were significantly worse at remembering specific source information (which of four people said a to-be-remembered item) and partial source information (the gender of the person who said a to-be-remembered item). The evidence

---

1   The cited paper is not of course concerned with this idea, but instead is a very scholarly work on the influence of the relationship between the body's glucose regulation ability and cognitive decline.

collected by Simons *et al.* implies that memory for partial and specific information is equally affected.

In a related theme, older adults are similarly poor at editing out irrelevant information. In a technique they named 'externalized free recall' Kahana *et al.* (2005) gave participants a free recall task, but during the recall phase told participants to produce not only the to-be-remembered words but also any other words that 'appeared in the head' (i.e. distracters). Participants were instructed to press a button indicating if they knew a word to be a distracter. Whilst older and younger adults produced distracters, the older participants were significantly worse at identifying distracters. Even allowing for older adults being poorer at doing concurrent tasks such as button pressing and recalling words, the findings of Kahana *et al.*'s study further indicate that older people's episodic memory is seriously hampered by a failure to organise and keep in check.

It follows from studies such as these that if older adults are less able to recall contextual information and are more willing to accept distracters as targets that they are also more prone to false memories – and that generally appears to be the case, at least in laboratory studies (see Dehon and Brédart, 2004). Which raises further concerns for the reliability of older adults' eyewitness memory (see section on eyewitness testimony).

Although semantic and episodic memory are often contrasted with each other, it appears that the two skills are correlated with each other and even may become more strongly related in later life. In a longitudinal study over five years, Lövdén *et al.* (2004) found that although episodic memory performance fluctuated over time more than semantic (a finding echoed by Nyberg *et al.*, 2003), the two types of memory were strongly correlated, and this relationship tended to increase over time. This is perhaps not surprising, as it is known that changes in episodic memory are a good guide to general changes in cognitive skills and other memory processes such as working memory (Hertzog *et al.*, 2003). However, although episodic and semantic memory are associated with each other, there is still room for each to have unique properties (Allen *et al.*, 2002).

Implicit memory

Evidence on implicit memory points to there being no significant age difference, or, at worst, only a slight decline (Craik and Jennings, 1992; Fleischman *et al.*, 2004; Gaudreau and Peretz, 1999; Light and Singh, 1987; Mitchell and Bruss, 2003; Salthouse, 1991b). Park and Shaw (1992) argue that in studies that have found an age difference, it has not been established if the younger participants had realised that they were taking part in a memory test, and so deliberately concentrated harder on the TBR items. Park and Shaw cite the work of Light and Albertson (1989) which found that, if aware participants were excluded from the analysis, an age difference in implicit memory performance disappeared. Park and Shaw's own study found no evidence for an age difference on a word completion task 'regardless of whether [participants] aware of the memory test were included or excluded' (Park and Shaw, 1992, p.632). Jennings and Jacoby (1993) demonstrated that implicit memory was preserved, even when a distracter task was employed (though explicit memory worsened).

Some manipulations of implicit memory tasks do induce age differences, however. For example, Harrington and Haaland (1992) gave participants the task of performing various hand movements. These were either performed in a repetitive set sequence or were done in random sequences. It was anticipated that the regular repetition should aid implicit memory far more than the random sequences. The researchers found that this was true for younger participants, but older adults showed no difference between the two conditions. This implies that older people are less able to make use of implicit information, although note that another study showed that placing an explicit order on a physical act through list organisation *improved* older participants' explicit memory for the act (Norris and West, 1993). Again, as was seen in Chapter 2, although subject to experimental artefacts, it has been found that older people are less capable of implicitly learning that a target will appear with greater frequency in some locations than in others in a visual search task. However, countering this is the finding that older people are disadvantaged to the same extent as younger adults when a regular predictable sequence of stimuli in a reaction time task is replaced with a random sequence (Howard and Howard, 1992).

Another caveat is raised by McEvoy *et al.* (1992), who found an apparent worsening of ability to *use* implicit information. In one of their experiments, they gave participants a set of words to remember, and then tested recall using cues (in this case, words related in meaning – e.g. if the TBR word was 'butter' then the cue might be 'bread'). For the younger participants, recall was worse if the TBR word had a lot of potential associates (e.g. 'car' has lots of associates, 'basilisk' very few). This was also true for the older participants, but the size of the effect was significantly diminished. This, it is argued, indicates that older people are less able to make use of implicit associations. It is probable, however, that the older participants took longer to respond (no response latencies are recorded by McEvoy *et al.*). Therefore, the effect of the implicit associations may be diluted by the extra processing time.

Although implicit memory may in many instances be unaffected by ageing, there would appear to be other occasions where it is not (although this is not true for every instance of the same general experimental paradigm). This may provide support for Salthouse's (1991b) suggestion that age differences may be found in implicit memories for some materials but not for others (see also Cohen, 1996). However, it may also be the case that implicit memory is better preserved where the participants simply have to receive information passively, and that a decline occurs only when some additional processing has to be done to make use of the implicit information. In other words, an age difference only appears when processing demands increase beyond a certain level, which is a familiar refrain in psychogerontology. However, until more evidence is gathered, this is a moot point.

Autobiographical memory and ageing

Several major problems beset autobiographical memory research. The most often-cited of these is the issue of reliability. For example, an older participant may reminisce about a picnic in 1936, held with her now-dead parents. How can one possibly verify the accuracy of this recollection? This is not to say that the participant is deliberately lying but usually reminiscences have been recalled many times over a person's lifetime, and with each retelling, details alter to improve the flow of the narrative (Bartlett, 1932). Thus, the recounting of a story five years after the event in question may have the same basic plot as a retelling 50 years on, but the details of the two narratives are likely to be different. This argument is supported by the findings of a longitudinal study by Field (1981). Comparing reminiscences of the same events 30 and 70 years, on, there was a reasonably high correlation for points in the basic plot ($r = 0.88$), but only a 16 per cent concordance for recall of more peripheral details ($r = 0.43$).

Another serious methodological flaw concerns how the memories are elicited. Asking participants for their most *vivid* memories produces a glut of reminiscences from the early part of their lives. So does giving participants a cue word, and asking them to produce a reminiscence associated with it (e.g. jam – 'Oh yes, I remember helping my mother make jam when I was a child'), provided the participant has to put a date to each memory after producing it. However, if the participant is allowed to produce a whole list before any dating of memories is done, then the bias shifts in favour of a preponderance of memories from the recent past (Cohen, 1989). To further muddy the waters, words which are rated highly in imagery-provoking properties tend to generate older memories (Rubin and Schulkind, 1997b). Thus, how the participant is asked determines the age of memories produced, and there is certainly no evidence to support the cliché that older people live in the past. Indeed, many studies have shown that younger and older adults produce equal numbers of reminiscences from childhood (e.g. Cohen and Faulkner, 1988; Rubin and Schulkind, 1997a). This is not necessarily due to participants wallowing in nostalgia. Rabbitt and Winthorpe (1988) found that, when memories are divided into 'pleasant' and 'unpleasant', reminiscences from early life fall predominantly into the latter category. Berntsen and Rubin (2002) using a different technique for eliciting memories found a higher proportion of happy memories, but unpleasant memories were nonetheless reported in appreciable numbers.

In addition, smell also can play an important role. Smell and taste are both noted anecdotally to be excellent prompters of long-forgotten memories. The best-known example is perhaps Proust's madeleine,[2] but practically everyone has experienced unexpectedly strong memories stirred by a scent or taste. This is probably because scent and taste cannot be easily rehearsed and mentally revived in the memory – what is needed is the genuine article, and so presumably the awakening of memories by smell/taste is so much the stronger because they are unexpected and less often encountered. Maylor, Carter and Hallett (2002) found that for both younger and older adults, presenting a cue word in combination with an odour attached to the word (e.g. the word 'rose' in combination with the smell of rose oil) doubled the number of memories produced. The finding is interesting in its own right, but it also questions whether other autobiographical memory tests have accidentally biased results by the smell of the test room, scent worn by the researcher, etc.

Another problem is that participants may censor their memories. It is a reasonable assumption that, human nature being what it is, people's most vivid memories include a largish proportion of sexual experiences. Curiously, these seem to be rarely mentioned by participants.

Notwithstanding the above considerations, the **reminiscence peak** (a.k.a. **reminiscence bump**) has been reported by many researchers. This is the phenomenon that when due allowance is made for testing methods, most autobiographical memories are likely to come from the period when the individual was between 10 and 30 years old (e.g. Berntsen and Rubin, 2002; Rubin, Rahhal and Poon, 1998). This is not surprising, since this is the time when most of the key life events (first forays into sex, employment, exams, marriage, parenthood, and so forth) usually occur (see Jansari and Parkin, 1996). However, the largest proportion of memories tend to be from the most recent decade of a person's life (Rubin and Schulkind, 1997a). In contrast, autobiographical memories from the very early years are scarce or non-existent (**childhood amnesia**). Freud and his followers believed that this was due to suppression of unpleasant memories and psychoanalytic conflicts, but it is now felt to be because young children lack the mental facilities to encode retrievable autobiographical memories.

An issue related to what is remembered is the vividness of the recall. Introspection shows that some memories are clearer than others, and, generally, earlier memories are perceived as 'dimmer' than later ones (Cohen and Faulkner, 1988). This was also demonstrated by Nigro and Neisser (1983), who found that distant memories are usually

2   For the uninitiated: man revives a long-suppressed childhood memory from the taste of a biscuit dunked in herbal tea. This is the start of Marcel Proust's *A la Recherche du Temps Perdu*, a multi-volume novel with memory as a central theme that is, depending on one's viewpoint, either the height of literary genius or the oh-so-precious ramblings of a cosseted epicene who should have got out more.

perceived as if watching the events taking place as a bystander (i.e. as though watching oneself), while more recent events are remembered from one's viewpoint at the time. Furthermore, the reasons why an event is perceived as vivid change across the lifespan. Cohen and Faulkner (1988) found that younger and middle-aged adults were affected by how emotionally charged the event was – the greater the feelings, the greater the vividness. For older adults, the biggest cause of vividness was how often they had thought about the event subsequently. Cohen and Faulkner suggest that, because ageing blunts the vividness of memories, it is only by rehearsing them that their details can be retained (rather like taking pieces of silverware out of the cupboard to polish them, to prevent them tarnishing). Rabbitt and Winthorpe (1988) found that older people gave poorer quality responses in autobiographical memory tests (and were also generally slower to produce reminiscences). For example, they provide vague rather than specific answers (e.g. 'I remember going on a picnic when I was a child' as opposed to 'I remember going on a picnic on Salisbury Plain on my seventh birthday'). However, Winthorpe and Rabbitt (1988) demonstrated that this was not due to ageing *per se*, but to the coincidental decline in fluid intelligence and working memory (which is used to keep track of what has been said and what needs to come next in the narrative). In a subsequent study by the researchers, it was found that detail in the reminiscences was determined by age, fluid intelligence and crystallised intelligence (Holland [née Winthorpe] and Rabbitt, 1990; Phillips and Williams, 1997, report analogous results). This was interpreted as meaning that, although the ageing process and the fall in fluid intelligence cause a decline in reminiscence skills, the age-invariant crystallised skills may to some extent compensate for this. These findings are complemented by more recent research by Levine *et al.* (2002). They found that younger adults provided details specific to the memory being recalled, whereas older adults tended to recall general semantic information that could be applicable across many situations. This phenomenon persisted even after the participants were probed for further details.

Moving away from consideration of quantities of autobiographical memories, there is the issue of their function. A study by Cappeliez and O'Rourke (2002) identified a link between production of autobiographical memories and personality type. Using the five-factor theory of personality (see Chapter 5), they found production of autobiographical memories to be correlated with extraversion, neuroticism and openness to experience. Perhaps unsurprisingly, extraversion was associated with producing memories for use in conversations and neuroticism with ruminating about unpleasant past events. Openness to experience was correlated with seeking a meaning for both life and death. Because of its association with finding meaning in life, reminiscence has been used in therapeutic contexts. Many commentators believe that 'reminiscence therapy' for older people should be encouraged, since it enables them to come to terms with their lives (see Kermis, 1983; Pasupathi and Carstensen, 2003). There is also evidence that eliciting auto-biographical memories can be an effective component in the treatment of older adults' depression for roughly the same reason (Serrano *et al.*, 2004). However, for many older people, reminiscence may simply be a response to boredom:

> Older people may experience an increasing contrast between an unmemorable present and an eventful past. Remote events may be more often researched and rehearsed in memory as the theatre of the mind becomes the only show in town. (Rabbitt and Winthorpe, 1988; p.302)

Prospective memory

As many recent textbooks have noted, one of the principal functions of memory is not to remember the past but to plan for the future. In part this means learning from one's experiences and mistakes in order to cope better with situations when they next arise. This can be considered as part of wisdom/crystallised intelligence. Another, more literal aspect is prospective memory, or the ability to remember to do something in the future. It might be supposed that prospective memory is simply another form of LTM, since it involves retaining information over a long time period. However, there is ample evidence to disprove this notion. First, on theoretical grounds the two memory types are distinct. In retrospective memory, it is sufficient to recall an item or event for the action to be considered a success. In prospective memory, however, the item can be recalled any number of times, but it is only successful if the person remembers to do it at the right time and acts upon it (West, 1988). A second consideration is that the memory types are empirically distinct, with little correlation either in accuracy or in types of mnemonic strategies used (Jackson, Bogers and Kerstholdt, 1988; Kvaviloshvili, 1987; Wilkins and Baddeley, 1978).

Methods of recall in prospective memory vary greatly between individuals, but, broadly speaking, they can be divided into two classes – **internal** and **external** **strategies/cues**. External cues are such familiar things as entries in a diary or the knot in the handkerchief. In other words, prompts which the person places in the external environment. Some experiments test use of these strategies through **event-based tasks** (where the participant must retrieve and act on a memory when given a particular prompt). Internal cues, on the other hand, are purely mental strategies, where the person hopes to prompt him- or herself at the appropriate time. This may be measured through **time-based tasks** (the participant must respond at a particular point in time). This division is not as clear cut as some commentators seem to suppose, however. For example, a common strategy is to remember to do something in conjunction with a familiar daily routine, such as the habitual breakfast coffee (Maylor, 1990a, Appendix A). Is this an internal strategy (simply remembering to add another action onto the end of a familiar sequence) or an external one (the sight of the coffee acting as an *aide memoire*)? Similarly, an external cue such as a diary entry requires an internal strategy to remember to look in the diary. Therefore, the functional distinctions between the mnemonic methods are blurred, and certainly are too ambiguous to bear deep analysis. Therefore, for the rest of this section, internal and external methods will be treated purely as practical strategies, avoiding the question of how they work.

In certain kinds of prospective memory tasks, there is either no age difference or even an ageing superiority. For example, a 'traditional' prospective memory task requires participants to remember to phone the experimenter at prearranged times. Poon and Schaffer (1982, cited West, 1988) and Moscovitch (1982) found that the older participants remembered to phone more often and they were more punctual. However, this could in part be a cohort effect. Older people may lead more sedate lives and thus have less to distract them from making phone calls. Again, they might have been brought up to place greater emphasis on punctuality and keeping appointments than younger people and thus were more motivated to make the calls. This latter supposition is supported by Poon and Schaffer's finding that increasing the monetary reward for making a call improved the older people's performance, but not the younger people's. One method of minimising the cohort effect is to take participants in their fifties as the younger adult group. This age group will still intellectually perform more or less on a par with adults in their twenties (the age of a typical 'younger adult' group) but are more similar to older adults in their upbringing. Maylor (1990a) did this, and furthermore selected participants who had similar lifestyles. The participants had to phone once per day for five days, either at a specific time (the 'exact' condition) or between two specified times (the 'between' condition). Maylor found no significant difference between age groups in punctuality nor in number of calls remembered. She also found no age difference in the cues used to remember to make the calls. This contradicts earlier findings that older adults tend to use more external cues (e.g. Jackson *et al.*, 1988; Moskovitch, 1982). Possibly this reflects a cohort effect. Studies other than Maylor's have often used students as younger participants, who may be forced to take part in experiments as part of their degree programme (much psychological research takes place under the guise of practical classes). Given the typical undergraduate enthusiasm for practicals, the younger participants may be apathetic, and they may use internal cues because it is less effort than creating external reminders. Maylor's study used younger participants who were all active volunteers in an ongoing large-scale programme into the effects of ageing, and thus they were probably more motivated.

Maylor did find an age effect, however, in the efficiency with which participants used external and internal cues. Namely, internal cue users who made errors were significantly older, and external cue users who made errors were significantly younger. Thus, those participants who continue to rely solely on their memories worsen, whilst those who turn to external aids improve (probably because they become more practised). However, to some extent participants use strategies according to the task at hand. Maylor found that the 'between' condition generated greater use of external cues than did the 'exact' condition. She suggests that this is because of the perceived difficulties of the two tasks (i.e. the condition thought to be harder demands a more positive response in the shape of preparing an external cue). West (1988) has reported similar links between cue use and task demands.

However, under other circumstances, there are considerable age differences in prospective memory. For example, Cockburn and Smith (1988) found that older participants were worse on tests of remembering an appointment and remembering to deliver a message. Again, West (1988) demonstrated that older participants were significantly worse at remembering to deliver a message during a test session. Indeed, in general, if participants must remember to do something as part of other measures, then there is an age difference. Furthermore, age declines tend to increase with the increased complexity of the task (e.g. Einstein, McDaniel and Guynn, 1992) and/or its attentional demands (Einstein *et al.*, 1998). Why older people should be better at some prospective memory tasks than others remains an open issue. It has been suggested that older adults are better at event-based tasks than time-based tasks. However, ignoring the criticism of this classification presented above, the findings of several studies militate against a simplistic interpretation of this. For example, Maylor (1998) found significant age differences in a task requiring participants to identify pictures of famous people, with a prospective memory component requiring participants to identify those people wearing spectacles. Thus, the experiment provided strong event-based cues, but there was an age difference. Again, Park *et al.* (1997) has plausibly argued that, under some circumstances, time-based tasks may be measuring time monitoring rather than memory *per se.* And finally, Henry *et al.* (2004) demonstrated that younger adults significantly outperform older adults on both time- and event-based tasks (and the age difference on the latter significantly increases if the processing demands are increased).

Perhaps a more satisfying explanation is derived from Craik *et al.*'s (1995) observation that prospective memory tasks tend, perversely enough, to be most prone to age differences over relatively short time frames. Thus, if asked to do something as part of a fairly complex ongoing task, then this is more likely to be forgotten than, for example, remembering to do a single act in a week's time. It is questionable whether the relatively long-term and naturalistic and relatively short-term and laboratory-based paradigms are assessing the same types of prospective memory. For example, suppose a person is asked to play a particularly taxing video game of the 'shoot 'em up' variety, and told that every time they shoot a red monster, they should shout out 'bananas'. If they forget to call out every time they kill a red monster, is this due to forgetting to do something in the future or a lapse in performing just another component of the ongoing task (akin to forgetting that, for example, shooting the yellow monsters gets double the points of shooting the blue monsters?). In comparison, forgetting to phone the experimenter at a particular time on a particular day is more likely to be a memory lapse rather than distraction by a large number of demands competing for the participant's attention at *precisely* the same moment in time. It should be noted that the demands of the short-term prospective memory tasks need not (in subjective terms) be onerous to induce an age difference. For example, Maylor's (1998) task could not exactly be described as difficult. Again, Maentylae and Nilsson (1997) found older people were significantly less likely to remember to do the even simpler task of asking an experimenter to sign a paper at the end of a two-hour test session. Another consideration is that longer-term tasks, such as remembering to phone someone on a particular day and time can be integrated into the general routine of daily life and thus become part of a well-practised procedure. However, doing concurrent tasks or delivering messages during meetings with researchers is not something at which older adults have had much practice.

In short, current research on prospective memory in ageing may be encompassing two rather different phenomena under a blanket heading. 'Prospective Memory I', used in a naturalistic setting, is remembering a future appointment or responsibility. This is almost inevitably tested under realistic conditions. 'Prospective Memory II' is the ability to remember to perform an action during concurrent processing of other tasks. This is almost inevitably tested under laboratory conditions. This difference appears to be borne out by a meta-review of the research literature by Henry *et al.* (2004). They found that, whilst older adults outperform younger adults on naturalistic tasks, the reverse applies for laboratory-based tasks. Intelligence, however, is not a particularly strong predictor for either type of study (Cockburn and Smith, 1988; Maylor, 1998).

Metamemory and ageing

To what extent can older people gauge their mental abilities? The answer to this question seems to depend very much on the type of memory being considered.

One method of gauging one's own memory abilities is **metaknowledge**, or **feeling of knowing (FOK)**. A typical FOK experiment might require participants to look at a question and then declare how confident they are that their answer is correct. For example, a participant might be confronted with the following:

QUESTION: What is a pangolin?

HOW CONFIDENT ARE YOU ABOUT GIVING THE CORRECT ANSWER TO THIS QUESTION?

1. Complete guess

2. Educated guess

3. Fairly confident

4. Completely confident

PLEASE GIVE YOUR ANSWER

Several researchers have shown that participants are quite accurate in their judgements. Namely, the more confident they are that they are right, the greater the probability that they *are* right (though a curious exception is eyewitness memory, where FOK scores are uncorrelated with accuracy – Perfect and Hollins, 1999). There appears to be no age difference in FOK accuracy (e.g. Allen-Burge and Storandt, 2000; Fozard, 1980; Perlmutter, 1978). However, although this may be the case, older people do not necessarily believe it. For example, Camp (1988) reported that older adults thought their semantic memory had declined. In other instances, FOK may be related to the level of confidence in the subject matter being memorised. For example, Marquié and Huet (2000) demonstrated that older participants' FOK levels were only lower than younger adults' for information about computing, but were not significantly different on general knowledge items. Arguably this is part of a larger trend of age-related pessimism, since researchers have long reported lowered self-confidence in older participants (e.g. Botwinick, 1967).

There is little effect of ageing when judging relatively abstract features of memory, such as deciding on which types of TBR items are easiest to remember and the best mnemonic strategies to use (Perlmutter, 1978). However, other aspects of metamemory *do* show an age-related decline. Principally, age differences occur when: (a) judgements are asked on a memory act which is incomplete, or (b) global judgements on past and future performance are required. Furthermore, as will be seen below, methodological problems with the test of the latter in any case make much of the research literature uninterpretable.

A prime example of an incomplete memory act is the **tip of the tongue (TOT)** state (for readers pursuing matters further, note that some commentators classify TOT as part of semantic memory rather than metamemory). This is a familiar experience for most people. The word one is searching for cannot quite be recalled, yet one can remember some features of it, such as the first letter, the number of syllables, words which sound like it, and so forth. Brown and McNeill (1966) were the first to investigate this phenomenon intensively, by giving participants definitions of obscure words, and asking them to provide the words. Often, participants either knew the word or simply had no idea, but on some occasions a TOT state was generated. Typically, participants could indeed provide details of the word (e.g. 57% per cent of the time they could identify the first letter). The TOT state is nothing more than an annoyance when confined to defining rare words. However, if it creeps into everyday speech, then it is a potential disability. Burke, Worthley and Martin (1988) decided to study the TOT state in older people, in part because older volunteers in a study the experimenters were running had complained about it being a problem. Indeed, in general older people can be bad at remembering words, and especially names (Crook and West, 1990). Burke *et al.* asked their participants to keep diary records of all TOTs over a four-week period. They were asked to record all the details of the word they could remember whilst in the TOT state, and whether they ever discovered what the word they were searching for actually was (i.e. whether the TOT resolved itself). Burke *et al.* found that the older participants reported significantly more TOTs, although there was no age difference in the proportion of resolved TOTs (over 90% of the time both age groups eventually found the word they were looking for). However, whilst in the TOT state, the younger participants could report significantly more details of the word (a finding echoed by Maylor, 1990b). Subsequent research has indicated that younger people's TOTs contain more information and are closer to the recognition threshold than older people's. For example, White and Abrams (2002) found that if participants were asked general knowledge questions that generated the occasional TOT state, a phonological prime (e.g. the initial sound of the word the participants were searching for) would resolve the TOT state for younger but not older adults.

Burke *et al.* also found an age difference in the types of words which generated TOTs. Both younger and older participants had the greatest difficulty with proper nouns, but for the remainder, older people had the greatest difficulty with the names of everyday objects and younger people with abstract nouns. A final difference the researchers noted was that younger volunteers tended actively to search mentally for the desired word, or even ask someone else for help, whilst the older participants usually simply hoped that the word would 'pop up' (though some did try the same strategies as the younger participants). In a similar study, Cohen and Faulkner (1986) had participants complete a two-week diary of TOTs for proper nouns (i.e. names). Surprisingly, the majority of these (68%) turned out to be for names of friends and acquaintances. Perhaps, as Cohen (1989, p.104) notes, 'there are more opportunities to forget names that are in frequent use' (though it seems unlikely that memory for names is *disproportionately* disadvantaged in later life, as a careful analysis by Maylor, 1997, demonstrates). It should also be noted that in general, older adults are significantly and disproportionately worse than younger adults at remembering new names than new details about people, such as their occupation (James, 2004), probably due to a lowered efficiency of mental processing (simplistically, it is easier to remember a semantic category such as 'farmer' than the precise name 'Mr Farmer'). Again, older people seemed to rely on a strategy of waiting for the name to 'pop up'. Given these findings, one can surmise that older people have a problem with retrieving faint memory traces. This can be seen in the facts that they have more TOT states and that, when in a TOT state, they have fewer details of the word. Because they lack many details of the target word, it is probably not worth their while to search for it on the basis of the little information they have available (the product of a metamemory strategy?). Conversely, younger people, who can identify more about the word in a TOT state, and thus have more information to act upon, will probably find it worthwhile to indulge in a search of their memories.

A further aspect of metamemory is what a person knows about the general state of his or her memory. Typically, this is assessed by requesting participants to complete a self-report questionnaire. This includes assessments of everyday memory competence (e.g. from 1 for 'poor' to 5 for 'excellent'), and asks participants to estimate how often they forget things from the important (such as an appointment) to the trivial (such as going into a room to fetch something and forgetting what one went in for). Results from such studies have been conflicting. Some studies have found older people reporting a decline in their abilities and a concomitant rise in acts of absent-mindedness, and so forth (e.g. Perlmutter, 1978). Other researchers have found the reverse – namely, it is the *younger* participants who report a greater number of memory lapses (e.g. Baddeley, 1983; Rabbitt and Abson, 1990). To gauge the accuracy of participants' metamemories, scores on questionnaires are often correlated with a battery of tests of memory spans and often other psychological measures as well. The relationship between questionnaire scores and memory spans is similarly muddled. Many researchers report a poor correlation between self-predicted performance and actual memory skills (e.g. Herrman, 1984; Rabbitt and Abson, 1990; Zelinski, Gilewski and Shaie, 1993). However, others have found a correlation (e.g. Maylor, 1990a). Taylor, Miller and Tinklenberg (1993), in a longitudinal study, found a correlation at a group level between some memory scores and self-report (but not with a measure of fluid intelligence). However, when individuals were considered, then no significant effect was found.

Why is there this confusion? The answer lies in the methodologies used. First, people are notoriously bad at quantifying their abilities (hence the need for professional psychologists!). Second, as Rabbitt (1984) observes, a person can only judge how his or her memory is by comparing it with that of other people. But whom? Younger people (or him- or herself when younger)? Contemporaries? An idealised hyper-intelligent being? Participants may differ markedly in their value judgements because they are using a variety of models to form their judgements, and, hence, they are not being gauged against a common scale. Third, a variety of factors may be used by a person in making a judgement and different factors may underlie different aspects of belief about one's memory. For example, Lane and Zelinski (2003) found that in a longitudinal study of changes in metamemory, a variety of factors including personality, actual memory change and general beliefs about what memory is all affected an individual's belief about their own memories. Pearman and Storandt (2004) found that a combination of three personality measures (conscientiousness, self-esteem and neuroticism – see Chapter 5) predicted about a third of the total variance in older adults' subjective memory evaluations.

It follows from the above that self-image may be a key factor in shaping metamemory. Older people often expect to be forgetful, younger people do not. Accordingly, older people may be more sensitive to memory lapses, and so unrealistically downgrade their abilities. It is not surprising to find there is a correlation between older people's self-ratings of forgetfulness and their level of depression (Collins and Abeles, 1996; Cipolli et al., 1996; Rabbitt and Abson, 1990; Thompson et al., 1987). However, if metamemory is being downgraded by poor self-image then it follows that by encouraging older adults to break out of a pessimistic outlook, self-belief and perhaps performance can be improved. West and Yassuda (2004) demonstrated that if older adults were encouraged to set higher goals for what they wanted to attain in a memory test, then both subjective opinions about memory and actual memory performance improved (this echoes an earlier study by West, Welch and Thorn, 2001). However, this was not a panacea, since younger adults motivated by goals still outperformed older participants.

Another frequent criticism is that, perversely, questionnaires may still overestimate the memory skills of the least-skilled participants. Information about a participant's memory comes only from them; there is usually no corroborating evidence. However, with the self-confessed forgetful, how can they remember all that they have forgotten? This is an ingenious and untestable argument. However, there are some indications that it is overly pessimistic, since several studies involving the spouses of participants have found a good correlation between self-reported memory skills and spouses' estimates of the same (Cohen, 1989). However, even the most fervent supporter of the questionnaire method would admit that there will inevitably be some inaccuracies in self-ratings.

The generally poor correlations between self-ratings and actual memory spans probably arise because usually questionnaires ask participants how their memories are in real life, whilst spans are taken from tests run under laboratory conditions. For example, most 'standard' memory tests assess a single type of memory in quiet, unstressful conditions. In real life, such opportunities rarely arise (Cohen, 1989; Rabbitt and Abson, 1990), and Jonker, Smits and Deeg (1997) have noted that for many older people simple anxiety about taking a memory test may be as important a predictor as metamemory.

It is also worth observing that, under realistic conditions, many memory lapses may not be due to memory at all. For example, Tenney (1984) found that a frequent cause of older people misplacing items was that they had literally overlooked the said items in a systematic search for them. In other words, the problem is often one of misperception rather than memory *per se* (though note that memory for spatial location for anything but the shortest time intervals (Olson *et al.* 2004) is significantly worse in later life – Uttl and Graf, 1993; see Craik, 2000 for a brief review). Rabbitt and Abson also note that, in general, the correlations between memory tasks are poor anyway. For example, training participants to be good at one type of memory task in no manner improves their performance on others, as noted above. Therefore, expecting to find a general all-embracing metamemory measure which will simultaneously predict all types of memory is a misplaced ideal: there is no memory equivalent of intelligence's *g*. In studies such as Maylor (1990a), which *have* reported a correlation between self-report and degree of failure, the effect is usually due to specific items on the questionnaire, rather than overall score.

Summary and overview – how *does* ageing affect memory?

Alas, the familiar complaint of many older people that their memories 'aren't what they used to be' seems in the main to be justified. Memory *does* decline in later life, and despite a few areas of relative preservation (e.g. 'basic' STM span and some aspects of metamemory), the outlook is downwards. Decline in one memory type is usually associated with declines in other memory types that show decline, even if the relationship is not in all cases strong. For example, it has already been noted that the decline in episodic and semantic memory in later life is linked, but nonetheless, the two types of memory do not decline exactly in tandem. Again, Dumas and Hartman (2003) demonstrated that ageing changes in temporal and item memory are correlated with each other, but possibly through a shared dependence on a declining ability to memorise context (see the research on episodic memory above).

It is intuitively implausible that the various types of memory decline totally independently. Therefore, what are the factors underlying the ageing changes? The list of candidates is a long one. For example, emotional state, socio-economic background and level of education have been suggested as plausible determinants of intellectual skill (see Chapter 2). Some commentators have suggested that having a positive image of ageing may offset memory loss; a not wholly implausible idea, given some of the findings on metamemory and self-image presented above. Earles *et al.* (2004) found that imposing tight time constraints or making the task harder led to a disproportionate decline in older adults' performance. This was attributed by the researchers at least in part to induced anxiety and lowered self-image. In contrast, Yoon *et al.* (2000) considered a group of Chinese Canadians with very positive images of ageing and found no evidence for the argument, beyond a higher level of recall of items that were strongly related to Chinese culture (which may be attributable to a specific cohort effect). Rahhal, Hasher and Colcombe (2001) argued that perhaps older people's negative images of their memory skills pre-set them to perform badly on memory tasks. The researchers manipulated the instructions given at the start of a memory task so that the memory aspects of it were emphasised or were underplayed. Where memory instructions were explicit, there was a significant difference between younger and older participants; where no emphasis on memory was made, there was no significant age difference. This implies that many studies of ageing and memory may have exaggerated the size of memory loss. What was being examined was not the genuine memory skills of older adults, but rather the degree to which manipulating older people's self-esteem can mar their performance.

Murphy *et al.* (2000) found that the performance of younger adults in memorising items under noisy conditions was functionally similar to that of older adults memorizing under quiet conditions, leading to the argument that perhaps part of the decline in ageing memory is attributable to degraded sensory input (basically, because the to-be-remembered items lack sensory fidelity, and mental effort that could have been spent on memorising has to be diverted to basic perception). Other physical changes in the body can also have an effect. For example, West *et al.* (2002) found that the time of day of testing can also have an effect on memory performance. Older adults tend to report being relatively more alert in the morning, younger adults in the evening. Testing at the 'wrong' time of day can accentuate age differences.

West, Crook and Barron (1992), in an impressively large study of nearly 2500 participants, assessed performance on a wide variety of 'realistic' memory tasks (remembering people's names, face recognition, and so on). The researchers also took measures of chronological age, 'vocabulary, education, depression, gender, marital status, and employment status' (West *et al.*, 1992, p.72). Perhaps not surprisingly, vocabulary level (also indicative of general intelligence, and crystallised intelligence in particular) accounted for a measure of prose recall, and also generally accounted for some of the variability in performance of other memory tasks. Gender proved a significant predictor of memory tasks in which participants had to memorise a grocery list. Women participants were better, though given traditional gender roles, this is not surprising (note that Larrabbee and Crook, 1993, found that memory for such stereotypically 'female' tasks showed a gender bias across the lifespan, and was not disproportionately altered in later life). However, with these exceptions, chronological age was the best predictor of memory performance, and overall was unquestionably the best.

In a three-year longitudinal study, Zelinski *et al.* (1993) took a rather smaller sample (508 men and women, of whom 227 were available for retesting) and assessed the relationship between memory, vocabulary and tests of 'higher reasoning' (essentially, fluid intelligence). Measures of length of schooling and other biographical data were also taken. The researchers found a less clear-cut picture than West *et al.* Although age was a good predictor of performance on some memory tasks (especially for participants who displayed a very marked decline), 'higher reasoning' also had a significant effect independent of any influence of age. This should not be surprising, if one recalls Rabbitt's caveat, cited in Chapter 2, that practically any intellectual decline can be linked to a fall in fluid intelligence (as Zelinski *et al.* acknowledge). However, the authors found that age had a strong relationship with memory decline which could not be attributed to the coincidental effects of changes in fluid intelligence. Probably the most parsimonious explanation of the results is that there is no parsimonious explanation of the results.

It would, however, be surprising if ageing and fluid intellectual decline were not at least partly responsible for memory decline. However, this begs the question – what is the nature of the link?

It has been suggested that memory decline may in part be due to the selective physiological changes in the brains of ageing people, and that the decline in neural functioning is reflected in a concomitant decline in both fluid intelligence and memory. On *a priori* grounds, this is a reasonable assumption. The decline in both the numbers and efficiency of neurons (see Chapter 1) means that the physical memory storage system is inevitably compromised, leading to the possibility that this will have psychological consequences (see Rosenzweig, 1996). For example, using PET scans, Cabeza *et al.* (1997) and Madden *et al.* (1999) found significant differences in the patterns of activity in the brains of older and younger adults during memory tasks. This could be the product of different strategies using different areas of the brain rather than a physical decline. However, at a more fundamental level, animal studies of ageing rodents have demonstrated that older neurons often show a decline in efficiency in learning and memory tasks (e.g. Russell, 1996; Shen *et al.*, 1997), and formation of memory traces in the elderly rat hippocampus are significantly delayed (Wilson *et al.*, 2004a). Statistical modelling indicates that there is probably more neural noise in older human brains, interfering with accurate processing of signals (Allen *et al.*, 1998). At a broader anatomical level, studies have related ageing memory decline to anatomical and functional changes in the frontal lobes (e.g. Haenninen *et al.*, 1997; Purcell *et al.*, 1998; Rypma *et al.* 2001; Stebbins *et al.* 2002; Stuss *et al.*, 1996) and the hippocampus (e.g. Golomb *et al.*, 1996; de Leon *et al.*, 1997), as well as more general indices such as ventricular size (McArdle *et al.*, 2004). Decline in these areas can neatly explain many of the memory deficits experienced by older adults. Since the hippocampus, amongst its other roles, acts as a 'relay station' between STM and LTM, a deficit in its functioning will have particularly severe consequences. Likewise, a deficit in frontal lobe functioning may severely disrupt planning and ordering of memories.

Other measures of brain function have similarly been correlated with age-related changes in memory performance, such as significant age differences in event-related brain potentials (ERPs – essentially, measures of electrical activity in specific parts of the brain) in a prospective memory task (West, Herndon and Covell, 2003); a greater ERPs response to priming in younger adults (Wegesin, Ream and Stern, 2004); slower ERPs response to names and faces in older participants (Pfütze, Sommer and Schweinberger, 2002); and qualitatively different patterns of brain activity (as measured by a PET scan) during face recognition (Grady *et al.*, 2002).

Taking a slightly different approach, it can be observed that memory skills which do not decline are very much part of crystallised intelligence (knowledge of facts, procedures, and so forth). Problems tend to occur when participants have to process novel information and concurrently deal with other tasks (this is most clearly seen in working memory tasks). Thus, it is not surprising to find that such tasks are strongly correlated with fluid intelligence and general neural efficiency, as was noted above. Similarly, Rabbitt (1988b) noted that scores on various tests of STM and LTM did not correlate with each other if intelligence test performance was partialled out. This indicates that declines in memory, like declines in intellectual performance, tend to occur in processes which are especially sensitive to the status of neural functions. However, it is once again important not to assume automatically that these changes are inevitable or totally physically based. For example, Rabbitt (1988b) is at pains to point out that not all of the memory decline can be attributed to changes in fluid intelligence (nor in participants' choice reaction times, which were also measured). Again, it is possible that at least in part, lack of practise of mental skills causes some neural systems to decline through disuse. Furthermore, general lifestyle may have serious consequences. For example, long-term stress elevates some hormone levels which may accentuate hippocampal atrophy (Bremner and Narayan, 1998).

Suggested further reading

Baddeley (1983) provides an immensely readable introduction to the general psychology of memory, and the book is warmly recommended. Baddeley (1995) is a more advanced text, but is still reasonably accessible to a non-specialist. Good introductions to studies of ageing and memory are provided by Chapter 11 of Schaie and Willis (1991a), Chapter 8 of Perlmutter and Hall (1992), Cohen (1996), Craik (2000), Craik *et al.* (1995) and Rabbitt (1998). A discussion of the basic neurological aspects of memory change is provided by Woodruff-Pak (1997).

CHAPTER 4

Ageing and Language

Introduction

Linguistic skills encompass the production and comprehension of speech and writing. Before examining the effects of ageing on these, there is a primer on basic aspects of language processing. Those already familiar with these concepts may wish to skim read the next few paragraphs.

It is perhaps easiest to introduce the area through an examination of the psychological processes involved in reading (which in any case is the linguistic skill perhaps most often studied by psychologists and educational gerontologists). Introspectively, reading is perceived as being a fairly automatic and instantaneous process (e.g. try not reading *don't read this*) but in fact it involves the co-ordination of a variety of different skills, from the very basic to the very complex. On *a priori* grounds, normal reading must involve at the very least the following processes. First, there must be a mental mechanism for identifying individual letters, to distinguish them from, say, random splodges of ink, or items from a foreign alphabet. Furthermore, there must be a method of identifying whether sequences of letters form real words or whether they are merely nonsense strings (e.g. *aslkdhf*), and also of judging how to pronounce the word (i.e. of converting the printed into a spoken representation). Following from these stages must be a skill of judging if sequences of words form meaningful phrases. These have to be judged for both their **syntactic** and **semantic** acceptability. For example, the phrase:

goldfish make suitable pets

is sensible, if banal. The phrase:

hypotheses make sensible pets

is more interesting, but is obviously nonsense, and is said to be semantically unacceptable (loosely, semantics is the expression of meaning). However, the phrase's syntax (loosely, its grammar) is acceptable. Conversely, a phrase such as:

> goldfish makes suitable pets

is syntactically unacceptable (because it is grammatically incorrect), but it could be argued that it still conveys a meaning, and thus is semantically acceptable. A final stage in the reading process must involve extracting meaning from the phrases. Introspection shows that one does not remember every word of what has been read – instead, one recalls the gist of the story. Thus, readers must possess a method of extracting the key features of a piece of text.

It must not be supposed that all the processing is in one direction from the basic skill of letter recognition to the relatively complex one of meaning extraction, since the latter operations can send information back down the processing chain to speed up reading. For example, suppose one is reading a passage of text written in an appallingly untidy hand, and suppose that some letters are completely unrecognisable, represented below by *x*s:

> Ix is xoutful if anx moxe axxixtance is rexxired. Remxmbxr the xroverb: txo maxy coxks xpoil the xxxxh.

Most readers should have little difficulty in decoding this message. There are several reasons for this. First, some words like *xoutful* and *xroverb* can only be *doubtful* and *proverb.* Thus, the reader makes use of knowledge of which letter combinations make real words to work out what the indecipherable letters stand for. In other instances, semantic knowledge is used. For example, *Ix* alone could be *If, It, In* or *Is.* However, *Ix is* only makes sense if *Ix* is *It.* The final word of the passage – *xxxxh* – is unrecognisable by itself, but is easily recognised as broth because it is the last word of a well-known saying. This is an example of **semantic facilitation**, where the semantic content of a passage enables one to predict the words coming up. This does not just apply to reading sloppy handwriting. For normal print, one uses one's expectations to facilitate word recognition, and it has been demonstrated that words which are logically linked to what has just been read are read faster than less predictable words. Thus, if one had been reading about animals, then one would read *tiger* faster than *chair.* In formal experimental situations, the phenomenon is tested by presenting participants with a word or sentence (the 'prime') and then presenting them with a word which may or may not be semantically related to the prime. Participants are usually asked to decide if the word is a word or not, or to say the word out loud. In both instances, responses are faster if the prime is semantically related. How facilitation occurs is still hotly contested, but generally it appears that the mind in effect places mental representations of semantically related words on 'standby' so that if they appear in print, their meaning is accessed faster.

A final consideration is the role of memory. Obviously, without LTM (long-term memory), it would be impossible to read a story and understand it, simply because one would keep forgetting the plot. Less obvious is the need for working memory (see

Chapter 2, or the Glossary), but one must be able to keep in mind what has just been read, otherwise by the time one reaches the end of the sentence, one would have forgotten the point of it, and this would be especially true of long convoluted sentences such as this.

Thus, reading involves the active integration of a number of perceptual, cognitive, linguistic and memory skills. It will not have escaped some readers' attention that the processes involved in the comprehension of spoken language are similar. There must be the capacity for recognising individual letters or words; for identifying they are correctly pronounced; for identifying meaning and whether phrases are syntactically acceptable; and, finally, for extracting the gist of a spoken message. Obviously, there are differences – reading is accessed visually, speech acoustically, so readers can (and do) look back at something they have not understood, whilst listeners usually have fewer opportunities to do an analogous thing, and instead have to ask a speaker to repeat something they have difficulty with. Speech and writing also have different conventions. Writing, for example, tends to be more formal and grammatically correct. Indeed, there has been a debate whether speech and writing share *any* processes in common (Olsen *et al.*, 1985). In this chapter, this will not be addressed, but given that reading and listening have functionally analogous processes, examination of the effects of ageing on the two skills will be conducted in tandem. It is not necessarily implied, however, that a change in a reading sub-skill is automatically linked to a change in the analogous listening sub-skill. It should also be noted that the effects of ageing on the skills of speech production and writing have received relatively little attention, but such experimental findings as there are will be placed at appropriate points in the commentary.

Although each section that follows is reasonably self-contained, researchers do not devise their work with the express aim that it can be neatly compartmentalised under sub-headings in textbooks, so there is some overlap between sections. Indeed, it is fair to say that studies of ageing and linguistic skills provide a more disjointed picture than for example intelligence or memory. In all sections it should be noted that research has almost always used cross-sectional studies. Where longitudinal research has been conducted on linguistic changes, then, as with measurements of cognitive performance (see Chapter 2), it has generally found smaller-scale changes than have cross-sectional studies (e.g. Connor *et al.*, 2004). To take a more specific example, in a cross-sectional study of vocabulary size, Alwin and McCammon (2001) found that differences within an age group were significantly greater than differences between age groups (probably reflecting radical differences in educational experiences and other cohort effects). Thus, some caution should be exercised in interpreting data from cross-sectional studies.[1] It

---

1   Verhaeghen (2003) raises the rather technical point that because of the **Flynn effect** (see Glossary) comparing different age groups matched on some verbal skills test scores is not matching like with like, and accordingly yet further caution is advised.

should also be noted that the interaction between different skills involved in reading is very complex and still far from understood, and considerable portions of variance in ability may be specific to a particular situation, person or group (see Stine-Morrow *et al.*, 2001).

The degree to which changes are identified also to some extent depends upon the level of focus. Burke *et al.* (2000) argue that age-related decline in reception of language is practically non-existent in comparison with problems in the production of language. In overall and relative terms this is arguably true, but it can give the impression that reception of linguistic information is totally unaffected by ageing, and that is not the case.

The sections that follow begin with general considerations of reading – as part of lifestyle and in conjunction with general cognitive change. Then different aspects of linguistic skills are considered in a (loosely) hierarchical manner, beginning with word recognition and proceeding 'up' to comprehension.

The role of reading in older people's lifestyles

Because reading is a sedentary activity, it is often assumed that older people spend more time engaged in it than younger people. In fact, some evidence points in the opposite direction (e.g. National Council on Aging, 1975). Despite worthy intentions, people generally do not read more once retirement presents the opportunity to do so through increased leisure time. Older adults who read a lot were almost invariably voracious readers when they were younger. Likewise, young adult readers who hover around the level of functional literacy (i.e. barely capable of reading all but the most basic textual information such as signs and simple instructions) are unlikely to improve their skills in later life, compounding a variety of problems associated with low reading ability (see Roman, 2004).

If solely those older adults who are active readers are considered, then there are some intriguing differences between them and their younger counterparts. The older active readers spend more time reading (e.g. Rice, 1986a), but significantly more of this time is spent on newspapers and magazines (e.g. Ribovich and Erikson, 1980; Rice, 1986a). This means that the reading 'practice' older people obtain may be of a poorer quality, because the content of newspapers may be facile compared with the demands of, for example, a 'heavyweight' novel. In the same manner that failure to train strenuously reduces an athlete's performance, so a failure to read sufficiently demanding texts may cause a decline in reading skills. Why this change in reading habits should occur is open to debate. Reduced mental resources may mean that some older people no longer have the intellectual rigour to plough through works by Dostoevsky or similar authors. Alternatively, when old age is reached, many people may feel that they have read most of the fiction they wanted to read, and have no desire to reread works for which they already know the plot. A more cynical view is that older people feel that there is too little time left to waste it on wading through tedious 'classics'. Younger adults may read 'heavy' works to 'improve' themselves. Older people may no longer have this competitive urge. For whatever reason, older people select 'easy' reading over 90 per cent of the time, be it periodicals, newspapers or 'light' fiction. Furthermore, they appear to get the same level of enjoyment out of reading as do younger adults (Bell, 1980; Rice, 1986a).

Physical constraints

As was noted in Chapter 1, the eyesight of most older people worsens, and visual acuity ('focusing power') is reduced. One study (Bell, 1980) estimates that about 23 per cent of community resident older people are incapable of reading normal print. A solution to this problem is to print books in a larger typeface (for the technically minded, 18–20 point, which is about the size of the main chapter titles in this book). Perhaps the best-known example of this in the UK is the Ulverscroft series. The larger print makes easier reading for those with poor sight, but a study has shown that in the UK at least there are disadvantages. The first arises from the fact that large print books have a relatively small market. Younger visually impaired adults tend to use magnifying equipment, enabling them to cope with normally sized print. Therefore, the principal market is older people. This is further restricted by the fact that few readers buy large print books – most borrow from the local library. These considerations mean that publishers tend to stick to fairly 'safe' lightweight fiction that will appeal to the largest readership, such as that by James Herriot, Agatha Christie, Catherine Cookson and so forth. Whilst there is nothing wrong with these authors *per se*, this policy means that an older person with eyesight problems is restricted in his or her choice to texts which are unlikely to stretch his or her reading abilities. An additional consideration is that many older people are limited in the amount they can read. Large print books are heavy, and older people may take fewer books home from the library than when they were younger, simply because they cannot carry more (Bell, 1980). Furthermore, there is some evidence that while large print size may increase the rate at which words can be read aloud, it may decrease the speed with which they are read silently (Bouma *et al.*, 1982). However, Lovie and Whittaker (1998) found limited evidence that print size had an effect on reading rate. As noted in Chapter 2, adjusting print size of intelligence tests lessened, but did not remove, age differences (Storandt and Futterman, 1982), whilst Rosenstein and Glickman (1994) found increased print size had no effect on performance of a personnel selection test. The font face used can also affect reading speed (Vanderplas and Vanderplas, 1980), although note that Cerella and Fozard (1984) found that making print harder to read did not differentially affect older people relative to younger people.

Considerations about print size may eventually become outmoded because of the rise in availability of talking books. For example, Bouchard Ryan *et al.* (2003) observed that older adults with visual problems such as macular degeneration (see Chapter 1) were more likely to change from reading newspapers and magazines (which typically have small print and poor contrast) to listening to talking books. The authors also noted that circa a quarter of their sample used computer technology to enlarge print. However, although talking books offer a solution to people with sight difficulties, they are not, as is commonly supposed, a direct substitute for reading. Three reasons can be cited. First, the narrator will almost certainly place emphases upon what is being read out that may not match what the listener would emphasise were he or she reading for themselves. Second, listening to a talking book involves hearing every word. As noted above, reading does not involve reading every word (studies of eye movements in reading show that necessary but predictable words such as 'the' and 'and' are usually skipped over). Third, in reading it is easy to move back over a passage of print just read, or to skim read through a section of prose. This is either very difficult or impossible to do when using a talking book.

It should be noted that many older people are unaware that they have problems with their vision. Holland and Rabbitt (1989) noted that all participants from the age of 50 onwards gave near-identical subjective ratings of their vision, though in reality there was a marked deterioration in the older participants. A decline in perceptual abilities does not just mean that older people need larger print and/or hearing aids, however. A sensory loss can directly affect the efficiency with which information is processed. For example, Rabbitt (1989) noted that older people with mild hearing loss (35–50 dB) had great difficulty remembering lists of spoken words, even though they were earlier able to repeat them all perfectly as they were spoken to them. It appears that hearing impaired older people can perceive words, but it takes greater effort to do this, leaving fewer mental resources to encode and remember them. That there is nothing especially wrong with their memories can be shown by the fact that if the participants were shown *printed* lists of words, then there was no difference between their and normal hearing controls' performance (i.e. the effect was confined to when hearing was part of the processing chain). Similarly, Schneider (1997) demonstrated that cochlear degeneration and relatively small changes in the fidelity of signal transmission can have much broader effects on, for example, following conversations in a noisy environment or rapidly spoken prose. Schneider *et al.* (2000) found that older adults only demonstrated a failing of memory for discourse (both in terms of the details and the gist of what had been heard) when differences in hearing levels were not controlled for. If volume levels of the stimuli were presented at what was appropriate for the individual participant's hearing abilities, then older and younger participants could recall aspects of discourse equally well both with and without background noise (only in a very high background noise condition did the younger participants show an advantage in recall of details). Schneider, Daneman and Murphy (2005) found that altering parameters of the speech signal that minimised its auditory degradation likewise removed age differences. Thus, peripheral changes in hearing can account for a large proportion of the ageing decline in linguistic skills involving auditory input.

The voice also undergoes changes. The obvious superficial alterations, in a raising of pitch and a weakness of projection, arise from a variety of factors, including muscle wastage and a reduction in lung capacity. Other changes may result from relatively modern phenomena, such as (ill-fitting) dentures and smoking (Thompson, 1988). However, whatever the reason, vocal output is generally poorer in older people (Xue and Deliyski, 2001). This loss of vocal efficiency also shows itself in a slowing of articulation rate for normal impromptu speech, reading a passage of prose and reaction times to pronouncing words (e.g. Laver and Burke, 1993; Oyer and Deal, 1989; Ryan, 1972). However, it should also be noted that slower speech rate correlates significantly with memory span (Multhaup, Balota and Cowan, 1996) implying a cognitive connection as well.

Handwriting undergoes changes (see Miller, 1987), largely tied to physical deterioration. Aside from the effects of conditions such as the early stages of dementia (Slavin et al., 1999) and Parkinson's disease (e.g. Contreras-Vidal, Teulings and Stelmach, 1995), 'normal' ageing too presents its problems. For example, fine control over the spatial co-ordination of finger and wrist movements involved in handwriting declines in later life (Contreras-Vidal, Teulings and Stalmach, 1998) and generally older writers are less efficient in using visual feedback (Slavin, Phillips and Bradshaw, 1996). However, not all age differences are necessarily due to physical factors. For example, it is worth noting that many older adults who are 'naturally' left-handed use their right (i.e. less efficient) hand for writing, simply because until relatively recently, many schools forced all children to write with their right hands (see Beukelaar and Kroonenberg, 1986). This may distort findings on some age differences in handwriting skill. The effects of these changes, other than in the aesthetic appearance of the writing itself, are mixed. Dixon, Kutzman and Friesen (1993) found that overall, writing speed decreases with age across a wide variety of writing tasks. However, to some extent this is shaped by the level of familiarity of the tasks: the more familiar the task, the less the age difference. In addition, the more tasks were practised, the less the age difference became (recalling Rabbitt's findings on the effect of practice on reaction times reported in Chapter 2).

General cognitive constraints

Given the findings reported elsewhere in this book, it might be intuitively supposed that anything that increases processing load or otherwise makes a linguistic task 'harder' will be disproportionately disadvantageous for older adults. However, the results are surprisingly mixed. For example, Smiler, Gagne and Stine-Morrow (2003) found that reading speed was unaffected by a concurrent load placed by having to perform another distractor task simultaneously. An analogous finding was reported by Stuart-Hamilton and Rabbitt (1997b) who found that manipulating aspects of text (e.g. syntactic complexity and/or amount of the text that could be seen at any one time) did not affect the reading speed of older adults relative to younger adult controls. However, with regard to eye movements, Kemper, Crow and Kemptes (2004) found relatively few age differences in eye movements except that older adults tended to look back over ambiguous text (e.g. to use one of the authors' examples, *The experienced soldiers warned about the dangers conducted the midnight raid*) more than did younger adults. This implies that older adults can process less information in a single 'bite' and thus need to re-check complex text more often than younger adults.

Other manipulations produce rather more straightforward ageing effects. For example, Speranza, Daneman and Schneider (2000) presented participants with sentences to read that were obscured by an overlying pattern of 'visual noise'. The researchers found that the older adults needed a significantly lower level of noise in order to perform at the same level as younger adult readers. However, older readers were disproportionately advantaged over younger readers when the sentences offered semantic facilitation (thus echoing the findings of other studies – see below). Again, measurements of EEG responses by older and younger participants engaged in reading whilst attempting to ignore distractors demonstrate that older adults' mental processes are significantly more disrupted by the extraneous stimuli (Phillips and Lesperance, 2003). Kemper, Herman and Lian (2003) provided participants with the task of giving spoken responses to questions whilst engaged in another activity (walking and finger tapping). The researchers found that older participants produced less fluent and syntactically less complex speech than younger participants, thus supporting the argument that older adults have a lowered working memory span (see Chapter 3). Interestingly, the researchers also found that younger adults adopted a different strategy from older participants; namely, they used grammatically simpler and shorter sentences, whereas the older adults slowed their speech rate.

Other effects are more complex and not uniform across all types of linguistic activity. For example, DeDe *et al.* (2004) found that working memory's influence varied according to which aspect of reading skills was being considered. The paper is very difficult to summarise, but in essence, using structural equation modelling, the researchers found that the mediating effect of working memory shifted from a marginal role to central importance depending upon the specific reading task being considered.

Thus, although there are instances where linguistic skills are affected by general cognitive decline and a lowering of cognitive capacity, the effects are not always clear cut, with some skills apparently largely immune to these effects. This is something of a recurrent theme in ageing and language, with some instances of decline that fit with the general findings of intellectual and memory changes and others where there is a surprisingly well-preserved skill that goes against intuitive expectations. So far no overarching theory has been devised to explain these dichotomies, but as noted above, linguistic skills tend in any case to be multi-faceted and surprisingly resistant to reduction to basic explanations.

Word recognition

There are a variety of ways to test the ability to read single words, but two of the commonest are the **lexical decision** and the **naming latency** tasks. The former requires participants simply to decide if a group of letters forms a word (note that the participants do not have to identify what the word 'says'). A naming latency task measures how quickly a participant can read a word aloud. Generally, older people are no worse at these tasks than younger adults when the task is presented in its conventional form (e.g. Bowles and Poon, 1985; Cerella and Fozard, 1984). However, if the tasks are made harder or more complex, then often an age decrement appears. For example, Ratcliff *et al.* (2004) found that in two lexical decision tasks, older adults were slower but more accurate than younger participants. This was accounted for using the **Ratcliff diffusion model** (see Glossary) which argued that older adults were slower at some aspects of processing but adopted more conservative decision criteria.[2]

Bowles and Poon (1981) found further evidence of age-related decline when they gave participants a modified lexical decision task. Participants had to judge pairs of letter groupings, both of which had to form real words for a 'yes' response to be given. Allen *et al.* (1993) manipulated the difficulty of the words used in a lexical decision task in ways likely to strike at relatively peripheral (such as altering the ease with which stimuli could be encoded) and relatively central (such as word frequency) aspects of processing. The researchers concluded that age differences tend to arise in peripheral rather than central mental processes (e.g. there were no age differences induced by word frequency). This is echoed in the findings of Madden (1992) who found age differences were greater when the visual appearance of the words (likely to be a fairly peripheral effect) was manipulated. Evidence of lack of differences at a central level is provided by, amongst others, Karayanidis *et al.* (1993), who found no differences between the EEG patterns of older and younger adults during a lexical decision task (though there were some differences when encountering words seen earlier, this is essentially a memory rather than word recognition effect). Spieler and Balota (2000) found that in a naming latency task, older adults made significantly greater relative use of word frequency information,

2   In comparison, the same research group found older adults to be slower and less accurate at a letter discrimination task (Thapar, Ratcliff and McKoon, 2003). These findings too were accounted for by the diffusion model.

whereas younger adults made significantly greater use of orthographic features of the word. The authors concluded that this denotes an age-related shift from primary reliance on features within the word to features of the word itself.

Generally, as lexical decision task difficulty increases, then so does the size of the age difference. Myerson *et al.* (1997) found that this can be reduced to a Brinley plot – in other words, the general phenomenon may be explained in terms of the general slowing hypothesis (for further discussion, see Chapter 2). However, Allen *et al.* (2004) found in a study of older and younger adults' lexical decision speeds that Brinley plots for errors and response times were significantly different and in effect contradicted each other. Using a very complex mathematical technique (for those interested – error values were converted into entropy and then response speeds predicted from these transformed data) the authors demonstrated that components of the response associated with peripheral processes were significantly affected by ageing, but those associated with central processes were relatively unaffected; thus, by a circuitous route, supporting the earlier findings cited above. However, another study by the same group of researchers (Allen *et al.*, 2002) points to a rather more complex state of affairs. Participants were given a lexical decision task in which the words were either conventionally printed all in the same case (e.g. 'same case'), or were mixed case (e.g. 'MiXed CaSe') and in either instance could be printed in one colour or in several colours. It was predicted that conventionally printed words would be processed faster since the mind would process them holistically (basically, they primarily would be processed by shape and outline with relatively little reliance on the more laborious method of reading letter by letter). On the other hand, mixed case words present unusual outlines, and thus cannot be processed holistically, but instead must be processed analytically (in essence, letter by letter). It was thus predicted that processing of mixed case words would be slower. It was felt that use of different colours would have no effect on holistic processing of words but it would speed up processing of mixed case words. The researchers found that these predictions were borne out by the performances of young adult participants, but older participants had a different pattern of responses, suggesting that ageing does not affect holistic processing, but causes a decrement in analytic processing. This is reflected in a study by Logan and Balota (2003). They gave participants the task of studying a group of words and then doing a task in which they had to complete a word from a fragment of it. If the word fragment was preceded by a blocking word that was orthographically related (loosely, had a lot of letters in common) then older participants were disproportionately disadvantaged and were more likely to complete the fragment by erroneously using the blocking word. The authors concluded that this was because older adults may have problems in suppressing activity of rival (but inaccurate) alternatives in processing words. This recalls the research on frontal lobe deficits discussed in Chapter 2.

In semantic facilitation experiments, older people are generally slower (as with many reaction time experiments – see Chapter 2). However, older participants gain a disproportionately greater advantage from this, when compared with recognising words seen in isolation (Laver and Burke, 1993; Myerson *et al.*, 1992; though note that earlier commentators, such as Craik and Rabinowitz, 1984, found no difference). At one level the explanation for this phenomenon is simple – 'a slow horse will save more time than a fast horse when the distance is reduced by a constant amount' (Laver and Burke, 1993, p.35). If one horse runs at 40 kilometres per hour, and another at 20 kph, then cutting the race distance from 40 to 20 kilometres will save 30 minutes for the faster horse and an hour for the slower one. In a similar manner, if older people are reacting less quickly, then facilitation (which in effect decreases the computational 'distance') will be of greater benefit to older participants (see also Bennett and McEvoy, 1999).

Spelling

Spelling skills in later life might be supposed to experience the same fate as word recognition. Knowledge of spelling rules is a crystallised skill, and as such should be relatively immune from ageing effects. However, there is evidence that this is not the case. MacKay, Abrams and Pedroza (1999) observed that older participants were as adept as younger participants at detecting misspellings in a list of words. However, there was an age difference involved in being able subsequently to retrieve the correctly and incorrectly spelt words from memory. MacKay and Abrams (1998) also found that misspellings increased in later life, as did Stuart-Hamilton and Rabbitt (1997a). These age-related deficits are not directly attributable to general slowing, crystallised intelligence or education level. Stuart-Hamilton and Rabbitt found fluid intelligence to be a good predictor of spelling skills, whilst MacKay and co-researchers link the decline to a more specific linguistic coding deficit (see MacKay *et al.*, 1999). In part it is predicated on the transmission deficit hypothesis (MacKay and Burke, 1990) which argues that concepts are stored in interconnected 'nodes'. Ageing weakens these connections and the ease with which nodes may be activated, though this can be compensated for by regular practice, and/or stimulation by more prompts. Hence, *inter alia*, new pieces of information are more prone to inefficient processing than older pieces, and recognition is easier than recall.

Pronunciation

Knowledge of pronunciation of words might also be expected to be preserved in later life, and indeed this would appear to be generally the case (though note that the *speed* with which words can be pronounced may decrease – see above). Typically, pronunciation is tested by presenting participants with a list of irregularly spelt words (e.g. *yacht, dessert*), and asking them to say them out loud. Because the words do not obey conventional spelling rules, their pronunciation cannot be calculated from first principles. For example, pronouncing *dessert* by conventional spelling rules would yield the spoken presentation of *desert* (and vice versa). Those readers who have already read Chapter 2 will appreciate that pronunciation abilities are therefore part and parcel of crystallised intelligence (loosely speaking, general knowledge), which is largely ageing-proof. It follows from this that pronunciation ability should remain stable in later life. Nelson and O'Connell (1978) examined the pronunciation abilities of 120 adults aged 20–70 years, and found no significant correlation between test score and chronological age (Nelson and McKenna, 1973). This word list was developed into the **National Adult Reading Test**, or **NART**. A subsequent study by Crawford *et al.* (1988) found a slight negative correlation between age and NART score, but this disappeared when either length of education or social class was partialled out of the equation. Hence, concluded the authors, 'age has little or no effect on NART performance' (p.182). Because of such arguments, the NART has become widely used as a quick assessor of crystallised intelligence, particularly where older participants with dementia or some other kinds of brain damage have retained the ability to read whilst being incapable of some other intellectual tasks (e.g. Brayne and Beardsall, 1990; Carswell *et al.*, 1997; O'Carroll, Baikie and Whittock, 1987; O'Carroll and Gilleard, 1986; however, this is now disputed – see Chapter 6). The NART is not necessarily a totally accurate guide, however. When words from the NART are placed in the context of a sentence, then performance generally improves (Conway and O'Carroll, 1997, who developed this format into a new test – the Cambridge Contextual Reading Test (CCRT) – see Beardsall, 1998). In other instances, the NART may overestimate intelligence levels (Mockler, Riordan and Sharma, 1996), whilst researchers using an American version of the NART (called, not surprisingly, the American NART or AMNART or ANART) found somewhat different patterns of results within groups of White-American and African-American older people who were either non-demented or suffering from dementia (Boekamp, Strauss and Adams, 1995). It is difficult to get a clear overall picture from these and similar studies simply because different samples of people have been used (e.g. some have dementia, some have not; amongst studies of dementia, different grading criteria have been used, and so forth). The general conclusion of many researchers is that the NART is a fair *general* predictor of intellectual status (and breakfast consumption: cereal eating and test score are positively correlated; Smith, 1998), even if the shortened (and quicker) format arguably lacks accuracy (Bucks *et al.*, 1996) and the full test is not absolutely precise (see Law and O'Carroll, 1998).

Semantic processing

In addition to recognising words and knowing how they are spelt and pronounced, it is also necessary to know what the words mean. In Chapter 2, it was demonstrated that knowledge of word meaning is the key component of many measures of crystallised intelligence, and it is known that, although age does not affect crystallised intelligence (and thus knowledge of word meanings) as much as, for example, tasks heavily based on fluid intelligence, nonetheless there is a decline in later life. Principally, older adults are slower to produce responses and definitions offered are likely to be less precise than younger people's. For example, McGinnis and Zelinski (2000) gave participants the task of providing definitions of unfamiliar words that could be gleaned from the context in which they were presented. The researchers found that older adults picked up fewer of the available pieces of information available in the text, and produced more vague generalised definitions. In a second experiment, McGinnis and Zelinski provided four definitions for each unfamiliar word and asked participants to choose the correct definition. One definition was rigorously correct; one was more generalised (thus, not quite 'wrong' but certainly vague); one was a generalised interpretation of the story; and one was irrelevant. Younger adults relatively favoured the exact definitions, whilst the oldest old participants (those aged 75 years and over) were more likely to select the generalised definitions. In a follow-up study, the authors gave participants the task of reading a passage of prose that contained an unfamiliar word. Whilst reading, the participants were asked to 'think aloud' about what they were reading, and afterwards were asked to rate a set of definitions derived from the passage for accuracy (McGinnis and Zelinsky, 2003). The researchers found that the older participants produced more generalised comments about the passages whilst thinking aloud, and rated generalised and irrelevant definitions more highly. Overall, McGinnis and Zelinski concluded that older adults have appreciable problems processing the relatively complex information required to extract meaning from context. More specifically, they fail to think at a sufficiently abstract level and thus fail to draw adequate inferences. This echoes the findings of Albert *et al.* (1987) cited in Chapter 2, in which it was noted that older adults have especial problems providing definitions of sayings and proverbs. This failure too can be seen as a reduced ability to see beyond the literal to the underlying symbolic structure.

It should be noted, however, that semantic processing almost invariably is predicated on the use of other skills, and thus age differences may be the result of a wide variety of potential factors. It is rather like judging the worth of different brands of flour in cake recipes. Whilst a reasonable estimate of differences may be gauged, the influence of the other ingredients will always be there and will vary from recipe to recipe. Similarly, whilst semantic skills can be measured, participants have by definition to use other skills (e.g. phonological processing) to perform a semantic task. Thus, the field is wide open for other variables to have an effect. For example, Taylor and Burke (2002) presented participants with pictures of objects. The participants had to name these objects, whilst distracting words were read out. In some instances, the object was a homophone (i.e. had more than one meaning – the authors cite the example of *ball*). If the participant was looking at a picture of an item and a word semantically related to its other meaning was spoken (e.g. the participant sees a picture of a ball and hears the word 'dance' spoken) then this aided the response times of younger participants, but not older participants. Other distractors generally did not differentially affect the responses of the age groups. Taylor and Burke use this finding to develop an interesting and rather complex connectionist model in which ageing has an asymmetric effect on phonological and semantic mechanisms. In contrast, Mayr and Kliegl (2000) gave participants the task of producing members of either (1) the same semantic category or (2) a member of one semantic category alternating with a member of another semantic category (i.e. member of category A, then a member of category B, then a member of category A, then B, etc.). The researchers used the parameters of the experiment to estimate performance at semantic retrieval itself and performance at the peripheral skills necessary for semantic retrieval to take place. Mayr and Kliegl concluded that semantic retrieval was relatively intact – it was the peripheral factors that showed a significant decline.

Interesting as the findings of Taylor and Burke and Mayr and Kliegl are in their own right, of concern here is the fact that, under different circumstances, semantic processing in older adults can be made to appear good, bad or indifferent according to the experimental design used. In addition, what is meant by 'semantic processing'? Relatively basic semantic processes appear to be age-resistant. For example, Lahar, Tun and Wingfield, 2004, demonstrated that filling in a missing word in a sentence where the answer can be gauged from the context appears to be relatively unaffected by ageing (though there may be differences in EEG activity – see Federmeier and Kutas, 2005). Again, presented with the relatively uncomplicated task of providing a definition of a new word just encountered in a passage of prose, older adults produced more complete definitions (Long and Shaw, 2000). It is only with more complex semantic skills that the evidence is more circumspect. However, if the 'mugging analogy' made in Chapter 2 is recalled, it may be argued that no matter what the 'real' state of something is after all extenuating variables have been accounted for, at the end of the day it is how a skill presents itself for immediate inspection that is usually of paramount concern.

Syntactic processing

Relatively little research has been conducted on semantic or syntactic processing independent of the concurrent considerations of text recall. However, one notable exception is a series of excellent papers and articles by Susan Kemper on changes in syntactic processing in older people. Kemper (1986) requested younger and older adults to imitate sentences by creating new ones with the same syntactic structure. She found that the older participants could only reliably imitate short sentences: long sentences, particularly those containing embedded clauses, were the hardest to imitate. Baum (1993) likewise found that increasing the syntactic complexity of sentences resulted in age group differences in a sentence repetition task; this also occurred when the sentences were used in a lexical decision task. Obler *et al.* (1991) found similar effects of syntax on sentence comprehension. This syntactic decline is also reflected in spontaneous everyday language. Kynette and Kemper (1986) noted that the diversity of syntactic structures declines with age, whilst there is an increase in errors such as the omission of articles and the use of incorrect tenses. In a similar vein, Kemper (1992) found that older and younger adults had the same number of sentence fragments in their spontaneous speech. However, the younger adults' fragments tended to be of 'better quality', being false starts to statements, whereas older adults tended to produce these incomplete statements as 'filler' during a pause.

Kemper and Rush (1988) reported other examples of this decline. For example, the average number of syntactic clauses per sentence fell from 2.8 for those aged 50–59 to 1.7 for those aged 80–89. The researchers also assessed the **Yngve depth** of the syntax. This is a fairly complex technique which gives a syntactic complexity 'score' to a phrase or sentence (the higher the score, the more sophisticated the construction). Yngve scores declined with age, but more intriguingly, they correlated well ($r = 0.76$) with digit span. Thus, the better the memory, the better the syntax. There is an attractively simple explanation for this finding. Syntactically complex sentences are almost invariably longer than simple ones and to construct or comprehend them, greater demands are placed on memory. Or, put simply, more words have to be remembered at one time. This is a plausible explanation of why older people simplify their syntax – they know that their working memory no longer has its youthful capacity, so sentences are simplified and shortened to cope with this. However, as Kemper herself has acknowledged, this is an overly simplistic explanation. More probable is that declines in spans and syntax are both manifestations of a general intellectual decline.

Comparable results are reported by Gould and Dixon (1993). They asked younger and older married couples to describe a vacation they had taken together, and analysed their descriptions for linguistic content. The general finding was that the younger couple produces a greater amount of detail. The researchers attributed the older couples' 'failure' to do this to a decline in working memory. However, they also acknowledge it is possible that the age-related change is due to a shift in attitude – 'the younger couples... May have given less consideration to being entertaining than did the older couples' (Gould and Dixon, 1993; p.15). Arbuckle, Nohara-LeClair and Pushkar (2000) argue that off-target verbosity is indicative of poor processing skills (e.g. poor inhibition – see Chapter 2). They identified people who had particularly high levels of off-target verbosity and found that they were significantly worse at providing accurate descriptions (in this instance, in a task where they were required to provide a description of an abstract figure to a listener) even when they did not stray off-target. A further study by the same research group (Pushkar *et al.*, 2000) also noted that being high in off-target verbosity generally brought less satisfaction to those listening to it (thus countering the argument made above that discursion may be more entertaining). However, the same study also found that verbosity was unrelated to age or cognitive level, thereby arguing against the case that verbosity necessarily reflects an age-related decline.

Related to Gould and Dixon's findings is a study by Adams (1991), which noted that compared with a group of younger controls, older adults' written summaries of stories tended to interpret the text at a more abstract level, and placed emphasis on a *précis* of the story's structure. This qualitative difference may arise because of a loss of processing capacity. For example, if the older participants cannot remember as much about the story, then talking about it in abstract terms might be a wise option. Kemper and Anagnopoulos (1993) likewise argue that older people may use various discourse strategies to circumvent deficiencies or discrepancies in their syntactic processing skills. Pasupathi, Henry and Carstensen (2002) also note that in telling a narrative, older adults are more likely to emphasise positive emotional aspects of the story (i.e. there may be more than simply a cognitive change at work).

Kemper (1987a and b) examined six diaries kept by people for most of their adult lifespans. Drawn from museum archives, the diaries commenced between 1856 and 1876, and finished between 1943 and 1957. Kemper found that the language used became simpler over the writers' lifespans. Sentence length decreased, as did complexity of syntax. For example, the number of embedded clauses declined, and there was an increase in the failure of **anaphoric reference** (e.g. referring to 'he' without adequately specifying which of two previously cited males is meant). At the same time, the sophistication of the narrative declined, and increasingly events were described as a catalogue of facts rather than as a 'story' with a plot and a conclusion. In a similar vein, Bromley (1991) gave participants aged 20–86 years the task of writing a description of themselves. Analysing the results, he found that the syntactic complexity and breadth of vocabulary exhibited in the writing was related to the participant's age, but that other factors, such as word length and readability, were affected by the participant's educational level and level of vocabulary (as measured by the Mill Hill test, a common crystallised intelligence measure – see Chapter 2). Interestingly, fluid intelligence did not play a significant role.

There are other grounds for assuming that a decline in writing cannot automatically be attributed to an intellectual failing. As anyone who has kept a diary for some time will know, writing it can be a chore. Thus, the older they got, the less motivated the writers may have felt to write a 'story' (or perhaps less happened in their lives which might have motivated them to describe it in more elaborate prose). Again, rereading their attempts at creative writing might have so embarrassed the writers that they decided to resort to a less florid style. Furthermore, the purpose of the journal may change over years and become for example a method of empowerment at a time of changes in self-perception (see Brady and Sky, 2003). This might also necessitate a change in writing style. It may also be the case that, as the writers grew older, general attitudes to writing styles relaxed, and thus a simpler style was deliberately adopted (e.g. when the diaries began, the massive Victorian novel was in its heyday, and when they ended F. Scott Fitzgerald and Hemingway were contemporary figures). Indeed, Kemper (1987b) could identify a cohort difference even within her small sample. The writers born earliest in her group used significantly more infinitives ('to go', 'to do', etc.) than did the younger ones.

However, more recent research tends to support the argument that writing changes reflect a decline in ability rather than a stylistic shift. For example, an ingenious study of the letters of King James VI/I[3] by Williams *et al.* (2003) demonstrates a cognitive-related decline that furthermore can be correlated with well-documented bouts of illness that can be reasonably assumed to have had deleterious intellectual effects on the king. In a slightly more prosaic format (no pun intended) Kemper, Thompson and Marquis (2001) conducted a longitudinal study of the writing of older volunteers. Annual samples of language were taken and cognitive tests were also administered. The researchers demonstrated an age-related decline (particularly after the mid-seventies) in grammatical complexity and propositional content and this was linked to cognitive changes. Kemper and Sumner (2001) demonstrated that grammatical complexity was linked to working memory, and sentence length to verbal intelligence (see also Kemper, Herman and Liu, 2004).[4] Kemtes and Kemper (1997) found that processing of syntactically complex sentences was correlated with working memory performance both at the 'on-line' level of reading the text and the 'off-line' level of comprehending the text (see also Waters and Caplan, 2001). Thus, although there may be stylistic and cohort effects to account for some syntactic changes in later life, the principal factor would be appear to be general ageing intellectual decline.

A related argument concerns how the changes in older people's language can be linked to linguistic usage in childhood. In other words, do older people regress to a childlike linguistic state? This is known as the **regression hypothesis**. The argument in a strong form does not seem plausible, because the grammatical usage of older people is still far more sophisticated and varied than that of children (see Kemper, 1992). Although

---

3   He was first crowned King James VI of Scotland and then on the death of Elizabeth I became King James I of England as well, thereby (nominally at least) uniting Scotland with England.
4   A more technical discussion of statistical techniques appropriate to this kind of analysis is provided by Kemtes and Kemper (2001).

language may in some sense be simplified in later life, it does not simplify itself *that* much. At a weaker level, the theory is more plausible, since *some* linguistic usage may be superficially similar to children's language, in that both use simplified forms; but this does not prove much beyond the fact that older people at times use simpler language (Hemingway used simpler language than Thomas Hardy, but nobody thought Hemingway had regressed). However, beyond general considerations such as this, it is difficult to make very firm statements.

From these arguments, it is plausible to link syntactic change to alterations in the general intellect. However, there is also evidence that the effects are confounded by crystallised skills, cohort effects, and possibly a deliberate change in linguistic style (though whether this is a response to a lowered mental processing capacity is a moot point). Thus, as with much in research on ageing and language, the results are not totally clear cut.

Story comprehension

Until relatively recently, story comprehension arguably attracted more research than any other linguistic topic in gerontology.[5] This is not surprising, because ultimately the efficacy of listening and reading must be judged by how much information can be absorbed and comprehended. Because of the large number of studies, it is perhaps most convenient to itemise this field of research.

General aspects

The basic 'story comprehension' paradigm is simple – a participant listens to or reads a short passage of text (usually 300–400 words long) and then in one form or another either repeats back as much as possible, or is given a multiple-choice recognition test. Most studies have shown that older people remember less (e.g. Byrd, 1985; Light and Anderson, 1985; and Petros *et al.*, 1983 in cross-sectional studies; Zelinski and Burnight, 1997 and Zelinski and Stewart, 1998 in longitudinal studies) and may generalise more (e.g. Zelinski and Hyde, 1996). However, whilst this is a general finding, it is not a universal truth, and varying the types of experimental participants and/or test materials can have a crucial effect, as can be surmised from some of the findings already reported in this chapter, and as shall be demonstrated further in the following sections.

---

5   An author inevitably tempts fate by making such statements, but in researching for this edition, very few new studies of ageing and comprehension could be found. Instead, there appeared to be an upsurge of interest in other linguistic skills.

Choice of participants

Some experimenters, using groups of 'old' participants with an average age in their sixties, have failed to find a younger–older age group difference (e.g. Mandel and Johnson, 1984). Age differences are only reliably found when the 'old' participants are in their mid seventies or older (Meyer, 1987). Another important consideration is the education or prior knowledge level of the participants. Studies have sometimes found no age difference when older people with a high verbal ability (and hence high IQ/education level) have been used as participants (e.g. Taub, 1979). Soederberg Miller (2003) gave participants various texts to read, some of which related to cookery. The readers varied in cookery expertise, and the greater their knowledge (not surprisingly) the greater their encoding and memory of cookery-related items. However, the age of the participants had no effect on this phenomenon.

Thus, as has been noted in previous chapters, those with a well-preserved intellect can maintain a youthful level of performance. The findings of Rice and Meyer (1986) criticise this assumption, however. They found that the quantity of reading practice declined in later life, and tended to concentrate on simpler reading materials. Rice, Meyer and Miller (1988) demonstrated that although quantity and quality of reading practice were important in determining level of text recall, chronological age *per se* and intelligence were still the best predictors. Holland and Rabbitt (1990) found that, among a battery of measures, the best predictors were age, and fluid and crystallised intelligence scores; Brebion *et al.* (1997) demonstrated a correlation with working memory capacity.

Cavanagh and Murphy (1986) noted that personality type and level of anxiety also significantly influenced level of text recall. Dixon and Hultsch (1983) also found that emotion levels affected the performance of older participants. These findings are reflected in a study by Riggs, Lachman and Wingfield (1997). They gave older participants the task of repeating back a spoken passage, which they could pause when and where they wanted. In other words, they could divide the task into segments they felt most comfortable with working with. The researchers found that participants who felt that their intellectual status was principally beyond their control set themselves longer segments of speech than they could remember, and were less good at predicting their memory skills than participants who felt they did have principal control over their intellectual functioning.

The choice of intended listener can also make a difference. Adams *et al.* (2002) gave older and younger women the task of remembering a story which they were told had to be told to either an adult or a child. Although both younger and older adults simplified the story and did more elaborations of key points when retelling the story to a child, older adults did this to a greater extent. When an adult was the listener, the retelling was more 'sophisticated' and younger adults produced a significantly higher proportion of propositions from the original story. This does not necessarily indicate a superiority of older adults in the child as listener condition (arguably it is easier and the additional elaboration may represent a different level of pragmatic awareness rather than a cognitive superiority). However, as Adams *et al.* point out, it does mean that social context may be a confounding variable of some importance in this area of research, and researchers should be careful over choice of the 'listener' when participants are recalling stories and other information. In connection with this, it is also worth noting that there may be a further cohort effect in many studies. Ratner *et al.* (1987) observe that many studies compare a group of younger adults recruited from students with older adults recruited from a broader demographic base. The researchers found a group of non-student younger adults matched for verbal ability with a group of students and compared the two groups with a group of older people on a prose recall task. The students performed better than the other two groups (the non-student younger and older adults performed reasonably similarly to one another). This implies that a considerable part of the age difference in many studies of story recall and comprehension may be attributable to using younger participants who not only are different in age but also radically different in skill at memorising and interpreting text.

Choice of presentation of materials

The findings within this field have been mixed. Even an apparently simple procedure, such as examining prose comprehension following simplification of the text, has met with nebulous results. For example, Walmsley, Scott and Lehrer (1981) found that simplifying a passage of prose improved comprehension when the simplification was done by the subjective opinion of experienced writers. However, more objective measures, such as simplifying according to a readability formula, had no significant effect on recall.

Cohen (1981) found that older people were significantly worse at recalling spoken than written materials, whilst for the younger participants there was no difference (Zacks *et al.*, 1987). This is what would be predicted from Rabbitt's (1990) findings on auditory versus visual recall of word lists reported previously. Presumably the decline in hearing is in this instance more disadvantageous to the older people than is the decline in their sight. Attempts to manipulate the presentation of the story itself have met with variable results. Some alterations have no effect. For example, requiring participants to read aloud versus reading silently does not affect the quantity of information recalled (Taub and Kline 1978), nor does giving people the choice of subject matter for the to-be-read text (Taub, Baker and Kline, 1982).

Varying the speed of presentation of the story has yielded mixed results. Where participants are free to read at their own speed, usually no age difference is reported, but there have been exceptions (Meyer, 1987). Participants can be forced to read text faster by setting time limits on how long they have to read a piece of text. Auditory presentation rate can be increased simply by the narrator speaking faster. Obviously the faster the presentation rate, the faster one has to process information to comprehend it, and one would logically expect older participants to be disadvantaged. Indeed, there are several studies supporting this argument, but a sizeable minority have failed to find an age difference. Furthermore, Petros *et al.* (1983) found that when both presentation and semantic difficulty were varied, there was no appreciable disadvantage to older participants beyond that experienced by the younger participants. Conversely, Tun *et al.* (1992) found that older people were differentially disadvantaged when recalling quickly spoken passages. However, this age difference was not affected by having to perform a concurrent task of picture recognition (in other words, the magnitude of the difference remained the same).

Stine, Wingfield and Poon (1989) demonstrated a significant age difference in recall of spoken words when they were 'jumbled up' so they made no sense, and this difference increased the faster the rate at which the words were presented. However, the difference diminished when the words made syntactic sense (e.g. 'bright deep gorillas fructate omnivorously'), and disappeared for all but the very fastest presentation rate when the words formed conventional phrases (i.e. that made both syntactic and semantic sense). This implies that older people may be limited in processing the spoken output (e.g. through poorer hearing, a lowered capacity in working memory, and so forth), but that they can compensate for this by making greater use of the semantic facilitation provided by normal phraseology. But this is predicated on the false assumption that processing jumbled prose is the normal way in which speech comprehension takes place, and that participants make use of semantic and syntactic information only as extra help when it is needed. However, the unusual combinations are the syntactic and jumbled sentences. If older people do less well on these, it may be because they normally make greater use of semantic and syntactic facilitation, but it could also be because they cannot attune to a different (and artificial) manner of speech comprehension as well as the younger participants can. It has already been noted in this chapter and elsewhere in this book that older people are particularly disadvantaged on novel tasks, but given practice at them, the age difference diminishes. Thus, it is possible that extended practice at the jumbled conditions might lessen the age difference.

Because of these issues, probably the safest conclusion is that the issue of age and presentation rates is as yet unresolved, and it is very much an artefact of the experimental method used.

Some other manipulations of text have an effect. For example, Connelly, Hasher and Zack (1991) gave participants short passages of prose to read. Interspersed in the to-be-read prose were segments of distracting prose, printed in a different font, which the participants were told to ignore. Both younger and older participants read the passage more slowly and correctly answered fewer comprehension questions, but the older group were disproportionately disadvantaged. Again, Dywan and Murphy (1996) found that when sections of italicised to-be-ignored text were interleaved with to-be-read text, older adults were more likely to make false starts and read out bits of the italicised text (before correcting themselves), and were also more likely to miscomprehend the to-be-read text by erroneously incorporating information from the italicised text. However, when later tested, younger participants were better able to recognise words from the italicised text, in spite of apparently being better at ignoring it. This implies that the younger adults were better at shutting out *responses* to the text rather than not reading it. It also implies that there is a difference in the degree to which readers of different ages are able to control the early stages in the reading process. This is supported by the findings of Stine-Morrow, Loveless and Soederberg (1996) that in reading text for subsequent recall, younger readers place relatively greater emphasis on the immediate features of the text, whilst older readers put greater store in contextual information.

Generally, complexity increases the age difference. For example, Byrd (1985) found older people were impaired on straightforward recall of a passage of text, but were disproportionately disadvantaged when asked to *summarise* it. In other words, when the passage had to be simultaneously remembered and processed, older people were at a severe disadvantage. Again, Hamm and Hasher (1992) found that older people had greater difficulty in drawing inferences from ambiguous stories in which the text began by implying one thing before finally resolving itself in a different direction from the one initially anticipated. They attributed the age-related decline to a lessening ability to process information in working memory (i.e. to keep the initial story 'in mind' whilst resolving the contradiction introduced at the end of the story). Light and Albertson (1988) found that ability to draw inferences from sentences was only marred when the sentences were complex and/or concurrent processing of another task was required. Cohen and Faulkner (1984) demonstrated that older participants were especially disadvantaged at a recognition task when they had to integrate separate facts gleaned from the story to answer correctly. Smith *et al.* (1989) tested memory for prose of three types: 'standard' (self explanatory), 'scrambled' (sentences with no coherent links) and 'interleaved' (two or more stories alternating with each other sentence by sentence). The older and younger participants performed qualitatively the same for the standard and the scrambled texts. However, for the interleaved condition, the younger participants treated it qualitatively as they had done for the standard prose, and the older participants treated it qualitatively as they had done for the scrambled prose. In other words, the younger participants had sufficient processing capacity to untangle the interleaved prose and treat it as a standard text, whilst the older participants could not do this.

It is tempting to ascribe the above changes to a decline in the memory skills of older people. However, it should be noted that some researchers have found a poor correlation between text recall and other memory measures, such as digit span (Light and Anderson, 1985). Other, more linguistic factors may also contribute. For example, Kemper and Rush (1988), reviewing their own and others' studies, found that the quantity of information recalled varied directly with the syntactic complexity of the to-be-remembered passage. Given the evidence on syntactic changes presented in the previous section, this is not a surprising finding. More remarkable perhaps is the contrast between the recall of details versus main points of the text. Another reported finding is that older participants remember as many main points of a story as younger adults, but that they are significantly worse at remembering details (Cohen, 1989). For example, in remembering a story, an older person might remember that it involved a girl entering a shop and buying a dress, but he or she might not recall the colour of the purchase. A failure of memory for details is not surprising if one argues that they require more processing to be remembered, and thus are less likely to be memorised than the main points, which are modest in their processing requirements (Cohen, 1988; Holland and Rabbitt, 1990). However, as the next section will demonstrate, this phenomenon is not universally true.

Interaction between participant type and reading materials

It might be supposed that if the prior experience of participants was relevant to the reading matter, then this might have an effect, but Morrow, Von Leirer and Altieri (1992) did not find this to be the case. They tested groups of older and younger participants (who were a mixture of airline pilots and non-pilots), on stories, some of which had a flying theme and some did not. There was a significant age difference in ability to recall items (specifically, participants were asked which character was being referred to as 'he' or 'she' in a sentence they had just read). However, level of flying experience had no effect on the age differences.

In an excellent review of the literature, Meyer (1987), drawing principally on work by Dixon *et al.* (1984), observes that age differences in recall of main points and details is not as clear cut as some commentators have supposed. Instead, the main points–details balance seems to depend upon the (verbal) intelligence of the participants and the type of text being used. Normally, well-structured prose with a clear, logical text is used. When younger and older adults with high verbal abilities are tested on this sort of prose, then typically age differences are small or non-existent on main points but larger for details. However, for those with lower verbal ability, the reverse is true – in other words, the age difference is in main points of the text rather than the details. This whole pattern is turned on its head when unstructured text is used (i.e. where there is no clear narrative thread to the story). In this instance, high verbal ability participants show an age difference on main points, and lower ability participants show an age difference on details. This is summarised in Table 4.1.

Table 4.1 Relative differences in recall of main points and details

		Prose type	
		Well structured	*Ill structured*
Level of participants' ability	Higher verbal	Difference bigger for details	Difference bigger for main points
	Lower verbal	Difference bigger for main points	Difference bigger for details

Source: Adapted from Meyer, 1987.

Two major explanations have been proposed to account for age declines in story recall. The first, introduced above, it that it is simply due to a decline in processing capacity. This can comfortably explain why in some instances main points are better remembered, because they are less demanding of mental resources. However, without modification, the theory cannot explain the qualitative differences in performance across types of text. The second explanation is that differences between higher and lower verbal ability participants are due to different reading strategies. Thus, the lower ability participants have chosen a strategy which is diametrically opposed to that of the higher ability participants. However, this theory in its 'strong' form is difficult to defend, because it implies that lower ability participants go out of their way to choose the wrong strategy (Cohen, 1988). By combining elements of the capacity and strategy theories, however, it is possible to gain an insight into why age changes affect story recall in such an intriguing fashion.

The higher verbal ability participants will be considered first. Meyer (1987) plausibly argues that they are more likely than lower ability participants to be responsive to an author's intentions. If someone writes a passage of prose with a relatively obscure plot, then it is probably the case that the author expects readers to pay more attention to details. An extreme example of this is a telephone directory, but more commonly, authors of many textbooks employ this strategy when wishing to impress the reader with the range of the topic being covered. Murder 'whodunits' provide another example where, to resolve the issue, the details must be attended to and the plot, such as it is, is merely a device for accruing clues. Conversely, where there is a strong narrative thread to the story, the author clearly intends the reader to attend to this, with details intended to add a little local colour, and little else. It therefore follows that in well-structured prose, higher verbal ability participants attend primarily to the main points, and details are only processed for storage if there is any spare processing capacity left over after the main points have been gathered (please note that this is an analogy – the reader does not necessarily have conscious awareness of the process). Given that the processing capacity of older people is generally less than that of younger people, it follows that older participants will have less capacity for picking up details. The finding by Stine and Wingfield (1988) that older and younger adults tend to have a similar pattern of recall of text when there is a low 'density' of information, and that the age difference widens the denser the information becomes, supports this argument. Conversely, in ill-structured prose, the details hog the attention, and it is main points which are processed only if there is spare processing capacity.

Hence, for higher ability participants, the points–details balance shifts according to what the participants think the author is stressing as more important. For lower ability participants, a different explanation is required, which hinges on the likelihood that they have relatively inefficient reading strategies. There is some evidence from child and adolescent readers that lower verbal abilities are associated with poor or ill-coordinated general reading strategies (e.g. Fredericksen, 1978; Stuart-Hamilton, 1986), and Hartley (1988) has provided some tentative evidence that this also applies to older people. Note that it is not being argued that poorer readers have chosen a strategy which is the reverse of better readers' – only that they are *less efficient.* Lower ability participants, just like the higher ability participants, know to some degree that they must concentrate on the main points in a well-structured text, and on details in an ill-structured one. However, they are less efficient at searching out and encoding information, and thus do not take in their fill. This would appear to be a fairly profound deficit. As part of a larger study, Taub (1984) gave older participants a comprehension test in which the prose they had read was in front of them, with key passages and phrases underlined. The higher ability participants made use of this, but the lower ability participants did not.

Because structured text places greater emphasis on main points, participants tend to notice more of them. The difference in the processing capacities of younger and older adults means that the former encode more of them than the latter. For ill-structured text, the reverse applies. An objection to this argument is that, in terms of numbers, there may be an equal number of details and main points in well- and ill-structured texts. However, this ignores **pragmatics** (the understanding of intent as opposed to explicit meaning). Thus, simply counting the numbers of details and main points ignores their relative subjective importance.

The above arguments are perhaps made clearer by an analogy. Suppose that the lower and higher verbal participants are like riflemen on a shooting range. Targets appear, and the riflemen have a limited time in which to shoot as many targets as possible. In the same manner, readers have only a limited time in which to take in as much information as possible. Suppose that some targets are worth twice the points of others (in the same manner that main points and details can be more important than each other in different types of text). Higher ability readers are like good marksmen, who pick off the high value targets first, and then in the remaining time shoot at as many of the lesser value targets as possible. The older skilled marksmen may be slower at shooting, and thus although in the time available they hit as many of the prime targets as younger shooters, they have less time for the remaining lesser targets. The higher ability readers behave in a similar manner – each gets roughly the same number of 'important' pieces of information, the difference only appearing in secondary factors. The lower ability readers are like poor shooters – they will aim at anything, and hit much less often than the good marksmen. However, the law of averages means that the more prominent targets will be hit more often by chance then the less prominent ones. In a similar manner, different types of text will cause some features to be more salient than others. The younger shots will hit more targets than will the older people, not because they are better at aiming, but simply because they can fire more shots in the time available.

More recently newer types of analysis have begun, if not to question the above arguments, then to view the process of text recall/comprehension in a different light. For example, the authors of a recent study argued that their results 'showed that during memory retrieval, younger adults showed superior memory for surface form and textbase knowledge (what the text was), whereas older adults had equivalent or superior memory for situation model information (what the text was about)' (Radvansky *et al.*, 2001, p.145). However, the authors concluded that higher-level abilities remained relatively unaffected by ageing. There is thus a point of similarity with the above studies.

Ecological validity

The above findings have to be weighed against the argument that the experiments reported above lack ecological validity (in other words, they are not very realistic). The standard story recall test – of reading a passage of 300–400 words then attempting to regurgitate it whole – is hardly an everyday activity. Rice (1986b) observes that the only activity where anything approaching this skill is required is studying for exams, an activity which few older people indulge in. The experience is probably more central to the younger participants, thus creating an experimental bias. However, even in hardened exam takers, attempts at verbatim recall do not consist of attempting to learn 300–400 words in one reading. A far saner strategy would be to learn such a length of prose sentence by sentence (and evidence for age differences in this activity is more equivocal). In short, the text recall paradigm is unrealistic, and much of the age difference may be a cohort effect. Another consideration is the length of the prose passage used. Experimenters have usually chosen items of about the same length as magazine or newspaper articles – the commonest items read by older people (Rice, 1986b). However, they do not accord with other reading experiences. Meyer (1987) observes that a 'very long text' used in only a minority of studies is about 1600 words. Given that a moderately sized novel is circa 60,000 words, even the longest texts currently being used in standard experiments fall well short of a realistically long piece of prose. The reason for this observation is that, as librarians know to their cost, older adults are often appallingly bad not only at remembering the plots of books, but also *which* books they have read before. Clive James, the writer and television presenter, once worked as a librarian and describes the phenomenon thus:

> I ran out of answers for the little old ladies who wanted to know if they had already read the books they were thinking about taking out. The smart ones used personalised coding systems... There were hundreds of them at it all the time. If you picked up a book by Dorothy L. Sayers or Margery Allingham and flicked through it, you would see a kaleidoscope of dots, crosses, blobs, circles, swastikas, etc. (James, 1983, Ch. 8, p.243)

The phenomenon seems to be widespread. The author has spoken to a number of librarians who practically gave a paraphrase of Mr James's observations. However, this shining failure of recall for lengthy passages of prose seems to have escaped researchers' attention.

Summary

The study of language changes in older people is currently fragmented. Some areas have been covered in depth, whilst others have barely been touched upon (e.g. there is a woeful lack of studies of writing skills). Because of this, interpretations must be guarded.

It should first be noted that declines in sight and hearing will affect linguistic skills. More generally, a decline in physical health may generally lessen access to the 'outside world', and with it conversational opportunities, library visits, and so forth. Within the home, reading habits change, with a general shift towards 'lightweight' reading materials. Whether this is due to declining intellectual skills or changing motivation is a moot point, but nonetheless for many older people there is an appreciable alteration in the practice of reading and other linguistic skills. This may in part account for the more general changes in language. However, the usual suspects of general slowing and intelligence must also be cited (though, surprisingly, crystallised intelligence may not play a particularly major role).

Other researchers have argued for other models to explain the phenomena. For example, as noted earlier, Burke *et al.* (2000) argue that it is production of language that is primarily affected by ageing – in relative terms, the ability to receive language is unscathed. This creates problems for models of general cognitive change such as slowing, since the decline might be expected to be more widespread. Burke *et al.* argue in favour of the **transmission deficit hypothesis**. This is a model of language production and reception that argues that the process is underpinned by priming of possible alternatives. The speed and efficiency with which these primes are produced will greatly facilitate the speed and accuracy of recognition/production. Ageing is assumed to lower the speed and efficiency with which the priming takes place (more so for production than recognition). For this author at least, there is an unresolved issue concerning the relative difficulty of reception and production tasks and the degree to which other skills may offer compensation. However, the authors present an ingenious justification of the model, and, although there arguably needs more empirical examination of some of the details, it provides a plausible direction for further research.

Concentrating on specific skills such as word recognition, syntactic processing and story recall, it can be seen that there are age-related declines. One study (Hale and Myerson, 1995) estimates that, overall, older readers may be as much as 50 per cent slower than younger adults. However, the magnitude of the age difference is probably inflated by experimental artefacts such as the types of test materials used, cohort effects, and so forth. Perhaps the biggest criticism is that many reading tests are unrealistic – people do not normally spend their time learning very short stories verbatim, pronouncing obscure words or deciding if a string of letters on a computer screen forms a word or not. Thus, a loud note of caution needs to be sounded over these results, since the measures used probably do not directly match real-life experiences.

Suggested further reading

Light and Burke's (1988) edited collection of papers on ageing linguistic skills is probably the most comprehensive review currently available. However, there is a great deal of repetition between chapters, and many authors assume a detailed prior knowledge of technical terms. Kemper (1988, 1992) provides an excellent overview of her own work. For those interested in the general mechanics of reading, Ellis (1993) is recommended. Although outside the remit of this book, there is a useful sociolinguistic study of older people's language by Coupland, Coupland and Giles (1991) which some readers may find of interest. The chapter by Burke et al. (2000) is also recommended.

CHAPTER 5

Ageing, Personality and Lifestyle

Introduction

This chapter considers how older people present themselves to others and interact with them. We will examine age-related changes in personality and also the related issues of the lifestyles of older people, change of status, attitudes people hold about ageing and older people, and how these factors affect physical and psychological status. The central question will be: what benefits and disadvantages do these confer on older people? Although united by a common thread, these topics are disparate in many ways, with different research traditions, predicated on different assumptions, and generally with radically different agendas and goals. Nonetheless, as shall be seen, some common themes emerge.

Personality

Personality can be defined in many ways, but a useful general definition is: 'the individual characteristics and ways of behaving that, in their organization or patterning, account for an individual's unique adjustments, to his or her total environment' (Hilgard, Atkinson and Atkinson, 1979, p.541). Elsewhere in this book, the efficiency of the psychological skills under discussion can usually be gauged by a simple scale: for example, how many questions are correctly answered, how syntactically complex an utterance is, or how many list items are correctly recalled. Personality assessment is less clear cut, since how can one judge what is a 'good' or a 'bad' personality? Obviously, people who behave like Mother Teresa or, conversely, Adolf Hitler, are easily categorised, but most people fall into a 'grey area' in between, and exhibit a mixture of attractive and quite unappealing behaviours. To complicate matters further, what is appealing to some is appalling to others. For example, someone who is the life and soul of the party to one group of people may be seen by another group as a loud-mouthed airhead. Accordingly, a single objective measure of personality 'goodness' is impossible to construct. The best one can hope for is to look for qualitative differences between the personalities of individuals, and, where possible, to measure these against 'real-life' behaviours.

Because personality measurement is relatively resistant to objective measures, much work in this field is descriptive and cannot be easily abbreviated. The solution to this problem is either to devote an entire textbook to the subject or to present a general overview in the form of a thumbnail sketch. For obvious reasons, the latter solution is adopted here. However, the reader should be aware that behind many of the apparently simplistic arguments presented lie often sophisticated theories and descriptions (for more detailed discussions, Coleman and O'Hanlon, 2004; Pratt and Norris, 1994 and Turner and Helms, 1994 are particularly recommended). A further reason for erring on the side of brevity is that much of ageing personality and lifestyle research draws heavily on work in other areas (particularly sociology) and thus falls outside the ambit of this book.

Trait models

Perhaps the area of personality research with the strongest links to mainstream psychology is the study of the **personality trait**. This may be defined as an enduring characteristic of a person's personality which is hypothesised to underpin his or her behaviour. The concept sounds complicated, but in fact it is often used in everyday life. For example, if one is told that a person is 'very nervous' then one can predict how he or she will behave when watching a horror film (in other words, one assumes that the trait of 'nervousness' will cause that person to display a characteristic behaviour pattern). A number of trait models, which seek to explain behaviour by means of a few disposing factors, have been developed by psychologists. Perhaps the best known is Eysenck's measure of **extraversion–introversion, neuroticism** and **psychoticism**. Eysenck argued that people's personalities are principally determined by the degree to which they display these three traits. The extraversion–introversion (E) trait measures the degree to which a person is outgoing and assertive. Someone who tends towards these characteristics is said to be an extravert, and the stronger they possess the attributes, the more extraverted they are said to be. Conversely, someone who is shy and retiring is an introvert, and again, the more shy and retiring they are, the more introverted they are. Eysenck argued that the extraversion–introversion measure is a continuum: people are never purely extraverted or purely introverted. Instead, they possess features of both attributes, although overall they tend to be one kind or the other. For example, a person who is extravert and can go to a karaoake bar without the slightest worry (even when sober) may nonetheless be racked with embarrassment using a public changing room. The psychoticism (P) trait is a measure of the degree to which a person is emotionally 'cold' and antisocial, and the neuroticism (N) trait gauges the extent to which a person is anxious and emotionally unstable. High scores on the P and N scales do not necessarily mean that a person is mentally disturbed, but rather that under stress, they are likely to display psychotic or neurotic characteristics. Eysenck measured the E, P and N traits using the **Eysenck Personality Questionnaire (EPQ)**. Participants are asked to give 'yes' or 'no' answers to a series of statements designed to elicit how strongly individuals identify with each particular trait. For example, one of the questions designed to assess the strength of extravert tendencies is 'Are you a talkative person?' (Eaves, Eysenck and Martin, 1989; Appendix B).

According to Eysenck, E, P and N alter as people get older, and gender also has an important influence. P declines with age, but the rate of decline is much greater for men than women. At 16 years, male P scores are almost double those of females, but by the age of 70, this difference is practically non-existent. More curious is the change in E. Both men and women become more introverted as they get older. Males in their late teens are more extraverted than females, but thereafter, their extraversion declines at a much greater rate, so that by their sixties, males are more *introverted* than females (the crossover point, where the two sexes are equally introverted, occurs in the forties). The changes in N are less spectacular. There is a decline in neuroticism for both sexes, but at all ages female scores remain higher than male scores (Eysenck, 1987; Eysenck and Eysenck, 1985). Eysenck (1987) argues these findings predict that older people should be less prone to violent swings of mood and hence calmer. Note that Eysenck was not arguing that older people should necessarily be happier in later life. If anything, people should become more indifferent about the world, with only relatively small swings in mood in either direction. At an ideal best, such indifference might be cultivated into calmness and serenity, but, equally, an undesirable apathy or sloth might be produced. Eysenck argued that personality changes across the lifespan are primarily the result of physiological changes altering levels of excitation with the nervous system. This argument is disputed by many other psychologists and a plausible case can be made for changes in lifestyle being the prime causes of shifts in E, P and N. For example, older people may become more introverted, not because of changing levels of neural excitation, but because, as they age, society becomes less geared to their needs. This causes older people to withdraw in upon themselves, and this in turn engenders feelings of reserve and hence increased introversion. Because men more than women define themselves by their role in society (see below), men will show a disproportionately bigger loss of assertiveness as they age, reflected in their declining E score.

Other researchers have tended to disagree with Eysenck's findings. For example, in a longitudinal study of Dutch people, Steunenberg *et al.* (2005) found a mild decrease in N between the mid fifties and seventy and then a slight rise. Butcher *et al.* (1991) found no appreciable changes in the pattern of personality using another common measure of personality (the **Minnesota Multiphasic Personality Inventory** or **MMPI**), and generally, longitudinal studies of self-reported personality measures have found little alteration, even though participants often feel they have changed dramatically (Perlmutter and Hall, 1992). Kogan (1990) reviewed a number of longitudinal studies of changes in personality traits across the lifespan. His general finding was that in many instances there were significant shifts in personality which were commensurate with changing lifestyles (e.g. the transition from college to paid employment). However, he also found that generally there was less change in the latter half of adult life.[1]

Another popular trait model of personality is the **Big Five** model (a.k.a. five factor personality model) by Costa and McCrae (see Costa and McCrae, 1980, 1982). This is predicated, as its name implies, on the assumption that personality is best described using five basic personality traits – conscientiousness (how reliable a person is), agreeableness (how compliant with others' wishes), openness (how willing to cope with the unfamiliar), extraversion and neuroticism (see Stuart-Hamilton, 1999a for further discussion). Research has demonstrated that scores on the Big Five traits (sometimes called OCEAN after the initial letters) remain remarkably stable throughout life (see Costa and McCrae, 1980, 1982 and Small *et al.*, 2003). This initially seems counter-intuitive, since nearly everyone can think of acquaintances whose personality and lifestyle have changed dramatically. However, there are three principal rejoinders to this. The first is that isolated examples do not deny a general rule (one swallow does not a summer make, etc.). The second is that the model allows for drastic change in vulnerable individuals following very serious life events such as divorce (Costa *et al.*, 2000). The third is that the same traits under different circumstances may express themselves in different ways. As Hoyer and Roodin (2003, p.396) neatly summarise it, 'Individuals who rated high in neuroticism found new things to complain, worry, and become dissatisfied about'. Likewise, people with a high level of openness may markedly change their manner of behaviour throughout their lifespan as they seek out new experiences and ways of living.

However, not all research points to the relative stability of personality across the lifespan. Field and Millsap (1991) found that extraversion declined slightly in a longitudinal study of older adults. Again, Mroczek and Spiro (2003) conducted a longitudinal study on a group of 1600 men (initially aged 43–91) over a 12-year period. They found considerable variability in E and N scores over this time. They also found that significant life events (e.g. death of spouse) were related to these changes. Again, there is

1   Note also that as for IQ, individuals maintain the same general position relative to their age
    peers – it is the raw scores on measures which change.

evidence that personality traits have shifted towards being more flexible and accommodating across birth cohorts in the twentieth century (see Schaie and Willis, 1991a and also Mroczek and Spiro, 2003). This may explain the stereotype that older adults become more conservative and hidebound. It is not ageing that makes someone hidebound – rather, ageing presumably throws into relief personality characteristics of the birth cohort that have always been there. As younger cohorts with more liberal personalities grow older, presumably this myth will disappear.

Notwithstanding these caveats (which in any case generally report relatively small changes) it seems that the majority view is that personality traits are largely invariant for the majority of people across the adult lifespan (see Hoyer and Roodin, 2003).

It was stated that one personality type is not necessarily more morally worthy than another, and that is arguably true. However, there is evidence that some personality types may be more advantageous in particular situations. For example, Jerram and Coleman (1999) analysed the health behaviour of older adults using the Big Five personality model. They found that people possessing a higher level of openness, agreeableness, extraversion and conscientiousness and lower levels of neuroticism had fewer health problems and generally led healthier lifestyles. Other studies have tended to support this finding. Wilson *et al.* (2004b) also conducted a study of the relationship between the Big Five and mortality in a longitudinal study of circa five years (the precise time differed between individual participants). The researchers found a strong correlation between neuroticism and mortality, with those with the top 10 per cent of N scores having double the risk of dying compared with the scorers with the lowest 10 per cent of N scores. A high conscientiousness score was associated with a lowered risk of death. Again, Lauver and Johnson (1997) demonstrated that higher levels of neuroticism may be disadvantageous in coping with chronic pain in later life, whilst Spiro *et al.* (1995), reporting on a longitudinal study, found it to be correlated with high blood pressure. Generally, researchers have homed in on neuroticism as it has so consistently been found to be adversely related to general health status in older people (Kempen, Jelicic and Ormel, 1997). Again, a higher level of extraversion appears to be advantageous in recovering from a stroke (Elmstahl, Sommer and Hagberg, 1996) and more generally in maintaining a high level of morale (Adkins, Martin and Poon, 1996) and feeling of well-being (Francis and Bolger, 1997). However, it should be noted that there is some danger of a chicken and egg problem with the above research. The issue will be returned to later in this chapter, but it must be remembered that, whilst a person may have better health or quality of life because of their personality, equally, their personality could have shifted in response to their changing health and quality of life. A recent study by Caplan and Schooler (2003) found that a higher level of fatalism predicted the later development of illness and disability, suggesting that personality can predispose to illness, but more research needs to be conducted before a firm answer can be given to this question.

Psychoanalytic theory and the ageing personality

Some of the earliest attempts to codify the ageing personality came from psychoanalysis. It is difficult to give a concise definition of this term. In its usual sense, it means any treatment regime which is based upon an integrated theory of the subconscious and its effects on behaviour. However, the term sometimes applies (particularly with later practitioners) to broader-based models that, whilst having roots in psychoanalysis, also integrate findings from the behavioural sciences. Often psychoanalytic theories are named after their author (e.g. 'Freudian' after Sigmund Freud, 'Jungian' after Carl Jung). Strictly speaking, psychoanalysis is not part of mainstream psychology (see Stuart-Hamilton, 1999a), and many psychologists have questioned its efficacy (e.g. Eysenck, 1952). However, from a historical viewpoint at least, a brief examination is necessary. The founding father of psychoanalysis, Sigmund Freud, was sceptical about the value of therapy being administered to older patients, because they had relatively little remaining life in which to enjoy the benefits of treatment (generally, the treatment of older people has been a minority subject within the psychoanalytic literature, though this position is changing – see Gorusch, 1998; Settlage, 1996). The crux of Freud's theory is that personality is made up of a mixture of three components – the **id**, **ego** and **superego**. The id describes basic appetitive urges, the ego people's rational selves, and the superego a set of moral dictums (often unrealistically harsh). For reasons too complex to describe here, Freudian theorists felt that the id's efficiency and strength were drawn from the state of a person's smooth (i.e. involuntary) muscle, whilst the ego's strength is dependent on the state of the central nervous system (CNS). Because the CNS declines more rapidly in later life than does smooth muscle, the ego becomes relatively weaker than the id. A tenet of Freudian theory is that the ego strives to keep the id in check. To prevent the id getting the upper hand, the ego starts to conserve its energy by rationalising resources. In psychoanalytic terms, this means adopting a relatively unvarying and conservative set of attitudes and responses, even though they may not be entirely appropriate to the situations older people find themselves in. This perceived inflexibility of older people is specious, however. For example, Pratt *et al.* (1991) found no age differences on measures of moral reasoning, and as shall be seen here, the ageing personality varies greatly across individuals (in other words, there is no single typical 'older personality'). It is worth noting that, although he did little formal work on ageing, in his private life and correspondence Freud appears to have had a very melancholy and illogical attitude towards ageing (Woodward, 1991).

Erikson (1963, 1982; see also Wolf, E.S. 1997) felt that personality developed throughout the lifespan – unlike other psychoanalysts, who felt that it was essentially determined by childhood habits. He argued that at different ages different conflicts had to be resolved. For example, in infancy, individuals must resolve the conflicting impulses to trust or to mistrust by developing a sense of trust. There are eight of these conflicts to resolve, of which only the final one occurs in later life. The goal of this stage is **ego integration** – the acceptance that earlier goals have been satisfied or resolved, and there are no 'loose ends'. A person who feels that not everything has been achieved can feel a sense of despair because, with death approaching, it is too late to make amends. Thus, the despairing individual also comes to fear death, and he or she ends life feeling anxious and depressed. Hannah *et al.* (1996) present evidence that ego integration is usually only attained by people who have successfully resolved the earlier Eriksonian stages of conflict. In other words, personality in later life is as much a product of early behaviour as the current situation. A criticism of Erikson's theory might be that, taken simplistically, it portrays ageing as a passive preparation for death. However, this is not what Erikson intended. He viewed the final stage of development as a learning process, and in 'such final consolidation, death loses its sting' (Erikson, 1963; p.268).

Peck (1968) expanded on Erikson's theory, and argued that, in later life, three conflicts need to be resolved. The first of these is **ego differentiation versus work-role preoccupation**. Many working people (particularly men) establish their status and self concept through their work. Thus, a professional person may develop a high self-esteem simply because they have an occupation which society regards favourably. However, when a person retires, this status disappears with the job. Thus, retirees must find something in themselves which makes them unique or worthy of an esteem previously conferred on them by a job title. The second conflict is **body transcendence versus body preoccupation**. For most individuals, ageing brings a decline in health and general physical status. If an older person overemphasises bodily well-being in extracting enjoyment from life, then disappointment will almost inevitably result. Successful ageing involves an ability to overcome physical discomfort, or at least finding enjoyable activities where bodily status is unimportant. The third of Peck's conflicts is **ego transcendence versus ego preoccupation**. This essentially means that a person comes to terms with the fact that he or she will inevitably die. This is obviously an unpleasant thought, but Peck argues that, by attempting to provide for those left after a person has died, and continually striving to improve the surroundings and well-being of loved ones, an overweening concern for the self and the self's fate can be overcome.

Levinson's view of ageing is akin to Erikson's and Peck's but concentrates rather more on the role of the older person in family and society (e.g. Levinson, 1980). Changing physical and occupational status means that in the early to mid-sixties (the **late adult transition**), people must come to terms with the fact that they are no longer the prime movers in either work or in family life (this may be affected by lowering of typical retirement age – see Settersen, 1998). To remain content, older people must therefore learn to shed leadership and take a 'back seat' (other researchers have reported similar conflicts – e.g. Settersen and Haegestad, 1996). This does not mean that all cares and duties can be avoided, since, aside from assuming the role of wise counsellor to family and younger friends, older people must come to terms with their past (in a manner similar to that described by Erikson). Levinson refers to this process as the '**view from the bridge**'.

Do these theoretical personality types really exist outside the confines of a psychotherapist's office? Levinson's work just cited was founded on in-depth interviews with participants, but it should be noted that much of the key research was based on a relatively small sample of men only, most of whom were engaged in fairly 'elite' occupations. Other research has tended to support psychoanalytic descriptions, at least in broad terms. For example, Reichard *et al.* (1962) interviewed 87 American men aged 55–84, half of them in retirement and half in full- or part-time employment (note that for some jobs in the USA there is no compulsory retirement age). Many points raised by Reichard *et al.* support the psychoanalytic theories. For example, participants approaching retirement seemed to be particularly 'on edge' and self-deprecatory, indicating that the period in question was perceived as being one of change and of anxiety. Overall, five main personality types were identified. **Constructiveness** is akin to the optimal resolution envisaged by Erikson's and Peck's theories – people possessing this trait had come to terms with their lives, and were relatively free from worries, while striving to interact with others. The **dependent** or '**rocking chair**' type created some contentment, but individuals were dissatisfied with products of their own efforts, and relied on others to help or serve them, regarding later life as a time of leisure. The **defensiveness** or '**armoured approach**' type is essentially neurotic. Participants possessing it carried on working or were engaged in a high level of activity as if to 'prove' that they were healthy and did not need other people's help. The fourth type – **hostility** – involves blaming others for personal misfortune. Participants unrealistically attributed failures throughout their lives to factors other than themselves. In part this sprang from a failure to plan adequately. The final type identified by Reichard *et al.* was **self-hatred**. The self-hating individuals were akin to the hostile type possessors, except that they turned their hatred and resentment inwards. Reichard *et al.* found that people possessing the first three types were well adjusted towards later life, whilst those possessing one of the latter two were less successful. However, given that the researchers' personality descriptions contain implicit value judgements of quality of lifestyle, this is not surprising.

Other personality type studies

Reichard *et al.* also observed that people's personalities had developed long before the onset of later life. In other words, the types are not the result of 'being old' *per se*. It follows from this that, in order to enjoy later life, one must prepare for it. This argument is somewhat supported by the findings of a longitudinal study reported by Haan (1972).

Participants were studied from their teens to the onset of middle age. Various personality types were identified, but these can be principally divided into the stable and secure, those akin to Reichard *et al.*'s defensive personalities, and the insecure who blamed others for their misfortunes and who often had disorganised lifestyles. These types are remarkably similar to those found in studies of older people, and it is reasonable to conclude that those found in later life are probably those which have been there since early adulthood (Kermis, 1986). However, this may not be entirely true. In a review of the literature, Aiken (1989) notes that while some of the more stable personality types may not alter greatly over the lifespan, the less stable types may be more labile in response to age changes. Again, it can be shown that older people become more inward looking (Neugarten, 1977). This is not necessarily surprising. Unstable personalities might be expected to change, and stable people may always have been stable because circumstances have always been consistent and relatively rewarding. Older people may become inward looking, not because of an intrinsic compulsion, but because the death of friends and a world which caters primarily for younger people leaves few attractions for previously outward-going older people.

It is interesting to note that some personality types may be better adapted to early rather than late adulthood and vice versa. **Type A personalities** are very hard-edged, competitive types who find it difficult to relax – in Eighties parlance, they are ideal 'yuppie' material. **Type B personalities** are the opposite – easy-going, carefree, and so forth. It might be expected that Type As will be best suited to early adulthood when there are perhaps the greatest chances to exhibit competitiveness in career chasing, sport, and so forth. Later life should not suit Type As because of its emphasis on a sedentary lifestyle. For Type Bs, the reverse should hold true. Strube *et al.* (1985) measured the psychological well-being of a group of people aged 18–89, and found that in general Type A and B personalities fulfilled this prediction, although the results were mediated by factors such as the social environments of individuals. Again, Shimonaka, Nakazato and Homma (1996) found Type B personalities to be more prevalent amongst centenarians.

Returning to studies of the measurement of personality types within older people, Neugarten, Havinghurst and Toibin (1961, 1968) studied a sample of people in their seventies. Four principal personality types (with subdivisions) were identified, which bore great similarity to the traits uncovered by other studies already mentioned. The most desirable type was the **integrated personality**. People in this category were **reorganisers** (as one activity became physically impossible, another was found), were **focused** (activities were limited to a small set of feasible and highly rewarding ones) or they were **disengaged** (the deliberate abnegation of many responsibilities). Another major type was the **armoured-defensive** personality. People in this category were either **holding on** types, who felt that they could stave off decay by maintaining a high level of activity, or they were **constricted**, and dwelt on what they had lost as a result of ageing.

The armoured-defensive individuals were less satisfied than those with integrated per-sonalities. A third group possessed **passive-dependent** personalities. Like Reichard *et al.*'s dependent/'rocking chair' types, such people relied on others to help them (the **succourant-seeking**), or they withdrew from interaction with others as much as possible (the **apathetic**). The fourth and final group comprised the **disorganised** personalities. These unfortunate people had serious problems (possibly early dementia?) and could not be classified as functioning conventionally.

As has been noted, there is much similarity between the various type studies. All emphasise that personality is largely fixed long before the first grey hairs appear, and that, essentially, older people can adjust their personalities but not alter them radically. There is more than one way to age successfully, but all essentially involve accepting limitations and renouncing responsibilities without suffering a feeling of loss. A slightly less successful strategy is to maintain a fear of the ravages of ageing, and to fight them by keeping as active as possible. However, as this involves a failure to come to terms with ageing, it is ultimately less satisfying. The worst option is to have no strategy at all and to blame all the wrong factors for one's present state. Many commentators have arrived at the same general conclusions (e.g. Aiken, 1989; Kermis, 1983; 1986; Turner and Helms, 1987; Whitbourne, 1987). However, the argument presented is a generalisation and a potentially misleading one. Successful ageing involves accepting limitations and abnegating responsibility, but this may be because of societal pressure to hand over the reins of power. Accepting this change willingly may be akin to surrendering gracefully to a stronger opponent on the principle that if one is going to lose, one may as well do so with the minimum of hurt. In other words, the 'successfully' aged older person has not gained a philosophical insight as much as grasped a point of pragmatics. Another important consideration is socio-economic class. The 'unsuccessful' aged person may rant and rail about external forces precisely because his or her social position has yielded them fewer privileges and 'lucky breaks' (often researchers note that such individuals are downwardly socially mobile). In contrast, someone who has known the good things in life will be more likely to have a relaxed view of life. Accordingly, the older personality may be as much a product of social and economic circumstances as of any internally motivating factors. This consideration does not refute the theories described, but one should be careful not to consider personality as a purely internally driven entity.

Another approach to the above argument is to question whether 'losing' independence is necessarily such as bad thing. Cordingly and Webb (1997) note that the whole issue is imbued with major questions of status in many societies (particularly western ones) where individualism and 'standing on one's own feet' is a key measure of societal approval. Older people are seen as being dependent and as such their status is diminished. Societal forces, though well meaning, tend to emphasise the role of dependent older people and play down the idea of older independence. For example,

Baltes and Wahl (1996) make the telling point that older people's requests or needs for help (which of course help define their role as dependent) tend to be met, whilst independent behaviour is ignored. Baltes (1996) examined the issue of dependency in detail and argued that it can be both good and bad, depending upon the type of dependency and the circumstances in which it is acquired. Bad dependency might result from bad motives. Thus, an institutional environment in which older residents are denied any autonomy is a clear example of this. However, bad dependency can also be produced from good intentions. For example, a social worker might provide an older person not just with the specific help they need, but then swamp them with lots of other forms of assistance (even though the older person has neither asked for them nor needs them), because they are seen as a generous aid package. Of course at one level they are, but this largesse is also forcing an older person to become dependent on a system to a much greater extent than they need. However, not all dependency is bad. Baltes notes that increased dependency can be good, if, for example, it liberates an older person from trivial cares or tasks which are too problematic. It should also be noted that bad dependency can be reversed or at least lessened through intervention. Thus, dependency is in itself neither good nor bad — it is how and why it is used which matters. Some researchers have found that increased dependency is predictive of subsequent illness (e.g. Willis *et al.*, 1997), but the degree to which this is 'good' or 'bad' dependency is often uncertain.

It will not have escaped the reader's attention that some researchers have argued for the relative stability of personality across the lifespan, whilst others have argued that it changes. There are several possible explanations for this. The first is that it is due to differences in measurement techniques (Kogan, 1990). This is plausible, but it hardly bodes well for research if a factor as important as personality can behave so capriciously when measured. However, it is worth noting that many longitudinal studies have only found personality changes when the participants are compared over several decades — relatively short periods do not yield large changes. Also, there may be a cohort effect — older participants may be less 'open' about their responses than younger people, not because of their personalities *per se*, but because they wish to be 'polite' (Stokes, 1992). A further factor is that different studies have measured different aspects of personality. This is a psychological facet which cannot be measured on a single scale as intelligence can be gauged by the IQ measure. Which of a wide range of measures are taken as representative of the personality and at what level (e.g. traits versus types) may lie behind many of the discrepancies between studies.

Attitudes towards ageing and older adults

It follows from the caveat given above that, to understand personality in later life, external forces impinging on older people's self-image and life satisfaction must also be considered. A general consideration is the effect of the stereotype of the 'typical' older person. As was noted in Chapter 1, society expects people to behave appropriately for their age. Kite, Deaux and Miele (1993) found that stereotypes of older people are stronger than those of gender differences, and that the archetypal 'masculine' attributes are felt to be particularly prone to decline in later life. Because the terms 'old' and 'elderly' are usually derogatory in western culture, it is small surprise to discover that in one study, only 20 per cent of people in their sixties and 51 per cent of people in their seventies labelled themselves as being 'old' (Ward, 1984). The author of this study also notes that, ironically, older people are often hoisted by their own petard, since when they were younger they formed the illogical stereotypes of ageing which now haunt them. Stereotyping seems to affect older people's confidence and generally, the more older people believe in stereotypes, the lower their self-esteem (Ward, 1977). However, given that many older people are likely to be inward looking, might it not be the case that they come to think that everyone of their age is like themselves, and thus, the lower their opinion of others, the lower their self-regard? Again, perhaps self-image and stereotypes are self-reinforcing, creating a vicious circle. The exact relationship remains unclear, but for whatever reason, the majority of studies find that self-image declines in later life in most people (Aiken, 1989).

This argument is reinforced by a study by Ryff (1991). She asked younger, middle-aged and older adults to rate their past, present and future selves and well-being. She found that the younger and middle-aged adults tended to see themselves on a path of self-improvement – they were better than their past selves, and in the future would get even better. The older participants, on the other hand, saw the best as being behind them and saw a decline in front of them. Graham and Baker (1989) examined two groups of (Canadian) participants: a group of older people (mean age 67 years) and a group of younger adult students. Participants were asked to grade imaginary people of different ages (e.g. '40-year-old man') for their level of status within society. The researchers found that, for both groups of participants, children were graded at a low level, status rose through the teens, twenties and thirties, and then began to decline once again, so that 80-year-olds were perceived to have roughly the same status as five-year-olds. A subsequent study by Garstka *et al.* (2004) indicates that this is even more damaging than first thought. Younger people who are denigrated in this way tend not to feel discriminated against because they feel it is a temporary state of affairs they will (literally) grow out of, whereas for older people, this is seen as a permanent state. Returning to Graham and Bakers' study, although older participants gave the same relative balance of judgements as the students, the difference between the highest and lowest ratings was significantly less. Thus, although different generations have the same general pattern in their view of ageing and status, the researchers argued that older people are apparently 'slightly more egalitarian than the young' (Graham and Baker, 1989; p.255). This finding was echoed in a study by Laditka *et al.* (2004), which found that older participants were more likely to rate older adults positively (though arguably this could be through self-interest).

Less egalitarianism was found in a later study by Igier and Mullet (2003). They asked participants of different ages to describe how well different age groups epitomised each personality trait of the Big Five model. The researchers found that the older adults were seen as more conscientious, less open, not markedly neurotic, and moderately introverted and agreeable. The ratings are not particularly anti-ageing, but of interest is that, across the whole study, the age of the person being graded accounted for circa two thirds of the total variance, whilst the age of the participant accounted for only circa one tenth. Studies on level of self-esteem across the lifespan tell a similar tale with regard to ageing. Robins *et al.* (2002) found that self-esteem was high in childhood, dipped during adolescence, then rose again, only to decline in old age. These findings applied across gender, socio-economic and national groups. Likewise, whilst younger adults felt that the future would bring an increase in their subjective well-being, older adults saw only further decline (Staudinger, Bluck and Herzberg, 2003). Overall the evidence implies that most people have a consensus of opinion about what constitutes 'typical' signs and status of ageing.

The above studies paint a bleak picture of ageing, both for older people's images of themselves and younger people's images of older people. However, it must not be assumed that such views are irrevocably fixed. For example, Guo, Erber and Szuchman (1999) demonstrated that exposing participants to positive reports about ageing can improve subsequent judgements of older people's skills. Likewise, Schwartz and Simmons (2001) reported that positive experiences of older adults (rather than simple frequency of meetings) was a significant determinant of younger adults' positive opinions of older people. In a similar vein, Stuart-Hamilton (2000) found that altering a set of five questions at the beginning of a questionnaire on attitudes from neutral to very slightly negative (the latter questions drew attention to the financial problems of some UK pensioners) was sufficient to create a significantly more negative set of judgements about older people in the latter group. Again, Polizzi and Millikin (2002) found that asking participants to rate the characteristics of people aged '70–85 years of age' resulted in significantly more favourable ratings than when asked to rate the characteristics of 'old' people.

The ease with which views can be manipulated implies that to some extent negative views of ageing may be a product of experimental design. Certainly in the studies which have found strongly negative views of ageing, participants have been asked to more or less make a direct comparison between an older and a younger person (Stuart-Hamilton, 2000). Under such circumstances, older people will be almost inevitably regarded in a negative light. It is not being ageist to say that on average older people have more physical and psychological problems than younger people, any more than it is sexist to say that on average women are shorter than men. However, such statements can easily predispose a person to ageist or sexist views. Thus, if participants are asked to compare younger versus older adults, the older adults will almost certainly come off the worse. This is indicated by Stuart-Hamilton (1998), who conducted a (UK) nationwide survey of women's attitudes to ageing. Women of all ages were questioned, and were simply asked what they thought of older people on their own terms (in other words, without comparisons being drawn with younger adults). The responses were much more positive about ageing than those in many other studies. Therefore, at least some of the negative views of ageing are probably a result of how the questions have been asked.

However, how deeply these attitudes are changed by such manipulations, and the degree to which they express true opinions is open to question. Harris and Dollinger (2001) found that students taking a course on the psychology of ageing improved their knowledge of ageing but their own anxieties about growing old had not significantly altered. Stuart-Hamilton and Mahoney (2003) conducted a study in which younger adult participants (employees of a local government district in the UK) were given a half-day training session intended to increase awareness of ageing and older adults. Prior to the session, participants were given two questionnaires – one measured attitudes to ageing (the **Fraboni Scale of Ageism** – Fraboni, Saltstone and Hughes, 1990) and the other knowledge of ageing. Two months after the training session, participants were given the same tests again. Not surprisingly, it was found that knowledge of ageing improved following training. However, attitudes to ageing and older adults remained unaffected, except for an increased awareness of not to use ageist language. This is a potentially worrying finding. Many studies of anti-ageism training use a measure of knowledge of ageing as a gauge of whether training has been successful (see Stuart-Hamilton and Mahoney, 2003). However, as can be seen, *knowledge* can change without significant changes in the underlying *attitudes* (in the same way that an army general can learn a great deal about the state of the opposing forces without changing his or her dislike for them). The degree to which attitudes can truly change is therefore still open to question, and it may therefore be assumed that anti-ageing stereotypes are still strong in many instances.

Indeed, ageing stereotypes appear even when views are not directly measured by questionnaire. For example, Hummert, Garstka, and Shaner (1997) found that participants attributed significantly fewer positive attributes to pictures of older people (there is also an interesting rebuttal of Graham and Baker's claims of egalitarianism cited above, since photos of very old people were rated significantly less positively by older participants). A later study by the same group (Hummert *et al.*, 2002) further reinforces this, finding that implicit associations about older adults and ageing are often less ageing-positive than overt statements. Use of implicit attitude measures should prove to be a fruitful area of research in the future. Again, participants giving instructions to people of different ages tended to 'talk down' to older people, and, although this was done less if it were emphasised that the older person was 'competent', nonetheless, speech was still different from when providing instructions to a younger adult (Thimm, Rademacher and Kruse, 1998).

Cross-cultural differences

In practically any discussion of attitudes to ageing in the popular media, a sharp contrast is drawn between attitudes in the East and West. A visual cliché of documentary makers is to contrast shots of an impoverished pensioner in a British planning blight apartment block with serene octogenarians doing communal Tai Chi exercises. Generally in the Far East, later life *is* revered to a greater extent than in the West. However, this is a generalised statement. First, it is generally active old age that is prized, where the older adult can still make a contribution (see Okamoto and Tanaka, 2004). A later life of infirmity and reliance is regarded less positively. Again, as globalisation continues its seemingly inexorable progress, there are signs of some change towards western values in eastern countries – in other words, a more negative view of older people in general (see Ingersoll-Dayton and Saengtienchai, 1999). Also, not all eastern cultures have the same strengths of attitude. For example, Levy (1999) reports that Japanese people tend to have less negative attitudes towards older people than do Chinese. Also, note that even at best the view of ageing is still often negative in absolute terms – it is merely the *strength* of the view's expression which differs between cultures.

Tangential to this, in general, non-industrialised and developing societies have a higher regard for later life, according it a special status. This may be because later life is relatively rare in such groups, and in peoples lacking a written language system older people may be especially valued for their memories of the past. However, as with many eastern countries, the very elderly and physically and mentally infirm are often regarded far less favourably (see Perlmutter and Hall, 1992). It is also important to recognise that, within developing countries, just as with eastern ones, attitudes to ageing are not in stasis. For example, Aboderin (2004) has identified significant shifts in attitudes to ageing amongst urban Ghanaians, with an increasing expectation that older adults show self-reliance rather than (as was traditional) relying on younger members of the family to provide a high level of support. Aborderin attributes this sea change in attitudes to the increasingly materialist culture of Ghana.

Ethnic minority groups within industrialised countries tend to have a higher regard for, and more inclusive treatment of, older adults. This may in part be attributed to a higher proportion of multigenerational households and closer-knit families (for majority culture Europeans, the social support systems in different countries are broadly similar – Wenger, 1997). Even where the traditional family unit is becoming less common, a support system may still remain in place that leaves older adults satisfied with the level of support from younger family members and their social network (e.g. Cornman *et al.*, 2004). In addition, for some ethnic minorities (e.g. African-Americans) the church may play a greater role in providing social and unifying support (Jackson, Antonucci and Gibson, 1990) and specific cultural expectations and practices may significantly shape interactions and their success (e.g. the outcomes of caring for a sick older relative – see Dilworth-Anderson, Goodwin and Wallace Williams, 2004).

However, it is dangerous to overgeneralise such arguments and assume that cultural differences are uniquely the product of particular cultures and are fundamentally different to the core. Almost inevitably there are confounding factors, such as the fact that ethnic minorities tend to have a lower socio-economic standing and thus may be forced to be more inter-reliant through economic necessity, and these are difficult to tease apart from other factors (see Rosenthal, 1986, for a discussion of the methodological implications of ethnicity research). For example, Fung, Lai and Ng (2001) demonstrated that the life expectancy of an ethnic group can significantly shape matters. In comparing social preferences of older Taiwanese people against those of typically shorter-lived mainland Chinese people, statistically controlling for differences in life expectancy also removed cultural differences. In addition, studies across different ethnic/cultural groups have found common themes and expectations, such as recognising the importance of mutual assistance and reciprocity between generations, even if the relative emphasis placed on individual factors within the system varies between groups (e.g. Becker *et al.*, 2003).

Notwithstanding these comments, older people within an ethnic minority face what has been termed **double jeopardy** – the problem that not only will they be treated prejudicially because they are older, but also because of their ethnic identity. It is certainly true that older people from ethnic minorities under-use health and social care programmes (e.g. Gallagher-Thompson *et al.*, 1997). Norman (1985) states the case more strongly, and argues that many older members of ethnic minorities are in fact faced with a **triple jeopardy** because, in addition to the aforementioned issues, they also, through the prejudice of others and often through communication problems, cannot get the help they need and deserve from the local or state authorities (other commentators such as Paz and Aleman, 1998, have identified the three factors as age, poverty and ethnicity, but the import of the term is the same). Norman makes a strong case based on the practical problems faced by older ethnic minorities in claiming services and amenities. However, other measures, such as well-being and living conditions, provide more equivocal support (see Perlmutter and Hall, 1992). This is not surprising, since many of the effects of the host country will be ameliorated by the practices of the minority community to which the older people belong. It should also be noted that some health authorities (though alas not all) are making demonstrable efforts to encompass the needs of minority older groups (e.g. Hart *et al.*, 1996; Tennstedt, Chang and Delgado, 1998). However, these may still be in need of improvement. For example, White-Means (2000) found that older African-Americans are less likely to use various medical services, and this explanation holds even after financial differences have been accounted for. Dunlop *et al.* (2002) found similar findings, also on a sample of American older patients. Finally, it is very important to bear in mind that in discussing ethnic minority groups (as with any groups) that there will be considerable individual differences within the group (see Whitfield and Baker-Thomas, 1999), and discussions of ethnic minority problems are descriptive, not prescriptive.

Acute causes of change in later life

A range of treatments, from cosmetic to medical intervention, can often alleviate at least some of the physical problems of ageing, but other changes – in societal roles and relationships – are irrevocable. Of these, some are chronic whilst others are significant single events. Of the latter, probably the biggest are retirement from full-time employment and widowhood.

Retirement

Herzog, House and Morgan (1991) studied older adults who were working or were in semi-retirement. They found that well-being was not related as much to how *much* work they did as whether the work was what they wanted to do. This finding was the same for a group of slightly younger workers (aged 55–64 years). The degree of control over retirement is also important. For example, an older person who is made redundant has generally a lower chance of being re-employed and so in effect is given involuntary retirement. A longitudinal study by Gallo *et al.* (2000) found significant negative effects on mental and physical health of being involuntarily retired (in contrast, older workers made redundant and then fortunate enough to be re-employed showed a marked improvement in mental and physical health, independently of how long they had been out of work). These findings applied even after prior health and socio-economic status were controlled for (see also Szinovacz and Davey, 2004). With regard to voluntary retirement, the decision to retire is often made for the obvious pragmatic reasons. For example, in a study of British civil servants (basically, government officials) opting for early retirement, Mein *et al.* (2000) found that the principal reasons were high income (i.e. could afford to retire early on a good pension), ill health or dislike of the job. Older workers who had material difficulties (e.g. debts) usually felt compelled to carry on working.

Related to the above, it is important to note that with changing employment patterns, retirement is no longer synonymous with 'old age' in the cut and dried way it perhaps once was. For example, Settersen (1998) found that for many people age is now an irrelevant criterion on which to judge retirement. However, if current proposals to make people work longer before they are entitled to a full pension are enacted, this may again change.

With regard to retirement itself, it has been noted that people approaching it tend to be more apprehensive and self-deprecatory but in most instances, once people have stopped working, the experience is pleasurable. However, there are some instances of people suffering psychological problems because they no longer feel useful. For example, Swan, Dame and Carmelli (1991) reported in their study of American retired persons that those who felt that they had been 'forced' to retire had generally lower levels of well-being, and (perhaps not surprisingly) that people with Type A personalities were more likely to complain that they had retired against their will. However, it is difficult to exclude the possibility that such people would have suffered problems and complained in any case. Sharpley (1997) identified three factors – missing work, health and relationships – and, once again, it is tempting to argue that the latter two problems might have arisen regardless of retirement. For the majority, retirement brings little change in life satisfaction. However, other factors may impinge on this. For example, in couples with traditional gender roles, marital satisfaction is higher where the husband is working and the wife is retired than in the reverse situation (Myers and Booth, 1996; Szinovacz, 1996). Perhaps not surprisingly, marital satisfaction can be improved by retirement from a stressful occupation, but health problems may cause a worsening (Myers and Booth, 1996). Again, there is generally an increase in satisfaction among very healthy retirees (Parnes, 1981). White collar workers tend to enjoy retirement more than blue collar workers, but this can probably be attributed to better health and finances (Bengston and Treas, 1980; Ward, 1984). The full picture may thus be complicated by individual differences and circumstances (Moen, 1996). As an illustration of this, van Solinge and Henkens (2005), examining Dutch people approaching retirement, found that a combination of several factors (length of time in the same full-time job, degree of control over when and how to retire, level of anxiety and expectations about the process of retirement, level of self-efficacy) predicted success at adjusting to retirement, and that these factors varied considerably between individuals. Kim and Moen (2002) make a similar case for observing a wide variety of factors.

Widowhood

The state of widowhood (loss of one's partner of either gender) more commonly affects women than men, because of the differing life expectancies of the two sexes. There is some evidence that the impact of the loss depends upon how anticipated it was. For example, Eisdorfer and Wilkie (1977) found that the loss was less stressful if the deceased had been ill for some time (see also Wells and Kendig, 1997). Also, it is known that older people tend to have a milder reaction than younger adults (Cook and Oltjenbruns, 1989), because older people are better primed to accept the death of a partner. However, Carr *et al.* (2001) contradict these findings. In their longitudinal study, they found that the degree to which the death was expected had no significant effect on factors such as grief or depression. A sudden death slightly increased feelings of yearning in a bereaved woman, but *lowered* it in a bereaved man. These contradictory findings may depend on the sensitivity of measures taken and also the age spread of the participants tested. Carr *et al.*'s study was confined to people aged at least 65, so arguably even in the case of sudden death, the demise of a partner cannot be wholly unexpected, whereas in studies that have included younger adults, a sudden death may have greater impact.

Again, the level of loss (and anxiety) is positively correlated with how reliant a person was on the deceased for support (Carr *et al.*, 2000). It is also known that a belief in a good spiritual afterlife results in lower levels of hypertension amongst the bereaved (Krause *et al.*, 2002). Bereavement is also associated with poorer health, but a longitudinal study by Williams (2004) argues that this is due to a decline in health maintaining behaviours, and that bereaved people who maintain health maintenance behaviours do not show a health decline. In the majority of cases, adjustment to loss is reported as being at least satisfactory or robust (see Bonanno, Wortman and Nesse, 2004), though there are some residual signs of grief and other negative feelings 30 months after the bereavement (Thompson *et al.*, 1991), and a sizeable proportion (20%) of widowed persons report a failure to cope adequately (Lopata, 1973). Furthermore, the number of negative aspects of personal relationships within a widow's social circle has been found to increase in the years following bereavement (Morgan, Neal and Carder, 1997). A study by van Baarsen (2002) echoes this. However, changing friends and acquaintances after bereavement can also create problems. Zettel and Rook (2004) demonstrated that, following bereavement, the greater the change in a widow's social network, the greater the damage to psychological health.

Carey (1979) argued that men are better able to adjust post-bereavement than women. This may be because in traditional sex(ist) roles, a married woman's status is determined by the presence of her husband, while the reverse does not apply as strongly. Also, a widowed man is likely to be financially more secure, and may have greater opportunities to find another partner. Other studies, however, have contradicted this viewpoint (Cook and Oltjenbruns, 1989), possibly because more men than women are inept at looking after themselves, and also because widowhood is primarily a woman's experience. Lee *et al.* (2001) found that men became more depressed than women following bereavement, but argued that prior to this they were less depressed, and the level of increase simply brought them on a par with the typical depressed level of older women. Factors underlying this included a greater dislike of domestic chores and a feeling of being less able to give assistance to younger relatives. However, Lee *et al.*'s study had a sampling method that found bereaved men who had been widowed for less time than the women, and this may potentially distort the results.

It thus appears that the reaction to bereavement is dictated by a multitude of factors, and the waters are muddied further when one considers cross-cultural comparisons. For example, in one study it was found that social networks had a direct influence on some features of bereavement in Germany and Japan, were mediated by gender and age in France, and had no effect in the USA (Antonucci *et al.*, 2001). As with many aspects of ageing research, it is difficult to make comfortable generalisations about the effects of bereavement beyond a superficial gloss.

Chronic causes of change in later life

Although retirement and widowhood are the two principal acute factors influencing self-image and life satisfaction, other, often chronic, factors also take their toll. For example, insidious physical changes, from the relatively minor (e.g. greying hair) to the more serious (e.g. arthritis) can all cause a re-evaluation of self-concepts (Ward, 1984). Some studies have found that health and concomitant changes in mobility are the biggest predictors of satisfaction in later life, but others have failed to replicate this (e.g. Bowling, Farquhar and Grundy, 1996) and findings may depend upon what measures the health gauge is weighed against.

The chronic issue of monetary worries figures large in most researcher's lists. Krause, Jay and Liang (1991) demonstrated that financial problems (common in many older people) are a prime factor in reducing feelings of self-worth and in the increase of depressive symptoms. This is true of many cultures. Krause *et al.*'s study found the same basic phenomenon in samples of both American and Japanese older people. Zhang *et al.* (1997) found financial problems to be a major negative factor amongst older people in China. Ferraro and Su (1999) similarly found financial problems increased psychological distress in participants from three different cultures (Fijian, Korean and Philippino, though note that Malaysian participants were an exception). However, the authors also noted that the level of social and family support can at least ease some of these problems. This is reflected in a longitudinal study by Russell and Catrona (1991), who found that, the less social support the older person experienced at the start of the study, the higher his or her depressive symptoms were one year later (and the greater his or her experience of 'daily hassles'). Again, personality factors may play an important role. For example, a well-integrated individual can cope with stress far better than someone who is disorganised. Conversely, a person in bad health and with poor finances may be better able to cope with the declines of health and wealth because they are already used to it (Ward, 1977; 1984). It is also worth noting that in addition to personality types, other psychological factors such as intellectual changes can dent self-esteem. For example, in Chapter 3 it was noted that a high self-report of memory lapses is correlated with level of depression. Perlmutter *et al.* (1987) note that this may create a vicious circle – an older person who perceives his or her performance on a memory task to be poor may suffer a lowering of morale, which may further hamper his or her abilities.

It is also important to note that episodes in a person's past can impinge on their attitudes to later life. Obviously, decisions about careers, relationships, whether to have children, and so forth have a direct impact. Stallings *et al.* (1997) found that negative events in a person's life tend to affect the negative aspects of the mood of a person and positive events the positive aspects, with minimal crossover influences (supporting the so-called **two-factor theory of well-being**). Taking a different approach, Caspi and Elder (1986) examined feelings of life satisfaction in a group of older women who in their thirties had experienced the American Great Depression. Middle-class women who endured hardship at this time now had demonstrably higher ratings of life satisfaction as a result. However, the reverse applied to working-class women in the same situation – they had a lower life satisfaction. Perhaps this is because the middle-class women had demonstrably 'won through' to a better material lifestyle, while the working-class women perceived themselves as being still 'at the bottom'. In an analogous manner, people rated as high in wisdom who experienced the Great Depression had better psychological health in later life than people rated low in wisdom (Ardelt, 1998). However, regardless of background, women on the whole demonstrate a lower level of subjective well-being, as a meta-analysis of the research literature by Pinquart and Sörensen (2001) demonstrated.

Other factors also may contributed to life satisfaction. For example, Cook (1998) found that participating in organised group reminiscence sessions improved the level of life satisfaction amongst older women in a residential home. This should not be taken as support for the stereotype that older people long to live in the past. Although there is evidence that at least some groups of older people would like their past achievements and status to be recognised more (Ghusn *et al.*, 1996), when asked the question 'Looking back, what period of your life brought you the most satisfaction?' the commonest response from older people was, 'Right now' (Field, 1997). Generally, and perhaps unsurprisingly, social activities and friendships have been found to be beneficial by almost all researchers (though in the case of friendships, it is probably quality rather than quantity of friendships that is more important; Pinquart and Sörensen, 2000). An interesting twist on this is provided by Greenwood (1999), who found that where there are problems in a changing social life in later years then men are less likely to report decreased satisfaction, because in general they may have lower expectations of interpersonal relations than women. Again, it is not sufficient to group older people together and expect satisfaction to increase as a result. For example, in a telling phrase, Kovach and Robinson (1996) reported that being given a roommate in a residential home 'predicted life satisfaction only for those who talked to their roommates' (p.627). Participation in exercise activities or non-energetic leisure activities also is correlated with greater life satisfaction (and health). The authors of one study (Menec and Chipperfield, 1997) attribute this to an enhanced feeling of being in control of events (see also McConatha *et al.*, 1998). However, although sociable activities are undoubtedly beneficial, pastimes do not necessarily have to be gregarious to enhance life satisfaction. For example, Sherer (1996) demonstrated that being allowed access to personal computers had a beneficial effect on the self-esteem and life satisfaction of older nursing-home residents and day patients (it is perhaps worth noting in passing that the women in the study tended to use educational software, whilst the men played video games). Generally speaking, purposeful activity is beneficial to life satisfaction (Madigan, Mise and Maynard, 1996).

The above findings suggest that a rich tapestry of factors determine later life satisfaction. In part, this may be because many studies have an air of 'seek and ye shall find' about them. By asking a limited set of questions or focusing on a narrow range, then some factors can be made to appear more important than they perhaps are. For example, using a more qualitative interview technique, Glass and Jolly (1997) found that their sample of participants did not raise good health or finance as key factors contributing to life satisfaction. Not all studies are equally 'guilty' of this selectivity, but it is difficult to move beyond a fairly general statement that intuitively obvious factors such as health, finance, bereavement and retirement have some influence on both self-esteem and general life satisfaction, but these are undoubtedly not the only factors, and all of them may interact with each other and be mediated by personality variables. Unfortunately, this statement is not far removed from what a non-psychologist might produce if asked for an intuitive summary of the issue.

Psychosocial factors and health

Psychosocial factors such as personality, social environment, etc., are all related to health and health is linked to feelings of well-being (more so than age *per se* – see Kunzmann, Little and Smith, 2000). However, how different factors within this equation are linked precisely is less clear-cut. Some connections, such as choosing to live a healthy lifestyle and level of health, are relatively straightforward. Others, such as level of disability and behaviour, are not. The following section attempts an overview of this complex and often contradictory area.

As anyone living in the developed world knows, governments are keen that people pursue a 'healthy' lifestyle, and thus live a longer, healthier life without being a burden to the health services and thus the taxpayer. The links between smoking, diet, exercise and health and health/life expectancy are too well known to need reiterating here, and it may be assumed that a healthy lifestyle is a good thing. How, though, can older adults be persuaded to adopt it if they are not already? Certainly some of the signs are not propitious. For example, several studies have noted that older adults have poorer eating habits (e.g. Quandt and Chao, 2000; Quinn *et al.*, 1997; Souter and Keller, 2002). Other factors may have roots much further in a person's past. People rarely take up 'bad habits' in later life (e.g. older smokers have usually been abusing their bodies for several decades) and accordingly, attempts to make older people change their ways may in some instances be fighting decades of maladaptive behaviour. In addition, older adults may be more reluctant to take up exercise because they fear the risks outweigh the benefits, such as having a heart attack through over-exertion (O'Brien Cousins, 2000; Wilcox *et al.*, 2003). This is not helped by the finding that older adults have fewer people to encourage (or nag) them about their health-related behaviour (Tucker, Klein and Elliott, 2004). However, once past this barrier of taking up exercise and healthier behaviour, several studies have reported that older and younger adults respond to health education equally well (see Elias, Elias and Elias, 1990, for further discussion). With regard to the physical benefits of exercise, undoubtedly peak physical performance declines with age, and this is more pronounced for activities requiring sudden bursts of energy (e.g. athletics throwing-events) than for activities requiring lower, but sustained, levels of energy (e.g. middle- and long-distance running). However, several (though not all) studies have found that older people who follow an exercise regime have faster reaction times and better psychomotor performance (Spirduso and MacRae, 1990). This is not surprising, but of greater interest is that well-exercised older people's performances would put many people in their twenties to shame (see the excellent review by Spirduso and MacRae, 1990, for further details). But getting people to *maintain* healthy behaviour is not easy, and other researchers have reported that getting older people to comply with and maintain an exercise programme may require some effort (see Resnick, 2001). However, if an older person chooses to, they can considerably improve their life expectancy and physical and (in part) psychological well-being.

Considering a more direct relationship between personality and lifestyle on the one hand and psychological and physical well-being on the other, there appears to be a positive correlation between the two (e.g. Bookwala, Harralson and Parmelee, 2003) though note that studies using people's self-reports generally produce higher correlations than when objective measures of physical health are taken (e.g. Whitbourne, 1987). Note also that the strength of the relationship tends to weaken in the oldest of older people (Pinquart, 2001).

However, this correlation does not give an indication of causation. At the most simplistic, we can ask: does having the right personality/lifestyle make a person healthy? Or does being healthy make a person be healthy? Both these simple questions have evidence in their favour. For example, it can be demonstrated that certain psychological characteristics affect physical health. Kermis (1986) argues that depression and/or stress can cause a worsening of health (e.g. by suppressing the immune system). In a seven-year longitudinal study, Ostir, Ottenbacher and Markides (2004) found that positive affect was associated with a significantly lowered risk of frailty amongst older Mexican Americans. Again, exposure even to subliminal presentations of negative stereotypical statements about older adults and ageing can raise blood pressure and other physiological measures of stress in older participants (Levy, *et al.*, 2000). Therefore, over the long term, exposure to persistent negative comments about ageing and older people may have a deleterious effect on health (thus refuting the adage about sticks and stones). Conversely, there is evidence that physical health affects psychological functioning. For example, Druley *et al.* (2003) found that the more severe the response to the physical pain of osteoarthritis in older married women, the greater the negative impact on both their and their husbands' behaviour.

However, it would be naïve to assume that such an issue as this can be explained simply in terms of '*A* causes *B*' or '*B* causes *A*' arguments. A far more probable explanation is that the effects are multidirectional, and that in effect 'vicious circles' of maladaptive functioning can be created (e.g. physical decline causes a rise in stress and depression, which makes the physical decline worse, which in turn...etc.). A case in point is falls in older adults. A fall is unpleasant at any age, but it brings with it increased health risks in later life. This is principally because more brittle bones mean that breaks of the hip and leg bones are a distinct possibility, and if not these, then other unpleasant injuries are likely; one study found that an older person has a one in three chance of suffering a functional decline following a fall (Stel *et al.*, 2004). Older people who have fallen over once are understandably unwilling to repeat the experience, but the added caution this feeling engenders may perversely may make matters worse. A longitudinal study by Delbaere *et al.*, (2004) found that older adults who had fallen were more frightened of falling again and had lower levels of daily activity. But this greater fear and lower activity were the best predictors of having a fall in the subsequent year (on a more positive note, methods for reducing fear of falling are available – see Li *et al.*, 2005). Findings such as this must be treated with some degree of caution as it is possible that an underlying physical cause may be causing people to fall, and it is not difficult to find evidence of physical causes of falls (see Vassallo *et al.*, 2003). However, on *a priori* grounds, the vicious circle argument must hold true for at least some instances of fall behaviour. Nor can it be denied that a fear of falling can have negative consequences not only for quality of life but also general health if mobility is unduly restricted (Li *et al.*, 2003).

It would also be unwise to assume that a relationship between psychosocial and physical factors need be purely causal. In many instances factors appear to alter the strength of expression of another factor rather than simply causing it to be present or absent. For example, Bailis and Chipperfield (2002) argue that if an older person has a strong sense of social identity, this may cushion (but not remove) the negative effects of a decline in physical health when there is little the individual can do about preventing the decline itself happening. A complex statistical regression analysis of circa 1200 older female patients supported this hypothesis. Femia, Zarita and Johansson (2001) found that psychosocial factors mediated the impact of illness on the ability of old old people's daily living activities. Indeed, in general the presence of a support network appears to enhance health in older adults. Kempen *et al.* (2001) found that individuals who reported a high level of social support also showed significantly better recovery from fall-related injuries both at five and twelve months after the injury. Again, Duke *et al.* (2002) found that size of social support network was related to the probability that a person forced to give up one activity because of illness or disability would take up another to replace it. Socio-economic factors can also have an effect. The most striking examples of these are arguably the social class and regional differences in life expectancy noted in Chapter 1. However, there are other notable instances. For example, Melzer *et al.* (2001) found that education level is a significant predictor of mobility disability in later life, with people with a low level of education (six years or less) being circa 1.7 times more likely to be movement disabled that people with over twelve years of education.

A related topic is that of **hostility** and ageing. Hostility has already been mentioned as a personality type, but it can also be defined as 'a negative orientation toward others that has cognitive, affective and behavioral manifestations' (Barefoot, 1992, p.13). Some studies have reported higher levels of hostility amongst younger adults and older elderly people, with a drop in hostility between these two ages (see Barefoot *et al.*, 1993). This may in part be adaptive, because a healthy cynicism is arguably a useful tool for both younger adults first finding their way in the world, and older people in increased dependence on health and social welfare services. Comijs *et al.* (1999) found that hostility was also associated with being mistreated. However, as many commentators have argued, it can also be disadvantageous, because high hostility levels are associated with an increased risk of heart disease (see Meesters, Muris and Backus, 1996) and other illnesses (see Ranchor *et al.*, 1997).

However, it is also possible to over estimate the relationship between physical health and psychosocial factors. For example, a good predictor of physical health in later life is physical health in earlier life. Maas and Kuypers (1974) observed that many illnesses of later life are preceded by related physical complaints earlier in life. In turn this may be related to socio-economic status – low childhood SES is significantly related to lower health status in later life. In part this is because of the long-term effects of childhood illness, but also because of lower income and living standards in adult life (Luo and Waite, 2005). Again, Krause, Shaw and Cairney (2004) found that suffering trauma in early adulthood is strongly correlated with worse health in later life. This means at the very least that, if there is a change in personality in response to illness, it may not just be the illness in later life which is causing this – it could be an effect accumulated across the lifespan. However, the links between illness and personality can be exaggerated. For example, the Type A personality has been associated with a significantly higher heart attack rate. However, a review by Elias *et al.* (1990) observes that whilst this may be true for younger people, having a Type A personality *after* the age of 65 does not increase the risk of coronary problems (the finding cannot be simply attributed to most people with Type A dying before they reach this age).

It should also be noted that throughout this section, much of the discussion has centred on quantitative methods of research that emphasise reducing complex data to an underlying numerical pattern. However, although it can appear a trite cliché, we should remember that it is the health and suffering of *individuals* that is ultimately the focus of these studies. Recent research by Black and Rubinstein (2004) has conducted a qualitative analysis of older adults' experience of illness, and notes that many of their findings can only be treated at an individual level, and defy simple reductionist techniques. Therefore, global statements about this topic potentially overlook important details.

Before leaving this section, it is also important to note that attitudes towards older people by members of the caring professions can also have an important effect on the standard of care experienced by older adults. For example, Helmes and Gee (2003) found that, when presented with a (fictional) description of a patient presenting with symptoms of depression, both psychologists and counsellors were significantly less optimistic about the prognosis for the patient if they were described as 'elderly'. Peake and Thompson (2003) followed the progress of circa 1600 patients diagnosed with lung cancer. They found that treatment was directed more intensively towards the younger patients, even when other health factors were equal. For example, one commonly-used surgical treatment was given to 37 per cent of younger patients versus only 15 per cent of patients aged over 75 years. Six months after diagnosis, the mortality rate for patients aged under 65 was 42 per cent versus 57 per cent in those aged over 75 – a difference that arguably cannot be accounted for simply by differences in other health indices.

In part, this inequality may reflect an ignorance of the full facts about ageing and the attitudes of practitioners. For example, Knapp, Beaver and Reed (2002) found that church ministers and students for the ministry were surprisingly unaware of very basic facts about ageing and later life. Schiller Schigelone and Ingersoll-Dayton (2004) studied two groups of medical students – one with an interest in specialising in geriatric medicine, the other with no interest. In a counter-intuitive finding, the authors report that the 'interested' group had stronger positive *and negative* feelings about ageing and later life than the 'not interested' group, and also had significantly higher levels of anxiety about growing old. These findings may indicate a source of fuel for some of the less desirable attitudes to ageing in practitioners, but caution must be exercised since Schiller Schigelone and Ingersoll-Dayton's sample was relatively small (ten in each group). A further study demonstrates that, even when exposed to situations that should increase knowledge and awareness of older adults, this may not occur. Hakamies-Blomqvist *et al.* (2002) examined Swedish and Finnish general practitioners' (GPs') knowledge of ageing and driving. Under Finnish law, older adults must be assessed by a GP before they are allowed to drive. The same is not true in Sweden. It might therefore be assumed that Finnish GPs would be more knowledgeable about ageing and driving than their Swedish counterparts, but this is not the case. The authors suggest that this may be because of undue complacency by Finnish doctors, convinced of the efficacy of their screening procedures, but it seems remarkable that little additional knowledge seems to have been acquired during repeated exposure.

Marriage

Generally, older married couples are found to be as happy or even more content than younger married adults (Cunningham and Brookbank, 1988) and generally report a reduction in negative interactions with increasing age (see Akiyama *et al.*, 2003). This may in part be due to reduced work and parenting responsibilities (Orbuch *et al.*, 1996). Levenson, Cartensen and Gottmann (1993) assessed younger (40–50 years) and older (60–70 years) married couples on a variety of measures. They found that the older couples displayed greater equanimity of aims and sources of pleasure (and fewer sources of disagreement) and also tended to have more equal standards of health. There results are encouraging, in that it would appear that older married people are not simply clinging to the wreckage because the prospect of living apart is financially and/or emotionally too awful to contemplate. In another sense, the results are uninformative, because they do not indicate whether happily married older couples have always been happily married or whether today's happiness is the result 'of a process in which old wars are diminished' (Levenson *et al.*, 1993, p.312) to the point where a truce has been called.

Other research suggests a rather less cosy picture. For example, Chipperfield and Havens (2001) observed older adults over a seven-year period and observed changes in life satisfaction for those whose marital status remained unchanged over the period versus those for whom there had been a marital change (principally, loss or divorce of a partner). The basic finding of the study was that men benefited more from marriage than women. Thus, if there was no change in marital status, women's life satisfaction tended to diminish, whilst men's remained relatively stable. Loss of a partner affected both genders badly, but men more than women. If a couple married, then the man's satisfaction tended to rise, whilst the woman's was unaffected. Reasons for the relative levels of satisfaction may be dependent on a number of factors; for example, the degree to which each partner relies on the other for support. Gurung, Taylor and Seeman (2003) found that older husbands relied principally on their wives for emotional support, whilst wives were more likely to use friends and close family members. As older friends die and families move further apart, it is easy to see how women could lose many of their sources of support.

Discussion so far has concentrated on married couples. It might be tempting, given today's social mores, to assume that the findings will be true for cohabiting couples as well. However, this may not be the case. For example, Brown, Roebuck Bulanda and Lee (2005) found that the male partners in cohabiting couples had significantly higher levels of depression than husbands in married couples, even after controlling for socio-economic factors, health and levels of social support. At the time of writing these are still relatively new findings and further studies may reveal causal factors underlying this. However, on functional grounds alone, it would be wrong to treat married and cohabiting groups as being automatically synonymous. The findings further support the argument that marriage favours men – Brown *et al.* found that there were increased levels of depression in married and cohabiting women; only the married men appeared to benefit in relative terms.

Sexuality and ageing[2]

It is a commonplace observation that the media portray sex as being for the young and slim, and ageist humour dictates that older people wanting a sex life are either 'dirty old men' or ugly and desperate (see Walz, 2002). Even those older people whom the media have labelled 'sexy' are chosen because, generally, they do not 'look their age' (see Walz, 2002). Accordingly, older people do not receive support from everyday sources that wanting a sex life in later adulthood is normal and healthy. It is therefore unsurprising to find that people's professed interest in sex decreases after the age of 50 (Segrave and Segrave, 1995) and in part this is attributed to negative societal views (though illnesses and medical treatments affecting sex drive are also major contributors). Perversely enough, this may not be altogether bad. Some loss of sexual opportunity is almost

---

2   This section deals with ageing rather than middle age, but the related issue of the menopause is clearly of importance. See e.g. Dennerstein, Alexander and Kotz (2003); Palacios, Tobar and Menendez (2002). It is also, *purely* for the sake of space, devoted to majority heterosexual practices. For an excellent survey of gay behaviour and ageing, see Heaphy, Yip and Thompson (2004).

inevitable in later life due to death of partners, loss of physical functioning, etc. A stereotype that informs older adults that less (or even no) opportunity for sex in later life is to be expected may therefore act as a comfort. Examinations of older adults' reactions to a loss of sexual functioning and/or partner shows that the negative effects may be lessened or negated by the expectation that this is part of 'normal ageing' (Gott and Hinchliff, 2003). This does not mean that older adults should be discouraged from an enjoyable sex life (far from it), but arguing too vociferously that sex is an automatic right may be misinterpreted by those who lack the opportunity (or physical means) that they have 'failed'.

There are a variety of problems associated with studying sexuality in the later years. One is a cohort effect – older people were brought up in less permissive times, and are not accustomed (and indeed may lack the vocabulary) to talk about sexual issues. Surveying the history of studies of sexual activity in later life, Gibson (1992) observes that the more recent the study, the more often older people admit to having sexual relations. Non-compliance is a traditional problem with sex surveys (conversely, participants who are rather *too* willing to participate may also provide biased data). Therefore, older groups may provide less information, not because they have sex less often, but because they are less willing to talk about it. Another problem often cited by researchers concerns what constitutes 'sex'. If penetrative intercourse is taken as the only measure of sex, then older people may show a greater decline in activity than if a wider range of activities is considered. It is worth noting, however, that sexually active older people generally report great satisfaction in whatever activity they indulge in (see Gott, 2004; Matthias *et al.*, 1997; Skoog, 1996).

A further problem is one of opportunity. Since women on average live longer than men, there are a lot more older women than men. Thus, older women's opportunities for heterosexual contact are diminished, and activity may cease not because of lack of capability or willingness, but because of lack of a suitable partner. For men, the biggest problems are usually inability to sustain an erection and/or lacking the physical stamina for intercourse. Extrapolating from Gibson (1992), between 10 and 20 per cent of older men and 35 per cent (or more) of older women have no sex life (though note that figures vary enormously across studies). For those older people who attempt to find sexual contact through higher-risk behaviours, such as using prostitutes, there is an increased risk of contracting sexually transmitted diseases, including AIDS (Gott, 2004). A study of circa 800 Swiss people aged over 45 found that they had behaviours presenting an increased risk of contracting AIDS compared with younger adults (Abel and Werner, 2003). An additional factor is that the 'baby boomers' generation, which was arguably the first to embrace substance abuse on a widespread scale, has shown less reluctance to drop their habits as they have grown older, relative to previous generations of substance abusers (Topolski *et al.*, 2002). Continued intravenous drug use of course drastically raises the risk of HIV/AIDS, but, in addition, the lifestyle associated with substance abuse is also probabilistically linked to a higher level of risky sexual practices. But older adults are no less vulnerable than any other age group when it comes to infection by AIDS – as proof of this, circa 15 per cent of all HIV/AIDS cases in the USA are in people aged over 50 (Emlet, 2004).

A final problem to be mentioned here is the relative under-treatment by health professionals, who may undervalue or ignore older people's sexuality (see Gussaroff, 1998; Mayers and McBride, 1998) and may be unaware of the prevalence of HIV/AIDS in older adults (Emlet, 2004); generally, a high proportion of cases of sexual dysfunction in older adults remains untreated (see Godschalk, Sison and Mulligan, 1997). In many instances, there is a clear and pressing need for health care professionals to become far better versed in issues surrounding sexuality and sexual behaviours in later life (see Sharpe, 2004).

Generally, in addition to limitations of physical health, the level of sexual activity is dependent upon the level of activity in early adulthood (e.g. Martin, 1981). This implies that, once again, the state of one's later life is determined by one's earlier behaviour. However, it is worth remembering that sexual drives differ markedly between individuals (e.g. Masters and Johnson, 1966). In later life, a key determinant of sexual activity is the level of importance of sex to the individual (DeLamater and Sill, 2005). Although this may to some extent be a circular argument (e.g. if a person cannot have sex then arguably it may become less important, especially with a stereotype that loss of libido is 'normal' in later life), it cannot *all* be circular. Put simply, it is wrong to assume that there is a 'correct' level of sexual activity, or indeed, that sexual activity is necessary at all, for successful ageing to occur.

Preferences for lifestyle

So far, older personality and lifestyle have been conceived principally in terms of changes *within* the individual. In this and the following section, attention is turned to the question of how older people choose to interact with others. It has been tacitly acknowledged in various parts of the research literature that part of ageing is a preparation for death. Nowhere is this made more explicit than in the **disengagement theory** by Cumming and Henry (1961), based on a large study of residents in Kansas City. This argued that as people get older, their contact with the world lessens. At one level this is through a decline in the senses. At a social level, the loss of spouses and friends, and other social estrangements such as retirement, cause older people to disengage from contact with others. This was seen by Cumming and Henry as a rational process, initiated by older people and aided and abetted by societal conventions. It is as if older people are preparing to die by shedding their links with the physical world.[3] The theory can be criticised (and indeed was) for presenting the behaviour of passively waiting for the Grim Reaper as a good role model for older people. This is perhaps being a little harsh on Cumming and Henry, who were talking about relative rather than total disengagement. In addition, as Coleman and O'Hanlon (2004) observe, the prevailing societal attitude (in the USA at least) was that old age 'should' ideally be like middle age – therefore, old age was seen as an unhealthy decline from the norm.[4] Rather than denigrating later life, Cumming and Henry were in fact making a vigorous stand celebrating the separate identity of later life and in effect empowering people in senescent decline as undergoing a natural rather than aberrant experience. In any case, later evidence indicated that disengagement was largely confined to individuals who were always reclusive (e.g. Maddox, 1970b) or in some cases to people who had loneliness thrust upon them by force of circumstances. In other instances it was linked to level of economic hardship. For example, Magai *et al.* (2001) found that the greater the hardship, the greater the isolation, and this in turn was probabilistically related to racial grouping (African-Americans were on average poorer and more isolated than European Americans). It has also been argued that people who disengage from society have probably been doing so for most of their lives – in other words, it is not purely a response to ageing (Maddox, 1970a). This is supported by a longitudinal study by Barnes *et al.* (2004), which found that such behaviour was present before participants entered old age. In other words, the phenomenon may be a 'natural' extension of a particular personality type or the result of specific events, not a universal feature, or even product of ageing. Another criticism is that disengagement is a very rare phenomenon in many developing countries, where older people are kept in an active role in the community (e.g. Merriman, 1984).

Researchers and commentators responding to Cumming and Henry's work argued that the best policy for older people is to keep as active as possible. Their argument is roughly as follows. Older people usually want to keep active, and life satisfaction is found to be greatest in those with an active involvement (see above). In addition, greater social involvement (or at least, a more supportive social network) appears to lessen the impact of negative social exchanges (Rook, 2003) and be associated with a lower level of cognitive decline (Holtzman *et al.*, 2004). Thus, greater social involvement is associated with beneficial things, and it is not surprising that a theoretical stance that older people should be encouraged to be socially active developed. However, in its extreme form this **activity theory** is as unattractive as the argument it tried to replace. The image of hordes of social

---

3   The process of physically 'downsizing' when moving into a smaller home in later life and disposing of larger possessions is examined by Ekerdt *et al.* (2004).

4   This echoes a criticism of current 'successful ageing' models – see Chapter 7.

workers forcing older people to mix with others 'for their own good', with compulsory whist drives and so forth, is not a pleasant one. Nor is it necessarily effective. Social activity is often confounded by level of health (i.e. an older person has to be relatively healthy in order to engage in social activities, so the finding that older adults who engage in social activities are also the healthiest may not be surprising). Lennartsson and Silverstein (2001) found that when health was statistically controlled for, the most beneficial activities with regard to older people's further life expectancy were solitary activities.

The modern consensus is that disengagement and activity theories describe the optimal strategies for some but not all older individuals, and which is better, depends on a variety of factors, such as financial circumstances (e.g. can one afford an active lifestyle?), health (e.g. does one still have the vigour for some hobbies?) and personality types (e.g. introverts may hate a socially active lifestyle). To some extent, level of activity in later life is explained by behaviour in earlier life. For example, in a longitudinal study, Holahan and Chapman (2002) found that level of purposiveness at age 40 predicted the goals being actively sought from activities at age 80. It is also worth noting that a number of studies have found increased social involvement only appreciably improves well-being in lower income groups (e.g. Caspi and Elder, 1986; Larson, 1978). However, it should also be noted that disengagement can also be indicative of encroaching illness and is correlated with mortality level (e.g. Bennett, 2002). Hence, although caution should be exercised in labelling particular behaviours as undesirable, withdrawal may in some instances be an early warning of serious health problems.

The role of the family

Many people, given the choice, would probably like to combine aspects of the disengagement and activity lifestyles. This is shown in research on preferences for family relationships. It would appear that in western nations at least, older people prefer to live independently, but also to have their children or close relatives living nearby. In about 80 per cent of cases, older parents live within 30 minutes' travel of at least one of their offspring (Bengston and Treas, 1980).[5] Thus, older people seem to like to combine the opportunity for activity through interaction with family members with disengagement through the privacy of their own homes.

The family can have distinct advantages. For example, as has been seen in the studies of financial problems cited above, the effects of hardship can be at least partly offset by

---

5   For an overview of residence patterns across cultures, see Bongaarts and Zimmer (2002).

family factors (e.g. Ferraro and Su, 1999; Zhang *et al.*, 1997). However, family members can be a more ambiguous asset in times of an acute rather than a chronic problem. In a masterly review of the literature, Bengston and Treas observed that, while family members were the usual and preferred source of comfort and help in a crisis, older people were more depressed the greater their expectations of assistance from their relatives. In other words, expect too much and disappointment will almost inevitably follow (though note that the proportion of older people with unrealistically high expectations is relatively low). This is further supported by a study by Bengston and Kuypers (1986), who found that when a crisis occurs and help is needed, this may damage familial relations because family members may feel that they have not adequately coped.

A detailed analysis of family intervention is provided by McCubbin and Patterson's (1982) **double ABCX model**, where *A* is the event causing the crisis, *B* the familial resources for coping, *C* the familial perception of the crisis and *X* the perceived stress. Variations in *A*, *B*, and *C* will determine the overall level of stress the family and older person experience (see Clark, 1999, for an example of an application of the model). Gatz, Bengston and Blum (1990) created a similar model, comprising a sequence of *event-stressor-appraisals-mediators-outcomes*. The *event* is the crisis, and the *stressor* the deleterious effect of the event. *Appraisals* refers to the process whereby the family caregivers decide the degree to which they feel they can control the situation, and the *mediators* are the available aid and caring skills. The *outcomes* process refers to the degree to which the family feel stressed and/or adapt to the change in the situation.

Both these models of family care in a crisis are essentially descriptive, and there is a considerable research literature available to describe each stage of either model. The tone of this is rather uniform – most aspects of caring and adaptation are potentially stressful and have negative effects. Detailed reviews are provided by Gatz *et al.* (1990) and Wenger (1990). A caveat to these observations is that the majority of caregiving duties fall on the spouses or offspring of older people (Qureshi and Walker, 1989) – thus, most caregivers are themselves older or middle-aged. Accordingly, caregivers themselves may experience physical problems in nursing sick patients, and increased incidences of ill-health in caregivers have (unsurprisingly) been reported (see Gatz *et al.*, 1990).

As was noted in Chapter 1, in westernised nations at least, the proportion of the population aged over 60 has risen dramatically over the past 100 years. At the same time, for a variety of reasons the birth rate has dropped. This means that older people today have fewer relatives to seek support from than did older people in the historical past (though about 80% of older people have at least one living son or daughter; see also Johnson and Troll, 1996). However, does this mean that the older person's plight (if there is one) has worsened? The answer is probably not. First, because the general improvement in living standards and pension schemes means that older people can be self-sufficient more often than their ancestors could. The workhouse, the refuge of working-class older people, no longer looms like the dire punishment it did only a few decades ago. It is also worth observing that the extended family (where three generations live under the same roof) was the exception rather than the rule in pre-twentieth century Europe (e.g. Laslett, 1976). In short, there has not been a 'golden age' in the past where greater pastoral care was given to older people (see Thane, 2000).

In addition, perceptions of family harmony seem to be greater the smaller the family – a study by Fingerman and Birditt (2003) found that people who cited a smaller number of family members tended to rate these relatives as being 'closer' and the incidence of problematic relationships to be lower. Interestingly, older adults were less likely to report problematic relationships than were younger members of the same family. It is possible to offer a cynical interpretation of these results – namely, that the smaller the family, the more obliged members feel to get along, and, simultaneously, the older one gets, the more oblivious one becomes to problems within the family. However, this is perhaps an unduly bleak view.

It should also be noted that in the case of childless older adults, where there may be no younger generation to interact with, greater psychological stress is not inevitable but may depend on specific circumstances (e.g. men without a living partner had higher levels of loneliness and often depression, but men with a living partner did not – see Zhang and Hayward, 2001).

It is also important to note that findings on the role of familial support can vary according to the social class of the family.[6] For example, Sundstrom's (1986) Swedish study notes that the geographical distance between older adults and their offspring is typically greater in the middle than in the working classes (although when this is controlled for, there is little class difference in level of care). This is perhaps accounted for by the finding from Qureshi and Walker's (1989) English study that members of 'higher' social classes tended to use the phone and postal services more frequently. Other class differences are perhaps due to material opportunity rather than motivation. For example, Qureshi and Walker also found that 'higher' social class older people were more likely to visit other members of their families. However, measures of level of emotional closeness between family members were roughly the same across all social classes.

Religion and ageing

To the best of the author's knowledge, the majority of research on religious practice and ageing has looked at the Christian faith as practised in industrialised nations, and particularly in the USA. No offence is intended to other belief systems by the concentration of discussion on Christianity in the following section.

---

6   And culture – see the 'Cross-cultural differences' section of this chapter.

It has already been noted that the role of organised religion may play a greater role in the lives of older members of some ethnic minorities, providing a social network and material as well as spiritual support. However, what of spiritual belief itself? Evidence generally supports the argument that a high level of spiritual belief can be beneficial in ageing. The role of religion in a time of crisis is something known to many people, and its beneficial nature is well documented. For example, it is known that strength of religious faith is negatively correlated with depression (see Braam *et al.*, 1997) and faith is of value in lessening the negative effects of caregiving for an elderly sick relative with, for example, dementia (see Chapter 6). More generally, religiousness is strongly correlated with well-being even after controlling for gender, birth cohort and socio-economic group (Wink and Dillon, 2003). It may also be associated with better health, possibly through the intermediary step of increasing optimism and thereby presumably lowering stress (Krause, 2002).

However, the relationship between religiousness and ageing is not as clear cut as may be first supposed. For example, it might be intuitively supposed that religious belief, with its emphasis on the afterlife, might be crucial in helping people to come to terms with their mortality and thus might be especially useful in a time of illness. However, the onset of potentially life-threatening illnesses, or harbingers of a serious decline in health such as cancer, a broken hip or serious cardiovascular problems, are responded to with a *decline* in attendance at religious services (Benjamins *et al.*, 2003). Although use of more easily accessible religious media, such as television evangelists, regular reading of the Bible and similar, are unaffected by illness, the decline in church attendance, which lies at the heart of most Christians' lives, is singular. However, this does not mean that religious belief is of no value in times of illness. For example, Kirby, Coleman and Daley (2004) found that level of spirituality helped lessen the effects of illness and physical frailty on the well-being of very old adults. Again, a longitudinal study by Idler, Kasl and Hays (2001) found that level of religious feeling remained stable or even increased in the last year of life, even though attendance at religious services declined (perhaps because of physical limitations). Therefore, attendance at services is not necessarily a good indicator of belief.

The precise nature of the reasons for the beneficial effects of religious observance and belief on subjective feelings of well-being in later life are not fully understood and perhaps move beyond a reductionist psychological approach. However, Krause (2003) in a study of differences between Black and White American older adults, found that Black older adults gained greater meaning from religion and applied it to their everyday life experiences. This in turn was associated with greater self-esteem and life satisfaction. To explain this further is perhaps to encroach on matters of faith. Some Christian groups might argue that attaining a belief rooted in everyday life is a step closer to spiritual grace, but other Christian groups, and certainly some other religions, might find a move towards the earthly a regressive step. Arguably what is important is that either the application of religious belief to everyday life or (more probably) a correlate of this brings with it greater life satisfaction to some people.

Summary

The findings of research on personality and lifestyle are varied. Studies of personality types and traits indicate that older people usually 'receive' their personalities in early adulthood, and any shifts thereafter tend to be a diminution of strength relative to younger adults. Certainly, there is not a personality type unique to later life. On the other hand, some types of personality enable people to cope with later life better than others. The identification of these comes primarily from psychoanalysis rather than mainstream psychology, but there is considerable empirical support for them. However, all these arguments must be weighed against the considerable criticisms of personality testing and research methodologies. Again, it should be noted that many personality taxonomies incorporate implicit value judgements. For example, a successfully ageing person is held to have a placid and almost stoic attitude towards life. However, this conforms to the stereotype that older adults should be quiet, wisdom-dispensing, archetypal grandparent figures – or, in other words, people who make little fuss and make themselves available to others. This may be pragmatically the best way to grow old, but it is not the only way.

Having acknowledged that personality traits are largely born in early adulthood, and that some traits are more appropriate than others, older people still have a number of methods at their disposal for improving their lot, such as adopting a healthier lifestyle. The relationship between lifestyle and well-being is more complicated than it may first appear, however. Socio-economic class, ethnicity, widowhood, familial relations, finances and many other factors interact to provide a complex web of events and pressures whose effects are far from fully mapped.

Suggested further reading

An excellent overview of many of the issues covered in this chapter (particularly psychoanalytic theories) is provided by Coleman and O'Hanlon (2004). Perlmutter and Hall (1992) provide excellent additional commentaries on many of the topics covered in this chapter (see particularly Chapter 16 on American ethnic minorities). An overview of personality research in general is provided by Caspi, Roberts and Shiner (2005). The general issues of social factors in ageing are well addressed by Pratt and Norris (1994). Turner and Helms (1994) provide a useful overview of general adult development, and are particularly strong on discussions of personality and social development in later life. A more detailed discussion of the level of dependency exhibited by older people is an excellent book by the late Margaret Baltes (Baltes, 1996). Gibson (1992, 1997) provides an intelligent overview of sexual and emotional changes (see also Schlesinger, 1996). Although death and dying are not covered in this book, it is perhaps worth noting at this point two useful books on thanatology for those interested: Kübler-Ross (1970) is rightly acknowledged as a classic (see also Kübler-Ross, 1997) and Stroebe, Stroebe and Hansson (1993) provides a more recent overview.

CHAPTER 6

Mental Illness and Ageing

Introduction

Older people are less likely to suffer from mental illness than any other age group (Smyer and Qualls, 1999). All conditions, other than cognitive impairment, are at a lower level. This does not of course mean that mental illness in later life can be dismissed. It is a serious problem at any age, but in older people may be compounded by generally poorer health and lowered intellectual skills. The number of chronic conditions an average person suffers from increases over the lifespan, and the problem is greater the lower the socio-economic group being considered (House *et al.*, 1992). When further problems, such as double jeopardy (see Chapter 5) and declining intellect and memory are added into the equation, it can be appreciated that the problems facing older adults with mental illness may be considerable. Not surprisingly, there is a considerable literature on mental health in later life (see e.g. Murphy and Alexopoulos, 1995; Parks, Zec and Wilson, 1993; Smyer and Qualls, 1999; Woods, 1996, for more detailed discussions). In the present chapter, an overview will be presented of some of the key features. We will begin with discussion of an illness, which, although not unique to later life, is certainly most commonly found in older people; namely, dementia. This will occupy a large proportion of the chapter. A final section will introduce the reader to some of the key concepts and findings in studies of older patients suffering from mental illnesses of other causes.

Dementia

Introduction

Dementia describes the global deterioration of intellectual functioning resulting from atrophy of the central nervous system. Although many people (and not a few textbooks) have the impression that the disease has only a few causes, in fact at least 50 have been identified (Haase, 1977), although admittedly a lot of these are extremely rare. It is also not true that dementia is synonymous with later life. This is wrong on two counts – first, only a minority of older adults develop dementing symptoms, and second, dementia can be contracted at any age. It is the *probability* of developing the illness which increases with age. A useful rule of thumb by White *et al.* (1986) states that the incidence of dementia starts at 1 per cent at age 60, then doubles every five years (i.e. becoming 2% at 65, 4% at 70, 8% at 75, 16% at 80 and 32% at 85). This roughly concurs with the figures of other researchers (e.g. see Hestad, Ellersten and Klove, 1998; Smyer and Qualls, 1999). It is also worth bearing in mind that many individuals will only show relatively mild symptoms, and, cold comfort as this is, they will probably die from other causes before the disease has gained a firm hold. This means that only 2–3 per cent of older adults are institutionalised because of dementing symptoms (Kermis, 1983). In other words, although these are noteworthy figures, developing dementia is not an inevitable feature of later life.

However, although an individual older person's fears of becoming 'senile' are often unrealistic, this does not mean that dementia is not a serious problem. From a demographic viewpoint, the illness poses a challenge to industrialised nations. As was noted in Chapter 1, both the actual number of older people and the proportion they form of the total population are increasing. This means that the number of cases of dementia is also rising. The principal concern, however, should not be the degree to which health services are affected but the hideous nature of the illness itself. The patient is, after the early stages of the illness, usually (though not inevitably) mercifully unaware of most aspects of his or her condition (though patients with some forms of MID for example – see below – retain awareness). On the other hand, the effect on those left to care for the patient can be devastating. Usually, until the terminal stages of the illness, patients are not institutionalised. This means that the burden of care falls on the patient's spouse or children. These caregivers (whom, it should be remembered, are often themselves middle-aged or older) have the task of tending to the needs of someone who has no memory, and is incontinent and subject to temper tantrums and other irrational behaviours. As an added bonus, many demented patients cannot even recognise their own spouse, children or close friends. Thus, the reward for a lifetime's love, affection and sharing can be to tend for a person who, whilst outwardly resembling a loved one, has lost all indication of being a sentient being. No one deserves to die in such an undignified fashion, and no one should have to witness it happen to someone they have loved. Such an end would be tragic if it lasted several weeks, but for most patients the decline is gradual and takes place over *years*. To this should be added that, in the UK at least, there will be precious little government help until the final stages of the illness, whereupon the local authorities are empowered to seize most of the patient's estate to pay for the care. Thus, for example, a spouse may have to sell the family home in order to meet the bills (note also that few private health insurance schemes cover dementia). So the reward to caregivers for taking on a job which, most would agree, should be undertaken by the welfare state is not only to see their personal lives blighted but then to see financial security removed. Presumably this is what is meant by the modern 'caring society'.

Dementia is thus a cause for major concern, doubly so since there are no known cures for its commonest forms. In this chapter, we shall examine the principal psychological features of the main types of dementia, although lengthy discussions of diagnostic procedures have been avoided because they would occupy a disproportionately large part of the text (which is not in any case a guide to how to practise clinical psychology). For those interested in such considerations, a useful starting point is Parks *et al.* (1993) or Wasylenki (1987).

Classifying dementias

The first step in diagnosing dementia is to discover the extent of the disability suffered by the patient when they first seek help. This may be hampered by the age of the individual in question. Younger adults with early symptoms of dementia are likely to go to a medical practitioner much sooner, because memory loss and other signs of intellectual decline are considered atypical in their age group. The decline may have to reach a rather more pronounced stage in older adults before anything unusual is noticed, simply because the early symptoms of decline may be taken as no more than 'typical' age-related loss.

Once the patient's problem has been noticed, there are a number of basic measures of intellectual functioning to provide a rough guide to the degree of impairment. A widely used British test of this type is the **Blessed Dementia Scale** (Blessed, Tomlinson and Roth, 1968). In the USA, the equivalents are the **Mental Status Questionnaire** or **MSQ** (Kahn *et al.*, 1960) and the **Mini-Mental State Examination (MMSE)**. These ask the patient such memory questions as 'Who is the current prime minister/president?', 'What is the day today?' and 'What is your name?'. In short, these are questions which no non-demented person should get wrong. The more questions the patient answers incorrectly, the greater the degree of their impairment and the more pronounced their illness is held to be. In addition, a questionnaire on the patient's behaviour may be given to a caregiver. This determines the extent to which the patient is still functionally independent, by asking questions such as the degree of help he or she requires in getting dressed. This has the dual advantage of not only giving a further gauge of the patient's degree of impairment but also judging the level of nursing care the patient requires. Scales such as the Blessed and the MSQ can also be used as the illness progresses, to keep a useful check on the general status and needs of the patient.

A more detailed method of describing the level of functioning of the demented patient is provided by Reisberg *et al.*'s (1989a) Functional Assessment Stages, or **FAST**. The method was originally devised to describe the functional status of Alzheimer's disease patients (see later in this chapter). Patients are placed into one of seven categories, with Stages 6 and 7 divided into sub-stages. Stage 1 describes normal functioning. In Stage 2, there are subjective feelings of loss of intellectual power, although these are not perceived as serious by other people. In Stage 3, intellectual impairment (particularly in memory) is evident in complex tasks that previously posed no problems, and in Stage 4 this has extended to relatively complex everyday tasks (e.g. 'ability to handle finances'). Stage 5 is defined as 'deficient performance in choosing the proper clothing to wear', and in Stage 6, the patient is no longer able to dress him- or herself or properly attend to personal hygiene (the stage is divided into five hierarchical sub-stages, ranging from problems with dressing through to faecal incontinence). Stage 7 describes the loss of motor and speech skills (with six sub-stages, beginning with the loss of speech through to 'loss of ability to hold up head'). The authors also place estimates of the length of time a patient is likely to remain in a particular stage if he or she does not die during it (Stage 3 = 7 years; 4 = 2 years; 5 = 18 months; 6 = 2 years 5 months; 7 = 6 years +). A slightly simpler assessment is provided by the **Clinical Dementia Rating (CDR)**, which is a checklist of level of functioning on a variety of tasks (e.g., memory, orientation, behaviour in the home). Based on the scores, the patient is graded as having no dementia, or 'questionable', 'mild', 'moderate', or 'severe' forms of the illness (Berg, 1988). The American Psychiatric Association periodically produces a taxonomy of mental illnesses, which is highly influential. The most recent edition of the **Diagnostic and Statistical Manual of Mental Disorders (DSM-IV)** (American Psychiatric Association, 1994) indicates that in addition to perceptual, intellectual and/or memory impairment sufficient to interfere with daily activities these must be present when the patient is fully awake and with no evidence of intoxication (from alcohol or drugs). The illness is graded by its functional effect: *mild* (no supervision necessary) *moderate* (some supervision necessary) or *severe* (constant supervision required).

It is also worth noting that incidences of **agitation** increase in demented individuals (*c.*60% of all demented patients exhibit it – Eisdorfer, Cohen, and Paveza, 1992). The term refers to a group of symptoms drawn from a large set of agitated behaviours, including aggression (physical and verbal), lack of co-operativeness, shouting, grabbing, restless behaviour, etc. Level of cognitive impairment appears to be a principal predictor (Vance *et al.*, 2003). To some extent agitated behaviour can be controlled by caregivers being trained to respond in an appropriate way (see Roth *et al.*, 2002), including offering positive verbal responses. Certainly this is preferable simply to tranquillising 'difficult' patients.

The different types of dementia (sometimes called dementias of different **aetiologies** or **etiologies**) all have the general characteristics described above. However, within this general decline, each has a unique pattern of dysfunction. We shall now consider the principal forms the illness takes.

Dementia of the Alzheimer type (DAT)

Dementia of the Alzheimer type (DAT) was first diagnosed in 1907 by Alois Alzheimer in a case study of a 51-year-old woman, and is also known as **Alzheimer's disease (AD)**, senile dementia of the Alzheimer type (SDAT), and **primary degenerative dementia (PDD)** as well as dementia of the Alzheimer type (DAT). For the sake of convenience, the latter term is principally used in this book. DAT can occur at any age in adult life, but is incredibly rare before the age of 50, and thereafter the probability rises, following the general rise in incidence for dementia described above. Commentators agree that DAT is the commonest of the dementias, but estimates of the precise proportion of dementias caused by DAT vary considerably, from circa 40 to 80 per cent or more (see Cohen and Dunner, 1980; Hestad *et al.*, 1998; Smyer and Qualls, 1999). In part this variation is due to different regional and national diagnostic techniques, but a figure of about 70 per cent is a not unreasonable average figure.

As with dementia in general, the older the patient, the more advanced the illness usually is when he or she first presents for treatment. The reason for initially seeking help is typically severe memory failure well beyond the scope of everyday experience. This may include forgetting very simple lists or instructions, or getting lost in familiar surroundings, such as a local shopping centre or streets around the home. Standardised memory tests will typically show a gross failure to remember new information for more than a few minutes or even seconds, and short-term memory (STM) measures for digit span and similar may also show a decline. Patients may also show other symptoms, such as **apraxia** (inability to perform skilled movements) or **visual agnosia** (inability to recognise by sight). In some cases, these alone are the cause of the original referral, and the patient's memory may be relatively unscathed. Language may also be intact, although vocabulary may be impoverished. Patients may have difficulty in producing the appropriate words, and may fail to comprehend abstract phrases, such as proverbs. Patients' responses to their symptoms vary. Some are depressed, others apathetic and unconcerned; others are aware of a problem, but either discount it or underestimate its severity. Others develop a paranoia that people are deliberately hiding things.

As the illness progresses, so the severity of the above symptoms increases (though as a longitudinal study by Wilson *et al.*, 2000, notes, there is large individual variability in the rate at which this occurs). Memory for new items is now severely curtailed, often even for items in STM. Memory for remote events, learnt before the onset of the illness, also worsens. Recognition declines, even to the point of being incapable of recognising friends and family (which obviously causes great distress). Language worsens considerably, and **aphasia** (language failure) becomes a key feature of the latter stages of DAT. The patient can have problems producing speech (**Broca's aphasia**), understanding speech (**Wernicke's aphasia**), or both. Speech can be reduced to a few words and a series of garbled speech-like sounds, or can consist of recognisable words produced in a nonsensical order. Sometimes the ability to read aloud is remarkably well preserved, with proper observation of punctuation and intonation (see Raymer and Berndt, 1996). However, patients have typically very poor recall of what they have read (**demented dyslexia**). The external appearance of the patients reflects their inward decline. Without the aid of dedicated helpers, the patients' grooming and general demeanour inevitably worsen. Movement begins to appear crabbed and awkward. A shuffling gait, characteristic of **Parkinsonism** (see Glossary) becomes commonplace. In the terminal stages of the illness, the patient usually falls into an uncommunicative state. Incontinence becomes habitual. Often patients display **Kluver-Bucy syndrome.** This is a set of bizarre behaviours, including **hyperorality** (the urge to put everything seen into the mouth) and the associated problem of **bulimia** (the urge to eat vast quantities of food). The other symptoms of Kluver-Bucy syndrome are visual agnosia, **hyper-metamorphosis** (the compulsive urge to touch everything) and a loss of **affect** (emotion). Death typically occurs about five years or more after the appearance of the first 'major' symptoms (though note there are huge variations between studies, depending on what is counted as a 'major symptom', etc.).[1] Certainly, length of survival after being admitted to institutional care has increased in recent decades (Wood, Whitfield, and Christie, 1995), probably reflecting improvements in general medical care. Death is most commonly ascribed to respiratory failure, presumably exacerbated by the relative immobility of patients in the later stages of the disease (see Burns, 1995).

The description of the stages of the disease has been deliberately kept loose. There is immense variation between patients in the severity of their symptoms, the relative sparing of individual functions, and the length of time patients remain in each stage of the illness. However, a DAT patient who reaches the terminal phase of the disease will at some stage endure all the listed stages. A diagnostic test, specifically designed for DAT, is provided by the **NINCDS-ADRDA criteria**. The initials refer to the 'National Institute of Neurological and Communicative Disorders and Stroke' and the 'Alzheimer's Disease and Related Disorders Association of America', the two bodies who jointly devised the scheme. It provides three levels of certainty about the diagnosis: 'probable', 'possible' or 'definite'. The final judgement can only be given when there is physiological proof from a biopsy or autopsy, so most researchers content themselves with a 'probable' diagnosis. This requires, amongst other factors, proof of functional disability (as measured by the Blessed Dementia Scale and similar), memory loss, 'deficits in two or more areas of cognition', and an absence of indicators of other causes, such as tumour, delirium (see below) and so forth. Katzman *et al.* (1988) note that the DSM criteria are probably equivalent in accuracy.

---

1   A model for predicting whether a DAT patient is likely to die in the following 12 months has been developed by Newcomer *et al.* (2003).

Some older textbooks restrict the use of DAT to cases arising before the age of 60 and use the term **senile dementia** to describe those occurring after this age. Others distinguish between a pre-senile and senile form of DAT (often using the terms 'early onset' and late onset'). It is generally true that the illness is more pronounced (particularly in linguistic deficits – Seltzer and Sherwin, 1983) and progresses faster through the early stages in younger patients (Reisberg *et al.*, 1989a), although, perversely enough, younger patients tend to survive longer in the later stages (e.g. Nielsen *et al.*, 1977). However, the set of symptoms of the two forms, though differing in strength of expression, are arguably equivalent, and many researchers have argued that the older–younger division is specious (see Sulkava, 1982; Sulkava and Amberia, 1982; see Lezak, 1995, for an overview). Other researchers, however, have argued that there is more than one form of DAT. Depending upon the author in question, this can mean that either: (a) there is more than one cause of the same symptoms; (b) the same cause can yield more than one set of symptoms, though they all bear sufficient in common to merit being given the same label; or (c) a permutation of (a) and (b). Added to this is the possibility that patients classified as suffering from DAT in fact have several conditions, which present diagnostic techniques are incapable of teasing apart. For example, at one stage there was thought to be one form of cancer – with improvements in medical science, it is now known that there are many different forms. Likewise, it is now known that the same type of cancerous cells can produce different symptoms in different bodies, and that the same cancer can have several different causes. Thus, the term 'DAT' may be covering a multitude of factors – small wonder, then, that there is such a variability in symptoms. To complicate matters yet further, there is also the issue of the age and intellectual status of the patient. We have seen that younger patients tend to have more pronounced decline. In addition, it is known that patients with higher levels of intellectual and/or linguistic skills are less prone to dementia (see Butler, Ashford and Snowdon, 1996; Hestad *et al.*, 1998; Snowdon *et al.*, 1996). Therefore, in addition to possibly different types of DAT, the progression of the illness may be shaped by the age and IQ of the patient.

Those unfamiliar with neurophysiology are advised to consult Chapter 1 before proceding.

The reason for introducing this element of confusion is more than just demonstrating that there are no easy answers to the question of DAT (or indeed any of the other dementias). It is also to point to extreme caution in interpreting findings of studies of the psychological characteristics of DAT patients. For example, suppose that we take what should be the most objective of measures – namely, the incidence of tissue decay in the brains of DAT patients – and gauge this against their psychological status. DAT patients, by the classical definitions, display characteristic patterns of brain cell decay. Aside from cell loss, some of the cell death leaves behind characteristic bodies, including **neuro-fibrillary tangles** and **senile plaques**, which are groups of dead brain cells which look like tangled string and solid lumps respectively (for some excellent illustrations and a more complete explanation of the same, see Hyman *et al.*, 1993). Cell loss is fairly selective, and is concentrated in the cortex (though the occipital region remains relatively undamaged) and some subcortical regions, principally the amygdala, the hippocampus and the brain stem (Moss and Albert, 1988). It is worth noting that some areas of the central nervous system are often spared, notably the basal ganglia, cerebellum and spinal cord (Petit, 1982). Given this pattern of damage, one would expect intellectual and memory functions to be affected, and indeed, early studies supported this, finding that there was a negative correlation between cell loss and level of intellectual functioning – in other words, as cell death increases, intellectual performance decreases (e.g. Tomlinson, Blessed and Roth, 1968). However, Katzman *et al.* (1988) found that some patients have a high number of plaques but no discernible signs of DAT. Conversely, other studies have found some patients with DAT symptoms in the absence of obvious neurological damage (see Hestad *et al.*, 1998, for a review).

Again, it is known that the output of neurotransmitters from the cholinergic system is severely depleted (Kermis, 1986). Since it is known that deliberately suppressing cholinergic activity impairs memory, it is tempting to assume that the cause of DAT patients' problems is lack of this transmitter. This is called the **cholinergic hypothesis**. However, there is ample evidence that cholinergic depletion does not usually cause *all* the types of memory loss shown in DAT (see Gottfries, 1996; Moss and Albert, 1988). Furthermore, neurotransmitters other than those in the cholinergic system are also known to be significantly depleted (Rossor and Iversen, 1986). Therefore, the cholinergic hypothesis cannot provide a full explanation (although cholinergic therapy may nonetheless be beneficial – see Sirvio, 1999). Taken as a whole, these results could mean one of several things. First, neurological decay may be unrelated to demented symptoms. However, this is so improbable that it can be dismissed. Second, neurological decay may be offset by other factors. For example, it is known that people with higher levels of education are less likely to develop dementing symptoms (it was thought that this was true for all types of dementia, but a study by Gatz *et al.*, 2001, suggests that the phenomenon may only apply to DAT). The preservative effects of a higher level of education may mean that the brain is better 'structured' and so can endure more decay before symptoms manifest themselves. Alternatively, perhaps vulnerable individuals have neural networks that have *always* been less efficient and more vulnerable to damage, causing poorer intellectual performance and thus an early exit from formal education. However, this cannot explain dementing symptoms where there is *no* evidence of decay. Also, Gilleard (1997) argues that the higher the education level, the better the patient may be able to *mask* the symptoms – in other words, the protection afforded by education may not be as great as some other commentators have argued. This suggests a third reason – namely, that underlying the same set of symptoms may be several different causes.

The search for the causes of DAT has an obvious importance, since it may in turn indicate a cure or at least some prophylactic treatments. Given that the illness has several manifestations, it is reasonable to assume that there may be more than one cause. Undoubtedly there is a genetic component in at least *some* cases of DAT, probably caused by the unfortunate combination of several genes rather than a single aberrant gene (Kidson and Chen, 1986). The search for the faulty genetic code is an area of active research. Early research in this area (e.g. Schweber, 1989a; St George-Hyslop *et al.*, 1987) found a flawed structure in chromosome 21, at a location close to that of the damage found in patients with Trisomy 21, the commonest cause of Down syndrome. Many commentators have noted that Down syndrome patients develop DAT-like symptoms in middle age, and that the neuropathology of the patients' brains is very similar to that of DAT patients (e.g. Schweber, 1989b). More recently, several more precise genetic factors have been identified. For example, the **Apoliproprotein E (apoE)** gene[2] based on chromosome 19 has attracted considerable attention. More specifically, a variant of apoE known as apoE e4 appears to confer a significantly greater risk of developing late onset DAT, and even in non-dementing people is associated with a significant worsening of memory in later life (Hofer *et al.*, 2002; Small *et al.*, 2004). However, note that apoE does not account for the majority of late onset DAT cases. Several genetic links to early onset DAT have been found: **amyloid precursor protein (APP)**, a gene located on chromosome 21; **presenilin-1**, a gene located on chromosome 14 and **presenilin-2** located on chromosome 1 (see Bertram and Tanzi, 2004, for a review).

However, although there may be a genetic component to DAT, this does not mean that this is the sole cause. For example, if an early onset form of DAT develops within a family, then transmission of the illness is not automatic. If the son or daughter of a DAT patient develops dementia, then there is approximately a 50 per cent chance that his or her siblings will do likewise. These cases are likely to develop at a pre-senile age (i.e. < 60 years) and develop faster (Heston *et al.*, 1981; see Lezak, 1995, for an overview). Thus, DAT can develop in people with a particular genetic make-up, but it would be wrong to move further from this position to argue that people with 'DAT genes' will *inevitably* become demented provided they live long enough. For example, there is an under evens chance of only one of a pair of identical twins developing DAT (Jarvik, 1988). Since identical twins have an identical genetic structure, clearly more than just genes must cause the disease to occur. The most likely explanation is the **threshold model of dementia**, which states that a person's genetic make-up may predispose them to develop DAT, but it requires something in the environment to trigger the onset of the disease.

2   Note that some authors write apoE as APOE.

A number of candidates for this lurking menace in the environment have been suggested. In recent years, aluminium has been suggested as a likely culprit. This is because brain cells in DAT patients have been found to contain tiny grains of the metal. Some worried people stopped using aluminium cooking utensils and similar; probably a futile gesture, since aluminium is a very common element, present in a great many 'natural' things and foodstuffs. Why DAT patients are especially vulnerable to aluminium is still something of a mystery. It is possible that the aluminium uptake is a symptom rather than a cause of the decline. For example, dying cells within a DAT patient's brain may just happen to absorb aluminium, rather than the aluminium causing the cells to die. This is illustrated by the finding that attempting to restrict aluminium uptake into the brains of DAT patients does not affect the progression of the illness (Shore and Wyatt, 1983). Another proposal is that the illness is caused by a slow-acting virus. It is known that some dementing illnesses such as **kuru** (which affects a few native tribes in Papua New Guinea) can be caught by handling diseased nervous tissue. However, generally the evidence on DAT is inconclusive (Lezak, 1995). A severe blow to the head *may* trigger *some* cases of DAT, but again, the evidence is inconclusive. A final point regarding causes of DAT is worth noting. Even if the causes are identified, they do not necessarily predict the rate of progression of the illness. A longitudinal study by Bäckman *et al.* (2003) found that the only reliable predictor of rate of change in demented patients was the number of other illnesses the patient suffered from.

Vascular dementia

Vascular dementia (VaD) is an umbrella term referring to dementia caused by damage to the blood vessels within the brain. This may be due to a blood vessel becoming blocked by the formation of a clot (**thrombosis**); a detached clot lodging in an artery (causing an **embolism**); or a rupture in the wall of a blood vessel (a **haemorrhage**) causing damage to the surrounding tissue. The damage in turn causes the surrounding brain tissue to die, the dead tissue being called an **infarct**. VaD is the second commonest form of dementia, and together with DAT makes up about 90 per cent of all cases of dementia (Lezak, 1995; Smyer and Qualls, 1999). Nearly all cases of VaD come from a sub-group called **multi-infarct dementia (MID)**. This is characterised by the patient's brain suffering a succession of infarcts, none of which in themselves may cause noticeable changes in behaviour, but which taken together cause dementia to occur. These infarcts can be anywhere in the brain and be relatively random. In some cases they can be concentrated into particular regions of the brain. In **cortical atherosclerotic dementia (CAD)** the damage is largely in the cortex, whilst in **subcortical arteriosclerotic dementia (SAD)** damage is principally in the subcortical regions. As might be predicted, CAD is associated with greater intellectual impairment and SAD with movement disorders (see Metter and Wilson, 1993). Two common forms of SAD are **lacunar strokes** and **Binswanger's disease**, which have similar symptoms though their origins are in damage to different subcortical areas. The identification of MID as a condition distinct from **stroke** (a single **infarction**) is relatively recent (Hachinski *et al.*, 1974). It is worth noting, however, that misdiagnosis of MID patients as stroke victims and vice versa is not unknown (Funkenstein, 1988). The causes of MID are not fully known. Not surprisingly, patients often have a history of cardiovascular (**CV**) problems, and there may also be some familial tendency to MID or stroke. It is also known that a number of CV illnesses can be the trigger for MID (Funkenstein, 1988). The illness is extremely rare before the age of 55, with average onset at 65. A common method of testing for MID is the **Hachinski Ischaemic Score (IS)**, after its inventor (Hachinski *et al.*, 1975). This awards points to the patient based upon the number of symptoms they display, with particularly salient symptoms being weighted to reflect their greater importance.

Because infarcts occur reasonably randomly in MID, the course of the illness is difficult to predict, and symptoms can vary greatly between patients. For example, as with DAT, the simple quantity of brain tissue destroyed by MID bears little relationship to the symptoms produced (see Metter and Wilson, 1993). To quote one researcher, 'there are few findings that can be considered *consistent with* a diagnosis of MID' (LaRue, 1992, p.236 [author's italics]). This is because the areas of the brain controlling different mental functions may decay at different rates (according to where the infarcts most frequently strike). To take an example: suppose that there are areas of the brain called A, B, C, D and E, controlling abilities X, Y, Z, P and Q respectively. One MID patient may show a decline in areas A, B and C, and thus in abilities X,Y and Z. Another patient may have well-preserved areas A and B, but show decline in areas C, D and E, and thus in abilities Z, P and Q. Thus, two patients with the same basic complaint may have radically different symptoms. It will have not escaped some readers' notice that, because infarcts can occur relatively randomly, in some instances the damage they inflict can by chance mimic the effects of dementias of other aetiologies, and thus misdiagnosis is common. Largely because of this, a precise estimate of the incidence of MID is difficult to obtain (see Metter and Wilson, 1993). The problem is confounded by the existence of some forms of dementia in which symptoms of MID, or more generally VaD, coexist with symptoms of DAT – together these are known as **AD-MID**. Alafuzoff *et al.* (1989) suggest that patients with AD-MID display symptoms which are more than just a combination of DAT and MID, but it is possible that the more pronounced of these symptoms are simply the products of an interaction between the two conditions. To even further muddy the waters, some patients with DAT may also have infarcts, which although they appear to occur separately from the atrophy of tissue associated with 'pure' Alzheimer's patients, may exacerbate the condition (see Snowdon *et al.*, 1997).

Nonetheless, there are aspects of 'pure' MID which make it distinguishable from other dementing disorders. For example, the onset of the symptoms can in some cases be quite sudden: there may not be the insidious development seen in other dementias.

However, some MID patients (e.g. Binswanger's disease patients) display a progressive onset, so this is not an infallible identifying feature. MID patients also almost invariably have a history of CV illness. This can be true of other demented patients, but a lengthy history of strokes, high blood pressure and similar will provide a strong indication that MID or another form of VaD is probable. However, the cardinal difference is in MID's development. While patients suffering from other dementias typically show a steady rate of decline, MID patients show a steplike, jerky decline. In other words, they tend to stay at one level of ability (and may even show some temporary improvement) for weeks or months, before suddenly worsening to a lower level. This process then repeats itself, with each decline removing more of the patient's intellectual powers. Because the infarcts tend to occur relatively randomly, the progression of symptoms is hard to predict, although memory is typically an early victim. Progressively more of the patient's intellectual status is whittled away until he or she is reduced to a vegetative state. Death usually occurs from a CV-related illness (such as a heart attack) or opportunistic infection, on average about four years after initial diagnosis.

Other dementias

Although MID and VaD between them account for most cases of dementia, as mentioned above there are nearly 50 other known causes. Of these, the following are perhaps the most often encountered. **Pick's disease** (named after its discoverer) is not commonly a disease of later life, with the average age of onset in the late forties. Atrophy begins and is concentrated in the frontal lobes, spreading to the thalamus, basal ganglia and amygdala (see Lezak, 1995). At a cellular level, neurons often degenerate into **Pick's bodies**, which have a characteristic swollen appearance. Note that some patients can have the same *general* pattern of atrophy as Pick's disease, but lack Pick's bodies. Recent clinical practice is to classify such patients as suffering from **frontal lobe dementia** (which includes other dementias centred on frontal lobe atrophy). The patient usually first presents with problems expected of frontal lobe damage, such as loss of planning skills, ability to think in the abstract, and so forth. Kluver-Bucy syndrome usually manifests itself early in the course of the illness (as opposed to the late stages of DAT). It may also incorporate compulsive sexual behaviour, often without regard for social propriety. As the disease progresses, dementing symptoms akin to DAT begin to manifest themselves. Often language is more impaired than memory, but this is not an infallible rule. Pick's patients are also more prone to **confabulating** (essentially, making up stories or implausible explanations to cover up gaps in memory or other skills), something rarely seen in MID or DAT patients. In the terminal stages, the patient is reduced to a vegetative state. Death is typically about four years after the onset of the first symptoms.

Creutzfeldt-Jakob disease (CJD) is a very rare illness, affecting approximately one in a million people. The illness typically manifests itself first as a movement disorder before intellectual deterioration begins. The illness is atypical of dementias in two main respects – first, death is usually swifter (c.one year after onset of symptoms), and second, it is known that it is contracted via an infection. At the time of writing, CJD is of especial interest because a new variant of the disease (nvCJD) was discovered in the 1990s. So far, only about 120 or so individuals have contracted it. There is strong evidence that the infection source may be beef contaminated with **bovine spongiform encephalopathy (BSE)**, an infective agent which produces symptoms similar to CJD in cattle. Although some of the more excitable media speculations about an epidemic of nvCJD have so far proved unfounded and now even seem unrealistic, the fact that dementia may be contracted through eating a common foodstuff is clearly alarming.

Huntington's disease (a.k.a. Huntington's chorea) is not considered to be a dementia by all commentators. Like CJD it is relatively rare, but it tends to cluster in families, indicating a strong genetic component. Also like CJD, the early symptoms of the illness are disturbances of movement, often taking the form of writhing and twitching. Subsequently, patients develop dementing symptoms, although the decline can also mimic schizophrenia (Kermis, 1986). Patients with Huntington's disease tend to last longer than patients with other dementias, typical life expectancy after the appearance of the first symptoms being circa 15 years. The illness can strike at any age, but onset in middle age is commonest.

Parkinson's disease (PD) is also chiefly characterised by movement disorders, including a characteristic shuffling gait and tremors. However, there is a higher than average risk that PD patients will also develop dementia (about 10–15%: Lezak, 1995; Moss and Albert, 1988). It should be noted that many DAT patients develop PD-like symptoms as their illness progresses. The most salient difference between PD and DAT patients is that linguistic skills are usually considerably better preserved (or even unaffected) in PD (LaRue, 1992).

Dementia can also appear as a symptom of other illnesses, such as **normal pressure hydrocephalus** (where cerebrospinal fluid gets trapped in the brain instead of draining away, putting destructive pressure on the brain tissue), brain tumours and AIDS; and also as a result of long-term exposure to toxic chemicals and chronic alcohol abuse.

Cortical and subcortical dementias

Some commentators prefer to categorise dementias according to whether the principal atrophy is in the cortex (the **cortical dementias**) or in the subcortical regions (the **subcortical dementias**). By this reckoning, the commonest cortical dementias are DAT and Pick's disease, and the commonest subcortical dementias are PD and Huntington's disease (with types of VaD belonging to either group, depending upon the particular form in question). Since the cortex is principally concerned with higher intellectual functions and the subcortex with the control of movement, emotion and so forth (see Chapter 1), there should be a functional division between the two groups, and this is what is typically found. Thus, cortical dementias manifest themselves most strikingly as disorders of thought, memory and language, with some movement disturbances as relatively minor symptoms, whereas subcortical dementias are very much characterised by problems with movement (for this reason amongst others, some commentators have argued that subcortical dementias are not 'true' dementias). Subcortical dementias also tend to strike before the onset of later life. There is an excellent review of the issue by Peretz and Cummings (1988).

Illnesses which can be confused with dementia

An assortment of conditions can give the appearance of dementia but in fact have other causes. The two commonest of these are both treatable, unlike the dementias, and for this reason are sometimes called the **reversible dementias**. The first of these is **pseudodementia**. This can arise in some older people who suffer severe depression (see below). In becoming depressed, the patient loses motivation and this is reflected in very poor scores on tests of memory and intellect. This, and their general lack of interest in their surroundings, can provide an excellent imitation of dementia. Indeed, some commentators argue that the impersonation is so good that the term 'pseudodementia' is misleading and that the illness should be classified as a form of 'true' dementia. However, there are several key differences between pseudodementia and the genuine article. First, pseudodemented patients are usually well orientated in time and space; for example, they know where they are, what day of the week it is, why they are being tested, and so forth. Second, they are also typically aware that they are performing badly on memory and intellectual tests. Third, pseudodemented patients' intellectual performance typically fluctuates in tandem with their level of depression, and improves as their depression is treated (Jenike, 1988; LaRue, 1992). However, it would be misleading to suppose that depression and 'genuine' dementia have no connection. Between 20 and 30 per cent of patients with DAT, MID, or other dementing symptoms caused by atrophy also have some symptoms of depression (e.g. Marsden and Harrison, 1972; see also Boland et al., 1996; Carlson, Sherwin and Chertkow, 2000) which follow a relatively predictable pattern (Gilley et al., 2004). Again, it is salient to note that one study found that 57 per cent of older patients referred for treatment for depression subsequently developed dementia (Reding, Haycox and Blas, 1985). In other words, severely depressed older people may display pseudodementia, but, equally, a high proportion of 'genuinely' demented patients may also display depression.

The other major impersonator of dementia is **delirium**, also known as **acute confusional state (ACS)**. Delirium is typically rapid in onset (usually a matter of hours or days). The age groups most at risk are children and older adults. There are many possible causes, including fever, infection, (legally prescribed) drug intoxication, stroke and inadequate diet (particularly one with a deficit of vitamin B12). Most cases of delirium are cured by treating the underlying causes. Delirious patients display poor intellectual and memory skills, and also tend to be either excessively languid (**hypoactive delirium**), agitated or anxious (**hyperactive delirium**) or a mixture of both (**mixed delirium**). It is also possible for the patient to exhibit no 'obvious' behavioural symptoms. However, generally, rambling or incoherent speech is also a common feature. To this extent, a patient with delirium can resemble, for example, a demented patient, a depressed patient or a very anxious patient, and misdiagnosis is relatively common (see Foreman and Milisen, 2004). This can have serious consequences. For example, a hyperactive delirium patient may have a serious underlying physical condition that needs urgent treatment; mistaking this for a severe anxiety attack and sedating the patient could be life threatening. However, a major difference between delirium and dementia, other than the rapid onset of the former, is that many delirious patients suffer from **illusions** (distorted perceptions of the world around them). Illusions are relatively rare in dementia, in spite of some popular misconceptions on this subject. In addition, attention span in delirium is limited, whereas (surprisingly) it is often reasonably well preserved in demented patients. Various diagnostic tests, which act as a checklist of symptoms (e.g. the **Delirium Rating Scale**) are available. Note, however, that delirium can, and does, occur in demented patients (see Cole, 2004; Marengoni, Calíbrese and Cossi, 2004). Delirium in an older adult indicates a higher probability of serious illness and imminent mortality. For example, Pitkala *et al.* (2005) found that older patients suffering from delirium had an almost 75 per cent greater chance of dying in the subsequent year than did non-delirious controls.

Problems with diagnosis and testing

Clinicians tend to diagnose dementia by default. In other words, a patient is labelled as demented after other possibilities (depression, fever, tumours, etc.) have been ruled out. Discrimination between dementia and pronounced (but non-dementing) ageing change is fraught with problems when dementia is only in its early stages (see Woods, 1999, for an excellent discussion of this). To illustrate this, consider the following remarkable fact: a study by Löppönen *et al.* (2003) found that a sample of Finnish doctors responsible for primary health care had failed to identify *over half* of the cases of dementia amongst the patients in their care. However, even once dementia has been identified, diagnosis of the *type* of dementia is fraught with equal, if not larger, problems. Because different dementias can share similar sets of symptoms, accuracy is often low, with a rate of 30–50 per cent of misdiagnosed cases being not unknown (see Gurland and Toner, 1983; Lezak, 1995; Roth, 1979). It might be supposed that brain scanning techniques might improve identification, and to some extent they do, but it has already been seen that first, some patients' physical and psychological symptoms do not 'match up', and second, within the same disease several patterns of atrophy may be found, which may be confused with dementias of different aetiologies (see Charletta, Bennett and Wilson, 1993). This raises problems for treatment. If diagnosis is uncertain, then the treatment given may be inappropriate. Since drug therapy for dementia is still in its fledgeling stages, this means that getting accurate feedback on the efficacy of treatments is very difficult indeed. Aside from this, there is the equally important consideration that the relatives of demented patients cannot be given an accurate prognosis of the expected length of survival, the likely path of the decline, and so forth.

From a researcher's viewpoint, the lack of accurate diagnoses means that it is very difficult, if not downright impossible, to assemble a group of patients and know for certain that they are all suffering from the same form of dementia. Thus, finding a difference between a group of patients suffering from DAT and another suffering from MID on a particular test may mean there is a genuine difference between DAT and MID patients on the skill measured by that test. However, this conclusion must be weighed against the consideration that at least some of the DAT group may be suffering from MID and vice versa. Another problem is in matching patients with different forms of dementia. It is not really sufficient to assemble a group of DAT patients, a group of MID patients and compare them, without also considering how long the patients in each group have been diagnosed as suffering from their respective illnesses. If, for example, the MID patients have had the illness longer than the DAT patients, how can we be sure that any difference between the groups is not due simply to the length of having the illness rather than any intrinsic difference between DAT and MID? Again, are the groups of the same average age – if not, any difference might be due simply to ageing rather than the illness. Conversely, if the groups are of the same average age, are they typical of their illness groups? For example, suppose that on average dementia A strikes at 60 years of age, and dementia B at 70. If we test an A group and B group, and both have an average age of 70, how can we be sure that there is not something slightly unusual about the A group (in other words, is it truly representative?). To take yet another possible problem, suppose that it is found that patients with, for example, DAT, are very bad at remembering spoken words. It might be supposed that this indicates a poor verbal memory. However, dementia, and particularly DAT, is Murphy's Law applied to intellectual functioning – in other words, whatever can go wrong *will* go wrong. Thus, finding a failure of verbal memory may mean there is a decline in verbal memory, but perhaps a decline in linguistic skills meant that the patient simply did not understand the test instructions.

None of these problems is necessarily insurmountable, but they do indicate that extreme caution must be taken in interpreting the results of studies of dementia. Certainly it is nearly always unwise to pursue points in any great detail, simply because the initial diagnosis and the problems of accurately comparing different patient groups are too problematic for more than fairly general statements to be made with any certainty.

Memory changes in dementia

Since memory loss is a defining feature of most forms of dementia, it is unsurprising to note that many studies have found general deterioration of memory in patients with dementia, and that generally, the more advanced the disease, the worse the memory. Indeed, one recent study has argued that the majority of appreciable memory loss in older adults is indicative of the pre-clinical stages of dementia (Sliwinski *et al.*, 2003). However, general changes in memory are not in other instances particularly interesting, since this is simply restating the definition of dementia. Of greater interest are differences between dementias in the severity of memory loss and the degree to which different types of memory are spared or lost relative to each other within the same illness. Unsurprisingly, most of this research has concentrated on DAT.

It can be readily established that, as for non-dementing older people, DAT patients' performance on short-term memory (STM) tasks worsen the harder the memory task set (e.g. Nebes, 1992). A sizeable cause of this deficit may be an encoding problem. For example, Kopelman (1985) found that DAT patients could retain memories as well as non-dementing participants, provided they were given (a lot) more opportunities to rehearse the to-be-remembered (TBR) items. Thus, if information can get into a long-term store in DAT patients' memories, then there is a reasonable possibility that it will be retained. Further evidence for this assumption comes from Becker *et al.* (1987), who found that, within 30 seconds of being given a set of TBR items, DAT patients had forgotten a significant proportion of them. However, those items which *were* remembered after 30 seconds had the same probability of being remembered 30 *minutes* later, as did items which non-dementing control participants remembered after 30 seconds (see also Hulme, Lee and Brown, 1993). Again, there is evidence that memory stores are still functioning in the same qualitative manner as those of non-dementing participants'. For example, memory of verbal materials is presumed by most commentators to be stored on a phonological loop. This mental mechanism is believed to work not unlike a 'voice in the head' talking on to a continuous tape loop. As has been demonstrated on many occasions in non-dementing participants (see Baddeley, 1986), if given a set of TBR items which sound similar (e.g. *B*, *C*, *D*, *V*, *G*), the phonological loop stores them less well than when faced with dissimilar-sounding items (e.g. *H*, *W*, *J*, *Y*, *E*). DAT patients remember less overall, but are relatively speaking just as prone to having memory lowered by phonological similarities in TBR items (Morris, 1984).

An optimistic interpretation of this is that if encoding problems could be overcome, DAT patients' amnesia could be overcome. However, studies such as Kopelman's have tended to use patients in the very early stages of the illness. What is being stated is that encoding is the first aspect of memory to decline – where it has led, other aspects of memory may follow. For example, Collette et al. (1999) report that, whilst the phonological loop is unimpaired in early DAT, there is a decline in patients with more advanced forms of the disease. The same general finding of inexorable worsening is true for most other dementing illnesses. For example, Martone et al. (1984) found comparable encoding problems in Huntington's disease patients. Perhaps not surprisingly, patients with pseudodementia behave like non-dementing older participants, though with an overall lower memory span (e.g. Gibson, 1981; Miller and Lewis, 1977).

At least in the early stages of DAT, Baddeley (1986) and other commentators have argued that the slave systems in working memory are functioning relatively unscathed, and that the deficit is in the central executive. There is considerable evidence that when given a STM task and a simultaneous distracting task, DAT patients' memory spans get disproportionately worse the harder the distracting task is made (Morris, 1986). This strongly indicates a deficit in the central executive, since one of its main functions is to control and co-ordinate intellectual and memory tasks (Baddeley et al., 1991; Morris, 1994; Morris and Kopelman, 1986). The central executive is felt to be anatomically based in the frontal lobes (Baddeley, 1986), an area known to be badly affected in DAT.

An important caveat to the above concerns the apparent similarity between dementing and non-dementing ageing effects on working memory. In both cases, a decline in memory capacity seems to be attributable to failings in the central executive and more generally, the frontal lobes. However, as Baddeley (1986) and other commentators have pointed out, the decline in non-dementing older people is largely quantitative only – in other words, the processes at work in non-dementing older adults are largely the same as those at work in younger adults. An illustration of this is provided by Stuart-Hamilton, Rabbitt and Huddy (1988), who tested groups of MID, DAT and non-dementing older adults with very low IQ test scores. The researchers gave the participants the task of remembering sequences of movements in which an array of shapes had to be tapped in the order prescribed by the experimenter. MID and non-dementing participants remembered longer sequences when the shapes were coloured and had different outlines than when the shapes were all black squares of identical size. For DAT patients, the reverse was true. This indicates that the variety introduced by the colour and shape aids non-dementing people but hinders DAT patients. It is hypothesised that this was because colour and shape can be used as extra memory cues by non-dementing people, but the DAT patients cannot cope with the extra information this presents, and so in effect get confused. However, of key interest here is that DAT patients and non-dementing older participants performed in qualitatively different ways.

Remote memory is also affected by dementia. Although it is sometimes popularly supposed that demented patients have no memory for yesterday but a pin-sharp recall of events from their childhood, this is not the case (except in the very early stages of the illness when the memory problem may be for new information alone). Formal laboratory studies have demonstrated that remote memory for famous names and events is significantly worse than for non-dementing older people (e.g. Corkin *et al.*, 1984; Wilson, Kaszniak and Fox, 1981), and declines at a greater rate than autobiographical memory (Greene and Hodges, 1996b). Some studies have found that memory for more distant events is better than for recent ones (see Nebes, 1992), but others (e.g. Corkin *et al.*, 1984; Greene and Hodges, 1996a) have found memory to be better for recent events, or for items from different time periods to be remembered equally well (Wilson *et al.*, 1981). The pattern of recall produced may rest on the types of names and events used, and may simply be an experimental artefact. However, what is certain is that, overall, remote memory is worse in demented patients. Whilst such findings do not completely disprove the argument that storage and retrieval mechanisms are intact in demented patients, and that the principal deficit is in encoding, they certainly raise interesting questions about why events stored long before the onset of illness can now not be retrieved if storage and retrieval are intact. Greene, Hodges and Baddeley (1995) attributed their finding of a decline in autobiographical memory in DAT patients to a retrieval problem, in turn linking this to a failure of the central executive.

The above studies raise the question of whether demented patients' memory problems can be alleviated. Certainly some common-sense procedures seem to help. For example, priming the patient with the first letter of a TBR item produces a disproportionate improvement in the memory performance of demented patients (e.g. Davis and Mumford, 1984; Miller, 1975). However, priming has to be fairly unsubtle to be efficacious. For example, priming with a word semantically related to the TBR item, or giving lists of words semantically related to each other, has no advantageous effect on dementing patients, though non-dementing older adults are advantaged by this (e.g. Davis and Mumford, 1984).

Linguistic skills and semantic processes

One of the commonest measures of linguistic skills is a simple naming task in which the patient must identify pictures of common objects. Failure to name objects (**anomia**) is a common first symptom of DAT, and DAT patients are notably disadvantaged when compared with not only non-dementing controls but also patients with Huntington's disease, and PD and MID patients (Bayles and Tomoeda, 1983; Chan *et al.* 1995; Schram, Rubert and Loewenstein, 1995). It is suggested that this deficit is in part due to the degeneration of the storage of this information. In a similar vein, Chan *et al.* (1995) found that the manner in which semantic interrelationships are stored is radically different in DAT patients compared with non-dementing participants and patients with Huntington's disease. Several researchers (e.g. Martin and Fedio, 1983; Schwartz, Marin and Saffran, 1979; Warrington, 1975) found that, as DAT progresses, words for specific items and events tend to be lost before more general words, implying a loss of detail from the system. A recent ingenious study by Garrard *et al.* (2005) plots the decline in the linguistic skills of Iris Murdoch, the noted novelist, as she gradually succumbed to the effects of DAT. The researchers note that a striking deficit was the gradual impoverishment of vocabulary (Murdoch's early works were noted for their rich vocabulary).

A cautionary note about measuring the size of the decline in DAT patients is raised by Nicholas *et al.* (1996), who argue that the disproportionate deficit may be due to the method chosen to score errors, and that another arguably equally viable method shows no especial disadvantage. Other researchers have also argued that the size of the difference can be ameliorated by the test methods used (see Nebes, 1992; Nebes and Brady, 1990). However, this is largely a debate about the magnitude of the effect, not the effect itself. Certainly an especial problem with semantic memory may explain the failure of semantic cues to facilitate memory in DAT patients (though see Carlesimo *et al.*, 1995). The semantic deficit may also in part be due to a decline in working memory, particularly in judgements of phrases or similar, where several words must be kept in mind simultaneously (see Kemper, 1997). Brain scans reveal a complex pattern of atrophy associated with different linguistic deficits (see Harasty *et al.*, 1999; Hirono *et al.*, 1998; Keilp *et al.*, 1999).

Linguistic problems are not confined to anomia and related semantic problems, however, and, generally, linguistic skills worsen as DAT progresses. For example, Grossman *et al.* (1995) found that DAT patients were significantly poorer on a range of linguistic tasks (sentence–picture matching, judgements of the grammatical acceptability of sentences, sentence completion), which was not explicable by memory deficits nor indeed the supposed severity of the illness (though note that linguistic deficits in DAT do not appear with the same severity at the same stage in all patients). Common symptoms include **intrusions** (inserting inappropriate words or phrases), **perseverations** (repeating the same phrase, word, or part of a word) and **circumlocution** (talking around the subject). Note, however, that Waters and Caplan (2002) found no especial problems in syntactic processing in their study of DAT patients (though it should also be noted that the patients were in the relatively early stages of the illness).

Not all linguistic skills will decline at the same rate, however. For example, **phonology** (awareness of speech sounds, as shown, for example in correct pronunciation), and **morphology** (knowledge of the roots of words) are generally well preserved in DAT (e.g. Appell, Kertesz and Fisman, 1982). Again, reading (at least of single words) is assumed to be relatively well-preserved in at least the early stages of DAT. This is countered by Patterson, Graham and Hodges (1994) and Storandt, Stone and LaBarge (1995), who found significant deficits in NART performance (see Chapter 4) in a group of patients with very mild DAT. This contradicts the accepted wisdom of using the NART as a gauge of pre-illness intelligence. However, other researchers (e.g. Law and O'Carroll, 1998) have found relatively little change. Glosser, Grugan and Friedman (1999) suggest that what deficit there is may be due to other intellectual and/or memory problems rather than a specific reading deficit, whilst Strain *et al.* (1998) concluded from their study that a reading deficit only occurs when there has been an appreciable decline in semantic memory.

Visuo-spatial skills

Declines in visuo-spatial skills have been found in patients with very mild DAT, even when memory demands of the task are minimised (Bucks and Willison, 1997; Kaskie and Storandt, 1995). Armstrong and Cloud (1998) attribute the decline to the reduced efficiency of components of the working memory system. Some visuo-spatial skills are not reliable discriminators between DAT and non-dementing people, however. For example, a commonly used task is the **clock drawing test (CDT)**, in which the participant must copy an analogue clock face. Lee *et al.* (1996) found that, although DAT patients' performance declined the more severe their dementia became, in the very early stages of the illness their performance was not always distinguishable from non-dementing participants. Cahn *et al.* (1996) also question the use of the CDT as a screening test when used on its own. However, such concerns over diagnostic accuracy of one test should not blind the observer to the simple general truth that visuo-spatial skills are generally very poor in DAT (see Lezak, 1995). This can be seen in skills as diverse as copying simple displays of crosses (Grossi and Orsini, 1978) and iconic memory (Coyne, Liss and Geckler 1984; Moscovitch, 1982; Schlotterer *et al.*, 1984). Nor should it be supposed that problems are only at a relatively complex level of processing. For example, Neargarder *et al.* (2003) demonstrated that DAT patients show a significant decline in a process as 'basic' as the contrast sensitivity function (see Chapter 1). Again, Pache *et al.* (2003) found that DAT patients had significantly lower scores on measures of colour vision tests than did age-matched controls. Interestingly, the level of deficit was independent of degree of dementing decline.

Olfaction

Olfactory functions (i.e. smell) worsen in DAT. For example, Nordin and Murphy (1996) found that DAT patients had a higher odour threshold (i.e. the smell had to be more powerful before it was detected) and poorer memory for smells. In a review of the literature, Thompson, Knee and Golden (1998) conclude that olfactory problems are effective in distinguishing between DAT patients and non-dementing older adults, and may also be effective in distinguishing DAT from some other forms of dementia (e.g. Huntington's disease: see Murphy, 1999; though not e.g. Parkinson's disease: see Mesholam *et al.*, 1998).

Predicting dementia

Since patients with dementia show progressive deterioration it is intuitively obvious that this deterioration must have a beginning and from this it may be deduced that at some point an unfortunate individual may be displaying the very early symptoms of dementia without realising it. Andel *et al.* (2001) conducted a longitudinal study in which older identical twins were tested on a variety of cognitive measures and then followed up. In some cases, one twin developed dementia whilst the other did not. In these instances, the demented twin's cognitive scores were significantly lower than the non-demented twin's at the first test session (i.e. when everything still appeared 'normal'). More specifically, the authors of the study argue that it is mental processes requiring conscious control that show especial decline. Moreover, if the non-dementing twins' scores are compared with age-matched controls, then they show a decline, suggesting that the non-dementing twins may also be on the edge of developing dementia as well. Some researchers (e.g. Meguro *et al.*, 2001) have argued that the very early decline in dementia is also distinct from that of senescent ageing. Balsis, Carpenter and Storandt (2005) present evidence that personality changes may also occur very early in the course of DAT. Using data from a longitudinal study, they found that personality changes were often observable before a clinical diagnosis of DAT had been made. Kemper *et al.* (2001), in a longitudinal study of writing across the lifespan in a group of nuns, found that those who developed dementia had an initially less complex style of written language. There is thus clear evidence from a variety of sources that dementia is preceded by notable psychological changes. However, it is difficult to see what diagnostic value much of this information provides. At an individual level, early changes *may* indicate dementing change, but can still functionally fall within normal parameters. And since by definition early changes are slight, it is difficult to see how an individual or a health care professional would notice them unless everyone was tested and retested at regular intervals so that any change could be objectively identified.

The effect on caregivers

All forms of illness can have negative effects not just on patients but also on those family members and friends who look after them. However, the effect may be particularly strong on caregivers for demented patients, because the nature of the illness means that the patient cannot give adequate feedback. It takes little imagination to envisage the unique stress induced by looking after a spouse or a parent who needs constant attention and yet who cannot even recognise their caregiver. Levesque, Ducharme and Lachance (1999) demonstrated in a large-scale study of caregivers that the stresses experienced by people looking after demented patients are significantly greater than in caring for patients with other illnesses. Also, the caregiver burden is generally higher with younger than older demented patients (Freyne et al., 1999), and VaD patients present greater problems than DAT patients in the early stages of the illnesses, with a reversal in the later stages (Vetter et al., 1999).

Not surprisingly, there is a large body of evidence that caring for a demented relative usually results in significantly higher levels of depression, stress and other related health problems (e.g. Coppel et al., 1985; Kennedy, Kiecold-Glaser and Glaser, 1988; Morrisey et al., 1990). This tends to worsen the more severe the patient's problem behaviours become (Hooker et al., 2002; Neundorfer et al., 2001). Suicide risk is also higher (Fry, 1986). It should also be noted that because of the immense pressure the caregiver is placed under, elder abuse is not uncommon (e.g. Compton, Flanagan and Gregg, 1997; Cooney and Wrigley, 1996; see Wolf, R.S., 1997, for an overview). Note that this does not necessarily imply violence, but may include nonetheless undesirable behaviours such as neglect (see Pritchard, 1995).

The social role of the caregiver is a key determinant of the level of adverse effects experienced. Morrisey et al. (1990) found that spousal caregivers who did not have paid employment (they were homemakers) cited loss of social contacts and disruption to household chores (as well as the severity of the spouse's disability) as the chief causes of depression. Caregivers in paid employment cited the severity of the spouse's disability as less serious, and the disruption to household chores as more serious than the homemakers. Curiously, a large number of friends and relatives alleviated the homemaker's depression, but made it worse for the paid workers. Morrisey et al. concluded that this was because the paid workers' friends included workplace colleagues who may inadvertently add stress by offering social interaction, but not practical help. Schulz and Williamson (1991), in a two-year longitudinal study, found that male caregivers tended to get more depressed as time passed, whilst female caregivers remained at the same level. These findings might be compromised by not knowing the levels of depression prior to the onset of the illness, but Dura, Stukenberg and Kiecolt-Glaser (1991), with greater baseline measures, also found that depression increased over time.

Some factors can make a difference to the well-being of caregivers. For example, practical assistance and financial security (e.g. Pruchno and Kleban, 1993) are obvious examples. Again, providing training for caregivers can be advantageous (see Teri, 1999; and commentary by Gilhooly, 1999). Again, there are probable cultural differences. In a review of the literature, Connell and Gibson (1997) found that in non-white communities, caregiving is more likely to be by a younger relative or friend rather than the spouse, and that generally, a lower negative state is reported. Religious faith and practice also played a stronger role.

However, at the level of individuals, the relationship is not necessarily clear cut. For example, Rivera et al. (1991) found no difference between depressed and non-depressed caregivers in their level of satisfaction with the support offered. This indicates that individual differences in the psychological characteristics of the caregivers may also play a role. For example, Cicirelli (1993) found that daughters caring for their mothers who felt a strong feeling of emotional attachment reported a lower level of burden, whilst feelings of obligation increased this. Again, Rapp et al. (1998) found that the level of social resourcefulness displayed by individual caregivers was significantly related not only to their level and type of social interaction, but also their level of well-being.

It is perhaps worth finally noting the arguably more pressing matter that generally caregivers living in countries such as the UK must endure health and welfare systems that will often happily bleed them white before paying out for any treatment themselves. The simple truth is that the main reason for caregiver burden is that unless a caregiver is very rich, he or she cannot afford to pay for others to share the load.

Summary and overview

Dementia is a progressive loss of memory, intellectual and linguistic skills, usually accompanied by radical changes in personality and sometimes in motor skills. Symptoms vary markedly between patients, but generally the different dementias are distinguishable by their patterns of development. Several illnesses can be confused with dementia because of a superficial similarity of symptoms, but these can usually be easily identified. At a physical level, dementias often differ in patterns and type of atrophy, but, as has been seen, the correlation between damage and psychological symptoms is far from watertight. Almost all intellectual functions decline in dementia (particularly DAT, where research has been most concentrated). Although there are some interesting qualitative differences in functioning, it should be noted that these are usually only found in patients in the very early stages of the illness – as the disease progresses, patients usually lack sufficient psychological skills to comprehend or perform the tasks presented to them. It must also be remembered that in dementia, like many other illnesses, it is not only the patient who suffers, and that the disease can be a great source of stress and burden to caregivers.

In closing this section, it is worth noting that the severity and awfulness of dementia's symptoms can lead to an exaggerated view of its prevalence. Thus, it is worth repeating that only 5–6 per cent of all older people will develop dementing symptoms, and that many will be only mildly demented at death. It is also inaccurate to perceive dementia as solely a disease of later life, as though it is an inevitable consequence of ageing. As has been seen, all dementias can begin prior to the onset of later life, and some, indeed, are rarely seen past the age of 65. Furthermore, the psychological performances of demented patients are qualitatively different from those of non-dementing older people, thereby demonstrating that dementia is not a natural extension of the ageing process. Woods (1999) amongst others (e.g. Cohen, 1996) has suggested that, because dementia in the very early stages is hard to distinguish from non-dementing ageing, a continuum exists. This is plausible, but one could equally argue that at the start of many illnesses, a patient still shares many of the characteristics of a well person. However, that does not stop them having a distinctly different state of health.

Depression

Depression is a condition which almost all people experience in a relatively mild form many times in their lives. In most cases, the feeling of melancholy is in reaction to a specific event, disperses in a few days, and would not typically be considered a mental illness. Depression meriting clinical attention is long-lasting, and severe enough to interfere with normal functioning. It is important to stress that clinical depression is not solely 'feeling down' – the patient is in effect incapacitated by the condition. In addition to a depressed mood, he or she is typically lacking in both mental and physical energy to an extreme degree, has irrational feelings of worthlessness and/or guilt, and may have preoccupations with dying and suicide (generally, older patients have a greater preponderance of physical symptoms – Caine *et al.*, 1994). Depression of this magnitude is far less common in later life than in any other age group; however, isolated *symptoms* of depression are far more frequent (Kasl-Godley, Gatz and Fiske, 1998; Smyer and Qualls, 1999).[3] The latter finding is probably due to older people being exposed to a higher proportion of depressing events, such as bereavement, painful illness, and so on. It is also worth noting that, although some of the key features of depression experienced by sufferers are reasonably similar across the lifespan (Nolen-Hoeksema and Ahrens, 2002),

---

3   Freudenstein *et al.* (2001) argue that depression amongst non-responders to population surveys (which obviously goes unreported) may lead to an underestimate of the true size of the problem.

older depressed people carry the unique risk of developing pseudodementia (see above; estimates of the prevalence of pseudodementia vary wildly between studies; however, Kasl-Godley, Gatz and Fiske's estimate of *c.*11% is a plausible average). This can hamper making an accurate diagnosis (see above and also Lezak, 1995).

Causes of depression in later life are often attributed (unsurprisingly) to stressful and negative events. For example, bereavement is known to cause depressive symptoms (see Chapter 5), though these in most instances are relatively short-lasting and are not typically apparent after one year (see Kasl-Godley *et al.*, 1998; Smyer and Qualls, 1999; Woods, 1999). Again, illness and medical treatment side-effects can cause or exacerbate depression in some patients (see Sadavoy *et al.*, 1995). Penninx *et al.* (1996) report that depressive symptoms increase with the number of illnesses from which the patient suffers. In addition, some diseases seems to be more conducive to depression than others: perhaps unsurprisingly, conditions which create chronic pain, such as arthritis, were found to be more likely to be associated with depression than were serious but less painful conditions such as diabetes. Beekman *et al.* (1997) argue that an even stronger predictor of depression is level of physical health as opposed to disease; in a similar vein, Palinkas, Wingard and Barrett-Connor (1996) found depression to be significantly greater in obese older people. Psychological status may also be an important factor in some cases, with various real or imaginary declines in capabilities, such as dementia (e.g. Forsell and Winblad, 1998; also see above) and memory loss (e.g. Collins and Abeles, 1996; see also Chapter 3) correlated with depressive symptoms.

More generally, factors such as perceived level of social support (Taylor and Lynch, 2004), financial problems (e.g. West, Reed and Gildengorin, 1998), genetic inheritance (Carmelli *et al.*, 2000), perceived (rather than actual) health (Hong, Zarit and Malmberg, 2004), perceived level of informal care (Wolff and Agree, 2004), apparent failure or stalling of recovery after an injury (Scaf-Klomp *et al.*, 2003), level of physical activity (Fukukawa, Nakashima, Tsuboi, Kozakai *et al.*, 2004), having to give up an activity because of failing health (Benyamini and Lomranz, 2004), low level or lack of religious faith (see Braam *et al.*, 1997), negative life events (Kraaij, Arensman and Spinhoven, 2002) or long-term social and relationship problems (e.g. Kraaij, Kremers and Arensman, 1997) also contribute to the level of depression.. Factors can act individually or in combination. For example, Harris *et al.* (2003) found that level of disability, health, socio-economic status, feeling of control and social support all were separate predictors of depression. As evidence for more complex effects, Fukukawa, Nakashima, Tsuboi, Niino *et al.* (2004) demonstrated that the quality of familial relations could act as a buffer between health problems and depressive symptoms. Furthermore, there is a danger of the depression interacting with the cause (e.g. a person may become depressed because of relationship difficulties, but their depression may in turn make the relationship worse, thereby increasing the depression, and so on). A caveat to this is that evidence from a longitudinal study by Meeks, Murrell and Mehl (2000) argues that for depression to have an effect on health, it must be long-lasting – a relatively short bout of depression does not have an appreciable effect. Another point is raised by a longitudinal study by Fiske, Gatz and Pedersen (2003) which found that (unsurprisingly) negative life events in the past were related to current depression levels. However, of greater interest is that level of depression predicted the number of negative life events likely to occur in the future. In other words, once a person was depressed, a higher number of bad things were likely to happen to worsen the situation still further.

Also (perhaps unsurprisingly) institutionalised older adults have major depression in much higher proportions: for example, in the USA, rates run at circa 10 per cent (see Blazer, 1993, 1994), compared with the national average of approximately 1 per cent for non-institutionalised older people. Other studies have found higher rates of incidence of depression in non-institutionalised older people in the general population (e.g. c.4% – Forsell and Winblad, 1998; Lindesay, Briggs and Murphy, 1989), probably because of differences in samples chosen and the diagnostic criteria used.

There is little age difference in responsivity to treatment, with the majority of both younger and older depressed patients recovering (approximately 60% permanently, 20% with a relapse – Kasl-Godley, Gatz and Fiske, 1998; see also Alexopoulos et al., 1996; Burvill, Stampfer and Hall, 1995; Tuma, 1996).[4] Increased exercise also appears to be beneficial to older depressed people (Penninx et al., 2002). However, the outlook on suicides, which typically are preceded by depression, is far less optimistic. With the exception of Poland, the highest suicide rates in all World Health Organization countries are in the over-75s (De Leo, 1997). This may come as a surprise to some readers, as a strong impression created by the media is that suicide is a younger person's death. To some extent this is true – suicide is one of the commonest causes of death in teenagers. However, this is a matter of proportions – because the death rate amongst teenagers is very low (in industrialised countries at least), the percentage of suicides is striking, but in absolute terms, the figures are far less dramatic (see MacLeod, Williams and Linehan, 1992 for US figures; Lester, Cantor and Leenaars, 1997 for British and Irish statistics; and Gulbinat, 1996, for a global comparison). Furthermore, suicide attempts by older people are more likely to 'succeed' than younger adults' efforts (Conwell, 1997), where there is over a 50 per cent 'failure' rate (Cook and Oltjenbruns, 1989). In part this because of differences in the physical robustness of the age groups, but also because of methods chosen. Older adults are more likely to select a method which practically guarantees death, such as shooting (see Adamek and Kaplan, 1996a and 1996b) or

---

4   The acceptability of a therapy type for an older adult may vary according to the precise
    symptomatology – see Landreville et al. (2001).

asphyxiation, whereas younger adults are more likely to choose less certain methods, such as taking an overdose in a place where they are likely to be found by friends or relatives before the drugs can take effect (see Woods, 1999). This difference also applies on a relative scale within the older age group, with the oldest old electing more 'definite' methods than younger older adults (Erlangsen, Bille-Brahe and Jeune, 2003).

In part the method chosen may be a reflection of the reason for the suicide attempt. Older adults are often attempting suicide to *escape* from a life of pain and suffering. Younger adults may want to *change* their situation and the suicide attempt is a response to this (see Fremouw, Perezel and Ellis, 1990). However, it will not suffice to say that suicides amongst older people are purely a response to suffering, since there is also a notable racial and sexual difference in suicide rates (though note there are no gender or racial differences in *attitudes* to suicide – Parker, Cantrell and Demi, 1997). Namely, older women and older black men do not show an increase in suicide in later life (in fact, if anything, there is a decline). The increase in suicide rate is principally due to older white men. The most parsimonious explanation of this phenomenon is that white men are more accustomed to power and a high standard of living, and a loss of or a decline in these is too much for some individuals to cope with (e.g. Miller, 1979). This is suggested in the findings of a longitudinal study by Barefoot *et al.* (2001). They found that from the age of 60 to 80 men show an increase in depressive symptoms whilst women do not (though note that Fiske, Gatz and Pedersen, 2003, did not find such a pronounced gender difference). Again, Leenaars and Lester (1998) found that, in Canada, suicides amongst older people were higher in provinces where there was general affluence, but a higher percentage of older people were on low incomes. However, this is not a full explanation. Other factors have also been identified, such as medical problems and relationship loss (Florio *et al.*, 1997), (for the oldest old) bereavement within the past year (Erlangsen *et al.*, 2004), depression (see Johnston and Walker, 1996), low extraversion and high neuroticism scores (Duberstein *et al.*, 2000) and social isolation (see Draper, 1996). One ingenious study (Salib, 1997) has suggested that suicide amongst the over-65s of north Cheshire (a relatively affluent area of northern England) is positively correlated with hours of sunshine and humidity (though see Godber, 1998, for a critique).

Related to depression is **bipolar disorder**, better known by its original name of **manic depression**. The disorder is characterised by episodes of depression alternating with episodes of extreme and unrealistic elation and hyperactivity (mania). Cases of patients showing manic behaviour episodes *for the first time* in later life are rare (see Shulman, 1997), and it is suggested that such behaviour is not 'true' bipolar disorder, but may instead be indicative of an organic cause, possibly related to dementia, though the links are as yet tenuous (see Broadhead and Jacoby, 1995).

Anxiety

The term 'anxiety', rather like 'depression', is something which most people can understand from their own experience. Practically everyone has at some time felt anxious about a situation they have found themselves in. The level of anxiety experienced by a person seeking clinical treatment is far greater than this, and is often identified by the term **anxiety disorder**. This refers to a long-lasting state of anxiety characterised by symptoms such as extreme restlessness, insomnia and fatigue, producing distress and impairment of function. It can manifest itself in many forms, including **phobias** (an irrational or inappropriately high fear of an item or event, such as open spaces, spiders, and so on), **generalised anxiety** (according to Wetherell, Le Roux and Gatz (2003) characterised in older adults by a perpetual or frequent feeling of uncontrollable anxiety, sleep disturbance, and muscle rigidity), **obsessive-compulsive disorder** (a condition in which to relieve anxiety feelings, the patient is compelled to repeat the same act – e.g. repeatedly washing the hands to remove anxiety-invoking dirt, and so on; see Gupta, Austin and Black's 1997 case study of a 93-year-old patient), and **panic disorder** (characterised by repeated **panic attacks** – sudden attacks of overwhelming apprehension, shortness of breath, feeling of loss of control, and so on). Anxiety is relatively rare in older adults in comparison with the younger population (Smyer and Qualls, 1999), but this does not mean it is not a cause for concern, since within any one age group it is one of the commonest mental illnesses (Scogin, 1998), and is often found in tandem with depression (e.g. Flint and Rifat, 1997; though note anxiety symptoms are generally more stable than depression – see Wetherell, Gatz and Pedersen, 2001) and dementia (see Scogin, 1998).

Researchers are generally agreed that about 10 per cent of older adults report some form of anxiety disorder, the majority of these being a phobia (Lindesey *et al.*, 1989; Manela, Katona and Livingston, 1996; Scogin, 1998; Woods, 1999). Of the phobias, a commonly reported one is **agoraphobia** (fear of open spaces), which tends to be conflated with a more specific fear of 'leaving the house'. Other commonly reported sources of concern include falling, dying and social situations (see Woods, 1999). These can undoubtedly be sources of anxiety, but one cannot help feeling that calling them 'phobias' may be perhaps a little harsh, since they are palpably more rational than more stereotypical phobias. For example, an often-cited paradox is that older people are the least likely victims of crime but are the age group which most fears crime. Therefore, does this mean that older people are being illogical in fearing crime or in going out for fear of being mugged? Statistically, the answer to this simplistic interpretation must be 'yes'. However, as Woods (1999) and others have observed, this statistic applies to crimes overall, and for certain types of misdemeanour, older people are not much less at risk. The most plausible explanation is that a phobia may arise because a heightened level of anxiety 'fixes' onto a tangible and rational topic of concern.

Substance abuse

The term 'substance abuse' refers to the use of either illegal substances or licit substances with an addictive quality (such as alcohol) in excessive quantities to the point where everyday functioning is severely affected. The stereotype of older people militates against an image of them as addicts, but health authorities are becoming increasingly concerned at the prospect of a significant proportion of older adults suffering from one or more addictive behaviours (Blow and Oslin, 2003; Stewart and Oslin, 2001). Often in the past health care providers have been arguably under-trained to recognise and deal with these problems (see Finlayson, 1995; Schonfeld *et al.*1993).

The idea of 'addiction' immediately brings to mind alcohol and drug abuse, but it can also include gambling. In the USA in particular, casinos are widespread and offer not only gambling but a social experience, with organised visits (often sponsored or encouraged by the casinos – see McNeilly and Burke, 2001) by seniors groups a common feature. This means that gambling presents both an attractive and an unattractive face. On the negative side, McNeilly and Burke (2002) report case studies of older adults who had developed gambling problems. A slightly more recent study found that circa 3% of older American adults are gambling at a level probably meriting treatment (Wiebe and Cox, 2005). However, on the positive side, researchers have reported that, for some older individuals, participating in gambling (visits to casinos, etc.) is a key social activity with no notably negative effects (e.g. Hope and Havir, 2002; Vander Bilt *et al.*, 2004). Stitt, Giacopassi and Nichols (2003) also concur that gambling appears on the whole to have little negative effect on older people in general, but make the pragmatic point that further research is needed to test this assumption at an appropriate depth.

Even someone with very egalitarian views of ageing would find it hard to imagine older people using psychoactive drugs, but in fact they are heavy consumers of (legitimately prescribed) hypnotic (i.e. sleep inducing) and sedative drugs. In a survey of older Canadian women, Graham, Carver and Brett (1995) found that the group was the largest user of (prescription) psychotropic drugs (use tended to be associated with negative factors such as being widowed, less educated and in poorer health). Misuse (accidental or deliberate) of these drugs is the single commonest cause for admission to the casualty department/emergency room of a US hospital (LaRue, Dessonville and Jarvik, 1985). In many instances, the reason for this is that the ageing body cannot adequately metabolise the drug in question even when on the dosage schedule prescribed by the doctor, leading to serious health problems. However, an appreciable proportion of older adults are taking prescription sedatives and similar, and have become dependent on them (e.g. Gomberg and Zucker, 1998). The problem is exacerbated by the fact that patients may be unaware of the risks associated with many psychoactive drugs, reasoning that if a medical professional has prescribed them, then 'they must be all right', and thus, deterioration in, for example, alertness and cognitive abilities is ignored.

Ironically, in many instances the drugs should probably never have been prescribed in the first place. For example, a study by Avorn *et al.* (1992) demonstrated that the proportion of residential older adults on psychotropic drugs could be drastically reduced without any effect on behaviour or psychological symptoms. McGrath and Jackson (1996) found that 88 per cent of older residents with behavioural problems were being inappropriately prescribed **neuroleptic drugs** (in effect, major tranquillisers – see Glossary). This is of concern not only because use of a 'chemical cosh' is a morally dubious method of controlling undesirable behaviour but also because neuroleptic drugs may lower cognitive functioning (Brown, Chobor and Zinn, 1993) or, in the case of patients with dementia, accelerate the rate of decline (McShane *et al.*, 1997). Although the precise rate of over-prescribing of such drugs can be questioned and may not be applicable across all settings, nonetheless *any* mis-prescribing of this type is a cause for concern. Alas, a more recent study (Fahey *et al.*, 2003) demonstrates that, in the UK at least, poor prescribing is still taking place for older adults in both residential and community settings.

However, drug use in older adults is not simply confined to misuse of legal drugs, but involves use of illicit drugs as well. Whilst absolute numbers are not on a par with young adults, nonetheless older drug addicts can be found. It might be intuitively assumed that older addicts form a rump of younger adults who through some medical miracle have survived into old age. Certainly there are such people, and the available evidence suggests that those who have used drugs throughout their lives will not give up their habit with any ease. For example, Levy and Anderson (2005) found that the older drug users they studied (aged 50–68 years) would only give up use of illicit injection drugs for two things – serious illness or death. Given that long-term drug abuse is associated with a hugely increased risk of early death at worst and serious physical and mental health problems at best (Hser *et al.*, 2001) this is an eventuality likely to happen sooner than is desirable. In addition, such behaviour is likely to lead to imprisonment, either for drug use or for crimes committed to pay for the habit. Arndt, Turvey and Flaum (2002), in a study of US prison inmates, found that 71 per cent of older (defined here as 55 years and over) prisoners had a substance abuse problem (drugs and/or alcohol) and a third had never received any treatment at all for it. For those older drug users who avoid prison, they may nonetheless find themselves marginalised by the drug-using community, which is predominantly composed of much younger adults (Anderson and Levy, 2003). This problem is likely to get worse. The ageing 'baby boomer' generation will bring with it a higher amount of drug abuse, not only because of an increase in absolute numbers but also because amongst drug users of that cohort, abuse has not abated as has been the case with earlier generations. Gfroerer *et al.* (2003) estimate that, in the USA alone, the number of older adults requiring treatment for substance abuse will rise from the 2001 figure of 1.7 million to 4.4 million by 2020. The attendant health issues (including a raised danger of contracting HIV/AIDS) present health care services with a new range of problems for the future (see Topolski et al., 2002).

It is also worth noting that not all drug habits start in youth. For example, a study by Lofwall et al. (2005) found that the older drug users in their study (a group of 41 adults aged 50–66 years) had begun using opioid drugs later in life. But this is probably not a case of middle-aged adults suddenly succumbing after a lifetime of drug-free living. Lofwall et al. found that the participants had a prior history of other forms of substance abuse and psychiatric problems. Research by Rosen (2004) explains the likely course of events. His study found that amongst older (aged over 50) methadone users, there was a willingness to try other illicit drugs if they were available within their social network. Accordingly, one addictive behaviour can lead to another.

Another common form of substance abuse is excessive alcohol consumption. Generally, it is assumed that alcohol consumption declines in later life. In part this may be explained by the macabre argument that heavier drinkers are likely to die before they reach old age, either through the effects of alcohol or because in general they have led unhealthier lives (see Fillmore et al., 1998; Leino et al., 1998), thereby accounting for at least some of these statistics. Gilhooly (2005) has further argued that much of our knowledge of changes in drinking across the lifespan are based on cross-sectional studies, and it is possible that a cohort effect accounts for the observed 'decline' in drinking – quite simply, older cohorts have always drunk less and thus it coincidentally appears that as people get older they consume less alcohol. A careful analysis of evidence across three countries (the UK, the USA, and the Netherlands) indicated that drinking does seem to decline as people get older, but there are also cohort effects. As Gilhooly notes, this is potentially a serious problem because the 'baby boomer' generation, who have been relatively heavy drinkers, may lack the prudence to lower their alcohol levels as much as is medically desirable, thereby creating problems, not least of which is the added burden on health care services.

However, regardless of the rate of change, it is estimated that circa 5 per cent of older American adults living independently have an alcohol problem (Emlet, Hawks and Callahan, 2001; Stoddard and Thompson, 1996). Hajat et al. (2004) report similar data for UK older adults (c.5% of men and c.2.5% of older women). However, there appear to be national differences in reasons for drinking. In the USA, Stoddard and Thompson found that over-drinking appears to be prompted by feelings of loneliness, underpinned by numerous factors encompassing (perhaps not surprisingly) negative life events, health problems, and similar. In the UK study, however, the over-drinkers were generally people who were financially secure (i.e. could afford to buy alcohol) and tended to have more active social lives. Before too much is made of this comparison it is perhaps worth noting that like may not be being compared with like (and different methods of measuring alcohol consumption may not tally with each other, especially in cases of over-drinking – see Wilcox and King, 2000) and so caution is advised.

DeHart and Hoffmann (1995) and O'Connell *et al.* (2003) note the problems in identifying alcohol problems in older adults. Many of the current diagnostic measures are designed for younger adults, since in general the research literature has assumed that over-drinking is largely a younger person's problem – one has only to consider the current preoccupation of health authorities with binge drinking in teenagers and twenty-somethings to appreciate this. O'Connell *et al.* argue that current screening methods may underestimate the level of the problem in older people. DeHart and Hoffmann also note that alcohol abuse may be linked with a myriad of health problems in older adults (see Stoddard and Thompson's findings above), and this also makes a simple identification of likely precursors of increased drinking problematic.

In general, studies find that older men are more prone to alcohol abuse than women (e.g. Graham *et al.*, 1996; Hajat *et al.*, 2004). Emlet *et al.* (2001) found that men were three times more likely to drink than women. Note however that precise figures can vary between studies (e.g. Hajat *et al.*, found that men were 'only' twice as likely), depending upon the particular culture tested and measurement method used, and may also to some extent be dependent on cohort effects.

Regardless of what percentage of the population have a problem with alcohol, the health risks for alcoholics and heavy drinkers are greater (O'Connell *et al.*, 2003). However, there is a danger that a 'killjoy' attitude can be extrapolated from this, implying that all alcohol consumption must have a negative effect. In many instances, the association between alcohol consumption and illness and injury in later life is not clear cut (Reid *et al.*, 2002). It should also be noted that alcohol consumption is not necessarily injurious to psychological functioning. Richards, Hardy and Wadsworth (2005) found that in men and women in their fifties, alcohol consumption was associated with a slower decline in memory for the men and a significant worsening of psychomotor skills in the women. These findings beg for a follow-up study, but at the very least create the possibility that alcohol may not always be an evil.

Before leaving this section, it is perhaps worth inserting a reality check. Although substance abuse problems are a serious matter and are undoubtedly growing, they still affect only a small minority of older adults. This should not lessen our level of concern for these people, but it is also worth noting that, amongst healthy older adults, substance abuse is at its lowest for any adult age group (Satre *et al.*, 2004).

Personality disorder

Whilst it has been seen in Chapter 5 that there are a wide variety of personality types which can legitimately be seen as of equal value, there are nonetheless some patterns of behaviour which are sufficiently extreme and at odds with societal norms to cause distress to the patient and/or those whom he or she comes into contact with. It is important to note that these personalities go beyond the bounds of what might be considered 'eccentric' but nonetheless tolerable behaviour. The incidence of personality disorder is believed to be low in later life, but there is a danger that clinicians are willing to overlook patterns of behaviour which would be considered unusual in a younger person because of different expectations about how older adults 'should' behave. Certainly there is a lower tendency for older adults to be diagnosed as having a personality disorder (Rayburn and Stonecypher, 1996). Amongst the types of personality disorder most commonly described in the literature from the UK and USA (see Smyer and Qualls, 1999) are the *avoidant* (low self-image and avoidant of company) and *dependent* (over-willingness to let others decide everything). Since these concur with the stereotype of the retiring older person, it is conceivable that they could be falsely identified as 'normal' behaviour. Again, Sadavoy (1996) argues that personality disorders could be masked by other behaviours associated with other mental or even physical illnesses. Because of considerations such as these, the true level of personality disorder may be higher than has been supposed (see the meta-review of this subject by Abrams and Horowitz, 1996). However, the level is felt to be particularly high in patients with depression (see Abrams *et al.*, 1998). Note that there are possible cultural differences in the relative frequency of these disorders. For example, some Croatian researchers report the highest prevalence in their country was for sadistic and antisocial disorders in men, and self-defeating, borderline and schizotypal disorders in women (Mandic and Barkic, 1996).

Schizophrenia

The final illness to be considered in this chapter is **schizophrenia**. The term means 'cloven mind' in the sense of a broken or fragmented self, rather than the popular misconception of a 'split personality'. In essence, it is a profound disorder of thought, perception and language in the absence of intellectual disability, characterised by a severe distortion of perception of reality and concomitant changes in emotions and behaviour. There are various forms of the illness, each with a distinct set of symptoms. The commonest of these symptoms include irrational beliefs about the way the world functions, often with a central theme that the patient is being persecuted. There may also be hallucinations (such as 'voices in the head'). Language can often be best described as 'surreal', with unusual expressions and ideas, and invented words (see Stuart-Hamilton, 1999a).

Most commonly, schizophrenia first appears in early adulthood (**early onset schizophrenia**, or **EOS**), but about a quarter of cases arise in middle age or later (**late** onset schizophrenia, or LOS), and some studies have estimated about a tenth of schizophrenic patients first show symptoms in their sixties or older (see e.g. Bartels and Mueser, 1999; Karon and VandenBos, 1998). Thus, older schizophrenic patients can be divided into EOS and LOS groups, depending upon the length of time they have had the illness. It would be misleading to create the impression that LOS suddenly appears without warning. Studies often report that LOS patients have led fairly reclusive, undemanding lives, with few social contacts. They have typically been protected either consciously or tacitly by parents or friends, and it is often the death or incapacitation of the latter which precipitates the onset of the illness. In other words, LOS may have been an illness waiting to happen.

Straightforward comparisons of these groups are not always easy, however. For example, because EOS patients have received radically different treatments for their illness than LOS patients, there may be a strong cohort effect. Again, the age at which patients are first introduced to antipsychotic drugs appears to have an effect, with older patients reporting significantly more adverse reactions (though these can be ameliorated – see Bartels and Mueser, 1999). There would appear to be little difference in the symptoms found in EOS and LOS (Lacro, Harris and Jeste, 1995; Reicher-Roessler, Loeffler and Munk-Jorgensen, 1997; though see Jeste et al., 1997), although some EOS–LOS differences have been identified in such measures as EEG patterns in response to auditory stimuli (Olichney et al., 1998). It has also been noted that a disproportionate number of schizophrenic patients develop dementia or at least dementing symptoms (see Arnold and Trojanowski, 1996). However, after some early histological studies supporting a link, more recent work has failed to find DAT-like atrophy in the brains of older schizophrenic patients (Arnold et al., 1998; Purohit et al., 1998). Notwithstanding these comments, the prognosis for treating patients with either form of the illness is reasonably optimistic (Karon and VandenBos, 1998).

Overview

It should be recalled that mental illness in older adults is often lower than for the population as a whole. The problems faced by older patients can of course be grave, but, in many instances, evidence points to these not being appreciably worse in themselves than those faced by younger patients with the same illnesses. Of course, contracting a mental illness in later life does not absolve the patient from becoming ill with common age-related physical complaints such as arthritis or hearing impairment, and of course it may be anticipated that these will exacerbate the problem (see e.g. Smyer and Qualls, 1999).

Suggested further reading

Several books can be warmly recommended. An excellent general overview of ageing and mental health is provided in a book chapter by Woods (1999) and, on a larger scale, Smyer and Qualls (1999) and Nordhus *et al.* (1998). Lezak's *Neuropsychological Assessment* (Lezak, 1995) is a vast and comprehensive review of its subject, and includes an excellent section on the dementias. Parks, Zec and Wilson (1993) is an edited volume of papers on the neuropsychology of the dementias. Like Lezak, it is a specialist work and has a high concentration of technical terms. Tallis and Fillit (2003) is an embarrassment of riches on all matters connected with mental illness in later life as well as physical health. However, some chapters are perhaps a little 'technical' for some readers. More accessible perhaps is Manthorpe and Iliffe's (2005) book on depression in later life, which also takes a more applied approach that some readers may find useful. Leentjens and van der Mast (2005) provide a useful overview of studies of delirium. Stuart-Hamilton (1999a) provides an overview of mental illnesses, their classification and treatment.

CHAPTER 7

Problems in Measuring the Psychological Status of Older People

Introduction

The chapters so far have attempted to present the psychology of ageing as a narrative, representing, as far as possible, a consensus view of the discipline. This is a general introduction to the topic, and it would be unfair to present a more critical view of the literature as the 'correct' one to students discovering the basic facts about psychogerontology for the first time. However, it is also unrealistic to expect students to accept that the findings reported are without criticism, or that the research is so cut and dried that any future discoveries can only be footnotes on what has already been written. Of course the subject is still developing and expanding.[1] Various new methods are constantly being suggested. Some attempt a radical break with the old methods. For example, approaching the topic from a radically different angle and set of research traditions, Calasanti (2004) makes a case for feminist gerontology. Other researchers essentially accept the status quo but look for ways to develop the existing methodology to explore new areas. For example, for those readers with a degree-level background in psychology, Dixon, Backman and Nilsson's (2004) edited volume exploring potential new directions in cognitive ageing research will be of great interest.

Notwithstanding Chapter 8, the current book is intended to be a survey of what is, rather than speculate too much on what may develop (and with the greatest of respect to

---

1   For example, without adding an appreciable number of new topics or sections, this book is c.50 per cent larger than the previous edition of six years ago, reflecting the enormous growth in recent studies.

Dixon *et al.* and other researchers, if experience of research in the past is any guide, some areas suggested as trailblazers in recent publications will almost certainly lead up blind alleys). It is however appropriate that at least some criticisms are offered of the general assumptions and methodologies underlying a lot of current research on the psychology of ageing. These are intended to stimulate the reader, who, having acquired the basic facts, must now begin to look at the subject critically for themselves. But no claim is made that this is anything but the beginning of a long process. There are other possible critiques and the author makes no claim that what follows is the only possible approach to the issue.

The view from without

Simone de Beauvoir divided her classic study *Old Age* (de Beauvoir, 1970) into two main sections: one was the view from without, and the other the view within later life. This book has taken the view from without for the simple reason that research on ageing is almost solely the work of young or at least pre-retired adults. The simple and pragmatic reason for this is that most published research is the work of paid academics who almost always are aged under 60. At times, an unfortunate impression is created by this. Researchers sensibly need to take a detached view of their subject matter, but by discussing age-related phenomena in a dispassionate way, there are times when the *person* appears to have been lost from the discussion. A reading of any of the major psychology of ageing journals creates an impression that ageing is nothing more than a testing ground for how senescence or dementia affects models of memory, intelligence, personality or caregiver stress. The concept that the subject is about studying real people in real-life situations is conspicuously absent. However, the criticism really only stands if one is prepared to accept a rather naïve view of research. Practically any academic topic at the level of individual journal papers can appear divorced from reality. Individual pieces of research should be seen on their own merits, nothing more. It is up to commentators and the individual reader to decide what these findings mean when taken as a whole.

However, if the field of the psychology of ageing is viewed at a broad level, it creates a curious picture. It can be readily demonstrated that later life is, on the whole, a time of decline. It can also be shown that there are so many caveats to this summary that it is difficult if not impossible to make a definitive statement about a *typical* older person. It is quite possible that this is the correct summation of the field. Social sciences study individuals and by definition, this means accepting greater variability than in, say, the physical sciences. Making a statement about the properties of a typical older adult means accepting that the said person will come equipped with a wide range of options. In comparison, a test tube of mercury is the same the world over. However, an acknowledgement that 'people are different' does not absolve a researcher from making as accurate an assessment as possible. Perhaps part of the reason for the general woolliness of findings is that experimental protocols and philosophies have not been accurately pinned down in the first place. In the rest of the chapter, some of the potential flaws in current experimental practices will be examined. For the sake of simplicity, this will be done principally with reference to a single topic within the psychology of ageing – namely, intellectual skills. However, the arguments could be easily applied to other topics.

Confounding variables and the search for 'pure' ageing

Research on ageing is predicated on the assumption that we can measure something called 'pure' ageing. This is not always explicitly stated by researchers, but it is at least a tacit assumption. It is essentially the belief that after cohort effects have been accounted for, any age difference which is left 'must' be due to ageing alone. In Chapter 2, it was noted that to a certain extent, age differences on fluid and crystallised intelligence tests depend upon the test methods used. Fluid intelligence test performance, for example, is partly governed by the speed at which a person can write down their answers. Older people, because of arthritis, rheumatism and similar conditions, generally write less quickly, and this can affect how many answers they can produce in a paper-and-pencil test against the clock. In short, test artefacts may be underestimating the true mental state of an older person. Conversely, the absence of age differences in crystallised tests may be due to the reverse reason – namely, that tests are generally untimed and that, were time limits imposed, an age difference would display itself.

Writing speed and issues about whether a test should be timed or not are far from the only issues shaping age differences. Simply reading from a pile of journal abstracts to hand on the author's desk, the following potential confounding variables may be identified: level of education (Anstey, Stankov and Lord, 1993; Christensen, Hendersen et al., 1997; Christensen, Korten et al., 1997; Compton, Bachman, and Logan, 1997; Jones and Gallo, 2002), genetic inheritance (Deary et al., 2004; McGue and Christensen, 2001), general health (Horn, 1982; Riegel and Riegel, 1972), level of exercise (Powell, 1974), level of motivation (Bauer, 1966), degree to which skills are practised (Charness, 1979; 1981; Milne, 1956; Plemons et al., 1978), sensory functioning (Lindenberger and Baltes, 1994), quality of social networks (Holtzman et al., 2004) and socio-economic status[2] (Rundinger and Lantermann, 1980). The above list is just the tip of the iceberg: a very long list of possible confounding variables can be devised by a person with the time and will to do it. Note that it is not necessarily the case that all of these items are of equal

---

2   Though note that the findings of Rabbitt et al. (2004) found no relationship.

importance, but the sheer magnitude of the list makes it likely that a significant proportion of the difference between older and younger adults may be due to cohort effects rather than 'pure' ageing.

Salthouse (1991b), in a meta-analysis of the ageing literature, found that removing health or education level lessened, but did not remove, age differences. However, with the greatest respect to Salthouse, who is a scrupulous researcher, these are just two variables from a potential list of hundreds. What if instead of two variables, a larger number were chosen? In theory, we could decide to measure what is left of an age difference after 5, 10, 20 or 100 confounding variables are accounted for. There is no 'law' to stop researchers doing this. We could, for example, continue to add in more confounding variables until an age difference completely disappeared. Statistically speaking, this would be a dubious practice, but the point is that we really have no clear grounds for knowing what constitutes a valid cohort effect which should be accounted for, and what constitutes an invalid one. Consider the following example.

Suppose that it is decided to control for effects of cardiovascular disease, since it is plausible that people with heart and circulation problems may perform less well on intellectual tasks. Thus, patients with these conditions are excluded from the experiment. However, why stick at cardiovascular problems? Why not also exclude people with arthritis, or rheumatism, or cancer? All these conditions could plausibly influence intellectual performance. Taking this policy to extremes, one would finish with a sample solely consisting of 'A1' fit older adults. This may satisfy the criteria to exclude any illness-based cohort effects, but it would be hopelessly unrepresentative of the older population (see Stuart-Hamilton, 1995). And this is solely considering health. What if we now also decide to balance older and younger adults on education levels? Older adults generally received fewer years' education. Therefore, this should be controlled for. However, how do we now control for differences in the type of education received? Older adults tended to receive rather more rigid forms of teaching with greater emphasis on rote learning, and many older adults (in the UK at least) received greater training in practical skills, such as needlework and woodwork, than younger people. How is this controlled for?

Clearly it is impossible to control for all possible confounding variables. Inevitably, some will have to be left in the analysis, and they will inevitably contaminate the data to a greater or lesser extent. As can be seen by a perusal of gerontology journals, many researchers do not even bother to start correcting for possible cohort effects, others only control for one or two. This might not matter if all researchers drew their volunteers from the same group of people, since in that case, comparisons between experiments would be based upon a common ground. However, the people upon whom the tests are conducted vary enormously. To take an example of this, the author chose a single edition of a psychology of ageing journal and recorded the way in which volunteers were recruited for studies of non-dementing ageing. Two of the papers gave insufficient details, but the remainder listed the following: newspaper advertisements in New York; newspaper adverts in Canada, plus 'various community organisations'; advertisements in the media; advertisement in senior centres and senior apartment complexes; members of an older volunteer pool maintained by the university in question; people originally recruited in a 1960s national survey; local volunteer groups; a sample of those aged over 70 on the electoral roll in part of Australia; and healthy community resident volunteers. The level of screening for other conditions (particularly health, which was often left to self-report) was extremely variable, from a rigorous exclusion of anyone not 'A1' fit to no real barriers to participation. It takes little contemplation to realise that the list of participants in the above studies could potentially be enormously different. Some studies will have physically healthier participants than others, some will have people from higher socio-economic groupings, and so forth.

It might be argued that the above argument is unnecessarily pedantic. However, as has been demonstrated throughout the previous chapters, variability increases considerably in later life, and any practices which are enhancing this variability and blocking sensible direct comparisons between studies are doing little to clear the picture. Added to this is the further problem that when younger adults are included for comparison purposes, studies nearly always use students recruited from undergraduate participation pools. Given that older people are almost certainly being recruited from a much broader intellectual base (i.e. the undergraduates are almost bound to be smarter on average, since not all of the older participants will have studied for a degree), and will have different motivations for participating (e.g. the desire to participate in research as opposed to doing a boring task in order to get a degree), any comparisons between older and younger adults are coloured right from the start.

Given such criticisms, it is readily apparent that any experiment on older adults is bound to contain at least some cohort effects. However, something might be done to control at least the most striking cohort effects. This would involve establishing a benchmark measure of controls which all researchers would agree to abide by (similar controls exist in other sciences to great effect). This would consist of controlling for at least the most often-cited variables (education, general health, etc.), recruiting participants in a set manner (i.e. everyone agrees to recruit in the same way), and pragmatically accepting that inevitably some confounding variables will be left, so that some 'noise' will remain in the data. Regrettably, there is no 'industry standard' set of such variables that all researchers are expected to use (Stuart-Hamilton, 1995). Thus, different researchers are left free to have different policies, as has been seen, and this makes judgements about the true size of age differences very difficult to determine (Stuart-Hamilton, 1995, 1999b).

The above argument is predicated on the assumption that a measure of 'pure' ageing is submerged beneath the cohort effects, and, furthermore, that this measure is useful. However, this is debatable, and the following counter-argument might be proposed. A measure of 'pure' ageing is often tacitly assumed, but rarely explicitly explored. However, since cohort effects are removed by researchers in order to get a 'more accurate' view of ageing, it may be assumed be assumed that 'pure ageing' is a measure of ageing which is free of the influences of upbringing. In short, this is the nature–nurture debate, so beloved of individual differences researchers, being played out on a new field: pure ageing is nature, cohort effects are nurture (Stuart-Hamilton, 1999a). However, it is difficult if not impossible to see how intellectual development could occur if it were totally free of influences of upbringing and social interaction: *in extremis*, it is like arguing that only a person raised in an isolation tank can experience pure ageing. Most intellectual skills shown in later life occur *because* of these, not *in spite* of them (see Pratt and Norris, 1994). Cohort effects may thus be more than just inconveniences which distorts the 'true' results – they could be part and parcel of an older person's intellect to the extent that they cannot be removed without denying part of that person's intellectual status. It may thus be argued that each age cohort is inevitably different, and if part of the difference is due to differences in upbringing, then so be it.

Neither of these views – 'all cohort effects are bad' versus 'cohort effects are ageing' – is in itself satisfactory. However, finding a compromise between the two is fraught with difficulties as well. This would involve finding a limited set of cohort effects which would be controlled for, but, as has already been seen, defining this in itself is a daunting and perhaps impossible task. We are thus left with only one certain statement: older people tend to be worse at intelligence tests. However, the degree to which this is a reflection of 'pure' ageing is left open for debate – as is what we mean by 'true' ageing.

The relevance of findings to everyday life

A further problem for ageing research is that it often is at odds with everyday life. Throughout this book, psychological tests (and intelligence tests in particular) have been presented as if they were 'pure' measures of intellectual skills. If this is so, then one would logically expect psychological tests to correlate well with abilities at 'everyday' skills. For example, intelligence test scores should be excellent predictors of scholastic ability, job status, ability at chosen job, and so on. However, this is not the case. An old psychological chestnut is that the best correlation ever found between IQ and a real-life measure was 0.7. The real-life measure was the number of real (as opposed to false) teeth possessed by the participants. Usually, IQ tests are poor predictors of real-life performance – correlations are usually of the order of 0.2–0.3: in other words, about 10 per cent of the variance on the real-life measure is predicted by IQ. This is not to say that intelligence tests are useless. Even their detractors acknowledge that they are good at identifying extremes of ability. Thus, IQ tests can identify the exceptionally intellectually gifted and deprived (though it can also be argued that one really does not need an IQ test to do this). What intelligence tests cannot do with any real accuracy is identify performance of people between the extremes (i.e. the majority). This raises an uncomfortable question for psychogerontology: if intelligence tests are not an accurate reflection of everyday skills, then of what value is the bulk of work on ageing intellectual changes?

Salthouse (see Chapter 2) provides one answer to this question: namely, that although intelligence is a poor predictor of absolute ability, it is vital as a control process. This may be so, but one might wonder why psychologists have indulged in so much research on measures which have at best only a minor relevance to everyday life. An uncharitable view might be that although IQ tests are poor predictors, they are still the best measure available and thus they continue to be used, until, to quote the song, 'the real thing comes along'. By this reckoning, the psychology of ageing is very well versed in what happens to 10 per cent of older people's intelligence, but, like the iceberg, 90 per cent of it remains hidden. This is too severe a judgement, however. At a *general* level, IQ tests are probably perfectly adequate indicators of intellectual change. Throughout this book, it can be seen that changes in specific memory, linguistic and intellectual skills are correlated with a decline in intelligence test performance. Admittedly, the correlations have often been small, but nonetheless they are statistically significant and have fallen in the expected direction. For example, there have been no instances where overall the older people have got higher fluid intelligence scores than younger participants, or where memory has improved the lower the intelligence test score of the participant. IQ tests are quite adequate, indeed they are remarkably consistent, at predicting *trends*.

It would be unfair to blame psychogerontology for this failure to find the IQ test of more than general descriptive use. The problem is one which has beset **psychometrics** (the study of psychological differences) since its inception. What is at stake is convenience. In an ideal psychometric world, participants could take a single IQ test, and this score would perfectly predict their ability on any intellectual task they could ever encounter. A single test score would thus tell one all one needed to know about a person's intellectual abilities. Unfortunately for psychometricians, this test does not exist, and it is virtually impossible that one could ever be devised. The reason for this is that psychological research has shown that intellectual skills are not determined by a single factor, but rather by several intellectual skills, each of which is at least partly autonomous of the others. The general intelligence test is really only an expression of the aggregate of performance on all of these sub-skills, and hence can only hope to give an overall impression of an individual's abilities.

The situation is akin to predicting the performance of a football team. A team consists of different players with different specialist abilities. A league table gives an overall gauge of how good a particular team is, by showing its position relative to other teams. However, league position tells one little about the abilities of individual players in the team. Of course, good teams will tend to have better players than bad teams, but this is not an inevitable rule. For example, a particular side might have the best forward in the history of the game, but the side may be languishing at the bottom of the league table because the rest of the team is poor. In a similar manner, the overall score on an IQ test can give an indication of the overall intellectual performance of an individual, but it cannot accurately predict how well a person will perform a specific task. Nor can it be said that measures of sub-skills are necessarily more informative. There is a double bind in psychometrics which is as follows. General intelligence measures are poor predictors of everyday skills. Measures of sub-skills give better predictions, because they assess abilities which are more akin to those used in 'real life'. However, there is a danger that the tests of sub-skills may be so like real-life problems that one might as well cut out the middle man and use the real-life ability as a measure. Thus, at one extreme a measure fails because it is too general, whilst at the other it flounders because it is too specific.

A further criticism of lack of realism comes from the observation made in Chapter 2 that the difference between younger and older adults on many intelligence tests amounts to nearly two standard deviations. Readers with a background in education research will recognise this as a very meaningful figure, since in the case of children, performing at 2 standard deviations below average would mark a child down as potentially in need of remedial (or 'special') education. If the way older people perform on intelligence tests is genuinely indicative of the way they behave in everyday life, then a large proportion of older adults should be on a par or worse than younger adults or children unfortunate enough to fall within the 'special needs' bracket. Clearly this is not the case. In other words, a simple reading of psychological tests underestimates older people's 'real-life' skills.

Indeed, psychogerontologists seem tacitly to acknowledge this with practically every paper they publish. Researchers are rightly concerned about any reports on racial differences which imply a 'genuine' difference between races. However, even the largest differences between racial groups ever reported pale into insignificance next to the findings of a large number of studies of ageing. Report after report catalogues declines which should mark down an average older person as barely capable of functioning without remedial help, and yet scarcely a comment on the practical implications of what has been found is made. It is as if psychogerontologists find age-related declines, but do not want them to matter.

The above is of course a rather exaggerated argument; at the very least, declines in skills may be compensated for by other strategies or the skills may be ones which older people do not use very much in everyday life. However, if that is the case, then why study skills which may be important to younger adults but which have little relevance to older people? In part the answer is that it is important to map out mental changes using these measures because they give a good indication of the extent to which some skills alter or decline. One cannot judge if an older person is compensating unless it is known what he or she is compensating for. However, it is also arguable that many intellectual skills are studied because of tacit assumptions made by academics about ideal ageing and ideal intellectual life. Academics have a tendency to judge events by their own standards, and to expect others to do the same. Thus, we are sporadically treated to polemics from commentators arguing that people lack the skills taught by their discipline. Thus, representatives of the arts argue that people are insensitive to aesthetics in a mechanistic world, whilst scientists counter-argue that too much time is spent on teaching 'easy' artistic subjects, and, as a result, the general public is typically illogical and lacks the necessary knowledge about scientific matters to make informed decisions. It is neither necessary nor timely to enter further into this debate here. However, the general issue makes it apparent that academics have an established interest in the types of learning and knowledge people should acquire, and this inevitably contains a value judgement that some forms of knowledge are better than others.

Which leads back to the psychology of ageing. The measures of intellectual skills which psychogerontologists use are typically not developed just for studying older people. Generally, they have already been devised for testing younger adults and then are simply given to older people to see how they perform relative to this younger age group. In other words, intellectual ageing is being set up as a measure of how far older people have fallen from the ideal standard set by younger adults. In other words, 'successful ageing' in most psychogerontologists' eyes is the degree to which an older adult maintains the same level of performance he or she had in younger days (Stuart-Hamilton, 1999b). Thus, it is assumed that older people should not develop as much as remain in a kind of mental stasis once they hit their intellectual peak in the late teens or early twenties. Although some commentators note that older adults may attain greater depths of wisdom or become more adept at integrating pragmatic considerations with pure logic, matters are still largely couched in terms of the degree to which decay from a youthful ideal is either accelerated or diminished.

However, this begs a rather obvious, if contentious, question. Why should later life be seen negatively if one does not analyse things as analytically or know as much as they would in a youthful ideal? Such things matter to academics, but not everyone would consider it a disaster if one day their verbal skills had declined from a previous level and they could no longer spell *charisma* or *liaison*, or remember what *manumit* means. The pursuit of high intellectual ideals is very important to some people, academics included, but they are not necessary nor desirable for everyone. The days of most older people are not filled with reading books favourably reviewed in one of the more highbrow newspapers, watching subtitled films or doing *The Times* crossword. To assume that a high intellect, or rather a particular set of intellectual skills, is a necessary part of life, is both patronising and divisive. Indeed, the goal of an intellectually powered old age bears little resemblance to anyone's ideal beyond that of university lecturers contemplating what they will do in retirement. To assume that this should be set as the goal by which all older people must be judged is foolhardy, to say the least. We have seen that psychogerontology has structured views of ageing in terms of how the older mind differs from the younger. It is assumed that both age groups perform tasks using the same set of mental skills. To take an analogy, the older and younger people are akin to two soccer teams made to compete against each other. However, what if one of the teams has given up soccer and gone off to play bowls instead? In other words, psychogerontology's view of intellectual change is predicated on the view that older adults are still using the same set of intellectual skills that younger adults use. However, the evidence for this, as has been seen, is far from compelling.

This has been demonstrated in Chapter 2 by the studies of older adults' performance on traditional measures of child development, such as Piaget's experiments. Put simply, older adults often appear to have chosen to adopt 'primitive' methods of thought in preference to more complex 'academic' problem solving. Further evidence for this is provided by Klaczynski and Robinson (2000), who found that older adults on the whole shifted towards using heuristics rather than first principles analysis to solve some types of problems. Again, Allaire and Marsiske (2002) found that problems based on everyday situations predicted older adults' everyday functioning significantly better than traditional psychometric measures.

If older adults are rejecting the skills many researchers think older adults 'should' be using, and this may in part be linked to choice of lifestyle or motivation, then it is difficult to continue comparing older and younger adults by the same rigid criteria. However, this still leaves the necessity of explaining how the shift in mental styles occurs. The following is one possible explanation. We begin with the premise that development consists of the accumulation of knowledge and problem-solving strategies, determined by both genetic inheritance and the environment in which one lives (none of this should be contentious). The knowledge and problem-solving strategies can (with tongue only slightly in cheek) be described as 'idea species'. Whether an idea species thrives depends upon the conditions in which it finds itself. Species will only be acquired if the person can integrate them into an existing mental framework, and they will only be maintained if effectively stored and rehearsed. Thus, acquisition of skills in childhood and their loss in later life are governed by the same basic mechanism. Existing psychogerontological models map cross-sections of processes at one point in time – they add a depth to the model whilst developmental studies add breadth. Much of this has been voiced in one way or another before. The key difference is that in the past it has been tacitly assumed that development and ageing were essentially directed towards specific goals. Arguably this ultimately replays the homunculus problem which plagued computer modelling studies for years. The difference here is that the whole process is essentially blind – the individual has no truly conscious awareness of these processes, and whether a mental process is gained or lost is ultimately down to probabilistic odds. We can stack the odds in particular directions through planning, but essentially the process is removed from the concerns of current studies, which tacitly assume a single desirable path of development. Note that this theory does not negate either the disuse or general slowing theories – both provide possible mechanisms to drive changes. For example, Singer *et al.* (2003a) finding that skills in extreme old age show greater reliance on fluid-based skills (thus fuelling the argument for general slowing) may in turn account for older adults embracing relatively primitive heuristics in response to failing skills in other cognitive domains.

Unwitting ageism

The above argument creates a case for arguing that ageing is essentially what a person makes it, and that defining it in simple terms of being worse or better at tests is rather missing the point. Many researchers, even if they disagree with the model presented, would probably concur with this conclusion. However, it is still very easy to create an artificial barrier between age groups, even armed with an egalitarian philosophy. This raises the topic of **ageism** (an irrational prejudice against older adults and/or ageing). Deliberate ageism is a vile condition and unusually stupid, even by the low standards of other prejudices. A racist may be a vile piece of pond slime, a male chauvinist may sully the name of as noble a creature as the pig, but both can attack their objects of hate in the sound knowledge that they will never change race or sex. Ageists, on the other hand, have a high chance of turning into that which they hate – namely, that they will them-selves grow old. Thankfully, few ageist people take careers in caring for, or researching into, older adults. Even so, gerontology is not free of all ageist philosophies.

It is *not* ageist to say that older adults are more prone to physical ailments than younger people, that they are more likely to get dementia, or that that they are generally less able at intelligence tests. It is likewise not sexist to say that on average women are shorter than men, that they on average cannot lift weights as heavy, or run as quickly. However, if these measures are taken as value judgements rather than simple statements of *average* difference on measures of dubious importance, then this paves the way towards viewing one group as intrinsically inferior to another. This can be done for the most egalitarian of motives. For example, it might begin with a laudable general declaration that older adults need greater care because, on average, they have greater needs. It is a short step from this to regarding older people as automatically being weaker and less adept on a wide range of measures. A person holding these views can still be doing so for the very best of reasons, but a stigma is being created. For example, consider the following statement in an instructional video for nurses concerning sexual abuse of patients. The presenter reports that there have been cases of older patients being sexually abused, demonstrating that 'even the elderly are not immune from attack'. At one level this of course raises a very proper level of concern; sexual abuse is a very serious matter. However, the phrase 'even the elderly' carries a striking value judgement that older people are enfeebled and sexually unattractive: a strong piece of stereotyping which has arisen from what was undoubtedly a genuine and laudable concern.

CHAPTER 8

What is the Future of Ageing?

Introduction

In this final brief chapter, the ways in which older adults will react to and behave within a future, more technologically driven society will be considered. This will be done by bringing to bear arguments and information described in earlier chapters.

What will constitute being 'old'?

At the current time, judgements about what makes a person 'old' are based on several criteria, including appearance, attitudes and amount of leisure time. However, a variety of developments is likely to change all of these in the future. Appearance may well be the most fundamental factor to be affected. Already, plastic surgery and hormone replacement therapy can remove a decade or more from a person's appearance. These are of course largely cosmetic changes. There is little reason to doubt that techniques in this field will improve and possibly become more affordable, so that a wider range of people can make use of them. This is aside from the possibility that advances in medical services may find further ways of retarding the ageing process. It is already well established that some animals can live much longer by simple manipulations of their environment and diet. The leap from such results with animals to humans is not a simple one, but at some point the change will almost certainly come, and the over-60s will no longer look 'old' in the stereotypical meaning of the term. However, will this necessarily change matters? Might it not be the case that people will look for different indicators of age, so that instead of looking for wrinkles or greying hair, attention will shift to, for example, the brightness of the eye? It can be demonstrated that cultures differ in their perception of key physical attributes in other respects, such as erogenous zones. Heterosexual males of different cultures might be most attracted by breasts, buttocks, legs or the nape of the neck. Why should the prime indicator of age not similarly shift across cultures separated by time?

Alternatively, ageing retardation may be very successful, so that no one can tell how old an adult is. This raises a series of possible dilemmas. Will some individuals deliberately select to grow older 'naturally' and choose to make themselves outcasts? Perhaps anti-ageing treatments may be very expensive, so that only particular social castes can afford them. Again, perhaps a new neurosis will arise, afflicting people who feel 'trapped' in a body which is the wrong age for their thoughts and attitudes. Perhaps treatments might delay the onset of signs of ageing, but nonetheless it will eventually arrive (i.e. at the point when the treatment 'fails'), albeit at a later age. Might this physical change (which the individual has taken deliberate steps to avoid) be more traumatic than for a person who has aged naturally and passively allowed his or her body to undergo the ageing process? Before voting too hastily in favour of anti-ageing treatments, it would be wise to consider the potentially serious psychological consequences. It should also be noted that, whatever the outcome, images of ageing are still likely to be predicated on the assumption that the process is synonymous with physical decline. Warren (1998), in an interesting review of the history of identifying markers of ageing, identifies this as the prime marker of the ageing process in the future.

Attitudes are supposedly a good indicator of age. The popular conception of the older person is that he or she is conservative and cantankerous – a thoroughly erroneous view, as was noted in Chapter 5. However, there is a further reason for doubting this assumption. There has been a radical sociological shift in the past 50 years towards a far more liberal and permissive society, which has allowed young adults to express and celebrate being young, rather than attempting to become carbon copies of their parents' generation as quickly as possible. The first rock 'n' roll generation has now reached retirement age, and the flower power generation is in its fifties. The full ramifications of this are complex and are more properly dealt with by a sociological text, but an important psychological prediction emerges from this. Namely, that older people of the future are unlikely to fit into the niches which have been established by societal expectations with quite the same willingness as previous cohorts. They have seen that conventions can be flouted and that protest can work. Accordingly, if younger generations do not change societal mores to better cater for older people, then older people are more likely to do it themselves.

A final consideration concerns leisure time. Perversely, in industrial societies where leisure is treasured, an excess of it is usually greeted with distaste, since it often indicates unemployment or retirement. However, the increased automation of work (particularly computerisation) may well change this attitude. Shorter working weeks, and an increase in flexihours and home offices may lead to more people of working age spending a greater proportion of time in their homes than in traditional workplaces. This means that retired and older people may no longer be marked out simply because they are not 'at work'.

Older people and the technological society

It is a cliché to note the immense changes in lifestyles of people in industrialised nations which have resulted from the technological and scientific advances of the past hundred or so years. It is tempting to imagine that older people will be swept up in this tidal wave of change, and this raises the issue of how well they will cope.

Intuitively, one might suppose that the greatest impact will be in improved medical care, and that people will live longer because of this. However, as was noted in Chapter 1, this is not necessarily so. The increase in the average life expectancy has primarily resulted from fewer people dying in infancy rather than a lengthened life expectancy *per se*. Indeed, the older the age group considered, the less the increase in life which modern medicine can provide. Many of the illnesses which afflict older adults, such as cancers and cardiovascular complaints, are as incurable now as they were in 1900 (though modern palliative care can certainly alleviate the suffering more efficiently and may be able to prolong life expectancy slightly further). Again, if a cure for a disease is found, this need not prolong life by a significant degree. Finding a cure for one form of cancer, for example, does not cure all the other varieties. Furthermore, curing an older person of one illness does not necessarily improve their life expectancy to a significant degree. As has already been noted, older adults (particularly those aged over 75) may have several physical symptoms on the verge of collapse. Preventing a disease striking one of these down does not make the others any less immune to degradation. In short, curing a fatal heart disease may simply make a failing liver the cause of death instead (please note this is *not* an argument in favour of denying older adults medical care because it is a 'lost cause'; although it may apply to a proportion of older adults, it is not a universal truth).

Because of these considerations, it is unlikely that people aged 70 or over are likely to display an appreciable rise in life expectancy in the future. This is simply because although cures for individual illnesses may be found, methods of overcoming widespread ageing decline will have to be discovered before much benefit can be reaped. This raises a further, more controversial issue – will there be the impetus to pursue this? The financial burden imposed by the greying population was noted in Chapter 1. Any appreciable lengthening of the lifespan will simply compound this problem. There is also a moral issue – if a method is found to prolong life, it carries with it the question of whether the quality of life makes the effort worthwhile. In addition, the procedure may be hazardous – current medical thinking assumes that, for example, lengthening telomeres may also increase the risk of contracting cancer (see Concar, 1996, and Chapter 1). What if a person considers the prospect of an artificially longer life and decides, for whatever reason, that they do not want it? Will this refusal be counted as voluntary euthanasia? Again, what if the treatment is expensive and thus only within the reach of the very wealthy? Should they be allowed to enjoy extra life just because they have more money? Mercifully, such questions can for the foreseeable future remain the preserve of science fiction writers (e.g. John Wyndham's (1960) excellent *Trouble With Lichen*), as the imminent advent of truly effective life-prolonging drugs seems unlikely.

Another major impact of technological change is the automation of tasks. It is a commonplace of science fiction to envisage a time when manual tasks have become the preserve of machines, and the marked decline in manual labour as a proportion of the workforce is testament to this. However, the advent of word processors, copiers, and so forth has also seen a decline in 'white collar' occupations (copy typists, to give one example). These changes are not likely to be limited to relatively routine occupations. The use of 'expert systems', which seek to emulate the diagnostic abilities of a specialist, is also likely to come to the fore. Large investment and banking firms already use computers to monitor changes in stock market prices, and can automatically initiate the buying and selling of shares, as witnessed by the popularity of tracker accounts. In the future, it may be possible to consult a computerised doctor, which will perform the same role as a general practitioner by analysing the patient's responses to a series of questions, using algorithms based on the diagnostic processes of a real doctor. The impact of automation is almost certain to affect the lives of future cohorts of older people. One of the most basic issues (and one already touched upon) concerns shifts in working practices. There will undoubtedly be changes in the socio-economic backgrounds of retired persons. As noted in Chapter 5, social class and occupation type are predictive of attitudes towards later life, and, accordingly, there may be a shift in the pattern of behaviour and lifestyle in the older population as a whole.

However, any consideration of future trends based on technological innovation is inevitably highly speculative, and a perusal of future predictions in 1960s textbooks provides a suitable warning. In the 1960s, there were authoritative predictions that, by the 1990s, everyone would have died from pollution, nuclear war, famine and/or overpopulation. Alternatively, everyone would be living a life of luxury, with every whim catered for by robots. It is highly probable that the predictions made here will be similarly ludicrous. Humanity has a strange habit of finding more work when old employment opportunities are replaced by automation.

Of greater interest to the psychologist are the likely direct effects of technology on older people. The effects of this can be somewhat anticipated from the impact of previous technological innovations. The by now almost ubiquitous telephone, television and radio allow older people access to an outside world which would have been unthinkable for all but the very wealthy 50 years ago. In shaping leisure activities, the impact of television on modern life is difficult to underestimate. Besides being entertaining, television enables older people to see places, plays, concerts and other cultural events which they perhaps are no longer physically or financially robust enough to attend in person. Often older people (especially those living alone) report using the television or radio as a comforting background noise without especially attending to the programme. However, there are disadvantages as well. The programmes on television and radio are primarily geared to the needs and demands of younger adults. Programmes may be presented in a manner too lurid for an older person's tastes, or possibly even the basic content may be unappealing (e.g. 'youth'-orientated programmes). The advent of 'niche television' afforded by the multi-channel delights of satellite and cable television has not yielded much which could be said to be of especial interest to older adults. Certainly there is no channel dedicated to older people (though there are tens of channels specifically for children and a certain kind of lobotomised teenager), and few programmes of special interest, other than an occasional worthy (and usually rather dull) magazine programme by a community television unit filling up the off-peak hours. The majority of programming is aimed solidly at younger audiences. However, older people are generally the heaviest consumers of television programmes, a finding echoed across different countries (e.g. Dubois, 1997; Grajczyk and Zoellner, 1998). Perhaps (as was suggested in the first edition of this book more than nine years ago) there will eventually be an outlet for smaller, community-led television stations which will allow air time for a significant proportion of programmes by and for older viewers, but as yet there is no real evidence of this outside a few pockets of activity in the USA, where it appears to have met with some success (Burns, 1988). Printed outlets for older adults, such as magazines, have met with greater success, and several specialist publications are commercially successful. However, these can be seen as appealing to a particular niche within the older community, such as the affluent middle classes interested in expensive holidays and investment advice (see Featherstone and Wernicke, 1997). For a variety of demographic and socio-economic reasons, a publication with wider appeal is unlikely to be a viable commercial proposition.

There may be similar demographic limits to the degree to which older adults use the Internet. The medium should hold especial benefits to many older people. For example, there is a vast range of information available, there are opportunities to join discussion groups, there is not the feeling of being 'rushed' which there may be in an oral discussion, and all without needing to leave the safety and comfort of one's house. In the previous edition of the book, it was noted that Internet use was far commoner in the USA than in the rest of the world, but the difference between countries is shrinking year by year as computers and phone links become increasingly affordable. However, even in the USA, older adults are the age group least likely to use a computer (Cutler, Hendricks and Guyer, 2003).

In part, older people may be deterred from using a computer through feelings of lack of control, dehumanisation (Czaja and Sharit, 1998) and anxiety, though this may be unrelated to real computing ability (Laguna and Babcock, 1997). The degree to which people succeed during their initial training also plays a key role in determining future participation in computing (Kelley et al., 1999). Others may perceive that there is little of interest to them. Lurid media reports of prosecutions of individuals possessing child pornography downloaded from the Internet do little to enhance the image that surfing the Web is a suitable activity for a respectable older person.

When older adults do use the Internet, then in the USA at least, they are most likely to use it for emails (Hilt and Lipschultz, 2004). Whilst this serves a clearly useful social function, potentially the Internet could be especially useful for older adults in such areas as health education and perhaps this should be promoted more strongly to older people. Older adults are also more likely to find use of the Internet a positive experience (Chen and Persson, 2002). Other studies have likewise found that, once older adults take to computers, they are an empowering or at least enjoyable experience. However, resistance to starting use and/or drop-out from training may be high (Namazi and McClintic, 2003). In addition, Priest, Nayak and Stuart-Hamilton (in press) demonstrated that the biggest barrier to Web use was typically poor Web design rather than intelligence or prior experience of the older user. This indicates that many of the blocks to effective Web use may be illusory and the products of poor design rather than an intrinsic age-related deficit.

Other technological changes might also bring mixed blessings, in part because, although they should in theory be a boon to older adults, lack of relevant prior experience may militate against their successful use (see Charness and Schaie, 2003). Modern household appliances take much of the strain out of cooking and general housework. These items are financially available to most if not all older people, and undoubtedly are immensely advantageous. For example, refrigeration and better methods of preserving food reduce the risk of food poisoning when an older person's senses become blunted to the point where they cannot detect something which has 'gone off'. Furthermore, the imminent arrival of 'smart' fridges (which will read bar codes on pre-wrapped foods and warn when something is unsafe to eat) will further enhance this. Simultaneously, labour-saving devices and safety checks may encourage some older adults to avoid exercise and become too complacent. Thus, their health may decline through lack of physical activity and a misplaced optimism in food safety may lead to poisoning.

Other technological changes may still be prone to misuse. For example, use of microchip-controlled medicine dispensers have been mooted (see Kapur, 1995). The time at which some drugs are taken is vital for their efficacy, and because some older people are forgetful, the automated dispenser emits a beep when it is time for the patient to take the next dose. There is of course one minor snag with this device, which is that it relies upon a forgetful person remembering to keep the dispenser within earshot and to remember what to do when the device goes beep. This is a problem which pervades most of the gadgetry designed to help mentally disadvantaged people – they have to remember to use it. *Aides memoires*, be they beeping pillboxes, palm-held computers or electronic diaries, clearly fall foul of this problem. The problems created by a declining memory show the magnitude of the problem facing designers. Other technological innovations do not face these problems, and seem at first sight to be quite benevolent, such as the expert systems described earlier. However, expert systems require a computer, and where will the computer be located? We have noted above that computer use may be limited amongst older adults. If an older person has had to make the effort to travel to somewhere where there is a computer (e.g. the doctor's surgery in the case of a medical expert system), then they will surely want to see a real person as a reward for their efforts. Assuming there is a computer and a doctor programme in the house, there are still problems. An expert system only works as well as the information it is fed. What if people choose to lie or gloss over some symptoms? A human doctor, by observing voice tone and body language, should be better at detecting subterfuge than a computer, unless both hardware and software improve considerably beyond their present limits. In short, the system is open to serious, and potentially fatal, abuse.

A further consideration is that new technology is largely designed for younger adults. Miniaturised electronic gadgets are no doubt a tribute to the designer's art, but they are often too small for an older person to see or handle efficiently. In Chapter 1, it was noted that the ageing perceptual system loses its ability to process fine detail in any sensory modality, and it thus appears that many pieces of modern technology are designed to impair the older person. The Centre for Applied Gerontology at Birmingham University in the UK has a notable slogan – 'Design for the young and you exclude the old; design to the old and you include the young'. It is not being argued that every item should be designed to be age-impartial, but it is hard to see why manufacturers seem to want to exclude at least 20 per cent of their potential market by making things difficult. It should also be noted (and this is not intended to be an ageist statement) that in designing with older people in mind, it is also aiding many younger adults with physical problems, such as people with poor vision or limited dexterity. On the reverse side of this argument, there is a danger that in making such pronouncements one is presenting a view of older people being disadvantaged to a greater extent than they are. For example, several publications and websites give advice on designing computer interfaces which as first priority stress the need for adequate wheelchair access, simple instructions and very large print. Of course these are necessary pieces of advice (for a small proportion of older adults), but at times one might wish that these pieces of advice were given a little less prominence.

Accordingly, technological advances are a mixed blessing to older people. While they promise great hope, many of the details of their operation have not been sufficiently thought through. Machines which are designed to help save labour may be impossible to operate, or may create more harm than good. Medical advances will cure some illnesses but still leave older adults vulnerable to others. A medical breakthrough which could delay the ageing process is a mixed blessing because it invites people to extend the time in which they can suffer as well as enjoy life. To imagine that older people will automatically be made happier by such advances is foolishly optimistic.

Conclusion

A view of the future almost inevitably stems from a criticism of the present, and many of the predictions and arguments raised in this and the previous chapter are fuelled by the current problems with gerontological research and with the lot of older people in industrialised societies. However, it would be unfair to conclude from this that something is rotten in the state of psychogerontology. The area shows a healthy growth and an agreeably wide range of interests. The predictions presented in these final two chapters can be divided into two sorts – those which ought to come true and those which might. In the former camp fall those born of criticisms of existing research methods. Researchers *must* stop treating older people as if they are a race apart. Not only is it unscientific; it is also patronising and divisive. On a milder note, although some moves have been made in this direction, the ageing mind needs to be seen more as an interactive process and less as a set of single systems. The approach of isolating a single aspect of ageing and analysing it in great detail is analogous to the old chestnut about three blind men examining an elephant – depending upon which part of the animal they felt, the men identified the animal as being like a snake, a tree or a bird (there are other, often ruder versions of the same tale, in case this one is unfamiliar to the reader). Inevitably, changing to a multifactorial model leads to problems and a single-figure result is never likely to suffice. However, as the inestimable Mr Wilde wrote, the truth is never pure and rarely simple. The second set of predictions concerns possible future changes in technology and attitudes, and how these might affect older people. It is improbable that many of the changes described will be readily apparent for several years at least. It is always tempting to think that technology will inevitably shape lives. A possibility rarely considered is that people will simply ignore it. Older people may resist new inventions, not because of inbuilt conservatism (which in any case Chapter 5 demonstrated to be an ageist conceit), but because they cannot see the worth of adopting new practices which are likely to be of only limited use. Perhaps in many ways this is the most optimistic vision one could have of future generations of pensioners – older adults standing up for what *they* want, rather than what younger adults are foisting on them 'for their own good'.

If there is a message to be taken from this book it is this:

Whether an older person is mentally advantaged or disadvantaged, content with life or suicidal, healthy or housebound, principally or solely depends upon their genetic inheritance and how he or she behaved earlier in life. A content later life is a reward, not an automatic right. It can only be reached by approaching the prospect of ageing with a clear and open mind. Some changes, such as those to the intellect, can only be partially controlled, but even though there may be some decline, this should never, with the exception of dementia, be sufficient to mar a productive and happy later life. For those unmoved by this argument, who still insist on stereotyping older people as an homogeneous, inferior group, there remains a final thought. All older people are survivors: this is an accolade which not all their younger detractors will live long enough to proclaim for themselves. This is the one fact that describes every older person.

Glossary of Technical Terms

The glossary contains definitions of the technical terms printed in bold type in the main body of the text. In addition, it includes definitions of terms not mentioned in the text, but in common or relatively common use in the gerontological literature.

Italicisation of a word or term within a definition indicates that it has its own entry in the glossary.

A-68 Protein found in abnormally high concentration in patients with *dementia of the Alzheimer type* (DAT).

AAMI *age-associated memory impairment.*

acceptance of prospect of dying stage See *Kübler-Ross's stages of dying.*

accommodation (vision) The ability to focus at different distances.

acetylcholine Type of *neurotransmitter.*

acquired dysgraphia A profound difficulty in writing (particularly spelling) resulting from brain damage.

acquired dyslexia A profound difficulty in reading resulting from brain damage.

ACS *acute confusional state.* See *delirium.*

active life expectancy The average number of years remaining in which an individual, or more generally members of an *age cohort*, can expect to lead an active life.

activity theory The counter-argument to *disengagement theory*, which argues that older people should be kept involved and active in the community.

acuity (vision) Ability to focus clearly.

acute brain disorder *delirium.*

acute brain dysfunction *delirium.*

acute confusional state (ACS) *delirium.*

acute crisis phase (of dying) See *Pattison's stages of dying.*

AD *Alzheimer's disease.* See *dementia of the Alzheimer type.*

AD-MID A *dementia* in which the patient displays symptoms of *dementia of the Alzheimer type* and *multi-infarct dementia* simultaneously.

ADL *assessment of daily living.*

aetiology The origin and causes (particularly of disease).

affect Emotion.

afferent (neurons) Carrying signals from the *peripheral* nervous system to the *central nervous system.*

age-appropriate behaviour *social age.*

age-as-leveller The argument that later life diminishes the perceived differences between socioeconomic/ethnic groups.

age-associated memory impairment (AAMI) Pronounced memory decline in later life, which is associated with ageing, rather than *dementia* or similar.

age bias *age discrimination.*

age cohort A group of people born and raised in the same period of time/history.

age discrimination Unfair bias against a person because of his or her age.

age-equivalent scale Test scores expressed in terms of the proportion of an age group who typically possess them. Thus, whether a person is advanced or less able for their age can be assessed.

age grading The societal pressures which determine what is considered appropriate for different *social ages.*

age norm The mean score on a test for a given age group, and hence a gauge of what is typical for that age group.

age-normative effect A factor which influences the majority of people at the same point in their lives.

age scale *age-equivalent scale.*

age set *age cohort.*

age-specific mortality rate Proportion of people in an age group likely to die before they get too old to be in the said group.

age stratification Dividing the lifespan into a series of *social ages.*

age × complexity effect The phenomenon that the difference between older and young adults gets disproportionately larger the more complex the task set. See *age × treatment interaction.*

age × process interaction *age × treatment interaction.*

age × treatment interaction The phenomenon that some psychological skills decline more than others in later life (see *differential preservation* and *preserved differentiation*). Thus: if skill 1 requires mental process *X* and skill 2 process *Y*, but skill 1 declines disproportionately more than skill 2 in later life, then process *X* must be more affected by ageing than is process *Y*. This is not the same as the *age × complexity* effect, which argues that changing the complexity of items which the same skill has to process has a disproportionate effect on older participants.

AGECAT A computerised package for assessing the mental state of older patients.

ageing Process of change occurring with the passage of time. Usually restricted to changes (often perceived as negative) which occur after adolescence. See *anatomical age, biological age, carpal age, chronological age, distal ageing effects, physiological age, primary ageing, probabilistic ageing, proximal ageing effects, secondary ageing, social age* and *universal ageing.*

ageing/aging Either spelling is acceptable. However, citizens of the USA tend to use 'aging' and UK inhabitants 'ageing'.

ageism *age discrimination* (usually refers to discrimination against older people).

agerasia Compare with *Hutchinson-Gilford syndrome.*

aging See *ageing/aging.*

Aging Semantic Differential (ASD) Method of measuring attitudes to ageing by Rosencranz and McNevin (1969) asking people to judge older adults in terms of pairs of adjectives, deciding in each case which adjective is preferred. Rosencranz and McNevin identified three traits in their original study – competence, autonomy and acceptability. Subsequent researchers have sometimes failed to find these and Intrieri *et al.* (1995) argue for a modified four-factor model.

agitation Term covering a set of symptoms indicative of restlessness and dissatisfaction, including acts of physical aggression, grabbing, complaining, shouting, verbal abuse, etc. Often used to describe a range of problematic behaviours found in institutionalised older adults, particularly those who are intellectually compromised or suffering from *dementia*.

agoraphobia Fear of open spaces.

AIDS dementia Form of *dementia* found in some patients in the terminal stages of acquired immune deficiency syndrome (AIDS).

alcoholic dementia (1) Old (and misleading) synonym for *Korsakoff's syndrome*. (2) A *dementia* resulting from long-term alcohol abuse, and similar to *Korsakoff's syndrome* although with a different neuroanatomical pattern of decay (this distinction is controversial and not universally accepted).

ALE Average *life expectancy*.

alexia A complete failure to read or to recognise words or letters (in *dyslexia* there is a partial ability). Only usually seen in brain-damaged individuals.

alpha waves A pattern of electrical activity detected by *EEG* (see *electroencephalograph*) with a frequency between 8 and 12 Hz.

aluminium theory of dementia of the Alzheimer type Brain cells of Alzheimer patients show unusually large concentrations of aluminium, leading to the theory that the principal cause of *dementia of the Alzheimer type* is the 'poisoning' of the brain with aluminium contamination. However, recent work suggests that this may be an artefact of the manner in which the cells are analysed.

alumni education US term for education schemes for former students (alumni) of an institution of higher education. The courses are typically intended for intellectual enrichment, rather than for specific postgraduate qualifications such as a Master's or PhD degree.

Alzheimer-type dementia *dementia of the Alzheimer type (DAT)*.

Alzheimer's disease (AD) *dementia of the Alzheimer type.*

ambiguous loss Phenomenon usually encountered in severely *demented* patients, that the afflicted individual exists only physically – there is no sign of a sentient being occupying the body.

amenity migration Moving from one country or area of the country to another because it offers better amenities/lifestyle, etc. The term is often used to describe retired people moving to a 'nice place in the country'.

amnesia A failure of memory. Usually arises as a result of *stroke*, head injury, illness (e.g. *dementia*) or poisoning (e.g. chronic alcoholism).

amyloid precursor protein (APP) A gene located on chromosome 21 associated with some forms of early onset *dementia of the Alzheimer type*.

anaphoric reference Referring to a previously named person, persons, thing or things by the appropriate noun (e.g. mentioning 'the man' and then in the next sentence citing the same character as 'he').

anatomical age *Biological age*, measured through relatively gross state of body (e.g. bone structure, body build, etc.) rather than through *physiological age*. See *carpal age*.

anger at prospect of dying stage See *Kübler-Ross's stages of dying.*

anniversary reaction Negative feelings engendered by it being the anniversary (or general time of year) of an event distressing to a person (e.g. death of a close friend or relative).

Anomalous Sentences Repetition Test (ASRT) Test designed to identify patients in early stages of *dementia* from those with *pseudodementia*. Participants are required to repeat sentences spoken by the tester.

anomia A failure to name objects.

antagonistic pleiotropy theory The theory that many of the deleterious changes found in later life are the products of genes that in earlier life conferred advantages.

antediluvian ageing myth Myth that at some distant time ('antediluvian' means 'before the flood') a (usually virtuous and pious) race of people existed, who had incredibly long lifespans. Also known as *hyperborean ageing myth*.

anticholinergic Anything which blocks the action of the cholinergic system. This can lead to severe memory loss, and this information is one of the cornerstones of the *cholinergic hypothesis*.

anticipatory grief Preparing for the death of a loved one.

anxiety disorder A long-lasting state of anxiety characterised by symptoms such as extreme restlessness, insomnia and fatigue, producing distress and impairment of function. It can manifest itself in many forms, including *phobias* (an irrational or inappropriately high fear of an item or event, such as open spaces, spiders, etc); *generalised anxiety* (a perpetual feeling of anxiety, often accompanied by physical symptoms such as sweating, being aware of a pounding pulse, etc.); *obsessive-compulsive disorder* (a condition in which to relieve anxiety feelings, the patient is compelled to repeat the same act – e.g. repeatedly washing the hands to remove anxiety-invoking dirt, etc.); and *panic disorder* (characterised by repeated *panic attacks* – sudden attacks of overwhelming apprehension, shortness of breath, feeling of loss of control, etc.).

apathetic (personality) See *passive-dependent personality*.

aphasia A failure of language. See *Broca's aphasia* and *Wernicke's aphasia*.

Aphasia Screening Test Sub-test of the *Halsted-Reitan Neuropsychological Battery*, used to assess for signs of *aphasia*.

apnoea Temporary suspension of breathing, usually in sleep. Commoner in infants and older people. Several possible causes.

apoE *Apoliproprotein E.*

apoliproprotein E (apoE) A gene found on chromosome 19 believed to be linked to *dementia of the Alzheimer type* (and also *vascular dementia*). The gene comes in several forms, the commonest being e2, e3 and e4. It is e4 that is believed to be associated with a higher possibility of developing late-onset DAT. Interestingly, the e2 variant seems to carry a lower risk of developing DAT.

apoptosis Programmed cell death.

APP *amyloid precursor protein.*

apportioned grandmother See *Robertson's taxonomy of grandmothers.*

apraxia An inability to perform skilled movements.

armoured approach personality *defensiveness personality.*

armoured-defensive personality *Personality* type found in Neugarten *et al.*'s (1961, 1968) studies. Possessors of this type were either *holding on* (maintaining a high level of activity to 'defeat' ageing); or *constricted* (dwelling on what they had lost through ageing).

articulatory loop Previous term for the phonological loop.

ASD *Aging Semantic Differential.*

ASRT *Anomalous Sentences Repetition Test.*

assessment of daily living (ADL) Any method of measuring daily activities, usually with the purpose of identifying memory slips, ability to cope independently, etc.

attention The ability to concentrate on a target item(s) despite distracting stimuli. See *divided attention, selective attention* and *sustained attention*.

autobiographical memory Memory for events peculiar to one's own life, as opposed to past events which everyone has experienced (i.e. events which have been 'in the news' such as general elections, train crashes). See *flashbulb memory* and *observer memory*.

autoimmune theory of ageing Theory that the ageing body's autoimmune system falters and begins to attack the body's own cells as if they were infections. See *disposable soma theory of ageing, Hayflick phenomenon* and *somatic mutation theory of ageing*.

autonomic (neuron) Carrying signals from the *central nervous system* to bodily systems over which there is little conscious control (e.g. glands, smooth and cardiac muscle).

awareness of dying The degree to which a person is aware he or she has a fatal illness.

baby boom Strictly speaking, any period of time in which there has been a notable increase in the birth rate (generally, following the end of a war and the return home of troops after a long absence). However, the term usually refers to the *age cohort* of people born between the mid-1940s and 1960s, when there was an appreciable increase in the birth rate in the USA and other westernised nations.

baby boomer Person born during the *baby boom* period.

backward masking A method used in *iconic memory* experiments. A *to-be-remembered* item is presented for a brief period of time on a display screen, and is immediately supplanted by a different image (a 'mask') which has the potential (depending upon its appearance, intensity, etc.) to destroy the memory of the to-be-remembered item. This process of disrupting the *memory trace* is called backward masking.

backward span A *short-term memory* task in which a list of items is presented to the participant, who must repeat them back in reverse order of presentation – a more sadistic form of the *ordered recall* task.

Baltes's theory of lifespan development A rich and complex theory, devised by psychologist P. Baltes. Argues that development is determined by three factors – purely environmental, purely biological, and mixtures of biological and environmental. These influences express themselves through three strands of development: (1) *normative age-graded development* is the basic developmental pattern one would expect to find in any normal individual (e.g. in terms of *biological ageing*, the onset of puberty, in terms of *social ageing*, the effects of retirement on behaviour and attitudes); (2) *normative history-graded development* charts the effects of historical events which would normally be experienced by the whole of the *age cohort* (e.g. experience of food rationing would be normal for most English people born before 1940, but would be unusual for people in their twenties); (3) 'non-normative life development' measures the effects of major events unique to an individual's life.

bargaining at prospect of dying stage See *Kübler-Ross's stages of dying*.

BDI *Beck Depression Inventory*.

BDS *Blessed Dementia Scale*.

Beck Depression Inventory (BDI) A multiple choice questionnaire, where the participant is required to indicate which of a choice of responses best describes him or herself in relation to a range of potentially depressive attributes.

Behaviour Rating Scale (BRS) See *Clifton Assessment Procedure for the Elderly*.

benign senescent forgetfulness *age-associated memory impairment*.

beta waves A pattern of electrical activity detected by *EEG* with a frequency above 12 Hz.

Big Five (personality) Model of personality which identifies five basic personality traits: conscientiousness (how reliable a person is), agreeableness (how compliant with others' wishes), openness (how willing to cope with the unfamiliar), *extraversion* and *neuroticism*.

Binswanger's disease Form of *vascular dementia*.

biographical approach The analysis of the lives of pre-eminent members of professions, etc., to see if there are any common factors to explain their greatness. Has been widely used in *creativity* research.

biological age The body's state of physical development/degeneration. This is gauged against the state of an average person of the same *chronological age*. See *anatomical age, physiological age*.

bipolar disorder Mental illness characterised by alternate episodes of extreme and unrealistic elation and hyperactivity (mania) and depression. Better known by its older name of *manic depression*.

birth cohort A group of people born in the same period of time. See *cohort*.

Blessed Dementia Scale (BDS) A measure of intellectual impairment and functioning, usually employed in the assessment of *demented* patients. The test requires the patient to answer some simple memory questions (e.g. 'What is your name?', 'Who is the current prime minister?') and to perform some simple intellectual tasks (e.g. 'Count backwards in steps of three'). Details of how capable the patient is of looking after him- or herself are collected from a *caregiver*. The test provides a useful 'ready reckoner' of how intellectually impaired a patient is, and how much professional nursing care and assistance is required. The Blessed Dementia Scale (named after its author, Dr Blessed) is a British test. The American equivalent is the *Mental Status Questionnaire* which has a similar format.

blood–brain barrier A physiological mechanism which prevents potentially damaging chemicals in the bloodstream from entering the brain.

body transcendence versus body preoccupation In Peck's theory, realising that in later life, bodily fitness and health can no longer be a prime cause of self esteem.

BOLD-fMRI (Blood-Oxygen-Level-Dependent fMRI) Commonly-used *fMRI* technique.

bovine spongiform encephalopathy (BSE) Degenerative disease of the nervous system in cattle, colloquially known as *mad cow disease*. The cause is unknown – the most popular theory is that it is due to cattle eating infected feed, possibly accidentally contaminated with remains of humans who died from a form of *dementia*.

bradykinesia Very slow movement; a common feature of *Parkinsonism*.

bradylexia Very slow (but not necessarily inaccurate) reading.

brainstem Section of the brain which is the meeting place between the spinal cord and the brain. Besides acting as a relay station between the spinal cord and other areas of the brain, the brain stem controls many life support mechanisms (e.g. blood pressure, respiration).

brick test Semi-serious term for a *creativity* test in which the participant must think of novel uses for an everyday object (often a house brick, hence the name).

Brinley plot Plot of older adults' response times versus younger adults' response times on the same set of tasks. For both age groups, times get slower the more complex the task, but the plot of the older versus the younger times is linear (i.e. it appears as a straight line on a graph). This supports the *general slowing hypothesis*.

Broca's aphasia A specific problem with producing speech, resulting from brain damage.

Brown-Peterson task Named after its inventors, the task presents participants with a list of *to-be-remembered* items, then gives them a distracting task (usually counting backwards in units of 2 or 3), before asking participants to recall the *to-be-remembered* items.

BRS *Behaviour Rating Scale.* See *Clifton Assessment Procedure for the Elderly.*

BSE *Bovine spongiform encephalopathy.*

bulimia The uncontrollable urge to overeat.

CAD *cortical atherosclerotic dementia.*

CAMDEX Cambridge Mental Disorders of the Elderly Examination – a *test battery* of measures for assessing older people for *dementia* and other aspects of mental health and psychological well-being.

CANTAB Cambridge Automated Neuropsychological Test Battery. A *test battery* of measures assessing neuropsychological functioning and thus assessing for signs of brain damage.

CAPE *Clifton Assessment Procedure for the Elderly.*

caregiver A person who looks after a patient or child. In the context of this book, the term usually refers to the relative of an older patient who is principally responsible for the latter's welfare.

Caregiver Strain Index (CSI) Measure of stress and strain in *caregivers* (usually caregivers of older patients).

caretaker (1) *caregiver* (2) For the benefit of American readers, 'caretaker' is commonly used in British English to denote a janitor, particularly of a school.

carpal age *chronological age* calculated through the state of the wrist (carpal) bones.

CAS *Cognitive Assessment Scale.* See *Clifton Assessment Procedure for the Elderly.*

cascade model of ageing Model of ageing which argues that changes begin in a relatively slight fashion, and then gather momentum and accelerate in severity.

cataracts A progressive opaqueness of the lens, ultimately causing blindness.

catastrophe theory *error catastrophe theory.*

CBS *chronic brain syndrome.*

CDR *Clinical Dementia Rating.*

CDT *clock drawing test.*

cellular garbage theory Model of ageing which argues that the decline of the older body is attributable to the accumulation of 'waste products' from the cells' metabolic processes.

central executive The section of the *working memory* model which controls and oversees the specialist *slave systems*. The central executive is itself a memory store (though of limited capacity).

central nervous system (CNS) The collective term for *neurons* forming the brain and the spinal cord.

cerebellum Area of the brain primarily responsible for balance and co-ordinating movement.

cerebral cortex Usually known by its abbreviated name of *cortex*. The cerebral cortex is the characteristic wrinkled surface of the brain. It is divided into two linked *hemispheres* and can be divided into four regions or lobes which display different functions. The cerebral cortex is responsible for the majority of higher intellectual functioning.

cerebral haemorrhage *Bleeding in the brain.*

cerebrospinal fluid Fluid which cushions and in part supplies the brain with nutrients.

CFQ *Cognitive Failures Questionnaire.*

changing environment effect *cohort effect.*

childhood amnesia Phenomenon that *autobiographical memories* of early childhood are scarce or non-existent.

choice reaction time (CRT) The time taken for a participant to make the correct response when there is more than one stimulus, and each stimulus requires a different response. Compare with *simple reaction time.*

cholinergic hypothesis Theory that much of the memory loss in *dementia of the Alzheimer type* can be attributed to depletion of the *cholinergic system*. See *ganglioside, ondansetron,* and *tacrine.*

cholinergic system Shorthand for the network of *neurons* which use the chemical *acetylcholine* as their *neurotransmitter*. About 90 per cent of neurons in the brain are cholinergic.

chronic brain syndrome (CBS) Long-term degeneration of brain tissue, resulting in severe impairment of personality and/or intellectual functioning.

chronic living–dying phase (of dying) See *Pattison's stages of dying.*

chronological age The length of time a person has been alive.

chunking A *mnemonic* strategy for making long lists of items easier to remember. Items are grouped ('chunked') into sub-groups of 3 or 4 instead of being treated as a continuous list. Thus, the sequence 1789675401 might be 'chunked' into 178 967 5401.

CI *cognitive impairment.*

circumlocution Talking around the topic in question because the appropriate word cannot be recalled (found to spectacular effect in some *demented* patients).

CJD *Creutzfeldt-Jakob Disease.*

classic ageing curve (Erroneous) belief of some early researchers that intelligence peaked in early adulthood and then gently declined across the rest of the lifespan.

classic ageing decline Pattern of relative preservation of *crystallised intelligence*-based skills and decline of *fluid intelligence*-based skills in older people.

Clifton Assessment Procedure for the Elderly (CAPE) Test battery consisting of two 'sub-batteries' - the *Cognitive Assessment Scale (CAS)* and the *Behaviour Rating Scale (BRS)*, measuring intellectual skills and personality respectively, in

older participants (particularly hospital patients and institutionalised older people).

Clinical Dementia Rating (CDR) A 'checklist' for assessing the level of functioning a patient suspected of *dementia* is capable of on various tasks. From this his or her level of impairment, and hence the severity of the dementia, can be calculated.

clock drawing test (CDT) Measure of visuospatial skills in which the participant is required to copy an analogue clock face.

CNS *central nervous system.*

cognition The study of thought processes (including memory and problem solving).

cognitive Pertaining to *cognition.*

Cognitive Assessment Scale (CAS) See *Clifton Assessment Procedure for the Elderly.*

Cognitive Failures Questionnaire (CFQ) A test which asks participants to report instances of memory failure in recent everyday life (e.g. forgetting to buy items when shopping).

cognitive impairment (CI) An appreciable impairment of *cognitive* abilities sufficient to interfere with the norms of independent living. Often used as a general term for the declining intellectual skills in patients suffering from *dementia, delirium* and other illnesses with similar effects.

cohort A group of people with a shared characteristic. Usually describes a group of people raised in the same environment and/or period of time, and thus is often used as a synonym for *age cohort.*

cohort effect A difference between age groups which is better attributed to differences in the ways they were raised and educated rather than to their ages *per se.*

cohort sequential design *overlapping longitudinal study.*

compensation General and often ill-defined theory that older people can compensate for failings in one (usually *fluid intelligence*-based) skill by increasing their reliance on another (usually *crystallised intelligence*-based). See *molar equivalence (ME)*.

complexity effect *age × complexity effect.*

component efficiency hypothesis Hypothesis that the decline in a skill is due to a decline in one or more of the 'basic' sub-skills governing it.

compression of morbidity theory Theory that *healthy life expectancy* has increased or can increase because: (1) with the advent of inoculation programmes, better treatments, etc., people are on average older before they contract a disease or condition that medical science cannot cure and (2) the time spent suffering from a terminal disease has decreased relative to earlier generations.

computed tomography (CT scan) A method of electronically scanning the body (in the context of this book, the brain) and taking the equivalent of X-rays of narrow slices of tissue.

conceptual organisation The ability to treat items at an abstract level in order to uncover basic rules and principles and group items accordingly.

concurrent processing Holding items in *working memory* while performing a potentially distracting task at the same time (a common everyday experience is remembering a telephone number while dialling). By changing the nature and/or level of difficulty of the distracting task, the degree of memory loss can be affected. A technique frequently used to test how well participants can retain information in memory. In the working memory model, concurrent processing is held to be controlled by the *central executive*.

confabulating Condition in which the patient makes up stories or other implausible explanations to cover up gaps in his or her memory or other skills. Generally, the term is reserved for situations in which there is no conscious attempt to deceive.

confounding variable A variable which may distort the finding of primary interest. In psychology of ageing, this nearly always means the *cohort effect*.

constraint seeking strategy In solving a problem (e.g. in a '20 questions' game), seeking answers which progressively reduce the set size of all possible answers.

constricted (personality) See *armoured-defensive* personality.

constructiveness *Personality* type discovered by Reichard *et al.* (1962). Older people possessing it had come to terms with their lives, and were prepared to help others.

contextual perspective The belief that ageing effects are in a large part attributable to social and environmental effects rather to a biological process.

contrast sensitivity function (CSF) A measure of the changing ability to focus clearly on a fine pattern of dark and light parallel lines when the relative darkness and lightness and thickness of the lines is altered.

corpus callosum The principal link between the left and right *hemispheres* of the brain.

correlation A statistical term which, technically speaking, means how much of the variance in one variable can be predicted by variance in another. In layperson's terms, a correlation describes the strength of the relationship between two variables, and the extent to which a change in one is met by a change in the other. Correlations are represented by the symbol r. Correlations can be positive (i.e., as one variable increases, so does the other) or negative (i.e., as one variable increases, the other decreases). Correlations also vary in strength – a value of 0 means that no relationship exists between the variables, a value of 1 indicates perfect positive correlation (i.e., for every increase in one variable, there is exactly the same increase in the other) and a value of -1 indicates perfect negative correlation (i.e., every rise in one variable is met with exactly the same fall in the other). In 'real life', correlations fall somewhere between these extremes. The closer the figure is to 1 or -1, the stronger the correlation (typically, a value of 0.3 or better is taken to be a good indicator). 'Correlation' is not synonymous with 'causation'. There is no method of deciding whether one variable is causing the other to alter. It should also be considered if both might not be governed by a third party (see *partial correlation*). A correlation can only show that two variables are associated with each other. For the mathematically minded: the percentage of the variance in one variable which the other predicts can be easily calculated by squaring *r* and multiplying the result by 100 (e.g. variables *A* and *B* correlate at 0.6; *A* predicts 36% of *B*'s variance).

Corsi blocks task A test of *visuo-spatial memory*. Participants are shown an array of blocks positioned on a table. The experimenter taps on some of these blocks in a sequence which the participant is asked to copy. The experimenter gradually increases the length of sequence until the subject's *memory span* is discovered.

cortex See *cerebral cortex*.

cortical Pertaining to the *cerebral cortex*.

cortical atherosclerotic dementia (CAD) *Vascular* dementia whose primary damage occurs in the *cortex*.

cortical dementias *Dementias* whose principal focus of damage is in the *cerebral cortex*.

creativity The ability to produce novel and appropriate ideas and solutions.

Creutzfeldt-Jakob Disease (CJD) A very rare *dementia*, contracted through contact with diseased nervous tissue. In addition to archetypal *demented* symptoms, there are severe disturbances of gait and movement. A new variant (*nvCJD*) has appeared in recent years, and has been plausibly (though not conclusively) linked to consuming beef or other products infected with *bovine spongiform encephalopathy*.

critical loss Pertaining to the *terminal drop model*, the theory that a decline in some intellectual abilities can be endured, but that a fall in others constitutes a 'critical loss' which heralds death.

cross-linking theory of ageing Theory that the physical decline of the older body can be attributed to a loss of elasticity of tissues (skin, muscle etc.).

cross-sectional research/samples/study An experimental method where age differences are measured by testing different age groups in the same test period. Contrast with *longitudinal research/samples/study*, and see *overlapping longitudinal study*.

CRT *choice reaction time.*

crystallised intelligence The amount of factual (as opposed to autobiographical) knowledge a person has acquired during a lifetime – this roughly corresponds to the lay term 'general knowledge'.

CSI *Caregiver Strain Index.*

CT/CT scan See *computed tomography.*

cued recall Experimental technique for assessing memory in which the participant is given information about the item he or she is supposed to recall (i.e. he or she is given a 'hint', such as the first letter of a *to-be-remembered* word).

CV Cardiovascular (i.e., pertaining to the heart and blood vessels).

cytologic theory Theory of ageing that bodily decline can be attributed to 'poisoning' by toxins (including the waste products of metabolic processes). Compare with *wear and tear theory*.

DAT *dementia of the Alzheimer Type.*

death preparation Preparing for the psychological and practical impact of the death of oneself or of a loved one. Usually helps to lessen the negative effects of the event. To some extent, 'passive' death preparation increases with age, as the probability of dying increases.

defensiveness personality *Personality* type discovered by Reichard *et al.* (1962). Older people possessing it had a strong urge to carry on working to 'prove' they were still young.

delirium A major disturbance (usually temporary) in intellect and perception resulting from a general deleterious change in the central nervous system's metabolism (e.g. through fever, intoxication, drug overdose). Can be confused with *dementia*, but its very rapid onset is in itself a sufficiently distinguishing feature. Occurs in three basic forms: *hyperactive delirium* is characterised by an agitated level of behaviour; *hypoactive delirium* by an unusually subdued level of behaviour; and *mixed delirium* by a mixture of hyperactive and hypoactive symptoms. Delirium may also occur without any 'obvious' behavioural symptoms.

Delirium Rating Scale (DRS) A test assessing the likelihood that a patient's symptoms indicate *delirium* (*acute confusional state*) rather than an illness with which it can be easily confused (e.g. *dementia*).

delta waves A pattern of electrical activity detected by *EEG* with a frequency between 0 and 4 Hz.

demented Describing the state associated with *dementia*.

demented dyslexia A condition found in some *demented* patients, where they can read aloud perfectly normally, and yet have no understanding of what they are reading.

dementia A global deterioration of intellectual function, resulting from atrophy of the *central nervous system*. The illness takes many forms: the commonest are *dementia of the Alzheimer type* and *multi-infarct dementia*. In some (older) textbooks, 'dementia' refers purely to those cases arising in pre-*senile* patients and *senile dementia* to cases in senile patients. This distinction is now largely disregarded.

dementia of the Alzheimer type (DAT) Form of *dementia* whose symptoms have a characteristic

pattern, first described by Alois Alzheimer in the 1900s.

dementia praecox Outmoded term (invented by Emil Kraeplin 1883) for the illness now known as *schizophrenia*. The term means 'pre-senile dementia', but should not be confused with the condition now graced with that name.

dementia pugilistica *pugilistic dementia.*

dementia syndrome of depression (DSD) *pseudodementia.*

denial of dying stage See *Kübler-Ross's stages of dying.*

dental age Calculation of *chronological age* from the state of the subject's teeth. Useful for dead humans and live horses.

dependency ratio The ratio of working to non-working members of the population.

dependent personality *Personality* type discovered by Reichard *et al.* (1962). Older people possessing it had some life satisfaction, but relied on others to help them.

depression at prospect of dying stage See *Kübler-Ross's stages of dying.*

depression-related cognitive dysfunction *pseudodementia.*

depression with cognitive impairment *pseudodementia.*

depressive pseudodementia *pseudodementia.*

deterioration quotient (DQ) Measure of rate of intellectual decline associated with ageing. Sections of the *Wechsler Adult Intelligence Scale (WAIS)* (or indeed many other intelligence test batteries) can be divided into those measuring *crystallised intelligence* (held to be unaffected by ageing), and those measuring *fluid intelligence* (held to decline with ageing). These can also be referred to as *hold tests* and *don't hold tests* respectively. The DQ is calculated as {[(score on hold tests) – (score on don't hold tests)]/(score on hold tests)} × 100. A phenomenon of the WAIS is that hold and don't hold scores are equal in early adulthood. Hence the bigger the gap in an older person's hold and don't hold test scores, the greater the deterioration. The DQ expresses this change as a percentage. See *efficiency quotient*.

Dewey's paradox of ageing John Dewey, philosopher, argued that 'we are…in the unpleasant and illogical condition of extolling maturity and depreciating age' (Dewey, 1939, p.iv).

diabetic retinopathy Disorder of vision resulting from diabetes-created damage to the retina's blood vessels.

Diagnostic and Statistical Manual of Mental Disorders (DSM) Usually known by its abbreviation, followed by the suffix of the edition in question. At the time of writing, the current edition is the fourth (*DSM IV*). The DSM is the American Psychiatric Association's (1994) classification of all mental illnesses and disabilities. It is a hugely influential publication, not only in the USA, but also worldwide. The DSM lists the major symptoms which characterise and distinguish between different mental illnesses and disabilities. It also takes note of life events and physical illnesses which may exacerbate or ameliorate the condition a patient is suffering from.

dichotic listening task A measure of divided attention. Participants hear (via stereo headphones) different messages in either ear, and must then report what they have heard in either ear.

diencephalon Also called the *interbrain*. A collective term for a number of key segments of the brain 'sandwiched' between the *brain stem, cerebellum and cortex*. More important areas include the *thalamus, hypothalamus* and *hippocampus*.

differential preservation The theory that some intellectual skills may be preserved better than others in ageing. See *preserved differentiation* and *age × treatment interaction*.

digit span *Memory span* for numbers.

digit-symbol test A member of the *Wechsler Adult Intelligence Test* battery, which assesses the ability to learn an arbitrary matching of abstract symbols and numbers.

Diogenese syndrome A condition of extreme self-neglect found in some patients with *dementia*, characterised by a very pronounced lack of personal hygiene, lack of awareness of the filthy and untidy state of their surroundings, etc.

disease cohort A group of people suffering from the same disease. See *cohort, patient cohort*.

disengaged (personality) See *integrated personality*.

disengagement theory The theory that older people seek to lose much of their contact with the outside world, in preparation for death. See *activity theory*.

disorganised personalities *Personality* type found in Neugarten *et al.*'s (1961, 1968) studies. Possessors of this type were not capable of normal functional behaviour.

disposable soma theory of ageing The theory that the body 'sacrifices' replacing all somatic (non-reproduction) cells lost through natural 'wear and tear' to concentrate on reproductive fitness. This, it is argued, is the evolutionary force which 'causes' ageing. See *autoimmune theory of ageing, free radical theory of ageing, Hayflick phenomenon* and *somatic mutation theory of ageing*.

distal ageing effects Ageing changes attributable to relatively distant events (e.g. poor self-image in later life because of childhood bullying) or events which are only felt through several intermediaries. See *proximal ageing effects*.

distracters Items which are included along with *targets* and which the participant may erroneously choose.

disuse theories (of ageing) Theories which argue that intellectual skills worsen in later life because they are not practised frequently enough.

divergent thinking Usually associated with *creativity*. The ability to create ideas and solutions stemming from a simple proposition or problem.

divided attention The ability to attend to and process information from more than one source simultaneously.

don't hold tests See *deterioration quotient (DQ)*.

dopamine Type of *neurotransmitter*.

double ABCX model An attempt to account for the stress induced in a family by a major crisis befalling one of its older members. The letters refer to variables expressing the seriousness of the crisis, the amount of available help etc.

double jeopardy Term denoting the problem faced by older members of an ethnic minority who face not only *ageism* but racism as well.

drop-out effect Phenomenon that in a *longitudinal study*, participants who perceive themselves as performing badly tend to withdraw from further participation, leaving a rump of 'better preserved' volunteers, thereby artificially minimising the measurements of ageing change.

DRS *Delirium Rating Scale*.

DSD *dementia syndrome of depression*. See *pseudodementia*

DSM-IV *Diagnostic and Statistical Manual of Mental Disorders*, 4th edition.

Duke Longitudinal Study 20 years' *longitudinal study* of community residents aged 50+ years in Raleigh-Durnham, North Carolina, USA.

dying trajectory (1) The speed with which a person is likely to die. (2) The emotional and intellectual states associated with dying.

dynamic equilibrium theory Theory that as *life expectancy* has increased, the time spent experiencing mild disability has increased, but the time spent experiencing severe disability has decreased.

dysarthria Disorder of muscular control of speech (and often of skills associated with the same muscles, such as eating and drinking).

dyscalculia A profound problem with arithmetic skills. Can be developmental or acquired as the result of brain damage in adulthood.

dyslexia A profound reading problem (though note there is evidence of some reading ability). The syndrome can be inherited (developmental dyslexia) or can be acquired through brain damage (acquired dyslexia).

dyslogia Poor spoken articulation.

dysphasia A profound spelling problem.

dysphonia Disorder of voice production.

E *extraversion–introversion*.

early onset schizophrenia (EOS) *schizophrenia* which first manifests itself before middle age.

echolalia Abnormal repetition of what has just been said.

ecogenic An event not tied to a particular historical epoch. See *epogenic*.

ecological validity The degree to which a study's findings bear any relevance to everyday life.

educational gerontology Broadly speaking, the study of education in later life. Chiefly concerned with the benefits and practicalities of education for older people and the real or illusory barriers to learning they may experience.

EEG See *electroencephalograph*.

efferent (neurons) Carrying signals from the *central nervous system* to the *peripheral nervous system*.

efficiency quotient (EQ) Measure of an older person's intellectual abilities relative to those of younger adults (who are assumed to be at their peak). Basically, it is the IQ which the younger adult would be recorded as possessing if he or she had the same *raw score* as the older person. For example, an older man has a raw test score of 95, which is good for his age group, and gives him an IQ of 130. A score of 95 would be poor for a younger adult, and would give him/her an IQ of e.g. 70. The older person's EQ is therefore classed as 70. By comparing EQ with IQ, a measure of age-related decline can thus be calculated. However, a more useful single measure is probably the *deterioration quotient*.

ego In Freudian theory, a person's rational self. See also *id* and *superego*.

ego differentiation versus work-role preoccupation In Peck's theory, coming to terms with retirement, and realising that status is no longer conferred by one's employment.

ego integration See *integrity versus despair*.

ego transcendence versus ego preoccupation In Peck's theory, coming to terms with the fact that one is inevitably going to die.

elder abuse Abuse of older people, particularly those who are mentally enfeebled. The abuse can be physical, but also psychological and/or financial (e.g. extorting money).

eldering Ageing in terms of *social age*.

elderspeak The use of patronising 'baby talk' when talking to older adults.

electroencephalograph Often (understandably) shortened to *EEG*, this is a device which measures the pattern of electrical activity on the scalp and by extrapolation of the *cerebral cortex* underneath. The rate of activity and where on the scalp it occurs can give some insight into how active and healthy an individual's brain is.

embolism Caused by a blood clot becoming detached and being sent around the blood vessels until it becomes 'stuck', causing a blockage.

encoding The process of creating a *memory trace*.

encopresis Faecal incontinence. See *enuresis*.

enuresis Urinary incontinence. See *encopresis*.

EOS *early onset schizophrenia*.

episodic memory Memory for personal experiences.

epogenic An event unique to a particular historical epoch. See *ecogenic*.

EPQ *Eysenck's Personality Questionnaire*.

EQ *efficiency quotient*.

error catastrophe theory Model of ageing which attributes bodily decline in later life to faulty replication of proteins.

ethnogerontology Study of ageing in different ethnic/cultural groups.

etiology See *aetiology*.

event-based task In *prospective memory* experiments, a task which requires a response which is prompted by an event or other 'sign'.

excitatory (neurons) An excitatory *neuron* either (a) causes (almost invariably in combination with other excitatory neurons) another neuron to become active, and/or (b) makes a neuron already active send signals at a faster rate.

expansion of morbidity theory Theory that *life expectancy* has increased because modern medical treatments can extend the lives of those suffering from diseases that would in earlier generations have been fatal at an earlier age. This usually carries the implication that suffering in later life is increasing.

explicit memory Memory which is consciously retrieved/searched for. Contrast with *implicit memory*, which is the recall of items or the use of memorised information which the person is unaware of recalling or even possessing.

external cue See *internal cue*.

extraversion–introversion A *personality trait* from *Eysenck's personality model*, measuring the degree to which a person is outgoing and self-confident (extraversion) or shy and retiring (*introversion*).

Eysenck's personality model A model of personality which argues that personality is composed of a mix of three personality traits – *extraversion–introversion, neuroticism* and *psychoticism.*

Eysenck's Personality Questionnaire (EPQ) A test assessing the degree to which a person possesses the *personality traits* of *Eysenck's personality model.*

FAD *familial Alzheimer's disease.*

familial Alzheimer's Disease (FAD) Relatively rare form of *dementia of the Alzheimer type* which invariably has its onset before old age, and where the patient has close older relatives who also had the condition. Children of a FAD patient usually have a 50 per cent chance of contracting the disease themselves. See *sporadic Alzheimer's disease.*

Famous Names Test (FNT) A measure of *remote memory.* Participants are presented with a list of names of people famous for brief periods of time since the 1920s and are asked to identify those names which they can remember. Included in the list are some fictitious names, designed to prevent participants from simply replying 'yes' to every item.

FAST model Model by Reisberg *et al.* (1989a) which describes seven stages of progressively worsening intellectual deterioration found in patients suffering from *dementia of the Alzheimer type.*

feeling of knowing (FOK) A person's understanding of his or her own level of knowledge (i.e. how good he or she feels his or her knowledge is).

flashbulb memory An *autobiographical memory* of a key event in one's life which is perceived as being unusually vivid (like a photograph taken with a flashbulb). There is a debate over whether such events are qualitatively different from others, or whether they simply subjectively appear to be more vivid.

fluid intelligence The ability to solve problems for which there are no solutions derivable from formal training or cultural practices. There is usually an added assumption that to have a high level of fluid intelligence, a person must be able to solve the problems quickly.

Flynn effect The phenomenon that IQ test scores have increased with each generation of the population in the twentieth century (Flynn, 1987). The reasons are not completely understood – in part it may reflect an increase in ability to think in abstract terms as a result of changes in education and lifestyle, but the effect is certainly not applicable to all types of intellectual performance, and a full explanation of the phenomenon has proved elusive.

fMRI Functional *magnetic resonance imaging* – scanning technique that assesses structure and activity within the body simultaneously.

FNT *Famous Names Test.*

focused (personality) See *integrated personality.*

FOK *feeling of knowing.*

formal operations In Piaget's theory of cognitive development, the period from the age of 11 years + when the child begins to think in genuinely abstract terms.

fourth age Period of later life (usually during terminal illness, *dementia,* etc.) when a person is dependent on others for basic welfare provision. See *third age.*

Fraboni Scale of Ageism (FSA) Scale devised by Fraboni *et al.* (1990) measuring attitudes to ageing, and yielding three measures: antilocution (speaking negatively about older adults), avoidance (avoiding contact with older people), and discrimination (feeling that older adults are inferior). The FSA consists of a set of 29 statements – for each one the respondent indicates his or her strength of agreement/disagreement.

free radical theory of ageing Free radicals are ions (charged atomic particles) produced in chemical reactions in the body. The theory argues that free radicals damage cells and their chromosomes, thereby causing physical decline. Some theorists argue that consuming extra daily quantities of vitamin C will offset these effects. See *autoimmune theory of ageing, disposable soma theory of ageing, Hayflick phenomenon* and *somatic mutation theory of ageing.*

free recall A memory task in which items can be recalled in any order (i.e. the order in which they were originally presented does not have to be reproduced). Compare with *ordered recall.*

frontal lobe dementia *Dementia* whose origin and primary focus is the *frontal lobes.* The principal form is *Pick's disease.*

frontal lobes The front section of the *cerebral cortex* extending back to the temples. Primarily involved in planning and controlling actions and thoughts (e.g. by getting words in the correct order whilst speaking, producing socially appropriate behaviour).

fronto-temporal dementia *Dementia* originating in the *frontal lobes* and/or the *temporal lobes.* In practice, the term is used interchangeably with *frontal lobe dementia.*

FSA *Fraboni Scale of Ageism.*

functional age The average age at which a particular set of abilities are found (i.e. it measures how well an individual performs relative to his or her age group).

g General intellectual capacity; the general intellectual ability felt by many researchers to underpin all intellectual skills to a greater or lesser extent (though researchers differ considerably over the extent to which g exerts an influence and the degree to which it is genetically determined).

ganglioside Drug whose effects included the enhanced release of *acetylcholine* (see *cholinergic hypothesis*). Has been cited as a possible treatment for patients suffering from *dementia.* See *ondansetron* and *tacrine.*

Gc/gc Symbol for *crystallised intelligence.*

GDS *Geriatric Depression Scale.*

general ageing effect An effect which is known to be related to ageing, but whose precise nature is unknown. The effect is most commonly found in studies of correlation, where a significant part of the variance is attributable to *chronological age.* Since chronological age is essentially an arbitrary measure (how many time the Earth has been around the sun since you were born) in and of itself is meaningless, there must be as yet unknown or unidentified processes that are associated with chronological age that account for the effect.

general slowing hypothesis Theory that age changes in intellectual tasks are attributable to a general slowing of neural transmission speeds. Generally used more specifically to denote the argument that performance on all tasks, regardless of complexity, is affected by a constant (as opposed to a disproportionately increasing deficit the more complex the task), as witnessed by *Brinley plots.*

generalised anxiety See *anxiety disorder.*

generationally biased stimuli Stimuli (or other test materials) which will only be recognised by, or be most familiar to, a particular *age cohort.*

Geriatric Depression Scale (GDS) A 'yes–no' questionnaire measuring the level of depression in the respondent. The questions are geared to match the symptoms and lifestyles typically found in depressed older people.

Geriatric Mental State (GMS) A standardised interview package for assessing the mental status of older patients.

geriatrics Medical treatment and study of older people. See *gerontology.*

geronting Ageing in terms of *psychological ageing.*

gerontologists Practitioners of *gerontology*.

gerontology The study of ageing and later life. The term is often restricted to psychological, sociological and more generally the social-scientific aspects of ageing.

gerontopsychology *psychogerontology*.

geropsychology *psychogerontology*.

Gf/gf Symbol for *fluid intelligence*.

Gibson Spiral Maze A test of *psychomotor* skill, in which the participant is required to trace a pencil line around a spiral shaped path as quickly and accurately as possible.

glaucoma An excess accumulation of fluid in the eyeball, increasing pressure on retinal cells, leading to their (permanent) destruction.

GMS *Geriatric Mental State*.

Gorham Proverb Interpretation Test Measure of intelligence through ability to interpret proverbs. See *proverb interpretation*.

graceful degradation The phenomenon that the considerable cell loss which typically accompanies ageing is reflected in a gentle loss of memories and level of skill (rather than a wholesale and absolute loss).

granny dumping Slang term for the process whereby caregivers (usually adult children) who cannot cope with an older relative abandon him or her to the local authorities (sometimes literally leaving him or her on the doorstep of the local hospital/social services office).

granulovacuolar degenerations Malformed dead neurons which under a microscope look like dense granules.

grey matter The cell bodies, synapses, etc., of nerve cells of the *central nervous system*, responsible for neural processing. Contrast with *white matter*, which is principally composed of the parts of the cells responsible for transmitting the information.

greying population A population in which there is an appreciable increase in the proportion of older adults within it.

Hachinski Ischaemic Score (IS) A diagnostic technique identifying *vascular dementias*. Patients are scored on the number of symptoms they display, with strongly indicative symptoms being weighted.

HALE *healthy life expectancy*.

haemorrhage Rupture of a blood vessel wall.

Halsted-Reitan Neuropsychological Battery (HRNB) A battery of neuropsychological tests, assessing abstract reasoning and linguistic, sensory, visuo-spatial and motor skills.

Harvard Alumni Study A study of the relationship between disease risk and level of exercise, diet, lifestyle, etc. in over 11,000 Harvard alumni (mean age late fifties).

Hayflick limit See *Hayflick phenomenon*.

Hayflick phenomenon Named after its discoverer, L. Hayflick. Living cells taken from a body can be reared in a laboratory and will reduplicate a limited number of times (the *Hayflick limit*). The older the animal from which the cells are taken, the lower this number is. This implies that the upper limit of life expectancy may be due to the simple fact that the body's cells only reduplicate a limited number of times (which in turn may be affected *inter alia* by the length of the *telomeres*).

health transition A radical change in the general health of a group. In the context of ageing, the term is often used to denote the radical changes in the pattern of health and social care brought about by the decline in infectious diseases and the rise in the proportion of older adults in the populations of developed countries.

healthy life expectancy (HALE) The amount of remaining *life expectancy* that can be expected to be lived free of poor health.

hearing impairment (HI) Loss of auditory sensitivity sufficient to cause disability. Often measured in terms of the minimum volume (measured in decibels, or dB) which can be reliably heard (the higher the figure the worse the impairment). For example, a hearing loss of 90 dB means that the quietest sound which a person can hear is over 90 dB (i.e. about the same noise level as heavy traffic). See *profound hearing impairment.*

hemispheres (cortex) The *cerebral cortex* is divided into two equally sized halves, or hemispheres, along a vertical axis running from the front to the back of the head. In most individuals, the left hemisphere tends to specialise in linguistic and the right in visuo-spatial skills. The hemispheres are linked by several pathways, of which the most important is the *corpus callosum.*

HI *hearing impairment.*

hierarchical approach (intelligence) The theory that intelligence comprises a general intellectual ability (*g*) and a range of more specialised skills.

hippocampus Area of the brain particularly concerned with memory and the transfer of information from short- to long-term memory. Damage to this area can result in a particularly debilitating amnesia, characterised by failure to retain any new information.

hold tests See *deterioration quotient (DQ).*

holding on See *armoured defensive personality.*

hostility An irrational level of antagonism towards others for real (or imagined) acts that have acted adversely on a person.

Huntingdon's disease Genetic disorder resulting in neural decay. Early symptoms include disturbances of movement and jerking movements. There is also a severe decline in cognitive abilities.

Hutchinson-Gilford syndrome Extremely rare disease with onset in infancy characterised by accelerated physical (though not mental) ageing.

Patients have a characteristic 'bird-like' appearance of large hooked nose and bulging eyes. Death is typically in the early teens.

hyperactive delirium See *delirium.*

hyperactivity An inappropriately high level of activity, which either cannot be controlled, or can be, but only with difficulty. Characteristic of some patients with *dementia*, who may pace up and down or begin *wandering.*

hyperborean ageing myth Myth that there is a distant land where people have incredibly long lifespans. Also known as *antediluvian ageing myth.*

hyperlexia Reading accurately but with no or little comprehension of what is being read. See *demented dyslexia.*

hypermetamorphosis The compulsive urge to touch everything.

hyperorality The urge to put everything seen into the mouth.

hypoactive delirium See *delirium.*

hypokinesia Difficulty in imitating a movement.

hypothalamus *Subcortical* section of the brain, whose primary task is to assist in the control of bodily drives (e.g. hunger and satiety, anger, sex).

hypothesis scanning Asking specific questions to seek verification of a specific hypothesis.

iatrogenic illness Describes any complaint induced by medical treatment (e.g. drug side-effects).

iconic memory Memory for items which appear for a fraction of a second and disappear before there is time for them to be fully processed and recognised.

id The basic appetitive urge that Freud argued underpinned human behaviour. See *ego* and *superego.*

illusions Distorted perceptions.

immune system theory of ageing *autoimmune theory of ageing.*

implicit memory See *explicit memory.*

individualised grandmother See *Robertson's taxonomy of grandmothers.*

infarct (a) The cell death caused by damage to the blood vessels supplying the cells in question. (b) The whole process of blood vessel damage and resulting cell death (though strictly speaking this is *infarction*).

infarction The creation of an *infarct.*

inhibition deficit Generally, a failure to inhibit: can refer to an age-related problem of failing adequately to inhibit unnecessary pieces of information or actions. For example, in trying to remember a list of words, failing to 'block out' items from a now-redundant list learnt earlier.

inhibition theory A theory of cognitive ageing which argues that older people become less proficient at inhibiting extraneous information and concentrating on the task at hand.

inhibitory (neurons) An inhibitory neuron (almost invariably in combination with many other inhibitory neurons) either slows or prevents the activation of another neuron.

inhibitory deficit hypothesis Theory that a cause of ageing decline is due to a failure to inhibit irrelevant information; for example, failing to reject items from memory from earlier lists of *to-be-remembered* items that are not part of a current *to-be-remembered* list.

inhibitory functioning Inhibiting (i.e. preventing) alternative course of action so that only the correct action is executed. The phrase is often applied to one of the principal functions of the frontal lobes.

initial letter priming Providing participants with the initial letters of words which the participants are trying to recall.

institutionalised behaviour Nebulous term for deleterious changes in some individuals, resulting from a (usually lengthy) spell in an institution (e.g. hospital, retirement home). Such afflicted individuals tend to have poor social skills, lack of 'individuality', lowered intelligence test scores, and so forth.

integrated personality *Personality* type found in Neugarten *et al.*'s (1961, 1968) studies. Possessors of this type were of three kinds: *reorganisers* (finding new things to do as old ones became impractical), *focused* (activities were restricted in scope, but were rewarding) or *disengaged* (deliberately avoiding responsibilities).

integrity versus despair In Erikson's theory, a conflict which has to be resolved in later life – whether to come to terms with one's past (*ego integration*) or to feel that past events cannot be amended.

intellectual realism Term (first used by Luquet, 1927) describing drawings or pictures in which the 'true' state of the object is represented rather than what can be seen ('perceptual realism').

intelligence quotient (IQ) Often (erroneously) used as an exact synonym of 'intelligence'. IQ denotes a person's intellectual skills relative to his or her *age cohort* (traditionally, a score of 100 denotes average, and scores less than 70 or greater than 130 fairly exceptional). Thus, the same number of questions answered correctly (the *raw score*) means different things to different age groups. For instance, an older person with a raw score of e.g. 40 is probably more gifted than a younger adult with a raw score of 40 on the same test. Hence, the older adult's IQ is higher than the younger adult's. IQ tends to stay reasonably constant throughout life (i.e. a person remains in the same position relative to his or her age peers) – it is the raw score which declines in later adulthood.

interbrain See *diencephalon.*

internal cue A mental prompt ro something that is produced within the mind without an external reminder such as an alarm. Compare with an *external cue*, which is a physical prompt to do something (e.g. an alarm clock, a note in a diary).

introversion See *extraversion-introversion.*

intrusions When referring to linguistic errors, an inappropriate segment of language (e.g. a repetition of an earlier phrase in an inappropriate place in the current statement).

IQ *intelligence quotient.*

irregular spelling A word whose pronunciation disobeys the normal rules of spelling-to-sound correspondence. Irregular words abound in English (e.g. 'quay', 'misled').

IS *Hachinski Ischaemic Score.*

KDCT *Kendrick Digit Copying Test.*

Kendrick Battery for the Detection of Dementia in the Elderly Early version of the *Kendrick Cognitive Tests for the Elderly.*

Kendrick Cognitive Tests for the Elderly Test battery for identifying *dementia* in participants aged 55 years and over. Consists of two tests. The *Kendrick Object Learning Test (KOLT)* is a memory test for arrays of pictures and the *Kendrick Digit Copying Test (KDCT)* measures the speed at which the participant copies a set of numbers.

Kendrick Digit Copying Test (KDCT) See *Kendrick Cognitive Tests for the Elderly.*

Kendrick Object Learning Test (KOLT) See *Kendrick Cognitive Tests for the Elderly.*

Kluver-Bucy syndrome A collection of abnormal behaviours, including *hyperorality, bulimia, visual agnosia, hypermetamorphosis* and loss of *affect.*

KOLT *Kendrick Object Learning Test.*

Korsakoff's syndrome (KS) Severe amnesia (particularly for new information) resulting from brain damage caused by long-term alcohol abuse coupled with vitamin deficiency through poor diet. Damage is particularly centred in the *hippocampus.*

Kübler-Ross's stages of dying Psychological stages exhibited by dying people, according to the work of E. Kübler-Ross (e.g. 1970). Consist of *denial of death stage,* followed by *anger. Bargaining* follows (pleas to the deity, fate, etc.), followed by *depression* and finally, *acceptance.* See *Pattison's stages of dying.*

Kuru Type of *prion disease* found in New Guinea. Probably orginated in burial practices that included eating brain tissue.

lacunar deficits The phenomenon sometimes encountered in brain-damaged patients, where some intellectual functions are almost completely destroyed, whilst others remain relatively intact.

lacunar strokes Form of *subcortical arteriosclerotic dementia.*

late adult transition The period surrounding retirement.

late life psychosis Any psychosis (any mental illness characterised by a severe loss of contact with reality in the absence of *dementia* or *delirium;* principally the term describes *schizophrenia*) which manifests itself in later life. The condition can appear in tandem with dementing symptoms, but need not do.

late onset schizophrenia (LOS) *Schizophrenia* which first manifests itself in middle age or later.

late paraphrenia Mental disorder of later life, characterised by symptoms of feelings of persecution and elaborate fantasies of the same. Commoner in women. Can have a variety of causes, including cardiovascular problems and previous episodes of mental illness.

letter strings Groups of letters which may or may not form real words.

Lewy body A form of brain cell damage found in some patients with *dementia;* the damage comprises a dense round body surrounded by looser filaments.

Lewy body disease A proposed (though not yet universally accepted) category of *dementia* attributable to the presence of *Lewy bodies*.

lexical decision task Participants are shown *letter strings* and must decide as quickly as possible if they form words.

life crisis A set of profoundly negative feelings created by the transition from one *social age* to another.

life expectancy How much longer a person can expect to live. Typically describes the average remaining life for a particular *age cohort*, and is often formally defined as the age at which half the cohort will be predicted to have died. Contrast with *lifespan*.

lifespan The maximum age which a member of a species can expect to live. Contrast with *life expectancy*.

living will Usually signed and witnessed declaration that in the event of becoming so ill as to be placed on a 'life support' system, that such apparatus be switched off if there is no prospect of a satisfactory recovery.

long-term memory (LTM) Memory for events of more than a few minutes ago. Long-term memory is often sub-classified according to the nature of what is being remembered; see *autobiographical*, *episodic*, *prospective*, *remote* and *semantic memory*.

longitudinal research/samples/study Experimental method in which the same participants are tested at different ages. Compare with *cross-sectional research/samples/study*. See overlapping *longitudinal study* and *sequential research design*.

LOS *late onset schizophrenia*.

loudness recruitment Problem found in some forms of hearing impairment in which sounds in certain frequency bands are (mis)perceived as being louder than normal, sometimes to the point of being painful.

LTM *long-term memory*.

macular degeneration Degeneration and ultimately loss of the eye's 'yellow spot' or macula, which is responsible for the highest resolution of focus in the eye.

mad cow disease *bovine spongiform encephalopathy*.

magnetic resonance imaging (MRI scan) Method of obtaining cross-sectional or three-dimensional images of body parts (including the brain). Essentially works by detecting the resonance of cell molecules in a magnetic field and extrapolating an image from these.

manic depression *bipolar disorder*.

matching (participants) Process of ensuring that groups of participants have equivalent scores on certain essential measures, thereby ensuring that any group differences found on other tests are not due to differences on the measures which have been matched. For example, if groups of older and younger adults have been chosen for identical scores on intelligence tests, and an age group difference is then found on Test *X*, then this difference cannot be due to differences in intelligence, but must be due to something else (e.g. age).

ME *molar equivalence*.

ME-MD strategy See *molar equivalence*.

mechanistic intelligence Term devised by Baltes to describe the current state of a person's intellectual abilities. This is contrasted with *pragmatic intelligence*, which is the knowledge a person has accumulated in the past.

memory span The longest list of items which a participant can reliably remember. Researchers vary in their interpretation of 'reliably' – e.g. some hold that span is the longest list length consistently remembered, others that it is the length remembered on 50 per cent of occasions.

memory trace The storage of memory.

mental capacity The limit on how much information a mind can process at any one time, and/or how quickly it can process information.

Mental Status Questionnaire (MSQ) Devised by Kahn *et al.* (1960), a simple gauge of a (usually demented) patient's intellectual status and degree of functional independence. See *Blessed Dementia Scale.*

metaknowledge A person's understanding of the quantity and accuracy of what he or she knows.

metamemory A person's knowledge about their own memory abilities.

method of loci A technique for improving memory. Participants imagine a familiar scene and juxtapose images of *to-be-remembered* items onto it. By taking a 'mental walk' through the scene, participants should be able to remember the items.

MID *multi-infarct dementia.*

Mill Hill Vocabulary Test A measure of vocabulary – the test requires participants to provide definitions of words, whose obscurity increases as the test progresses (there is no time limit).

Mini Mental State Examination (MMSE) A quickly-administered assessment of the general intellectual state of a patient. Questions include measures of orientation for time and place, basic tests of *short-term memory*, and ability to name common objects.

Minnesota Multiphasic Personality Inventory (MMPI) Personality test, yielding scores on ten scales, which are indices of (principally abnormal) personality traits.

mixed delirium See *delirium.*

MMPI *Minnesota Multiphasic Personality Inventory.*

MMSE *Mini Mental State Examination.*

mnemonic (a) Memory aid. (b) More generally, pertaining to memory and its workings.

molar equivalence (ME) A *molar skill* is one which can be broken down into a number of sub-skills (*molecular decomposition*). If a molar skill is performed equally well by groups of differing ages, then 'molar equivalence' is said to have occurred. However, a skill is performed equally well but some of the sub-skills are performed better by some groups than others, then an *ME-MD strategy* (*or compensation*) has occurred.

molar skill See *molar equivalence.*

molecular decomposition See *molar equivalence.*

morphology Strictly speaking, the science of form. More generally, an awareness and knowledge of word meanings and word structure.

motor (neurons) Carrying signals from the *central nervous system* to skeletal muscle.

motor skills Ability to control bodily movements. 'Fine motor skills' describes control of relatively delicate movements, such as manual dexterity.

MRI scan *magnetic resonance imaging.*

MSQ *Mental Status Questionnaire.*

multi-infarct dementia (MID) Form of *dementia* characterised by the brain suffering a large number of *infarcts*. Patients typically suffer a steplike rather than progressive decline.

multiple regression Statistical technique for predicting the value of a variable given the value of several others. The technique can also be used to see which variable of several is the best predictor of another variable and whether once the best predictor's performance has been taken into account, the remaining variables can add any further predictive value to the equation.

mutation accumulation theory The theory that many of the deleterious changes found in later life have evolved because it is a period of life after breeding has taken place and in any case few animals reach this stage 'in the wild'. Thus, there is no or little evolutionary pressure preventing ageing.

myelin Fatty insulating layer found around many neurons. Acts in a manner akin to the insulating plastic around electrical wires.

N *neuroticism.*

naming latency The speed with which a new word can be read aloud.

NART *National Adult Reading Test.*

National Adult Reading Test (NART) A list of words, most with *irregular spellings*, which participants must read out loud (i.e. pronounce).

need for cognition A measure of the drive to pursue intellectually demanding tasks.

negative correlation A value of *r* falling below zero and greater than -1. In other words, a relationship in which as one variable increases in value, the other declines (e.g. number of sweets eaten and desire to eat more). See *correlation.*

negative priming Creating the conditions so that performance on a subsequent task is marred. This generally involves swapping which items are used as targets and distractors, but other methods are possible.

nerve See *neuron.*

neural noise Concept that neural signals lose some of their fidelity because of interfering signals from neighbouring neurons (loosely, akin to poor radio reception because of interference from other stations). This is assumed to increase in later life, making mental processing less efficient and hence lowering intellectual ability.

neuritic plaque *senile plaque.*

neurofibrillary tangles (NFT) Clumps of dead brain neurons which (under a microscope and with some artistic licence) look like knotted string. Common feature of the brains of patients with *dementia of the Alzheimer type.*

neuroleptic drug Drug primarily designed to lessen the disturbed behaviours seen in many forms of psychosis, but because of its calming effects is sometimes (and often inappropriately) used as a tranquilliser for patients presenting 'awkward' behaviours.

neuron/neurone An individual 'nerve' or 'nerve cell' (strictly speaking, a *nerve* is a collection of neurons forming a common path for sending messages in the *peripheral nervous system;* a similar structure in the *central nervous system* is called a *tract*).

neuroticism As used in this book a *personality trait* from *Eysenck's personality model.* Generally, neuroticism measures how anxious and emotionally unstable a person is.

neurotransmitters Chemicals transmitted between neurons at *synapses,* and hence the means by which neurons communicate with each other.

new learning deficit Relative difficulty in learning new information, in comparison with older information and/or another group of people. Used by some commentators to describe the relative weakness of older people in learning a new piece of information and/or task.

NFT *neurofibrillary tangle.*

NINCDS-ADRDA criteria A set of criteria for evaluating the probability that a patient is suffering from *dementia of the Alzheimer type.* The initials refer to the organisations who jointly devised the scheme. It provides a diagnosis of 'probable', 'possible' or 'definite'.

nocturnal delirium *sundown syndrome.*

noise in nervous system *neural noise.*

non-normative life development Aspects of a person's life unique to them (i.e. as opposed to experiences held in common with others alive at the same time, such as major news events, etc.).

noradrenaline A *neurotransmitter.*

noradrenergic system Network of neurons using *noradrenaline* as their *neurotransmitter.* Primarily used in the control of smooth muscle.

normal distribution A distribution of scores/measurements which has a characteristic bell-shaped curve with a peak above the horizontal axis, and which is symmetrical about its vertical midpoint. The peak of the curve represents the mean (i.e. average), median (the score which is bigger than 50 per cent of the values represented by the curve) and the mode (the commonest score). Because the distribution is found for many types of measurement, it is termed 'normal' and many types of statistical test are predicated on the assumption that data are drawn from normally distributed populations.

normal pressure hydrocephalus Caused by a failure of *cerebrospinal fluid* to drain away, leading to a destructive pressure on brain tissue. The complaint can lead to *dementia*.

normative age-graded development See *Baltes's theory of lifespan development*.

normative history-graded development See *Baltes's theory of lifespan development*.

nun study A longitudinal study of a group of American nuns who have agreed to be tested on a battery of psychological and medical tests each year, and have agreed that on death their brains will be made available for autopsy.

nvCJD See *Creutzfeldt-Jakob Disease*.

Object Memory Evaluation (OME) Measure of memory for objects at different gaps of time and employing learning trials.

observer memory The phenomenon that one's distant *autobiographical memories* are usually recalled as if one were a bystander.

obsessive-compulsive disorder See *anxiety disorder*.

obsolescence effect Theory that some age-related deterioration may be because older people's memories may no longer be attuned to the contemporary world (i.e. are obsolete rather than lost).

occipital lobes Regions of the *cerebral cortex* roughly in the region of the back of the head. Their principal function is in vision.

old age dependency ratio The number of people aged 60 and over divided by the number aged 20–64. This gives an indication of the proportion of people drawing pensions and other welfare and health benefits to those in employment who will be the principal financial supporters of this through taxation.

old elderly Most commonly defined as those people aged over 75 years (though note commentators differ over the precise figure). See *young elderly*.

OME *Object Memory Evaluation*.

ondansetron Drug whose effects include the enhanced release of acetylcholine (see *cholinergic hypothesis*) and thus a potentially beneficial treatment of some forms of *dementia*. See *ganglioside* and *tacrine*.

ordered recall A memory task in which items have to be recalled in exactly the order in which they were originally presented. Compare with *free recall*.

overlapping longitudinal study Type of *longitudinal study* in which several *age cohorts* are tested at regular intervals on the same body of tests. Cross-cohort comparisons can be made at each test session (as in a *cross-sectional study*); ageing change within the same individuals can be measured (as in a longitudinal study), and by comparing performance of different cohorts as they reach the same age at different calendrical times, it is possible to assess the strength of *cohort effects*.

P *psychoticism*.

paired associate learning Remembering which item was previously presented with which (e.g. the participant sees the words 'cat' and 'briefcase' presented together, and later when shown 'cat' must recall 'briefcase').

panic attack See *anxiety disorder.*

panic disorder See *anxiety disorder.*

parietal lobes The region of the *cerebral cortex* which occupies an area contiguous with an Alice band (or headphones strap) across the head. Their role is hard to define concisely, but they can be said to be involved in maintaining an awareness of the body's state and location, and in interpreting symbols.

Parkinsonian dementia *dementia* in which *Parkinsonism* is present.

Parkinsonism Set of symptoms, including a shuffling gait and trembling hands, *bradykinesia* and *hypokinesia*, found in *Parkinson's Disease* and also in several other brain disorders, including some of the *dementias.*

Parkinson's disease (PD) Illness caused by a decline in the substantia nigra (an area of the brain responsible for producing *dopamine*). Characteristic symptoms are known collectively as *Parkinsonism.*

partial correlation A statistical technique for assessing how much of the *correlation* between two variables is due to the coincidental effect of a third variable (the removal of whose influence is known as *partialling out*).

partialling out See *partial correlation.*

passive-dependent personality *Personality* type identified by Neugarten *et al.*'s (1961, 1968) studies. Possessors of this type rely on others to help them (*succourant seeking*) or withdraw from human interaction as much as possible (*apathetic*).

passive euthanasia Allowing someone to die by not administering life-saving or life-prolonging treatment.

patient cohort Group of patients with not only an illness in common but also a set of attitudes (e.g. feeling 'unhealthy'). Compare with *disease cohort.*

Pattison's stages of dying Psychological stages which a dying patient passes through according to E.M. Pattison (1977). (1) *acute crisis phase* – great anxiety upon realising that death is imminent; (2) *chronic living-dying phase* – a period of mourning for what is being lost; (3) *terminal phase* – an inward withdrawal and resignation/acceptance. See *Kübler-Ross's stages of dying.*

PD *Parkinson's disease.*

PDD *primary degenerative disorder.* See *dementia of the Alzheimer type.*

peg board task Several variants of this task, but all have the central feature of requiring the participant to put pegs into holes as quickly as possible.

peripheral nervous system (PNS) Neurons connecting the *central nervous system* to the rest of the body.

perseverations Inappropriate repetition (e.g. repeating the same phrase or keeping at a particular problem-solving strategy after it has been demonstrated to be inappropriate).

personality 'The individual characteristics and ways of behaving that, in their organisation or patterning, account for an individual's unique adjustments, to his or her total environment' (Hilgard *et al.*, 1979, p.541).

personality trait An enduring characteristic of *personality* which is hypothesised to underpin all or most behaviour.

PET scan See *positron emission tomography.*

PHI *profound hearing impairment.*

phobia See *anxiety disorder.*

phoneme The smallest unit of speech whose substitution or removal from a word causes a change in the word's sound. More loosely, the basic sounds which make up words (and even more loosely, the verbal equivalent of letters).

phonological Pertaining to *phonemes.*

phonological loop *Slave system* in the *working memory model* responsible for the temporary storage of any information capable of being stored *phonologically*.

phonology Strictly speaking, the study of phonetics. Sometimes used to denote a person's awareness and understanding of phonological structure.

physiological age *Biological age* expressed through the state of the body's physiological processes, such as metabolic rate. See *anatomical age*.

Piagetian conservation tasks A series of tests (named after their inventor, Piaget) intended to demonstrate the illogicality of children's thought processes.

Piaget's 'kidnapping' Anecdote by Piaget (the famous developmental psychologist) illustrating the fallibility of *autobiographical memory*. Piaget had a distinct memory of a kidnap attempt on himself when aged two years, which his nurse successfully repulsed. Years later, he discovered that the nurse had invented the whole episode, and therefore his memory was an elaboration of her story rather than the recall of a real event.

Pick's bodies Damaged neurons, found in *Pick's disease* patients, and possessing a characteristic swollen appearance.

Pick's disease A form of *dementia* characterised by a progressive deterioration of the frontal lobes and other subcortical areas of the brain. Psychologically, there are often disturbances in personality before intellect or memory.

PMA See *Primary Mental Abilities Test*.

PNS *peripheral nervous system*.

positive correlation A value of *r* greater than 0 and less than 1. In other words, a relationship where as one variable increases, so does another. See *correlation*.

positron emission tomography (PET) An electronic scanning method which measures how a section of the body (in the context of this book, typically the brain) metabolises a (mildly radioactive) tracer injected into the blood. This gives an indication of the relative level of activity, and by implication, health, of the area of the body being surveyed.

post-developmental A phrase used by some gerontologists to denote that changes in later life are often detrimental rather than developmental and/or beneficial.

postformal thought Theory that in adulthood, people develop the ability to combine subjective and objective criteria in resolving a problem. The term refers to the concept that it develops after *formal operations*.

potential lifespan *lifespan*.

practice effect The phenomenon that the more times a person takes part in psychological tests, the better their performance on them. This can apply even when the tests are not particularly similar (i.e. it is not simply the case that the person is remembering the correct answers from a previous test session). It is probably attributable to becoming increasingly familiar with the general methods used, being less tense, etc.

pragmatic intelligence See *mechanistic intelligence*.

pragmatics The understanding of the intent of an utterance rather than its literal interpretation. More generally, the ability to grasp the most satisfactory solution rather than the one which is necessarily logically correct.

pre-morbid IQ The *IQ* level (usually estimated) of a person before the onset of an illness (usually one which has affected the intellect, such as *dementia*).

pre-senile dementia *dementia* where onset is before the patient's sixtieth birthday.

presby- Prefix denoting old or ageing.

presbyacusis *presbycusis.*

presbycusis Hearing loss which worsens with ageing, typically characterised by loss of ability to hear high frequency sounds.

presbyo- *presby-.*

presbyopia Inability to focus on near objects.

presenilin-1 Gene located on chromosome 14 associated with a variant of early onset *dementia of the Alzheimer type.*

presenilin-2 Gene located on chromosome 1 associated with a variant of early onset *dementia of the Alzheimer type.*

preserved differentiation Theory that some skills are better preserved than others in later life because they have always been better. The argument is implausible for the general population, but may be feasible for specific samples of the population with very specialised skills (e.g. professional musicians).

primary ageing Age changes which all older people can expect to experience to some degree (e.g. skin wrinkling). See *secondary ageing* and *universal ageing.*

primary degenerative dementia (PDD) *dementia of the Alzheimer type.*

primary memory *short-term memory.*

Primary Mental Abilities Test (PMA) An intelligence *test battery* devised by Thurstone.

primary vascular dementia *multi-infarct dementia.*

priming In memory experiments, providing hints about features of the items a participant is trying to recall.

prion disease Group term for a range of degenerative brain disorders, such as *bovine spongiform encephalopathy* and *Creutzfeldt-Jakob Disease*, which some commentators believe are due to an abnormal protein metabolism. 'Prion' is an abbreviation of 'proteinaceous infectious particle'.

probabilistic ageing Aspects of ageing likely to affect most (but not necessarily all) older people (e.g. cardiovascular problems). Similar to *secondary ageing.* See *universal ageing.*

processing resources theory of ageing Any theory which argues that changes in ageing intellectual skills are attributable to a lowered capacity for mental calculations (e.g. of *working memory*), lowered speed of processing, etc.

profound hearing impairment (PHI) *Hearing impairment* of > 90 dB.

progeria Disease characterised by the symptoms of abnormally rapid ageing (patients typically die in their teens).

programmed cell death A method by which cells can keep control of total cell growth by in effect destroying themselves. The phenomenon is well documented in non-ageing aspects of cell activity. Some theories of ageing argue that programmed cell death may be the root cause of ageing. For example, the *Hayflick limit* is marked by the onset of programmed cell death.

programmed senescence Belief that the body is genetically programmed to age, usually with the implication that this is the result of evolutionary pressure. See *programmed theory of ageing.*

programmed theory of ageing Theory that cells may be predestined to die because of inbuilt faults in the replication system (see e.g. *Hayflick limit*). Not to be confused with *programmed senescence*, which more often denotes that these problems are the result of evolutionary pressure.

progressive (illness) Description of an illness in which the symptoms appear and then get worse over time.

progressive supranuclear palsy (PSP) Illness characterised by disturbances of motor function and mild to moderate *dementia.*

prospective memory The ability to remember to do something in the future.

proverb interpretation Measure of the understanding of the meaning of proverbs (e.g. *Gorham Proverb Interpretation Test*). Patients in the early stages of *dementia* may give very literal interpretations of proverbs meant to be taken at symbolic value (e.g. 'a rolling stone gathers no moss').

proximal ageing effects Ageing changes directly attributable to changes in another process (e.g. a *stroke*). Compare with *distal ageing effects.*

PSEN1 *presenilin-1.*

PSEN2 *presenilin-2.*

pseudodementia Severe lowering of cognitive abilities to *dementia*-like levels caused by severe depression in some older patients.

PSP *progressive supranuclear palsy.*

psychogenic mortality Psychological factors leading to physical symptoms which in turn cause death.

psychogerontology The study of the psychology of ageing.

psychological age A person's psychological state compared to that of an average person of the same *chronological age.*

psychometrics Strictly speaking, the measurement of psychological traits and skills, but more generally, the study of psychological differences.

psychomotor skill A physical skill in which there is a strong component of intellectual prowess or vice versa.

psychotherapy Any treatment regime based on an integrated theory of mind.

psychoticism A personality trait in *Eysenck's personality model* measuring the degree of emotional 'coldness' a person possesses.

pugilistic dementia *Dementia* induced by repeated blows to the head, often over some period of time (has been observed in some older boxers, hence the name).

pyramidal society Society in which there are far more younger than older people (the population can be envisaged as successively smaller age groups stacked one on top of another, forming a pyramid). This contrasts with a *rectangular society,* in which there are roughly equal numbers of people in each age group (and hence the layers stacked on each other look more like a rectangle than a pyramid).

quality ratio In studies of creativity, the ratio of good to indifferent or poor works produced by a person within a particular time period.

r Symbol for *correlation.*

RAGS *Relatives' Assessment of Global Symptomatology.*

Ranschburg effect The phenomenon that lists of *to-be-remembered* items are less well remembered if some of the items are repeated within the list.

Ratcliff diffusion model A model of decision-making devised by Ratcliff (1978) that assumes in making a decision involving two choices (e.g. accept versus reject), evidence accumulates in favour of both until one reaches a threshold and is accepted over the other (e.g. a person decides to accept rather than reject, or vice versa). Speed of accumulation of evidence, the level of the threshold and the discriminability between the two alternatives can all vary (e.g. through practice, the general efficiency of mental processing, the degree of conservatism exhibited in setting thresholds, etc.). The situation is analogous to two rival cattle drovers trying to persuade a cow to pass through their respective gates. The proximity of the gate to the starting point (analogous to the threshold) the degree to which the cow can tell the drovers apart (akin to the discriminability of the two choices) and the speed and strength of the drover's cajoling (akin to the speed of accumulation of evidence) can all vary. The model (rather more complex and elegant than this description makes it sound) has been widely used in studies such as memory and reaction time tasks, in part because of its high level of correspondence with the empirical evidence, but also because it allows for different components of a response to a stimulus to be statistically separated and examined.

Raven's Progressive Matrices A test of *fluid intelligence*, in which participants are given a series of problems (against the clock) which have a common theme of a logically governed sequence from which one member is missing (the participant must find the missing member from a set of choices).

raw score The actual score on a test, as opposed to an adjusted or weighted figure, such as the *intelligence quotient*.

re-engagement theory *activity theory.*

reaction time (RT) Time taken for a person to respond to the appearance of a stimulus. See *choice reaction time* and *simple reaction time.*

recall The ability to remember items in memory without any prompting. See *ordered recall* and *free recall.*

recognition The ability to identify which items have been previously encountered when given a list of alternatives to choose from.

rectangular society See *pyramidal society.*

rectangular survival curve Hypothesised graph of percentage of *survivors* in an *age cohort* in a future of very effective medical care. By this reckoning, very few people will die until their *lifespan* is reached, when most will die within a few years of each other. A graph of the percentage of the age cohort alive at different ages (with percentage of

the vertical axis and age on the horizontal) would thus look rectangular.

reflex arc A simple connection between *afferent* and *efferent neurons* in the spinal cord. The mechanism is responsible for several reflexes (e.g. the famous knee-jerk reflex).

regression Statistical technique predicting the value of one variable from the value of another. See *multiple regression.*

regression hypothesis Theory that older people's linguistic skills revert to the qualitative state of a child's.

rehearsal (memory) The process of repeating *to-be-remembered* items 'in the head' in an effort to remember them better.

Relatives' Assessment of Global Symptomatology (RAGS) Questionnaire measure of symptoms of the patient observed by his or her *caregivers.*

reminiscence bump *reminiscence peak.*

reminiscence peak Phenomenon that the bulk of *autobiographical memories* stem from when people were 10–30 years old.

remote grandmother See *Robertson's taxonomy of grandmothers.*

remote memory Memory for non-autobiographical events which have occurred during a person's lifetime. A frequent proviso is that these events must exclude famous incidents which have been aired in the media so often that they are part of general knowledge.

reorganisers See *integrated personality.*

reversible dementia An illness which produces symptoms of *dementia*, but which can be cured and in the process reverse or at least lessen the dementing symptoms.

reversible dementia of depression *pseudodementia.*

Ribot's hypothesis Theory that in damaged or decaying mental systems, memories for recent events are worse than memories for remote events.

Rivermead Behavioural Memory Test Set of memory tasks analogous to everyday situations where memory is required (e.g. face recognition, remembering a route).

Robertson's taxonomy of grandmothers J.F. Robertson (1977) categorised grandmothers into four types: (1) *apportioned grandmother* – has both a social and a personal set of expectations for her grandchildren; (2) *symbolic grandmother* – has a social set of expectations; (3) *individualised grandmother* – has a set of personal expectations; (4) *remote grandmother* – relatively detached from the whole idea of being a grandmother.

rocking chair personality See *dependent personality*.

Roseto effect The effect on health of changing a lifestyle. Named after an Italian-American community in Roseto, Pennsylvania, whose susceptibility to heart disease increased as it became more 'Americanised'.

RT *reaction time.*

SAD *subcortical arteriosclerotic dementia.*

SATSA *Swedish Adoption/Twin Study on Aging.*

schema Collection of memories about an event or item which enable one to plan responses and to interpret information surrounding the said event or item.

schizophrenia A profound disorder of thought, perception and language in the absence of mental retardation, characterised by a severe distortion of perception of reality and concomitant changes in emotions and behaviour. There are various forms of the illness, each with a distinct set of symptoms. The commonest of these symptoms include irrational beliefs about the way the world functions, often with a central theme that the patient is being persecuted. There may also be hallucinations (such as 'voices in the head'). Language can often be best described as 'surreal', with unusual expressions and ideas and invented words.

Seattle Longitudinal Aging Study *Longitudinal study* of psychological ageing, run by K.W. Schaie and colleagues. The first participants were tested in 1956 and have been retested (along with new cohorts of participants) at regular intervals ever since.

secondary ageing Age changes associated with, but not necessarily an inevitable consequence of, ageing (e.g. arthritis). See *primary ageing* and *probabilistic ageing.*

selective attention The ability to attend to one stimulus set against distracting stimuli.

self-hatred personality Personality type identified by Reichard *et al.* (1962) characterised by unrealistic self-blame for misfortune.

semantic Pertaining to meaning.

semantic deficit hypothesis Model of ageing which argues that age-related deficits in intellectual functioning are attributable to a failure adequately to process incoming items (e.g. items to be memorised) for the information they contain.

semantic facilitation Phenomenon that items are identified faster if preceded by items related in meaning (e.g. 'bread' is identified faster if the participant has just seen 'butter' as opposed to 'car').

semantic memory Memory for facts; compare with *episodic memory.*

semantic priming *semantic facilitation.*

senescence Later life, with the implication of ageing free from *dementia* and other impairments of psychological functioning.

senescing Ageing in terms of *biological age.*

senile Medical term for 'old'; *never* to be used as a synonym for later life.

senile dementia See *dementia*.

senile plaque (SP) Amorphous clumps of dead *neurons* found in high concentrations in the brains of some patients with *dementia*.

sentential grouping A (typically inefficient) method of classifying objects on the grounds that they can be included in the same sentence or story.

sequential research design *Longitudinal study* in which different *age cohorts* are tested at intervals over several years. In addition, age cross-sections of the population are tested in tandem with the longitudinal test panel, to gain an insight into possible *cohort effects*.

SETOF *speed-error-tradeoff function*.

short-term memory (STM) Temporary memory for events which have occurred in the past few seconds/minutes. Has a limited capacity (typically between five and nine items, depending upon the task and the individual), is easily disrupted and items are quickly forgotten unless a conscious effort is made to remember them. See *long-term memory* and *working memory*.

silent stroke *Stroke* which produces no symptoms, and is only discovered by either a brain scan or at autopsy. The term is sometimes used to describe a stroke which is unnoticed at the time of occurrence, but which subsequently causes a significant alteration in behaviour or functioning.

simple reaction time (SRT) Time taken to respond when there is only one choice of response to the stimulus. See *choice reaction time*.

slave systems Term derived from computing to denote systems (usually capable of one type of operation only) which cannot operate unless under the command of a master controller.

SOA *stimulus onset asynchrony*.

social age A set of behaviours and attitudes considered to be socially appropriate for the *chronological age* of the individual.

social clock Hypothesised mechanism which an individual 'consults' to determine the most appropriate behaviour for his or her *social age*.

somatic (peripheral nervous system) Information from joints, skin and skeletal muscle transmitted to the *central nervous system*.

somatic mutation theory of ageing Theory that as cells are lost through natural 'wear and tear' they are replaced by imperfect copies because of genetic errors, and thus are less likely to function efficiently. See *autoimmune theory of ageing, disposable soma theory of ageing, free radical theory of ageing* and *Hayflick phenomenon*.

source memory Memory for the circumstances under which an item was learnt as opposed to memory for the item itself.

SP *senile plaque*.

span Abbreviation of *memory span*.

speed-error-tradeoff function (SETOF) Measure of the degree to which an individual is prepared to trade speed at performing a task (i.e. slow down) in order to reduce the number of errors made. A measure often used in *reaction time* experiments.

speed hypothesis *general slowing hypothesis*.

spinal cord The principal meeting point between *peripheral* and *central nervous system* neurons.

sporadic Alzheimer's disease *Form of dementia of the Alzheimer type* in which the patient developing the disease has no 'obvious' genetic predisposition to develop the illness such as a parent who contracted the same disease at an early age. The term is slightly misleading since there may in fact be a genetic cause (hence why it is avoided in the main body of the book). It is used to distinguish the condition from *familial Alzheimer's disease*.

SRT *simple reaction time*.

standard deviation Statistical measure used, *inter alia*, to indicate the range of scores in a sample. A useful rule is that for a *normal distribution* the range of scores between the mean minus two standard deviations and the mean plus 1.96 standard deviations accounts for 95 per cent of the sample's scores.

statistical theory of ageing The theory that ageing occurs because of random cumulative damage and loss. Most such events are relatively minor in themselves but it is their combined impact that is of importance.

stimulus onset asynchrony (SOA) In a *backward masking* experiment, the difference between the length of time the *to-be-remembered* item has to be presented alone and the length of time it has to be presented when it is followed by a mask for it to be correctly recognised.

STM *short-term memory.*

stroke Damage to brain tissue caused by the cessation of its blood supply. The psychological effect of the stroke depends upon the location of the injury.

subcortical Pertaining to the areas of the brain other than the *cerebral cortex*.

subcortical arteriosclerotic dementia (SAD) *Vascular dementia* whose primary damage occurs in regions of the brain other than the *cortex*.

subcortical dementia *Dementia* whose principal focus of damage is not in the *cerebral cortex*.

subdural haematoma Blood clot in the brain. See *cerebral haemorrhage*.

subitization The ability to count the number of items in an array 'at once' without counting the individual items. Most people can count between two and four items in this manner, though larger numbers are possible.

successful ageing Rather nebulous term describing (1) older people whose lifestyles are successful, or at least trouble-free and/or (2) more specifically, the retention of youthful levels of performance of the skill in question.

succourant-seeking See *passive-dependent personality*.

Sullivan method Method of calculating the proportion of remaining *life expectancy* that can be expected to be free of significant disability.

sundown syndrome The phenomenon observed in some patients with *dementia*, who get up during the night and wander about, without regard for the propriety of the time or place. See *wandering*. The term may also refer to increased confusion, aggressive or erratic behaviour at the close of day.

superego In Freudian theory, a person's set of (often over-harsh) moral dictums. See *ego* and *id*.

supraspan learning Learning lists of items whose number exceeds one's *memory span*.

survival curve Graph plotting the numbers of people within an *age cohort* still living at different ages.

survivors Members of an *age cohort* who have lived past a particular age.

sustained attention The ability to concentrate on a set task without being distracted.

Swedish Adoption/Twin Study on Ageing (SATSA) *Longitudinal study*, commenced in 1979, of Swedish identical and non-identical twins reared apart or together.

symbolic grandmother See *Robertson's taxonomy of grandmothers*.

synapse The junction between two neurons, in the form of a microscopic gap across which *neurotransmitters* can be sent.

syntax Grammar.

tacrine Drug whose effects include the enhanced release of *acetylcholine* (see *cholinergic hypothesis*), and thus a possible treatment for some forms of *dementia*.

talking book Cassette or other audio recording of a person reading a book. Most talking books are readings of edited versions of the originals to keep the size of the package down to one or two cassettes, discs, etc.

target (1) In *recognition* tasks, the item which has been previously encountered and which must be distinguished from any *distracters* present; (2) in *attention* tasks, the item to be located from amongst the distracters.

TBR *to-be-remembered.*

telomerase Enzyme responsible for maintaining the length of *telomeres* in some specific cell types (principally, egg and sperm cells). Telomerase is not used in all cells, probably because there would be a too-high risk of cancerous cell production.

telomere Section of DNA felt to be involved in ageing. When a cell duplicates itself, the length of the telomere is shortened; after several duplications, it reaches its shortest length and cell duplication can no longer take place.

temporal lobes Section of the *cerebral cortex* occupying (roughly speaking) the areas of the right and left temples. Chief function is in interpretation of information; in most people, the left temporal lobe is essential in language comprehension and production. Also strongly involved in the storage of memory.

terminal drop model The theory that in older individuals, there is a sudden and marked decline in intellectual skills a few months/years before their death.

terminal phase (of dying) See *Pattison's stages of dying.*

tertiary ageing A rapid deterioration during the process of dying.

tertiary memory *remote memory.*

test battery A group of tests designed to assess the same skill (e.g. intelligence).

test wise The condition of becoming attuned to the general design of psychological tests (particu-larly intelligence tests) and improving in perfor-mance as a result. The phenomenon usually arises from using the same panel of volunteers too often, thereby artificially elevating their apparent skills. The problem is of particular concern in *longitudinal studies.*

thalamus Area of brain co-ordinating and chan-nelling information and executing motor move-ments. Damage to this area is heavily involved in *Parkinsonism.*

thanatology The study of death and dying.

theta waves A pattern of electrical activity de-tected by *EEG* with a frequency between 4 and 8 Hz.

third age Active and independent later life. Con-trast with *fourth age.*

threshold age The *chronological age* which (arbi-trarily) denotes the division between one age group and another.

threshold model of dementia The theory that individuals have a genetically fixed predisposition to develop *dementia,* but whether they actually do depends upon a trigger in the environment. In people with a low predisposition, a large environ-mental input is required, and vice versa.

thrombosis Blood vessel blocked due to clotting.

time-based task In *prospective memory* experi-ments, a task requiring a response which must be self-initiated at the appropriate time.

time-lag comparison Comparing different *age cohorts* at the same age in a *longitudinal study.*

time-lag effect *cohort effect.*

time-sequential design An 'extended' *cross-sectional study* design now generally no longer practised. Two or more groups are compared at one time period, and then several years later, different participants are tested, who are the same ages as the participants were in the original study.

tinnitus A hearing complaint characterised by a (usually permanent) irritating noise (often akin to a 'ringing in the ears', and sometimes painful) which interferes with normal hearing.

tip of the tongue (TOT) Phenomenon of recalling features of an item (e.g. what it sounds like, number of syllables, and so forth) but not its identity. Often induced in experiments by providing people with the definition of a word and asking them to name it.

to-be-remembered (TBR) Items in a memory task which the participant is asked to remember.

TOT *tip of the tongue.*

tract See *neuron.*

Trail Making test Sub-test of the *Halsted-Reitan Neuropsychological Battery,* assessing ability to follow sequences. The participant must make a pencil trail between particular numbers (or in another version, numbers and letters) printed on a sheet of paper.

transient ischaemic attack *Stroke* where effects are usually relatively trivial, and are gone within 24 hours.

transmission deficit hypothesis Model of linguistic functioning that argues that activation of words (either in recognition or production) is underpinned by priming of possible alternatives. The speed and efficiency with which these primes are produced will greatly facilitate the speed and accuracy of recognition/production. Ageing is assumed to lower the speed and efficiency with which the priming takes place (more so for production than recognition).

triple jeopardy Term illustrating that older people facing *double jeopardy* often also face a third problem of prejudice and/or communication problems barring them from the help they need and deserve.

two-factor theory of well-being In essence, the theory that positive events tend to influence the positive aspects of one's mood and negative events the negative aspects of one's mood.

Type A personality A personality type prone to being competitive and 'hard edged'. Contrasts with *Type B personality,* which is prone to being (over)easy-going and relaxed.

Type B personality See *Type A personality.*

Ulverscroft large print series Series of popular books in large print size intended for people with visual impairments. Traditional patrons are older users of public libraries.

universal ageing Aspects of ageing held to affect everyone who reaches later life (e.g. wrinkling skin). See *probabilistic ageing.*

VaD *vascular dementia.*

vascular dementia (VaD) *Dementia* caused by damage to the blood vessels within the brain.

verbal span *Memory span* for words.

view from the bridge Title of an Arthur Miller play. Also, in Levinson's theory, the desired state in late life when older people have come to terms with their past.

viscera Intestines.

visual agnosia Inability to recognise objects by sight.

visual marking In a *visual search task,* the inhibition of old items (with the effect of speeding up the search for the target).

visual search task Test of *selective attention.* The participant must find a *target* item which is located in an array of distracter items.

visuo-spatial Pertaining to visual appearance and spatial characteristics (e.g. where items in a display are relative to each other).

visuo-spatial memory The ability to remember visual and/or spatial information.

visuo-spatial sketchpad A *slave system* of the *working memory* model: a temporary store of visuo-spatial information.

WAIS See *Wechsler Adult Intelligence Scale.*

wandering (dementia) Nebulous term describing any inappropriate walking behaviour. This can manifest itself as part of *hyperactivity*, but may also describe walking about apparently aimlessly or 'wandering off' on a walk for no apparently obvious reason (see also *sundown syndrome*).

wear and tear theory Theory of ageing that parts of the body gradually 'wear out' with use. Compare with *cytologic theory*.

Wechsler Adult Intelligence Scale (WAIS) Intelligence *test battery* covering all commonly assessed areas of intelligence.

Wechsler Memory Scale Memory sub-tests from the *Wechsler Adult Intelligence Scale.*

Werner's syndrome Extremely rare disease with onset in teens (though first symptoms may not become 'obvious' for some years), characterised by accelerated physical ageing, notably the skin, hair and cardiovascular system. Death is typically in the forties.

Wernicke's aphasia Specific failure to understand speech, resulting from brain damage.

Wernicke's dementia *Dementia* caused by vitamin deficiency (particularly vitamin B). Often there is an associated motor impairment.

white matter See *grey matter.*

Winston Churchill argument The argument that some individuals (such as Winston Churchill) have lifestyles that modern medical opinion insists are unhealthy and yet lead long productive lives.

Wisconsin Card Sorting Task Measure of hypothesis formation and the ability to reject or not persevere with an invalid one. Participants must discover the correct rule for matching up cards of different patterns and colours (e.g. a yellow card must always be matched with a red card). Once participants have discovered the correct rule, the experimenter changes it, and how quickly the participants stop using the old rule and search for the new one is measured, as well as how quickly they solve the new problem. Abnormally persevering with an old rule can be indicative of brain damage, particularly to the *frontal lobes.*

wisdom Somewhat nebulous concept, with several separate though related definitions, depending upon the researcher in question. Most agree in essence that it refers to an ability to judge and resolve real-life problems which require a balance of logical and pragmatic factors, tempered by experience. However, within this broad remit, individual authors have used the term loosely, ranging from a synonym of *crystallised intelligence* to psychoanalytic theories.

word completion task Task in which the participant is required to complete a word given the first letter(s).

word span *Memory span* for words.

working memory Popular and influential model of *short-term memory*, first described by Baddeley and Hitch (1974). The model argues that short-term memory is controlled by a *central executive*, which delegates memory tasks to specialist *slave systems*, principally the *phonological loop* and *visuo-spatial sketchpad.*

Yngve depth An analytic technique which gives a 'score' for the syntactic complexity of a sentence or phrase.

young elderly The commonest definition is the age group between 60 and 75 years (though lower and higher boundaries are not unknown). See *old elderly.*

young–old plot Plotting a graph of the performances of younger adults against older adults on the same task. Best known example is the *Brinley plot.*

zeitgeist Spirit of the (historical) age.

References

Abel, T. and Werner, M. (2003) HIV risk behaviour of older persons. *European Journal of Public Health, 13*, 350–2.

Aboderin, I. (2004) Decline in material family support for older people in urban Ghana, Africa: Understanding processes and causes of change. *The Journals of Gerontology Series B: Psychological Sciences and Social Sciences, 59*, 128–37.

Abrams, R.C. and Horowitz, S.V. (1996) Personality disorders after age 50: A meta-analysis. *Journal of Personality Disorders, 10*, 271–81.

Abrams, R.C., Spielman, L.A., Alexopoulos, G.S. and Klausner, E. (1998) Personality disorder symptoms and functioning in elderly depressed patients. *American Journal of Geriatric Psychiatry, 6*, 24–30.

Adamek, M.E. and Kaplan, M.S. (1996a) The growing use of firearms by suicidal older women, 1979–1992: A research note. *Suicide and Life-Threatening Behavior, 26*, 71–8.

Adamek, M.E. and Kaplan, M.S. (1996b) Firearm suicide among older men. *Psychiatric Services, 47*, 304–6.

Adams, C. (1991) Qualitative age differences in memory for text: A life-span developmental perspective. *Psychology and Aging, 6*, 323–36.

Adams, C., Smith, M.C., Pasupathi, M. and Vitolo, L. (2002) Social context effects on story recall in older and younger women: Does the listener make a difference? *The Journals of Gerontology Series B: Psychological Sciences and Social Sciences, 57*, 28–40.

Adams, R.D. (1980) The morphological aspects of aging in the human nervous system. In J.E. Birren and R.B. Sloane (eds), *Handbook of Mental Health and Aging*. Englewood Cliffs, NJ: Prentice-Hall, 149–62.

Adams-Price, C. (1992) Eyewitness memory and aging: Predictors of accuracy in recall and person recognition. *Psychology and Aging, 7*, 602–8.

Adkins, G., Martin, P. and Poon, L. (1996) Personality traits and states as predictors of subjective well-being in centenarians, octogenarians and sexagenarians. *Psychology and Aging, 11*, 408–16.

Aihie Sayer, A. and Cooper, C. (1997) Undernutrition and aging. *Gerontology, 43*, 203–5.

Aiken, L.R. (1989) *Later Life*. Hillsdale, NJ: Lawrence Erlbaum Associates.

Akiyama, H., Antonucci, T., Takahashi, K. and Langfahl, E.S. (2003) Negative interactions in close relationships across the life span. *The Journals of Gerontology Series B: Psychological Sciences and Social Sciences, 58*, 70–9.

Alafuzoff, I., Iqbal, K., Friden, H., Adolfsson, R. and Winblad, B. (1989) Histopathological classification of dementias by multivariate data analysis. In K. Iqbal, H.M. Wisniewski and B. Winblad (eds), *Alzheimer's Disease and Related Disorders*. New York: Alan R. Liss.

Albert, M.S. (1988) Cognitive function. In M.S. Albert and M.B. Moss (eds), *Geriatric Neuropsychology*. New York: Guilford.

Albert, M.S., Duffy, F.H. and Naeser, M.A. (1987) Nonlinear changes in cognition and their non-psychological correlation. *Canadian Journal of Psychology, 41*, 141–57.

Albert, M.S. and Stafford, J.L. (1988) Computed tomography studies. In M.S. Albert and M.B. Moss (eds), *Geriatric Neuropsychology*. New York: Guilford.

Alexopoulos, G.S., Meyers, B.S., Young, R.C., Kalayam, B., Kakuma, T., Gabrielle, M. and Sirey, J.A. (1996) Recovery in geriatric depression. *Archives of General Psychiatry, 53*, 305–12.

Allaire, J.C. and Marsiske, M. (2002) Well- and ill-defined measures of everyday cognition: Relationship to older adults' intellectual ability and functional status. *Psychology and Aging, 17*, 101–15.

Allen, P.A., Hall, R.J., Druley, J.A., Smith, A.F., Sanders, R.E. and Murphy, M.D. (2001) How shared are age-related influences on cognitive and noncognitive variables? *Psychology and Aging, 16*, 532–49.

Allen, P.A., Kaufman, M., Smith, A.F. and Propper, R.E. (1998) A molar entropy model of age differences in spatial memory. *Psychology and Aging, 13*, 501–18.

Allen, P.A., Madden, D.J., Weber, T.A. and Groth, K.E. (1993) Influence of age and processing stage on visual word recognition. *Psychology and Aging, 8*, 274–82.

Allen, P.A., Murphy, M.D., Kaufman, M., Groth, K.E. and Begovic, A. (2004) Age differences in central (semantic) and peripheral processing: The importance of considering both response times and errors. *The Journals of Gerontology Series B: Psychological Sciences and Social Sciences, 59*, 210–9.

Allen, P.A., Sliwinski, M., Bowie, T. and Madden, D.J. (2002) Differential age effects in semantic and episodic memory. *The Journals of Gerontology Series B: Psychological Sciences and Social Sciences, 57*, 173–86.

Allen, P.A., Smith, A.F., Groth, K.E., Pickle, J.L., Grabbe, J.W. and Madden, D.J. (2002) Differential age effects for case and hue mixing in visual word recognition. *Psychology and Aging, 17*, 622–35.

Allen-Burge, R. and Storandt, M. (2000) Age equivalence in feeling-of-knowing experiences. *The Journals of Gerontology Series B: Psychological Sciences and Social Sciences, 55*, 214–23.

Alpaugh, P.K. and Birren, J.R. (1977) Variables affecting creative contributions across the adult life span. *Human Development, 20*, 240–8.

Alwin, D.F. and McCammon, R.J. (2001) Aging, cohorts and verbal ability. *The Journals of Gerontology Series B: Psychological Sciences and Social Sciences, 56*, 151–61.

American Psychiatric Association (1994) *Diagnostic and Statistical Manual of Mental Disorders*. 4th edition. Washington, DC: American Psychiatric Association.

Amorim Cruz, J.A., Haveman-Nies, A., Schlettwein-Gsell, D. and De Henauw, S. (2002) Gender, cohort and geographical differences in 10-year mortality in elderly people living in 12 European towns. *Journal of Nutrition, Health and Aging, 6*, 269–74.

Andel, R., Gatz, M., Pedersen, N.L., Reynolds, C.A., Johansson, B. and Berg, S. (2001) Deficits in Controlled Processing May Predict Dementia: A Twin Study. *The Journals of Gerontology Series B: Psychological Sciences and Social Sciences, 56*, 347–55.

Anderson, T.L. and Levy, J.A. (2003) Marginality among older injectors in today's illicit drug culture: Assessing the impact of ageing. *Addiction, 98*, 761–70.

Anstey, K.J., Dain, S., Andrews, S. and Drobny, J. (2002) Visual abilities in older adults explain age-differences in Stroop and fluid intelligence but not face recognition: Implications for the vision-cognition connection. *Aging, Neuropsychology and Cognition, 9*, 253–65.

Anstey, K.J., Hofer, S.M. and Luszcz, M.A. (2003) A latent growth curve analysis of late-life sensory and cognitive function over 8 years: Evidence for specific and common factors underlying change. *Psychology and Aging, 18*, 714–26.

Anstey, K.J., Luszcz, M.A. and Sanchez, L. (2001) A reevaluation of the common factor theory of shared variance among age. *The Journals of Gerontology Series B: Psychological Sciences and Social Sciences, 56*, 3–11.

Anstey, K., Stankov, L. and Lord, S. (1993) Primary aging, secondary aging and intelligence. *Psychology and Aging, 8*, 562–70.

Antonucci, T.C., Lansford, J.E., Schaberg, L., Smith, J., Baltes, M., Akiyama, H., Takahashi, K., Fuhrer, R. and Dartigues, J.F. (2001) Widowhood and illness: A comparison of social network characteristics in France, Germany, Japan and the United States. *Psychology and Aging, 16*, 655–65.

Appell, J., Kertesz, A. and Fisman, M. (1982) A study of language functioning in Alzheimer patients. *Brain and Language, 17*, 73–91.

Arbuckle, T.Y., Nohara-LeClair, M. and Pushkar, D. (2000) Effect of off-target verbosity on communication efficiency in a referential communication task. *Psychology and Aging, 15*, 65–77.

Ardelt, M. (1997) Wisdom and life satisfaction in old age. *Journal of Gerontology B: Psychological Sciences and Social Sciences, 52*, 15–27.

Ardelt, M. (1998) Social crisis and individual growth: The long-term effects of the Great Depression. *Journal of Aging Studies, 12*, 291–314.

Arenberg, D. (1982) Changes with age in problem solving. In F.M. Craik and A.S. Trehub (eds), *Aging and Cognitive Processes*. New York: Plenum.

Armstrong, C.L. and Cloud, B. (1998) The emergence of spatial rotation deficits in dementia and normal aging. *Neuropsychology, 12*, 208–17.

Arndt, S., Turvey, C.L. and Flaum, M. (2002) Older offenders, substance abuse and treatment. *The American Journal of Geriatric Psychiatry, 10*, 733–40.

Arnold, S.E. and Trojanowski, J.Q. (1996) Cognitive impairment in elderly schizophrenia: A dementia (still) lacking distinctive histopathology. *Schizophrenia Bulletin, 22*, 5–9.

Arnold, S.E., Trojanowski, J.Q., Gur, R.E., Blackwell, P., Han, L. and Choi, C. (1998) Absence of neurodegeneration and neural injury in the cerebral cortex in a sample of elderly patients with schizophrenia. *Archives of General Psychiatry, 55*, 225–32.

Auden, W.H. (1979) *Selected Poems*. London: Faber.

Avorn, J., Soumerai, S.B., Everitt, D.E. and Ross-Degna, D. (1992) A randomized trial of a program to reduce the use of psychoactive drugs in nursing homes. *New England Journal of Medicine, 327*, 168–73.

Bäckman, L., Jones, S., Small, B.J., Agüero-Torres, H. and Fratiglioni, L. (2003) Rate of cognitive decline in preclinical Alzheimer's disease: The role of comorbidity. *The Journals of Gerontology Series B: Psychological Sciences and Social Sciences, 58*,
228–36.

Bäckman, L., Laukka, E.J., Wahlin, A., Small, B.J. and Fratiglioni, L. (2002) Influences of preclinical dementia and impending
death on the magnitude of age-related cognitive deficits. *Psychology and Aging, 17*, 435–42.

Baddeley, A.D. (1983) *Your Memory: A User's Guide.* London: Penguin.

Baddeley, A.D. (1986) *Working Memory.* Oxford: Oxford Scientific Publications.

Baddeley, A.D. (1995) *Memory.* 2nd edition. London: Lawrence Erlbaum.

Baddeley, A.D., Bressi, S., Della Sala, S., Logie, R. and Spinnler, H. (1991) The decline of working memory in Alzheimer's
disease: A longitudinal study. *Brain, 114*, 2521–42.

Baddeley, A.D. and Hitch, G. (1974) Working memory. In G.H. Bower (ed.), *Attention and Performance VI.* New York:
Academic Press.

Bai, U., Seidman, M.D., Hinojosa, R. and Quirk, W.S. (1997) Mitochondrial DNA deletions associated with aging and
possibly presbycusis: A human archival temporal bone study. *American Journal of Otology, 18*, 449–53.

Bailis, D.S. and Chipperfield, J.G. (2002) Compensating for losses in perceived personal control over health: A role for collective self-esteem in healthy aging. *The Journals of Gerontology Series B: Psychological Sciences and Social Sciences, 57*, 531–9.

Bakker, S.L., de Leeuw, F., de Groot, J.C., Hofman, A., Koudstall, P. and Breteler, M.M.B. (1999) Cerebral vasomotor reactivity and cerebral white matter lesions in the elderly. *Neurology, 52*, 578–83.

Balsis, S., Carpenter, B.D. and Storandt, M. (2005) Personality change precedes clinical diagnosis of dementia of the
Alzheimer type. *The Journals of Gerontology Series B: Psychological Sciences and Social Sciences, 60*, 98–101.

Baltes, M. (1996) *The Many Faces of Dependency in Old Age.* New York: Cambridge University Press.

Baltes, M. and Wahl, H.W. (1996) Patterns of communication in old age: The dependence-support and independence-ignore
script. *Health Communication, 8*, 217–31.

Baltes, P.B. and Lindenberger, U. (1997) Emergence of a powerful connection between sensory and cognitive functions
across the adult life span: A new window to the study of cognitive aging? *Psychology and Aging, 12*, 12–21.

Baltes, P.B. and Reese, H.W. (1984) The lifespan perspective in developmental psychology. In M.H. Boornstein and M.E.
Lamb (eds), *Developmental Psychology.* Hillsdale, NJ: Lawrence Erlbaum.

Baltes, P.B. and Smith, J. (1990) Toward a psychology of wisdom and its ontogenesis. In R.J. Sternberg (ed.), *Wisdom: Its
nature, origins and development.* Cambridge: Cambridge University Press, 87–120.

Band, G.P.H., Ridderinkhof, K.R. and Segalowitz, S. (2002) Explaining neurocognitive aging: Is one factor enough? *Brain
and Cognition, 49*, 259–67.

Barefoot, J.C. (1992) Developments in the measurement of hostility. In H. Friedman (ed.), *Hostility, Coping and Health.* Washington DC: American Psychological Association, 13–31.

Barefoot, J.C. Beckham, J.C., Haney, T.L., Siegler, I.C. and Lipkus, I.M. (1993) Age differences in hostility among
middle-aged and older adults. *Psychology and Aging, 8*, 3–9.

Barefoot, J.C., Mortensen, E.L., Helms, M.J., Avlund, K. and Schroll, M. (2001) A longitudinal study of gender differences in
depressive symptoms from age 50 to 80. *Psychology and Aging, 16*, 342–5.

Barnes, L.L., Mendes de Leon, C.F., Bienios, J.L. and Evans, D.A. (2004) A longitudinal study of black–white differences in
social resources. *The Journals of Gerontology Series B: Psychological Sciences and Social Sciences 59*, 146–53.

Bartels, S.J. and Mueser, K.T. (1999) Severe mental illness in older adults: Schizophrenia and other late-life psychoses. In
M.A. Smyer and S.H. Qualls (eds), *Aging and Mental Health.* Oxford: Blackwells, 182–207.

Bartlett, F.C. (1932) *Remembering.* Cambridge: Cambridge University Press.

Barton, E.M., Plemons, J.K., Willis, S.L. and Baltes, P.B. (1975) Recent findings on adult and gerontological intelligence:
Changing a stereotype of decline. *American Behavioral Scientist, 19*, 224–36.

Basak, C. and Verhaeghen, P. (2002) Subitizing speed, subitizing range, counting speed, the Stroop effect and aging:
Capacity differences and speed equivalence. *Psychology and Aging, 18*, 240–9.

Bashore, T.R., Ridderinkhof, K.R. and van der Molen, M.W. (1997) The decline of cognitive processing speed in old age.
Current Directions in Psychological Science, 6, 163–9.

Bauer, B. (1966) Results and problems of intelligence testing of aging subjects. [English translation] *Probleme und Ergebnisse der
Psychologie, 16*, 21–39.

Baum, S.R. (1993) Processing of center-embedded and right-branching relative clause sentences by normal elderly individuals. *Applied Psycholinguistics, 14*, 75–88.

Bayles, K.A. and Tomoeda, C.K. (1983) Confrontation naming impairment in dementia. *Brain and Language, 19*, 98–114.

Bayley, N. (1968) Behavioral correlates of mental growth: Birth to thirty-six years. *American Psychologist, 23*, 1–17.

Beardsall, L. (1998) Development of the Cambridge Contextual Reading Test for improving the estimation of premorbid verbal intelligence in older persons with dementia. *British Journal of Clinical Psychology, 37,* 229–40.

de Beauvoir, S. (1970) *Old Age.* London: Penguin Books.

Becker, G., Beyene, Y., Newsom, E. and Mayen, N. (2003) Creating continuity through mutual assistance: intergenerational reciprocity in four ethnic groups. *The Journals of Gerontology Series B: Psychological Sciences and Social Sciences, 58,* 151–9.

Becker, J.T., Boller, F., Saxton, J. and McConigle-Gibson, K.L. (1987) Normal rates of forgetting of verbal and non-verbal material in Alzheimer's Disease. *Cortex, 23,* 59–72.

Beekman, A.T.F., Penninx, B.W., Deeg, D.J., Ormel, J., Braam, A.W. and van Tilburg, W. (1997) Depression and physical health in later life: Results from the Longitudinal Aging Study Amsterdam (LASA). *Journal of Affective Disorders, 46,* 219–31.

Beers, M.H. and Berkow, R. (eds) (2000) *The Merck Manual of Geriatrics.* 3rd edition. Whitehouse Station, NJ: Merck and Co.

Beier, M.E. and Ackerman, P.L. (2001) Current-events knowledge in adults: An investigation of age, intelligence and nonability determinants. *Psychology and Aging, 16,* 615–28.

Bell, L.J. (1980) *The Large Print Book and Its User.* London: Library Association.

Belmont, J.M., Freeseman, L.J. and Mitchell, D.W. (1988) Memory and problem solving: The cases of young and elderly adults. In M.M. Gruneberg, P.E. Morris and R.N. Sykes (eds) *Practical Aspects of Memory, Current Research and Issues, Volume 2.* Chichester: Wiley.

Benedetti, F., Vighetti, S., Ricco, C., Lagna, E., Bergamasco, B., Pinessi, L. and Rainero, I. (1999) Pain threshold and tolerance in Alzheimer's disease. *Pain, 80,* 377–82.

Bengston, U.L. and Kuypers, J. (1986) The family support cycle: Psychosocial issues in the aging family. In J.M.A. Munnichs, P. Mussen and E. Olbrich (eds), *Life Span and Change in a Gerontological Perspective.* New York: Academic Press.

Bengston, U.L. and Treas, J. (1980) The changing family context of mental health and aging. In J.E. Birren and B. Sloane (eds), *Handbook of Mental Health and Aging.* New Jersey: Prentice Hall.

Benjamins, M.R., Musick, M.A., Gold, D.T. and George, L.K. (2003) Age-related declines in activity level: The relationship between chronic illness and religious activities. *The Journals of Gerontology Series B: Psychological Sciences and Social Sciences, 58,* 377–85.

Bennett, D.J. and McEvoy, C.L. (1999) Mediated priming in younger and older adults. *Experimental Aging Research, 25,* 141–59.

Bennett, K.M. (2002) Low level social engagement as a precursor of mortality among people in later life. *Age and Ageing, 31,* 165–8.

Bent, N., Rabbitt, P. and Metcalfe (2000) Diabetes mellitus and the rate of cognitive ageing. *British Journal of Clinical Psychology, 39,* 349–63.

Berg, C.A. and Sternberg, R.J. (1992) Adults' conceptions of intelligence across the adult life span. *Psychology and Aging, 7,* 221–31.

Berg, L. (1988) Mild senile dementia of the Alzheimer type: Diagnostic criteria and natural history. *Mount Sinai Journal of Medicine, 55,* 87–96.

Bergeman, C.S. (1997) *Aging: Genetic and Environmental Influences.* Thousand Oaks: Sage.

Bergman, M., Blumenfeld, V.G., Casardo, D., Dash, B., Levett, H. and Margulies, M.K. (1976) Age-related decrement in hearing for speech: Sampling and longitudinal studies. *Journal of Gerontology, 31,* 533–8.

Berkowitz, B. (1964) Changes in intellect with age: IV. Changes in achievement and survival. *Newsletter for Research in Psychology, 6,* 18–20.

Bernaducci, M.P. and Owens, N.J. (1996) Is there a fountain of youth? A review of current life extension strategies. *Pharmacotherapy, 16,* 183–200.

Berntsen, D. and Rubin, D.C. (2002) Emotionally charged autobiographical memories across the life span: The recall of happy, sad, traumatic and involuntary memories. *Psychology and Aging, 17,* 636–52.

Bertram, L. and Tanzi, R.E. (2004) The current state of Alzheimer's disease genetics. What do we tell the patients? *Pharmacological Research, 50,* 385–96.

Beukelaar, L.J. and Kroonenberg, P.M. (1986) Changes over time in the relationship between hand preference and writing hand among left-handers. *Neuropsychologia, 24,* 301–3.

Bherer, L. and Belleville, S. (2004) Age-related differences in response preparation: The role of time uncertainty. *The Journals of Gerontology Series B: Psychological Sciences and Social Sciences, 59,* 66–74.

Binstock, R.H. and George, L.K. (eds) (1990) *Handbook of Aging and the Social Sciences.* London: Academic Press.

Birren, J.E., Butler, R.N., Greenhouse, S.W., Solokoff, L. and Yarrow, M.R. (1963) *Human Aging.* Washington Public Health Service Publication No. 986.

Birren, J.E. and Fisher, L.M. (1995) Aging and speed of behavior: Possible consequences for psychological functioning. *Annual Review of Psychology, 46,* 329–53.

Birren, J.E. and Schaie, K.W. (eds) (1990) *Handbook of the Psychology of Aging.* San Diego, CA: Academic Press.

Birren, J.E., Woods, A.M. and Williams, M.V. (1980) Behavioral slowing with age: Causes, organization and consequences. In L.W. Poon (ed.), *Aging in the 1980s: Psychological Issues. Washington DC: American Psychological Association.*

Bischmann, D.A. and Witte, K. (1996) Food identification, taste complaints and depression in younger and older adults. *Experimental Aging Research, 22,* 23–32.

Black, H.K. and Rubinstein, R.L. (2004) Themes of suffering in later life. *The Journals of Gerontology Series B: Psychological Sciences and Social Sciences, 59,* 17–24.

Blackburn, J.A. and Papalia, D.E. (1992) The study of adult cognition from a Piagetian perspective. In R.J. Sternberg and C. Berg (eds), *Intellectual Development.* Cambridge: Cambridge University Press.

Blazer, D.G. (1993) *Depression in Late Life.* 2nd edition. St Louis, MO: Mosby.

Blazer, D.G. (1994) Epidemiology in late-life depression. In L.S. Schneider, C.F. Reynolds, B.D. Lebowitz and A.J. Friedhoff (eds), *Diagnosis and Treatment of Depression in Late Life.* Washington, DC: American Psychological Association, 9–19.

Blessed, G., Tomlinson, B.E. and Roth, M. (1968) The association between quantitative measures of dementia and senile changes in the cerebral grey matter of elderly subjects. *British Journal of Psychiatry, 114,* 797–811.

Blow, F.C. and Oslin, D.W. (2003) Late-life addictions. *Geriatric Psychiatry, 22,* 111–43.

Blum, J.E., Clark, E.T. and Jarvik, L.F. (1973) The NYS Psychiatric Institute Study of aging twins. In L.F. Jarvik, C. Eisdorfer and J.E. Blum (eds), *Intellectual Functioning in Adults.* New York: Springer.

Boekamp, J.R., Strauss, M.E. and Adams, N. (1995) Estimating premorbid intelligence in African-American and White elderly veterans using the American version of the National Adult Reading Test. *Journal of Clinical and Experimental Neuropsychology, 17,* 645–53.

Bohr, V.A. and Anson, R.M. (1995) DNA damage, mutation and fine structure DNA repair in aging. *Mutation Research, 338,* 25–34.

Boland, R.J., Diaz, S., Lamdan, R.M., Ramchandani, D. and McCartney, J.R. (1996) Overdiagnosis of depression in the general hospital. *General Hospital Psychiatry, 18,* 28–35.

Bonanno, G.A., Wortman, C.B. and Nesse, R.M. (2004) Prospective patterns of resilience and maladjustment during widowhood. *Psychology and Aging, 19,* 260–271.

Bongaarts, J. and Zimmer, Z. (2002) Living arrangements of older adults in the developing world: An analysis of demographic and health survey household surveys. *The Journals of Gerontology Series B: Psychological Sciences and Social Sciences, 57,* 145–57.

Bookwala, J., Harralson, T.L. and Parmelee, P.A. (2003) Effects of pain on functioning and well-being in older adults with osteoarthritis of the knee. *Psychology and Aging, 18,* 844–50.

Bosma, H., van Boxtel, M.P.J., Ponds, R.W.H.M., Houx, P.J.H. and Jolles, J. (2003) Education and age-related cognitive decline: The contribution of mental workload. *Educational Gerontology, 29,* 165–73.

Bosman, E.A. (1993) Age-related differences in the motoric aspects of transcription typing skill. *Psychology and Aging, 8,* 87–102.

Botwinick, J. (1967) *Cognitive Processes in Maturity and Old Age.* New York: Springer.

Botwinick, J. (1973) *Aging and Behavior.* New York: Springer.

Botwinick, J. (1977) Intellectual abilities. In J.E. Birren and K.W. Schaie (eds), *Handbook of the Psychology of Aging.* New York: Van Nostrand Reinhold.

Botwinick, J. and Storandt, M. (1974) Vocabulary ability in later life. *Journal of Genetic Psychology, 125,* 303–8.

Botwinick, J., West, R. and Storandt, M. (1978) Predicting death from behavioral performance. *Journal of Gerontology, 33,* 755–62.

Bouchard Ryan, E., Anas A.P., Beamer, M. and Bajorek, S. (2003) Coping with age-related vision loss in everyday reading activities. *Educational Gerontology, 29,* 37–54.

Bouma, H., Legein, C.P., Melotte, H.E. and Zabel, L. (1982) Is large print easy to read? Oral reading rate and word recognition of elderly subjects. *IPO Annual Progress Report, 17,* 84–90.

Bouras, C., Riederer, B.M., Kovari, E., Hof, P.R. and Giannakopoulos, P. (2005) Humoral immunity in brain aging and Alzheimer's disease. *Brain Research, 48,* 477–87.

Bowles, N.L. and Poon, L.W. (1981) The effect of age on speed of lexical access. *Experimental Aging Research, 7,* 417–25.

Bowles, N.L. and Poon, L.W. (1985) Aging and retrieval of words in semantic memory. *Journal of Gerontology, 40,* 71–7.

Bowles, R.P. and Salthouse, T.A. (2003) Assessing the age-related effects of proactive interference on working memory tasks using the Rasch model. *Psychology and Aging, 18,* 608–15.

Bowling, A., Farquhar, M. and Grundy, E. (1996) Associations with changes in life satisfaction among three samples of elderly people living at home. *International Journal of Geriatric Psychiatry, 11*, 1077–87.

Braam, A.W., Beekman, A.T.F., van Tilburg, T.G., Deeg, D.J.H. and van Tilburg, W. (1997) Religious involvement and depression in older Dutch citizens. *Social Psychiatry and Psychiatric Epidemiology, 32*, 284–91.

Brady, E.M. and Sky, H.Z. (2003) Journal writing among older learners. *Educational Gerontology, 29*, 151–63.

Brattberg, G., Parker, M.G. and Thorslund, M. (1996) The prevalence of pain among the oldest old in Sweden. *Pain, 67*, 29–34.

Brayne, C. and Beardsall, L. (1990) Estimation of verbal intelligence in an elderly community: an epidemiological study using NART. *British Journal of Clinical Psychology, 29*, 217–24.

Brebion, G., Smith, M.J. and Ehrlich, M.F. (1997) Working memory and aging: Deficit or strategy differences. *Aging, Neuropsychology and Cognition, 4*, 58–73.

Bremner, J.D. and Narayan, M. (1998) The effects of stress on memory and the hippocampus throughout the life cycle: Implications for childhood development and aging. *Development and Psychopathology, 10*, 871–85.

Brewer, G.J. (1999) Regeneration and proliferation of embryonic and adult hippocampal neurons. *Experimental Neurology, 159*, 237–47.

Brink, J.M. and McDowd, J.M. (1999) Aging and selective attention: An issue of complexity or multiple mechanisms? *Journal of Gerontology Series B: Psychological Sciences and Social Sciences, 54*, 30–3.

Brinley, J.F. (1965) Cognitive sets, speed and accuracy in the elderly. In A.T. Welford and J.E. Birren (eds), *Behavior, Aging and the Nervous System.* New York: Springer-Verlag.

Broadhead, J. and Jacoby, R. (1995) Mania in old age: a first prospective study. In E. Murphy and G. Alexopoulos (ed.), *Geriatric Psychiatry: Key Research Topics for Clinicians.* Chichester: Wiley, 217–29.

Brody, J.A. (1988) Changing health needs of the ageing population. *Research and the Ageing Population.* Ciba Foundation Symposium 134. Chichester: Wiley.

Bromley, D.B. (1958) Some effects of age on short-term learning and memory. *Journal of Gerontology, 13*, 398–406.

Bromley, D.B. (1988) *Human Ageing. An Introduction to Gerontology.* 3rd edition. Harmondsworth: Penguin.

Bromley, D.B. (1991) Aspects of written language production over adult life. *Psychology and Aging, 6*, 296–308.

Brooks, D.N. and Hallam, R.S. (1998) Attitudes to hearing difficulty and hearing aids and the outcome of audiological rehabilitation. *British Journal of Audiology, 32*, 217–26.

Brown, J.W., Chobor, A. and Zinn, F. (1993) Dementia testing in the elderly. *Journal of Nervous and Mental Disorders, 181*, 695–8.

Brown, R. and McNeill, D. (1966) The 'tip-of-the-tongue' phenomenon. *Journal of Verbal Learning and Verbal Behavior, 5*, 325–37.

Brown, S.L., Roebuck Bulanda, J. and Lee, G.R. (2005) The significance of nonmarital cohabitation: marital status and mental health benefits among middle-aged and older adults. *The Journals of Gerontology Series B: Psychological Sciences and Social Sciences, 60*, 21–9.

Bryan, J. and Luszcz, M.A. (1996) Speed of information processing as a mediator between age and free-recall performance. *Psychology and Aging, 11*, 3–9.

Bucks, R., Scott, M.I., Pearsall, T. and Ashworth, D.L. (1996) The short NART: Utility in a memory disorders clinic. *British Journal of Clinical Psychology, 35*, 133–141.

Bucks, R.S. and Willison, J.R. (1997) Development and validation of the Location Learning Test (LLT): A test of visuo-spatial learning designed for use with older adults and in dementia. *Clinical Neuropsychologist, 11*, 273–86.

Bunce, D., Kivipelto, M. and Wahlin, A. (2005) Apolipoprotein E, B vitamins and cognitive function in older adults. *The Journals of Gerontology Series B: Psychological Sciences and Social Sciences, 60*, 41–8.

Bunce, D.J., Barrowclough, A. and Morris, I. (1996) The moderating influence of physical fitness on age gradients in vigilance and serial choice responding tasks. *Psychology and Aging, 11*, 671–82.

Burke, D.M., Mackay, D.G. and James, L.E. (2000) Theoretical approaches to language and aging. In T.J. Perfect and E.A. Maylor (eds), (2000) *Models of Cognitive Aging.* Oxford: Oxford University Press, 204–237.

Burke, D.M., White, H. and Diaz, D.L. (1987) Semantic priming in young and old adults: Evidence for age constancy in automatic and attentional processes. *Journal of Experimental Psychology: Human Perception and Performance, 13*, 79–88.

Burke, D.M., Worthley, J. and Martin, J. (1988) I'll never forget what's-her-name: Aging and tip of the tongue experiences in everyday life. In M.M. Gruneberg, P.E. Morris and R.N. Sykes (eds), *Practical Aspects of Memory: Current Research and Issues.* Chichester: Wiley.

Burns, A. (1995) Cause of death in dementia. In E. Murphy and G. Alexopoulos (ed.), *Geriatric Psychiatry: Key Research Topics for Clinicians.* Chichester: Wiley, 95–101.

Burns, R. (1988) A two-way TV system operated by senior citizens. *American Behavioral Scientist, 31*, 576–87.

Burnside, I.M. (1976) The special sense and sensory deprivation. In I.M. Burnside (ed.) *Nursing and the Aged*. New York: McGraw Hill, 380–97.

Burnside, I.M., Ebersole, P. and Monea, H.E. (eds) (1979) *Psychosocial Caring Throughout the Lifespan*. New York: McGraw Hill.

Burville, P.W., Stampfer, H.G. and Hall, W.D. (1995) Issues in the assessment of outcome in depressive illness in the elderly. In E. Murphy and G. Alexopoulos (eds), *Geriatric Psychiatry: Key Research Topics for Clinicians*. Chichester: Wiley, 177–90.

Butcher, J.N., Aldwin, C.M., Levenson, M.R., Ben-Porath, Y.S., Spiro, A.III. and Bossé, R. (1991) Personality and aging: A study of the MMPI-2 among older men. *Psychology and Aging, 6*, 361–70.

Butler, R.N. (1967) *Creativity in Old Age*. New York: Plenum.

Byrd, M. (1985) Age differences in the ability to recall and summarise textual information. *Experimental Aging Research, 11*, 87–91.

Byrne, M.D. (1998) Taking a computational approach to aging: The SPAN theory of working memory. *Psychology of Aging, 13*, 309–22.

Cabeza, R., Grady, C.L., Nyberg, L., McIntosh, A.R., Tulving, E., Kapur, S., Jennings, J.M., Houle, S. and Craik, F.I. (1997) Age-related differences in neural activity during memory encoding and retrieval: A positron emission tomography study. *Journal of Neuroscience, 17*, 391–400.

Cahn, D.A., Salmon, D.P., Monsch, A.U., Wiederholt, W.C., Corey-Bloom, J. and Barrett-Connor, E. (1996) Screening for dementia of the Alzheimer type in the community: The utility of the clock drawing test. *Archives of Clinical Neuropsychology, 11*, 529–39.

Caine, E.D., Lyness, J.M., King, D.A. and Connors, B.A. (1994) Clinical and etiological heterogeneity of mood disorders in elderly patients. In L.S. Schneider, C.F. Reynolds, B.D. Lebowitz and A.J. Friedhoff (eds), *Diagnosis and Treatment of Depression in Late Life*. Washington: American Psychological Association. 23–53.

Calasanti, T. (2004) Feminist gerontology and old men. *The Journals of Gerontology Series B: Psychological Sciences and Social Sciences, 59*, 305–14.

Calvaresi, E. and Bryan, J. (2001) B vitamins, cognition and aging. *The Journals of Gerontology Series B: Psychological Sciences and Social Sciences, 56*, 327–39.

Camp, C.J. (1988) Utilisation of world knowledge systems. In L.W. Poon, D.G. Rubin and B.A. Wilson (eds) *Everyday Cognition in Adulthood and Later Life*. Cambridge: Cambridge University Press.

Caplan, L.J. and Schooler, C. (2003) The roles of fatalism, self-confidence and intellectual resources in the disablement process in older adults. *Psychology and Aging, 18*, 551–61.

Cappeliez, P. and O'Rourke, N. (2002) Personality traits and existential concerns as predictors of the functions of reminiscence in older adults. *The Journals of Gerontology Series B: Psychological Sciences and Social Sciences, 57*, 116–23.

Carey, R.G. (1979) Weathering widowhood: Problems and adjustment of the widowed during the first year. *Omega, 10*, 263–74.

Carlesimo, G.A., Fadda, L., Marfia, G.A. and Caltagirone, C. (1995) Explicit memory and repetition priming in dementia: Evidence for a common basic mechanism underlying conscious and unconscious retrieval deficits. *Journal of Clinical and Experimental Neuropsychology, 17*, 44–57.

Carlson, L.E., Sherwin, B.B. and Chertkow, H.M. (2000) Relationships between mood and estradiol (E2) levels in Alzheimer's disease (AD) patients. *Journals of Gerontology Series B: Psychological Sciences and Social Sciences, 55*, 47–53.

Carmelli, D., Swan, G.E., Kelly-Hayes, M., Wolf, P.A., Reed, T. and Miller, B. (2000) Longitudinal changes in the contribution of genetic and environmental influences to symptoms of depression in older male twins. *Psychology and Aging, 15*, 505–10.

Carr, D., House, J.S., Kessler, R.C., Nesse, R.M., Sonnega, J. and Wortman, C. (2000) Marital quality and psychological adjustment to widowhood among older adults: a longitudinal analysis. *The Journals of Gerontology Series B: Psychological Sciences and Social Sciences, 55*, 197–207.

Carr, D., House, J.S., Wortman, C., Nesse, R. and Kessler, R.C. (2001) Psychological adjustment to sudden and anticipated spousal loss among older widowed persons. *The Journals of Gerontology Series B: Psychological Sciences and Social Sciences, 56*, 237–48.

Carswell, L.M., Graves, R.E., Snow, W.G. and Tierney, M.C. (1997) Postdicting verbal IQ of elderly individuals. *Journal of Clinical and Experimental Neuropsychology, 19*, 914–921.

Carter, J.H. (1982) The effects of aging on selected visual functions: Color vision, glare sensitivity, field of vision and accommodation. In R. Sekuler, D. Kline and K. Dismukes (eds), *Aging and Human Visual Function*. New York: Alan R. Liss, 121–30.

Casey, B. (2004) Discussion Paper PI-0503: Why people don't choose private pensions: the impact of 'contagion'. London: The Pensions Institute.

Caspary, D.M., Milbrandt, J.C. and Helfert, R.H. (1995) Central auditory aging: GABA changes in the inferior colliculus. *Experimental Gerontology, 30*, 349–60.

Caspi, A. and Elder, G.H. (1986) Life satisfaction in old age: linking social psychology and history. *Journal of Psychology and Aging, 1*, 18–26.

Caspi, A., Roberts, B.W. and Shiner, R.L. (2005) Personality development: Stability and change. *Annual Review of Psychology, 56*, 453–84.

Cattell, R.B. (1971) *Abilities: Their Structure, Growth and Action.* Boston, MA: Houghton Mifflin.

Cavallini, E., Pagnin, A. and Vecchi, T. (2003) Aging and everyday memory: The beneficial effect of memory training. *Archives of Gerontology and Geriatrics, 37*, 241–57.

Cavanagh, J.C. and Murphy, N.Z. (1986) Personality and metamemory correlates of memory performance in younger and older adults. *Educational Gerontology, 12*, 385–94.

Cerella, J. (1985) Information processing rate in the elderly. *Psychological Bulletin, 98*, 67–83.

Cerella, J. (1990) Aging and information-processing rate. In J.E. Birren and K.W. Schaie (eds), *Handbook of the Psychology of Aging.* 3rd edition. San Diego, CA: Academic Press.

Cerella, J. and Fozard, J.L. (1984) Lexical access and age. *Developmental Psychology, 20*, 235–43.

Chan, A.S., Salmon, D.P., Butters, N. and Johnson, S. (1995) Comparison of the semantic networks in patients with dementia and amnesia. *Neuropsychology, 9*, 177–86.

Chandler, M.J. and Holliday, S. (1990) Wisdom in a post apocalyptic age. In R.J. Sternberg (ed.), *Wisdom: Its Nature, Origins and Development.* Cambridge: Cambridge University Press, 121–41.

Chao, L.L. and Knight, R.T. (1997) Prefrontal deficits in attention and inhibitory control with aging. *Cerebral Cortex, 7*, 63–9.

Charletta, D.A., Bennett, D.A. and Wilson, R.S. (1993) Computed tomography and magnetic resonance imaging. In R.W. Parks, R.F. Zec and R.S. Wilson (eds), *Neuropsychology of Alzheimer's Disease and Other Dementias.* New York: Oxford University Press, 534–61.

Charness, N. (1979) Components of skill in bridge. *Canadian Journal of Psychology, 133*, 1–16.

Charness, N. (1981) Aging and skilled problem solving. *Journal of Experimental Psychology: General, 110*, 21–38.

Charness, N., Kelley, C.L., Bosman, E.A. and Mottram, M. (2001) Word-processing training and retraining: Effects of adult age, experience and interface. *Psychology and Aging, 16*, 110–27.

Charness, N. and Schaie, K.W. (eds) (2003) *The Impact of Technology on Successful Aging.* New York, NY: Springer.

Chen, Y. and Persson, A. (2002) Internet use among young and older adults: Relation to psychological well-being. *Educational Gerontology, 28*, 731–44.

Chipperfield, J.G. and Havens, B. (2001) Gender differences in the relationship between marital status transitions and life satisfaction in later life. *The Journals of Gerontology Series B: Psychological Sciences and Social Sciences, 56*, 176–86.

Christensen, H., Henderson, A.S., Griffiths, K. and Levings, C. (1997) Does ageing inevitably lead to declines in cognitive performance? A longitudinal study of elite academics. *Personality and Individual Differences, 23*, 67–78.

Christensen, H., Korten, A.E., Jorm, A.F., Henderson, A.S., Jacomb, P.A., Rodgers, B. and Mackinnon, A.J. (1997) Education and decline in cognitive performance: Compensatory but not protective. *International Journal of Geriatric Psychiatry, 12*, 323–30.

Christensen, H., Mackinnon, A.J., Korten, A.E., Jorm, A.F., Henderson, A.S., Jacomb, P. and Rodgers, B. (1999) An analysis of diversity in the cognitive performance of elderly community dwellers. Individual differences in change scores as a function of age. *Psychology and Aging, 14*, 365–79.

Cicirelli, V.G. (1976) Categorization behavior in aging subjects. *Journal of Gerontology, 31*, 676–90.

Cicirelli, V.G. (1993) Attachment and obligation as daughters' motives for caregiving behavior and subsequent effect on subjective burden. *Psychology and Aging, 8*, 144–55.

Cipolli, C., Neri,. M., De Vreese, L.P., Pinelli, M., Rubichi, S. and Lalla, M. (1996) The influence of depression on memory and metamemory in the elderly. *Archives of Gerontology and Geriatrics, 23*, 111–27.

Clark, M.S. (1999) The double ABCX model of family crisis as a representation of family functioning after rehabilitation from stroke. *Psychology, Health and Medicine, 4*, 203–20.

Clarke, R., Grimley Evans, J., Schneede, J., Nexo, E., Bates, C., Fletcher, A., Birks, J., Whitlock, G., Breeze, E. and Scott, J.M. (2004) Vitamin B12 and folate deficiency in later life. *Age and Ageing, 33*, 34–41.

Clayton, V.P. and Birren, J.E. (1980) The development of wisdom across the life span: A reexamination of an ancient topic. In P.B. Baltes and O.G. Brim (eds), *Life-Span Development and Behavior, 3.* New York: Academic Press.

Cockburn, J. and Smith, P.T. (1988) Effects of age and intelligence on everyday memory tasks. In M.M. Gruneberg, P.E. Morris and R.N. Sykes (eds), *Practical Aspects of Memory: Current Research and Issues.* Chichester: Wiley.

Coffey, C.E., Saxton, J.A., Ratcliff, G., Bryan, R.N. and Lucke, J.F. (1999) Relation of education to brain size in normal aging: Implications for the reserve hypothesis. *Neurology, 53*, 189–96.

Cohen, D. and Dunner, D. (1980) The assessment of cognitive dysfunction in dementing illness. In J.O. Cole and J.E. Barrett (eds), *Psychopathology in the Aged.* New York: Raven.

Cohen, G. (1981) Inferential reasoning in old age. *Cognition, 9*, 59–72.

Cohen, G. (1988) Age differences in memory for texts: Production deficiency of processing limitations? In D.M. Burke and L.L. Light (eds), *Language, Memory and Aging.* New York: Cambridge University Press.

Cohen, G. (1989) *Memory in the Real World.* Hove: Lawrence Erlbaum Associates.

Cohen, G. (1996) Memory and learning in normal ageing. In R. Woods (ed.), *Handbook of the Clinical Psychology of Ageing.* Chichester: Wiley 43–58.

Cohen, G. and Faulkner, D. (1984) Memory for text. In H. Bouma and D. Bouwhuis (eds), *Attention and Performance X: Control of Language Processes.* Hillsdale, NJ: Lawrence Erlbaum.

Cohen, G. and Faulkner, D. (1986) Memory for proper names: Age differences in retrieval. *British Journal of Developmental Psychology, 4*, 187–97.

Cohen, G. and Faulkner, D. (1988) Life span changes in autobiographical memory. In M.M. Gruneberg, P.E. Morris and R.N. Sykes (eds), *Practical Aspects of Memory, Current Research and Issues, Volume 2.* Chichester: Wiley.

Cohen, G. and Faulkner, D. (1989) The effects of aging on perceived and generated memories. In L.W. Poon, D.C. Rubin and B.A. Wilson (eds), *Everyday Cognition in Later Life.* Cambridge: Cambridge University Press.

Cohn, E.S. (1999) Hearing loss with aging: Presbycusis. *Clinical Geriatric Medicine, 15*, 145–61.

Cole, M.G. (2004) Delirium in elderly patients. *The American Journal of Geriatric Psychiatry, 12*, 7–22.

Coleman, P.G. and O'Hanlon, A. (2004) *Ageing and Development: Theories and Research.* London: Arnold.

Collette, F., Van der Linden, M., Bechet, S. and Salmon, E. (1999) Phonological loop and central executive functioning in Alzheimer's disease. *Neuropsychologia, 37*, 905–18.

Collins, M.W. and Abeles, N. (1996) Subjective memory complaints and depression in the able elderly. *Clinical Gerontologist, 16*, 29–54.

Comijs, H.C., Jonker, C., van Tilburg, W. and Smit, J.H. (1999) Hostility and coping capacity as risk factors of elder mistreatment. *Social Psychiatry and Psychiatric Epidemiology, 34*, 48–52.

Compton, D.M., Bachman, L.D. and Logan, J.A. (1997) Aging and intellectual ability in young, middle-aged and older educated adults: Preliminary results from a sample of college faculty. *Psychological Reports, 81*, 79–90.

Compton, S.A., Flanagan, P. and Gregg, W. (1997) Elder abuse in people with dementia in Northern Ireland: Prevalence and predictors in cases referred to a psychiatry of old age service. *International Journal of Geriatric Psychiatry, 12*, 632–5.

Concar, D. (1996) Death of old age. *New Scientist, 150*, 24–9.

Cong, Y.S., Wright, W.E. and Shay, J.W. (2002) Human telomerase and its regulation. *Microbiology and Molecular Biology Review, 66*, 407–25.

Connell, C.M. and Gibson, G.D. (1997) Racial, ethnic and cultural differences in dementia caregiving: Review and analysis. *Gerontologist, 37*, 355–64.

Connelly, S.L., Hasher, L. and Zacks, R. (1991) Age and reading: The impact of distraction. *Psychology and Aging, 6*, 533–41.

Connor, L.T., Spiro, A., Obler, L.K. and Albert, M.L. (2004) Change in object naming ability during adulthood. *The Journals of Gerontology Series B: Psychological Sciences and Social Sciences, 59*, 203–9.

Contreras-Vidal, J.L., Teulings, H.L. and Stelmach, G.E. (1995) Micrographia in Parkinson's disease. *Neuroreport: An International Journal for the Rapid Communication of Research in Neuroscience, 6*, 2089–92.

Contreras-Vidal, J.L., Teulings, H.L. and Stelmach, G.E. (1998) Elderly subjects are impaired in spatial coordination in fine motor control. *Acta Psychologica, 100*, 25–35.

Conway, S.C. and O'Carroll, R.E. (1997) An evaluation of the Cambridge Contextual Reading Test (CCRT) in Alzheimer's disease. *British Journal of Clinical Psychology, 36*, 623–5.

Conwell, Y. (1997) Management of suicidal behavior in the elderly. *Psychiatric Clinics of North America, 20*, 667–83.

Cook, A.S. and Oltjenbruns, K.A. (1989) *Dying and Grieving.* New York: Holt, Rinehart and Winston.

Cook, E.A. (1998) Effects of reminiscence on life satisfaction of elderly female nursing home residents. *Health Care for Women International, 19*, 109–18.

Cooney, C. and Wrigley, M. (1996) Abuse of the elderly with dementia. *Irish Journal of Psychological Medicine, 13*, 94–6.

Coppel, D.B., Burton, C., Becker, J. and Fiore, J. (1985) Relationships of cognition associated with coping reactions to depression in spousal caregivers of Alzheimer's disease patients. *Cognitive Therapy and Research, 9*, 253–66.

Cordingly, L. and Webb, C. (1997) Independence and aging. *Reviews in Clinical Gerontology, 7*, 137–46.

Corkin, S., Growden, J.H., Nissen, M.J., Huff, F.J., Freed, D.M. and Sagar, H.J. (1984) Recent advances in the neuropsychological study of Alzheimer's disease. In R.J. Wurtman, S. Corkin and J.H. Growden (eds), *Alzheimer's Disease: Advances in Basic Research and Therapies.* Cambridge, MA: Center for Science and Metabolism Trust.

Cornelissen, F.W. and Kooijman, A.C. (2000) Does age change the distribution of visual attention? A comment on McCalley, Bouwhuis and Juola (1995). *The Journals of Gerontology Series B: Psychological Sciences and Social Sciences 55*, 187–90.

Cornman, J.C., Lynch, S.M., Goldman, N., Weinstein, M. and Lin, H.S. (2004) Stability and change in the perceived social support of older Taiwanese adults. *The Journals of Gerontology Series B: Psychological Sciences and Social Sciences 59*, 350–57.

Corran, T.M., Farrell, M.J., Helm, R.D. and Gibson, S.J. (1997) The classification of patients with chronic pain: Age as a contributing factor. *Clinical Journal of Pain, 13*, 207–14.

Corso, J.F. (1981) *Aging Sensory Systems and Perception.* New York: Praeger.

Corso, J.F. (1987) Sensory-perceptual processes and aging. *Annual Review of Gerontology and Geriatrics, 7.* New York: Springer.

Costa, P.T., Herbst, J.H., McCrae, R.R., Siegler, I.C. (2000) Personality at midlife: Stability, intrinsic maturation and response to life events. *Assessment, 7*, 365–78.

Costa, P.T. and McCrae, R.R. (1980) Still stable after all these years: Personality as a key to some issues of adulthood and old age. In P.B. Baltes and G.G. Brim (eds), *Life-span Development and Behaviour, Volume 3.* New York: Academic Press.

Costa, P.T. and McCrae, R.R. (1982) An approach to the attribution of aging: Period and cohort effects. *Psychological Bulletin, 92*, 238–50.

Coupland, N., Coupland, J. and Giles, H. (1991) *Language, Society and the Elderly.* Oxford: Blackwells.

Cowart, B.J., Yokomukai, Y. and Beauchamp, G.K. (1994) Bitter taste in aging: Compound-specific decline in sensitivity. *Physiology and Behavior, 56*, 1237–41.

Cowgill, D. (1970) The demography of aging. In A.M. Hoffman (ed), *The Daily Needs and Interests of Older People.* Springfield, IL: C.C. Thomas.

Coxon, P. and Valentine, T. (1997) The effects of the age of eyewitnesses on the accuracy and suggestibility of their testimony. *Applied Cognitive Psychology, 11*, 415–30.

Coyne, A.C., Liss, L. and Geckler, C. (1984) The relationship between cognitive status and visual information processing. *Journal of Gerontology, 39*, 711–7.

Craik, F.I.M. (1977) Age differences in human memory. In J.E. Birren and K.W. Schaie (eds), *Handbook of the Psychology of Aging.* New York: Van Nostrand Reinhold.

Craik, F.I.M. (1986) A functional account of age differences in memory. In F. Klix and H. Hagendorf (eds), *Human Memory and Cognitive Capabilities, Mechanisms and Performance.* Amsterdam: Elsevier, 409–22.

Craik, F.I.M. (2000) Age-related changes in human memory. In D.C. Park and N. Schwarz (eds), *Cognitive Aging A Primer.* Philadelphia: Taylor and Francis. 75–92.

Craik, F.I.M., Anderson, N.D., Kerr, S.A. and Li, K.Z.H. (1995) Memory changes in normal ageing. In A.D. Baddeley, B.A. Wilson and F.N. Watts (eds), *Handbook of Memory Disorders.* Chichester: Wiley, 211–42.

Craik, F.I.M. and Jennings, J.M. (1992) Human memory. In F.I.M. Craik and T.A. Salthouse (eds), *The Handbook of Aging and Cognition.* Hillsdale, NJ: Lawrence Erlbaum.

Craik, F.I.M. and Rabinowitz, J.C. (1984) Age differences in the acquisition and use of verbal information. In H. Bouma and D. Bouwhuis (eds), *Attention and Performance X: Control of Language Processes.* Hillsdale, NJ: Erlbaum, 471–99.

Crandall, R.C. (1980) *Gerontology. A Behavioral Science Approach.* Reading, MA: Addison-Wesley.

Crawford, J.R., Stewart, L.E., Garthwaite, P.H., Parker, D.M. and Bessan, J.A.O. (1988) The relationship between demographic variables and NART performance in normal subjects. *British Journal of Clinical Psychology, 27*, 181–2.

Crook, T.H. and West, R.L. (1990) Name recall performance across the adult life span. *British Journal of Psychology, 81*, 335–49.

Crosson, C.W. and Robertson-Tchabo, E.A. (1983) Age and preference for complexity among manifestly creative women. *Human Development, 26*, 149–55.

Cumming, E. and Henry, W.E. (1961) *Growing Old.* New York: Basic Books.

Cunningham, W.R. and Brookbank, J.W. (1988) *Gerontology: The Psychology, Biology and Sociology of Ageing.* New York: Harper and Row.

Cunningham, W.R., Clayton, V. and Overton, W. (1975) Fluid and crystallised intelligence in young adulthood and old age. *Journal of Gerontology, 30*, 53–5.

Cutler, S.J., Hendricks, J. and Guyer, A. (2003) Age differences in home computer availability and use. *The Journals of Gerontology Series B: Psychological Sciences and Social Sciences, 58*, 271–80.

Czaja, S.J. and Sharit, J. (1998) Age differences in attitudes towards computers. *Journal of Gerontology B: Psychological Sciences and Social Sciences, 53*, 329–40.

Dannifer, D. and Perlmutter, M. (1990) Development as a multidimensional process: Individual and social constituents. *Human Development, 33*, 108–37.

Daselaar, S.M., Veltman, D.J., Rombouts, S.A., Raaijmakers, J.G. and Jonker, C. (2005) Aging affects both perceptual and lexical/semantic components of word stem priming: An event-related fMRI study. *Neurobiology Learning and Memory, 83*, 251–62.

Davis, P.E. and Mumford, S.J. (1984) Cued recall and the nature of the memory disorder in dementia. *British Journal of Psychiatry, 144*, 383–6.

Dawkins, R. (1976) *The Selfish Gene.* Oxford: Oxford University Press.

De Jong, N., Mulder, I., de Graaf, C. and van Staveren, W.A. (1999) Impaired sensory functioning in elders: The relation with its potential determinants and nutritional intake. *Journal of Gerontology A, 54*, 324–31.

De Leo, D. (1997) Suicide in late life at the end of the 1990s: A less neglected topic? *Crisis, 18*, 51–52.

De Leon, M.J., George, A.E., Golomb, J., Tarshish, C., Convit, A., Kluger, A., de Santi, S., McRae, T., Ferris, S.H., Reisberg, B., Ince, C. and Rusinek, H. (1997) Frequency of hippocampal formation atrophy in normal aging and Alzheimer's disease. *Neurobiology of Aging, 18*, 1–11.

Deary, I.J. (2001) *Intelligence: A Very Short Introduction.* Oxford: Oxford University Press.

Deary, I.J., Leaper, S.A., Murray, A.D., Staff, R.T. and Whalley, L.J. (2003) Cerebral white matter abnormalities and lifetime cognitive change: A 67-year follow-up of the Scottish Mental Survey of 1932. *Psychology and Aging, 18*, 140–148.

Deary, I.J., Whalley, L.J., Lemmon, H., Crawford, J.R. and Starr, J.M. (2000) The stability of indicidual differences in mental ability from childhood to old age: Follow-up of the 1932 Scottish Mental Survey. *Intelligence, 28*, 49–55.

Deary, I.J., Whiteman, M.C., Pattie, A., Starr, J.M., Hayward, C., Wright, A.F., Visscher, P.M., Tynan, M.C. and Whalley, L.J. (2004) Apolipoprotein E gene variability and cognitive functions at age 79: A follow-up of the Scottish Mental Survey of 1932. *Psychology and Aging, 19*, 367–71.

Decker, D.L. (1980) *Social Gerontology.* Boston, MA: Little, Brown and Company.

DeDe, G., Caplan, D., Kemtes, K. and Waters, G. (2004) The relationship between age, verbal working memory and language comprehension. *Psychology and Aging, 19*, 601–16.

DeHart, S.S. and Hoffmann, N.G. (1995) Screening and diagnosis of 'alcohol abuse and dependence' in older adults. *International Journal of the Addictions, 30*, 1717–47.

Dehon, H. and Brédart, S. (2004) False memories: Young and older adults think of semantic associates at the same rate, but young adults are more successful at source monitoring. *Psychology and Aging, 19*, 191–7.

DeLamater, J.D. and Sill, M. (2005) Sexual Desire in Later Life. *Journal of Sex Research, 42*, 138–49.

Delbaere, K., Crombez, G., Vanderstraeten, G., Willems, T. and Cambier, D. (2004) Fear-related avoidance of activities, falls and physical frailty. A prospective community-based cohort study. *Age and Aging, 33*, 368–73.

Dennerstein, L., Alexander. J.L. and Kotz, K. (2003) The menopause and sexual functioning: A review of the population-based studies. *Annual Review of Sex Research, 14*, 64–83.

Denney, D.R. and Denney, N.W. (1973) The use of classification for problem solving: A comparison of middle and old age. *Developmental Psychology, 9*, 275–8.

Denney, D.R. and Denney, N.W. (1974) Modelling effects on the questioning strategies of the elderly. *Developmental Psychology, 10*, 458.

Denney, N.W. (1974) Evidence for developmental changes in categorization criteria for children and adults. *Human Development, 17*, 41–53.

Derwinger, A., Neely, A.S. and Bäckman, L. (2005) Design your own memory strategies! Self-generated strategy training versus mnemonic training in old age: An 8-month follow-up. *Neuropsychological Rehabilitation 15*, 37–54.

Dewey, J. (1939) Introduction. In E.V. Cowdrey, *Problems of Ageing.* Baltimore, MD: Williams and Wilkins.

Diehl, M., Willis, S.L. and Schaie, K.W. (1995) Everyday problem solving in older adults: Observational assessment and cognitive correlates. *Psychology and Aging, 10*, 478–91.

Dilworth-Anderson. P., Goodwin. P.Y. and Wallace Williams, S. (2004) Can culture help explain the physical health effects of caregiving over time among African American caregivers? *The Journals of Gerontology Series B: Psychological Sciences and Social Sciences, 59*, 138–45.

Dixon, R.A., Backman, L. and Nilsson, L.G. (2004) *New Frontiers in Cognitive Ageing.* Oxford: Oxford University Press.

Dixon, R.A. and Hultsch, D.F. (1983) Metamemory and memory for text relationships in adulthood: A cross-validation study. *Journal of Gerontology, 38*, 689–94.

Dixon, R.A., Hultsch, D.F., Simon, E.W. and Van Eye, A. (1984) Verbal ability and text structure effects on adult age differences in text recall. *Journal of Verbal Learning and Verbal Behavior, 23*, 569–78.

Dixon, R.A., Kurzman, D. and Friesen, I.C. (1993) Handwriting performance in younger and older adults: Age, familiarity and practice effects. *Psychology and Aging, 8*, 360–70.

Domey, R.G., McFarland, R.A. and Chadwick, E. (1960) Dark adaptation as a function of age and time. *Journal of Gerontology, 15*, 267–79.

Doty, R.L. (1990) Aging and age-related neurological disease: Olfaction. In F. Goller and J. Grafman (eds), *Handbook of Neuropsychology.* Amsterdam: Elsevier, 459–62.

Draper, B. (1996) Attempted suicide in old age. *International Journal of Geriatric Psychiatry, 11*, 577–87.

Druley, J.A., Stephens, M.A.P., Martire, L.M., Ennis, N. and Wojno, W.C. (2003) Emotional congruence in older couples coping with wives' osteoarthritis: Exacerbating effects of pain behavior. *Psychology and Aging, 18*, 406–14.

Duberstein, P.R., Conwell, Y., Seidlitz, L., Denning, D.G., Cox, C. and Caine, E.D. (2000) Personality traits and suicidal behavior and ideation in depressed inpatients 50 years of age and older. *Journals of Gerontology Series B: Psychological Sciences and Social Sciences, 55*, 18–26.

Dubno, J.R., Dirk, D.D. and Morgan, D.E. (1984) Effects of age and mild hearing loss on speech recognition in noise. *Journal of Acoustical Society of America, 76*, 87–96.

Dubois, L. (1997) La representation du vieillissement a la television: Des images de negation et d'exclusion dans une logique de mise en marche. *Canadian Journal on Aging, 16*, 354–72.

Dudley, N.J., Bowling, A., Bond, M., McKee, D., Scott, M.M., Banning, A., Elder, A.T., Martin, T. and Blackman, I. (2002) Age- and sex-related bias in the management of heart disease in a district general hospital. *Age and Ageing, 31*, 37–42.

Duffy, F.H. and McAnulty, G. (1988) Electrophysiological studies. In M.S. Albert and M.B. Moss (eds), *Geriatric Neuropsychology*. New York: Guilford Press.

Duke, J., Leventhal, H., Brownlee, S. and Leventhal, E.A. (2002) Giving up and replacing activities in response to illness. *The Journals of Gerontology Series B: Psychological Sciences and Social Sciences, 57*, 367–76.

Dulay, M. and Murphy, C. (2002) Olfactory acuity and cognitive function converge in older adulthood: Support for the common cause hypothesis. *Psychology and Aging, 17*, 392–404.

Dumas, J.A. and Hartman, M. (2003) Adult age differences in temporal and item memory. *Psychology and Aging, 18*, 573–86.

Duncan, J., Emslie, H., Williams, P., Johnson, R. and Freer, C. (1996) Intelligence and the frontal lobe: The organization of goal-directed behavior. *Cognitive Psychology, 30*, 257–303.

Dunlop, D.D., Manheim, L.M., Song, J. and Chang, R.W. (2002) Gender and ethnic/racial disparities in health care utilization among older adults. *The Journals of Gerontology Series B: Psychological Sciences and Social Sciences, 57*, 221–33.

Dura, J.R., Stukenberg, K.W. and Kiecolt-Glaser, J.K. (1991) Anxiety and depressive disorders in adult children caring for demented parents. *Psychology and Aging, 6*, 467–73.

Dwyer, J.T. (1988) Health aspects of vegetarian diets. *American Journal of Clinical Nutrition, 48*, 712–38.

Dywan, J. and Murphy, W.E. (1996) Aging and inhibitory control in text comprehension. *Psychology and Aging, 11*, 199–206.

Earles, J.L., Kersten, A.W., Mas, B.B. and Miccio, D.M. (2004) Aging and memory for self-performed tasks: effects of task difficulty and time pressure. *The Journals of Gerontology Series B: Psychological Sciences and Social Sciences 59*, 285–93.

Eaves, L.J., Eysenck, H.J. and Martin, N.G. (1989) *Genes, Culture and Personality*. London: Academic Press.

Eggermont, J.J. and Roberts, L.E. (2004) The neuroscience of tinnitus. *Trends in Neurosciences, 27*, 676–82.

Egolf, B., Lasker, J., Wolf, S. and Potvin, L. (1992) The Roseto effect: A 50-year comparison of mortality rates. *American Journal of Public Health, 82*, 1089–92.

Einstein, G.O., Earles, J.L. and Collins, H.M. (2002) Spared Inhibition for Visual Distraction in Older Adults. *The Journals of Gerontology Series B: Psychological Sciences and Social Sciences, 57*, 65–73.

Einstein, G.O., McDaniel, M.A. and Guynn, M.J. (1992) Age-related deficits in prospective memory: The influence of task complexity. *Psychology and Aging, 7*, 471–78.

Einstein, G.O., McDaniel, M.A., Smith, R. and Shaw, P. (1998) Habitual prospective memory and aging: Remembering instructions and forgetting actions. *Psychological Science, 9*, 284–88.

Eisdorfer, C., Cohen, D. and Paveza, G.J. (1992) An empirical evaluation of the Global Deterioration Scale for staging Alzheimer's disease. *American Journal of Psychiatry 149*, 190–4.

Eisdorfer, C. and Wilkie, F. (1977) Stress, disease, aging and behavior. In J.E. Birren and K.W. Schaie (eds), *Handbook of the Psychology of Aging*. New York: Academic Press.

Ekerdt, D.J., Sergeant, J.F., Dingel, M. and Bowen, M.E. (2004) Household disbandment in Later Life. *The Journals of Gerontology Series B: Psychological Sciences and Social Sciences, 59*, 265–73.

Ellis, A.W. (1993) *Reading, Writing and Dyslexia A Cognitive Analysis*. Hove: Lawrence Erlbaum.

Elias, M.F., Elias, J.W. and Elias, P. (1990) Biological and health influences on behavior. In J.E. Birren and K.W. Schaie (eds), *Handbook of the Psychology of Aging*. New York: Academic Press.

Elias, M.F., Elias, P.K. and Elias, J.W. (1977) *Basic Processes in Adult Developmental Psychology*. St Louis: C.V. Mosby.

Elmstahl, S., Sommer, M. and Hagberg, B. (1996) A 3-year follow-up of stroke patients: Relationships between activities of daily living and personality characteristics. *Archives of Gerontology and Geriatrics, 22*, 233–44.

Elwood, P.C., Gallacher, J.E.J., Hopkinson, C.A., Pickering, J., Rabbitt, P., Stollery, B., Brayne, C., Huppert, F.A. and Bayer, A. (1999) Smoking, drinking and other life style factors and cognitive function in men in the Caerphilly cohort. *Journal of Epidemiology and Community Health, 53*, 9–15.

Elwood, P.C., Pickering, J., Bayer, A. and Gallacher, J.E.J. (2002) Vascular disease and cognitive function in older men in the Caerphilly cohort. *Age and Ageing, 31*, 43–8.

Elwood, P.C., Pickering, J. and Gallacher, J.E.J (2001) Cognitive function and blood rheology: results from the Caerphilly cohort of older men. *Age and Ageing, 30*, 135–9.

Emery, C.F., Pedersen, N.L., Svartengren, M. and McClearn, G.E. (1998) Longitudinal and genetic effects in the relationship between pulmonary function and cognitive performance. *Journal of Gerontology B: Psychological Sciences and Social Sciences, 53*, 311–7.

Emlet, C.A. (2004) HIV/AIDS and aging: a diverse population of vulnerable older adults. *Journal of Human Behavior in the Social Environment, 9*, 45–63.

Emlet, C.A., Hawks, H. and Callahan, J. (2001) Alcohol use and abuse in a population of community dwelling, frail older adults. *Journal of Gerontological Social Work, 35*, 21–33.

Engen, T. (1977) Taste and smell. In J.E. Birren and K.W. Schaie (eds), *Handbook of the Psychology of Aging*. New York: Academic Press.

Erikson, E.H. (1963) *Childhood and Society*. New York: Norton.

Erikson, E.H. (1982) *The Life Cycle Completed: A Review*. New York: Norton.

Erlangsen, A., Bille-Brahe, U. and Jeune, B. (2003) Differences in suicide between the old and the oldest old. *The Journals of Gerontology Series B: Psychological Sciences and Social Sciences, 58*, 314–22.

Erlangsen, A., Jeune, B., Bille-Brahe, U. and Vaupel, J.W. (2004) Loss of partner and suicide risks among oldest old: a population-based register study. *Age and Ageing, 33*, 378–83.

Eysenck, H.J. (1952) The effects of psychotherapy: An evaluation. *Journal of Consulting Psychology, 16*, 319–24.

Eysenck, H.J. (1985) The theory of intelligence and the psychophysiology of cognition. In R.J. Sternberg (ed.) *Advances in Research in Intelligence, 3*. Hillsdale, NJ: Lawrence Erlbaum.

Eysenck. H.J. (1987) Personality and ageing: An exploratory analysis. *Journal of Social Behaviour and Personality, 3*, 11–21.

Eysenck, H.J. and Eysenck, M.W. (1985) *Personality and Individual Differences: A Natural Science Approach*. New York: Plenum.

Eysenck, H.J. and Kamin, L. (1981) *The Intelligence Controversy*. New York: Wiley.

Fahey, T., Montgomery, A., Barnes, J. and Protheroe, J. (2003) Quality of care for elderly residents in nursing homes and elderly people living at home: Controlled observational study. *British Medical Journal, 326*, 580–1.

Fahlander, K., Wahlin, A., Fastbom, J., Grut, M., Forsell, Y., Hill, R.D., Winblad, B. and Bäckman, L. (2000) The relationship between signs of cardiovascular deficiency and cognitive performance in old age. *The Journals of Gerontology Series B: Psychological Sciences and Social Sciences, 55*, 259–65.

Farkas, E. and Luiten, P.G. (2001) Cerebral microvascular pathology in aging and Alzheimer's disease. *Progress in Neurobiology, 64* 575–611.

Featherstone, M. and Wernicke, D. (eds) (1997) *Images of Ageing – Cultural Representations of Later Life*. London: Routledge.

Federmeier, K.D. and Kutas, M. (2005) Aging in context: Age-related changes in context use during language comprehension. *Psychophysiology, 42*, 133–41.

Femia, E.E., Zarita, S.H. and Johansson, B. (2001) The disablement process in very late life: A study of the oldest-old in Sweden. *The Journals of Gerontology Series B: Psychological Sciences and Social Sciences, 56*, 12–23.

Ferguson, S.A., Hastroudi, S. and Johnson, M.K. (1992) Age differences in using source-relevant cues. *Psychology and Aging, 7*, 443–52.

Ferraro, K. and Kelley-Moore, J.A. (2003) A half century of longitudinal methods in social gerontology: Evidence of change in the journal. *The Journals of Gerontology Series B: Psychological Sciences and Social Sciences, 58*, 264–70.

Ferraro, F.R. and Moody, J. (1996) Consistent and inconsistent performance in young and elderly adults. *Developmental Neuropsychology, 12*, 429–41.

Ferraro, K.F. and Su, Y. (1999) Financial strain, social relations and psychological distress among older people: A cross-cultural analysis. *Journal of Gerontology B: Psychological Sciences and Social Sciences, 54*, 3–15.

Ferrer, E., Salthouse, T.A., Stewart, W.F. and Schwartz, B.S. (2004) Modeling age and retest processes in longitudinal studies of cognitive abilities. *Psychology and Aging, 19*, 243–59.

Field, D. (1981) Retrospective reports by healthy intelligent people of personal events of their adult lives. *International Journal of Behavioral Development, 4*, 443–52.

Field, D. (1997) 'Looking back, what period of your life brought you the most satisfaction?' *International Journal of Aging and Human Development, 45*, 169–94.

Field, D. and Millsap, R.E. (1991) Personality in advanced old age: Continuity or change? *The Journals of Gerontology Series B: Psychological Sciences and Social Sciences, 46*, 299–308.

Fillmore, K.M., Golding, J.M., Graves, K.L., Kniep, S., Leino, E.V., Romelsjo, A., Shoemaker, C., Ager, C.R., Allebeck, P. and Ferrer, H.P. (1998) Alcohol consumption and mortality. III. Studies of female populations. *Addiction, 93*, 219–29.

Filoteo, J.V. and Maddox, W.T. (2004) A quantitative model-based approach to examining aging effects on information-integration category learning. *Psychology and Aging, 19*, 171–82.

Fingerman, K.L. and Birditt, K.S. (2003) Do age differences in close and problematic family ties reflect the pool of available relatives? *The Journals of Gerontology Series B: Psychological Sciences and Social Sciences, 58,* 80–7.

Finkel, D., Pedersen, N.L. and Larsson, M. (2001) Olfactory functioning and cognitive abilities. A twin study. *The Journals of Gerontology Series B: Psychological Sciences and Social Sciences, 56,* 226–33.

Finkelstein, J.A. and Schiffman, S.S. (1999) Workshop on taste and smell in the elderly: An overview. *Physiology and Behavior, 66,* 173–6.

Finlayson, R.E. (1995) Misuse of prescription drugs. *International Journal of the Addictions, 30,* 1871–901.

Fisk, J.E. and Warr, P. (1996) Age and working memory: The role of perceptual speed, the central executive and the phonological loop. *Psychology and Aging, 11,* 316–23.

Fiske, A., Gatz, M. and Pedersen, N.L. (2003) Depressive symptoms and aging: the effects of illness and non-health-related events. *The Journals of Gerontology Series B: Psychological Sciences and Social Sciences, 58,* 320–8.

Fleischman, D.A., Wilson, R.S., Gabrieli, J.D.E., Bienias, J.L. and Bennett, D.A. (2004) A longitudinal study of implicit and explicit memory in old persons. *Psychology and Aging, 19,* 617–25.

Flint, A.J. and Rifat, S.L. (1997) Anxious depression in elderly patients: Response to antidepressant treatment. *American Journal of Geriatric Psychiatry, 5,* 107–15.

Florio, E.R., Hendryx, M.S., Jensen, J.E., Rockwood, T.H., Raschko, R. and Dyck, D.G. (1997) A comparison of suicidal and nonsuicidal elders referred to a community mental health center program. *Suicide and Life-Threatening Behavior, 27,* 182–93.

Flynn, J.R. (1987) Massive IQ gains in 14 nations: What IQ tests really measure. *Psychological Bulletin, 101,* 171–91.

Foreman, M.D. and Milisen, K. (2004) Improving recognition of delirium in the elderly. *Primary Psychiatry, 11,* 46–50.

Forsell, Y and Winblad, B. (1998) Major depression in a population of demented and nondemented older people: prevalence and correlates. *Journal of the American Geriatrics Society, 46,* 27–30.

Foster, J.K., Black, S.E., Buck, B.H. and Bronskill, M.J. (1997) Ageing and executive functions: a neuroimaging perspective. In P. Rabbitt (ed.), *Methodology of Frontal and Executive Function.* Hove: Taylor and Francis, 117–34.

Fozard, J.L. (1980) The time for remembering. In L.C. Poon (ed.), *Aging in the 1980's: Psychological Issues.* Washington, DC: American Psychological Association.

Fozard, J.L., Wolf, E., Bell, B., McFarland, R.A. and Podolsky, S. (1979) Visual perception and communication. In J.E. Birren and K.W. Schaie (eds), *Handbook of the Psychology of Aging.* New York: Van Nostrand Reinhold.

Fraboni, M., Saltstone, R. and Hughes, S. (1990) The Fraboni scale of ageism (FSA): An attempt at a more precise measure of ageism. *Canadian Journal on Aging, 9,* 56–66.

Francis, L.J. and Bolger, J. (1997) Personality and psychological well-being in later life. *Irish Journal of Psychology, 18,* 444–7.

Fraser, S., Bunce, C. and Wormald, R. (1999) Risk factors for late presentation in chronic glaucoma. *Investigative Ophthalmology and Vision Science, 40,* 2251–7.

Frayne, A., Kidd, N., Coen, R. and Lawlor, B.A. (1999) Burden in carers of dementia patients: Higher levels in carers of younger sufferers. *International Journal of Geriatric Psychiatry, 14,* 784–8.

Fredericksen, J.R. (1978) Assessment of perceptual, decoding and lexical skills and their relation to reading proficiency. In A.M. Lesgold, J.W. Pellegrino, S.D. Fokkema and R. Glaser (eds), *Cognitive Psychology and Instruction.* New York: Plenum.

Fremouw, W.J., Perezel, W.J. and Ellis, T.E. (1990) *Suicide Risk.* Elmsfor: Pergamon.

Freudenstein, U., Arthur, A.J., Matthews, R.J. and Jagger, C. (2001) Community surveys of late-life depression: who are the non-responders? *Age and Ageing, 30,* 517–21.

Freyne, A., Kidd, N., Coen, R. and Lawlor, B.A. (1999) Burden in carers of dementia patients: Higher levels in carers of younger sufferers. *International Journal of Geriatric Psychiatry, 14,* 784–88.

Friedman, D. (2003) Cognition and aging: A highly selective overview of event-related potential (ERP) data. *Journal of Clinical and Experimental Neuropsychology, 25,* 702–20.

Friedman, D., Hamberger, M. and Ritter, W. (1993) Event-related potentials as indicators of repetition priming in young and older adults. *Psychology and Aging, 8,* 120–5.

Fries, J.F. (2000) Compression of morbidity in the elderly. *Vaccine, 18,* 1584–9.

Fry, P.S. (1986) *Depression Stress and Adaptations in the Elderly.* Rockville, MD: Aspen Publications.

Fukukawa, Y., Nakashima, C., Tsuboi, S., Kozakai, R., Doyo, W., Niino, N., Ando, F. and Shimokata, H. (2004) Age differences in the effect of physical activity on depressive symptoms. *Psychology and Aging, 19,* 346–51.

Fukukawa, Y., Nakashima, C., Tsuboi, S., Niino, N., Ando, F., Kosugi, S. and Shimokata, H. (2004) The impact of health problems on depression and activities in middle-aged and older adults: Age and social interactions as moderators. *The Journals of Gerontology Series B: Psychological Sciences and Social Sciences, 59,* 19–26.

Fung, H.H., Lai, P. and Ng, R. (2001) Age differences in social preferences among Taiwanese and mainland Chinese: The role of perceived time. *Psychology and Aging, 16,* 351–6.

Funkenstein, H.H. (1988) Cerebrovascular disorders. In M.S. Albert and M.B. Moss (eds), *Geriatric Neuropsychology*. New York: Guilford.

Gaeta, H., Friedman, D. and Ritter, W. (2003) Auditory selective attention in young and elderly adults: The selection of single versus conjoint features. *Psychophysiology, 40*, 389–406.

Gaeta, H., Friedman, D., Ritter, W. and Cheng, J. (2001) An event-related potential evaluation of involuntary attentional shifts in young and older adults. *Psychology and Aging, 16*, 55–68.

Gage, T.R. and O'Connor, K. (1994) Nutrition and the variation in level and age patterns of mortality. *Human Biology, 66*, 77–103.

Gallagher-Thompson, D., Leary, M.C., Ossinalde, C. Romero, J.J., Wald, M. and Fernandez-Gamarra, E. (1997) Hispanic caregivers of older adults with dementia: Cultural issues in outreach and intervention. *Group, 21*, 211–32.

Gallo, W.T., Bradley, E.H., Siegel, M. and Kasla, S.V. (2000) Health effects of involuntary job loss among older workers: findings from the health and retirement survey. *The Journals of Gerontology Series B: Psychological Sciences and Social Sciences, 55*, 131–40.

Gamboz, N., Russo, R. and Fox, E. (2002) Age differences and the identity negative priming effect: An updated meta-analysis. *Psychology and Aging, 17*, 525–30.

Gardner, J.P., Li, S., Srinivasan, S.R., Chen, W., Kimura, M., Lu, X., Berenson, G.S and Aviv, A. (2005) Rise in insulin resistance is associated with escalated telomere attrition. *Circulation, 111*, 2171–7.

Garrard, P., Maloney, L.M., Hodges, J.R. and Patterson, K. (2005) The effects of very early Alzheimer's disease on the characteristics of writing by a renowned author. *Brain, 128*, 250–60.

Garstka, T.A., Schmitt, M.T., Branscombe, N.R. and Hummert, M.L. (2004) How young and older adults differ in their responses to perceived age discrimination. *Psychology and Aging, 19*, 326–35.

Gates, G.A., Couropmitree, N.N. and Myers, R.H. (1999) Genetic associations in age-related hearing thresholds. *Archives of Otolaryngology Head and Neck Surgery, 125*, 654–9.

Gates, G.A. and Rees, T.S. (1997) Hear ye? Hear ye! Successful auditory aging. *West Journal of Medicine, 167*, 247–52.

Gatz, M., Bengston, V.L. and Blum, M.J. (1990) Caregiving families. In J.E. Birren and K.W. Schaie (eds), *Handbook of the Psychology of Aging*. New York: Van Nostrand Reinhold.

Gatz, M., Svedberg, P., Pedersen, N.L., Mortimer, J.A. Berg, S. and Johansson, B. (2001) Education and the risk of Alzheimer's disease: Findings from the study of dementia in Swedish twins. *The Journals of Gerontology Series B: Psychological Sciences and Social Sciences, 56*, 292–300.

Gaudreau, D. and Peretz, I. (1999) Implicit and explicit memory for music in old and young adults. *Brain and Cognition, 40*, 126–9.

Gavrilov, L.A. and Gavrilova, N.S. (2002) Evolutionary theories of aging and longevity. *The Scientific World Journal, 2*, 339–56.

Gescheider, G.A., Beiles, E.J., Checkosky, C.M., Bolanowski, S.J. and Verrillo, R.T. (1994) The effects of aging on information-processing channels in the sense of touch: II. Temporal summation in the P channel. *Somatosensory and Motor Research, 11*, 359–65.

Gfroerer, J., Penne, M., Pemberton, M. and Folsom, R. (2003) Substance abuse treatment need among older adults in 2020: The impact of the aging baby-boom cohort. *Drug and Alcohol Dependence, 69*, 127–35.

Ghiselli, E.E. (1957) The relationship between intelligence and age among superior adults. *Journal of Genetic Psychology, 90*, 131–42.

Ghisletta, P. and Lindenberger, U. (2003) Age-based structural dynamics between perceptual speed and knowledge in the Berlin aging study: Direct evidence for ability dedifferentiation in old age. *Psychology and Aging, 18*, 696–713.

Ghusn, H.F., Hyde, D., Stevens, E.S. and Hyde, M. (1996) Enhancing life satisfaction in later life: What makes a difference for nursing home residents? *Journal of Gerontological Social Work, 26*, 27–47.

Giambra, L.M. (1993) Sustained attention in older adults: Performance and processes. In: J. Cerella, J. Rybash, W. Hoyer and M.L. Commones (eds) (1993) *Adult Information Processing: Limits on Loss*. San Diego, CA: Academic Press, 259–72.

Gibson, H.B. (1992) *The Emotional and Sexual Lives of Older People*. London: Chapman and Hall.

Gibson, H.B. (1997) *Love in Later Life*. London: Peter Owen.

Gibson, S.J. and Farrell, M. (2004) A review of age differences in the neurophysiology of nociception and the perceptual experience of pain. *Clinical Journal of Pain, 20*, 227–39.

Gibson, S.J. and Helme, R.D. (1995) Age differences in pain perception and report: A review of physiological, psychological, laboratory and clinical studies. *Pain Reviews, 2*, 111–37.

Giles, L.C., Glonek, G.F., Luszcz, M.A. and Andrews, G.R. (2005) Effect of social networks on 10 year survival in very old Australians: The Australian longitudinal study of aging. *Journal of Epidemiological and Community Health, 59*, 574–9.

Gilhooly, M. (1999) 'Training families to provide care: Effects on people with dementia.' Commentary. *International Journal of Geriatric Psychiatry, 14,* 117–9.

Gilhooly, M.L.M. (2005) Reduced drinking with age: Is it normal? *Addiction Research and Theory, 13,* 267–80.

Gilleard, C.J. (1997) Education and Alzheimer's disease: A review of recent international epidemiological studies. *Aging and Mental Health, 1,* 33–46.

Gilley, D.W., Wilson, R.S., Bienias, J.L., Bennett, D.A. and Evans, D.A. (2004) Predictors of depressive symptoms in persons with Alzheimer's disease. *The Journals of Gerontology Series B: Psychological Sciences and Social Sciences, 59,* 75–83.

Gilmore, G.C., Tobias, T.R. and Royer, F.L. (1985) Aging and similarity grouping in visual search. *Journal of Gerontology, 40,* 586–592.

Glass, J.G. and Jolly, G.R. (1997) Satisfaction in later life among women 60 or over. *Educational Gerontology, 23,* 297–314.

Glass, J.M., Schumacher, E.H., Lauber, E.J., Zurbriggen, E.L., Gmeindl, L., Kieras, D.E. and Meyer, D.E. (2000) Aging and the psychological refractory period: Task-coordination strategies in young and old adults. *Psychology and Aging, 15,* 571–95.

Glosser, G., Grugan, P. and Friedman, R.B. (1999) Comparison of reading and spelling in patients with probable Alzheimer's disease. *Neuropsychology, 13,* 350–8.

Godber, C. (1998) Elderly suicide and weather conditions: Is there a link? *International Journal of Geriatric Psychiatry, 13,* 66.

Godschalk, M.F., Sison, A. and Mulligan, T. (1997) Management of erectile dysfunction by the geriatrician. *Journal of the American Geriatrics Society, 45,* 1240–6.

Goldstein, J.H., Cajko, L., Oosterbroek, M., Michielsen, M., van Houten, O. and Salverda, F. (1997) Video games and the elderly. *Social Behavior and Personality, 25,* 345–52.

Golomb, J., Kruger, A., de Leon, M.J. and Ferris, S.H. (1996) Hippocampal formation size predicts declining memory performance in normal aging. *Neurology, 47,* 810–3.

Gomburg, E.S.L. and Zucker, R.A. (1998) Substance use and abuse in old age. In I.H. Nordhus, G.R. VandenBos, S. Berg and P. Fromholt (eds), *Clinical Geropsychology.* Washington, DC: American Psychological Association, 189–204.

Gorin, S.H. and Lewis, B. (2004) The compression of morbidity: Implications for Social Work. *Health and Social Work, 29,* 249–55.

Gorusch, N. (1998) Time's winged chariot: Short-term psychotherapy in later life. *Psychodynamic Counselling, 4,* 191–202.

Gott, M. (2004) Are older people at risk of sexually transmitted infections? A new look at the evidence. *Reviews in Clinical Gerontology, 14,* 5–13.

Gott, M. and Hinchliff, S. (2003) How important is sex in later life? The views of older people. *Social Science and Medicine, 56,* 1617–28.

Gottfries, C.G. (1996) Neurochemistry and neurotransmitters. *International Psychogeriatrics, 8,* 225–31.

Gould, O.N. and Dixon, R.A. (1993) How we spent our vacation: Collaborative storytelling by young and old adults. *Psychology and Aging, 8,* 10–17.

Grady, C.L., Bernstein, L.J., Beig, S. and Siegenthaler, A.L. (2002) The effects of encoding task on age-related differences in the functional neuroanatomy of face memory. *Psychology and Aging, 17,* 7–23.

Graf, P. and Schachter, D.L. (1985) Implicit and explicit memory for new associations in normal and amnesic subjects. *Journal of Experimental Psychology: Learning, Memory and Cognition, 11,* 501–18.

Graham, I.D. and Baker, P.M. (1989) Status, age and gender: Perceptions of old and young people. *Canadian Journal on Aging, 8,* 255–67.

Graham, K., Carver, V. and Brett, P.J. (1995) Alcohol and drug use by older women: Results of a national survey. *Canadian Journal on Aging, 14,* 769–91.

Graham, K., Clarke, D., Bois, C., Carver, V., Dolinki, L., Smythe, C., Harrison, S., Marshman, J. and Brett, P. (1996) Addictive behavior of older adults. *Addictive Behaviors, 21,* 331–48.

Grajcyk, A. and Zoellner, O. (1998) How older people watch television: Telemetric data on the TV use in Germany in 1996. *Gerontology, 44,* 176–81.

Greene, J.D. and Hodges, J.R. (1996a) Identification of famous faces and famous names in early Alzheimer's disease: Relationship to anterograde episodic and general semantic memory. *Brain, 119,* 111–28.

Greene, J.D. and Hodges, J.R. (1996b) The fractionation of remote memory: Evidence from a longitudinal study of dementia of the Alzheimer type. *Brain, 119,* 129–42.

Greene, J.D., Hodges, J.R. and Baddeley, A.D. (1995) Autobiographical memory and executive function in early dementia of the Alzheimer type. *Neuropsychologia, 33,* 1647–70.

Greenwood, N.A. (1999) Androgyny and adjustment in later life: Living in a veterans' home. *Journal of Clinical Geropsychology, 5,* 127–37.

Gregoire, J. and Van der Linden, M. (1997) Effects of age on forward and backward digit spans. *Aging, Neuropsychology and Cognition, 4,* 140–9.

Griffiths, C. and Fitzpatrick, J. (2001) Geographical inequalities in life expectancy in the United Kingdom, 1995–97. *Health Statistics Quarterly, 9,* 16–27.

Grossi, D. and Orsini, A. (1978) The visual crosses test in dementia: An experimental study of 110 subjects. *Acta Neurologica, 33,* 170–4.

Grossman, M., Mickanin, J., Onishi, K. and Hughes, E. (1995) An aspect of sentence processing in Alzheimer's disease. *Neurology, 45,* 85–91.

Gulbinat, W.H. (1996) The epidemiology of suicide in old age. *Archives of Suicide Research, 2,* 31–42.

Guo, X., Erber, J.T. and Szuchman, L.T. (1999) Age and forgetfulness: Can stereotypes be modified? *Educational Gerontology, 25,* 457–66.

Gupta, S., Austin, R. and Black, D.W. (1997) Ninety-three – and washing. *American Journal of Geriatric Psychiatry, 5,* 354–5.

Gurland, B. and Toner, J. (1983) Differentiating dementia from nondementing conditions. In R. Mayeux and W.G. Rosen (eds), *The Dementias.* New York: Raven.

Gurung, R.A.R., Taylor, S.E. and Seeman, T.E. (2003) Accounting for changes in social support among married older adults: Insights from the MacArthur Studies of Successful Aging. *Psychology and Aging, 18,* 487–96.

Gussaroff, E. (1998) Denial of death and sexuality in the treatment of elderly patients. *Psychoanalysis and Psychotherapy, 15,* 77–91.

Haan, N. (1972) Personality development from adolescence to adulthood in the Oakland growth and guidance studies. *Seminars in Psychiatry, 4,* 399–414.

Haase, E.R. (1977) Diseases presenting as dementia. In C.E. Wells (ed.), *Dementia.* Philadelphia: Davis.

Hachinski, V.C., Iliff, L.D., Zilkha, E., Du Boulay, G.H., McAllister, V.L., Marshall, J., Russell, R.W. and Symon, L. (1975) Cerebral blood flow in dementia. *Archives of Neurology, 32,* 632–7.

Hachinski, V.C., Lassen, N.A. and Marshall, J. (1974) Multi-infarct dementia, a cause of mental deterioration in the elderly. *Lancet, 1978,* 207–10.

Haegerstrom-Portnoy, G., Schneck, M.E. and Brabyn, J.A. (1999) Seeing into old age: Vision function beyond acuity. *Optometry and Vision Science, 76,* 141–58.

Haenninen, T., Hallikainen, M., Koivisto, K., Partanen, K., Laakso, M.P. and Rickkinen, P.J. (1997) Decline of frontal lobe functions in subjects with age-associated memory impairment. *Neurology, 48,* 148–53.

Hajat, S., Haines, A., Bulpitt, C. and Fletcher, A. (2004) Patterns and determinants of alcohol consumption in people aged 75 years and older: results from the MRC trial of assessment and management of older people in the community. *Age and Ageing, 33,* 170–7.

Hakamies-Blomqvist, L., Henriksson, P., Falkmer, T., Lundberg, C. and Braekhus, A. (2002) Attitudes of primary care physicians toward older drivers: A Finnish–Swedish comparison. *Journal of Applied Gerontology, 21,* 58–69.

Hale, S. and Myerson, J. (1995) Fifty years older, fifty percent slower? Meta-analytic regression models and semantic context effects. *Aging and Cognition, 2,* 132–45.

Hamm, V.P. and Hasher, L. (1992) Age and the availability of inferences. *Psychology and Aging, 7,* 56–64.

Hannah, M.T., Domino, G., Figueredo, A.J. and Hendrickson, R. (1996) The prediction of ego integrity in older persons. *Educational and Psychological Measurement, 56,* 930–50.

Harasty, J.A., Halliday, G.M., Kril, J.J. and Code, C. (1999) Specific temporoparietal gyral atrophy reflects the pattern of language dissolution in Alzheimer's disease. *Brain, 122,* 675–86.

Harkins, S.W., Price, D.D. and Martelli, M. (1986) *Special Senses in Aging: A Current Biological Assessment.* Ann Arbor, MI: Institute of Gerontology at the University of Michigan.

Harrington, D.L. and Haaland, K.Y. (1992) Skill learning in the elderly: Diminished implicit and explicit memory for a motor sequence. *Psychology and Aging, 7,* 425–35.

Harris, L.A. and Dollinger, S. (2001) Participation in a course on aging: Knowledge, attitudes and anxiety about aging in oneself and others. *Educational Gerontology, 27,* 657–67.

Harris, T., Cook, D.G., Victor, C., Rink, E., Mann, A.H., Shah, S., DeWilde, S. and Beighton, C. (2003) Predictors of depressive symptoms in older people – a survey of two general practice populations. *Age and Ageing, 32,* 510–18.

Hart, V.R., Gallagher-Thompson, D., Davies, H.D., DiMinno, M. and Lessin, P.J. (1996) Strategies for increasing participation of ethnic minorities in Alzheimer's disease diagnostic centers: A multifaceted approach in California. *Gerontologist, 36,* 259–62.

Hartley, J.T. (1988) Aging and individual differences in memory for written discourse. In L.L. Light and D. Burke (eds), *Language, Memory and Aging.* New York: Cambridge University Press.

Hasher, L. and Zacks, R.T. (1979) Automatic and effortful processes in memory. *Journal of Experimental Psychology: General, 108,* 356–88.

Hausmann, M.F., Winkler, D.W., O'Reilly, K.M., Huntington, C.E., Nisbet, I.C.T. and Vleck, C.M. (2003) Telomeres shorten more slowly in long-lived birds and mammals than in short-lived ones. *Proceedings of the Royal Society of London: Biological Sciences, 270,* 1387–92.

Hawkins, H.L., Kramer, A.F. and Capaldi, D. (1992) Aging, exercise and attention. *Psychology and Aging, 7,* 643–53.

Hayflick, L.H. (1985) The cell biology of aging. *Clinical Geriatric Medicine, 1,* 15–27.

Hayflick, L.H. (1994) *How and Why We Age.* New York: Random House.

Hayflick, L.H. (1997) Mortality and immortality at the cellular level. A review. *Biochemistry, 62,* 1180–90.

Hayflick, L.H. (1998) How and why we age. *Experimental Gerontology, 33,* 639–53.

Hayslip, B. and Sterns, H.L. (1979) Age differences in relationships between crystallised and fluid intelligence and problem solving. *Journal of Gerontology, 34,* 404–14.

Heaphy, B., Yip, A.K.T. and Thompson, D. (2004) Ageing in a non-heterosexual context. *Ageing and Society, 24,* 881–902.

Hedden, T. and Park, D. (2001) Aging and interference in verbal working memory. *Psychology and Aging, 16,* 666–81.

Heidrich, S.M. and Denney, N.W. (1994) Does social problem solving differ from other types of problem solving during the adult years? *Experimental Aging Research, 20,* 105–26.

Helmes, E. and Gee, S. (2003) Attitudes of Australian therapists towards older clients: Educational and training imperatives. *Educational Gerontology, 29,* 657–70.

Hendricks, J. (1999) Creativity over the life course – a call for a rational perspective. *International Journal of Aging and Human Development, 48,* 85–111.

Henry, J.D., MacLeod, M.S., Phillips, L.H. and Crawford, J.R. (2004) A meta-analytic review of prospective memory and aging. *Psychology and Aging, 19,* 27–39.

Herbst, K.G. (1982) Social attitudes to hearing loss in the elderly. In F. Glendenning (ed.), *Acquired Hearing Loss and Elderly People.* Keele: Beth Johnson Foundation Publications.

Herrman, D.J. (1984) Questionnaires about memory. In J.E. Harris and P.E. Morris (eds), *Everyday Memory, Actions and Absent-mindedness.* London: Academic Press.

Herrman, D.J., Rea, A. and Andrzejewski, S. (1988) The need for a new approach to memory training. In M.M. Gruneberg, P.E. Morris and R.N. Sykes (eds), *Practical Aspects of Memory: Current Research and Issues.* Chichester: Wiley.

Hertzog, C. (1991) Aging, information processing speed and intelligence. In K.W. Schaie and P. Lawton (eds), *Annual Review of Gerontology and Geriatrics, 11,* 55–79.

Hertzog, C., Dixon, R.A., Hultsch, D.F., MacDonald, S. (2003) Latent change models of adult cognition: are changes in processing speed and working memory associated with changes in episodic memory? *Psychology and Aging, 18,* 755–69.

Hertzog, C. and Nesselroade, J.R. (2003) Assessing psychological change in adulthood: an overview of methodological issues. *Psychology and Aging, 18,* 639–57.

Herzog, A.R., House, J.S. and Morgan, J.N. (1991) Relation of work and retirement to health and well-being in old age. *Psychology and Aging, 6,* 202–11.

Hestad, K., Ellersten, B. and Klove, H. (1998) Neuropsychological assessment in old age. In I.H. Nordhus, G.R. VandenBos, S. Berg and P. Fromholt (eds), *Clinical Geropsychology.* Washington, DC: American Psychological Association, 259–88.

Heston, LL. Mastri, A.R., Anderson, V.E. and White, J. (1981) Dementia of the Alzheimer type. Animal genetics, natural history and associated conditions. *Archives of General Psychiatry, 38,*1085–90.

Hickson, J. and Housley, W. (1997) Creativity in later life. *Educational Gerontology, 23,* 539–47.

Hilgard, E.R., Atkinson, R.L. and Atkinson, R.C. (1979) *Introduction to Psychology.* 7th edition. New York: Harcourt Brace Jovanovich.

Hilt, M.L. and Lipschultz, J.H. (2004) Elderly Americans and the internet: E-mail, TV news, information and entertainment websites. *Educational Gerontology, 30,* 57–72.

Hirono, N., Mori, E., Ischii, K., Hirono, N. and Mori, E. (1998) Regional hypometabolism related to language disturbances in Alzheimer's disease. *Dementia and Geriatric Cognitive Disorders, 9,* 68–73.

Hofer, S., Berg, S. and Era, P. (2003) Evaluating the interdependence of aging-related changes in visual and auditory acuity, balance and cognitive functioning. *Psychology and Aging, 18,* 285–305.

Hofer, S.M., Christensen, H., Mackinnon, A.J., Korten, A.E., Jorm, A.F., Henderson, A.S. and Easteal, S. (2002) Change in cognitive functioning associated with ApoE genotype in a community sample of older adults. *Psychology and Aging, 17,* 194–208.

Hoffstein, V., Haight, J., Cole, P. and Zamel, N. (1999) Does snoring contribute to presbycusis? *American Journal of Respiratory Critical Care Medicine, 159,* 1351–4.

Hogan, M.J. (2003) Divided attention in older but not younger adults is impaired by anxiety. *Experimental Aging Research, 29,* 111–36.

Holahan, C.K. and Chapman. J.R. (2002) Longitudinal predictors of proactive goals and activity participation at age 80. *The Journals of Gerontology Series B: Psychological Sciences and Social Sciences, 57*, 418–25.

Holland, C. and Rabbitt, P. (1989) Subjective and objective measures of vision and hearing loss in elderly drivers and pedestrians. Talk at ESRC/General Accident Insurance Company Symposium on Road Traffic Accidents. University of Reading, 5 July.

Holland, C. and Rabbitt, P. (1990) Autobiographical and text recall in the elderly. *Quarterly Journal of Experimental Psychology, 42A*, 441–70.

Holtzer, R., Stern, Y. and Rakitin, B.C. (2004) Age-related differences in executive control of working memory. *Memory and Cognition, 32*, 1333–45.

Holtzman, R.E., Rebok, G.W., Saczynski, J.S., Kouzis, A.C., Doyle, K.W. and Eaton, W.W. (2004) Social network characteristics and cognition in middle-aged and older adults. *The Journals of Gerontology Series B: Psychological Sciences and Social Sciences, 59*, 278–84.

Hong, T.B., Zarit, S.H. and Malmberg, B. (2004) The role of health congruence in functional status and depression. *The Journals of Gerontology Series B: Psychological Sciences and Social Sciences, 59*, 151–7.

Hooker, K., Bowman, S.R., Coehlo, D.P., Lima, S.R., Kaye, J., Guariglia, R. and Lid, F. (2002) Behavioral change in persons with dementia: relationships with mental and physical health of caregivers. *The Journals of Gerontology Series B: Psychological Sciences and Social Sciences, 57*, 453–60.

Hooper, F.H., Fitzgerald, J. and Papalia, D. (1971) Piagetian theory and the aging process: Extensions and speculations. *Aging and Human Development, 2*, 3–20.

Hope, J. and Havir, L. (2002) You bet they're having fun! Older Americans and casino gambling. *Journal of Aging Studies, 16*, 177–97.

Horn, J.L. (1978) Human ability systems. In P.B. Baltes (ed.) *Life-span Development and Behavior, Volume 1*. New York: Academic Press, 211–56.

Horn, J.L. (1982) The theory of fluid and crystallised intelligence in relation to concepts of cognitive psychology and aging in adulthood. In F.I.M. Craik and S. Trehub (eds), *Aging and Cognitive Processes*. New York: Plenum.

Horn, J.L. and Cattell, R.B. (1967) Age differences in fluid and crystallised intelligence. *Acta Psychologia, 26*, 107–29.

House, J.S., Kessler, R.C., Herzog, A.R., Mero, R.P., Kinney, A.M. and Breslow, M.J. (1992) Social stratification, age and health. In K.W. Schaie, D. Blazer and J. House (ed.), *Aging, Health Behavior and Health Outcomes*. Hillsdale, NJ: Lawrence Erlbaum, 1–37.

Houston, D.K., Johnson, M.A., Nozza, R.J., Gunter, E.W., Shea, K.J., Cutler, G.M. and Edmonds, J.T. (1999) Age-related hearing loss, vitamin B-12 and folate in elderly women. *American Journal of Clinical Nutrition, 69*, 564–71.

Houx, P.J. and Jolles, J. (1993) Age-related decline of psychomotor speed: Effects of age, brain health, sex and education. *Perceptual and Motor Skills, 76*, 195–211.

Howard, D.V. and Howard, J.H. (1992) Adult age differences in the rate of learning serial patterns: evidence from direct and indirect tests. *Psychology and Aging, 7*, 232–41.

Hoyer, W.J. and Ingolfsdottir, D. (2003) Age, skill and contextual cuing in target detection. *Psychology and Aging, 18*, 210–18.

Hoyer, W.J. and Roodin, P.A. (2003) *Adult Development and Aging*. 5th edition. Boston, MA: McGraw Hill.

Hser, Y.I., Huffman, V., Grella, C.E. and Anglin, M. D. (2001) A 33-year follow-up of narcotics addicts. *Archives of General Psychiatry, 58*, 503–8.

Hubbard, R.E., Lyons, R.A., Woodhouse, K.W., Hillier, S.L., Wareham, K., Ferguson, B. and Majoe, E. (2003) Absence of ageism in access to critical care: A cross-sectional study. *Age and Ageing, 32*, 382–7.

Hubert, H.B., Bloch, D.A., Oehlert, J.W. and Fries, J.F. (2002) Lifestyle habits and compression of morbidity. *Journals of Gerontology: Series A: Biological Sciences and Medical Sciences, 57*, 347–51.

Hudson, L. (1987) Creativity. In R.L. Gregory and O. Zangwill (eds), *The Oxford Companion to the Mind*. Oxford: Oxford University Press.

Hulme, C., Lee, G. and Brown, G.D. (1993) Short-term memory impairments in Alzheimer-type dementia: Evidence for separable impairments of articulatory rehearsal and long-term memory. *Neuropsychologia, 31*, 161–72.

Hultsch, D.F., Hertzog, C., Small, B.J., McDonald-Miszczak, L. and Dixon, R.A. (1992) Short-term longitudinal change in cognitive performance in later life. *Psychology and Aging, 7*, 571–84.

Hultsch, D.F., MacDonald, S.W.S. and Dixon, R.A. (2002) Variability in reaction time performance of younger and older adults. *The Journals of Gerontology Series B: Psychological Sciences and Social Sciences, 57*, 101–15.

Hummert, M.L., Garstka, T.A., O'Brien, L.T., Greenwald, A.G. and Mellott, D.S. (2002) Using the implicit association test to measure age differences in implicit social cognitions. *Psychology and Aging, 17*, 482–95.

Hummert, M.L., Garstka, T.A. and Shaner, J.L. (1997) Stereotyping of older adults: The role of target facial cues and perceiver characteristics. *Psychology and Aging, 12*, 107–14.

Huntgeburth, M., Ten Freyhaus, H. and Rosenkranz, S. (2005) Alcohol consumption and hypertension. *Current Hypertension Reports, 7*, 180–5.

Hutchinson, K.M. (1989) Influence of sentence context on speech perception in young and older adults. *Journal of Gerontology B: Psychological Sciences, 44*, 36–44.

Hybertson, E.D., Perdue, J. and Hybertson, D. (1982) Age differences in information acquisition strategies. *Experimental Aging Research, 8*, 109–113.

Hyman, B.T., Arriagada, P.V., Van Housen, G.W. and Damasio, A.R. (1993) Memory impairment in Alzheimer's disease: An anatomical perspective. In R.W. Parks, R.F. Zec and R.S. Wilson (eds), *Neuropsychology of Alzheimer's Disease and Other Dementias*. New York: Oxford University Press, 138–50.

Iachine, I.A., Holm, N.V., Harris, J.R., Begun, A.Z., Iachine, M.K., Laitinen, M., Kaprio, J. and Yashin, A.I. (1998) How heritable is individual susceptibility to death? The results of an analysis of survival data on Danish, Swedish and Finnish twins. *Twin Research, 1*, 196–205.

Idler, E.L., Kasl, S.V. and Hays, J.C. (2001) Patterns of religious practice and belief in the last year of life. *The Journals of Gerontology Series B: Psychological Sciences and Social Sciences, 56*, 326–34.

Igier, V. and Mullet, E. (2003) Application of the five-factor model of personality to intergenerational perception. *The Journals of Gerontology Series B: Psychological Sciences and Social Sciences, 58*, 177–86.

Ingersoll-Dayton, B. and Saengtienchai, C. (1999) Respect for the elderly in Asia: Stability and change. *International Journal of Aging and Human Development, 48*, 113–30.

Intrieri, R. C., von Eye, A. and Kelly, J. A. (1995). The aging semantic differential: A confirmatory factor analysis. *The Gerontologist, 35*, 616–21.

Isingrini, M. and Vazou, F. (1997) Relation between fluid intelligence and frontal lobe functioning in older adults. *International Journal of Aging and Human Development, 45*, 99–109.

Izquierdo-Porrera, A.M. and Waldstein, S.R. (2002) Cardiovascular risk factors and cognitive function in African Americans. *The Journals of Gerontology Series B: Psychological Sciences and Social Sciences, 57*, 377–80.

Jack, C.R., Petersen, R.C., Xu, Y.G., Obrien, P.C., Smith, G.E., Ivnik, R.J., Boeve, B.F., Mizuno, K., Wakai, M., Takeda, A. and Sobue, G. (1997) Medial temporal atrophy on MRI in normal aging and very mild Alzheimer's disease. *Neurology, 49*, 786–94.

Jackson, J.L., Bogers, H. and Kerstholt, J. (1988) Do memory aids aid the elderly in their day to day remembering? In M.M. Gruneberg, P.E. Morris and R.N. Sykes (eds), *Practical Aspects of Memory, Current Research and Issues Volume 2*. Chichester: Wiley.

Jackson, J.S., Antonucci, T.C. and Gibson, R.C. (1990) Cultural, racial and ethnic minority influences on aging. In J.E. Birren and K.W. Schaie (eds), *Handbook of the Psychology of Aging*. 3rd edition. San Diego, CA: Academic Press.

Jaffe, G.J., Alvarado, J.A. and Juster, R.P. (1986) Age-related changes of the normal visual field. *Archives of Ophthalmology, 104*, 1021–5.

James, C. (1983) *Falling Towards England*. London: Jonathan Cape.

James, L.E. (2004) Meeting Mr. Farmer versus meeting a farmer: specific effects of aging on learning proper names. *Psychology and Aging, 19*, 515–22.

Jansari, A. and Parkin, A.J. (1996) Things that go bump in your life: Explaining the reminiscence bump in autobiographical memory. *Psychology and Aging, 11*, 85–91.

Jarvik, L.F. (1983) Age is in – is the wit out? In D. Samuel, S. Alegri, S. Gershon, V.E. Grimm and G. Toffanl (eds), *Aging of the Brain*. New York: Raven Press, 1–7.

Jarvik, L.F. (1988) Aging of the brain: How can we prevent it? *Gerontologist, 28*, 739–47.

Jarvik, L.F. and Falek, A. (1963) Intellectual stability and survival in the aged. *Journal of Gerontology, 18*, 173–6.

Jeffreys, M. (ed.) (1989) *Growing Old in the Twentieth Century*. London: Routledge.

Jenike, M. (1988) Depression and other psychiatric disorders. In M.S. Albert and M.B. Moss (eds), *Geriatric Neuropsychology*. New York: Guilford.

Jenkins, L., Myerson, J., Hale, S. and Fry, A.F. (1999) Individual and developmental differences in working memory across the lifespan. *Psychonomic Bulletin and Review, 6*, 28–40.

Jenkins, L., Myerson, J., Joerding, J.A. and Hale, S. (2000) Converging evidence that visuospatial cognition is more age-sensitive than verbal cognition. *Psychology and Aging, 15*, 157–75.

Jennings, J.M. and Jacoby, L.L. (1993) Automatic versus intentional uses of memory: Aging, attention and control. *Psychology and Aging, 8*, 283–93.

Jerram, K.L. and Coleman, P.G. (1999) The big five personality traits and reporting of health problems and health behaviour in old age. *British Journal of Health Psychology, 4*, 181–92.

Jeste, D.V., Symonds, L.L., Harris, M.J., Paulsen, J.S., Palmer, B.W. and Heaton, R.K. (1997) Nondementia nonpraecox dementia praecox? Late-onset schizophrenia. *American Journal of Geriatric Psychiatry, 5*, 302–17.

Johansson, B., Hofer, S.M., Allaire, J.C., Maldonado-Molina, M.M., Piccinin, A.M., Berg, S., Pedersen, N.L. and McClearn, G.E. (2004) Change in cognitive capabilities in the oldest old: the effects of proximity to death in genetically related individuals over a 6-year period. *Psychology and Aging, 19*, 145–156.

Johnson, C.L. and Troll, L. (1996) Family structure and the timing of transitions from 70 to 103 years of age. *Journal of Marriage and the Family, 58*, 178–87.

Johnson, F.B., Marciniak, R.A. and Guarente, L. (1998) Telomeres, the nucleolus and aging. *Current Opinions in Cell Biology, 10*, 332–8.

Johnson, P. and Falkingham, J. (1992) *Ageing and Economic Welfare*. London: Sage.

Johnston, M. and Walker, M. (1996) Suicide in the elderly: Recognizing the signs. *General Hospital Psychiatry, 18*, 257–60.

Jones, R.N. and Gallo, J.J. (2002) Education and sex differences in the mini-mental state examination: Effects of differential item functioning. *The Journals of Gerontology Series B: Psychological Sciences and Social Sciences, 57*, 548–58.

Jonker, C., Smits, C.H. and Deeg, D.J.H. (1997) Affect-related metamemory and memory performance in a population-based sample of older adults. *Educational Gerontology, 23*, 115–28.

Kahana, M.J., Dolan E.D., Sauder, C.L. and Wingfield, A. (2005) Intrusions in episodic recall: Age differences in editing of overt responses. *The Journals of Gerontology Series B: Psychological Sciences and Social Sciences, 60*, 92–7.

Kahn, R.L., Goldfarb, A.I., Pollack, M. and Peck, A. (1960) Brief objective measures for determination of mental status in the aged. *American Journal of Psychiatry, 117*, 326–8.

Kail, R. (1997) The neural noise hypothesis: Evidence from processing speed in adults with multiple sclerosis. *Aging, Neuropsychology and Cognition, 4*, 157–65.

Kail, R. and Pelligrino, J.W. (1985) *Human Intelligence: Perspectives and Prospects*. San Francisco, CA: Freeman.

Kapur, N. (1995) Memory aids in the rehabilitation of memory disordered patients. In A.D. Baddeley, B.A. Wilson and F.N. Watts (eds), *Handbook of Memory Disorders*. Chichester: Wiley, 533–56.

Karayanidis, F., Andrews, S., Ward, P.B. and McConaghy, N. (1993) Event-related potentials and repetition priming in young, middle-aged and elderly normal subjects. *Cognitive Brain Research, 1*, 123–34.

Karon, B.P. and VandenBos, G.R. (1998) Schizophrenia and psychosis in elderly populations. In I.H. Nordhus, G.R. VandenBos, S. Berg and P. Fromholt (eds), *Clinical Geropsychology*. Washington, DC: American Psychological Association, 219–27.

Karpel, M.E., Hoyer, W.J. and Toglia, M.P. (2001) Accuracy and qualities of real and suggested memories: Nonspecific age differences. *The Journals of Gerontology Series B: Psychological Sciences and Social Sciences, 56*, 103–10.

Kart, C.S. (1981) *The Realities of Aging*. Boston, MA: Allyn and Bacon.

Kart, C.S., Metress, E.S. and Metress, J.F. (1978) *Aging and Health: Biologic and Social Perspectives*. Menlo Park, CA: Addison-Wesley.

Kaskie, B. and Storandt, M. (1995) Visuospatial deficit in dementia of the Alzheimer type. *Archives of Neurology, 52*, 422–5.

Kasl-Godley, J.E., Gatz, M. and Fiske, A. (1998) Depression and depressive symptoms in old age. In I.H. Nordhus, G.R. VandenBos, S. Berg and P. Fromholt (eds), *Clinical Geropsychology*. Washington, DC: American Psychological Association, 211–7.

Katzman, R., Terry, R., Deteresa, R., Brown, T., Davies, P., Fuld, P., Renbing, X. and Peck, A. (1988) Clinical, pathological and neurochemical changes in dementia: A subgroup with preserved mental status on numerous neocortical plaques. *Annals of Neurology, 23*, 138–44.

Kaufman, A.S. and Horn, J.L. (1996) Age changes on tests of fluid and crystallised ability for women and men on the Kaufman Adolescent and Adult Intelligence Test (KAIT) at ages 17–94 years. *Archives of Clinical Neuropsychology, 11*, 97–121.

Kausler, D.H. (1982) *Experimental Psychology and Human Aging*. New York: Wiley.

Kawachi, I. and Kennedy, B.P. (1997) Socioeconomic determinants of health: health and social cohesion: Why care about income inequality? *British Medical Journal, 314*, 1037–40.

Kaye, J.A., Swihart, T., Howieson, D., Dame, A., Moore, M.M., Kamos, T., Camicioli, R., Ball, M., Oken, B. and Sexton, G. (1997) Volume loss of the hippocampus and temporal lobe in healthy elderly persons destined to develop dementia. *Neurology, 48*, 1297–304.

Keilp, J.G., Gorlyn, M., Alexander, G.E., Stern, Y. and Prohovnik, I. (1999) Cerebral blood flow patterns underlying the differential impairment in category vs letter fluency in Alzheimer's disease. *Neuropsychologia, 37*, 1251–61.

Kelley, C.L., Morrell, R.W., Park, D.C. and Mayhorn, C.B. (1999) Predictors of electronic bulletin board system use in older adults. *Educational Gerontology, 25*, 19–35.

Kempen, G.I.J.M., Jelicic, M. and Ormel, J. (1997) Personality, chronic medical morbidity and health-related quality of life among older persons. *Health Psychology, 16*, 539–46.

Kempen, G.I.J.M., Scaf-Klomp, W., Ranchor, A.V., Sanderman, R. and Ormel, J. (2001) Social predictors of recovery in late middle-aged and older persons after injury to the extremities: A prospective study. *The Journals of Gerontology Series B: Psychological Sciences and Social Sciences, 56*, 229–36.

Kemper, S. (1986) Limitation of complex syntactic construction by elderly adults. *Applied Psycholinguistics, 7*, 277–87.

Kemper, S. (1987a) Adults' diaries: Changes to written narratives across the life span. *Conference on Social Psychology and Language.* 20–24 July.

Kemper, S. (1987b) Life-span changes in syntactic complexity. *Journal of Gerontology, 42*, 3232–328.

Kemper, S. (1988) Geriatric psycholinguistics: Syntactic limitation of oral and written language. In L.L. Light and D.M. Burke (eds), *Language, Memory and Aging.* New York: Cambridge University Press.

Kemper, S. (1992) Adults' sentence fragments: Who, what, when, where and why. *Communication Research, 19*, 444–58.

Kemper, S. (1997) Metalinguistic judgments in normal aging and Alzheimer's disease. *Journal of Gerontology B: Psychological Sciences and Social Sciences, 52*, 147–55.

Kemper, S. and Anagnopoulos, C. (1993) Adult use of discourse constraints on syntactic processing. In J. Cerella, J. Rybash, W. Hoyer and M.L. Commons (eds), *Adult Information Processing: Limits on Loss.* San Diego, CA: Academic Press, 489–507.

Kemper, S., Crow, A. and Kemtes, K. (2004) Eye-fixation patterns of high- and low-span young and older adults: Down the garden path and back again. *Psychology and Aging, 19*, 157–70.

Kemper, S., Greiner, L.H., Marquis, J.G., Prenovost, K. and Mitzner, T.L. (2001) Language decline across the life span: Findings from the nun study. *Psychology and Aging, 16*, 227–39.

Kemper, S., Herman, R.E. and Liu, C.J. (2004) Sentence production by young and older adults in controlled contexts. *The Journals of Gerontology Series B: Psychological Sciences and Social Sciences, 59*, 220–4.

Kemper, S. and Rush, S.J. (1988) Speech and writing across the life span. In M.M. Gruneberg, P.E. Morris and R.N. Sykes (eds), *Practical Aspects of Memory, Current Research and Issues.* Chichester: Wiley.

Kemper, S. and Sumner, A. (2001) The structure of verbal abilities in young and older adults. *Psychology and Aging, 16*, 312–22.

Kemper, S., Thompson, M. and Marquis, J. (2001) Longitudinal change in language production: Effects of aging and dementia on grammatical complexity and propositional content. *Psychology and Aging, 16*, 600–14.

Kemtes, K.A. and Kemper, S. (1997) Younger and older adults' on-line processing of syntactically ambiguous sentences. *Psychology and Aging, 12*, 362–71.

Kemtes, K.A. and Kemper, S. (2001) Cognitive construct measurement in small samples of younger and older adults: An example of verbal working memory. *Experimental Aging Research, 27*, 167–80.

Kennedy, S., Kiecolt-Glaser, J.K. and Glaser, R. (1988) Immunological consequences of acute and chronic stressors: mediating role of interpersonal relationships. *British Journal of Medical Psychology, 61*, 77–85.

Kensinger, E.A. and Schachter, D.L. (1999) When true memories suppress false memories: Effects of ageing. *Cognitive Neuropsychology, 16*, 399–415.

Kermis, M.D. (1983) *The Psychology of Human Aging: Theory, Research and Practice.* Boston, MA: Allyn and Bacon.

Kermis, M.D. (1986) *Mental Health in Later Life. The Adaptive Process.* Boston, MA: Jones and Bartlett.

Kidson, A. and Chen, A. (1986) DNA damage, DNA repair and the genetic basis of Alzheimer's disease. *Progress in Brain Research, 70.* Amsterdam: Elsevier.

Kim, J.E. and Moen, P. (2002) Retirement transitions, gender and psychological well-being: a life-course, ecological model. *The Journals of Gerontology Series B: Psychological Sciences and Social Sciences, 57*, 212–22.

Kirby, S.E., Coleman. P.G. and Daley, D. (2004) Spirituality and well-being in frail and nonfrail older adults. *The Journals of Gerontology Series B: Psychological Sciences and Social Sciences, 59*, 123–9.

Kirkwood, T.B.L. (1988) The nature and causes of ageing. In *Research and the Ageing Population.* CIBA Foundation Symposium 134. Chichester: Wiley, 193–207.

Kite, M.E., Deaux, K. and Miele, M. (1993) Stereotypes of young and old: Does age outweigh gender? *Psychology and Aging, 8*, 19–27.

Klaczynski, P.A. and Robinson, B. (2000) Personal theories, intellectual ability and epistemological beliefs: Adult age differences in everyday reasoning biases. *Psychology and Aging, 15*, 400–16.

Kleemeier, R.W. (1962) Intellectual changes in the senium. *Proceedings of the Social Statistics Section of the American Statistical Association, 1*, 290–95.

Knapp, J.L., Beaver, L.M. and Reed, T.D. (2002) Perceptions of the elderly among ministers and ministry students: Implications for seminary curricula. *Educational Gerontology, 28*, 313–24.

Kogan, N. (1990) Personality and aging. In J.E. Birren and K.W. Schaie (eds) *Handbook of the Psychology of Aging.* 3rd edition. San Diego, CA: Academic Press.

Kopelman, M.D. (1985) Rates of forgetting in Alzheimer-type dementia and Korsakoff's syndrome. *Neuropsychologia, 23,* 623–38.

Korpelainen, H. (1999) Genetic maternal effects on human life span through inheritance of mitochondrial DNA. *Human Heredity, 49,* 183–5.

Kosslyn, S.M., Brown, H.D. and Dror, I.E. (1999) Aging and the scope of visual attention. *Gerontology, 45,* 102–9.

Kovach, S.S. and Robinson, J.D. (1996) The roommate relationship for the elderly nursing home resident. *Journal of Social and Personal Relationships, 13,* 627–34.

Kozora, E. and Cullum, C.M. (1995) Generative naming in normal aging: Total output and qualitative changes using phonemic and semantic constraints. *Clinical Neuropsychologist, 9,* 313–20.

Kraaij, V., Arensman, E. and Spinhoven, P. (2002) Negative life events and depression in elderly persons: a meta-analysis. *The Journals of Gerontology Series B: Psychological Sciences and Social Sciences, 57,* 87–94.

Kraij, V., Kremers, I. and Arensman, E. (1997) The relationship between stressful and traumatic life events and depression in the elderly. *Crisis, 18,* 86–8.

Kramer, A.F., Hahn, S., Cohen, N., Banich, M., McAuley, E., Harrison, C., Chason, J., Vakil, E., Bardell, L. and Colcombe, A. (1999) Ageing, fitness and neurocognitive function. *Nature, 400,* 418–9.

Kramer, A.F., Humphrey, D.G., Larish, J.F. and Logan, G.D. (1995) Aging and inhibition: Beyond a unitary veiw of inhibitory processing in attention. *Psychology and Aging, 9,* 491–512.

Kramer, A.F. and Strayer, D.L. (2001) Influence of stimulus repetition on negative priming. *Psychology and Aging, 16,* 580–7.

Krause, N. (2002) Church-based social support and health in old age: exploring variations by race. *The Journals of Gerontology Series B: Psychological Sciences and Social Sciences, 57,* 332–47.

Krause, N. (2003) Religious meaning and subjective well-being in late life. *The Journals of Gerontology Series B: Psychological Sciences and Social Sciences, 58,* 160–70.

Krause, N., Jay, G. and Liang, J. (1991) Financial strain and psychological well-being among the American and Japanese elderly. *Psychology and Aging, 6,* 170–81.

Krause, N., Liang, J., Shaw, B.A., Sugisawa, H., Kim, H.K. and Sugihara, Y. (2002) Religion, death of a loved one and hypertension among older adults in Japan. *The Journals of Gerontology Series B: Psychological Sciences and Social Sciences, 57,* 96–107.

Krause, N., Shaw, B.A. and Cairney, J. (2004) A descriptive epidemiology of lifetime trauma and the physical health status of older adults. *Psychology and Aging, 19,* 637–48.

Krmpotic-Nemanic, J. (1969) Presbycusis and retrocochlear structures. *International Audiology, 8,* 210–20.

Kübler-Ross, E. (1970) *On Death and Dying.* London: Tavistock Publications.

Kübler-Ross, E. (1997) *The Wheel of Life.* London: Bantam Press.

Kunzmann, U., Little, T.D. and Smith, J. (2000) Is age-related stability of subjective well-being a paradox? Cross-sectional and longitudional evidence from the Berlin Aging Study. *Psychology and Aging, 15,* 511–26.

Kvavilashvili, L. (1987) Remembering intention as a distinct form of memory. *British Journal of Psychology, 78,* 507–18.

Kwong See, S.T., Hoffman, H.G. and Wood, T.L. (2001) Perceptions of an old female eyewitness: Is the older eyewitness believable? *Psychology and Aging, 16,* 346–50.

Kynette, D. and Kemper, S. (1986) Aging and the loss of grammatical form: a cross-sectional study of language performance. *Language and Communication, 6,* 65–72.

Labouvie-Vief, G. (1992) A neo-Piagetian perspective on adult cognitive development. In R.J. Sternberg and C.A. Berg (eds), *Intellectual Development.* Cambridge: Cambridge University Press.

Labouvie-Vief, G. and Gonda, J.N. (1976) Cognitive strategy training and intellectual performance in the elderly. *Journal of Gerontology, 31,* 327–32.

Lacro, J.P., Harris, M.J. and Jeste, D.V. (1995) Late-life psychosis. In E. Murphy and G. Alexopoulos (ed.), *Geriatric Psychiatry: Key Research Topics for Clinicians.* Chichester: Wiley, 231–44.

Laditka, S.B., Fischer, M., Laditka, J.N. and Segal, D.R. (2004) Attitudes about aging and gender among young, middle age and older college-based students. *Educational Gerontology, 30,* 403–21.

Laditka, S.B. and Laditka, J.N. (2002) Recent perspectives on active life expectancy for older women. *Journal of Women and Aging, 14,* 163–84.

Laguna, K. and Babcock, R.L. (1997) Computer anxiety in young and older adults: Implications for human-computer interactions in older populations. *Computers in Human Behavior, 13,* 317–26.

Lahar, C.J., Tun, P.A. and Wingfield, A. (2004) Sentence–final word completion norms for young, middle-aged and older adults. *The Journals of Gerontology Series B: Psychological Sciences and Social Sciences, 59,* 7–10.

Lajoie, Y., Teasdale, N., Bard, C. and Fleury, M. (1996) Upright standing and gait: Are there changes in attentional requirements related to normal aging? *Experimental Aging Research, 22,* 185–98.

Landreville, P., Landry, J., Baillargeon, L., Guérette, A. and Matteaud, E. (2001) Older adults' acceptance of psychological and pharmacological treatments for depression. *The Journals of Gerontology Series B: Psychological Sciences and Social Sciences, 56*, 285–91.

Lane, C.J. and Zelinski, E.M. (2003) Longitudinal hierarchical linear models of the Memory Functioning Questionnaire. *Psychology and Aging, 18*, 38–53.

Lang, E., Arnold, K. and Kupfer, P. (1994) Women live longer–biological, medical and sociologic causes. *Zeitschrift fuer Gerontologie, 27*, 10–15.

Larrabee, G.J. and Crook, T.H. (1993) Do men show more rapid age-associated decline in simulated everyday memory than do women? *Psychology and Aging, 8*, 68–71.

Larson, R. (1978) Thirty years of research on the subjective well-being of older Americans. *Journal of Gerontology, 33*, 109–25.

LaRue, A. (1992) *Aging and Neuropsychological Assessment.* New York: Plenum.

LaRue, A., Dessonville, C. and Jarvik, L.F. (1985) Aging and mental disorders. In J.E. Birren and K.W. Schaie (eds), *Handbook of the Psychology of Aging.* New York: Van Nostrand Reinhold, 664–702.

Lasch, H., Castell, D.O. and Castell, J.A. (1997) Evidence for diminished visceral pain with aging: studies using graded intraesophageal balloon distension. *American Journal of Physiology, 272*, 1–3.

Laslett, P. (1976) Societal development and aging. In R.H. Binstock and E. Shanas (eds), *Handbook of Aging and the Social Sciences.* New York: Reinhold.

Latimer, J. (1963) The status of aging in intelligence. *Journal of Genetic Psychology, 102*, 175–88.

Laurence, M.W. and Arrowood, A.J. (1982) Classification style differences in the elderly. In F.I.M. Craik and S. Trehub (eds), *Aging and Cognitive Processes.* New York: Plenum.

Lauver, S.C. and Johnson, J.L. (1997) The role of neuroticism and social support in older adults with chronic pain behavior. *Personality and Individual Differences, 23*, 165–7.

Laver, G.D. and Burke, D.M. (1993) Why do semantic priming effects increase in old age? A meta-analysis. *Psychology and Aging, 8*, 34–43.

Law, R. and O'Carroll, R.E. (1998) A comparison of three measures of estimating premorbid intellectual level in dementia of the Alzheimer type. *International Journal of Geriatric Psychiatry, 13*, 727–30.

Lawton, M.P. and Salthouse, T.A. (eds) (1998) *Essential Papers on the Psychology of Aging.* New York: New York University Press.

Lee, G.R., DeMaris, A., Bavin, S. and Sullivan, R. (2001) Gender differences in the depressive effect of widowhood in later life. *The Journals of Gerontology Series B: Psychological Sciences and Social Sciences, 56*, 56–61.

Lee, H., Swanwick, G.R.J., Coen, R.F. and Lawlor, B.A. (1996) Use of the clock drawing task in the diagnosis of mild and very mild Alzheimer's disease. *International Psychogeriatrics, 8*, 469–76.

Lee, I.M. and Paffenberger, R.S. (1998) Physical activity and stroke incidence: The Havard Alumni Health Study. *Stroke, 29*, 2049–54.

Lee, I.M. and Paffenberger, R.S. (2000) Associations of light, moderate and vigorous intensity physical activity with longevity. The Harvard Alumni Health Study. *American Journal of Epidemiology, 151*, 293–9.

Lee, I.M., Sesso, H.D., Oguma, Y. and Paffenbarger, R.S. (2004) The 'weekend warrior' and risk of mortality. *American Journal of Epidemiology, 160*, 636–41.

Leenaars, A.A. and Lester, D. (1998) Predicting suicide rate among elderly persons in Canadian provinces. *Psychological Reports, 82*, 1202.

Leentjens, A.F.G. and van der Mast, R.C. (2005) Delirium in elderly people: An update. *Current Opinion in Psychiatry, 18*, 325–30.

Leino, E.V., Romelsjoe, A., Shoemaker, C., Ager, C.R., Allebeck, P., Ferrer, H.P., Fillmore, K.M., Golding, J.M., Graves, K.L. and Kniep, S. (1998) Alcohol consumption and mortality. II. Studies of male populations. *Addiction, 93*, 205–18.

Lennartsson. C. and Silverstein, M. (2001) does engagement with life enhance survival of elderly people in Sweden? The role of social and leisure activities. *The Journals of Gerontology Series B: Psychological Sciences and Social Sciences, 56*, 335–42.

Lester, D., Cantor, C.H. and Leenaars, A.A. (1997) Suicide in the United Kingdom and Ireland. *European Psychiatry, 12*, 300–4.

Levenson, R.W., Cartensen, L.L. and Gottman, J.M. (1993) Long-term marriage: Age, gender and satisfaction. *Psychology and Aging, 8*, 310–3.

Levesque, L., Ducharme, F. and Lachance, L. (1999) Is there a difference between family caregiving of institutionalized elders with or without dementia? *Western Journal of Nursing Research, 21*, 472–97.

Levine, B., Stuss, D.T. and Milberg, W.P. (1995) Concept generation: Validation of a test of executive functioning in a normal aging population. *Journal of Clinical and Experimental Neuropsychology, 17*, 740–58.

Levine, B., Svoboda, E., Hay, J.F., Winocur, G. and Moscovitch, M. (2002) Aging and autobiographical memory: Dissociating episodic from semantic retrieval. *Psychology and Aging, 17*, 677–89.

Levinson, D. (1980) Conception of the adult life course. In N. Smelser and E. Erikson (eds), *Themes of Work and Love in Adulthood.* Cambridge, MA: Harvard University Press.

Levy, B.R. (1999) The inner self of the Japanese elderly: A defense against negative stereotypes of aging. *International Journal of Aging and Human Development, 48,* 131–44.

Levy, B.R., Hausdorff, J.M., Hencke, R. and Wei, J.Y. (2000) Reducing cardiovascular stress with positive self-stereotypes of aging. *The Journals of Gerontology Series B: Psychological Sciences and Social Sciences, 55,* 205–13.

Levy, J.A. and Anderson, T. (2005) The drug career of the older injector. *Addiction Research and Theory, 13,* 245–58.

Lezak, M.D. (1995) *Neuropsychological Assessment.* New York: Oxford University Press.

Li, F., Fisher, K.J., Harmer, P. and McAuley, E. (2005) Falls self-efficacy as a mediator of fear of falling in an exercise intervention for older adults. *The Journals of Gerontology Series B: Psychological Sciences and Social Sciences, 60,* 34–40.

Li, F., Fisher, K.J., Harmer, P., McAuley, E. and Wilson, N.L. (2003) Fear of falling in elderly persons: association with falls, functional ability and quality of life. *The Journals of Gerontology Series B: Psychological Sciences and Social Sciences, 58,* 283–90.

Li, K.Z.H. and Lindenberger, U. (2002) Relations between aging sensory/sensorimotor and cognitive functions. *Neuroscience and Biobehavioral Reviews, 26,* 777–83.

Light, L.L. and Albertson, S.A. (1988) Comprehension of pragmatic implications in young and older adults. In L.L. Light and D.M. Burke (eds), *Language, Memory and Aging.* New York: Cambridge University Press.

Light, L.L. and Albertson, S.A. (1989) Direct and indirect tests of memory for category exemplars in young and older adults. *Psychology and Aging, 4,* 487–92.

Light, L.L. and Anderson, P.A. (1985) Working memory capacity, age and memory for discourse. *Journal of Gerontology, 40,* 737–47.

Light, L.L. and Burke, D. (eds) (1988) *Language, Memory and Aging.* New York: Cambridge University Press.

Light, L.L. and Singh, A. (1987) Implicit and explicit memory in young and older adults. *Journal of Experimental Psychology: Learning, Memory and Cognition, 13,* 531–41.

Lindenberger, U. and Baltes, P. (1994) Sensory functioning and intelligence in old age: A strong connection. *Psychology and Aging, 9,* 339–55.

Lindenberger, U. and Baltes, P. (1997) Intellectual functioning in old and very old age: Cross-sectional results from the Berlin Aging Study. *Psychology and Aging, 12,* 410–32.

Lindenberger, U., Kliegl, R. and Baltes, P.B. (1992) Professional expertise does not eliminate age differences in imagery-based memory performance during adulthood. *Psychology and Aging, 7,* 585–93.

Lindenberger, U., Marsiske, M. and Baltes, P.B. (2000) Memorizing while walking: Increase in dual-task costs from young adulthood to old age. *Psychology and Aging, 15,* 417–436.

Lindenberger, U., Mayr, U. and Kliegl, R. (1993) Speed and intelligence in old age. *Psychology and Aging, 8,* 207–20.

Lindenberger, U., Scherer, H. and Baltes, P.B. (2001) The strong connection between sensory and cognitive performance in old age: Not due to sensory acuity reductions operating during cognitive assessment. *Psychology and Aging, 16,* 196–205.

Lindesay, J., Briggs, K. and Murphy, E. (1989) The Guy's/Age Concern survey: Prevalence rates of cognitive impairment, depression and anxiety in an urban elderly community. *British Journal of Psychiatry, 155,* 317–29.

Lofwall, M.R., Brooner, R.K., Bigelow, G.E., Kindbom, K. and Strain, E.C. (2005) Characteristics of older opioid maintenance patients. *Journal of Substance Abuse Treatment, 28,* 265–72.

Logan, J.M. and Balota, D.A. (2003) Conscious and unconscious lexical retrieval blocking in younger and older adults. *Psychology and Aging, 18,* 537–50.

Long, L.L. and Shaw, R.J. (2000) Adult age differences in vocabulary acquisition. *Educational Gerontology, 26,* 651–64.

Lopata, H. (1973) *Widowhood in an American City.* Cambridge: Schenkman.

Löppönen, M., Räihä, I., Isoaho, R., Vahlberg, T. and Kivela, S.L. (2003) Diagnosing cognitive impairment and dementia in primary health care – a more active approach is needed. *Age and Ageing, 32,* 606–12.

Lövdén, M., Rönnlund, M., Wahlin, A., Bäckman, L., Nyberg, L. and Nilsson, L.G. (2004) The extent of stability and change in episodic and semantic memory in old age: Demographic predictors of level and change. *The Journals of Gerontology Series B: Psychological Sciences and Social Sciences, 59,* 130–4.

Lövdén, M. and Wahlin, A. (2005) The sensory-cognition association in adulthood: Different magnitudes for processing speed, inhibition, episodic memory and false memory? *Scandinavian Journal of Psychology, 46,* 253–62.

Lovie, K.J. and Whittaker, S. (1998) Relative size magnification versus relative distance magnification: Effect on the reading performance of adults with normal and low vision. *Journal of Visual Impairment and Blindness, 92,* 433–46.

Lowe, C. and Rabbitt, P. (1997) Cognitive models of ageing and frontal lobe deficits. In P. Rabbitt (ed.), *Methodology of Frontal and Executive Function.* Hove: Taylor and Francis, 39–59.

Luo, Y. and Waite, L.J. (2005) The impact of childhood and adult ses on physical, mental and cognitive well-being in later life. *The Journals of Gerontology Series B: Psychological Sciences and Social Sciences, 60,* 93–101.

Luquet, G.H. (1927) *Le Dessin Enfant*. Paris: Alcan.

Maas, M.S. and Kuypers, J.A. (1974) *From Thirty to Seventy*. San Francisco: Jossey-Bass.

MacDonald, S.W.S., Hultsch, D.F., Strauss, E. and Dixon, R.A. (2003) Age-related slowing of digit symbol substitution revisited: what do longitudinal age changes reflect? *The Journals of Gerontology Series B: Psychological Sciences and Social Sciences, 58*, 187–94.

Macintyre, S. (1994) Understanding the social patterning of health: The role of the social sciences. *Journal of Public Health Medicine, 16*, 53–9.

MacKay, D.G. and Abrams, L. (1998) Age-linked declines in retrieveing orthographic knolwedge: Empirical, practical and theoretical implications. *Psychology and Aging, 13*, 647–62.

MacKay, D.G., Abrams, L. and Pedroza, M.J. (1999) Aging on the input versus output side: Theoretical implications of age-linked assymetries between detecting versus retrieving orthographic information. *Psychology and Aging, 14*, 3–17.

MacKay, D.G. and Burke, D.M. (1990) Cognition and aging: A theory of new learning and the use of old connections. In T.M.Hess (ed.) *Aging and Cognition: Organization and Utilization*. Amsterdam: North-Holland, 1–51.

MacLeod, A.K., Williams, J.M.G. and Linehan, M.M. (1992) New developments in the understanding and treatment of suicidal behaviour. *Behavioural Psychotherapy, 20*, 193–218.

MacPherson, S.E., Phillips, L.H. and Della Sala, S. (2002) Age, executive function and social decision making: A dorsolateral prefrontal theory of cognitive aging. *Psychology and Aging, 17*, 598–609.

Madden, D.J. (1992) Four to ten milliseconds per year: Age-related slowing of visual word identification. *Journals of Gerontology, 47*, 59–68.

Madden, D.J. and Langley, L.K. (2003) Age-related changes in selective attention and perceptual load during visual search. *Psychology and Aging, 18*, 54–67.

Madden, D.J., Turkington, T.G., Provenzale, J.M., Denny, L.L., Hawk, T.C., Gottlob, L.R. and Coleman, R.E. (1999) Adult age differences in the functional neuroanatomy of verbal recognition memory. *Human Brain Mapping, 7*, 115–35.

Madden, D.J., Whiting, W.L., Cabeza, R. and Huettel, S.A. (2004) Age-related preservation of top-down attentional guidance during visual search. *Psychology and Aging, 19*, 304–9.

Maddox, G.I. (1970a) Persistence of life style among the elderly. In E. Palmore (ed.), *Normal Aging*. Durham: Duke University Press.

Maddox, G.I. (1970b) Themes and issues in sociological theories of human aging. *Human Development, 13*, 17–27.

Madigan, M.J., Mise, D.H. and Maynard, M. (1996) Life satisfaction and level of activity of male elderly in institutional and community settings. *Activities, Adaptation and Aging, 21*, 21–36.

Maentylae, T. and Nilsson, L.G. (1997) Remembering to remember in adulthood: A population-based study on aging and prospective memory. *Aging, Neuropsychology and Cognition, 4*, 81–92.

Magai, C., Cohen, C., Milburn, N., Thorpe, B., McPherson, R. and Peralta, D. (2001) Attachment styles in older European American and African American adults. *The Journals of Gerontology Series B: Psychological Sciences and Social Sciences, 56*, 28–45.

Mandel, R.G. and Johnson, N.S. (1984) A developmental analysis of story recall and comprehension in adulthood. *Journal of Verbal Learning and Verbal Behavior, 23*, 643–59.

Mandic, N. and Barkic, J. (1996) Psychosocial and cultural characteristics of personality disorders. *Psychiatrica Danubina, 8*, 29–33.

Manela, M., Katona, C. and Livingston, G. (1996) How common are the anxiety disorders in old age? *International Journal of Geriatric Psychiatry, 11*, 65–70.

Manetto, C. and McPherson, S.E. (1996) The behavioral-cognitive model of pain. *Clinical Geriatric Medicine, 12*, 461–71.

Manthorpe, J. and Iliffe, S. (2005) *Depression in Later Life*. London: Jessica Kingsley Publishers.

Marengoni, A., Calíbrese, A.P. and Cossi, S. (2004) Hospital admissions for acute onset of behavioral symptoms in demented patients: What do they want to say? *International Psychogeriatrics, 16*, 491–93.

Marquié, J.C. and Baracat, B. (2000) Effects of age, education and sex on response bias in a recognition task. *The Journals of Gerontology Series B: Psychological Sciences and Social Sciences, 55*, 266–72.

Marquié, J.C. and Huet, N. (2000) Age differences in feeling-of-knowing and confidence judgments as a function of knowledge domain. *Psychology and Aging, 15*, 451–61.

Marsden, C.D. and Harrison, M.J.G. (1972) Outcome of investigation of patients with presenile dementia. *British Medical Journal, 2*, 249–52.

Marsh, G.A. (1980) Perceptual changes with aging. In E.W. Busse and D.G. Blazer (eds) *Handbook of Geriatric Psychiatry*. New York: Van Nostrand Reinhold.

Marsh, G.R. and Watson, W.E. (1980) Psychophysiological studies of aging effects on cognitive processes. In D.G. Stein (ed.) *The Psychology of Aging. Problems and Perspectives*. New York: Elsevier North-Holland.

Marsiske, M., Klumb, P. and Baltes, M. (1997) Everyday activity patterns and sensory functioning in old age. *Psychology and Aging, 12*, 444–57.

Martin, A. and Fedio, P (1983) Word production and comprehension in Alzheimer's disease: the breakdown of semantic knowledge. *Brain and Language, 19*, 124–41.

Martin, C.E. (1981) Factors affecting sexual funcitoning in 60–79 year old married males. *Archives of Sexual Behavior, 10*, 339–420.

Martone, M., Butlers, N., Payne, M., Becker, J.T. and Sax, D.S. (1984) Dissociation between skill learning and verbal recognition in amnesia and dementia. *Archives of Neurology, 41*, 965–70.

Masoro, E.J. (1988) Food restriction in rodents: An evaluation of its role in the study of aging. *Journal of Gerontology, 43*, 59–64.

Masoro, E.J. (1992) Retardation of aging processes by food restriction: an experimental tool. *American Journal of Clinical Nutrition, 55*, 1250–2.

Masters, W.H. and Johnson, V.E. (1966) *Human Sexual Response.* Boston, MA: Little, Brown.

Masunaga, H. and Horn, J. (2001) Expertise and age-related changes in components of intelligence. *Psychology and Aging, 16*, 293–311.

Matthias, R.E., Lubben, J.E., Atchison, K.A. and Schweitzer, S.O. (1997) Sexual activity and satisfaction among very old adults: Results from a community-dwelling medicare population survey. *Gerontologist, 37*, 6–14.

Mayers, K.S. and McBride, D. (1998) Sexuality training for caretakers of geriatric residents in long term care facilities. *Sexuality and Disability, 16*, 227–36.

Maylor, E.A. (1990a) Age and prospective memory. *Quarterly Journal of Experimental Psychology, 42A*, 471–93.

Maylor, E.A. (1990b) Age, blocking and tip of the tongue state. *British Journal of Psychology, 81*, 123–34.

Maylor, E.A. (1997) Proper name retrieval in old age: Converging evidence against disproportionate impairment. *Aging, Neuropsychology and Cognition, 4*, 211–26.

Maylor, E.A. (1998) Changes in event-based prospective memory across adulthood. *Aging, Neuropsychology and Cognition, 5*, 107–28.

Maylor, E.A., Carter, S.M. and Halletta, E.L. (2002) Preserved olfactory cuing of autobiographical memories in old age. *The Journals of Gerontology Series B: Psychological Sciences and Social Sciences, 57*, 41–46.

Maylor, E.A. and Henson, R. (2000) Ranschburg effect: No evidence of reduced response suppression in old age. *Psychology and Aging, 15*, 657–670.

Maylor, E.A. and Lavie, N. (1998) The influence of perceptual load on age differences in selective attention. *Psychology and Aging, 13*, 563–73.

Maylor, E.A. and Rabbitt, P.M.A. (1994) Applying Brinley plots to individuals: Effect of aging on performance distributions in two speeded tasks. *Psychology and Aging, 9*, 224–30.

Maylor, E.A., Vousden, J.I. and Brown, G.D.A. (1999) Adult age differences in short-term memory for serial order: Data and model. *Psychology and Aging, 14*, 572–594.

Mayr, U. and Kliegl, R. (2000) Complex semantic processing in old age: Does it stay or does it go? *Psychology and Aging, 15*, 29–43.

McArdle, J.J., Hamgami, F., Jones, K., Jolesz, F., Kikinis, R., Spiro, A. and Albert, M.S. (2004) Structural modeling of dynamic changes in memory and brain structure using longitudinal data from the normative aging study. *The Journals of Gerontology Series B: Psychological Sciences and Social Sciences 59*, 294–304.

McConatha, J.T., McConatha, D., Jackson, J.A. and Bergen, A. (1998) The control factor: Life satisfaction in later adulthood. *Journal of Clinical Geropsychology, 4*, 159–68.

McCrae, C.S. and Abrams, R.A. (2001) Age-related differences in object- and location-based inhibition of return of attention. *Psychology and Aging, 16*, 437–49.

McCrae, R.R., Arneberg, D. and Costa, P.T. (1987) Declines in divergent thinking with age: Cross-sectional, longitudinal and cross-sequential analyses. *Psychology and Aging, 2*, 130–7.

McCubbin, H.I. and Patterson, J.M. (1982) Family adaptation to crises. In H.I. McCubbin, A.E. Cauble and J.M. Patterson (eds), *Family Stress, Coping and Social Support.* Springfield, IL: Thomas.

McDonald, L. and Stuart-Hamilton, I. (1996) Older and more moral? Age related changes in performance on Piagetian moral reasoning tasks. *Age and Ageing, 25*, 402–404.

McDonald, L. and Stuart-Hamilton, I. (2000) The meaning of life: Animism in the classificatory skills of older adults. *International Journal of Aging and Human Development, 51*, 231–42.

McDonald, L. and Stuart-Hamilton, I. (2002) Egocentrism in older adults – Piaget's three mountains task revisited. *Educational Gerontology, 28*, 35–43.

McDowd, J.M. and Filion, D.L. (1992) Aging, selective attention and inhibitory processes: A psychophysiological approach. *Psychology and Aging, 7*, 65–71.

McEvoy, C.L., Nelson, D.L., Holley, P.E. and Stelnicki, G.S. (1992) Implicit processing in the cued recall of young and old adults. *Psychology and Aging, 7*, 401–408.

McFarland, R.A. and Fisher, M.B. (1955) Alterations in dark adaptation as a function of age. *Journal of Gerontology, 10*, 424–8.

McGinnis, D. and Zelinski, E.M. (2000) Understanding unfamiliar words: The influence of processing resources, vocabulary knowledge and age. *Psychology and Aging, 15*, 335–50.

McGinnis, D. and Zelinski, E.M. (2003) Understanding unfamiliar words in young, young-old and old-old adults: Inferential processing and the abstraction-deficit hypothesis. *Psychology and Aging, 18*, 497–509.

McGrath, A.M. and Jackson, G.A. (1996) Survey of neuroleptic prescribing in residents of nursing homes in Glasgow. *British Medical Journal, 312*, 611–12.

McGue, M. and Christensen, K. (2001) The heritability of cognitive functioning in very old adults: Evidence from Danish twins aged 75 years and older. *Psychology and Aging, 16*, 272–80.

McIntyre, J.S. and Craik, F.I.M. (1987) Age differences in memory for item and source information. *Canadian Journal of Psychology, 41*, 175–92.

McNeilly, D.P. and Burke, W.J. (2001) Gambling as a social activity of older adults. *International Journal of Aging and Human Development, 52*, 19–28.

McNeilly, D.P. and Burke, W.J. (2002) Disposable time and disposable income: Problem casino gambling behavior in older adults. *Journal of Clinical Geropsychology, 8*, 75–85.

McShane, R., Keene, J., Gedling, K., Fairburn, C., Jacoby, R. and Hope, T. (1997) Do neuroleptic drugs hasten cognitive decline in dementia? Prospective study with necropsy follow up. *British Medical Journal, 314*, 266–7.

Meacham, J.A. (1990) The loss of wisdom. In R.J. Sternberg (ed.), *Wisdom: Its Nature, Origins and Development.* Cambridge: Cambridge University Press.

Medawar, P.B. (1952) *An Unsolved Problem of Biology.* London: H.K. Lewis.

Meeks, S., Murrell, S.A. and Mehl, R.C. (2000) Longitudinal relationships between depressive symptoms and health in normal older and middle-aged adults. *Psychology and Aging, 15*, 100–109.

Meesters, C.M.G., Muris, P. and Backus, I.P.G. (1996) Dimensions of hostility and myocardial infarction in adult males. *Journal of Psychosomatic Research, 40*, 21–8.

Meguro, K., Shimada, M., Yamaguchi, S., Ishizaki, J., Yamadori, A. and Sekita, Y. (2001) A 5-year retrospective examination of cognitive screening test stages in normal older adults and patients with Alzheimer's disease. The Tajiri Project. *The Journals of Gerontology Series B: Psychological Sciences and Social Sciences, 56*, 314–18.

Meier-Ruge, W. Gygax, P. and Wiernsperger, N. (1980) A synoptic view of pathophysiology and experimental pharmacology in gerontological brain research. In C. Einsedorfer and W.E. Fann (eds), *Psychopharmacology of Aging.* New York: S.P. Medical and Scientific Books, 65–98.

Mein, G., Martikainen, P., Stansfeld, S.A., Brunner, E.J., Fuhrer, R. and Marmot, M.G. (2000) Predictors of early retirement in British civil servants. *Age and Ageing, 29*, 529–36.

Melzer, D., Izmirlian, G., Leveille, S.G. and Guralnik, J.M. (2001) Educational differences in the prevalence of mobility disability in old age: the dynamics of incidence, mortality and recovery. *The Journals of Gerontology Series B: Psychological Sciences and Social Sciences, 56*, 294–301.

Memon, A., Bartlett, J., Rose, R. and Gray, C. (2003) The aging eyewitness: effects of age on face, delay and source-memory ability. *The Journals of Gerontology Series B: Psychological Sciences and Social Sciences, 58*, 338–45.

Menec, V.H. and Chipperfield, J.G. (1997) Remaining active in later life: The role of locus of control in senior's leisure activity participation, health and life satisfaction. *Journal of Aging and Health, 9*, 105–25.

Merriman, A. (1984) Social customs affecting the role of elderly women in Indian society. In D.B. Bromley (ed.), *Gerontology: Social and Behavioural Perspectives.* London: Croom Helm.

Mesholam, R.I., Moberg, P.J., Mahr, R.N. and Doty, R. (1998) Olfaction in neurodegenerative disease: A meta-analysis of olfactory functioning in Alzheimer's and Parkinson's disease. *Archives of Neurology, 55*, 84–90.

Metter, E.J. (1988) Positron emission tomography and cerebral blood flow studies. In M.S. Albert and M.B. Moss (eds), *Geriatric Neuropsychology.* New York: Guilford Press.

Metter, E.J. and Wilson, R.S. (1993) Vascular dementias. In R.W. Parks, R.F. Zec and R.S. Wilson (eds), *Neuropsychology of Alzheimer's Disease and Other Dementias.* New York: Oxford University Press, 416–37.

Meyer, B.J.F. (1987) Reading comprehension and aging. In K.W. Schaie (ed.), *Annual Review of Gerontology and Geriatrics, 7.* New York: Springer.

Midwinter, E. (1991) *The British Gas Report on Attitudes to Ageing.* London: British Gas.

Miller, D.B. and O'Callaghan, J.P. (2003) Effects of aging and stress on hippocampal structure and function. *Metabolism, 52,* 17–21.

Miller, E. (1975) Impaired recall and the memory disturbance in presenile dementia. *British Journal of Social and Clinical Psychology, 14,* 73–9.

Miller, E. and Lewis, P. (1977) Recognition memory in elderly patients with depression and dementia: a signal detection analysis. *Journal of Abnormal Psychology, 86,* 84–6.

Miller, L.S. (1987) Forensic examination of arthritic impaired writings. *Journal of Police Science and Administration, 15,* 51–5.

Miller, M. (1979) Suicides on a southwestern American Indian reservation. *White Cloud Journal, 1,* 14–18.

Milne, G.G. (1956) Deterioration and over-learning. *Australian Journal of Psychology, 8,* 163–72.

Minois, G. (1989) *History of Old Age.* Cambridge: Polity Press.

Mireles, D.E. and Charness, N. (2002) Computational explorations of the influence of structured knowledge on age-related cognitive decline. *Psychology and Aging, 17,* 245–59.

Mitchell, D.B. and Bruss, P.J. (2003) Age differences in implicit memory: Conceptual, perceptual, or methodological? *Psychology and Aging, 18,* 807–22.

Mitchell, K.J., Johnson, M.K., Raye, C.L., Mather, M. and D'Esposito, M. (2000) Aging and reflective processes of working memory: Binding and test load deficits. *Psychology and Aging, 15,* 527–41.

Moberg, P.J., Doty, R.L., Turetsky, B.I. and Arnold, S.E. (1997) Olfactory identification in elderly schizophrenia and Alzheimer's disease. *Neurobiology of Aging, 18,* 163–7.

Mockler, D., Riordan, J. and Sharma, T. (1996) A comparison of the NART (restandardized) and the NART-R (revised). *British Journal of Clinical Psychology, 35,* 567–72.

Moen, P. (1996) A life course perspective on retirement, gender and well-being. *Journal of Occupational Health Psychology, 1,* 131–44.

Mojet, J., Heidema, J. and Christ-Hazelhof, E. (2003) Taste perception with age: Generic or specific losses in supra-threshold intensities of five taste qualities? *Chemical Senses, 28,* 397–413.

Morgan, D.L., Neal, M.B. and Carder, P.C. (1997) Both what and when: The effects of positive and negative aspects of relationships on depression during the first three years of widowhood. *Journal of Clinical Geropsychology, 3,* 73–91.

Morra, S., Vigliocco, G. and Penello, B. (2001) M capacity as a lifespan construct: A study of its decrease in ageing subjects. *International Journal of Behavioral Development, 25,* 78–87.

Morris, R.G. (1984) Dementia and the functioning of the articulatory loop system. *Cognitive Neuropsychology, 1,* 143–57.

Morris, R.G. (1986) Short-term forgetting in senile dementia of the Alzheimer's type. *Cognitive Neuropsychology, 3,* 77–97.

Morris, R.G. (1994) Working memory in Alzheimer-type dementia. *Neuropsychology, 8,* 544–54.

Morris, R.G., Craik, F.I.M. and Gick, M.L. (1990) Age differences in working memory tasks. The role of secondary memory and the central executive system. *Quarterly Journal of Experimental Psychology, 42A,* 67–86.

Morris, R.G., Gick, M.L. and Craik, F.I.M. (1988) Processing resources and age differences in working memory. *Memory and Cognition, 16,* 362–6.

Morris, R.G. and Kopelman, M.D. (1986) The memory deficit in Alzheimer-type dementia: A review. *Quarterly Journal of Experimental Psychology, 38A,* 57–602.

Morrisey, E., Becker, J. and Rubert, M.P. (1990) Coping resources and depression in the caregiving spouses of Alzheimers patients. *British Journal of Medical Psychology, 63,* 161–171.

Morrow, D.G., Von Leirer, O. and Altieri, P.A. (1992) Aging, expertise and narrative processing. *Psychology and Aging, 7,* 376–88.

Morse, C.K. (1993) Does variability increase with age? An archival study of cognitive measures. *Psychology and Aging, 8,* 156–64.

Moscovitch, M. (1982) A neuropsychological approach to memory and perception in normal and pathological aging. In F.I.M. Craik and S. Trehub (eds), *Aging and Cognitive Processes.* New York: Plenum.

Moss, M.B. and Albert, M.S. (1988) Alzheimer's disease and other dementing disorders. In M.S. Albert and M.B. Moss (eds), *Geriatric Neuropsychology.* New York: Guilford.

Mroczek, D.K. and Spiro, A. (2003) Modeling intraindividual change in personality traits: Findings from the Normative Aging Study. *The Journals of Gerontology Series B: Psychological Sciences and Social Sciences, 58,* 153–65.

Multhaup, K.S., Balota, D.A. and Cowan, N. (1996) Implications of aging, lexicality and item length for the mechanisms underlying memory span. *Psychonomic Bulletin and Review, 3,* 112–20.

Murphy, C. (1985) Cognitive and chemosensory influences on age-related changes in the ability to identify blended foods. *Journal of Gerontology, 40,* 217–22.

Murphy, C. (1999) Loss of olfactory function in dementing disease. *Physiology and Behavior, 66,* 177–82.

Murphy, D.R., Craik, F.I.M., Li, K.Z.H. and Schneider, B.A. (2000) Comparing the effects of aging and background noise of short-term memory performance. *Psychology and Aging, 15*, 323–34.

Murphy, D.R., McDowd, J.M. and Wilcox, K.A. (1999) Inhibition and aging: Similarities between younger and older adults as revealed by the processing of unattended auditory information. *Psychology and Aging, 14*, 44–59.

Murphy, E.A. (1978) Genetics of longevity in man. In E.L. Schneider (ed.), *The Genetics of Aging*. New York: Plenum.

Murphy, E.A. and Alexopoulos, G. (1995) *Geriatric Psychiatry: Key Research Topics for Clinicians*. Chichester: Wiley.

Myers, S.M. and Booth, A. (1996) Men's retirement and marital quality. *Journal of Family Issues, 17*, 336–57.

Myerson, J., Emery, L., White, D.A. and Hale, S. (2003) Effects of age, domain and processing demands on memory span: Evidence for differential decline. *Aging, Neuropsychology and Cognition, 10*, 20–27.

Myerson, J., Ferraro, F.R., Hale, S. and Lima, S.D. (1992) General slowing in semantic priming and word recognition. *Psychology and Aging, 7*, 257–70.

Myerson, J., Hale, S., Chen, J. and Lawrence, B. (1997) General lexical slowing and the semantic priming effect: The roles of age and ability. *Acta Psychologica, 96*, 83–101.

Namazi, K.H. and McClintic, M. (2003) Computer use among elderly persons in long-term care facilities. *Educational Gerontology, 29*, 535–50.

Naramura, H., Nakanishi, N., Tatara, K., Ishiyama, M., Shiraishi, H. and Yamamoto, A. (1999) Physical and mental correlates of hearing impairment in the elderly in Japan. *Audiology, 38*, 24–9.

National Council on Aging (1975) *The Myth and Reality of Aging in America*. Washington, DC: National Council on Aging.

National Statistics Online, see http://www.statistics.gov.uk.

Naveh-Benjamin, M., Guez, J., Kilb, A. and Reedy, S. (2004) The associative memory deficit of older adults: further support using face-name associations. *Psychology and Aging, 19*, 541–6.

Neargarder, S.A., Stone, E.R., Cronin-Golomb, A. and Oross, S. (2003) The impact of acuity on performance of four clinical measures of contrast sensitivity in Alzheimer's disease. *The Journals of Gerontology Series B: Psychological Sciences and Social Sciences, 58*, 54–62.

Nebes, R.D. (1992) Cognitive dysfunction in Alzheimer's Disease. In F.I.M. Craik and T.A. Salthouse (eds), *The Handbook of Aging and Cognition*. Hillsdale, NJ: Lawrence Erlbaum.

Nebes, R.D. and Brady, C.B. (1990) Preserved organization of semantic attributes in Alzheimer's Disease. *Psychology and Aging, 5*, 574–79.

Nelson, H.E. and McKenna, P. (1973) The use of current reading ability in the assessment of dementia. *British Journal of Social and Clinical Psychology, 14*, 259–67.

Nelson, H.E. and O'Connell, A. (1978) Dementia: The estimation of premorbid intelligence levels using the New Adult Reading Test. *Cortex, 14*, 234–44.

Nesselroade, J.R. and Salthouse, T.A. (2004) Methodological and theoretical implications of intraindividual variability in perceptual-motor performance. *The Journals of Gerontology Series B: Psychological Sciences and Social Sciences, 59*, 49–55.

Nestle, M. (1999) Animal v. plant foods in human diets and health: is the historical record unequivocal? *Proceedings of the Nutrition Society, 58*, 211–18.

Neugarten, B.L. (1977) Personality and aging. In J.E. Birren and K.W. Schaie (eds), *Handbook of the Psychology of Aging*. New York: Reinhold.

Neugarten, B.L., Havinghurst, R.J. and Tobin, S.S. (1961) The measurement of life satisfaction. *Journal of Gerontology, 16*, 134–43.

Neugarten, B.L., Havinghurst, R.J. and Tobin, S.S. (1968) Personality and pattern of aging. In B.L. Neugarten (ed.), *Middle Age and Aging*. Chicago, IL: Chicago University Press.

Neundorfer, M.M., McClendon, M.J., Smyth, K.A., Stuckey, J.C., Strauss, M.E. and Patterson, M.B. (2001) A longitudinal study of the relationship between levels of depression among persons with Alzheimer's disease and levels of depression among their family caregivers. *The Journals of Gerontology Series B: Psychological Sciences and Social Sciences, 56*, 301–313.

Newcomer, R., Covinsky, K.E., Clay T. and Yaffe, K. (2003) Predicting 12-month mortality for persons with dementia. *The Journals of Gerontology Series B: Psychological Sciences and Social Sciences, 58*, 187–98.

Newson, R.S. and Kemps, E.B. (2005) General lifestyle activities as a predictor of current cognition and cognitive change in older adults: A cross-sectional and longitudinal examination. *Journals of Gerontology Series B: Psychological Sciences and Social Sciences, 60*, 113–120.

Ng, K., Woo, J., Kwan, M. and Sea, M. (2004) Effect of age and disease on taste perception. *Journal of Pain and Symptom Management, 28*, 28–34.

Nicholas, M., Obler, L.K., Au, R. and Albert, M.L. (1996) On the nature of naming errors in aging and dementia: A study of semantic relatedness. *Brain and Language, 54*, 184–95.

Nielsen, J., Homma, A. and Bjorn-Hendriksen, T. (1977) Follow-up 15 years after a geronto-psychiatric prevalence study: Conditions concerning death and life expectancy in relation to psychiatric diagnosis. *Journal of Gerontology, 32,* 554–61.

Nigro, G. and Neisser, U. (1983) Point of view in personal memories. *Cognitive Psychology, 15,* 465–82.

Nissen, N.J. and Corkin, S. (1985) Effectiveness of attentional cueing in older and younger adults. *Journal of Gerontology, 40,* 185–191.

Nolen-Hoeksema, S. and Ahrens, C. (2002) Age differences and similarities in the correlates of depressive symptoms. *Psychology and Aging, 17,* 116–24.

Nordhus, I.H., VandenBos, G.R., Berg, S. and Fromholt, P. (1998) *Clinical Geropsychology.* Washington, DC: American Psychological Association.

Nordin, S., Monsch, A.U. and Murphy, C. (1995) Unawareness of smell loss in normal aging and Alzheimer's disease: Discrepancy between self-reported and diagnosed smell sensitivity. *Journal of Gerontology Series B: Psychological Sciences and Social Sciences, 50,* 187–92.

Nordin, S. and Murphy, C. (1996) Impaired sensory and cognitive olfactory function in questionable Alzheimer's disease. *Neuropsychology, 10,* 113–19.

Nordin, S., Razani, L.J., Markison, S. and Murphy, C. (2003) Age-associated increases in intensity discrimination for taste. *Experimental Aging Research, 29,* 371–81.

Norman, A. (1985) *Triple Jeopardy: Growing Old in a Second Homeland.* London: Centre for Policy on Ageing.

Norris, M.L. and Cunningham, D.R. (1981) Social impact of hearing loss in the aged. *Journal of Gerontology, 36,* 727–9.

Norris, M.P. and West, R.L. (1993) Activity memory and ageing: The role of motor retrieval and strategic processing. *Psychology and Aging, 8,* 81–6.

Nyberg, L., Maitland, S.B., Rönnlund, M., Bäckman, L., Dixon, R.A., Wahlin, A. and Nilsson, L.G. (2003) Selective adult age differences in an age-invariant multifactor model of declarative memory. *Psychology and Aging, 18,* 149–160.

Obler, L.K., Fein, D., Nicholas, M. and Albert, M.L. (1991) Auditory comprehension and aging: Decline in syntactic processing. *Applied Psycholinguistics, 12,* 433–52.

O'Brien Cousins, S. (2000) 'My heart couldn't take it': Older women's beliefs about exercise benefits and risks. *The Journals of Gerontology Series B: Psychological Sciences and Social Sciences, 55,* 283–94.

O'Carroll, R.E., Baikie, E.M. and Whittick, J.E. (1987) Does the National Adult Reading Test hold in dementia? *British Journal of Clinical Psychology, 26,* 315–16.

O'Carroll, R.E. and Gilleard, C.J. (1986) Estimation of premorbid intelligence in dementia. *British Journal of Clinical Psychology, 25,* 157–8.

O'Connell, H., Chin, A.V., Cunningham, C. and Lawlor, B. (2003) Alcohol use disorders in elderly people – redefining an age old problem in old age. *British Medical Journal, 327,* 664–7.

OECD (1988) *Ageing Populations: The Social Policy Implications.* Paris: OECD.

OECD (2004) *Ageing and Employment Policies: United Kingdom.* London: OECD.

Okamoto, K. and Tanaka, Y. (2004) Subjective usefulness and 6-year mortality risks among elderly persons in Japan. *The Journals of Gerontology Series B: Psychological Sciences and Social Sciences, 59,* 246–9.

Oku, T. and Hasegewa, M. (1997) The influence of aging on auditory brainstem response and electrocochleography in the elderly. *Journal of Otorhinolaryngology and Related Specialities, 59,* 141–6.

Olichney, J.M., Iragui, V.J., Kutas, M., Nowacki, R., Morris, S. and Jeste, D.V. (1998) Relationship between auditory P300 amplitude and age of onset of schizophrenia in older patients. *Psychiatry Research, 79,* 241–54.

Olovnikov, A.M. (1996) Telomeres, telomerase and aging: Origin of the theory. *Experimental Gerontology, 31,* 443–8.

Olsen, D.R., Torrance, N. and Hildyard, A. (eds) (1985) *Literacy, Language and Learning.* Cambridge: Cambridge University Press.

Olshansky, S.J., Carnes, B.A., Hershow, R., Passaro, D., Layden, J., Brody, J., Hayflick, L., Butler, R.N. and Ludwig, D.S. (2005) Misdirection on the road to Shangri-La. *Science of Aging Knowledge Environment, 1,* 15.

Olson, I.R., Zhang, J.X., Mitchell, K.J., Johnson, M.K., Bloise, S.M. and Higgins, J.A. (2004) Preserved spatial memory over brief intervals in older adults. *Psychology and Aging, 19,* 310–17.

Orbelo, D.M., Grim, M.A., Talbot, R.E. and Ross, E.D. (2005) Impaired comprehension of affective prosody in elderly subjects is not predicted by age-related hearing loss or age-related cognitive decline. *Journal of Geriatric Psychiatry and Neurology, 18,* 25–32.

Orbuch, T.L., House, J.S., Mero, R.P. and Webster, P.S. (1996) Marital quality over the life course. *Social Psychology Quarterly, 59,* 162–171.

Ostir, G.V., Ottenbacher, K.J. and Markides, K.S. (2004) Onset of frailty in older adults and the protective role of positive affect. *Psychology and Aging, 19,* 402–408.

Owens, W.A. (1959) Is age kinder to the initially more able? *Journal of Gerontology, 14,* 334–7.

Oyer, H.J. and Deal, L.V. (1989) Temporal aspects of speech and the aging process. *Folia-Phoniatrica, 37,* 109–112.

Pache, M., Smeets, C.H.W., Gasio, P.F., Savaskan, E., Flammer, F., Wirz-Justice, A. and Kaiser, H.J. (2003) Colour vision deficiencies in Alzheimer's disease. *Age and Ageing, 32,* 422–26.

Palacios, S., Tobar, A.C. and Menendez, C. (2002) Sexuality in the climacteric years. *Maturitas, 43,* 69–77.

Palinkas, L.A., Wingard, D.L. and Barrett-Connor, E. (1996) Depressive symptoms in overweight and obese older adults: A test of the 'jolly fat' hypothesis. *Journal of Psychosomatic Research, 40,* 59–66.

Palmore, E. and Cleveland, W. (1976) Aging, terminal decline and terminal drop. *Journal of Gerontology, 31,* 76–81.

Papalia, D.E. (1972) The status of several conservation abilities across the life-span. *Human Development, 15,* 229–43.

Pardhan, S., Gilchrist, J., Elliott, D.B. and Beh, G.K. (1996) A comparison of sampling efficiency and internal noise level in young and old subjects. *Vision Research, 36,* 1641–48.

Park, D.C. and Shaw, R.J. (1992) Effect of environmental support on implicit and explicit memory in younger and older adults. *Psychology and Aging, 7,* 632–42.

Park, D.C., Hertzog, C., Kidder, D.P., Morrell, R. and Mayhorn, C. (1997) Effect of age on event-based and time-based prospective memory. *Psychology and Aging, 12,* 314–27.

Parker, L.D., Cantrell, C. and Demi, A.S. (1997) Older adults' attitudes toward suicide: Are there race and gender differences? *Death Studies, 21,* 289–98.

Parkin, A.J. and Java, R. (1999) Deterioration of frontal lobe function in normal aging: Influences of fluid intelligence versus perceptual speed. *Neuropsychology, 13,* 539–45.

Parkin, A.J. and Walter, B.M. (1992) Recollective experience, normal aging and frontal dysfunction. *Psychology and Aging, 7,* 290–8.

Parks, R.W., Zec, R.F. and Wilson, R.S. (1993) *Neuropsychology of Alzheimer's Disease and Other Dementias.* New York: Oxford University Press.

Parnes, H. (1981) *Work and Retirement: A Longitudinal Study of Men.* Cambridge, MA. MIT Press.

Partridge, L, Piper, M.D. and Mair, W. (2005) Dietary restriction in Drosophila. *Mechanisms of Ageing and Development, 126,* 121–30.

Pasupathi, M. and Carstensen, L.L. (2003) Age and emotional experience during mutual reminiscing. *Psychology and Aging, 18,* 430–42.

Pasupathi, M., Henry, R.M. and Carstensen, L.L. (2002) Age and ethnicity differences in storytelling to young children: Emotionality, relationality and socialization. *Psychology and Aging, 17,* 610–21.

Patterson, K.E., Graham, N. and Hodges, J.R. (1994) Reading in dementia of the Alzheimer type: A preserved ability? *Neuropsychology, 8,* 395–412.

Pattison, E.M. (1977) *The Experience of Dying.* New York: Prentice Hall.

Paz, J. and Aleman, S. (1998) The Yaqui elderly of Old Pascua. *Journal of Gerontological Social Work, 30,* 47–59.

Peake, M.D. and Thompson, S. (2003) Ageism in the management of lung cancer. *Age and Ageing, 32,* 171–7.

Pearman, A. and Storandt, M. (2004) Predictors of subjective memory in older adults. *The Journals of Gerontology Series B: Psychological Sciences and Social Sciences, 59,* 4–6.

Pearson, J.D., Morrell, C.H., Gordon-Salant, S., Brant, L.J., Metter, E.J., Klein, L.L. and Fozard, J.L. (1995) Gender differences in a longitudinal study of age-associated hearing loss. *Journal of the Acoustical Society of America, 97,* 1196–205.

Peck, R.C. (1968) Psychological developments in the second half of life. In B.L. Neugarten (ed.), *Middle Age and Aging: A Reader in Social Psychology.* Chicago, IL: University of Chicago Press.

Penninx, B.W., Beekman, A.T.F., Ormel, J., Kriegsman, D.M.W., Boeke, A.J.P., van Eijk, J.Th.M. and Deeg, D.J.H. (1996) Psychological status among elderly people with chronic diseases: Does type of disease play a part? *Journal of Psychosomatic Research, 40,* 521–34.

Penninx, B.W. J.H., Rejeski, W.J., Pandy, J., Miller, M.E., Di Bari, M., Applegate, W.B. and Pahora, M. (2002) Exercise and depressive symptoms: a comparison of aerobic and resistance exercise effects on emotional and physical function in older persons with high and low depressive symptomatology. *The Journals of Gerontology Series B: Psychological Sciences and Social Sciences, 57,* 124–32.

Peretz, J.A. and Cummings, J.L. (1988) Subcortical dementia. In U. Holden (ed.), *Neuropsychology and Ageing.* London: Croom Helm.

Perfect, T.J. (1994) What can Brinley plots tell us about cognitive aging? *Journal of Gerontology: Psychological Sciences, 49,* 60–64.

Perfect, T.J. and Hollins, T.S. (1999) Feeling-of-knowing judgments do not predict subsequent recognition performance for eyewitness memory. *Journal of Experimental Psychology: Applied, 5,* 250–64.

Perfect, T.J. and Maylor, E.A. (eds) (2000) *Models of Cognitive Aging.* Oxford: Oxford University Press.

Perlmutter, M. (1978) What is memory aging the aging of? *Developmental Psychology, 14,* 330–45.

Perlmutter, M., Adams, C., Berry, S., Kaplan, M. and Person, D. (1987) Aging and memory. In K.W. Schaie (ed.) *Annual Review of Gerontology and Geriatrics, 7.* New York: Springer. 57–92.

Perlmutter, M. and Hall, E. (1992) *Adult Development and Aging.* New York: Wiley.

Perlmutter, M. and Mitchell, D.B. (1982) The appearance and disappearance of age differences in adult memory. In F.I.M. Craik and S. Trehub (eds), *Aging and Cognitive Processes.* New York: Plenum.

Perlmutter, L.C. and Monty, R.A. (1989) Motivation and aging. In L.W. Poon, D.C. Rubin and B.A. Wilson (eds), *Everyday Cognition in Adulthood and Later Life.* Cambridge: Cambridge University Press.

Persad, C.C., Abeles, N., Zacks, R.T. and Denburg, N.L. (2002) Inhibitory changes after age 60 and their relationship to measures of attention and memory. *The Journals of Gerontology Series B: Psychological Sciences and Social Sciences, 57,* 223–32.

Petit, T.L. (1982) Neuroanatomical and clinical neuropsychological changes in aging and senile dementia. In F.I.M. Craik and S. Trehbub (eds), *Aging and Cognitive Processes.* New York: Plenum.

Petros, T., Tabar, L., Cooney, T. and Chabot, R.J. (1983) Adult age differences in sensitivity to semantic structure of prose. *Developmental Psychology, 19,* 907–14.

Pfütze, E.M., Sommer, W. and Schweinberger, S.R. (2002) Age-related slowing in face and name recognition: Evidence from event-related brain potentials. *Psychology and Aging, 17,* 140–60.

Phillips, L.H. (1999) Age and individual differences in letter fluency. *Developmental Neuropsychology, 15,* 249–67.

Phillips, L.H. and Della Sala, S. (1998) Aging, intelligence and anatomical segregation in the frontal lobes. *Learning and Individual Differences, 10,* 217–43.

Phillips, N.A. and Lesperance, D. (2003) Breaking the waves: Age differences in electrical brain activity when reading text with distractors. *Psychology and Aging, 18,* 126–39.

Phillips, S. and Williams, J.M.G. (1997) Cognitive impairment, depression and the specificity of autobiographical memory in the elderly. *British Journal of Clinical Psychology, 36,* 341–7.

Pichora-Fuller, M.K., Schneider, B.A. and Daneman, M. (1995) How young and old adults listen to and remember speech in noise. *Journal of the Acoustical Society of America, 97,* 593–608.

Pinquart, M. (2001) Correlates of subjective health in older adults: A meta-analysis. *Psychology and Aging, 16,* 414–26.

Pinquart, M. and Sörensen, S. (2000) Influences of socioeconomic status, social network and competence on subjective well-being in later life: A meta-analysis. *Psychology and Aging, 15,* 187–224.

Pinquart. M. and Sörensen, S. (2001) Gender differences in self-concept and psychological well-being in old age: a meta-analysis. *The Journals of Gerontology Series B: Psychological Sciences and Social Sciences, 56,* 195–213.

Pitkala, K.H., Laurila, J.V., Strandberg, T.E. and Tilvis, R.S. (2005) Prognostic significance of delirium in frail older people. *Dementia and Geriatric Cognitive Disorders, 19,* 158–63.

Pitts, D.G. (1982) The effects of aging on selected visual functions. In R. Sekuler, D. Kline and K. Dismukes (eds), *Aging and Human Visual Function.* New York: Alan R. Liss, 121–30.

Plemons, J.K., Willis, S.L. and Baltes, P.B. (1978) Modifiability of fluid intelligence in aging: A short-term longitudinal training approach. *Journal of Gerontology, 33,* 224–31.

Polich, J. (1997) On the relationships between EEG and P300: Individual differences, aging and ultradian rhythms. *International Journal of Psychophysiology, 26,* 299–317.

Polizzi, K.G. and Millikin, R.J. (2002) Attitudes toward the elderly: Identifying problematic usage of ageist and overextended terminology in research instructions. *Educational Gerontology, 28,* 367–77.

Poon, L.W., Fozard, J.L., Paushock, D.R. and Thomas, J.C. (1979) A questionnaire assessment of age differences in retention of recent and remote events. *Experimental Age Research, 5,* 401–411.

Poon, L.W. and Schaffer, G. (1982) Prospective memory in young and elderly adults. Paper presented at meeting of American Psychological Association, Washington, DC. Cited in West (1988).

Powell, R.R. (1974) Psychological effects of exercise therapy upon institutionalized geriatric mental patients. *Journal of Gerontology, 29,* 157–161.

Pratt, M.W., Diessner, R., Hunsberger, B., Pancer, S.M. and Savoy, K. (1991) Four pathways in the analysis of adult development and aging. *Psychology and Aging, 6,* 666–75.

Pratt, M.W. and Norris, J.E. (1994) *The Social Psychology of Aging: A Cognitive Perspective.* Cambridge, MA: Blackwells.

Priest, L., Nayak, U.S.L. and Stuart-Hamilton, I. (in press) Website task performance by older adults and the implications for website design. To appear in *Journal of Behaviour and Information Technology.*

Pritchard, J. (1995) *The Abuse of Older People: A Training Manual for Detection and Prevention.* 2nd edition. London: Jessica Kingsley Publishers.

Pruchno, R. and Kleban, M.H. (1993) Caring for an institutionalized parent: The role of coping strategies. *Psychology and Aging, 8,* 18–25.

Purcell, R., Maruff, P., Kyrios, M. and Pantelis, C. (1998) Cognitive deficits in obsessive-compulsive disorder on tests of frontal-striatal function. *Biological Psychiatry, 43,* 348–357.

Purdue, U. (1966) Age and mental abilities: A second adult follow-up. *Journal of Educational Psychology, 57,* 311–25.

Purohit, D.P., Perl, D.P., Haroutunian, V., Powchik, P., Davidson, M. and Davis, K.L. (1998) Alzheimer disease and related neurodegenerative diseases in elderly patients with schizophrenia. A postmortem neuropathologic study of 100 cases. *Archives of General Psychiatry, 55,* 205–11.

Pushkar, D., Basevitz, P., Arbuckle, T., Nohara-LeClair, M., Lapidus, S. and Peled, M. (2000) Social behavior and off-target verbosity in elderly people. *Psychology and Aging, 15,* 361–74.

Quandt, S.A. and Chao, D. (2000) Gender differences in nutritional risk among older rural adults. *Journal of Applied Gerontology, 19,* 138–50.

Quillan, D.A. (1999) Common causes of vision loss in elderly patients. *American Family Physician, 60,* 99–108.

Quinn, M.E., Johnson, M.A., Poon, L.W. and Martin, P. (1997) Factors of nutritional health-seeking behaviors. *Journal of Aging and Health, 9,* 90–104.

Qureshi, H. and Walker, A. (1989) *The Caring Relationship: Elderly People and Their Families.* London: Macmillan.

Rabbitt, P. (1979) Some experiments and a model for changes in attentional selectivity with old age. In F. Hoffmeister and C. Muller (eds), *Bayer Symposium VII. Evaluation of Change.* Bonn: Springer.

Rabbitt, P. (1980) A fresh look at reaction times in old age. In D.G. Stein (ed.), *The Psychology of Ageing: Problems and Perspectives.* New York: Elsevier.

Rabbitt, P. (1982) How do the old know what to do next? In F.I.M.Craik and S. Trehub (eds), *Aging and Cognitive Processes.* New York: Plenum.

Rabbitt, P. (1984) Memory impairment in the elderly. In P.E. Bebbington and R. Jacoby (eds), *Psychiatric Disorders in the Elderly.* London: Mental Health Foundation. 101–119.

Rabbitt, P. (1988a) The faster the better? Some comments on the use of information processing rate as an index of change in individual differences in performance. In I. Hindmarch, B. Aufdembrinke and H. Ott (eds), *Psychopharmacology and Reaction Time.* London: Wiley.

Rabbitt, P. (1988b) Does fast last? Is speed a basic factor determining individual differences in memory? In M.M. Gruneberg, P.E. Morris and R.N. Sykes (eds), *Practical Aspects of Memory, Volume 2.* Chichester: Wiley.

Rabbitt, P. (1989) Secondary central effects on memory and attention of mild hearing loss in the elderly. *Acta Neurologica Scandanavica, 40A,* 167–87.

Rabbitt, P. (1990) Applied cognitive gerontology: some problems, methodologies and data. *Applied Cogntiive Psychology, 4,* 225–46.

Rabbitt, P. (1993) Does it all go together when it goes? *Quarterly Journal of Experimental Psychology, 46A,* 385–434.

Rabbitt, P. (1996) Speed of processing and ageing. In R. Woods (ed.), *Handbook of the Clinical Psychology of Ageing.* Chichester: Wiley, 59–72.

Rabbitt, P. (ed.) (1997) *Methodology of Frontal and Executive Function.* Hove: Taylor and Francis.

Rabbitt, P. (1998) Aging of memory. In R.C. Tallis, S.H.M. Fillit and B.J.C. Brocklehurst (eds), *Brocklehurst's Textbook of Geriatric Medicine and Gerontology.* Edinburgh: Churchill Livingstone, 123–152.

Rabbitt, P. and Abson, V. (1990) 'Lost and found': Some logical and methodological limitations of self-report questionnaires as tools to study cognitive ageing. *British Journal of Psychology, 81,* 1–16.

Rabbitt, P., Diggle, P., Holland, F. and McInnes, L. (2004) Practice and drop-out effects during a 17-year longitudinal study of cognitive aging. *The Journals of Gerontology Series B: Psychological Sciences and Social Sciences, 59,* 84–97.

Rabbitt, P. and Goward, L. (1986) Effects of age and raw IQ test scores on mean correct and mean error reaction times in serial choice tasks: A reply to Smith and Brewer. *British Journal of Psychology, 77,* 69–73.

Rabbitt, P., Lowe, C. and Shilling, V. (2001) Frontal tests and models for cognitive ageing. *European Journal of Cognitive Psychology, 13,* 5–28.

Rabbitt, P., Osman, O., Moore, B. and Stollery, B. (2001) There are stable individual differences in performance variability, both from moment to moment and from day to day. *Quarterly Journal of Experimental Psychology: Human Experimental Psychology, 54,* 981–1003.

Rabbitt, P., Watson, P., Donlan, C., Mc Innes, L., Horan, M., Pendleton, N. and Clague, J. (2002) Effects of death within 11 years on cognitive performance in old age. *Psychology and Aging, 17,* 468–481.

Rabbitt, P. and Winthorpe, C. (1988) What do old people remember? The Galton paradigm reconsidered. In M.M. Gruneberg, P.E. Morris and R.N. Sykes (eds) *Practical Aspects of Memory, Volume 2.* Chichester: Wiley.

Radvansky, G.A., Zwaan, R.A., Curiel, J.M. and Copeland, D.E. (2001) Situation models and aging. *Psychology and Aging, 16,* 145–60.

Raguet, M.L., Campbell, D.A., Berry, D.T.R., Schmitt, F.A., *et al.* (1996) Stability of intelligence and intellectual predictors in older persons. *Psychological Assessment, 8,* 154–60.

Rahhal, T.A., Hasher, L. and Colcombe, S.J. (2001) Instructional manipulations and age differences in memory: Now you see them, now you don't. *Psychology and Aging, 16,* 697–706.

Rakerd, B., Van der Velde, T.J. and Hartmann, W.M. (1998) Sound localization in the median sagittal plane by listeners with presbyacusis. *Journal of American Academy of Audiology, 9,* 466–497.

Ranchor, A.V., Sanderman, R., Bouma, J., Buunk, B.P. and Heuvel, W.J. van de (1997) An exploration of the relation between hostility and disease. *Journal of Behavioral Medicine, 20,* 223–40.

Rapp, S.R., Shumaker, S., Schmidt, S., Naughton, M. and Anderson, R. (1998) Social resourcefulness: Its relationship to social support and wellbeing among caregivers of dementia victims. *Aging and Mental Health, 2,* 40–48.

Raskin, A. (1979) Signs and symptoms of psychopathology in the elderly. In A. Raskin and L.F. Jarvik (eds), *Psychiatric Symptoms and Cognitive Loss in the Elderly.* Washington, DC: Hemisphere.

Ratcliff, R. (1978) A theory of memory retrieval. *Psychological Review, 85,* 59–108.

Ratcliff, R., Thapar, A., Gomez, P. and McKoon, G. (2004). A diffusion model analysis of the effects of aging in the lexical-decision task. *Psychology and Aging, 19,* 278–289.

Ratcliff, R., Thapar, A. and McKoon, G. (2001) The effects of aging on reaction time in a signal detection task. *Psychology and Aging, 16,* 323–41.

Ratner, H.H., Schell, D.A., Crimmins, A., Mittelman, D. and Baldinelli, L. (1987) Changes in adults' prose recall: Aging or cognitive demands? *Developmental Psychology, 23,* 521–25.

Rayburn, T.M. and Stonecypher, J.F. (1996) Diagnostic differences related to age and race of involuntarily committed psychiatric patients. *Psychological Reports, 79,* 881–2.

Raymer, A.M. and Berndt, R.S. (1996) Reading lexically without semantics: Evidence from patients with probable Alzheimer's disease. *Journal of the International Neuropsychological Society, 2,* 340–9.

Rebok, G.W. (1987) *Life-Span Cognitive Development.* New York: Holt, Rinehart and Winston.

Receputo, G., Mazzoleni, G., Di Fazio, I., Alessandria, I., Savia, S., Scarpinato, R.R., Tomasello, F.B., Laurino, A. and Fornaro, D. (1996a) Study on the sense of taste in a group of Sicilian centenarians. *Archives of Gerontology and Geriatrics, 5,* 411–14.

Receputo, G., Mazzoleni, G., Rapisarda, R., Di Fazio, I., Restuccia, N., Di Stefano, S., Fornaro, D. and Dimora, A.L. (1996b) Sense of smell in centenarians from eastern Sicily. *Archives of Gerontology and Geriatrics, 5,* 407–411.

Reding, M., Haycox, J. and Blas, J. (1985) Depression in patients referred to a dementia clinic: A three-year prospective study. *Archives of Neurology, 42,* 894–6.

Reed, I.C. (2005) Creativity: Self-perceptions over time. *International Journal of Aging and Human Development, 60,* 1–18.

Reichard, S., Livson, F. and Peterson, P.G. (1962) *Aging and Personality: A Study of 87 Older Men.* New York: Wiley.

Reicher-Roessler, A., Loeffler, W. and Munk-Jorgensen, P. (1997) What do we really know about late-onset schizophrenia? *European Archives of Psychiatry and Clinical Neuroscience, 247,* 195–208.

Reid, M.C., Boutros, N.N., O'Connor, P.G., Cadariu, A. and Concato, J. (2002) The health-related effects of alcohol use in older persons: A systematic review. *Substance Abuse, 23,* 149–64.

Reimanis, G. and Green, R.F. (1971) Imminence of death and intellectual decrement in the aged. *Developmental Psychology, 5,* 270–72.

Reisberg, B., Ferris, S.H., de Leon, M.J., Kluger, A., Franssen, E., Borenstein, J. and Alba, R.C. (1989a) The stage specific temporal course of Alzheimer's disease. In K. Iqbal, H.M. Wisniewski and B. Winblad (eds) *Alzheimer's Disease and Related Disorders.* New York: Alan R. Liss.

Reisberg, B., Ferris, S.H., Franssen, E., Jenkins, E.C. and Wisniewski, K.E. (1989b) Clinical features of a neuropathologically verified familial Alzheimer's cohort with onset in the fourth decade. In K. Iqbal, H.M. Wisniewski and B. Winblad (eds), *Alzheimer's Disease and Related Disorders.* New York: Alan R. Liss.

Resnick, B. (2001) Prescribing an exercise program and motivating older adults to comply. *Educational Gerontology, 27,* 209–226.

Ribot, T. (1882) *Diseases of Memory.* London: Kegan, Paul, Tench and Co.

Ribovich, J.K. and Erikson, L. (1980) A study of lifelong reading with implications for instructional programs. *Journal of Reading, 24,* 20–6.

Riby, L.M., Meikle, A. and Glover, C. (2004) The effects of age, glucose ingestion and gluco-regulatory control on episodic memory. *Age and Ageing, 33,* 483–7.

Rice, G.E. (1986a) The everyday activities of adults: Implications for prose recall. Part I. *Educational Gerontology, 12,* 173–86.

Rice, G.E. (1986b) The everyday activities of adults: Implications for prose recall. Part II. *Educational Gerontology, 12,* 187–98.

Rice, G.E. and Meyer, B.J.F. (1986) Prose recall: Effects of aging, verbal ability and reading behavior. *Journal of Gerontology, 41,* 469–480.

Rice, G.E., Meyer, B.J.F. and Miller, D.C. (1988) Relation of everyday activities of adults to their prose recall performance. *Educational Gerontology, 14*, 147–158.

Richards, M., Hardy, R. and Wadsworth, M.E.J. (2005) Alcohol consumption and midlife cognitive change in the British 1946 birth cohort study. *Alcohol and Alcoholism, 40*, 112–17.

Riddle, D.R., Sonntag, W.E. and Lichtenwalner, R.J. (2004) Microvascular plasticity in aging. *Ageing Research Review, 2*, 149–68.

Riddle, T. (2001) I am Lord Voldemort. *If You're Reading This You've Too Much Time on Your Hands, 4*, 920–700.

Riegel, K.F. and Reigel, R.M. (1972) Development, drop and death. *Developmental Psychology, 6*, 306–319.

Riggs, K.M., Lachman, M.E. and Wingfield, A. (1997) Taking charge of remembering: Locus of control and older adults' memory for speech. *Experimental Aging Research, 23*, 237–56.

Rivera, P.A., Rose, J.M., Futterman, A., Lovett, S.B. and Gallagher-Thompson, D. (1991) Dimensions of perceived social support in clinically depressed and nondepressed female caregivers. *Psychology and Aging, 6*, 323–27.

Robbins, T.W., James, M., Owen, A.M., Sahakian, B.J., Lawrence, A.D., McInnes, L. and Rabbitt, P.M.A. (1998) A study of performance on tests from the CANTAB battery sensitive to frontal lobe dysfunction in a large sample of normal volunteers: Implications for theories of executive functioning and cognitive aging. *Journal of the International Neuropsychological Society, 4*, 474–90.

Roberge, R., Berthelot, J.M. and Wolfson, M. (1995) The Health Utility Index: measuring health differences in Ontario by socioeconomic status. *Health Report, 7*, 29–37.

Robertson, J.F. (1977) Grandmotherhood: A study of role concepts. *Journal of Marriage and the Family, 39*, 165–174.

Robins, R.W., Trzesniewski, K.H., Tracy, J.L., Gosling, D.S. and Potter, J. (2002) Global self-esteem across the life span. *Psychology and Aging, 17*, 423–34.

Rodgers, B. (1984) The trend of reading standards re-assessed. *Educational Research, 26*, 153–66.

Rogers, W.A. (2000) Attention and aging. In D.C. Park and N. Schwarz (eds), *Cognitive Aging: A Primer*. Philadelphia: Taylor and Francis, 57–74.

Rolls, B.J. (1999) Do chemosensory changes influence food intake in the elderly? *Physiology and Behavior, 66*, 193–7.

Roman, S.P. (2004) Illiteracy and older adults: Societal and individual implications. *Educational Gerontology, 30*, 79–93.

Rook, K.S. (2003) Exposure and reactivity to negative social exchanges: a preliminary investigation using daily diary data. *The Journals of Gerontology Series B: Psychological Sciences and Social Sciences, 58*, 100–111.

Rose, M.R. (1984) Laboratory evolution of postponed senescence in Drosophila-Melanogaster. *Evolution, 38*, 1004–1010.

Rose, M.R. (1999) Can human aging be postponed? *Scientific American, 281*, 6, 68–73.

Rosen, D. (2004) Factors associated with illegal drug use among older methadone clients. *The Gerontologist, 44*, 543–8.

Rosencranz, H.A. and McNevin, T.E. (1969) A factor analysis of attitudes toward the aged. *Gerontologist, 9*, 55–59.

Rosenstein, R. and Glickman, A.S. (1994) Type size and performance of the elderly on the Wonderlic Personnel Test. *Journal of Applied Gerontology, 13*, 185–92.

Rosenthal, C.J. (1986) Family supports in later life: does ethnicity make a difference? *The Gerontologist, 26*, 19–24.

Rosenzweig, M.R. (1996) Aspects of the search for neural mechanisms of memory. *Annual Review of Psychology, 47*, 1–32.

Rossor, M. and Iversen, L.L. (1986) Non-cholinergic neurotransmitter abnormalities in Alzheimer's disease. *British Medical Bulletin, 42*, 70–4.

Roth, D.L., Stevens, A.B., Burgio, L.D. and Burgio, K.L. (2002) Timed-event sequential analysis of agitation in nursing home residents during personal care interactions with nursing assistants. *The Journals of Gerontology Series B: Psychological Sciences and Social Sciences, 57*, 461–8.

Roth, M. (1979) The early diagnosis of Alzheimer's disease: An introduction. In A.I.M. Glen and L. Whalley (eds), *Alzheimer's Disease: Early Recognition of Potentially Reversible Deficits*. Edinburgh: Churchill Livingstone.

Rothermund, K. and Brandstädter, J. (2003) Coping with deficits and losses in later life: from compensatory action to accommodation. *Psychology and Aging, 18*, 896–905.

Rousseau, G.K. and Rogers, W.A. (2002) Effects of processing style and age on schema acquisition. *The Journals of Gerontology Series B: Psychological Sciences and Social Sciences, 57*, 11–18.

Rubens, A. and Benson, D.F. (1971) Associative visual agnosia. *Archives of Neurology, 24*, 305–16.

Rubin, D.C., Rahhal, T.A. and Poon, L.W. (1998) Things learned in early adulthood are remembered best. *Memory and Cognition, 26*, 3–19.

Rubin, D.C. and Schulkind, M.D. (1997a) The distribution of autobiographical memories across the lifespan. *Memory and Cognition, 25*, 859–66.

Rubin, D.C. and Schulkind, M.D. (1997b) Properties of word cues for autobiographical memory. *Psychological Reports, 81*, 47–50.

Rundinger, G. and Lantermann, E.D. (1980) Social determinants of intelligence in old age [English translation]. *Zeitschrift fuer Gerontologie, 13,* 433–41.

Russell, D.W. and Catrona, C.E. (1991) Social support, stress and depressive symptoms among the elderly: Test of a process model. *Psychology and Aging, 6,* 190–201.

Russell, R.W. (1996) Continuing the search for cholinergic factors in cognitive dysfunction. *Life Sciences, 58,* 1965–70.

Ryan, E.B. (1996) Psychosocial perspectives on discourse and hearing differences among older adults. *Journal of Speech Language Pathology and Audiology, 20,* 95–100.

Ryan, J.J., Lopez, S.J. and Paolo, A.M. (1996) Temporal stability of digit span forward, backward and forward minus backward in persons aged 75–87 years. *Nursopsychiatry, Neuropsychology and Behavioral Neurology, 9,* 206–208.

Ryan, W.J. (1972) Acoustic aspects of the aging voice. *Journal of Gerontology, 27,* 265–68.

Ryff, C.D. (1991) Possible selves in adulthood and old age: A tale of shifting horizons. *Psychology and Aging, 6,* 286–95.

Rypma, B., Prabhakaran, V., Desmond, J.E. and Gabrieli, J.D.E. (2001) Age differences in prefrontal cortical activity in working memory. *Psychology and Aging, 16,* 371–84.

Sabate, J. (1999) Nut consumption, vegetarian diets, ischemic heart disease risk and all-cause mortality: Evidence from epidemiologic studies. *American Journal of Clinical Nutrition, 70,* 500–503.

Sadavoy, J. (1996) Personality disorder in old age: Symptom expression. *Clinical Gerontologist, 16,* 19–36.

Sadavoy, J., Smith, I., Conn, D.K. and Richards, B. (1995) In E. Murphy and G. Alexopoulos (eds), *Geriatric Psychiatry: Key Research Topics for Clinicians.* Chichester: Wiley. 191–9.

Salib, E. (1997) Elderly suicide and weather conditions: Is there a link? *International Journal of Geriatric Psychiatry, 12,* 937–41.

Salthouse, T. (1982) *Adult Cognition.* New York: Springer.

Salthouse, T. (1985) *A Theory of Cognitive Aging.* Amsterdam: North-Holland.

Salthouse, T. (1991a) Mediation of age differences in cognition by reductions in working memory and speed of processing. *Psychological Science, 2,* 179–83.

Salthouse, T. (1991b) *Theoretical Perspectives on Cognitive Aging.* Hillsdale, NJ: Lawrence Erlbaum.

Salthouse, T. (1992a) Reasoning and spatial abilities. In F.I.M. Craik and T. Salthouse (eds), *The Handbook of Aging and Cognition.* Hillsdale, NJ: Lawrence Erlbaum.

Salthouse, T. (1992b) *Mechanisms of Age-Cognition Relations in Adulthood.* Hillsdale, NJ: Lawrence Erlbaum.

Salthouse, T. (1996) The processing-speed theory of adult age differences in cognition. *Psychological Review, 103,* 403–28.

Salthouse, T. (2000) Item analysis of age relations on reasoning tasks. *Psychology and Aging, 15,* 3–8.

Salthouse, T. (2001) Attempted decomposition of age-related influences on two tests of reasoning. *Psychology and Aging, 16,* 251–63.

Salthouse, T., Berish, D.E. and Miles, J.D. (2002) The role of cognitive stimulation on the relations between age and cognitive functioning. *Psychology and Aging, 17,* 548–57.

Salthouse, T. and Czaja, S.J. (2000) Structural constraints on process explanations in cognitive aging. *Psychology and Aging, 15,* 44–55.

Salthouse, T. and Ferrer-Caja, E. (2003) What needs to be explained to account for age-related effects on multiple cognitive variables? *Psychology and Aging, 18,* 91–110.

Salthouse, T., Fristoe, N. and Rhee, S.H. (1996) How localized are age-related effects on neuropsychological measures? *Neuropsychology, 10,* 272–85.

Samaras, T.T. and Elrick, H. (1999) Height, body size and longevity. *Acta Medica Okayama, 53,* 149–69.

Sanadi, D.R. (1977) Metabolic changes and their significance in aging. In C.E. Finch and L. Hayflick (eds), *Handbook of the Biology of Aging.* New York: Van Nostrand Reinhold.

Sasser-Coen, J.R. (1993) Qualitative changes in creativity in the second half of life: A life-span developmental perspective. *Journal of Creative Behavior, 27,* 18–27.

Satre, D.D., Knight, B.G., Dickson-Fuhrmann, E. and Jarvik, L.F. (2004) Substance abuse treatment initiation among older adults in the GET SMART program: Effects of depression and cognitive status. *Aging and Mental Health, 8,* 346–54.

Scaf-Klomp, W., Sanderman, R., Ormel, J. and Kempen, G.I.J.M. (2003) Depression in older people after fall-related injuries: A prospective study. *Age and Ageing, 32,* 88–94.

Schaie, K.W. (1983) The Seattle Longitudinal Study: A 21-year exploration of psychometric intelligence in adulthood. In K.W. Schaie (ed.), *Longitudinal Studies of Adult Psychological Development.* New York, Guilford Press, 64–135.

Schaie, K.W. (1989) Perceptual speed in adulthood: Cross-sectional studies and longitudinal studies. *Psychology and Aging, 4,* 443–53.

Schaie, K.W. (1994) The course of adult intellectual development. *American Psychologist, 49,* 304–313.

Schaie, K.W. and Hertzog, C. (1986) Toward a comprehensive model of adult intellectual development: Contributions of the Seattle Longitudinal Study. In R.J. Sternberg (ed.), *Advances in Human Intelligence, 3*. Hillsdale, NJ: Erlbaum, 79–118.

Schaie, K.W. and Willis, S.L. (1991a) *Adult Development and Aging*. New York: HarperCollins.

Schaie, K.W. and Willis, S.L. (1991b) Adult personality and psychomotor performance: Cross-sectional and longitudinal analyses. *The Journals of Gerontology Series B: Psychological Sciences and Social Sciences, 46*, 275–84.

Scharwey, K., Krzizok, T. and Herfurth, M. (1998) Night driving capacity of ophthalmologically health persons of various ages [English translation]. *Ophthalmologie, 95*, 555–8.

Scherer, M.J. and Frisina, D.R. (1998) Characteristics associated with marginal hearing loss and subjective well-being among a sample of older adults. *Journal of Rehabilitation Research and Development, 35*, 420–6.

Schiffman, S. (1977) Food recognition by the elderly. *Journal of Gerontology, 32*, 586–92.

Schiffman, S.S., Gatlin, L.A., Frey, A.E., Heiman, S.A., Stagner, W.C. and Cooper, D.C. (1995) Taste perception of bitter compounds in young and elderly persons: Relation to lipophilicity of bitter compounds. *Neurobiology of Aging, 15*, 743–50.

Schiller Schigelone, A. and Ingersoll-Dayton, B. (2004) Some of my best friends are old: A qualitative exploration of medical students' interest in geriatrics. *Educational Gerontology, 30*, 643–61.

Schlesinger, B. (1996) The sexless years or sex rediscovered. *Journal of Gerontological Social Work, 26*, 117–31.

Schliemann, A.D. (2000) Informal learning. In A.E. Kazdin (ed.) *Encyclopaedia of Psychology, Volume 4*. Washington, DC: American Psychological Association, 288–90.

Schlotterer, G., Moscovitch, M., Crapper, M. and McLachlan, D. (1984) Visual processing deficits as assessed by spatial frequency contrast sensitivity and backward masking in normal ageing and Alzheimer's disease. *Brain, 107*, 309–25.

Schmiedek, F. and Li, S.C. (2004) Toward an alternative representation for disentangling age-associated differences in general and specific cognitive abilities. *Psychology and Aging, 19*, 40–56.

Schneck, M.E., Haegerstrom-Portnoy, G., Lott, L.A. Braby, J.A. and Gildengorin, G. (2004) Low contrast vision function predicts subsequent acuity loss in an aged population: The SKI study. *Vision Research, 44*, 2317–25.

Schneider, B. (1997) Psychoacoustics and aging: Implications for everyday listening. *Journal of Speech Language Pathology and Audiology, 21*, 111–24.

Schneider, B.A., Daneman, M. and Murphy, D.R (2005) Speech comprehension difficulties in older adults: cognitive slowing or age-related changes in hearing? *Psychology and Aging, 20*, 261–71.

Schneider, B.A., Daneman, M., Murphy, D.R. and See, S.K. (2000) Listening to discourse in distracting settings: The effects of aging. *Psychology and Aging, 15*, 110–25.

Schneider, B., Speranza, F. and Pichora-Fuller, M.K. (1998) Age-related changes in temporal resolution: Envelope and intensity effects. *Canadian Journal of Experimental Psychology, 52*, 184–91.

Schonfeld, L., Rohrer, G.E., Zima, M. and Spiegel, T. (1993) Alcohol abuse and medication misuse in older adults as estimated by service providers. *Journal of Gerontological Social Work, 21*, 113–25.

Schooler, C. and Mulatu, M.S. (2001) The reciprocal effects of leisure time activities and intellectual functioning in older people: A longitudinal analysis. *Psychology and Aging, 16*, 466–82.

Schram, L.L., Rubert, M. and Loewenstein, D.A. (1995) A qualitative analysis of semantic intrusive errors in Alzheimer's Disease. *Archives of Clinical Neuropsychology, 10*, 255–63.

Schultz, R. and Williamson, G.M. (1991) A 2-year longitudinal study of depression among Alzheimer's caregivers. *Psychology and Aging, 6*, 569–78.

Schwartz, J.E., Friedman, H.S., Tucker, J.S., Tomlinson-Keasey, C. Wingard, D.L. and Criqui, M.H. (1995) Sociodemographic and psychosocial factors in childhood as predictors of adult mortality. *American Journal of Public Health, 85*, 1237–45.

Schwartz, L.K. and Simmons, J.P. (2001) Contact quality and attitudes toward the elderly. *Educational Gerontology, 27*, 127–37.

Schwartz, M.F., Marin, O.S.M. and Saffran, E.M. (1979) Dissociation of language function in dementia: A case study. *Brain and Language, 7*, 277–306.

Schweber, M.S. (1989a) Down Syndrome and the measurement of chromosome 21 DNA amounts in Alzheimer's Disease. In G. Miner, L. Miner, R. Richter and J.L. Valentine (eds) *Familial Alzheimer's Disease: Molecular Genetics and Clinical Prospects*. New York: Marcel Dekker.

Schweber, M.S. (1989b) Alzhimer's Disease and Down Syndrome. In K. Iqbal, H.M. Wisniewski and B. Winblad (eds), *Alzheimer's Disease and Related Disorders*. New York: Alan R. Liss.

Scialfa, C.T. (2002) The role of sensory factors in cognitive aging research. *Canadian Journal of Experimental Psychology, 56*, Ottawa: September, 153–64.

Scogin, F.R. (1998) Anxiety in old age. In I.H. Nordhus, G.R. VandenBos, S. Berg and P. Fromholt (eds), *Clinical Geropsychology*. Washington, DC: American Psychological Association, 205–209.

Searcy, J.H., Bartlett, J.C. and Memon, A. (1999) Age differences in accuracy and choosing in eyewitness identification and face recognition. *Memory and Cognition, 27*, 538–52.

Seeman, T.E., Huang, M.H., Bretsky, P., Crimmins, E., Launer, L. and Guralnik, J.M. (2005) Education and APOE-e4 in longitudinal cognitive decline: MacArthur studies of successful aging. *The Journals of Gerontology Series B: Psychological Sciences and Social Sciences, 60*, 74–83.

Segrave, R.T. and Segrave, K.B. (1995) Human sexuality and aging. *Journal of Sex Education and Therapy, 21*, 88–102.

Sekuler, R. and Blake, R. (1985) *Perception*. New York: Random House.

Sekuler, R., Hutman, L.P. and Owsley, C. (1980) Human aging and vision. *Science, 209*, 1255–6.

Sekuler, R. and Owsley, C. (1982) The spatial vision of older humans. In R. Sekuler, D. Kline and K. Dismukes (eds), *Aging and Human Visual Function*. New York: Alan R. Liss, 121–30.

Sekuler, R., Owsley, C. and Hutman, L. (1982) Assessing spatial vision of older people. *American Journal of Optometry and Physiological Optics, 59*, 961–8.

Selkoe, D.J. (1992) Aging brain, aging mind. *Scientific American, 267*, 97–103.

Seltzer, B. and Sherwin, I. (1983) A comparison of clinical features in early- and late-onset primary degenerative dementia: One entity or two? *Archives of Neurology, 40*, 143–6.

Serrano, A.L. and Andres, V. (2004) Telomeres and cardiovascular disease: Does size matter? *Circulation Research, 94*, 575–84.

Serrano, J.P., Latorre, J.M., Gatz, M. and Montanes, J. (2004) Life review therapy using autobiographical retrieval practice for older adults with depressive symptomatology. *Psychology and Aging, 19*, 272–7.

Seshamani, M. and Gray, A. (2004) Time to death and health expenditure: an improved model for the impact of demographic change on health care costs. *Age and Ageing, 33*, 571–6.

Sesso, H.D., Paffenbarger, R.S. and Lee, I.M. (2000) Physical activity and coronary heart disease in men: The Harvard Alumni Health Study. *Circulation, 102*, 975–80.

Settersen, R.A. (1998) Time, age and the transition to retirement: New evidence on life-course flexibility? *International Journal of Aging and Human Development, 47*, 177–203.

Settersen, R.A. and Haegestad, G.O. (1996) What's the latest? Cultural age deadlines for family transitions. *Gerontologist, 36*, 178–88.

Settlage, C.F. (1996) Transcending old age: Creativity, development and psychoanalysis in the life of a centenarian. *International Journal of Psycho-Analysis, 77*, 549–64.

Shan, Z.Y., Liu, J.Z., Sahgal, V., Wang, B. and Yue, G.H. (2005) Selective atrophy of left hemisphere and frontal lobe of the brain in old men. *Journals of Gerontology: Series A: Biological Sciences and Medical Sciences, 60*, 165–74.

Sharpe, T.H. (2004) Introduction to sexuality in late life. *Family Journal: Counseling and Therapy for Couples and Families, 12*, 199–205.

Sharpley, C.F. (1997) Psychometric properties of the self-perceived stress in retirement scale. *Psychological Reports, 81*, 319–22.

Sharps, M.J. (1998) Age-related change in visual information processing: Toward a unified theory of aging and visual memory. *Current Psychology, 16*, 284–307.

Shaw, C. (2004). Interim 2003-based national population projections for the United Kingdom and constituent countries. *Population Trends 118*, 6–16.

Shea, P. (1995) Ageing and wisdom. In F. Glendenning and I. Stuart-Hamilton (eds), *Learning and Cognition in Later Life*. Aldershot: Arena.

Shen, J., Barnes, C.A., McNaughton, B.L., Skaggs, W.E. and Weaver, K.L. (1997) The effect of aging on experience-dependent plasticity of hippocampal place cells. *Journal of Neuroscience, 17*, 6769–82.

Sherer, M. (1996) The impact of using personal computers on the lives of nursing home residents. *Physical and Occupational Therapy in Geriatrics, 14*, 13–31.

Shimamura, A.P., Berry, J.M., Mangels, J.A., Rusting, C.L. and Jurica, P.J. (1995) Memory and cognitive abilities in university professors: Evidence for successful aging. *Psychological Science, 6*, 271–77.

Shimonaka, Y., Nakazato, K. and Homma, A. (1996) Personality, longevity and successful aging among Tokyo metropolitan centenarians. *International Journal of Aging and Human Development, 42*, 173–87.

Shock, N.W. (1977) Biological theories of aging. In J.E. Birren and K.W. Schaie (eds), *Handbook of the Psychology of Aging*. 1st edition. New York: Van Nostrand Reinhold.

Shore, D. and Wyatt, R.J. (1983) Aluminium and Alzheimer's disease. *Journal of Nervous and Mental Disorders, 171*, 553–8.

Shulman, K.I. (1997) Disinhibition syndromes, secondary mania and bipolar disorder in old age. *Journal of Affective Disorders, 46*, 175–82.

Siegler, I.C. and Botwinick, J. (1979) A long-term longitudinal study of intellectual ability of older adults: The matter of selective subject attrition. *Journal of Gerontology, 34*, 242–5.

Siegler, I.C., McCarty, S.M. and Logue, P.E. (1982) Wechsler Memory Scale scores, selective attention and distance from death. *Journal of Gerontology, 37*, 176–81.

Simons, J.S., Dodson, C.S., Bell, D. and Schacter, D.L. (2004) Specific- and partial-source memory: effects of aging. *Psychology and Aging, 19*, 689–94.

Simonton, D.K. (1990) Creativity and wisdom in aging. In J.W. Birren and K.W. Schaie (eds) *Handbook of the Psychology of Aging.* 3rd edition. San Diego, CA: Academic Press.

Singer, T., Lindenberger, U. and Baltes, P.B. (2003a) Plasticity of memory for new learning in very old age: A story of major loss? *Psychology and Aging, 18*, 306–317.

Singer, T., Verhaeghen, P., Ghisletta, P., Lindenberger, U. and Baltes, P.B. (2003b) The fate of cognition in very old age: Six-year longitudinal findings in the Berlin Aging Study (BASE). *Psychology and Aging, 18*, 318–31.

Sirvio, J. (1999) Strategies that support declining cholinergic neurotransmission in Alzheimer's disease patients. *Gerontology, 45*, 3–14.

Skoog, I. (1996) Sex and Swedish 85-year-olds. *New England Journal of Medicine, 334*, 1140–1.

Slavin, M.J., Phillips, J.C. and Bradshaw, J.L. (1996) Visual cues and the handwriting of older adults: A kinematic analysis. *Psychology and Aging, 11*, 521–26.

Slavin, M.J., Phillips, J.C., Bradshaw, J.L., Hall, K.A. and Presnell, I. (1999) Consistency of handwriting movements in dementia of the Alzheimer's type: A comparison with Huntington's and Parkinson's diseases. *Journal of the International Neuropsychological Society, 5*, 20–5.

Slawinski, E.B., Hartel, D.M. and Kline, D.W. (1993) Self-reporting hearing problems in daily life throughout adulthood. *Psychology and Aging, 8*, 552–61.

Sliwinski, M. (1997) Aging and counting speed: Evidence for process-specific slowing. *Psychology and Aging, 12*, 38–49.

Sliwinski, M., Buschke, H., Kuslansky, G., Senior, G. and Scarisbrick, D. (1994) Proportional slowing and addition speed in old and young adults. *Psychology and Aging, 9*, 72–80.

Sliwinski, M. and Hall, C.B. (1998) Constraints on general slowing: A meta-analysis using hierarchical linear models with random coefficients. *Psychology and Aging, 13*, 164–75.

Sliwinski, M.J., Hofer, S.M., Hall, C., Buschke, H. and Lipton, R.B. (2003) Modeling memory decline in older adults: the importance of preclinical dementia, attrition and chronological age. *Psychology and Aging, 18*, 658–71.

Small, B.J., Fratiglioni, L., von Strauss, E. and Bäckman, L. (2003) Terminal decline and cognitive performance in very old age: Does cause of death matter? *Psychology and Aging, 18*, 193–202.

Small, B.J., Hertzog, C., Hultsch, D.F. and Dixon, R.A. (2003) Stability and change in adult personality over 6 years: findings from the Victoria Longitudinal Study. *The Journals of Gerontology Series B: Psychological Sciences and Social Sciences, 58*, 166–76.

Small, B.J., Rosnick, C.B., Fratiglioni, L. and Bäckman, L. (2004) Apolipoprotein E and cognitive performance: a meta-analysis. *Psychology and Aging, 19*, 592–600.

Smiler, A., Gagne, D.D. and Stine-Morrow, E.A.L. (2004) Aging, memory load and resource allocation during reading. *Psychology and Aging, 18*, 203–209.

Smith, A. (1998) Breakfast consumption and intelligence in elderly persons. *Psychological Reports, 82*, 424–26.

Smith, G.A. and Brewer, N. (1995) Slowness and age: Speed-accuracy mechanisms. *Psychology and Aging, 10*, 238–47.

Smith, J., Heckhausen, J., Kilegl, R. and Baltes, P.B. (1984) Cognitive reserve capacity, expertise and aging. *Meeting of Gerontological Society of America, San Antonio.* Cited in Rebok (1987).

Smith, S.W., Rebok, G.W., Smith, W.R., Hall, S.E. and Alvin, M. (1989) Adult age differences in the use of story structure in delayed free recall. *Experimental Aging Research, 9*, 191–5.

Smyer, M.A. and Qualls, S.H. (1999) *Aging and Mental Health.* Oxford: Blackwells.

Snowdon, D.A., Greiner, L.H., Riley, K.P., Markesbury, W.R., Greiner, P.A. and Mortimer, J.A. (1997) Brain infarction and the clinical expression of Alzheimer disease. *Journal of the American Medical Association, 277*, 813–17.

Snowdon, D.A., Kemper, S.J., Mortimer, J.A., Greiner, L.H., Wekstein, D.R. and Markesbury, W.R. (1996) Linguistic ability in early life and cognitive function and Alzheimer's disease in late life: Findings from the Nun Study. *Journal of the American Medical Association, 275*, 528–32.

Soederberg Miller, L.M. (2003) The effects of age and domain knowledge on text processing. *The Journals of Gerontology Series B: Psychological Sciences and Social Sciences, 58*, 217–23.

Sonnenschein, E. and Brody, J.A. (2005) Effect of population aging on proportionate mortality from heart disease and cancer, U.S. 2000–2050. *The Journals of Gerontology Series B: Psychological Sciences and Social Sciences 60*, 110–112.

Sorce, P. (1995) Cognitive competence of older consumers. *Psychology and Marketing, 12*, 467–80.

Souter, S. and Keller, C.S. (2002) Food choice in the rural dwelling older adult. *Southern Online Journal of Nursing Research, Issue 5, Volume 3*. See www.snrs.org/publications/SOJNR_articles/iss05vol03.htm (accessed on 13 January 2006).

Speranza, F., Daneman, M. and Schneider, B.A. (2000) How aging affects the reading of words in noisy backgrounds. *Psychology and Aging, 15*, 253–58.

Spieler, D.H. and Balota, D.A. (2000) Factors influencing word naming in younger and older adults. *Psychology and Aging, 15*, 225–31.

Spirduso, W.W. and MacRae, P.G. (1990) Motor performance and aging. In J.E. Birren and K.W. Schaie (eds), *Handbook of the Psychology of Aging*. 3rd edition. San Diego, CA: Academic Press.

Spiro, A., Aldwin, C.M., Ward, K.D. and Mroczek, D.K. (1995) Personality and the incidence of hypertenstion among older men: Longitudinal findings from the Normative Aging Study. *Health Psychology, 14*, 563–9.

Springer, M.V. McIntosh, A.R., Winocur, G. and Grady, C.L. (2005) The relation between brain activity during memory tasks and years of education in young and older adults. *Neuropsychology, 19*, 181–92.

St George-Hyslop, P.H., Tanzi, R.E., Polinsky, R.J., Haines, J.L., Nee, L., Watkins, P.C., Myers, R.H., Feldman, R.G., Pollen, D. and Drachman, D. (1987) The genetic defect causing familial Alzheimer's Disease maps on chromosome 21. *Science, 325*, 885–90.

Stallings, M.C., Dunham, C.C., Gatz, M., Baker, L. and Bengston, V.L. (1997) Relationships among life events and psychological well-being: More evidence for a two-factor theory of well-being. *Journal of Applied Gerontology, 16*, 104–19.

Stankov, L. (2005) Reductionism versus charting: Ways of examining the role of lower-order cognitive processes in intelligence. In R.J. Sternberg and J.E. Pretz (eds), *Cognition and Intelligence: Identifying the Mechanisms of the Mind*. New York: Cambridge University Press, 51–67.

Starr, J.M., Deary, I.J., Lemmon, H. and Whalley, L.J. (2000) Mental ability age 11 years and health status age 77 years. *Age and Ageing, 29*, 523–8.

Staudinger, U.M., Bluck, S. and Herzberg, P.Y. (2003) Looking back and looking ahead: Adult age differences in consistency of diachronous ratings of subjective well-being. *Psychology and Aging, 18*, 13–24.

Staudinger, U.M., Lopez, D.F. and Baltes, P.B. (1997) The psychometric location of wisdom-related performance: Intelligence, personality and more? *Personality and Social Psychology Bulletin, 23*, 1200–1214.

Staudinger, U.M., Maciel, A.G., Smith, J. and Baltes, P.B. (1998) What predicts wisdom-related performance? A first look at personality, intelligence and facilitative experiential contexts. *European Journal of Personality, 12*, 1–17.

Stebbins, G.T., Carrillo, M.C., Dorfman, J., Dirksen, C., Desmond, J.E., Turner, D.A., Bennett, D.A., Wilson, R.S., Glover, G. and Gabrieli, J.D.E. (2002) Aging effects on memory encoding in the frontal lobes. *Psychology and Aging, 17*, 44–55.

Stel, V.S., Smit, J.H., Plujm, S.M.F.. and Lips, P. (2004) Consequences of falling in older men and women and risk factors for health service use and functional decline. *Age and Ageing, 33*, 58–65.

Stephens, S. (1982) Some historical aspects of ototoxicity. *British Journal of Audiology, 16*, 76–80.

Sternberg, R.J. (1996) *Cognitive Psychology*. Fort Worth: Harcourt Brace.

Sternberg, R.J. (1998) A balance theory of wisdom. *Review of General Psychology, 2*, 347–65.

Steunenberg, B., Twisk, J.W.R., Beekman, A.T.F., Deeg, D.J.H. and Kerkhof, A.J.F.M. (2005) Stability and change of neuroticism in aging. *The Journals of Gerontology Series B: Psychological Sciences and Social Sciences, 60*, 27–33.

Stevens, J.C. (1996) Detection of tastes in mixture with other tastes: Issues of masking and aging. *Chemical Senses, 21*, 211–21.

Stevens, J.C., Cruz, L.A., Hoffman, J.M. and Patterson, M.Q. (1995) Taste sensitivity and aging: High incidence of decline revealed by repeated threshold measures. *Chemical Senses, 20*, 451–59.

Stevens, J.C. and Patterson, M.Q. (1996) Dimensions of spatial acuity in the touch test: Changes over the life span. *Somatosensory and Motor Research, 12*, 29–47.

Stevens, M. (1979) Famous personality test. A test for measuring remote memory. *Bulletin of the British Psychological Society, 32*, 211.

Stewart, D. and Oslin, D.W. (2001) Recognition and treatment of late-life addictions in medical settings. *Journal of Clinical Geropsychology, 7*, 145–58.

Stine, E.L. and Wingfield, A. (1988) Memorability functions as an indicator of qualitative age differences in text recall. *Psychology and Aging, 3*, 179–83.

Stine, E.L., Wingfield, A. and Poon, L. (1989) Speech comprehension and memory through adulthood: The roles of time and strategy. In L. W. Poon, D.C. Rubin and B.A. Wilson (eds), *Everyday Cognition in Adulthood and Everyday Life*. Cambridge: Cambridge University Press.

Stine-Morrow, E.A., Loveless, M.K. and Soederberg, L.M. (1996) Resource allocation in on-line reading by younger and older adults. *Psychology and Aging, 11*, 475–86.

Stine-Morrow, E.A.L., Milinder, L.-A., Pullara, O. and Herman, B. (2001) Patterns of resource allocation are reliable among younger and older readers. *Psychology and Aging, 16*, 69–84.

Stitt, B.G., Giacopassi, D. and Nichols, M. (2003) Gambling among older adults: a comparative analysis. *Experimental Aging Research, 29*, 189–203.

Stoddard, C.E. and Thompson, D.L. (1996) Alcohol and the elderly: Special concerns for counseling professionals. *Alcoholism Treatment Quarterly, 14*, 59–69.

Stokes, G. (1992) *On Being Old. The Psychology of Later Life*. London: The Falmer Press.

Storandt, M. (1976) Speed and coding effects in relation to age and ability level. *Developmental Psychology, 2*, 177–8.

Storandt, M. (1977) Age, ability level and scoring the WAIS. *Journal of Gerontology, 32*, 175–8.

Storandt, M. and Futterman, A. (1982) Stimulus size and performance on two subtests of the Wechsler Adult Intelligence Scale by younger and older adults. *Journal of Gerontology, 37*, 602–603.

Storandt, M., Kaskie, B. and Von Dras, D.D. (1998) Temporal memory for remote events in healthy aging and dementia. *Psychology and Aging, 13*, 4–7.

Storandt, M., Stone, K. and LaBarge, E. (1995) Deficits in reading performance in very mild dementia of the Alzheimer type. *Neuropsychology, 9*, 174–6.

Strain, E., Patterson, K., Graham, N. and Hodges, J.R. (1998) Word reading in Alzheimer's disease: Cross-sectional and longitudinal analyses of response time and accuracy data. *Neuropsychologia, 36*, 155–171.

Stroebe, M.S., Stroebe, W.S. and Hansson, R.O. (1993) *Handbook of Bereavement: Theory Research and Intervention*. Cambridge: Cambridge University Press.

Strouse, A., Ashmead, D.H., Ohde, R.N. and Grantham, D.W. (1998) Temporal processing in the aging auditory system. *Journal of the Acoustical Society of America, 104*, 2385–99.

Strube, M.J., Berry, J.M., Goza, B.K. and Fennimore, D. (1985) Type A behavior, age and psychological well-being. *Journal of Personality and Social Psychology, 49*, 203–18.

Stuart-Hamilton, I. (1986) The role of phonemic awareness in the reading style of beginning readers. *British Journal of Educational Psychology, 56*, 271–85.

Stuart-Hamilton, I. (1995) Problems with the assessment of intellectual change in elderly people. In F. Glendenning and I. Stuart-Hamilton (eds), *Learning and Cognition in Later Life*. Aldershot: Arena. 22–42.

Stuart-Hamilton, I. (1998) Women's attitudes to ageing: Some factors of relevance to educational gerontology. *Education and Ageing, 13*, 67–88.

Stuart-Hamilton, I. (1999a) *Key Ideas in Psychology*. London: Jessica Kingsley Publishers.

Stuart-Hamilton, I. (1999b) Intellectual changes in late life. In R.T. Woods (ed.), *Psychological Problems of Ageing*. Chichester: Wiley, 27–47.

Stuart-Hamilton, I. (2000) Attitudes to aging questionnaires: Some evidence for potential bias in their design. *Educational Gerontology, 26*, 1–11.

Stuart-Hamilton, I. (2003) Normal cognitive aging. In R. Tallis and H. Fillit (eds), *Brocklehurst's Textbook of Geriatric Medicine and Gerontology*. London: Churchill Livingstone.

Stuart-Hamilton, I. and Mahoney, B. (2003) The effect of ageing awareness training on knowledge of and attitudes towards, older adults. *Educational Psychology 29*, 251–60.

Stuart-Hamilton, I. and McDonald, L. (1996) Age and a possible regression to childhood thinking patterns. *British Psychological Society Psychologists Special Interest Group in the Elderly Newsletter, 58*, 13–6.

Stuart-Hamilton, I. and McDonald, L. (1998) Aging and the Bridges of Konigsberg problem: No age changes in perseverance. *Educational Gerontology, 24*, 225–32.

Stuart-Hamilton, I. and McDonald, L. (1999) Limits to the use of *g*. Paper presented at the International Conference on Lifelong Learning, University College Worcester, July.

Stuart-Hamilton, I. and McDonald, L. (2001) Do we need intelligence? Some reflections on the importance of *G*. *Educational Gerontology, 27*, 399–407.

Stuart-Hamilton, I., Perfect, T. and Rabbitt, P. (1988) Remembering who was who. In M.M. Gruneberg, P.E. Morris and R.N. Sykes (eds), *Practical Aspects of Memory, Volume 2*. Chichester: Wiley.

Stuart-Hamilton, I. and Rabbitt, P. (1997a) Age-related decline in spelling ability: A link with fluid intelligence? *Educational Gerontology, 23*, 437–41.

Stuart-Hamilton, I. and Rabbitt, P. (1997b) The decline of eye-voice span in elderly readers. *Educational Gerontology, 23*, 389–400.

Stuart-Hamilton, I., Rabbitt, P. and Huddy, A. (1988) The role of selective attention in the visuo-spatial memory of patients suffering from dementia of the Alzheimer type. *Comprehensive Gerontology B, 2*, 129–34.

Stuss, D.T., Craik, F.I.M., Sayer, L., Franchi, D. and Alexander, M.P. (1996) Comparison of older people and patients with frontal lesions: Evidence from word list learning. *Psychology and Aging, 11*, 387–95.

Sulkava, R. (1982) Alzheimer's disease and senile dementia of the Alzheimer type: a comparative study. *Acta Neurologica Scandanavica, 65,* 636–50.

Sulkava, R. and Amberia, K. (1982) Alzheimer's disease and senile dementia of Alzheimer type: a neuropsychological study. *Acta Neurologica Scandanavica, 65,* 651–60.

Sundstrom, G. (1986) Intergenerational mobility and the relationship between adults and their aging parents in Sweden. *The Gerontologist, 26,* 367–71.

Sunness, J.S., Gonzalez-Brown, J., Applegate, C.A., Bressler, N.M., Tian, Y., Hawkins, B., Barron, Y. and Bergman, A. (1999) Enlargement of atrophy and visual acuity loss in geographic atrophy form of age-related macular degeneration. *Ophthalmology, 106,* 1768–79.

Swan, G.E. and Carmelli, D. (2002) Impaired olfaction predicts cognitive decline in nondemented older adults. *Neuroepidemiology, 21,* 58–68.

Swan, G.E., Dame, A. and Carmelli, D. (1991) Involuntary retirement, Type A behavior and current functioning in elderly men: 27-year follow-up of the Western Collaborative Group Study. *Psychology and Aging, 6,* 384–91.

Szinovacz, M. (1996) Couple's employment/retirement patterns and perceptions of marital quality. *Research on Aging, 18,* 243–68.

Szinovacz, M.E. and Davey, A. (2004) Retirement transitions and spouse disability: effects on depressive symptoms. *The Journals of Gerontology Series B: Psychological Sciences and Social Sciences, 59,* 333–42.

Tallis, R.C. and Fillit, H.M. (eds) (2003) *Brocklehurst's Textbook of Geriatric Medicine and Gerontology,* 6th edition. London: Churchill Livingstone.

Taub, H.A. (1979) Comprehension and memory of prose materials by young and old adults. *Experimental Aging Research, 5,* 3–13.

Taub, H.A. (1984) Underlining of prose material for elderly adults. *Educational Gerontology, 10,* 401–405.

Taub, H.A., Baker, M.T. and Kline, G.E. (1982) Perceived choice of prose materials by young and elderly adults. *Educational Gerontology, 8,* 447–453.

Taub, H.A. and Kline, G. (1978) Recall of prose as a function of age and input modality. *Journal of Gerontology, 33,* 725–30.

Taylor, E. (1957) *Angel.* London: Peter Davies.

Taylor, J.K. and Burke, D.M. (2002) Asymmetric aging effects on semantic and phonological processes: Naming in the picture–word interference task. *Psychology and Aging, 17,* 662–76.

Taylor, M.G. and Lynch, S.M. (2004) Trajectories of impairment, social support and depressive symptoms in later life. *The Journals of Gerontology Series B: Psychological Sciences and Social Sciences, 59,* 238–46.

Taylor, J.L., Miller, T.P. and Tinklenberg, J.R. (1993) Correlates of memory decline: A 4-year longitudinal study of older adults with memory complaints. *Psychology and Aging, 8,* 185–93.

Tenney, Y.J. (1984) Ageing and the misplacing of objects. *British Journal of Developmental Psychology, 2,* 43–50.

Tennstedt, S.L., Chang, B. and Delgado, M. (1998) *Journal of Gerontological Social Work, 30,* 179–99.

Teri, L. (1999) Training families to provide care: Effects on people with dementia. *International Journal of Geriatric Psychiatry, 14,* 110–116.

Thane, P. (2000) *Old Age in English History.* Oxford: Oxford University Press.

Thapar, A., Ratcliff, R. and McKoon, G. (2003) A diffusion model analysis of the effects of aging on letter discrimination. *Psychology and Aging, 18,* 415–29.

Thimm, C., Rademacher, U. and Kruse, L. (1998) Age stereotypes and patronizing messages: Features of age-adapted speech in technical instructions to the elderly. *Journal of Applied Communication Research, 26,* 66–82.

Thompson, D.N. (1997) Contributions to the history of psychology: CVIII. On aging and intelligence: History teaches a different lesson. *Perception and Motor Skills, 85,* 28–30.

Thompson, I.M. (1988) Communication changes in normal and abnormal ageing. In U. Holden (ed.), *Neuropsychology and Aging.* London: Croom Helm.

Thompson, L.W., Gallagher-Thompson, D.G., Futterman, A., Gilewski, M.J. and Peterson, J. (1991) The effects of late-life spousal bereavement over a 30-month interval. *Psychology and Aging, 6,* 434–41.

Thompson, L.W., Gong, V., Haskins, E. and Gallagher, D. (1987) Assessment of depression and dementia during the later years. In K.W. Schaie (ed.), *Annual Review of Gerontology and Geriatrics, 7,* 295–324.

Thompson, M.D., Knee, K. and Golden, C.J. (1998) Olfaction in persons with Alzheimer's disease. *Neuropsychology Review, 8,* 11–23.

Thompson-Schill, S.L., Jondies, J., Marshietz, C., Smith, E.E., D'Esposito, M., Kan, I.P., Knight, R.T. and Swick, D. (2002) Effects of frontal lobe damage on interference effects in working memory. *Cognitive, Affective and Behavioral Neuroscience, 2,* 109–120.

Thornbury, J.M. and Mistretta, C.M. (1981) Tactile sensitivity as a function of age. *Journal of Gerontology, 36,* 34–39.

Thurstone, T.G. (1958) *Manual for the SRA Primary Mental Abilites.* Chicago, IL: Science Research Associates.

Tomlinson, B.E., Blessed, G. and Roth, M. (1968) Observations on the brains of nondemented old people. *Journal of Neurological Science, 7,* 331–56.

Topolski, J.M., Gotham, H.J., Klinkenberg, W.D., O'Neill, D.L. and Brooks, A.R. (2002) Older adults, substance use and HIV/AIDS: Preparing for a future crisis. *Journal of Mental Health and Aging, 8,* 349–63.

Tsai, H.K., Chou, F.S. and Cheng, T.J. (1958) On changes in ear size with age, as found among Taiwanese-Formosans of the Fukiense extraction. *Journal of the Formosan Medical Association, 57,* 105–111.

Tsuchiya, A. and Williams, A. (2005) A 'fair innings' between the sexes: Are men being treated inequitably? *Social Science and Medicine, 60* (2), 277–86.

Tucker, J.S. Klein, D.J. and Elliott, M.N. (2004) Social control of health behaviors: a comparison of young, middle-aged and older adults. *The Journals of Gerontology Series B: Psychological Sciences and Social Sciences, 59,* 147–150.

Tulving, E. (1972) Episodic and semantic memory. In E. Tulving and D.L. Horton (eds), *Verbal Behavior and General Behavior Theory.* New Jersey: Prentice-Hall.

Tuma, T.A. (1996) Effect of age on the outcome of hospital treated depression. *British Journal of Psychiatry, 168,* 76–81.

Tun, P.A., Wingfield, A. and Lindfield, K.C. (1997) Motor-speed baseline for the digit-symbol substitution test. *Clinical Gerontologist, 18,* 47–51.

Tun, P.A., Wingfield, A., Stine, E.A. and Mecsas, C. (1992) Rapid speech processing and divided attention: Processing rate versus processing resources as an explanation of age effects. *Psychology and Aging, 7,* 546–50.

Turner, J.S. and Helms, D.B. (1987) *Lifespan Development.* 3rd edition. New York: Holt, Rinehart and Winston.

Turner, J.S. and Helms, D.B. (1994) *Contemporary Adulthood.* 5th edition. Orlando, FL: Harcourt Brace.

Turner, J.S. and Helms, D.B. (1995) *Lifespan Development.* Fort Worth: Harcourt Brace.

Uttl, B. and Graf, P. (1993) Episodic spatial memory in adulthood. *Psychology and Aging, 8,* 257–73.

van Baarsen, B. (2002) Theories on coping with loss: the impact of social support and self-esteem on adjustment to emotional and social loneliness following a partner's death in later life. *The Journals of Gerontology Series B: Psychological Sciences and Social Sciences, 57,* 33–42.

van Solinge, H. and Henkens, K. (2005) Couples' adjustment to retirement: a multi-actor panel study. *The Journals of Gerontology Series B: Psychological Sciences and Social Sciences, 60,* 11–20.

Vance, D.E., Burgio, L.D., Roth, D.L., Stevens, A.B., Fairchild, J.K. and Yurick, A. (2003) Predictors of agitation in nursing home residents. *The Journals of Gerontology Series B: Psychological Sciences and Social Sciences, 58,* 129–137.

Vander Bilt, J., Dodge, H.H., Pandav, R., Shaffer, H.J. and Ganguli, M. (2004) Gambling participation and social support among older adults: A longitudinal community study. *Journal of Gambling Studies, 20,* 373–90.

Vanderplas, J.M. and Vanderplas, J.H. (1980) Some factors affecting legibility of printed materials for older adults. *Perceptual and Motor Skills, 50,* 923–32.

Vaneste, S. and Pouthas, V. (1999) Timing in aging: The role of attention. *Experimental Aging Research, 25,* 49–67.

Vassallo, M., Sharma, J.C., Briggs, R.S.J. and Allen, S.C. (2003) Characteristics of early fallers on elderly patient rehabilitation wards. *Age and Ageing, 32,* 338–42.

Verhaeghen, P. (2003) Aging and vocabulary score: A meta-analysis. *Psychology and Aging, 18,* 332–9.

Verhaeghen, P., Cerella, J., Semenec, S.C., Leo, M.A., Bopp, K.L. and Steitz, D.W. (2002) Cognitive efficiency modes in old age: Performance on sequential and coordinative verbal and visuospatial tasks. *Psychology and Aging, 17,* 558–70.

Verhaeghen, P. and De Meersman, L. (1998) Aging and the Stroop effect: A Meta-analysis. *Psychology and Aging, 13,* 120–6.

Verhaeghen, P., Steitz, D.W. Sliwinski, M.J. and Cerella, J. (2003) Aging and dual-task performance: A meta-analysis. *Psychology and Aging, 18,* 443–60.

Verillo, R.T. (1982) Effects of aging on the suprathreshold responses to vibration. *Perception and Psychophysics, 32,* 61–8.

Vetter, P.H., Krauss, S., Steiner, O., Kropp, P., Moeller, W., Moises, H.W. and Koeller, O. (1999) Vascular dementia versus dementia of Alzheimer's type: Do they have differential effects on caregiver's burden? *Journal of Gerontology B: Psychological Sciences and Social Sciences, 54,* 93–8.

Viskontas, I.V., Morrison, R.G., Holyoak, K.J., Hummel, J.E. and Knowlton, B.J. (2004) Relational integration, inhibition and analogical reasoning in older adults. *Psychology and Aging, 19,* 581–91.

Walker, N., Fain, W.B., Fisk, A.D. and McGuire, C.L. (1997) Aging and decision making: Driving-related problem solving. *Human Factors, 39,* 438–44.

Walmsley, S.A., Scott, K.M. and Lehrer, R. (1981) Effects of document simplification on the reading comprehension of the elderly. *Journal of Reading Behavior, 12,* 236–48.

Walsh, D.A. (1982) The development of visual information processes in adulthood and old age. In F.I.M. Craik and S. Trehub (eds), *Aging and Cognitive Processes.* New York: Plenum.

Walsh, D.A., Williams, M.V. and Hertzog, C.K. (1979) Age-related differences in two stages of central perceptual processes. *Journal of Gerontology, 34*, 234–41.

Walter, J.M. and Soliah, L. (1996) Sweetener preference among non-institutionalised older adults. *Journal of Nutrition for the Elderly, 14*, 1–13.

Walz, T. (2002) Crones, dirty old men, sexy seniors: Representations of sexuality of older persons. *Journal of Aging and Identity, 7*, 99–112.

Wang, J., Eslinger, P.J., Smith, M.B. and Yang, Q.X. (2005) Functional magnetic resonance imaging study of human olfaction and normal aging. *Journal of Gerontology A: Biological Sciences and Medical Sciences, 60*, 510–14.

Ward, R. (1977) The impact of subjective age and stigma on older persons. *Journal of Gerontology, 32*, 227–32.

Ward, R. (1984) *The Aging Experience*. Cambridge: Harper and Row.

Warren, C.A.B. (1998) Aging and identity in premodern times. *Research on Aging, 20*, 11–35.

Warrington, E. (1975) The selective impairment of semantic memory. *Quarterly Journal of Experimental Psychology, 27*, 635–57.

Wasylenki, D.A. (ed.) (1987) *Psychogeriatrics: A Practical Handbook*. London: Jessica Kingsley Publishers.

Waters, G.S. and Caplan, D. (2001) Age, working memory and on-line syntactic processing in sentence comprehension. *Psychology and Aging, 16*, 128–44.

Waters, G. and Caplan, D. (2002) Working memory and online syntactic processing in Alzheimer's disease: studies with auditory moving window presentation. *The Journals of Gerontology Series B: Psychological Sciences and Social Sciences, 57*, 298–311.

Watson, D.G. and Maylor, E.A. (2002) Aging and visual marking: Selective deficits for moving stimuli. *Psychology and Aging, 17*, 321–39.

Watson, D.G., Maylor, E.A. and Manson, N.J. (2002) Aging and enumeration: A selective deficit for the subitization of targets among distractors. *Psychology and Aging, 17*, 496–504.

Waugh, N.C. and Barr, R.A. (1982) Encoding deficits in aging. In F.I.M. Craik and S. Trehub (eds), *Aging and Cognitive Processes*. New York: Plenum.

Weg, R.B. (1983) Changing physiology of aging: Normal and pathological. In D.S. Woodruff and J.E. Birren (eds), *Aging: Scientific Perspectives and Social Issues*. Monterey, CA: Brooks-Cole.

Wegesin, D.J., Ream, J.M. and Stern, Y. (2004) Explicit contamination contributes to aging effects in episodic priming: behavioral and erp evidence. *The Journals of Gerontology Series B: Psychological Sciences and Social Sciences 59*, 317–24.

Weiffenbach, J.M., Baum, B.J. and Berghauser, R. (1982) Taste thresholds: Quality specific variation with human aging. *Journal of Gerontology, 37*, 372–7.

Weinstein, B.E. and Ventry, I.M. (1982) Hearing impairment and social isolation in the elderly. *Journal of Speech and Hearing Research, 25*, 593–9.

Weisberg, N. and Wilder, R. (eds), (2001) *Expressive Arts with Elders: A Resource*. 2nd edition. London: Jessica Kingsley Publishers.

Wells, Y.D. and Kendig, H.L. (1997) Health and well-being of spouse caregivers and the widowed. *Gerontologist, 37*, 666–74.

Wenger, G.C. (1990) Elderly carers: The need for appropriate intervention. *Ageing and Society, 10*, 197–219.

Wenger, G.C. (1997) Review of findings on support networks of older Europeans. *Journal of Cross-Cultural Gerontology, 12*, 1–21.

Weraarchakul, N., Strong, R., Wood, W.G. and Richardson, A. (1989) The effect of aging and dietary restriction on DNA repair. *Experimental Cell Research, 181*, 197–204.

West, R.L. (1988) Prospective memory and aging. In M.M. Gruneberg, P.E. Morris and R.N. Sykes (eds), *Practical Aspects of Memory: Current Research and Issues, Volume 2; Clinical and Educational Implications*. Chichester: Wiley, 119–225.

West, C.G., Reed, D.M. and Gildengorin, G.L. (1998) Can money buy happiness? Depressive symptoms in an affluent older population. *Journal of the American Geriatrics Society, 46*, 49–57.

West, R., Herndon, R.W. and Covell, E. (2003) Neural correlates of age-related declines in the formation and realization of delayed intentions. *Psychology and Aging, 18*, 461–73.

West, R., Murphy, K.J., Armilio, M.L., Craik, F.I.M. and Stuss, D.T. (2002) Effects of time of day on age differences in working memory. *The Journals of Gerontology Series B: Psychological Sciences and Social Sciences, 57*, 3–10.

West, R.L., Crook, T.H. and Barron, K.L. (1992) Everyday memory performance across the life span: Effects of age and noncognitive individual differences. *Psychology and Aging, 7*, 72–82.

West, R.L., Welch, D.C. and Thorn, R.M. (2001) Effects of goal-setting and feedback on memory performance and beliefs among older and younger adults. *Psychology and Aging, 16*, 240–50.

West, R.L. and Yassuda, M.S. (2004) Aging and memory control beliefs: performance in relation to goal setting and memory self-evaluation. *The Journals of Gerontology Series B: Psychological Sciences and Social Sciences 59*, 56–65.

Westerman, S.J., Davies, D.R., Glendon, A.I., Stammers, R.B. and Matthews, G. (1998) Ageing and word processing competence: compensation or compilation? *British Journal of Psychology, 89,* 579–97.

Wetherell, J.L., Gatz, M. and Pedersen, N.L. (2001) A longitudinal analysis of anxiety and depressive symptoms. *Psychology and Aging, 16,* 187–95.

Wetherell, J.L., Le Roux, H. and Gatz, M. (2003) DSM-IV criteria for generalized anxiety disorder in older adults: Distinguishing the worried from the well. *Psychology and Aging, 18,* 622–7.

Whelihan, W.M., Thompson, J.A., Piatt, A.L., Caron, M.D. and Chung, T. (1997) The relation of neuropsychological measures to levels of cognitive functioning in elderly individuals: A discriminant analysis approach. *Applied Neuropsychology, 4,* 160–164.

Whitbourne, S.K. (1987) Personality development in adulthood and old age. In K.W. Schaie (ed.) *Annual Review of Gerontology and Geriatrics, 7.* New York: Springer.

White, K.K. and Abrams, L. (2002) Does priming specific syllables during tip-of-the-tongue states facilitate word retrieval in older adults? *Psychology and Aging, 17,* 226–35.

White, L.R., Cartwright, W.S., Cornoni-Huntley, J. and Brock, D.B. (1986) Geriatric epidemiology. In C. Einsdorfer (ed.) *Annual Review of Gerontology and Geriatrics, 6.* New York: Springer.

White, N. and Cunningham, W.R. (1988) Is terminal drop pervasive or specific? *Journal of Gerontology, 43,* 141–4.

White-Means, S.I. (2000) Racial patterns in disabled elderly persons' use of medical services. *The Journals of Gerontology Series B: Psychological Sciences and Social Sciences, 55,* 76–89.

Whitfield, K.E. and Baker-Thomas, T. (1999) Individual differences in aging minorities. *International Journal of Aging and Human Development, 48,* 73–9.

Wickens, C.D., Braune, R. and Stokes, A. (1987) Age differences in the speed and capacity of information processing: A dual task approach. *Psychology and Aging, 2,* 70–8.

Wiebe, J.M.D. and Cox, B.J. (2005) Problem and probable pathological gambling among older adults assessed by the SOGS-R. *Journal of Gambling Studies, 21,* 205–21.

Wilcox, S., Bopp, M., Oberrecht. L., Kammermann, S.K. and McElmurray, C.T. (2003) Psychosocial and perceived environmental correlates of physical activity in rural and older African American and white women. *The Journals of Gerontology Series B: Psychological Sciences and Social Sciences, 58,* 329–37.

Wilcox, S. and King, A.C. (2000) Alcohol consumption in older adults: A comparison of two assessment methods. *Journal of Applied Gerontology, 19,* 170–180.

Wilkins, A. and Baddeley, A. (1978) Remembering to recall in everyday life: An approach to absent-mindedness. In M.M. Gruneberg, P.E. Morris and R.N. Sykes (eds), *Practical Aspects of Memory, Current Research and Issues, Volume 2.* Chichester: Wiley.

Wilkins, R. and Adams, O.B. (1983) Health expectancy in Canada, late 1970s: demographic, regional and social dimensions. *American Journal of Public Health, 73,* 1073–80.

Willett, J.A., Chisolm, T.H. and Lister, J.J. (2001) Modulation of presbycusis: Current state and future directions. *Audiology and Neuro-Otology, 6,* 231–49.

Williams, G.C. (1957) Pleiotropy, natural selection and the evolution of senescence. *Evolution, 11,* 398–411.

Williams, K. (2004) The transition to widowhood and the social regulation of health: consequences for health and health risk behavior. *The Journals of Gerontology Series B: Psychological Sciences and Social Sciences, 59,* 343–49.

Williams, K., Holmes, F., Kemper, S. and Marquis, J. (2003) Written language clues to cognitive changes of aging: An analysis of the letters of King James VI/I. *The Journals of Gerontology Series B: Psychological Sciences and Social Sciences, 58,* 42–4.

Williamson, G.M. and Schulz, R. (1992) Physical illness and symptoms of depression among elderly outpatients. *Psychology and Aging, 7,* 343–51.

Williamson, G.M. and Schulz, R. (1995) Activity restriction mediates the association between pain and depressed affect: A study of younger and older adult cancer patients. *Psychology and Aging, 10,* 369–78.

Willis, L., Goodwin, J., Lee, K-O., Mosqueda, L., Garry, P., Liu, P., Linn, R. and Waynes, S. (1997) Impact of psychosocial factors on health outcomes in the elderly: A prospective study. *Journal of Aging and Health, 9,* 396–414.

Wilson, I.A., Ikonen, S., Gureviciene, I., McMahan, R., Gallagher, M., Eichenbaum, H. and Tanila, H. (2004a) Cognitive aging and the hippocampus: How old rats represent new environments. *Journal of Neuroscience, 24,* 3870–8.

Wilson, R.S., Beckett, L.A., Barnes, L.L., Schneider, J.A., Bach, J., Evans, D.A., and Bennett, D.A. (2002) Individual differences in rates of change in cognitive abilities of older persons. *Psychology and Aging, 17,* 179–93.

Wilson, R.S., Gilley, D.W., Bennett, D.A., Beckett, L.A. and Evans, D.A. (2000) Person-specific paths of cognitive decline in Alzheimer's disease and their relation to age. *Psychology and Aging, 15,* 18–28.

Wilson, R.S., Mendes de Leon, C.F., Bienias, J.L., Evans, D.A. and Bennett, D.A. (2004b) Personality and mortality in old age. *The Journals of Gerontology Series B: Psychological Sciences and Social Sciences, 59,* 110–116.

Wink, P. and Dillon, M. (2003) Religiousness, spirituality and psychosocial functioning in late adulthood: Findings from a longitudinal study. *Psychology and Aging, 18*, 916–24.

Wishart, L.R., Lee, T.D., Murdoch, J.E. and Hodges, N.J. (2000) Effects of aging on automatic and effortful processes in bimanual coordination. *The Journals of Gerontology Series B: Psychological Sciences and Social Sciences 55*, 85–94.

Witte, K.L. and Freund, J.S. (1995) Anagram solutions as related to adult age, anagram difficulty and experience in solving crossword puzzles. *Aging and Cognition, 2*, 146–55.

Wolf, E.S. (1997) Self psychology and the aging self through the life curve. *Annual of Psychoanalysis, 25*, 201–215.

Wolf, R.S. (1997) Elder abuse and neglect: An update. *Reviews in Clinical Gerontology, 7*, 177–82.

Wolff, J.L. and Agree, E.M. (2004) Depression among recipients of informal care: the effects of reciprocity, respect and adequacy of support. *The Journals of Gerontology Series B: Psychological Sciences and Social Sciences, 59*, 173–180.

Wood, E., Whitfield, E. and Christie, A. (1995) Changes in survival in demented hospital inpatients 1957–1987. In E. Murphy and G. Alexopoulos (ed.), *Geriatric Psychiatry: Key Research Topics for Clinicians.* Chichester: Wiley, 85–93.

Woodruff-Pak, D.S. (1997) *The Neuropsychology of Aging.* Oxford: Blackwells.

Woods, R.L., Treagear, S.J. and Mitchell, R.A. (1998) Screening for ophthalmic disease in older subjects using visual acuity and contrast sensitivity. *Ophthalmology, 105*, 2315–26.

Woods, R.T. (1996) *Handbook of the Clinical Psychology of Ageing.* Chichester: Wiley.

Woods, R.T. (1999) Mental health problems in late life. In R.T. Woods (ed.), *Psychological Problems of Ageing.* Chichester: Wiley, 73–110.

Woodward, K. (1991) *Aging and its Discontents. Freud and Other Fictions.* Bloomington, IN: Indiana University Press.

Woodward, K.L. (1993) The relationship between skin compliance, age, gender and tactile discriminative thresholds in humans. *Somatosensory and Motor Research, 10*, 63–37.

World Health Organization (2004) *World Health Report 2000.* Geneva: World Health Organization.

Wyndham, J. (1960) *Trouble With Lichen.* London: Michael Joseph.

Xue, S.A. and Deliyski, D. (2001) Effects of aging on selected acoustic voice parameters: Preliminary normative data and educational implications. *Educational Gerontology, 27*, 159–168.

Yang, Z., Norton, E.C. and Stearns, S.C. (2003) Longevity and health care expenditures: the real reasons older people spend more. *The Journals of Gerontology Series B: Psychological Sciences and Social Science, 58*, 2–10.

Yarmey, A.D. and Yarmey, M.J. (1997) Eyewitness recall and duration estimates in field settings. *Journal of Applied Social Psychology, 27*, 330–44.

Yashin, A.I., De Benedictis, G., Vaupel, J.W., Tan, Q., Andreev, K.F., Iachine, I.A., Bonafe, M., DeLuca, M., Valensin, S., Carotenuto, L. and Franceschi, C. (1999) Genes, demography and life span: The contribution of demographic data in genetic studies on aging and longevity. *American Human Genetics, 65*, 1178–93.

Yong, H.H., Gibson, S.J., Horne, D. and Helme, R.D. (2001) Development of a pain attitudes questionnaire to assess stoicism and cautiousness for possible age differences. *The Journals of Gerontology Series B: Psychological Sciences and Social Sciences, 56*, 279–84.

Yoon, C., Hasher, L., Feinberg, F., Rahhal, T.A. and Winocur, G. (2000) Cross-cultural differences in memory: The role of culture-based stereotypes about aging. *Psychology and Aging, 15*, 694–704.

Zacks, R.T., Hasher, L., Doren, B., Hamm, V. and Attig, M.S. (1987) Encoding and memory of explicit and implicit information. *Journal of Gerontology, 42*, 418–22.

Zelinski, E.M. and Burnight, K.P. (1997) Sixteen-year longitudinal and time lag changes in memory and cognition in older adults. *Psychology and Aging, 12*, 503–513.

Zelinski, E.M., Gilewski, M.J. and Schaie, K.W. (1993) Individual differences in cross-sectional and 3-year longitudinal memory performance across the adult life span. *Psychology and Aging, 8*, 176–86.

Zelinski, E.M. and Hyde, J.C. (1996) Old words, new meanings: Aging and sense creation. *Journal of Memory and Language, 35*, 689–707.

Zelinski, E.M and Stewart, S.T. (1998) Individual differences in 16-year memory changes. *Psychology and Aging, 13*, 622–30.

Zettel, L.A. and Rook, K.S. (2004) Substitution and compensation in the social networks of older widowed women. *Psychology and Aging, 19*, 433–43.

Zhang, A.Y., Yu, L.C., Yuan, J., Tong, Z., Yang, C. and Foreman, S.E. (1997) Family and cultural correlates of depression among Chinese elderly. *International Journal of Social Psychiatry, 43*, 199–212.

Zhang, Z. and Hayward, M.D. (2001) Childlessness and the psychological well-being of older persons. *The Journals of Gerontology Series B: Psychological Sciences and Social Sciences, 56*, 311–20.

Zimprich, D. and Martin, M. (2002) Can longitudinal changes in processing speed explain longitudinal age changes in fluid intelligence? *Psychology and Aging, 17*, 690–5.

Zwaan, B.J. (1999) The evolutionary genetics of ageing and longevity. *Heredity, 82*, 589–97.

Index